DATE DUE

DEMCO 38-296

The Application of EC Law by National Courts

The Free Movement of Goods

The Application of EC Law by National Courts
The Free Movement of Goods

MALCOLM A. JARVIS
MA, LL M (Cantab.), LL D (Groningen)

CLARENDON PRESS · OXFORD
1998

at Clarendon Street, Oxford OX2 6DP
rd New York
ok Bogotá Buenos Aires Calcutta
Cape Town Chennai Dar es Salaam Delhi Florence Hong Kong Istanbul
Karachi Kuala Lumpur Madrid Melbourne Mexico City Mumbai
Nairobi Paris São Paolo Singapore Taipei Tokyo Toronto Warsaw
and associated companies in
Berlin Ibadan

Oxford is a registered trade mark of Oxford University Press

Published in the United States
by Oxford University Press Inc., New York

British Library Cataloguing in Publication Data
Data available

Library of Congress Cataloging in Publication Data
Jarvis, Malcolm A.
The application of EC law in national courts: the free movement
of goods / Malcolm A. Jarvis.
p. cm.
Includes bibliographical references and index.
1. Free trade—European Union countries.   2. International and
municipal law—European Union countries.   I. Title.
KJE5177.J37   1998   341.7'543'094—dc21   98–15091
ISBN 0–19–826595–6

1 3 5 7 9 10 8 6 4 2

Typeset by Hope Services (Abingdon) Ltd.
Printed in Great Britain
on acid-free paper by
Biddles Ltd., Guildford and King's Lynn

Contents

Preface

Selecting the appropriate balance in the title for this book was a difficult task. The dilemma was essentially whether the title should most reflect the emphasis in this work on the more general application of European Community law by national courts, or rather the accent on the specific area of the provisions within the EC Treaty concerning the free movement of goods. Since the issues arising from the application of the provisions concerning the free movement of goods by the national courts have such wide implications (being representative of the application of any of the other four freedoms and indeed the application of EC law by the national courts in general) it was felt that this should be reflected in the title. It is hoped that this work will add to the growing awareness of the pivotal role played by the national courts as the 'Community Courts', whilst also providing a thought-provoking analysis of the free-movement-of-goods provisions in the EC Treaty.

This book is based on a doctoral thesis conferred by the University of Groningen under the supervision of Professor Laurence Gormley. My thanks are due to him and to that institution. I also wish to express my gratitude to Professor Jacqueline Dutheil de la Rochère, Professor Jan Jans and Professor John Usher who comprised the reading committee for the thesis and to Professor Stephen Weatherill and Professor René Barents who acted as additional examiners for the award of the degree with distinction.

Thanks are also due to my parents for their ever present support and to Patrick Higgins, Paul McHugh, and Lambros Kilaniotis for their early encouragement of my academic endeavours. A special word of thanks must go to Frea Rijnsbergen and Fabian Amtenbrink for acting as my two 'paranymphs' and for our solidarity and friendship during my time in Groningen. Finally, I must thank my wife, Hilary, who forfeited much for what has resulted in this book.

MAJ
January 1998

Abbreviations

The following abbreviations have been used in relation to legal journals and periodicals, law reports, and French and Dutch courts.

AB	*Administratiefrechterlijke Beslissingen*
AC	*Appeal Cases*
Afd.	*Afdeling*
All ER	*All England Reports*
Amer. J. Comp. Law	*American Journal of Comparative Law*
AJDA	*Actualité juridique—droit administratif*
BGH	*Bundesgerichtshof*
BIE	*Bijblad bij de industriëele eigendom*
BNB	*Beslissingen in belastingzaken*
Bull. Cass. Civ.	*Bulletin des arrêts de la Cour de cassation, Chambre civile*
Bull. Cass. Crim.	*Bulletin des arrêts de la Cour de cassation, Chambre criminelle*
Bull. EC	*Bulletin of the European Communities*
CAA	Cour administrative d'appel
Camb. LJ	*Cambridge Law Journal*
CBB	*College van Beroep voor het Bedrijfsleven*
CDE	*Cahiers de Droit Européen*
ch. comm.	chambre commerciale
ch. corr.	chambre correctionnelle
ch. cr.	chambre criminelle
CLE	*Commercial Laws of Europe*
CMLR	*Common Market Law Reports*
CMLRev.	*Common Market Law Review*
Col. J. Transnat. Law	*Columbian Journal of Transnational Law*
Consum. LJ	*Consumer Law Journal*
Dalloz	*Receuil Dalloz, Receuil Dalloz-Sirey*
Dr. et pr. du com. int.	Droit et pratique de commerce internationale
EBLR	*European Business Law Review*
Ec.	*Economische*
ECC	*European Commercial Cases*
ECJ	European Court of Justice
ECLR	*European Competition Law Review*
ECR	*European Court Reports*
EIPR	*European Intellectual Property Review*

ELDig.	*European Law Digest*
ELRev.	*European Law Review*
EUI	European University Institute
EuLR	*European Law Reports*
EuR	*Europarecht*
Fordham Int. LJ	*Fordham International Law Journal*
FSR	*Fleet Street Reports*
Gaz. Pal.	*Gazette du Palais*
GRUR	*Gewerblicher Rechtsschutz und Urheberrecht*
IIC	*International Review of Industrial Property and Copyright Law*
ICLQ	*International and Comparative Law Quarterly*
ICR	*Industrial Cases Reports*
IER	*Intellectuele eigendom en reclamerecht*
ILRM	*Irish Law Reports Monthly*
Irish Rep.	*Irish Reports*
IRLR	*Industrial Relations Law Reports*
JCP	*Semaine juridique (Juriclasseur périodique), édition générale*
J. Environ. Law	*Journal of Environmental Law*
JORF	*Journal officiel de la République français*
KG	*Kort Geding*
LIEI	*Legal Issues of European Integration*
LQR	*Law Quarterly Review*
LS	*Legal Studies*
MLR	*Modern Law Review*
M & R	*Tijdschrift voor Milieu en Recht*
NJ	*Nederlandse Jurisprudentie*
NJB	*Nederlands-Juristenblad*
NLJ	*New Law Journal*
OJ	*Official Journal of the European Communities*
OJLS	*Oxford Journal of Legal Studies*
OLG	*Oberlandesgericht*
PIBD	*Propriété industrielle; bulletin documentaire*
PL	*Public Law*
QB	*Queen's Bench Reports*
RCC	*Reclame Code Commissie* [court]
RCC	Reclame Code Commissie [report]
RDP	*Revue du droit public et de la science politique en France et à l'étranger*
Rec. Lebon	*Receuil Lebon des décisions du Conseil d'Etat*
Rev. crit. dr. int. priv.	Revue critique de droit international privé
Rev. franç. dr. admin.	*Revue française de droit administratif*

Rev. int. prop. indus. art.	*Revue internationale de la propriété industrielle et artistique*
Rev. juris. comm.	*Revue de jurisprudence commerciale*
Rev. juris. fiscale	*Revue de jurisprudence fiscale*
Rev. juris. social	*Revue de jurisprudence social*
Rev. trim. de dr. civil	*Revue trimestrielle de droit civil*
RIDA	*Revue internationale du droit d'auteur*
RiW	*Recht der Internationalen Wirtschaft*
RMC	*Revue de Marché Commun (et de l'Union européenne)*
RMUE	*Revue du Marché Unique Européen*
RPC	*Reports of Restrictive Practices Cases*
RSC	Rules of the Supreme Court
RTDComm.	*Revue trimestrielle du droit commercial et de droit economique*
RTDE	*Revue trimestrielle de droit européen*
RvdW	*Rechtspraak van de Week*
Sc. Law Gaz.	*Scottish Law Gazette*
S. Ct.	Supreme Court
SEW	*Sociaal Economische Wetgeving*
SI	*Statutory Instruments*
SLT	*Scots Law Times*
Sol. Jo.	*Solicitors Journal*
Stb.	*Staatsblad*
Stcrt	*Staatscourant*
TGI	*Tribunal de grande instance*
UCB	*Uitspraken College van Beroep voor het Bedrijfsleven*
WLR	*Weekly Law Reports*
YEL	*Yearbook of European Law*
ZLR	*Zeitschrift für das gesamte Lebensmittelrecht*

Treaty of Amsterdam (revised articles)

The renumbering of the Articles of the EC Treaty (1957) which will take effect when the Treaty of Amsterdam (1997) enters into force (so far as is pertinent for the subject matter of this book):

EC Treaty Article	EC Treaty Article Renumbered
3b	5
5	10
6	12
7a	14
9	23
10	24
12	25
28	26
29	27
30	28
34	29
36	30
37	31
48	39
52	43
59	49
73b	56
85	81
86	82
90	86
92	87
93	88
95	90
100	94
100a	95
113	133
130r	174
169	226
170	227
171	228
173	230
175	232
177	234

EC Treaty Article	EC Treaty Article Renumbered
215	288
235	308

Table of Cases

THE NETHERLANDS

Table of cases

UNITED KINGDOM

AUSTRIA

BELGIUM

BENELUX COURT OF JUSTICE

GERMANY

GREECE

IRELAND

1

Introduction

The decentralized system for the application and enforcement of European Community (EC) law has the result that the national courts are the natural forum for its application. The need to entrust the application of EC law to the national courts of Member States of the European Community is not only a necessity, but also a reality. The volume of national court case law applying the provisions of substantive EC law confirms that the national judge is indeed the *'juge communautaire de droit commun'*.[1] This is by no means a new awakening. The early development by the European Court of Justice (ECJ) of the dual doctrines of supremacy and direct effect of EC law made the crucial role of the national courts in the Community's legal order inevitable. Furthermore, since individuals have only limited access to both the ECJ and the Court of First Instance, the national judges necessarily perform the role of 'Community courts'. The central theme of this work is thus to examine the position of the national courts within the judicial architecture of the European Community.

It is now almost a truism to state that a spirit of judicial co-operation between the ECJ and the national courts lies at the heart of the European Community's judicial structure.[2] The ECJ, and indeed the development of EC law more generally, relies heavily upon the co-operation of the national courts. The ECJ has stated that this duty of sincere co-operation 'is of particular importance *vis-à-vis* the judicial authorities of the Member States, who are responsible for ensuring that Community law is applied

---

[1] See Case T–51/89, *Tetra Pak Rausing SA* v. *Commission* [1990] ECR II–309 at para. 42 where this phrase is translated into English as 'Community courts of general jurisdiction', and Case T–219/95R, *Danialsson, Largenteau and Haoa* v. *Commission* [1995] ECR II–3051 at para. 77 where the same phrase in French is translated as 'the ordinary courts of Community law'. Temple Lang has written that '[e]very national court in the European Community is now a Community law court' and that 'in fact national courts probably interpret and apply Community law more often than the two Community courts do' ('The Duties of National Courts under Community Constitutional Law' (1997) 22 ELRev. 3 at 3). Similarly, Curtin has written that '[u]nder the Community system of decentralised control every national judge is considered to be a Community judge' ('The Decentralised Enforcement of Community Law Rights. Judicial Snakes and Ladders' in Curtin and O'Keeffe (eds.) *Constitutional Adjudication and National Law* at 34).

[2] Jacqué and Weiler have commented that 'the judicial co-operation between the European Court and national courts—at the very foundation of the constitutional order—has been one of the major success stories of European integration' ('On the Road to European Union—A New Judicial Architecture: An Agenda for the Intergovernmental Conference' (1990) 27 CMLRev. 185 at 186).

and respected in the national legal system'.[3] These observations only serve to underline the importance of the national courts in the system for the administration of justice in the EC legal order. Simply put, the national courts are the courts primarily responsible for the day-to-day application of EC law.[4]

The pivotal role played by the national courts, as the ordinary courts for the day-to-day application of EC law, has become increasingly apparent in recent years.[5] Interest in the national court perspective has to date centred itself on two areas. Firstly, the acceptance by the national courts of, or more usually their hostility to, the dual doctrines of the 'supremacy' and the 'direct effect' of Community law within the national legal systems. In this regard, attention has rightly been focused upon the mechanisms that have been employed by the national courts in the various legal jurisdictions that make up the European Community to accommodate EC law into the national constitutional contexts.[6] Secondly, interest has focused upon procedural questions which have arisen as a result of the split competence for the application of EC law between the European Community institu-

---

[3] Case C–2/88, *Imm. Zwartveld* [1990] ECR I–3365, [1990] 3 CMLR 457 at para. 18.

[4] Alter has commented that '[w]hile the European Court has played a decisive role in issuing expansive and important decisions on EC law, the linchpins of the European legal system are really the national courts of the Member States' ('The European Court and National Courts Doctrine and Jurisprudence: Legal Change in its Social Context. Explaining National Court Acceptance of European Court Jurisprudence. A Critical Evaluation of Theories of Integration' EUI, Working Paper RSC No. 95/27 at 2).

[5] See e.g. Kovar, 'Voies de droit ouverte aux individus devant les instances nationales en cas de violation des normes et décisions du droit communautaire' in *Les recours des individus devant les instances nationales* at 245; Steiner; 'The Application of EEC law in National Courts: Problems, Pitfalls and Precepts' (1980) 96 LQR 126; Usher, *European Community law and national law: the irreversible transfer?*; Barav, 'La fonction communautaire du juge national', unpub. Ph.D. thesis, Strasbourg University, 1983; idem, 'La plénitude de compétence du juge national en sa qualité de juge communautaire' in *L'Europe et le droit: mélanges en hommage à Jean Boulouis* at 1; Grévisse and Bonichot, 'Les incidences du droit communautaire sur l'organisation et l'exercice de la fonction juridictionnelle dans les Etats membres', ibid. at 297; Slynn, *European Law and the National Judge*; Tesauro, 'The Effectiveness of Judicial Protection and Co-operation between the Court of Justice and the National Courts' (1993) 13 YEL 1; Maher, 'National Courts as European Community Courts' (1994) 14 LS 226; Maher, 'A Question of Conflict: The Higher English Courts and the Implementation of European Community Law' in Daintith, *Implementing EC Law in the United Kingdom* at 303; Golub, 'The Politics of Judicial Discretion: Rethinking the Interaction between National Courts and the European Court of Justice' (1996) 19 *West European Politics* 360; Usher, 'Community Law and National Courts' in Vaughan (ed.), *Law of the European Communities Service*, pt. 3.

[6] See e.g. Simon, 'Les exigences de la primauté du droit communautaire' in *L'Europe et le droit* at 481; De Witte, 'Community Law and Constitutional Values' (1991) 2 LIEI 1; Haguenau, *L'Application effective du droit communautaire en droit interne: Analyse comparative des problèmes recontrés en droit français, anglais et allemand*; Thibaut de Berranger, *Constitutions nationales et construction communautaire*, and the Florence Project incorporating reports from various Member States under the title, 'The European Court and National Courts—Doctrine and Jurisprudence: Legal Change in its Social Context' pub. as EUI Working Papers RSC No. 95/24 to 95/31.

tions on the one hand, and the national courts on the other.[7] The focus of this work, however, is of a different nature. The point of departure for the discussion in this work is to assume that, broadly speaking and notwithstanding a few remaining difficulties, the national courts have now accepted the supremacy and direct effect of EC law into the national legal systems. This work thus attempts to shift the debate towards examining the actual application of the *substantive* rules of EC law by the national courts. In other words, now that the primacy and application of EC law in national courts has itself been secured, what may be termed the 'second generation' concern is emerging with an interest in the actual application of the substantive rules of EC law as interpreted in the case law of the ECJ.

The application of the free movement of goods rules contained in Articles 30 to 36 of the EC Treaty (EC) have been selected for the purposes of this analysis. This area of substantive EC law has been chosen since it forms one of the largest and most mature areas of EC law. Indeed, the free movement of goods may be described as the very foundation of the European Community.[8] Furthermore, the free movement of goods field also provides an interesting template since it is a central and characteristic testing ground for the division of powers between the Community and its Member States. The application of the free movement of goods provisions is also of great interest because of the extent of intervention that these provisions involve in national regulation of economic life.

The case law concerning the free movement of goods before the national courts of the United Kingdom, France and the Netherlands will be exhaustively analysed in this work. Additionally, the significant developments in the case law concerning the free movement of goods in all the other Member States will be referred to where appropriate. The Member States singled out for particular attention were selected on the following grounds: the United Kingdom to represent the common law tradition, France to focus on the reception of EC law in a civil law system, and finally the Netherlands, a fertile source given the extremely large body of case

---

[7] The most obvious example in this respect is the split jurisdiction between the European Commission and the national courts for the application of the EC Treaty's competition rules contained in Arts. 85 & 86 EC. In particular, the role of the national courts has been emphasized by the Court of First Instance in Case T–24/90 *Automec Srl* v. *Commission* (Automec II) [1992] ECR II–2223, [1992] 5 CMLR 431, by the ECJ in Case C–234/89 *Stergios Delimitis* v. *Henninger Brau* [1991] ECR I–935 and by Commission Notice on co-operation between national courts and the Commission in applying Articles 85 and 86, [1993] OJ C39/6, [1993] 4 CMLR 12. The role of the national courts in the field of State aid, and in applying Art. 93(3) EC in particular, has also been underlined by the ECJ's judgments in Case C–354/90 *Fédération Nationale du Commerce Extérieur des Produits Alimentaires* v. *France* [1991] ECR I–5505 and Case C–39/94 *Syndicat français de l'Express international* v. *La Poste* [1996] ECR I–3547.

[8] The ECJ has recently referred to the free movement of goods as 'one of the fundamental principles of the Treaty': Case C–265/95 *Commission* v. *France* [1997] ECR 1–nyr (judgt 9 Dec. 1997) at para. 24.

law in this field, emanating from a smaller Member State. In this way, the different legal traditions are covered whilst achieving a balance between the larger and smaller Member States.

Little work has been undertaken to analyse the application of substantive EC law by the national courts and it seems that the correct and loyal application of substantive EC law by these courts is all too often presumed with little verification as to whether this is actually the case in practice. This work seeks to redress this balance and aims to examine whether the experience of actual application of EC law by the national courts gives rise to confidence, or rather to dismay. In other words, the question which is posed is whether the decentralized structure for the application of EC law is functioning satisfactorily. Can the application of EC law be safely entrusted to the national courts? Is EC law being uniformly applied in all the Member States or is there a risk of divergent judgments?

The decentralized application of EC law by the national courts does not, however, work in one direction. A decentralized structure does not necessarily imply a one-way dialogue from the ECJ to the national courts. Rather, the process is, in line with the spirit of co-operation alluded to above, a two-way street. Therefore, a further question to which the examination of national court case law gives rise is the extent to which the approach of the ECJ itself should be adapted in order to take into consideration the problems of application of its own case law before the national courts. The analysis of the application of the free-movement-of-goods provisions before the national courts will thus also be used to prompt several suggestions for possible amendment of the ECJ's own interpretation of Articles 30 to 36 EC.

The structure of the discussion will broadly follow the structure of the free-movement-of-goods provisions themselves (Chapters 2 to 9). The discussion in each chapter will begin with a brief sketch of the applicable EC Treaty provisions and their interpretation in ECJ case law. Where appropriate, attention will also be drawn to the doctrinal difficulties which underlie the ECJ's case law, including references to discussion in the literature. In each chapter, this introduction to the interpretation of the free-movement-of-goods provisions at Community level will then be followed by a full analysis of the national case law applying these principles. Finally attention will also be devoted to the question of remedies for breach of EC law before the national courts and to preliminary references to the ECJ under Article 177 EC (Chapters 10 and 11 respectively).

The discussion of national case law in this work has two clear limitations which must be acknowledged at the outset. The first limitation is that it must be recognized that one is primarily reliant upon those cases concerning the application of the free-movement-of-goods provisions which have been reported. While it has been possible to obtain unreported judgments from other sources (such as from databases, from lawyers involved in such cases before the national courts and by writing to individual national courts requesting transcripts of judgments) the primary source has necessarily been those cases which have been reported. A second limitation arises from the fact that it is virtually impossible to identify those cases before the national courts in which neither the parties involved in the case, nor the national court of its own motion, raised a relevant point of EC law in circumstances where such a point ought to have been dealt with. Indeed, the effective application of EC law before the national courts depends not only upon the national judges, but also upon the advice of lawyers advising clients in the European Community. For this reason, the awareness of EC law amongst the legal professions plays a crucial role in the effective application of EC law.[9]

Finally, it may be noted that the judgments of the national courts discussed in this work are translated into the English language by the author except in those instances where an English translation has been available. In cases where difficulties have been encountered in reaching a satisfactory translation into English or when it has been considered necessary, the relevant excerpt from the judgment will be provided in a footnote in the original language version. The European Community Treaty will be referred to as the EC Treaty throughout (even when the national court judgment was handed down before the Treaty on European Union) except, of course, in direct quotations from the judgments themselves. The renumbering of the Articles of the EC Treaty which will take effect when the Treaty of Amsterdam enters into force is set out, so far as is pertinent for the subject-matter of this book, in a table at p. xix.

---

[9] In March 1997, the European Commission launched the 'Robert Schuman Project', which has the specific aim of encouraging further education of the legal professions as to the possibilities offered by EC law and to improve awareness and expertise in EC law; see amended proposal for a European Parliament and Council Decision establishing an action programme to improve awareness of Community law for the legal professions [1997] OJ C368/6. See also on this point, Darmon and Calvet, 'Les juristes français et le droit communautaire' Gaz. Pal. 1990, I Doctr. 197 and Pertek, 'L'enseignement du droit européen. Besoin et propositions' (1992) RMUE 159.

2

Article 30 and imports

1 LEGAL STRUCTURE AND SCOPE

Article 30 of the EC Treaty governs the import of goods from other Member States. That Article provides for a strict prohibition on import restrictions in the following terms:

Quantitative restrictions on imports and all measures having equivalent effect shall . . . be prohibited between Member States.

Two preliminary comments may be set out at this stage. Firstly, because of the fundamental importance of the principle of the free movement of goods, Article 30 has been strictly enforced. A common theme running throughout the European Court of Justice's (ECJ's) interpretation of Article 30 is that the prohibition contained in Article 30, as a basic freedom under the Treaty, must be interpreted as broadly as possible.[1] Secondly, the important issue of the direct effect of the provisions of Community law should not be overlooked. It will be recalled that sufficiently clear, precise, and unconditional Community provisions will have direct effect.[2] The consequence of this is that a provision, if directly effective, creates individual rights which national courts are bound to protect. All the Treaty provisions on the free movement of goods have been held by the ECJ to have direct effect[3] and the important practical consequence of this is that individuals may rely upon those provisions to enforce their rights before national courts.

(A) The definition of 'goods'

Although the wording of Article 30 refers only to 'imports' and makes no direct reference to 'goods' as such, it is clear from the position of this Article in Title 1 of the EC Treaty, concerning the 'free movement of goods', that Article 30 refers only to restrictions on the importation of 'goods'. The ECJ has defined 'goods' as 'products which can be valued in

---

[1] Correspondingly, as will be shown, the exceptions and justifications for breaches of Art. 30 have been narrowly construed; see Chs. 6 & 7. It should further be noted that the ECJ has always rejected any role for a *de minimis* principle for Art. 30: Case 177/82 *Van de Haar* [1984] ECR 1797, [1983] 1 CMLR 566. This will be discussed in detail in Ch. 3, sect. 2C).

[2] See Case 26/62 *Van Gend en Loos* [1963] ECR 1, [1963] CMLR 105.

[3] See, e.g., Case 74/76 *Ianelli and Volpi* [1977] ECR 557.

money and which are capable, as such, of forming the subject of commercial transactions'.[4] This has been held by the ECJ to extend to waste products[5] but not to means of payment, which fall to be considered under the Treaty provisions on the free movement of capital.[6]

(B) Goods from third countries 'in free circulation' in the Community

It will be apparent that the free movement of goods entails a great deal more than simply creating a free trade area. Unlike a free trade area, the European Community comprises a common market which entails the inclusion of a common customs tariff together with the abolition of customs duties for goods moving from one Member State to another.[7] The important consequence of this is that the EC Treaty provisions abolishing customs duties and restrictions on the free movement of goods apply not only to goods originating in Member States, but also to goods coming from non-member countries, so long as they have been duly imported into one Member State and any customs duties payable under the Common Customs Tariff have been accounted for.[8] The provisions on free movement of goods thus apply to all goods in free circulation in the Community.

The national courts have, on several occasions, held that goods in free circulation are entitled to free movement.[9] There have, however, been hints of difficulties before the national courts concerning the question of when the condition that particular goods have been 'put into circulation in

[4] Case 7/68 *Commission* v. *Italy* (Art Exports) [1968] ECR 423, [1969] CMLR 1.

[5] Case C–2/90 *Commission* v. *Belgium* (Walloon Waste Case) [1992] ECR I–4431 at para. 26, where it was held that 'objects which are shipped across a frontier for the purposes of commercial transactions are subject to Art. 30, whatever the nature of those transactions'.

[6] Case 7/78 *R.* v. *Thompson, Johnson and Woodiwiss* [1978] ECR 2247, [1979] 1 CMLR 47.

[7] Art. 9(1) EC provides, 'The Community shall be based upon a customs union which shall cover all trade in goods and which shall involve the prohibition between Member States of customs duties on imports and exports and of all charges having equivalent effect, and the adoption of a common customs tariff in their relations with third countries'.

[8] See Arts. 9(2) and 10(1) EC and the ECJ's judgment in Case 41/76 *Donckerwolcke* [1976] ECR 1921, [1977] 2 CMLR 535.

[9] For examples of early cases before the French courts concerning goods in free circulation, see *Ministère public* v. *Denise Cornet (née Deroche), Cour d'appel* Lyon, 4e ch. corr., 20 Nov. 1964, [1965] 1 CMLR 105; *Cour de Cassation,* ch. crim., 29 June 1966, Dalloz 1966, Jur. 596; Gaz. Pal. 1966, I Jur. 297, [1967] 1 CMLR 351; *Jacques Allion, Cour de Cassation,* ch. crim., 5 Dec. 1983, Dalloz 1984, Jur. 217 + 219–20; *Albert Lapeyre, Cour de Cassation,* ch. crim., 5 Jan. 1967, Dalloz 1967, Jur. 465; JCP 1967, II 15249; RTDE 1967, 699; [1967] 1 CMLR 362; *Ministère public et Direction général des douanes et droits indirects* v. *Stanislas Nowak, TGI,* la Seine, 11e ch. corr., 20 Oct. 1964, Gaz. Pal. 1965, I Jur. 40 and *Association des centres distributeurs Edouard Leclerc et SA des marchés et des usines Auchan, Conseil d'Etat,* 22 Nov. 1991, Rec. Lebon 1991, 400 (and 719). For an early case before the Dutch courts, see *International Fruit Company NV* v. *Producktschap voor Groenten en Fruit, CBB,* 30 July 1971, AB 1971, 256; SEW 1972, 308 and *CBB,* 5 May 1972, AB 1972, 189; SEW 1972, 503. For a full discussion of goods from third countries and intellectual property rights, see Ch. 8 sect. 9.

another Member State' has been satisfied. This was evident in a judgment of the Dutch *College van beroep voor het bedrijfsleven* (*CBB*) in *Hema BV* v. *Minister van Verkeer en Waterstaat*.[10] That case concerned the importation of telephones from Taiwan which did not comply with the applicable Dutch technical requirements.[11] The *CBB* held that the applicant had produced insufficient evidence to demonstrate that the telephones in question had been put into circulation in another Member State. What is of interest in the context of the present discussion is that the *CBB* explicitly went on to state that:

[T]he possibility cannot be excluded that in order to answer this question it will prove necessary to ask the EC Court under Article 177 EEC Treaty for a preliminary ruling concerning the applicability of Article 30 EEC Treaty in a situation in which a trade restriction affects a product which is put into circulation in another Member State *under limited conditions*.[12]

The *CBB* was thus unsure of the conditions of marketing in the other Member State that are required before it may be said that the goods in question are in circulation in that State. However, the *CBB* found it unnecessary to refer questions to the ECJ pursuant to Article 177 EC since it went on to find that the Dutch technical requirements were in any event justified for the protection of consumers under the rule of reason.[13] As Mortelmans has pointed out,[14] the judgment of the *CBB* is sensible since there is clearly no need to trouble the ECJ (and to put the parties to the expense and delay involved in a preliminary reference) when the case could be decided on other grounds. Nevertheless, there is a hint in the judgment of the *CBB* that the exact requirements in the condition that particular goods have been 'put into circulation in another Member State' will have to be clarified by the ECJ at some stage.[15]

---

[10] *CBB*, 30 Jan. 1991, SEW 1991, 489 (with note by Mortelmans); Ars Aequis 1991, 8.

[11] The technical requirements under Dutch law were set out in Art. 29, *Wet op de Telecommunicatievoorzieningen* (Telecommunications Act), Stb. 1988, 520. These technical requirements should have been notified to the Commission under Directive 89/189 [1983] OJ L109/8. See discussion of this aspect of the judgment at p. 362.

[12] Emphasis added.

[13] For a detailed discussion of this aspect of the judgment, see p. 186–7.

[14] n. 10 above.

[15] See discussion before the German courts of the question of whether it is necessary for a product to have been actually marketed (rather than capable of being marketed) in another Member State and whether the product must have been produced in the other Member State in *OLG*, Frankfurt, 14 May 1981, GRUR 1982, 58; *OLG*, Hamburg, 11 Nov. 1982, GRUR Int. 1983, 305 (both noted and discussed by Roth (1991) 28 CMLRev. 137 at 156. See also *OLG*, Karlsruhe, 28 Sept. 1988, 6U 145/88, ZLR 1989, 480; GRUR 1989, 697 (noted by Tegeder (1994) 19 ELRev. 86).

(C) Article 30 and other Articles in the EC Treaty

The relationship between Article 30 and various other Treaty Articles can be a complex question and the ECJ has maintained a strict division between the free-movement-of-goods provisions and other Treaty Articles. In *Ianelli and Volpi*[16] the ECJ held that 'however wide the field of application of Article 30 may be, it nevertheless does not include obstacles to trade covered by other provisions of the Treaty'.

With respect to the distinction between the goods and services provisions in the EC Treaty, Article 60 EC expressly provides that 'services shall be considered to be "services" within the meaning of this Treaty . . . in so far as they are not governed by the provisions relating to freedom of movement for goods'. However, the ECJ has approached the delimitation between the goods and services provisions by examining, in each case, whether the measure in question affects predominantly goods or services.[17] This was confirmed in the recent judgment of the ECJ in *Openbaar Ministerie* v. *J. G. C. van Schaik*.[18] The latter case concerned the compatibility of the Dutch Road Traffic Law with the provisions of Community law. On the facts of the case, van Schaik was prosecuted for driving along the A12 in the Netherlands in a car without a valid Netherlands *APK* (*Algemene Periodieke Keuring*) certificate[19] contrary to Article 9a(1)(d) of the *Wegenverkeerswet* (*WVW*: Road Traffic Act). With respect to the provisions on the free movement of goods, van Schaik argued that the *APK* regulations might have the effect that car owners might not avail themselves of the perhaps cheaper services of garage businesses in other Member States, and of the possibility of obtaining the requisite spare parts there, because it is practical to have maintenance and repairs carried out in a garage in which the periodic vehicle roadworthiness test can be carried out as part and parcel of a repair or a service. The ECJ refused to deal with the free-movement-of-goods point referred to it and held that the supply of goods (spare parts, oil etc.) during servicing in another Member State was 'incidental to the provision of services'; thus the ECJ dealt with the matter exclusively on the basis of the freedom to provide services.[20] While it is true that the services were the main activity in *van Schaik* and that the ECJ was merely being realistic as to the economic realities involved in that

---

[16] n. 3 above at para. 9.

[17] See, e.g., the ECJ judgments in Case 155/73 *Sacchi* [1974] ECR 409, [1974] 2 CMLR 177; Case 52/79 *Debauve* [1980] ECR 833 and Case C–275/92 *HM Customs and Excise* v. *Schindler* [1994] ECR I–1039.

[18] Case C–55/93 [1994] ECR I–4837.   [19] Vehicle roadworthiness test certificate.

[20] Case C–55/93 [1994] ECR I–4837, citing Case C–275/92, n. 17 above. The judgment was implemented by the *Hoge Raad* on 6 Dec. 1994, NJ 1995, 210, NJB Bijl. 1995, 186 where it was held that Art. 9a *WVW* was not contrary to EC law and the conviction of van Schaik was accordingly upheld.

case, it is submitted that it is regrettable that the ECJ passed over the Article 30 point. This is particularly the case when one considers that the *Hoge Raad* had, in its referring judgment,[21] found as a matter of fact that there was a potential effect on trade (albeit on a small scale in border regions). It is submitted that it would thus have been desirable for the ECJ to have addressed the Article 30 point referred to it by the national court regarding the 'actual or potential' effect on trade, rather than rejecting the application of Article 30 on the basis that the effect on trade was merely 'incidental to the provision of services'.[22] Such an interpretation would have been more consistent with the residuary role which is envisaged for the services provisions by Article 60 EC.

The national courts have occasionally unduly confused the provisions concerning the free movement of goods with those concerning competition law (Articles 85 and 86 EC). For example, in *Geniteau*[23] the French *Cour de Cassation* implicitly suggested that Article 36 (setting out justifications for breaches of Article 30) could be invoked to justify a breach of Article 85 EC (prohibiting anti-competitive agreements). Similarly, the *Tribunal de grande instance* of Paris held in *Fromagerie Bel—La vache qui rit* v. *SA Entremont*[24] that Article 36 could justify a breach of Article 86 EC (prohibiting abuse of dominant position).[25] It is beyond doubt that Article 36 provides for justifications for breaches of Articles 30 and 34 only, and cannot, contrary to what was suggested in the latter two national court judgments, be invoked to justify breaches of other Treaty Articles.[26]

With respect to the distinction between the provisions concerning free movement of goods and those concerning State aid (Articles 92 to 94 EC), the ECJ initially took the view that State aid could not be evaluated under Article 30. In *Ianelli*,[27] the ECJ held that:

The effect of an interpretation of Article 30 which is so wide as to treat an aid as such within the meaning of Article 92 as being similar to a quantitative restriction

---

[21] *Hoge Raad (Strafkamer)*, 16 Feb. 1993, NJ 1993, 368 (with note by ter Kuile); Verkeersrecht 1993, no. 120, p. 290

[22] See further discussion of this judgt at p. 105.

[23] *Cour de Cassation*, ch. crim., 17 June 1992, Bull. Cass. Crim. 1992, No. 244 p. 670; [1993] 1 CMLR 243.

[24] *TGI* Paris, 3e ch. II, 9 Jan. 1986, Annales de la propriété industrielle, artistique et littéraire 1988, 187.

[25] See also the judgments of the French courts to the same effect in *CSNRA* v. *Sodialfo—Rennes Ouest*, Trib. comm. Rennes (*Référés*), 12 July 1983, Gaz. Pal. 1983, II Jur. 585; *SARL Hoffmann* v. *Établissements Edouard Leclerc, TGI* Saint-Quentin (*Référés*), 4 Aug. 1983, Gaz. Pal. 1983, II Jur. 480; *Chambre syndicale nationale du commerce et de la réparation de l'automobile (CSNCRA)* v. *SA Allouette Distribution, Trib. comm.* Tours (*Référés*), 2 Aug. 1983, Gaz. Pal. 1983, II Som. 342 (summary).

[26] The very wording of Art. 36 confirms this by stating that 'The provisions of Articles 30 to 34 shall not preclude prohibition or restrictions'. See also the judgment of Whitford J to this effect in the Ch D, High Court in *Hoover Plc* v. *George Hulme* [1982] CMLR 186, [1982] FSR 565.

[27] Case 74/76, n. 3 above.

referred to in Article 30 would be to alter the scope of Articles 92 and 93 of the Treaty and to interfere with the system adopted in the Treaty for the division of powers by means of the procedure for keeping aids under constant review as described in Article 93.[28]

The ECJ proceeded in the *Ianelli* case to develop a so-called 'severability test' under which a national court should examine whether a measure under review is distinguishable from the aid itself. If so, Article 30 may, according to the ECJ, nevertheless apply to the severed part of the measure.[29] The foregoing analysis was applied by Oxford Crown Court and the Court of Appeal in *Potato Marketing Board* v. *Robertsons*[30] and *Potato Marketing Board* v. *Drysdale*[31] respectively. These cases concerned the Potato Marketing Scheme in the United Kingdom and the suit of registered potato producers for payment of a potato farming levy due under the Potato Marketing Scheme. The English courts established that the scheme constituted an existing State aid and the only question was whether the fact that the Scheme was covered by Articles 92 and 93 EC precluded the application of Article 34. Both courts answered the latter question in the affirmative, following and applying to the letter the ECJ's *Ianelli* judgment. Thus, the English courts accepted the argument that if Article 34 were to be applied in such circumstances, the State aid provisions would be superfluous or 'largely inoperable'. Very commendably, the English courts went on to apply the severability test outlined above and concluded that 'there are no aspects of the system of aid operated by the Board which are relevant to Article 34 and which are not necessary for the attainment of its object or for its proper functioning', and thus the issues concerning the free movement of goods were held not to be severable from the State aid elements.[32]

In more recent case law, the ECJ has however shifted its position since the *Ianelli* judgment and has moved more towards giving priority to the provisions concerning free movement of goods over those on State aid. In a series of cases since *Ianelli*, the ECJ has held that 'the fact that a national measure might be regarded as aid within the meaning of Article 92 is . . . not sufficient reason to exempt it from the prohibition contained in Article 30'.[33] It

---

[28] Para. 12 of judgt.

[29] See para. 14 of ECJ judgt. See also Case 249/81 *Commission* v. *Ireland* (Buy Irish) [1982] ECR 4005, [1983] 2 CMLR 104 at para. 18.

[30] [1983] 1 CMLR 93.   [31] [1986] 3 CMLR 331.

[32] [1983] 1 CMLR 93 at 116. The English courts proceeded to underline their conclusion in both these cases by holding that, in any event, Art. 34 would not be breached even if it were applied. See discussion of this aspect of these judgts at p. 136.

[33] Case 103/84 *Italy* v. *Commission* [1986] ECR 1759 at para. 15. See also Case 18/84 *Commission* v. *France* [1985] ECR 1339, [1986] 1 CMLR 605; Case C–21/88 *Du Pont de Namours* [1990] ECR I–889 and Case C–351/88 *Laboratori Bruneau* [1991] ECR I–3641.

appears therefore that the *Ianelli* judgment has, at least to a certain extent, been reversed.[34]

Finally, the ECJ has adhered to a strict distinction between the free-movement-of-goods provisions and those on, respectively, internal taxation (Article 95 EC) and charges having equivalent effect to Customs duties (Articles 9 to 16 EC). The classic case confirming this is *Officier van Justitie* v. *Kortmann*[35] which concerned a parallel importer of pharmaceutical products claiming that the cost incurred for registration of the pharmaceuticals in the Netherlands was contrary to Article 30 on the grounds that such registration, following the ECJ judgment in *de Peijper*,[36] was unnecessary since the official importer had already effected such registration. The ECJ held that, contrary to the assumption of the national court in the questions referred,[37] such costs, involving the payment of a sum of money, fell to be considered under Articles 9 and 95 rather than Article 30.

The national courts have a poor record in maintaining a clear distinction between Articles 30 to 36 EC and those of Articles 9 *et seq.* and Article 95. In *Zuid Vleeshandel BV* v. *Produktschap voor Vee en Vlees*,[38] the *CBB* held that charges imposed by the *Produktschap voor Vee en Vlees* (Cattle and Meat Board) did not breach Articles 30 to 34 EC. It is submitted that the charges in question should have been analysed under Articles 16 or 95 EC which the *CBB* did not even mention.[39] Equally the French *Cour de Cassation*[40] rejected an alleged breach of Article 30 by certain tariffs on road transport without mentioning Article 95, which would appear to have been the more correct Treaty Article on the facts in that case.[41] The clear delineation between these Articles established by the ECJ does not therefore seem to have been followed or respected to a satisfactory extent by the national courts.

---

[34] The apparent departure of the ECJ in these cases from the position in *Ianelli* has been criticized. See Fernandez Martin & Stehmann, 'Product Market Integration versus Regional Cohesion in the Community' (1990) 15 ELRev. 216 where they state, 'If one follows strictly the Court's reasoning of giving priority to the application of Article 30 which is moreover not subject to a *de minimis* rule, Articles 92 and 93 would lose much of their sense. From an economic point of view the Court's position leads to favouring market integration—represented by the free movement of goods provisions—to the detriment of regional cohesion—represented by the State aids provisions'.

[35] Case 32/80 [1981] ECR 252, [1982] 3 CMLR 46.

[36] Case 104/75 [1976] ECR 613, [1976] 2 CMLR 271.

[37] *Arrondissementsrechtbank* Roermond, 4 Dec. 1979, [1980] 3 CMLR 296. See also the ECJ judgments in Case 27/67 *Fink-Frucht* v. *Hauptzollamt München* [1968] ECR 223, [1968] CMLR 228 and Case 252/86 *Bergandi* v. *Directeur-Général des Impôts* [1988] ECR 1343.

[38] *CBB*, 2 May 1985 (transcr.: *CBB*).

[39] See also *Holland Champignons BV* v. *Produktschap voor Groenten en Fruit*, *CBB*, 10 Apr. 1987, SEW 1988, 486 (with note by Mortelmans).

[40] *Jandet*, *Cour de Cassation*, ch. crim., 23 Nov. 1987, Bull. Cass. Crim. 1987, no. 421 p. 1109.

[41] See Case 20/76 *Schottle* v. *Finanzamt Freudenstadt* [1977] ECR 247, [1977] 2 CMLR 98.

One final point needs to be raised concerning the relationship between Article 30 and Article 95. In *Commission* v. *Denmark*,[42] the ECJ was faced with an action brought by the Commission against Denmark for an infringement of Article 95 through the imposition of high internal taxation on personal motor vehicles in Denmark. Since there was no domestic production of cars in Denmark, the ECJ held that Article 95 could not be applied to such a tax because, in such circumstances, there is 'no basis for censuring the excessiveness of the level of taxation'.[43] Nevertheless, the ECJ went on to state that if the rate of taxation was so high that the free movement of goods within the common market would be impeded, 'appraising an adverse effect of that kind on the free movement of goods is by reference to the general rules contained in Article 30 *et seq.* of the Treaty'.[44]

The possibility of invoking Article 30 in circumstances when a form of taxation, though not contrary to Article 95, might nevertheless fall foul of Article 30 if its effect was to impede trade, arose before the English courts in *R.* v. *Cousins*. That case concerned excise duties on the importation of beer from France into the United Kingdom and the system for collecting such duties established by Directive 92/12.[45] It was argued *inter alia* that the latter Directive was incompatible with EC law. Both Southwark Crown Court[46] and the Court of Appeal (Criminal Division)[47] had little trouble in excluding the application of Article 95 since there was no evidence of any discriminatory or protective effect in the internal taxation. However, the argument that the system set up by the Directive might nevertheless infringe Article 30 was also raised before both courts. It was argued, relying on the ECJ judgment in *Commission* v. *Denmark*,[48] that although not contrary to Article 95, the system might nevertheless fall foul of Article 30 if its effect was to impede intra-Community trade.[49] Southwark Crown Court rejected this argument stating that the ECJ's judgment in *Commission* v. *Denmark* was 'in English terms' plainly *obiter dicta*. The Crown Court went on to state that:

---

[42] Case C–47/88 [1990] ECR I–4509.   [43] Ibid. at para. 10.

[44] Ibid. at para. 13. It may be noted that the Dutch *Hoge Raad* has applied this judgment and has held that the taxation of cars in the Netherlands fell to be considered under Art. 95 EC rather than Art. 30 EC since there was an (admittedly small) domestic production of cars in the Netherlands: *X* v. *Inspecteur der Omzetbelasting, Hoge Raad*, 23 Aug. 1996, *BNB* 1996, 403.

[45] [1992] OJ L76/1.   [46] [1995] 1 CMLR 654.

[47] [1995] 3 CMLR 220.   [48] n. 42 above.

[49] It was argued that the system of *reclaim* (as opposed to *suspension*) provided for in Directive 92/12, according to which an importer who buys beer and pays duty in the exporting State and also, on importation, the duty in the importing Member State, may subsequently reclaim the duty from the exporting State, is onerous and an impediment to the free movement of goods. In particular, it was pointed out that the importer would be out of pocket for a period and that Art. 7(5)(a) of the Directive requires that the importer make a declaration to the tax authorities of the Member State of importation.

[T]here is no reported decision of the European Court in which a fiscal measure—and I take the view that we are here dealing with a fiscal measure—there is no reported decision of the European Court holding that a fiscal measure is contrary to Article 30 of the Treaty of Rome.[50]

Irrespective of what may be the correct position as to the application of Article 30 to such measures, it is respectfully submitted that the reasoning of the Crown Court is flawed. In particular, the fact that there is 'no reported decision of the European Court holding that a fiscal measure is contrary to Article 30' is no reason to exclude such an application and, if anything, the absence of authority puts a greater presumption on the necessity to make a reference to the ECJ pursuant to Article 177 EC. The impact of the ECJ's *obiter* comment in *Commission* v. *Denmark*[51] concerning the possibility of invoking Article 30 in circumstances when a form of taxation, though not contrary to Article 95, might nevertheless fall foul of Article 30 if its effect was to impede trade, remains unclear. In this light, the conclusion of the Court of Appeal in *R.* v. *Cousins* that 'we do not refer a question to the European Court of Justice, as the answer is clear to us'[52] is regrettable.

2 QUANTITATIVE RESTRICTIONS

The first part of Article 30 provides for a prohibition on the imposition by Member States of quantitative restrictions on imports. Quantitative restrictions have been the subject of comparatively little litigation before either the ECJ or the national courts and have rarely been found to exist. This is largely due to the practical consideration that quantitative restrictions, unlike the more nebulous concept of 'measures having equivalent effect',[53] are transparent and difficult, if not impossible, for a Member State to maintain or conceal.

The imposition by a Member State of any import quotas will be considered to be a quantitative restriction and will therefore be unlawful. Equally, an outright import ban will also be prohibited. Such was made clear at an early stage by the ECJ. For example, in *Geddo* v. *Ente Nazionale Risi*,[54] the ECJ stated that 'The prohibition on quantitative restrictions covers measures which amount to a total or partial restraint of, according to

---

[50] n. 46 above at 663.   [51] Case C–47/88, n. 42 above.

[52] n. 47 above at 230.

[53] See discussion of the concept of 'measures having equivalent effect' under Art. 30 EC in sect. 3.

[54] Case 2/73 [1973] ECR 865. See also Case 7/61 *Commission* v. *Italy* [1961] ECR 633, [1962] CMLR 39; Case 7/68 *Commission* v. *Italy*, n. 4 above and Case 12/74 *Commission* v. *Germany* [1975] ECR 181, [1975] 1 CMLR 340.

the circumstances, imports, exports or goods in transit.' In spite of this clear statement by the ECJ that the term 'quantitative restrictions' includes 'total' restraints on imports, it is with some dismay that, in a judgment of the English Court of Appeal, such a clear interpretation was denied. In a well-known misapplication of Community law in the early days of the United Kingdom's membership of the European Community, Widgery LCJ in the Court of Appeal in *R.* v. *Henn and Darby*[55] held that a ban under section 42 of the Customs Consolidation Act 1876 on the importation of certain pornographic material from the Netherlands into the UK could not constitute a 'quantitative restriction' because '[T]he prohibition is total; the prohibition is on all obscene goods, not merely measured by quantity. At first blush . . . we would, I think, be inclined to say that Article 30 did not apply to this case because the restriction was not related to a quantitative measure.'[56] Widgery LCJ went on to add, 'We . . . find it extremely difficult to see how the adjective "quantitative" can appear in [Article 30] except in order to limit the prohibition to those concerned with quantity.'[57] Even allowing for the fact that the United Kingdom had, at the time of this judgment, only been a Member State of the EC for five years, this was, with respect, a poor application of Community law. The judgment of the ECJ in *Geddo* v. *Ente Nazionale Risi*[58] had, by referring to 'total' restraints on imports, made it clear that quantitative restrictions in Article 30 are not limited to numerical limits on importation to the exclusion of total bans (which involve no numerical limit). Rather, a total ban is, according to the interpretation of Article 30 by the ECJ, simply the lowest possible numerical ceiling (i.e. a quota of nil). In fairness to Widgery LCJ, it should be added that he did proceed to discuss Article 36 EC, and it was the fact that he was able to hold that the import ban would be justified under that Article, rather than the fact that he was 'inclined to say that Article 30 did not apply', that ultimately led him to decide not to refer the case to the ECJ under Article 177 EC. Nevertheless, the interpretation of 'quantitative restrictions' by the Court of Appeal is a classic example of the dangers of applying techniques of interpretation familiar to English law to Community legislation.[59] Gravells has described this literal interpretation of the adjective 'quantitative' as 'the very epitome of English law techniques of statutory interpretation, but applied to Community legislation which was not drafted in the manner of a UK statute and which is not,

---

[55] [1978] 2 CMLR 688, [1978] 1 WLR 1031, [1978] 3 All ER 1190.
[56] [1978] 2 CMLR 688 at 691.   [57] Ibid.   [58] Case 2/73, n. 54 above.
[59] The Common law tradition seeks to give effect to the literal meaning of legislation: the so-called 'rule of exclusion' binds judges to the letter of the statute, precluding consultation of *travaux préparatoires* to discover Parliament's intention at the time of the enactment of the legislation. By contrast, continental civil law systems proceed on the principle *ejus est interpretari cujus est condere* (it behoves he who makes the law to interpret it). See Van Caenegem, *Judges, Legislators and Professors. Chapters in European Legal History* (CUP, 1987) at 17–20.

therefore, susceptible to such techniques'.[60] On appeal, the House of Lords referred the matter to the ECJ and Lord Diplock warned against 'applying English canons of statutory construction' in the interpretation of Community legislation in the following terms:

The European Court in contrast to English courts, applies teleological rather than historical methods to the interpretation of the Treaties and other Community legislation. It seeks to give effect to what it conceives to be the spirit rather than the letter of the Treaties; sometimes, indeed, to an English judge, it may seem to the exclusion of the letter. It views the Communities as living and expanding organisms and the interpretation of the provisions of the Treaties as changing to match their growth.[61]

Thus, adopting a teleological approach, it is not surprising that the ECJ should find that the underlying aim in Article 30 is to promote the free movement of goods by prohibiting all measures that constitute an obstacle, *a fortiori* those which constitute a complete prohibition rendering free movement impossible. On this purposive view, import bans merely represent quantitative restrictions in their most extreme form.[62]

The judgment of the Court of Appeal in *Henn and Darby* may be considered as the low-water mark in the English courts' interpretation of 'quantitative restrictions' in Article 30. The subsequent judgment of the ECJ in that case, which unequivocally held that import bans constituted quantitative restrictions prohibited by Article 30, served the purpose, at least, of getting the message through: no similar error has been made in subsequent judgments by the English Courts. Thus, in *R. v. Bow Street Magistrates' Court and Martin Dubbey, ex. p. Noncyp Ltd*, both the High Court[63] and the Court of Appeal[64] held on similar facts to those in *Henn and Darby* that an absolute ban on the import from other Member States of obscene materials constituted a quantitative restriction, subject to justification under Article 36 EC.[65] That the message had firmly filtered through is further demonstrated by the words of Lord Denning in the Court of Appeal in *Allgemeine Gold- und Silberscheideanstalt v. Commissioners of Customs and Excise*[66] in a case concerning the forfeiture of imported coins:

---

[60] (1978) ELRev. 442 at 443.   [61] [1980] 2 CMLR 229 at 233.
[62] See Case 34/79 *R. v. Henn and Darby* [1979] ECR 3795; [1980] 1 CMLR 246 at para. 12. It may be noted that while the House of Lords had asked the ECJ whether the ban constituted a measure having equivalent effect, the ECJ held, without commenting on the matter, that the ban constituted a quantitative restriction.
[63] [1988] 3 CMLR 84; [1988] 3 WLR 827. Woolf LJ (as he then was) held (at [1988] 3 CMLR 87): 'It is not necessary to set out the provisions of Art. 30 because it is common ground that the seizure of the books would contravene Art. 30 and therefore be unlawful as being a quantitative restriction which is prohibited between Member States.'
[64] [1989] 1 CMLR 634; [1989] RTDE 716; [1989] 3 WLR 467; [1990] 1 QB 123 (CA). Croom-Johnson LJ held at [1989] 1 CMLR 637 that: 'there is no dispute about the effect of Art. 30'.
[65] See discussion of the 'public morality' justification under Art. 36 in Ch. 7, sect. 2.
[66] [1980] 2 CMLR 488; [1980] 1 QB 390 (CA); [1980] 2 WLR 555.

If we were to interpret the words 'quantitative' in the ordinary English way, Article 30 would seem to have something to do with quantity. But the European Court does not interpret the Treaty literally. They give the Article a much broader and more sensible interpretation. They interpret it as meaning that there are to be no restrictions on imports between Member States.[67]

The message in R. v. *Henn and Darby* was equally clear to the Irish High Court in *United States Tobacco (Ireland)* v. *Ireland*,[68] where Blayney J held that, following the ECJ judgment in *Henn and Darby*, it would be 'impossible' to argue that the words 'quantitative restrictions' in Article 30 did not cover a complete ban on the import of oral tobacco into the Irish Republic.

It appears therefore that it was the judgment of the ECJ in *Henn and Darby* which proved to be the most influential judgment for the national courts in interpreting the words 'quantitative restrictions' under Article 30. Nevertheless, national courts have not always taken care to specify whether the particular national measure found to be in breach of Article 30 is a 'quantitative restriction' or a 'measure having equivalent effect'.[69] While this may in theory be considered to be rather unsatisfactory, in practical terms, the result is not seriously objectionable since both types of measure are in any event prohibited by Article 30. Furthermore, the ECJ itself frequently states that national measures are contrary to Article 30 without specifying whether the national measures constituted 'quantitative restrictions' or 'measures having equivalent effect'.[70] It is submitted that, so long as the practical significance of the distinction between the two terms in an individual case is negligible, the lack of specificity in the case law of both the national courts and the ECJ is of little consequence.[71]

On the other hand, the practical significance of the distinction between 'quantitative restrictions' and 'measures having equivalent effect' will not, in all cases, be negligible. The loose distinction between these two terms

---

[67] [1980] 2 CMLR 488 at 489. See even more emphatically, Lord Diplock in R. v. *Goldstein* [1983] 1 CMLR 244 at 246 (concerning a ban on the import of Citizens' Band (CB) radios into the UK) who stated that: 'It is also well established, not surprisingly, by the jurisprudence (i.e. case law) of the European Court of Justice that a total prohibition upon imports is a quantitative restriction within the meaning of Art. 30'.

[68] [1993] 1 IR 241.

[69] See, e.g., the national court judgments in *SARL Les fils de Henri Ramel* v. *Ministre de l'interieur et Préfet de l'Hérault, Conseil d'Etat,* 7 Dec. 1979, Dalloz 1980, Jur. 303; Rec. Lebon 1979, 456; JCP 1981, II 19500 (with note by Pacteau); *Société Acopasa* v. *Ministre du Commerce extérieur, Conseil D'Etat,* 28 Mar. 1990, JCP 1990, IV 179; *Roland Perron* v. *Ministère public, Cour de Cassation,* ch. crim., 17 Feb. 1988, Bull. Cass. Crim. 1988, 207; Gaz. Pal. 1988, I Jur. 848; and note by Berr, La Semaine Juridique—éd. entreprise 1989, II 15556; *McAfee* v. *Smyth and Quigley,* Belfast Recorder's Court [1981] 1 CMLR 410 and R. v. *Thompson, Johnson and Woodiwiss* [1978] 1 CMLR 390; [1980] 2 All ER 102 (CA).

[70] See, e.g., the ECJ judgments in Case 40/82 *Commission* v. *United Kingdom* (Newcastle Disease) [1982] ECR 2793 and Case 194/85 *Commission* v. *Greece* [1988] ECR 1037.

[71] For further discussion of this point, see Oliver, *Free Movement of Goods in the European Community,* 67–8.

can lead to abuse. Three judgments by national courts illustrate this danger. Firstly, in two cases before the French *Conseil d'Etat*, the compatibility of Article L.162-38 of the French *Code de la securité sociale* (Social Security Act) and Article 30 EC was at issue. That Article of the *Code de la securité sociale* provided that the Ministers of Economics, of Health and of Social Security may, by means of *arrêtés*, fix the profit margins for the sale of certain medical products in France. In *SA Des Laboratoires Merck Sharp Dohme Chibret*[72] and *Lacombe*[73] pharmacies challenged certain such *arrêtés* on several grounds of French law but also on grounds that they infringed Article 30 EC. In both cases, the *Conseil d'Etat* rejected the Article 30 argument. In the *Laboratoires Merck* case, the *Conseil d'Etat* simply held that there was 'nothing in the file demonstrating that the lowering of the price of Zocor [the product at issue in that case] was of such a nature as to cause quantitative restrictions on importation or exportation of products'. In *Lacombe*, the *Conseil d'Etat* equally briefly dismissed the argument by holding that the *arrêté* under challenge in that case 'did not have the effect of reducing the quantities of imported medical products'. In the absence of fuller reasoning by the *Conseil d'Etat*, it is difficult to second-guess the *ratio* of these brief judgments. It is submitted that, even allowing for the brevity that is customary in decisions of the *Conseil d'Etat*, the perfunctory dismissal of the arguments in these cases which were based on EC law is too brief by any standards.[74] It appears that the *Conseil d'Etat* rejected the Article 30 argument on the basis that the national measures did not affect the quantity of imports and could not therefore constitute quantitative restrictions. There is in these judgments a conspicuous absence of discussion of measures having equivalent effect under Article 30. Under the ECJ's case law on measures having equivalent effect, it has been held that demonstrating an actual effect on imports is not a prerequisite for that Article to bite.[75] On the given facts it would seem that a more satisfactory approach would have been to have applied the ECJ's well-established case law on price-fixing and to hold that although national price-control rules applicable without distinction to both domestic and imported products cannot in general restrict imports, they may do so in certain specific cases where the profit margin in an individual *arrêté* is set at a level such that imported products are placed at a disadvantage in relation to identical domestic products, either because they cannot profitably be marketed in the conditions laid down, or because the competitive advantage conferred by lower cost

---

[72] *Conseil d'Etat*, 29 July 1994, Rev. juris. social 1994, 1186.

[73] *Conseil d'Etat*, 12 June 1992, Rec. Lebon 1992, 230.

[74] See discussion of the influence on the application of EC law by national courts of the style of judgments according to national legal traditions at p. 254.

[75] See, e.g., Case 249/81 *Commission* v. *Ireland* ('Buy Irish') n. 29 above. For further discussion of this point see Ch. 3.

prices is cancelled out.[76] If such was the case, Article 30 would be breached and the *arrêté* would have to be justified under the protection of health justification provided for in Article 36 EC.[77] The difficulty is that the judgments of the *Conseil d'Etat* in these cases are so brief that it is impossible to fathom whether, for example, the profit margins set resulted in importation of the medical products in question being made impossible or more difficult in practice. What is clear, however, is that the *Conseil d'Etat*'s reasoning is, with respect, incomplete since it mentioned only the possibility that the national measures may constitute a 'quantitative restriction' under Article 30 without proceeding to consider whether the measures may also constitute 'measures having equivalent effect' under that same Article. It is not suggested that the loose distinction between the concepts of 'quantitative restrictions' and 'measures having equivalent effect' in ECJ case law encourages such incomplete reasoning in the national courts. Nevertheless, a clearer distinction between, and definition of, each concept would be desirable. If the demarcation line between 'quantitative restrictions' and 'measures having equivalent effect' was more rigorously indicated and defined in ECJ judgments, the national courts would be more readily precluded from construing a national measure as a 'quantitative restriction' in cases where, as in these two cases before the French *Conseil d'Etat*, the measure is more properly to be construed as a 'measure having equivalent effect'.

A further judgment by a national court which provides support for the fact that further elaboration on the distinction between 'quantitative restrictions' and 'measures having equivalent effect' is both necessary and desirable, is the decision in interim proceedings of the President of the *Rechtbank* Haarlem in *Esge SA* v. *Alpha Trading BV and Wigo*.[78] Esge was the manufacturer of the 'Bamix' mixer (a food blender) in the Netherlands and brought an action for tort under Article 1401 *Burgerlijk Wetboek* (*BW*: Civil Code)[79] to prevent *slaafse nabootsing* (passing off) by Wigo GmbH who manufactured the 'K–24' mixer in Germany and imported it into the Netherlands. The *Rechtbank* held that the similarities between the two mixers were such that the passing-off action should succeed. With respect to the argument that this would result in an import restriction which would breach Article 30, the President held:

Quantitative import restrictions within the meaning of [Article 30] refer to legal or administrative provisions or administrative measures which restrict the import or export of one or more products with regard to their number or value. In our

---

[76] See discussion of price-fixing in sect. 5(B) (*vii*).
[77] See Case 65/75 *Tasca* [1976] ECR 291, [1977] 2 CMLR 183 and Case 82/77 *Van Tiggele* [1978] ECR 25, [1978] 2 CMLR 528.
[78] *Arrondissementsrechtbank*, Haarlem, 29 Jan. 1980, BIE 1982, 87.
[79] Now Art. 6:162 *Nieuw Burgerlijk Wetboek* (*NBW*).

interim judgment, judicial decisions holding that a ban such as that applied for in this case, are not covered by that term.

It is submitted that this statement is, with respect, an incomplete application of Article 30. As in the two *Conseil d'Etat* judgments discussed above, the *Rechtbank* Haarlem rejected the possibility of the existence of a quantitative restriction, but did not proceed to discuss whether judicial decisions fleshing out and elaborating on the wording in legislation could constitute a 'measure having equivalent effect' under Article 30. The ECJ's case law concerning intellectual property rights makes clear that judicial decisions interpreting national legislation in such a way that the free movement of goods is restricted, are capable of constituting measures having equivalent effect under Article 30.[80] Fortunately, an appeal against this judgment was allowed by the *Gerechtshof* Amsterdam[81] which had absolutely no hesitation in holding that 'it is in principle contrary to the free movement of goods within the common market that Esge AG relies on its right granted by Article 1401 *BW*'. Nevertheless, the judgment of the court below demonstrates that national courts are occasionally too quick to construe a national measure as a quantitative restriction to the exclusion of measures having equivalent effect. In individual cases, this may lead to incorrect applications of Article 30. Whether a more rigorous approach by the ECJ in its own case law, taking care to specify in each case whether a quantitative restriction rather than a measure having equivalent effect is at issue, would limit such 'misapplications' is open to question. Nevertheless, it is submitted that a more tightly defined concept of quantitative restrictions by the ECJ can only reduce the possibility that national courts will construe national measures as quantitative restrictions to the exclusion of measures having equivalent effect.

3 MEASURES HAVING EQUIVALENT EFFECT

The second limb of Article 30 provides that all 'measures having equivalent effect' to quantitative restrictions are prohibited. It is the definition of what exactly a 'measure having equivalent effect' is, that has been the subject of most ECJ case law. The ECJ has consistently held that a measure having equivalent effect to a quantitative restriction should be understood as covering:

---

[80] See discussion in Ch. 8. See also ECJ decisions in Case 6/81 *BV Industrie Diensten Groep* v. *J. A. Beele Handelsmaatschappij BV* [1982] ECR 707, [1982] 3 CMLR 102 and Case 58/80 *Dansk Supermarked* v. *Imerco* [1981] ECR 181, [1981] 3 CMLR 590.

[81] *Gerechtshof* Amsterdam, 25 Sept. 1980, BIE 1982, 87.

All trading rules enacted by Member States which are capable of hindering, directly or indirectly, actually or potentially, intra-Community trade.[82]

This classic exposition, which has become known as the *Dassonville* formula, is striking for its breadth. It remains the basic starting point for any legal analysis of the compatibility of a national measure with Article 30. The facts at issue in *Dassonville* concerned Belgian legislation which required importation of goods bearing a designation of origin to be accompanied by an official document certifying the origin and authenticity of the goods. Dassonville was prosecuted for importing Scotch whisky from France into Belgium without such a certificate. The ECJ held that the Belgian legislation was a measure having equivalent effect to a quantitative restriction, since only direct importers of Scotch from the United Kingdom were in a position to furnish certificates of origin without any difficulty, whereas importers of Scotch from a Member State other than the United Kingdom where the product had been put into free circulation, would have difficulty in adducing such certificates. Thus, the Belgian legislation was held 'capable of hindering, directly or indirectly, actually or potentially, intra-Community trade' and thus prohibited by Article 30 EC.

The facts of the *Dassonville* case give a flavour of the type of measures that will fall within the *Dassonville* formula. However, to provide a clearer picture of the broad scope of the measures caught by Article 30, a full analysis of the constituent parts of the *Dassonville* formula is instructive. To this end, national case law applying the first part of the *Dassonville* formula (*'all trading rules enacted by Member States which are capable of hindering directly or indirectly'*) will be discussed in the remainder of this chapter. In the following chapter, national case law concerned with the last part of the *Dassonville* formula (*'actually or potentially hindering intra-Community trade'*) will be discussed.

However, before moving on to discuss national case law on the constituent parts of the *Dassonville* formula, one interesting point concerning the meaning of measures having equivalent effect to quantitative restrictions which has arisen before the English courts merits brief discussion. In *R. v. H. M. Treasury and The Bank of England, ex. p. Centro-Com Srl*,[83] the question arose as to whether Article 30 applied in cases where the national measure, rather than restricting imports, actually increased imports from other Member States. The case concerned the implementation in the United Kingdom of Community Regulation 1432/92 (which was in itself the implementation of United Nations Security Council Resolution 757 of

---

[82] Case 8/74 *Procureur du Roi* v. *Dassonville* [1974] ECR 837, [1974] 2 CMLR 436, para. 5.

[83] [1994] 1 CMLR 109; CA (Civil Division), The Independent 3 June 1994 (transcr.: John Larking).

30 May 1992 imposing sanctions on trade with Serbia and Montenegro) in the Serbia and Montenegro (United Nations Sanctions) Order 1992.[84] The UN Resolution and the Community Regulation prohibited exports to Serbia and Montenegro, and payments for such exports from Serbian and Montenegran funds held in Member States, with the exception of exports (and related payments) of medicines or food notified to the United Nations Yugoslavia Sanctions Committee. This was implemented in the United Kingdom by freezing all Serbian bank accounts in the United Kingdom although they could be unfrozen for payments relating to authorized exports of medicines, provided that the export of the medicines was from the United Kingdom. Centro-Com Srl, an Italian company, had obtained authorization for such an export from Italy under the equivalent Italian legislation implementing the EC Regulation and sought payment from the National Bank of Yugoslavia's bank account in the United Kingdom. Approval for this was refused by the Bank of England since the exportation had not been from the United Kingdom but rather from Italy. Centro-Com challenged this refusal before the English courts on the grounds, *inter alia*, that it breached Article 30 EC. It was argued that that Article was breached because the United Kingdom implementation distorted the pattern or flow of trade by encouraging the manufacture in the United Kingdom of medical goods that were currently manufactured in other Member States, and by requiring manufacturers in other Member States seeking to export such goods to Serbia and Montenegro to route them via the United Kingdom, thus imposing on them greater costs than those which were borne by United Kingdom manufacturers. This argument was rejected by the High Court which held that rather than encouraging manufacture of medical products in the United Kingdom, the effect of the policy was in effect to encourage importation of the goods into the United Kingdom for re-exportation to Serbia and Montenegro.[85] This was upheld by the Court of Appeal, which distinguished the ECJ's judgment in *Generics* v. *Smith Kline and French*[86] on the basis that that case was concerned with a licensing system which tended to restrict imports from some Member States, whereas in the present case, the result was to route some goods from other Member States via the United Kingdom and this would tend to increase, not restrict, imports. Glidewell LJ concluded that 'I am confident that Article 30 has no application to the facts of this case'. The

---

[84] SI 1992/1302.

[85] The High Court distinguished the ECJ authorities in Case 434/85 *Allen and Hanburys* v. *Generics (UK)* [1988] ECR 1245, [1988] CMLR 701; Case C–30/90 *Commission* v. *United Kingdom* [1992] ECR I–829, [1992] 2 CMLR 709 and Case C–191/90 *Generics* v. *Smith Kline and French* [1992] ECR I–5335, [1993] 1 CMLR 89 where the encouraging of local manufacture or so-called 'local grab' measures, were held to breach Art. 30. See discussion of these judgments in Ch. 8, sect. 2.

[86] n. 85 above.

argument that the national policy would not have the effect of encouraging manufacture in the United Kingdom is, it is submitted, contestable on the facts. Nevertheless, what is of interest in the present context is the assumption by the English courts that if the consequence of national measures is to increase imports (to the extent that exports to third countries from other Member States had to be routed through the UK) the application of Article 30 will be excluded. It is submitted that the UK policy in this case, if it did not favour the manufacture of medical products in the United Kingdom, at the very least sufficiently affected the patterns or flow of trade within the single market for Article 30 to bite. While the High Court discussed the possibility, in the alternative, that the national measure could be justified under the public-policy head of justification under Article 36, the Court of Appeal was so certain that Article 30 was not breached that it did not judge it necessary even to discuss Article 36. It is submitted that the Article 30 point should have been referred to the ECJ for a preliminary ruling. Given that the Court of Appeal did in this case refer questions to the ECJ concerning the Common Commercial Policy and Article 113 EC, it is regrettable that it did not also attach questions concerning Article 30 for the ECJ.[87] For the moment, therefore, the English Courts are of the view that national measures which affect the channels and patterns of trade within the Community do not constitute measures of equivalent effect to quantitative restrictions under Article 30 if the de facto result is that imports into a Member State are increased as a result of a re-routing requirement in the national measure.

4 ALL TRADING RULES ENACTED BY MEMBER STATES

According to the first limb of the *Dassonville* definition of measures having equivalent effect, Article 30 concerns only 'trading rules enacted by Member States'. It has subsequently become clear that the specific reference to 'trading rules' is not a strict requirement: Article 30 applies to any rules that affect access to the market in the broad sense. Thus, in *Commission* v. *Ireland* ('Buy Irish'),[88] funds from public authorities provided to a private company in order to advertise national products were held by the ECJ to be contrary to Article 30. It is with difficulty that such action may be regarded as a 'trading rule' and the conclusion is clearly that this part of the *Dassonville* formula must be liberally interpreted. The latter point is further supported by the fact that, although the *Dassonville*

---

[87] The ECJ handed down its judgment in this case in C–124/95 [1997] ECR I–81 where it held that the measures adopted by the UK were not compatible with the Common Commercial Policy as set out in Art. 113 EC.
[88] n. 29 above.

formula has been repeated time and time again by the ECJ as the classic definition of measures having equivalent effect, the term 'trading rules' is sometimes omitted and often replaced by the words 'any measures'.[89]

While the reference to 'trading rules' may be a relatively unimportant ingredient in measures having equivalent effect, the phrase 'enacted by Member States' is, by contrast, of legal significance. These words in the *Dassonville* formula strongly suggest that Article 30 is concerned exclusively with State measures. In other words, for a measure to fall foul of Article 30 it must have been enacted by the State. It would seem that the rationale behind this requirement is to preserve the integrity of the system of the EC Treaty: while the competition rules contained in Articles 85 and 86 EC regulate the compatibility of the behaviour of individuals and undertakings with regard to the common market, Article 30 applies only to measures taken by Member States, thereby avoiding overlap with, or undermining of, the application of the competition rules.[90] It may be noted however, that there is academic discussion as to whether Article 30 should be limited to measures enacted by Member States.[91] Admittedly, some ECJ case law interpreting other Treaty Articles lends support to the contention that Article 30 should have 'horizontal direct effect' and so be capable of binding individuals.[92] In the field of the compatibility of the exercise by individuals of intellectual property rights with the provisions concerning

[89] See, e.g. Cases 266 & 267/87 *R.* v. *The Royal Pharmaceutical Society of Great Britain, ex p. Association of Pharmaceutical Importers* [1989] ECR 1295 at para. 17 & Cases C–267 & 268/91 *Keck and Mithouard* [1993] ECR I–6097, [1995] 1 CMLR 101 at para. 11, where the term 'trading rules' was replaced by 'any measures'. Cf. para. 12 of Case C–470/93 *Verein gegen gegen Unwesen in Handel und Gewerbe Koeln* v. *Mars GmbH* [1995] ECR I–1923 where the term 'trading rules' was repeated as part of the *Dassonville* formula.

[90] It should, however, be noted that the harmonious development of the Treaty free-movement rules with the competition rules has been somewhat distorted by developments in ECJ case law with respect to Arts. 85 or 86 in combination with Arts. 5 & 3(f). See, e.g., Case 311/85 *Vlaamse Reisbureaus* v. *Sociale Dienst* [1987] ECR 3801; Case 267/86 *Van Eycke* v. *ASPA* [1988] ECR 4769 and Case C–2/91 *Meng* [1993] ECR I–5751. In the latter case, the ECJ held that although Arts. 85 & 86 are directed at undertakings, there is an obligation on Member States, derived from Art. 5 EC, not to introduce measures that render ineffective the competition rules as applied to undertakings. In this way, it may be argued that the ECJ is blurring the harmonious development of the rules on free movement and competition which is the very *raison d'être* of restricting the application of Art. 30 to measures enacted only by Member States. See VerLoren van Themaat, 'Gaat de Luxemburgse rechtspraak over de vier vrijheden en die over het mededingingsbeleid uiteenlopen?' (1996) SEW 398.

[91] See, e.g., Quinn & MacGowan 'Could Article 30 Impose Obligations on Individuals?'; Gormley, *Prohibiting Restrictions on Trade Within the EEC*, 259–62; Oliver, above n. 72, 56–60; Temmink, 'Reclamezelfregulering mag, maar er zijn Europeesrechtelijke grenzen' at 231–3 and Mortelmans, 'Excepties bij non-tarifaire intracommunautaire belemmering: assimilatie in het nieuwe EG-Verdrag?'

[92] See esp. Case 36/74 *Walrave* v. *Union Cycliste Internationale* [1974] ECR 1405, [1975] 1 CMLR 320; Case 13/76 *Donà* v. *Mantero* [1976] ECR 1333, [1976] 2 CMLR 578; Case 43/75 *Defrenne* v. *Sabena* [1976] ECR 455, [1976] 2 CMLR 98; Case C–415/93 *Union Royale Belge des Sociétés de Football Association ASBL* v. *Bosman* [1995] ECR I–4921 and Case C–16/94 *Dubois and General Cargo Services* v. *Garonor Exploitation* [1995] ECR I–2421.

free movement of goods, the requirement that the measure be enacted by Member States becomes particularly difficult to maintain.[93]

It is submitted, however, that the ECJ is of the view that Article 30 should apply to State measures alone. This emerges from its recent judgment in *Commission* v. *France*[94] where the failure of the French State to adopt adequate measures to prevent obstacles to the free movement of goods arising from the actions of private individuals (*in casu*: French farmers who had systematically over a period of years intercepted lorries transporting agricultural produce from other Member States and had destroyed these lorries' loads and had treated their drivers violently) was held to breach Article 30. The ECJ held that:

Article 30 . . . does not prohibit solely measures emanating from the State which, in themselves, create restrictions on trade between Member States. It also applies where a Member State abstains from adopting the measures required in order to deal with obstacles to the free movement of goods which are not caused by the State.[95]

The ECJ makes plain in this passage that Article 30 may be invoked in the circumstances outlined above, not because of the actions of the private individuals (the farmers) themselves, but rather because of the Member States' failure to take adequate action against those private individuals. Moreover, the view is supported by other ECJ case law, which takes care to define the circumstances under which measures are to be considered to have been enacted by the State. In such case law, for example, the ECJ has held that local government regulations are clearly covered by Article 30.[96] With respect to national public bodies, the ECJ has tended to conclude that measures taken by a public body may be considered to have been enacted by the Member State if the body in question was set up by national legislation,[97] is funded and appointed by the government[98] or exercises disciplinary control over its members.[99]

National case law interpreting the term 'trading rules' and the term 'enacted by Member States' will be examined in turn.

(A) Trading rules

In spite of the fact that, as was noted above, the words 'trading rules' have been loosely interpreted by the ECJ to cover any measures that affect

---

[93] See Ch. 8 for further discussion.

[94] Case C–265/95 *Commission* v. *France* [1997] ECR I-nyr (judgt 9 Dec. 1997).

[95] Ibid. at para. 30.

[96] Case 45/87 *Commission* v. *Ireland* (Dundalk Water) [1988] ECR 4929.

[97] Case 222/82 *Apple and Pear Development Council* v. *Lewis* [1983] ECR 4083, [1984] 3 CMLR 733.

[98] Case 249/81 *Commission* v. *Ireland* ('Buy Irish'), n. 29 above.

[99] *Ex p. Association of Pharmaceutical Importers*, n. 89 above.

access to the market in the broad sense, the reference to 'trading rules' in the *Dassonville* formula has caused some confusion in the national courts. In most such cases, the confusion has arisen from a reluctance on the part of the national court to accord such a broad interpretation to Article 30. This is evident from the fact that it is usually in those cases where the effect on trade between Member States is tenuous, that the national court is inclined to attach significance to the fact that the national rule in question is not a 'trading rule' in the formal sense. A good example is provided by national case law concerning shop opening hours and Article 30. In *W. H. Smith Do-It-All and Payless DIY Ltd* v. *Peterborough City Council*,[100] Peterborough Crown Court held the following with respect to Section 47 of the Shops Act 1950:

We are told that the term 'trading rule' seems never to have been defined in any decision of the European Court after the *Dassonville* case; but it has never been rejected as a term in any subsequent decision of the European Court. We concluded that a 'trading rule' is a measure or enactment passed by a Member State for the specific purpose of regulating trade . . . Since Section 47 is a Section of an Act of Parliament enacted to regulate measures other than trade, for example, the working times and practices of employees and the lives of purchasers . . . we concluded that it cannot be said to be a 'trading rule'. We concluded that it was not intended that the effect of Article 30 should be so wide as to overtake national regulatory provisions of Member States which are not passed specifically to regulate trade and which are not specifically aimed at imports from Member States.[101]

It is evident from this passage that the Crown Court was influenced by the fact that the connection between the Shops Act 1950 and trade between Member States was tenuous. The national court thus invoked a narrow interpretation of 'trading rules' to ensure that the legislation fell outside the ambit of Article 30. Fortunately, the High Court allowed an appeal against this judgment since the ECJ had, in the interim, handed down its *Torfaen* judgment where it held that Article 30 *was* breached by the very same United Kingdom legislation unless 'the restrictive effects on Community trade which may result therefrom do not exceed the effects intrinsic to rules of that kind'.[102] Following this ECJ judgment, the High Court had no difficulty in concluding that 'the reliance on the concept of "trading rules", which the respondents had pushed on the Crown Court, and which the latter adopted, were unsound.'[103] Thus, although the restrictive interpretation of the term 'trading rules' by Peterborough

[100] Not reported, but quoted in the judgt on appeal of the QBD: [1990] 2 CMLR 577; [1991] 1 QB 304; [1990] 3 WLR 1131; [1991] 4 All ER 193.
[101] [1991] 4 All ER 193 at 204.
[102] Case C–145/88 *Torfaen BC* v. *B & Q* [1989] ECR 3851, [1990] 1 CMLR 337 para. 17. For a detailed discussion of the national case law concerning free movement of goods and Sunday-trading legislation, see Ch. 6, sect. 4.
[103] n. 101 above at 212.

Crown Court in this case was overturned on appeal, the Crown Court's judgment illustrates that the use of the words 'trading rules' in the *Dassonville* formula is open to abuse by national courts wishing to restrict the breadth of Article 30. This is all the more worrying since the Crown Court had stated, 'We are sure of our conclusion and had no doubt that Section 47 remains current English law so that no reference should be made to the European Court.' Such certainty was, with respect, clearly premature given that the Crown Court had itself conceded that 'the term "trading rule" seems never to have been defined in any decision of the European Court'.[104]

The views of Peterborough Crown Court were echoed by Advocate General Leijten in his opinion to the *Hoge Raad* in *Officier van Justitie* v. *Makro Zelfbedieningsgroothandel Nuth CV*.[105] With respect to the compatibility of the *Winkelsluitingswet* (Shop Closing Hours Act) 1951 with Article 30 EC, the Advocate General quoted the *Dassonville* formula and opined *inter alia* that the Dutch legislation was not a 'trading rule' that hinders intra-Community trade. The Hoge Raad went on to reject the Article 30 argument on different grounds,[106] but the reliance by its Advocate General on the term 'trading rules' is another warning that this part of the *Dassonville* formula is open to abuse by national courts wishing to reach an over-restrictive interpretation of Article 30.[107]

The story of national courts' interpretation of the words 'trading rules' is not, however, simply one of abuse. In certain cases, the necessity of some 'trade' between Member States before Article 30 will apply remains distinctly unclear. This lack of clarity surfaced in *Generics* v. *Smith Kline and French Laboratories Ltd (SKF)* before the Dutch courts. In that case, SKF held the patent in the Netherlands for the process of preparing the histamine-H–2 receptor which was used to make cimetidine and marketed in the Netherlands under the name 'Tagamet'. This patent expired on 4 September 1993. On two occasions in 1987 and one in 1989, Genafarma BV applied for registration with the Dutch Pharmaceutical Evaluation Authority (*College ter beoordeling van geneesmiddelen (CBG)*) of cimetidine tablets under Article 29 of the Law on the Provision of Pharmaceuticals (*Wet op de Geneesmiddelenvoorziening (WGV)*). Genafarma BV was granted the registrations applied for in 1990 and 1992 respectively. On 21 June 1993, Genafarma BV transferred the registrations to Generics. SKF brought

---

[104] n. 100 above.

[105] *Hoge Raad*, (*Strafkamer*), 4 Nov. 1986, NJ 1987, 384 (with note by Van Veen); SEW 1990, 674 (with note by A.M.); (1988) EL Dig. 14; (1989) CDE 481–2.

[106] See discussion of these grounds at p. 101.

[107] See also the judgt of the QBD in *R.* v. *Birmingham City Council, ex p. Wesson* where Rose J distinguished ECJ authorities adopting a broad interpretation to Art. 30 on the basis that those cases were concerned 'manifestly . . . with a trade measure': [1992] 3 CMLR 377 at 383. See further discussion of this case at pp. 99–100.

an action before the Dutch courts arguing that the application for registration, which had involved the submitting to the *CBG* of samples of cimetidine, was an infringement of its Dutch patent under Dutch law. The *Gerechtshof Den Haag*[108] held that under Dutch law, the submitting of samples to the *CBG* of the patented drug for registration was indeed (while the patent was still valid) a patent infringement.[109] With respect to the argument advanced by Generics that this would breach Article 30 EC and not be justified under Article 36 EC, the *Gerechtshof* held that:

[T]he Court is of judgment that such a prohibition—which would of course only be permitted during the validity of the patent—does not hinder intra-Community trade. The submitting of samples of medicines does not fall within the meaning of trade in Article 30 EEC . . . Article 36 EEC does not thus need to be applied.

It is evident that the *Gerechtshof* reached this conclusion by putting emphasis on the requirement that 'trade' is required for Article 30 to apply and that submitting samples to a national medicine registration bureau did not constitute such 'trade'. On appeal, the *Hoge Raad* referred the question as to whether the Dutch legislation (making the submitting of samples for registration of a patented drug a breach of that patent) was in breach of Article 30. The ECJ held that such a rule of national law did breach Article 30 (but could be justified under Article 36) and referred in its judgment only to 'any measure' rather than to 'all trading rules' in the *Dassonville* formula.[110] This confirms that the term 'trading rules' is of little, if any, significance in ascertaining a breach of Article 30 and that the interpretation of the *Gerechtshof* Den Haag was unduly restrictive.

(B) Enacted by Member States

It was submitted above[111] that the words 'enacted by Member States' in the *Dassonville* formula have the consequence that Article 30 applies exclusively to State measures.[112] The ECJ has never had the opportunity to address the question of whether Article 34, which prohibits restrictions on exports, similarly only applies to State measures.[113] It is submitted that the

[108] 19 May 1994, IER 1994, 30; BIE 1995 32.
[109] The *Gerechtshof* reached this conclusion interpreting Art. 30(1) & 30(3) of the *Rijksoctrooiwet* (Patent Act).
[110] Case C–316/95 [1997] ECR I–3929. [111] See pp. 24–5.
[112] This has been followed by the Queen's Bench Division of the High Court in *Meat and Livestock Commission* v. *Manchester Wholesale Meat & Poultry Market* [1997] EuLR 136, [1997] 2 CMLR 361 where Moses J held that an advertising campaign conducted by the Meat and Livestock Commission, a statutory corporation upon which is imposed the general duty to create greater efficiency in the livestock and livestock-products industry in the UK, was capable of falling within the scope of Art. 30. See further discussion of this judgt. in sect. 5 (A) (*vi*).
[113] For a detailed discussion of national case law on Art. 34 and exports, see Ch. 4.

arguments that were outlined above to support the contention that Article 30 should be limited to State measures, should apply *mutatis mutandis* to Article 34. The latter issue surfaced in two recent English cases concerning the export of live animals for slaughter in other Member States. In both cases, the English courts assumed that, in order for Article 34 to bite, the restriction must have its origin in a State measure. In *R. v. Chief Constable of Sussex, ex p. International Trader's Ferry*,[114] the Chief Constable of Sussex had issued decisions to the effect that the local police had insufficient resources to provide effective police support for lorries containing live animals destined for export via the port of Shoreham for more than two days a week. Lorry movements, and thus exports, were effectively banned on other days. On those facts, it was accepted as common ground before the English High Court that 'the Chief Constable was to be construed as an "emanation" of the United Kingdom government for the purposes of Community law—see *Johnston v. Chief Constable RUC* [1988] ECR 1651.'[115] Similarly, in *R. v. Coventry City Council, ex p. Phoenix Aviation and others*,[116] there were before the High Court three applications for judicial review of decisions of various public authorities which had the effect of banning the export of live calves. The relevant decisions were that of Coventry City Council suspending flights from their airport, Dover Harbour Board suspending cross-Channel services carrying live animals and Associated British Ports refusing to suspend the export of live calves. The High Court held that under the applicable English law, the public authorities had no discretion to refuse exports of live animals for slaughter,[117] and thus there was no need to discuss in any detail the points of EC law raised. It is important, however, that Simon Brown LJ in the High Court went on to identify the central questions of EC law that arose, which he described as 'difficult questions, very far from *acte clair*, and questions which we would have regarded as appropriate for reference to the Court of Justice of the European Communities had these challenges turned upon them'. One of the points identified concerned the question of whether the decisions in question could be said to have been 'enacted' by the United Kingdom State. Simon Brown LJ set out the issue thus:

Whether [the local public authorities] are caught by Article 34 depends in part on whether they can properly be considered as emanations of the State—see *Foster* v. *British Gas Plc* Case C–188/89 [1990] ECR I–3313—although in part too on the effect of the measures they take (which [counsel for the applicants] submits is more

---

[114] [1995] 3 CMLR 485.   [115] Ibid. at 495.   [116] [1995] 3 All ER 37.
[117] Air Navigation Order 1989, art. 78(3)2, Harbours, Docks and Piers Clauses Act 1847, s. 333; Harbours Act 1964, s. 404 respectively. The High Court held that under the respective statutory regimes there was no general discretion to distinguish between different lawful trades and no defence of necessity. Furthermore, the High Court added that even if there was a discretion, the Rule of Law did not allow public authorities to respond to unlawful protest and threats from pressure groups by surrendering to their dictates.

important even than the nature of the body taking them): see *Apple and Pear Development Council* v. *K. J. Lewis* Case 222/82 [1983] ECR 4083 and *R.* v. *Royal Pharmaceutical Society of GB, ex p. Association of Pharmaceutical Importers* Joined Cases 266 & 267/87 [1989] ECR 1295.

Since the case did not turn on the EC-law point, the High Court did not commit itself to a view on the issue. Nevertheless, it seems surprising that the High Court did not refer to the 'Dundalk Water' case in which the actions of the local authority in Dundalk were held to violate Article 30.[118] Since *Ex p. Phoenix Aviation* also concerned the actions of certain local public authorities, the Dundalk case was arguably the most useful authority. Instead, in both the *Ex p. Phoenix Aviation* case and the *Ex p. International Trader's Ferry* case, the High Court referred to ECJ authorities which dealt with the question of which bodies constitute the State for the purposes of the vertical direct effect of Community Directives.[119] It is questionable whether the ECJ would, or should, extend the *ratio* of those cases to the field of free movement of goods, particularly in view of the fact that the need to prevent a Member State from pleading its own wrong in failing to implement a Directive correctly is clearly absent in that field. Nevertheless, it is at the very least interesting to note that the English courts have, in these two cases at least, worked upon the assumption that the free movement of goods provisions apply exclusively to measures 'enacted by the State'.

The Dutch Association for Advertising Standards and the Advertising Standards Commission

One of the most intriguing examples of the application of the 'enacted by Member States' requirement in the national court context is to be found in the decisions of the Dutch Advertising Standards Commission (*Reclame Code Commissie* (*RCC*) and its Appeal Tribunal (*College van Beroep* (*CvB*). The background and status of the Dutch Association for Advertising Standards (*Stichting Nederlandse Reclame Code* (*SNRC*)) requires brief explanation. The *SNRC* is a foundation comprising all the main players involved with advertising in the Netherlands. For example, the Consumer Association (*Consumentenbond*), other consumer organisations (*Konsumenten Kontakt*), the Advertising Association (*Genootschap voor Reclame*), the Press Association (*de Nederlandse Dagbladpers*), the Dutch Society of Recognized Advertising Consultants (*de Nederlandse Vereniging van Erkende Reclame Adviesbureaus*) and the television advertising monopoly

---

[118] Case 45/87 *Commission* v. *Ireland*, n. 96 above.
[119] See Case 222/84 *Johnston* v. *Chief Constable RUC* [1988] ECR 4929 & Case C–188/89 *Foster* v. *British Gas Plc* [1990] ECR I–3313. See also Hecquard-Theron, 'La notion d'Etat en droit communautaire' (1990) RTDE 693.

(*de Stichting Ether Reclame* (*STER*)) are amongst its members.[120] The *SNRC* has the explicit aim of ensuring that advertising in the Netherlands is carried out in a responsible way by requiring its members to comply with its Advertising Standards Statutes (*Nederlandse Reclame Code* (*NRC*)). Members pledge that they will do 'everything possible'[121] to comply with these standards and furthermore to comply with any 'recommendation' of the *RCC* or *CvB* arising out of a specific complaint or an investigation of its own motion. The *SNRC* has no legislative foundation, being set up and funded entirely by its affiliated organizations, and is thus a classic example of industry self-regulation with the unwritten aim of keeping legislative intervention to a minimum.

The question which arises in the context of the present discussion is whether the decisions of such a self-regulating organization may be considered to have been 'enacted by Member States' and thus to fall within the ambit of Article 30. As was noted above, both the *RCC* and the *CvB* may, either on their own motion or acting on a complaint, issue a decision (formally only a 'recommendation') with the practical result that the advertising campaigns of individual undertakings are amended so as to comply with the interpretation given in an individual case.

The *RCC* and the *CvB* have been rather erratic with respect to their view of the application of Article 30 to the activities of the *SNRC*. On the one hand, the *RCC* and the *CvB* have in a number of cases themselves applied Article 30 EC and seem thus to have assumed that Article 30 is applicable when they have before them a case with an inter-State trade element. Thus in *Konsumentenkontakt* v. *L'Oréal Nederland BV*,[122] Article 30 was applied (but rejected on the facts[123]) in the context of the advertising campaign of L'Oréal of its 'Plenitude' product in the Netherlands. In *Alternatieve Konsumentenbond* v. *Mars BV*,[124] the claim that the import of 'Bounty' chocolate bars from Germany with the *'Der Grüne Punkt'* logo[125] would mislead Dutch consumers into thinking that the product was environmentally friendly, was held to result in a breach of Article 30 which would not be justified for the protection of consumers under the 'rule of

---

[120] A complete list of the organizations affiliated to the *SNRC* is set out in their handbook: *Informatie betreffende de werkwijze van de Reclame Code Commissie en het College van Beroep* (Amsterdam, Apr. 1993), 16. See also Vollebregt, 'De Reclame Code Commissie in Europees Perspectief: Artikel 85 van toepassing op de Reclame Code Commissie?'

[121] '*Al hetgeen in hun vermogen ligt*': Art. 10(2) of the Statutes of the *SNRC* (handbook cited in n. 120 above).

[122] *RCC*, 12 Sept. 1991, IER 1991, 58.

[123] See discussion of the substance of this case at p. 60.

[124] *RCC*, 15 June 1993, IER 1993, 38; BIE 1995, 22.

[125] Which, in Germany, signifies to consumers that the packaging may be recycled—Duales Systeem Deutschland (DSD) sells this logo in return for collecting and recycling the packaging material.

reason'.[126] In *Dommelsch België*,[127] both the *RCC* and the *CvB* upheld a complaint against Dommelsch for having labelled and marketed in the Netherlands beer with an alcohol content of 0.5 per cent as alcohol-free (*alcoholvrij*), while under the *Nederlandse Bierverordening* (Dutch Beer Regulation), beer with an alcohol content of less than 0.6 per cent should be labelled as 'low alcohol' (*alcoholarm*). The application of Article 30 (Dommelsch argued that beer could be labelled as alcohol-free (*alcoholvrij*) in Belgium if it contains less than 1 per cent alcohol) was rejected by the *CvB* on the facts, though not in principle. Finally, in *Ferrero BV* v. *STER*[128] the *RCC* upheld the refusal of the *STER* to broadcast an advertisement for 'Kinder-Chocolate' on the grounds that it infringed Article 17(2) of the *Voorschriften voor de Nederlandse Etherreclame* (Dutch Provisions for Advertising on Television). An infringement of Article 30 EC was rejected on the facts since Ferrero had not contested that the advert for the product in question had not already been broadcast in other Member States and 'it cannot be stated with certainty that the advertisement is indeed allowed in other Member States'.[129] The crucial aspect of all these decisions is that both the *RCC* and the *CvB* went ahead and applied (admittedly on at times extremely poor reasoning) Article 30 EC. In none of these decisions did either instance mention or consider the possibility that Article 30 EC might not be applicable on the grounds that the decisions were not 'enacted by Member States' or that they were issued as part of voluntary self-regulation rather than State legislation.[130]

In yet other decisions, however, the *RCC* and *CvB* have been more ambivalent about the role of Article 30 in their activities. The most explicit instance of a more 'stand-offish' approach arose in a case concerning a low alcohol drink 'Crodino' (0.7 per cent alcohol) imported into the Netherlands from Italy. While the drink in question could be labelled and

---

[126] For a discussion of the substance of this case see p. 186. See also the *ECO-fles* case, *RCC*, 3 Nov. 1993, *RCC* 1994, 60, where a similar claim that environmentally friendly packaging would mislead Dutch consumers under Art. 10 of the *Milieureclamecode* (Code for Environmental Advertising) was rejected on the facts since the products in question were manufactured and marketed in the Netherlands alone, and there was thus held to be no inter-State element for Art. 30 EC to apply. Finally, see also the *Panasonic* case, *CvB RCC*, 13 Feb. 1992, *RCC* 1992 nr. 680 91 7072, p. 69, where the application of Art. 30 EC was rejected on extremely poor reasoning in a case concerning the compatibility of the packaging of batteries (suggesting environmentally friendly properties) and Art. 7 of the *Milieureclamecode*.

[127] *RCC*, 10 Apr. 1991 & *CvB*, 28 Oct. 1991, *RCC* 1991, 663.

[128] *RCC*, 26 July 1991, IER 1991, 59.

[129] See discussion on the substance of this case at p. 60.

[130] See also the decision of the *Conseil d'Etat* in *Syndicat de l'Armagnac et des vins du Gers*, 17 Dec. 1986, AJDA 1987, 125; CDE 1989, 418 (summary); Rev. franç. dr. admin. 1987, 25 (note by Azibert and De Boisdeffre AJDA 1987, 80) where it was held that the schedule of conditions of a television channel prohibiting the advertisement of alcoholic drinks with an alcoholic content greater than 9% did not breach Art. 30 EC *on the facts* and was silent on the question of whether a schedule of conditions of a television channel could be construed as having been 'enacted by Member States' in the first place.

marketed as being alcohol-free in Italy, the same was not true in the Netherlands. With respect to the argument that this would constitute a restriction on the free movement of goods, the *CvB* held that Article 30 EC was not applicable because:

(a) Article 30 applies only to measures of State institutions which do not cover either the Advertising Standards Foundation or its affiliates, and
(b) a judgment of an advertising self-regulating organ that aims to recommend to advertisers amendments to its advertisements, does not have the character of a quantitative restriction or a measure having equivalent effect within the meaning of Article 30 of the EEC Treaty.

The *CvB* thus clearly, in contrast to the other cases discussed above where Article 30 was applied, rejected the role of that Article on the grounds that the measures that it was enforcing were not 'enacted by Member States'. The same formulation was subsequently repeated by the *CvB* in *L'Oréal SA v. Stichting Reclamecode*[131] where the *CvB* found a breach by L'Oréal of Article 7 of the *Nederlandse Code voor het Reclamewezen* (Dutch Code of Advertising) on misleading advertising in the advertising of its 'Plenitude' skin-care product. Once again, the *CvB* responded to the argument that this would constitute a breach of the provisions concerning the free movement of goods (by requiring L'Oréal to adopt a different advertising message than that which it used in other Member States) by repeating the formulation it used in the *Crodino* case set out above. An interesting feature of the present case was, however, that there was a subsequent appeal to the District Court in Amsterdam (Arrondissementsrechtbank Amsterdam) where it was claimed that the *CvB* had, by so deciding, committed an *onrechtmatige daad*[132] since such a conclusion was contrary to Article 30 EC. The *Arrondissementsrechtbank* rejected this claim explicitly on the grounds that the facts concerned a self-regulating complaints procedure which 'on the one hand is not set up or supervised by the State and, on the other hand, aims to prevent misleading advertising irrespective of the product or the nationality of the producer.'[133] It seems therefore that the Dutch civil courts (in the form of the *Arrondissementsrechtbank Amsterdam*) supported the conclusion of the *CvB* of the *SNRC* that there was no breach of Article 30 in part because of the absence of State involvement in the self-regulatory complaints procedure of the *SNRC*.

The position of the *SNRC* with regard to Article 30 EC is thus far from clear. On the one hand, we have seen a series of decisions handed down

---

[131] *CvB*, 9 Feb. 1990, IER 1994, 31.
[132] Under Art. 6:162 *NBW*; akin to a tort at common law.
[133] *Arrondissementsrechtbank* Amsterdam, 12 Oct. 1994, IER 1994, 31. The *Rechtbank* went on to add that, in any event, the claim that Art. 30 was breached lacked factual foundation since it could not be shown that the same campaign slogan had actually been used in other Member States. See discussion of this aspect of the judgt. at p. 60.

by the *RCC* and the *CvB* which apply Article 30 without even mentioning any conceptual difficulty in the application of that Article to the activities of this self-regulatory non-government organization. On the other hand, there are more ambivalent decisions where the application of Article 30 was rejected by these instances on the grounds, *inter alia*, that the measures were not 'enacted by Member States'. The fact that the tribunal of the *SNRC* itself seems to vacillate between these two positions perhaps suggests that it is not only undecided on the matter, but that it is also avoiding the issue. The matter is indeed one of considerable delicacy and is further complicated by the fact that it is unclear whether the *CvB* of the *RCC* is a tribunal which is competent to refer questions to the ECJ pursuant to Article 177 EC.[134]

It is submitted that the question, although a difficult one, should be answered so as to construe the activities of the *SNRC* as being 'enacted by Member States'. Although it is true that the Dutch State did not set up, appoint, or fund the *SNRC*, there are, it is submitted, sufficient links with the State to satisfy this requirement. It will have been noted that in *L'Oréal SA* v. *Stichting Reclamecode*,[135] an action had been brought before the *Arrondissementsrechtbank* Amsterdam claiming that a particular 'recommendation' from the *CvB* of the *RCC* constituted an *onrechtmatige daad* since it led to a breach of Article 30 EC. It will furthermore have been noted that the Arrondissementsrechtbank did not find this application inadmissible. It is submitted that the possibility of bringing an action before the civil courts, claiming that a decision of the *CvB* of the *RCC* breached Article 30, should be considered to constitute sufficient State involvement for the activities of the *SNRC* to be construed as 'enacted by Member States'. Such a conclusion is consistent with the judgment of the ECJ in *Ex p. Association of Pharmaceutical Importers*,[136] where the fact that The Pharmaceutical Society was able to exercise disciplinary control over its members clearly influenced the ECJ in reaching the conclusion that the activities of that Society could be construed to have been enacted by the Member State.[137] Furthermore, the links between the *SNRC* and the State are often closer than may appear at first sight. It is undoubtedly true that the *SNRC* has itself adopted certain tasks of the State such as that of ensuring that advertisements do not infringe the law.[138] Temmink has pointed out that there are also indications that the State supports the *SNRC*.[139] A good example

---

[134] See the ECJ judgments on this issue in Case 102/81 *Nordsee* v. *Reederei Mond* [1982] ECR 1095; Case 109/88 *Handels-og Kontorfunktionaerernes Forbund I Danmark* v. *Dansk Arbejdsgiverforing* [1989] ECR 3199; Case 61/65 *Vaassen* v. *Beambtenfonds Mijnbedrijf* [1966] ECR 261 & Case 246/80 *Broekmeulen* v. *Huisarts Registratie Commissie* [1981] ECR 2311.

[135] n. 133 above.   [136] n. 89 above.   [137] See esp. para. 14 of ECJ judgt.

[138] See Arts. 1 & 4 of the *Nederlandse Code voor het Reclamewezen* (Dutch Code of Advertising).

[139] Temmink, n. 91 above at 230.

illustrating the latter point may be seen in the context of the *Voorschriften voor de Nederlandse Etherreclame*.[140] While the *Voorschriften* can in no way be said to be State measures (they constitute a voluntary code of practice instituted by the *STER*), a closer look reveals that the application of Article 30 EC need not necessarily be excluded. For example, it may be noted that according to the Dutch *Mediawet* (Law on Broadcasting), the *STER* is given a monopoly in supervising television advertising. Furthermore, Article 6 of the *STER*'s statutes (which incidentally can only be amended with the approval of the Minister of Welfare, Health and Culture (*Welzijn, Volksgezondheid en Cultuur*)) provide that the *STER* is bound by the provisions concerning the content of advertisements set out by the *SNRC*.[141] Finally, Article 28 of the *Mediawet* provides that the income of *STER* should be available to the Minister of *Welzijn, Volksgezondheid en Cultuur*.[142] A combination of the latter features make it possible, if not likely, that according to the ECJ's existing case law, the enforcement of the *Voorschriften voor de Nederlandse Etherreclame* may be considered to be enacted by the State. The judgment of the ECJ in *Apple and Pear Council* v. *Lewis*[143] supports this conclusion; it will be remembered that in that case, the Apple and Pear Council was not funded by the State, but the fact that it was set up by legislation was sufficient for the ECJ to conclude that it was within the scope of Article 30. The same can be said in the present case: the *Voorschriften voor de Nederlandse Etherreclame* were not enacted by the State, but the links to legislation (the *Mediawet*) outlined above are, it is submitted, nevertheless sufficient to bring it within the scope of Article 30 EC. Finally, while it is clear that non-binding measures may nevertheless constitute measures having equivalent effect under Article 30,[144] and while it may be noted that decisions of the *RCC* or the *CvB* have only the formal status of 'recommendations', the practical effectiveness of these decisions should not be underestimated. It is true that neither instance can award damages to an injured party, but the *RCC* or its *CvB* may order a so-called *mediastop* which binds all the affiliated members to refrain from publishing or broadcasting the advertisement at issue.[145] In practice, therefore, these 'recommendations' are usually followed.

---

[140] This example is drawn from the note attached to the decision of the *RCC* in *Ferrero BV* n. 128 above.

[141] Under Arts. 25a(2)(c) & 52b. *Mediabesluit* (Media Order), 19 Dec. 1994, Stb. 914, commercial broadcasting organizations wishing to broadcast advertising messages are obliged to become members of the *SNRC*.

[142] It is also interesting to note that in the *Praktijkboek Reclamerecht* (*Handbook for Advertising Law*) it is suggested that the *STER* could, in cases where there is a connection with the *Mediawet*, make an Art. 177 EC preliminary reference to the ECJ (see Ch. 13, para. 15).

[143] Case 222/82, n. 97 above.   [144] See Case 249/81, n. 88 above.

[145] See *Praktijkboek Reclamerecht*, n. 142 above, XIIID–70.

Given the lack of certainty, it is perhaps not surprising that the *RCC* and the *CvB* have been somewhat inconsistent in their view of the role that Article 30 has to play in the activities of the *SNRC*.[146] It seems clear, however, that the application of Article 30 cannot be 'globally' excluded from the activities of the *SNRC*. It is submitted that in each individual case a functional test should be applied focusing on the nature and manner of exercise by the *SNRC* of its powers rather than focusing on the formal status of the institution itself. In the final analysis, one should not forget that if, in an individual case, the application of Article 30 is excluded because of the absence of a link with the State to enable the action to be construed as 'enacted by Member States', it is still possible that the EC Treaty's competition rules may be applicable.[147] Such an outcome would, it is submitted, be entirely in keeping with the system set up by the Treaty.

5 DIRECTLY OR INDIRECTLY

Article 30 prohibits measures which directly affect imports as well as those whose effects are indirect. Directly applicable measures are national measures which only apply to imports and are often also referred to as 'distinctly applicable' measures. Indirectly applicable measures refer to national measures that apply to both national products and imports and are often referred to as 'equally applicable' or 'indistinctly applicable' measures. In practice, this means that a measure may breach Article 30 even if it applies equally to imports as it does to domestic products. In other words, discrimination between the treatment of national products and that of imports is not a prerequisite for the application of Article 30. Although it would appear that the distinction between directly and indirectly applicable measures is unimportant, since both are capable of falling under Article 30, the distinction between the two remains pertinent since, as we shall see, justification of a restriction under the *Cassis de Dijon*[148] rule of reason is only possible if the measure in question is indirectly applicable; i.e. if it applies to both imports and domestic products alike.[149] It thus

---

[146] Indeed, the literature is divided on this point: see esp. Odle, 'Reclame en andere "verkoopmethoden" onder artikel 30 EG-Verdrag' at 69, criticized by Vollebregt, IER 1996, 98. See also Temmink, n. 91 above at 235, who notes that the matter is in need of settlement by the ECJ pursuant to a preliminary ruling under Art. 177 EC.

[147] See Vollebregt, n. 120 above.

[148] Case 120/78 *Rewe* v. *Bundesmonopolverwaltung für Branntwein* [1979] ECR 649, [1979] 3 CMLR 494. See discussion of the rule of reason in Ch. 6.

[149] See, e.g., Case 788/79 *Gilli & Andres* [1980] ECR 2071, [1981] 1 CMLR 146; Case 113/80 *Commission* v. *Ireland* [1982] ECR 1625, [1982] 1 CMLR 706; Case 207/83 *Commission* v. *United Kingdom* (Origin-marking) [1985] ECR 1201, [1985] 2 CMLR 259; Case 229/83 *Leclerc* v. *Au Blé Vert* [1985] ECR 1, [1985] 2 CMLR 286 at para. 30 & Cases C–321–324/94 *Pistre, Barthes, Milhau and Oberti* [1997] ECR I–2343, [1997] 2 CMLR 565 at para. 52.

remains useful to analyse the national case law in these two categories in the remainder of this chapter.[150]

(A) Examples of directly applicable measures

(i) *Import licences and obligations to make a declaration of origin*

The provisions on quantitative restrictions and measures having equivalent effect did not come into force until the end of the transitional period (i.e. 31 December 1969).[151] As of the date of entry into force of the Treaty of Rome (1 January 1959), there was in place only a 'standstill' requirement: Article 31 EC provided that Member States shall refrain from introducing new quantitative restrictions as between themselves, and Article 32 EC prohibited Member States from making existing restrictions more restrictive.[152] The question of the status of national import licences and declarations of origin during the transitional period arose before the French courts in *Ministère Public* v. *Denise Cornet (née Deroche)*. The facts of that case stemmed from 1961 and concerned the importation of certain colouring matter from Belgium into France. A check carried out by the French authorities subsequently established that the goods, which had been declared as being of Belgian origin, had in fact been imported into Belgium from Czechoslovakia, Poland, and the USSR. Cornet was prosecuted for false declaration of origin on the import licence on the basis of a circular of 14 June 1959[153] addressed to importers and issued by the French Government. The circular, which was itself based on Article 27 of Decree 47/1337 of 15 July 1947, provided that goods originating in third countries which had completed import formalities in another Member State, should carry an import licence upon which the importer should state the country of origin of the goods. The circular was introduced to meet 'a statistical need and economic and monetary purposes'[154] and explicitly provided that licences were to be issued automatically. The *Cour de Cassation* upheld the judgment of the *Cour d'appel of Lyon*[155] holding that the requirements set out in the circular for import licences, together with a declaration of origin, were not contrary to Article 30. The *Cour de*

---

[150] It may be noted that the ECJ's well-established position that the rule of reason is only applicable as a justification for indistinctly applicable measures is approved of by most commentators (see e.g. Mattera, *Le marché unique européen—Ses règles, son fonctionnement*, 274) but is cogently criticized by Oliver, n. 71 above at 110–14.

[151] Art. 32(2) EC.

[152] It may be noted that although these two Arts. are still in the EC Treaty, they are now, after the end of the transitional period, otiose.

[153] JORF 5914/59 (14 June 1959).

[154] See report of Judge Jean Mazard to the *Cour de Cassation*: [1967] 1 CMLR 351 at 355.

[155] *Cour d'appel* Lyon, 4e ch. corr., 20 Nov. 1964, [1965] 1 CMLR 105.

Cassation reached this conclusion by quoting from the judgment of the ECJ in *Albatros* v. *Sopeco*[156] where the ECJ had held that

none of the Articles of the Treaty mentioned [in the questions] implies the abrogation *ipso jure* at the date of the Treaty's entry into force of the quantitative restrictions, discriminations or measures of equivalent effect existing at that date, or
obliges the States to carry out their complete abolition as from 1959.[157]

On the basis of this, the *Cour de Cassation* concluded that 'the infliction of criminal penalties upon those who import, without licence, goods which are in free circulation does not constitute a measure having equivalent effect to a quantitative restriction'.[158] It is submitted that this was a correct application of Article 30 during the transitional period. The circular was based on a Decree of 1947 and thus pre-dated the entry into force of the Treaty of Rome. Accordingly, the only obligation upon the French State was to progressively suppress such existing restrictions.

New restrictions introduced during the transitional period, rather than existing restrictions, were at issue in a case before the French *Conseil d'Etat* in *Syndicat national des importateurs français en produits laitiers et avicoles et Decker et Cie.*[159] That case concerned a notice published in the *Journal officiel de la République français*[160] which established criteria according to which special licences for the importation of conserved milk from other Member States were to be granted during a period of temporary milk shortage in France. The licences were to be granted only to those importers who agreed not to take a windfall profit from the situation. Importers had to agree that at a later time they would export milk without an export sub-sidy to the extent that the amount of the export subsidy they waived would equal the difference between the current French price for milk and the lower price at which the importer would be able to purchase the con-served milk in the other Member States. The *Conseil d'Etat* held that

while the provisions of the notice under appeal thus reserved the import quota for
a determined category of importers, they did not have as their object, and it does
not appear from the file that they had as their effect, a reduction in the quantity of

---

[156] Case 20/64 [1965] ECR 29, [1965] CMLR 156.

[157] [1965] CMLR 156 at 178. Indeed, the ECJ held that 'the Treaty thus does not imply the immediate abrogation of all the measures for controlling imports existing when it entered into force, but does involve the prohibition of all new restrictions or discriminations, the obligation progressively to suppress the existing restrictions and discriminations, and the necessity that they should disappear totally at the latest by the end of the transitional period'.

[158] *Cour de Cassation*, ch. crim., 29 June 1966, [1967] 1 CMLR 351; Dalloz 1966, Jur. 596; Gaz. Pal. 1966, I Jur. 297. See note by Lauwaars (1966) CMLRev 339 and by Desmazières de Séchelles 'Experiences and Problems in Applying the Preliminary Proceedings of Art. 177 of the Treaty of Rome, as seen by a French advocate'.

[159] *Conseil d'Etat*, 27 Jan. 1967, Rec. Lebon 1967, 41; AJDA 1967, 284; RDP 1967, 788; RTDE 1967, 402; [1968] 1 CMLR 81; noted by Lecat and Massot AJDA 1967, 268.

[160] JORF, 28 Mar. 1962.

tinned milk imported from the member countries of the European Economic Community. Consequently, the provisions could not be assimilated to quantitative restrictions on importation or to measures of equivalent effect.

It is submitted that it would have been more proper for the *Conseil d'Etat* to have addressed a reference to the ECJ under Article 177(3) EC. As is outlined below, the ECJ has subsequently held that any import licence, even if granted automatically or as a mere formality, will be considered to be a measure having equivalent effect prohibited by Article 30.[161] Any actual reduction in the quantity of imports is thus irrelevant to this analysis. Article 31 EC provided that during the transitional period, Member States shall refrain from introducing *new* quantitative restrictions as between themselves. The import licence introduced by the notice in the present case was such a *new* quantitative restriction and it is submitted that at the time of the *Conseil d'Etat*'s judgment (1967), it was at least arguable that the ECJ's subsequent interpretation of Article 30 would, by virtue of Article 31 EC, have been applicable during the transitional period.

As of the end of the transitional period, it was clear that any requirement of an import licence for goods imported from another Member State will be contrary to Article 30, even in cases where such a licence is granted automatically. In *International Fruit Company*,[162] the ECJ held that the provisions of Article 30 'preclude the application to intra-Community trade of a national provision which requires, even as a formality, import or export licences or any other similar procedure.'[163] The ECJ reasons that the very existence of an exemption system is liable to create uncertainty in the minds of importers and thereby deter free trade. The unlawfulness of import licences after the end of the transitional period has largely been respected by the national courts. Thus, in *Syndicat national du commerce de la chaussure* v. *Ministère du commerce extérieur et Ministre de l'industrie et de la recherche*,[164] the French *Conseil d'Etat* annulled a circular of 29 June 1976 requiring importers of leather shoes into France to obtain an import licence on importation.[165] The *Conseil d'Etat* 'in a very straightforward fashion'[166] held that these measures had an effect equivalent to a quantitative restriction on imports and were thus prohibited by Article 30.[167]

---

[161] See text at n. 163, below.

[162] Cases 51–54/71 *International Fruit Company* v. *Produktschap voor Groenten en Fruit* [1971] ECR 1107. [163] Para. 9 of judgt.

[164] *Conseil d'Etat*, 18 Dec. 1981, Rec. Lebon 1981, 475; RTDE 1982, 201; CDE 1985, 214 (summary).

[165] The circular was issued against the background of economic problems in the shoe industry. The action before the *Conseil d'Etat* was brought by several trade associations. By way of defence, the Minister for Foreign Trade argued that the measures had been introduced for 'statistical purposes'.

[166] Servan-Schreiber 'EEC law in French Courts 1980–1984' (1986) at 174.

[167] It may be noted that this decision of the *Conseil d'Etat* is often quoted by commentators as an example illustrating that the *Conseil d'Etat* never had difficulty in according supremacy

More recently, in *Ministre de l'économie, des finances et du budget* v. *Société Lefebvre*, the *Cour administratif d'appel* of Nancy held that a Minister's refusal to grant import licences for the importation of bananas in free circulation in Belgium infringed Articles 30 and 33 EC.[168]

On the other hand, there also appear to be some rather alarming misapplications in the national courts. In a strange decision of the *Conseil d'Etat* in 1983, the *Conseil* held that a memorandum of 14 August 1977, providing that importers of certain textile products were subject to an import licence (*visa administratif préalable*), was not contrary to Article 30, since

it does not emerge from the file and it is not even alleged that the measure which requires prior administrative authorization of imports for which the decision under attack repeals the measures reimposing quotas previously in force would have the object or effect of delaying or limiting imports of the products concerned.[169]

It is submitted that the *Conseil d'Etat's* reasoning in this case is flawed in so far as it suggests that the slowing down or limiting of importation is a relevant consideration. As we have seen, the ECJ has held that any 'national provision which requires, even as a formality, import or export licences or any other similar procedure'[170] is prohibited under Article 30. As was noted above, it is the very existence of an exemption system which is held to be liable to create uncertainty in the minds of importers and thereby deter free trade and thus, the absence of any *actual* slowing down of importation should, it is submitted, have been an irrelevant consideration before the *Conseil d'Etat*.

While it is clear that import licences, even if granted automatically, are unlawful under Article 30, obligations to make a declaration of origin and to comply with other customs controls are, on the other hand, less clear cut. The ECJ has held in *Donckerwolcke* v. *Procureur de la République*[171] that

The requirement by the importing Member State of the indication of the country of origin on the customs declaration document for products in free circulation . . . would, however, fall under the prohibition contained in Article 30 of the Treaty if the importer were required to declare, with regard to origin, something other than what he knows or may reasonably be expected to know.

to EC law over subsequent national *administrative acts*. See e.g. Roseren, 'The Application of Community law by French Courts from 1980 to 1993' & Servan-Schreiber, n. 166 above.

[168] *CAA* Nancy, 9 July 1991, Rec. Lebon 1991, 741. Noted by Roseren (1994) 31 CMLRev. 315 at 338.

[169] *Syndicat des importateurs de vêtements et de produits artisanaux*, *Conseil d'Etat*, 29 July 1983, Rec. Lebon 1983, 640. In the original French: '*il ne ressort pas des pieces du dossier, et qu'il n'est même pas allegué, que la mesure consistant à soumettre à un regime de visa administratif préalable des importations pour lesquelles de décision attaquée abroge les mesures de recontingentement antérieurement édictées aurait eu pour objet ou pour effet de retarder ou de limiter les importations dont s'agit . . .*'

[170] n. 163 above.   [171] Case 41/76, n. 8 above.

Thus, requiring a declaration of origin is not *per se* unlawful under Article 30 unless it goes beyond information easily available to the importer.[172] This sits rather uneasily with the rationale of the ECJ's reasoning in *International Fruit Company*[173] where, as we have seen, the very existence of a formality is considered to be a restriction. The legitimacy of national requirements regarding customs clearance, although falling short of requiring an import licence in the strict sense, have been the subject of litigation before the French courts in *Hagege*.[174] In that case, the French *Cour de Cassation* upheld the convictions of certain French residents who imported from Germany postage stamp collections without first clearing them through a special clearance procedure with the French Customs as required by Article 38.1 of the *Code des douanes*. The *Cour de Cassation* held that

The principle of the free movement of goods in the customs territory of the Community set up by the Treaty of Rome does not have the effect of removing the said goods from the controls of the national customs authorities, which have the aim of verifying their nature, their value and their origin: elements upon which the application of the Community regime depends.

The requirement that the postage stamps should complete Customs clearance was thus held not to constitute a breach of Article 30 since such clearance sought only to verify the nature, value, and origin of the goods. While this judgment seems correct following the ECJ judgment in *Donckerwolcke*,[175] it is again submitted that this position sits rather uneasily with the rationale in *International Fruit Company*,[176] where, as was noted above, the very existence of a formality was considered to be a restriction. In any event, Oliver argues that as of 1 January 1993 (when Article 7A EC took effect) obligations to make a declaration of origin and all customs controls on goods moving between Member States would now constitute a measure having equivalent effect under Article 30.[177]

A further question which has arisen before the national courts is that of false declarations of origin. It was noted above that the ECJ had held in *Donckerwolcke*[178] that declarations of origin are not *per se* unlawful under Article 30 unless they go beyond information easily available to the importer.[179] The ECJ also held in that case that a disproportionately high penalty imposed by a Member State for a Customs irregularity would also

---

[172] See also Case 52/77 *Cayril* v. *Rivoira* [1977] ECR 2261, [1978] 2 CMLR 253 & Case 179/78 *Procureur de la République* v. *Rivoira* [1979] ECR 1147, [1979] 3 CMLR 456.

[173] n. 162 above.

[174] *Cour de Cassation*, ch. crim., 7 Oct. 1985, Dalloz 1986, IR 122 (summary); CDE 1989, 408 (summary).

[175] Case 41/76, n. 8 above.

[176] n. 162 above.

[177] Oliver, n. 71 above, 129, 134 and 136.

[178] Case 41/76, n. 8 above.

[179] See text at n. 172 above.

be a measure having equivalent effect prohibited by Article 30 'taking into account the purely administrative nature of the contravention'. In *Jacques Allion*, the French *Cour de Cassation* was faced with the question of the application of national law on fraud in the context of false declarations of origin.[180] The case concerned wine unloaded at French ports declared to be of Italian origin but which were subsequently found by the French authorities to be of Bulgarian and Maltese origin, and even synthetically produced wine of Dutch origin. The *Cour de Cassation* cited the ECJ's judgment in *Donckerwolcke* stating that penalties for failure should not be disproportionate, and upheld the convictions of the importers since it held that the application of national law on the prevention of fraud would not be disproportionate.[181]

(ii) Import inspections

The submission of imports to technical inspections (whether they be veterinary, phytosanitary or otherwise) will clearly be a measure of equivalent effect to a quantitative restriction under Article 30.[182] This is readily accepted and applied by the national courts.[183] In fact, the acknowledgement that an inspection will breach Article 30 is almost automatic as, in most cases, the national court will proceed immediately to the question of justification (which in practice is usually the justification on the grounds of the protection of public health in Article 36 EC). In such cases, the breach of Article 30 will only be mentioned in passing, if at all. Thus, for example, in *Michel Leclerc et Ministère public* v. *Jacques Restellini*, the *Cour d'appel* of Paris implicitly assumed that a compulsory roadworthiness test as a condition of vehicle registration, even where it related to an imported vehicle carrying a certificate of conformity and one which had not been placed on the road in another Member State before being registered in France, would breach Article 30.[184] Similarly, in both *Société Tresch-Alsacaves* v. *Ministre de l'economie, des finances et du budget*[185] and *Société vinicole Berard SA*[186] the respective *Tribunaux administratives* of Strasbourg and Dijon held that

---

[180] n. 9 above.
[181] See the subsequent judgment of the ECJ in C–212/88 *Felix Levy* v. *Ministère public* [1989] ECR 3511 which would seem to confirm the correctness of the decision of the *Cour de Cassation* in *Allion*. For cases dealing with declarations of origin in the context of transformation in the Community, see *Albert Lapeyre*, n. 9 above & *Stanislas Nowak TGI* La Seine, 11e ch. corr., 20 Oct. 1964, Gaz. Pal. 1965, I Jur. 40.
[182] See, e.g., Case 4/75 *Rewe-Zentralfinanz* v. *Landwirtschaftskammer* [1975] ECR 843, [1977] 1 CMLR 599.
[183] See, e.g., *Upjohn NV* v. *Veterinaire Dienst 's-Gravenhage*, Pres. *Raad van State* (*Afd. Rechtspraak*), 13 Oct. 1988, AB 1989, 200; KG 1988, 453.
[184] *Cour d'appel* Paris, 13e ch. corr., 19 Oct. 1988 (noted by Fourgoux, (1990) Revue de science criminelle et de droit pénal comparé 355).
[185] *Trib. admin.* Strasbourg, 5 June 1984, [1986] 2 CMLR 625.
[186] *Trib. admin.* Dijon, 15 Apr. 1986, Rec. Lebon 1986, 311; RTDE 1988, 112; (noted by Soler-Couteaux (1987) RTDE 109).

delays by the French Customs in clearing imports of wine from Italy,[187] allegedly for the purpose of making food analysis inspections, were excessive and not justified under Article 36 EC. The fact that food analysis inspections would breach Article 30 in the first place was simply assumed by the national court.[188]

(iii) Conditions imposed in relation to imports only

If it can be shown that certain conditions are imposed in relation to imports only, this would clearly constitute a directly applicable measure contrary to Article 30.[189] The important aspect to recognize is that even measures that, in the *formal* sense, appear to be equally applicable to domestic products and imports will nevertheless be found to be directly applicable measures if the *effect* of the measures is such that only imports are adversely affected. A well-known example is provided by the French alcohol advertising cases. French legislation restricted the advertising of grain spirits irrespective of whether they were nationally produced or imported. On the face of the legislation, therefore, there was no discrimination, preference, or advantage for domestic products. However, the legislation was found by the ECJ in *Commission* v. *France*[190] to be contrary to Article 30 since there was shown to be material discrimination: for, while it was prohibited to advertise grain spirits such as whisky and Geneva (mainly imported products), distilled spirits typical of French national produce (such as rums and spirits obtained from distillation of wines, ciders, or fruits), enjoyed completely unrestricted advertising. There was thus a material advantage for the advertising of nationally produced alcoholic beverages and, in *effect*, the conditions were imposed in relation to imports only. The French legislation was therefore held to constitute a directly applicable measure contrary to Article 30.[191]

---

[187] Delays rose from 40 days in 1978 to 180 days in 1981.

[188] These judgments essentially gave effect to the ECJ judgment in Case 42/82 *Commission* v. *France* [1983] ECR 1013, [1984] 1 CMLR 160 and also held that the breach gave rise to fault on the part of the French State giving rise to the obligation to pay damages. See Ch. 10, sect. 3 for further discussion of State liability for Member States' breaches of the free-movement-of-goods rules.

[189] See, e.g., Case 59/82 *Schutzverband gegen Unwesen in der Wirtschaft* v. *Weinvertriebs* [1983] ECR 1217.

[190] Case 152/78 [1980] ECR 2299, [1981] 2 CMLR 743.

[191] See also the French cases on resale price maintenance for books: Case 229/83 *Librairie 'Au Blé Vert'* v. *Sté Thouars Distribution SA & Association des centres distributeurs Leclerc* [1985] ECR 1; [1985] 2 CMLR 286 where the ECJ similarly held that the French legislation, which seemingly applied to all books intended for retail sale in France, *in effect* created a separate set of rules for imported books and thus in practice amounted to conditions imposed in relation to imports only, contrary to Art. 30. Both the 'alcohol' and the 'book' cases provoked a veritable wave of cases before the French national courts. These judgments are discussed at length in Ch. 10, sect. 2 (A).

Conditions imposed in relation to imports only were struck down by the English courts in *R. v. Secretary of State for Social Security, ex p. Bomore Medical Supplies Ltd*[192] in the context of new arrangements introduced in the United Kingdom for reimbursing retail chemists for the cost of medicines dispensed by them under the British National Health Service (NHS). Under the system prevailing before the new arrangements were introduced, a chemist received reimbursement of the tariff price of the medicines dispensed, less a discount calculated on a sliding scale starting at 0.46 per cent and rising to a maximum of 7.96 per cent, depending on the value of the prescriptions dispensed by the particular chemist in any month. The idea behind the old system was to limit NHS expenditure by reimbursing, not the full tariff price, but the tariff price less a discount. However, since parallel importers could in practice offer chemists a discount of about 20 per cent, chemists buying imported drugs at such large discounts were able to retain a very considerable profit under the old system when reimbursed by the NHS on the sliding scale set out above. Since the cost of such reimbursement fell ultimately upon the taxpayer, the Secretary of State for Health and Social Security was concerned to amend the scheme of discounts in such a way as to enable the taxpayer to share the benefits of low-cost imported products instead of having to reimburse chemists as if no such benefits existed. The scheme introduced by the Secretary of State[193] had two limbs: (a) medicines dispensed under a NHS prescription which had been obtained by the chemist at an overall discount of 12 per cent or less were reimbursed on the existing sliding scale ranging from 0.46 per cent up to 7.96 per cent; and (b) medicines similarly prescribed obtained by the chemist at an overall discount of more than 12 per cent of the current drug tariff price were reimbursed at a fixed discount of 20 per cent. These new arrangements were challenged before the English courts by way of judicial review proceedings initiated by Bomore Medical Supplies. It was common ground before the Court that in practice all domestic medicines were offered at less than 12 per cent discount and all imported medicines were offered at more than 12 per cent discount. The effect of the new arrangements in practice was thus to produce a 'no go' area of discounts between 12 per cent and 20 per cent: if a chemist stocked imported drugs which he had obtained at a discount of between 12 per cent and 20 per cent he would, under the new arrangements, only be able to dispense such drugs at a loss since a fixed discount of 20 per cent was not reimbursed by the NHS. It was only if the chemist stocked

---

[192] Before the QBD, High Court, 27 June 1985, [1986] 1 CMLR 34 & the CA, 29 Nov. 1985, [1986] 1 CMLR 228.

[193] The decision of the Secretary of State for Health and Social Security was issued under Reg. 28, National Health Service (General Medical and Pharmaceutical Services) Regulations 1974 and was formally announced by the Family Practitioner Notice FPN378 in Dec. 1984.

imported medicines obtained at a discount of over 20 per cent that he could dispense at a profit. In effect, parallel importers had a choice: they could either offer a smaller discount (i.e. a discount under 12 per cent) thereby nullifying their competitive advantage, or offer discounts of over 20 per cent which would mean that they could only penetrate the UK market at a loss. Both the High Court and the Court of Appeal held that, although the new reimbursement arrangements applied to all medicines dispensed by chemists irrespective of their origin, the *effect* of the measures was such that in practice, conditions were imposed only upon imports. This was thus, very commendably, held by the English courts to be contrary to Article 30 EC.[194]

The national courts have shown that there are, however, limits to the extent to which they will be prepared to conclude that particular national conditions apply only to imports. An extremely interesting example illustrating how the national courts will not allow this principle to be overstretched is provided by the facts of a case before the Dutch courts in *Openbaar Ministerie* v. *Autohandel- en sloperij J. R. BV*.[195] This case concerned the criminal prosecution of a defendant for being in possession of wrecked vehicles (*autowrakken*) without possessing a licence from the Dutch authorities for keeping and disposing of *autowrakken*, as required by Dutch law.[196] The defendant argued that the Dutch legislation discriminated against the importation of *autowrakken* from other Member States and was thus contrary to Article 30 EC. The essential thread of the argument was that damaged vehicles imported from other Member States did not in practice ever possess a valid registration plate and, under the definition of *autowrakken* in the relevant Dutch legislation (which defined *autowrakken* as damaged vehicles (*schade autos*) which did not have a valid registration plate) a vehicle demolition establishment importing damaged vehicles from other Member States would, in effect, always have to possess a licence for keeping and disposing of *autowrakken*. By contrast, a vehicle demolition establishment that only dealt with Dutch damaged vehicles, which would usually still have a valid registration plate, would not always need such a licence since vehicles with a registration plate do

---

[194] Both courts also rejected the possibility of the measures being justified under the *Cassis de Dijon* rule of reason since the new Regulations were distinctly applicable. It may be noted that these judgments of the English courts were criticized by Arnull, 'Use and Abuse of Art. 177 EEC', where he states that the conclusion reached 'although by no means untenable, was nonetheless a bold one to take in view of the indirect nature of the alleged restriction on the free movement of goods'. It is, with respect, submitted that this view is open to doubt since the effect on the free movement of goods was anything but indirect. In fact, as the English courts rightly held, the new reimbursement system was a directly applicable (discriminatory) measure imposing conditions on imports only.

[195] *Gerechtshof* Amsterdam (*Ec. Kamer*), 7 June 1994 & *Hoge Raad* (*Strafkamer*), 16 May 1995, NJ 1995, 567; M & R 1995, 108 (with note by Hendriks).

[196] Art. 33(1) & Art. 31(2) *Afvalstoffenwet* (Law on Waste).

not fall within the definition of *autowrakken*.[197] The defendant thus argued
that the owner of a vehicle demolition establishment in the Netherlands,
who did not possess a licence but who nevertheless wished to import
damaged vehicles from other Member States, would be put to the extra
expense of either re-registering the damaged vehicle in the Netherlands or
obtaining the requisite licence to possess and dispose of *autowrakken* in
the Netherlands. This defence was rejected by both the *Gerechtshof*
Amsterdam and the *Hoge Raad*.[198] Both courts refused to accept that the
national legislation imposed conditions in relation to imports only and
insisted that the provisions made no distinction as to the origin of the cars.
Both of these judgments may be criticized for having assumed that the fact
that a national measure is indistinctly applicable leads to the conclusion
that Article 30 has not been breached.[199] Putting this objection aside for a
moment, it is interesting in the context of the present discussion to note
that the national court thought that there were limits to what could be considered to be a condition imposed in relation to imports alone. On the facts
of the case, the defendant had been found to be in possession of wrecked
vehicles without the requisite licence under Dutch law. In using EC law as
a defence here, the defendant was attempting to avoid complying with the
national rules concerning licensing. It is clear from the opinion of
Advocate General van Dorst in this case that the distinction in the Dutch
legislation between *schade autos* (i.e. damaged vehicles with a valid registration plate) and *autowrakken* (i.e. damaged vehicles without a valid registration plate) stems from the desire to distinguish between vehicle
demolition establishment dealers (who dispose of the vehicles) and
garages (who take possession of the damaged vehicles with the intention
of repairing them and re-selling them). Dutch legislation intended to subject only the former to a licensing system. The nexus between the national
requirement that vehicle demolition establishments have a licence and the
national requirement that only damaged vehicles without a valid registration plate will be considered to be an *autowrak* is indeed tenuous. This
seems to be what the *Hoge Raad* was suggesting when it held that 'to have

[197] The defendant produced evidence that damaged vehicles imported from Germany
would never have a registration plate since under German law wrecked vehicles must be
notified to the *Kraftfahrt-bundesamt* (Federal Office for Motor Traffic) which then removes and
deletes the registration. Similarly, under Belgian law, which registration is attached to the
person rather than the car, so that the owner of a wrecked vehicle is obliged to surrender the
registration plate to the authorities with the result that wrecked vehicles imported from
Belgium would never be accompanied by a valid registration plate. On the facts, 54 of the 86
cars that the defendant was found to be in possession of were imported from other Member
States.

[198] n. 195 above.

[199] See discussion below of case law in national courts which (incorrectly) proceeds on the
assumption that Art. 30 EC only applies to national measures which *discriminate* against
imports.

a registration plate and valid registration certificate at one's disposal does not in any event apply as a requirement for running an installation to carry out such a business'. Thus, while these judgments of the national court may be criticized for assuming that non-discriminatory national rules cannot breach Article 30, the supposed 'condition' imposed in relation to imports only was extremely indirect. In the final analysis, it may have been true that imported damaged vehicles were almost never accompanied by valid registration plates, but to argue that this fact exempts an individual from a national rule that vehicle demolition establishment owners need a licence to dispose of vehicles and furthermore that it is a condition imposed in relation to imports only, is pushing the definition of directly applicable measures in the *Dassonville* formula to the limit. In this sense, it is regrettable that the *Hoge Raad*, as a court from which there is no further appeal, did not refer this question to the ECJ under the Article 177 preliminary-rulings procedure. Instead, the application of Article 30 was rejected and Article 177 EC was not even mentioned, let alone considered by the *Hoge Raad*.[200]

(iv) Limiting channels of distribution

National measures which by their operation limit the channels of distribution for imported products, will be found to be directly applicable measures contrary to Article 30. This was found by the ECJ to be the case in *de Peijper*,[201] which concerned Dutch legislation requiring importers of pharmaceutical products to supply certain information verified by the manufacturer of the products. The ECJ held that the information required by the Dutch authorities was more readily obtainable by the authorized distributors of the drug in the Netherlands, thus restricting the possibility for parallel importing. Thus, national measures which result in imports being channelled in such a way that only certain traders can effect the imports, while others cannot, constitute distinctly applicable measures having equivalent effect contrary to Article 30 EC. Full effect was given to this judgment when it was implemented by the *Kantongerecht Rotterdam* which held,

Naturally, the Dutch legislature ought to have realized at the time when the alleged offences were committed that the said provisions had a discriminatory effect and ought to have found a way to counteract this injustice. It is not apparent anywhere that the Dutch legislature took any steps at that time or endeavoured to

---

[200] The omission of the *Hoge Raad* in this case to make a reference to the ECJ for a preliminary ruling pursuant to Art. 177 EC has been criticized in the 'Thirteenth Report to the European Parliament on Commission Monitoring of the Application of Community Law (1995)' [1996] OJ C303/1 at 180.

[201] Case 104/75 *Openbaar Ministerie* v. *de Peijper* [1976] ECR 613, [1976] 2 CMLR 271.

find an adequate solution to remedy the situation now denounced by the Court of Justice.[202]

An interesting sequel to the *de Peijper* case came before the *CBB*, which is the court of last instance in matters of trade and industry in the Netherlands, in *Miedema* v. *Minister van Landbouw en Visserij*.[203] In the latter case however, the *CBB* held that there was on the facts no limit to the channels of distribution for the parallel importer. The case arose from a challenge by Miedema of the refusal by the Dutch Minister of Agriculture and Fisheries to grant a licence for certain plant protection products in the Netherlands. The products in question were parallel imports from the United Kingdom and had already been marketed in the Netherlands with the requisite licence by the producer (ICI). The *CBB* cited Article 30 EC and held that the plant protection product which had already been granted a licence was sufficiently different to the applicants' product such that a further investigation by the Ministry was necessary. Nevertheless, the *CBB* went on to hold that the Ministry was not free (following the ECJ's judgment in *de Peijper*) to require the applicant to provide information that can 'only be acquired with the assistance and support of the (foreign) manufacturer or its recognized importer in the Netherlands which results in the manufacturer and/or importer being given the power to hinder the parallel import of the product in question'. Applying this to the facts of the case, the *CBB* found that this was not the case here since Miedema 'could provide the information required by submitting invoices or correspondence with the wholesaler from which it ordered the products or equally by submitting a sample of the products'. This would, according to the *CBB*, ensure that the information was trustworthy and would not be known to the person who had already received permission to market the products in the Netherlands. In other words, the *CBB* held that Miedema could provide the information to the Ministry of Agriculture and Fisheries without the assistance and support of the foreign manufacturer or its recognized importer and thus did not result in the manufacturer or importer being given the de facto power to hinder the parallel import of the product in question. There was therefore no question of there being a limit to the channels of distribution on the facts of this case and the Ministry was held justified in having required such documentation from Miedema.[204]

---

[202] *Openbaar Ministerie* v. *de Peijper*, *Kantongerecht* Rotterdam, 6 Sept. 1976, NJ 1976, 549 (with note by Van Veen); [1977] 1 CMLR 321 and noted by Korte, Kellermann, Levelt-Overmars and Possen, *Primus Inter Pares: The European Court and National Courts* (1990 EUI Working Paper in Law no. 90/6), 14–15.

[203] *CBB*, 12 Aug. 1980, AB 1981, 34.

[204] Further examples of 'sequels' to the *de Peijper* case are to be found in the judgments of the Dutch courts in *Officier van Justitie* v. *Kortmann*, *Hoge Raad (Strafkamer)*, 1 Feb. 1983, NJ 1983, 402 (with note by Van Veen) and *Jacques George Henri H.* v. *Openbaar Ministerie*, *Hoge Raad (Strafkamer)*, 5 Nov. 1985, NJ 1986, 280 (with note by Van Veen); AB 1986, 309 (with note

In most cases before the national courts, the limitation to the channels of distribution are obvious. A very clear example presented itself before the English High Court in *Ex p. Bell Lines*.[205] Until 1983, the only milk imported into the United Kingdom was from Ireland, shipped into the two Irish Sea ports of Fleetwood and Newport. In 1983, however, following the judgment of the ECJ in *Commission v. United Kingdom* (Re UHT Milk),[206] all imports were banned unless they came in through seventeen designated United Kingdom ports, none of which was either Fleetwood or Newport or indeed any port convenient to Ireland. On an application by the shippers and exporters of Irish UHT milk and cream for a declaration that Fleetwood and Newport should be included as designated ports of entry, the High Court had no problem in finding a limitation to the channels of distribution and thereby a restriction on inter-State trade contrary to Article 30 and therefore granted the declaration sought. In such a case, the limitation was clear. The practical effect of the UK system of designated ports required sea-borne imports from Ireland to travel out of the sea in which their natural ports are situated and round the coast to another sea in order to reach the nearest designated port, thereby incurring uncompetitive extra costs.[207] By contrast, the English High Court in *Gillingham Borough Council v. Medway (Chatham) Dock Co*[208] was more reluctant to construe a proposed ban on the passage of heavy goods vehicles to and from a port between 7 pm and 7 am as a limitation to channels of distribution. Buckley J·held, *obiter dictum*, that such an injunction would 'not be designed to govern the patterns of trade between Member States' and that Article 30 would not apply. He added that he would be 'surprised and disappointed' if the ECJ did not reach the same result.[209]

(v) Obligatory origin-marking

It appears from ECJ case law that obligatory origin-marking requirements in national legislation will breach Article 30.[210] This was given full effect

---

by FHvdB). See also the decision of the English Court of Appeal in *R v. Licensing Authority, ex. p. Smith Kline and French Laboratories* [1988] 3 CMLR 301; [1988] 3 WLR 896 where the ECJ judgment in *de Peijper* was applied to conclude that the duty incumbent upon national authorities to use information already in their possession when considering an application for pharmaceutical licensing could not be affected by national law on confidentiality.

[205] *R. v. Minister of Agriculture, Fisheries and Food, ex p. Bell Lines Ltd and An Bord Bainne Co-operative Ltd (The Irish Dairy Board)* [1984] 2 CMLR 502.

[206] Case 124/81 [1983] ECR 203, [1983] 2 CMLR 1.

[207] See further discussion of this judgment in the context of the 'actual or potential' effect on trade between Member States at p. 91.

[208] [1992] 3 All ER 923; [1992] 4 J Environ. Law 251–71 (with note by Crawford).

[209] See further discussion of this judgment in the context of the 'actual or potential' effect on trade between Member States at p. 92.

[210] See e.g., Case 113/80 *Commission v. Ireland* ('Souvenirs') [1981] ECR 1625; [1982] 1 CMLR 706.

in a straightforward fashion by the President of the *Arrondissements-rechtbank* in the Hague in *Nederlandse Melkhandelaren Organisatie* v. *Konmar BV*.[211] The Dutch Milk Traders' Organization (*Nederlandse Melkhandelaren Organisatie (NMO)*) brought an action to prevent Konmar BV, a supermarket, from selling milk imported from Belgium without labelling stating that the milk in question was of that origin. Although Article 3(3)(f) and (g) and Article 14 of the General Labelling Decision under the Food and Drugs Act (*Algemeen Aanduidingenbesluit (Warenwet)*) provided that origin-marking was only obligatory if the absence of such marking would mislead the consumer as to the real origin, such was not the case according to Article 36(8) of the Milk Decision (*Melkbesluit*) 1974 which contained no such proviso. The President of the *Arrondissementsrechtbank* in the Hague held that there was, on the facts, no misleading of the consumer as to the real origin of the milk and that Article 36(8) *Melkbesluit* must be read in conjunction with Article 30 and the judgment of the ECJ interpreting that Article in *Commission* v. *United Kingdom*[212] with the result that the origin-marking requirement in the national rule was set aside.

Where the ECJ case law concerning obligatory origin-marking is less clear, however, and this was an underlying issue in the *Konmar* case before the Dutch courts, is whether it would ever be justified for national provisions to require the origin of goods to be marked on them, particularly in cases where the absence of such marking would mislead the consumer as to the real origin of the goods. This question has arisen before the German courts in *Re Labelling of Dutch Poultry*.[213] In that case, the defendants marketed Dutch chickens for retail sale in Germany. The chickens' labels were in the German language having been specially translated for the German market. Nothing in the wording or get-up indicated that they came from outside Germany. The plaintiff, a trade association of German poultry producers, sued for an injunction to prevent the sale of the Dutch chickens as so labelled, on the ground that the labelling was misleading since it induced the belief that the chickens were of German origin, a belief which apparently had marketing advantages. The *Oberlandesgericht* Köln held that the labels did indeed give the impression of German produce and that this was misleading under section 3 of the German Unfair Competition Act and granted an injunction to remove the impression of German origin (but not requiring positive identification as of Dutch origin). With respect to the Article 30 argument, the *Oberlandesgericht* Köln held that since the

---

[211] Pres. *Arrondissementsrechtbank* 's-Gravenhage, 17 Nov. 1986, KG 1986, 529.

[212] Case 207/83, n. 149 above. In that case, the ECJ held that the requirement in UK law that certain textile, electrical, and other goods be marked with or accompanied by an indication of their origin when offered for retail sale was prohibited by Art. 30.

[213] *OLG* Cologne, 29 Apr. 1988, GRUR 1989, 694; [1990] 2 CMLR 104 (concerning '*Pingo frisch*' chicken).

labels on the chicken had in any event been specially translated for the German market, requiring compliance with German law on unfair competition did not compel the defendant to adapt its usual get-up in the country of origin, and import was thus not made more difficult.[214] It is respectfully submitted that this judgment of the *Oberlandesgericht Köln* is at odds with the judgment of the ECJ in *Commission* v. *United Kingdom*[215] where the ECJ clearly stated that

> it has to be recognised that the purpose of indications of origin or origin-marking is to enable consumers to distinguish between domestic and imported products and this enables them to assert any prejudices which they may have against foreign products. As the Court has had occasion to emphasise in various contexts, the Treaty, by establishing a common market and progressively approximating the economic policies of the Member States seeks to unite national markets in a single market having the characteristics of a domestic market. Within such a market, the origin-marking requirement not only makes the marketing in a Member State of goods produced in other Member States in the sectors in question more difficult; it also has the effect of slowing down economic interpenetration in the Community by handicapping the sale of goods produced as the result of a division of labour between Member States.[216]

Thus, it seems that the requirement that the labelling of the Dutch chickens make clear that the chickens were not of German origin would have the purpose of enabling consumers to distinguish between domestic and imported products and thereby to 'assert any prejudices which they may have against foreign products'. The very *ratio* of the ECJ judgment is that this makes it more difficult to sell the imported goods which is anathema to the common market and 'economic interpenetration' in the Community. It is submitted that the *Oberlandesgericht* Köln should have hesitated long before it reached its conclusion that 'since . . . this judgment does not affect the commercial viability of the defendant's product in the German Federal Republic but only affects the get-up under which it is currently marketed . . . there is no need to stay the proceedings and refer to the European Court of Justice the legal questions raised by the Defendant'.[217] A reference to the ECJ is this case would, as Roth has pointed out,[218] have been more desirable given that the ECJ, rather controversially, went on to hold in the *Commission* v. *United Kingdom*[219] case that obligatory origin-marking, although formally equally applicable to

---

[214] See also, *OLG* Cologne, 30 Nov. 1984, GRUR 1986, 323 (concerning *Fleischwurst*); *OLG* Cologne, 20 Nov. 1981, GRUR 1983, 71 (concerning *Apfelkorn*). Cf. *OLG* Hamburg, 31 Aug. 1989, GRUR 1990, 55 (*obiter dicta* concerning *Buttergebäck*).

[215] n. 212 above.   [216] Para. 17 of judgt.

[217] [1990] 2 CMLR 104 at 114. It may also be noted that the *Bundesgerichtshof* did not accept the case for appeal, *BGH*, 11 May 1989.

[218] Roth, 'The Application of Community law in West Germany 1980–90' at 158–9.

[219] n. 212 above.

domestic and imported products, is de facto discriminatory because the consumer would give his preference to national products and cannot therefore be justified for the protection of consumers under the *Cassis de Dijon* rule of reason. An Article 177 reference by the *Oberlandesgericht* Köln in this case would have forced the ECJ to confront and perhaps reconsider this issue.[220]

(vi) Encouraging discrimination

The ECJ has held that campaigns conducted by public companies which encourage or attempt to persuade consumers to favour national products are capable of falling within the prohibition in Article 30.[221] Usually, the question which arises in such cases is whether the campaign may be considered to have been 'enacted by the Member State'.[222] However, it is also important to note that the ECJ has in such cases taken the view that Article 30 covers informal and merely persuasive action undertaken by Member States. In other words, mere recommendations, which have no binding legal status, may also breach Article 30.

The ECJ's approach to national campaigns which encourage consumers to prefer domestic goods over imports is however, more subtle. In *Apple and Pear Development Council* v. *Lewis*[223] it was held that national statutory companies are

under a duty not to engage in any advertising intended to discourage the purchase of products of other Member States or to disparage those products in the eyes of consumers. Nor must it advise consumers to purchase domestic products solely by reason of their national origin.[224]

The implications of this judgment were explained and elaborated on by the Commission which subsequently issued guidelines on Member States' involvement in the promotion of agricultural and fisheries products.[225] According to the Commission, it is permissible to promote a product by reference to its particular qualities, even if those qualities are typical of national production, but not simply because of national origin. The Commission stated its view that:

Identification of the producing country by word or symbol may be made providing that a reasonable balance between references, on the one hand to the qualities and varieties of the product and, on the other hand, to its national origin is kept. The references to national origin should be subsidiary to the main message put over to consumers by the campaign and not constitute the principal reason why consumers are being advised to buy the product.[226]

---

[220] For a discussion as to why it might be thought desirable for the ECJ to reconsider its position on this point, see in particular, Oliver, n. 71 above, 112–13.

[221] See e.g., Case 249/81, n. 29 above.

[222] See discussion of this question in sect. 4.   [223] Case 222/82, n. 97 above.

[224] Ibid. at para. 18.   [225] [1986] OJ C272/3.   [226] Ibid. at 4.

The national courts, charged with applying this case law, have a diffi-cult line to walk. These issues arose before the Queen's Bench Division of the English High Court in *Meat and Livestock Commission* v. *Manchester Wholesale Meat & Poultry Market*,[227] concerning a national television adver-tising campaign launched by the Meat and Livestock Commission, a statu-tory corporation upon whom is imposed the general duty to create greater efficiency in the livestock and livestock products industry in the United Kingdom. Moses J in the High Court reviewed the ECJ's test in the *Apple and Pear Development Council* case and the Commission's guidelines and held that

In my judgment, the appropriate test is whether the message conveyed by the cam-paign emphasises the domestic origin of the product to the extent that it may per-suade consumers to buy British meat because it is British or, if persuaded to buy meat, to buy British meat.[228]

In a thorough and detailed judgment, the High Court applied this to the facts and concluded that:

Looking at the campaign as a whole, the references to British meat are insignificant in comparison to the references to the quality of the meat and the usages to which it might be put . . . The advertisements seek to persuade the purchase of red meat by reference to the attractions of love or to the family or to versatility and health rather than to chauvinistic pride.[229]

The High Court thus concluded that the campaign in question centred on the quality rather than the national origin of the meat which it was pro-moting. It appears that this was a correct analysis on the given facts of this case. Nevertheless, as has already been noted, the line is an extremely fine one both for the national courts and for public corporations, such as the Meat and Livestock Commission, which are charged with promoting a product (*in casu* red meat) which does not possess a brand name with which consumers can identify.[230]

(B) Examples of indirectly applicable measures

The whole area of equally applicable measures is dominated by the land-mark decision of the ECJ in *Cassis de Dijon*.[231] Before proceeding to exam-ine national case law concerning equally applicable measures, that judgment needs to be briefly outlined here. German legislation precluded the sale of any spirits of the category into which the fruit liqueur Cassis

---

[227] n. 112 above, per Moses J.				[228] Ibid. at 147.				[229] Ibid. at 151.

[230] A brand-name developed on the basis of British origin would be contrary to Art. 30. This creates difficulties where third countries do take advantage of a brand name developed on the basis of origin (e.g. 'New Zealand Lamb').

[231] Case 120/78, n. 148 above.

fell, if the alcohol content of that spirit was below 25 per cent. The problem which arose was that the alcohol content of the Cassis de Dijon in question, which was lawfully produced and marketed in France, was between 15 and 20 per cent. Importers of the Cassis from France initiated proceedings since their application to the *Bundesmonopolverwaltung* (Federal Monopoly Administration for Spirits) for authorization to market the drink in Germany had been refused. The ECJ was thus faced with a non-discriminatory rule which applied to all fruit liqueurs marketed in Germany, without making any distinction according to origin. In other words, a product lawfully produced and marketed in France was excluded from the German market, not because of specific German legislation prohibiting the marketing of French Cassis in Germany, but simply because the rules in Germany differed from the rules in France. Different traditions in two Member States had led to an obstacle to trade and the partitioning of the common market. Faced with the question of whether the German legislation was compatible with Article 30, the ECJ replied that that provision was indeed breached. The Court held that 'There is . . . no valid reason why, provided that they have been lawfully produced and marketed in one of the Member States, alcoholic beverages should not be introduced into any other Member State'.[232] By holding that Article 30 applies to indistinctly applicable national rules, the ECJ succeeded in reinvigorating the common market by setting up a presumption on free trade.[233] Thus, a product lawfully marketed in one Member State should in principle be entitled to access to the market of another Member State and any measure preventing this, even if it applies to domestic and imported products alike, will be contrary to Article 30 and thus require justification.[234]

In national court case law, the single most striking 'error' which the courts make in applying Article 30 is to assume, contrary to the *Cassis de Dijon* case law, that a national measure which applies equally to national products and to imports is not capable of breaching Article 30. Time after time, these courts have expressly stated that the indistinctly applicable nature of a particular national measure is sufficient to exclude the application of Article 30. In the discussion which follows, concerning national case law dealing with indirectly applicable measures, frequent reference will be made to the instances where a national court has incorrectly

---

[232] Para. 14 of judgt.
[233] Additionally, the ECJ in its *Cassis de Dijon* judgment also fully enunciated the 'rule of reason' mandatory requirements approach which is discussed in Ch. 6.
[234] Well known examples of the application of the *Cassis de Dijon* approach to indistinctly applicable measures include: Case 178/84 *Commission* v. *Germany (Reinheitsgebot)* [1987] ECR 1227, [1988] 1 CMLR 780 & Cases 60 and 61/84 *Cinéthèque* v. *Fédération Nationale des Cinémas Français* [1985] ECR 2605, [1986] 1 CMLR 365. For a detailed discussion, see Oliver, n. 71 above, 92.

assumed that an indistinctly applicable national measure does not breach Article 30.[235]

The application of Article 30 and the *Dassonville* formula to indistinctly applicable measures has been substantially altered by the important judgment of the ECJ in *Keck and Mithouard*.[236] The impact of this judgment is discussed in detail in the following chapter. At this stage it may be noted that the ECJ held in *Keck and Mithouard* that:

In 'Cassis de Dijon' . . . it was held that, in the absence of harmonization of legislation, measures of equivalent effect prohibited by Article 30 include obstacles to the free movement of goods where they are the consequence of applying rules that lay down requirements to be met by goods (such as requirements as to designation, form, size, weight, composition, presentation, labelling, packaging) to goods from other Member States where they are lawfully manufactured and marketed, even if those rules apply without distinction to all products unless their application can be justified by a public interest objective taking precedence over the free movement of goods.

However, contrary to what has previously been decided, the application to products from other Member States of national provisions restricting or prohibiting certain selling arrangements is not such as to hinder directly or indirectly, actually or potentially, trade between Member States within the meaning of the *Dassonville* judgment . . . provided that those provisions apply to all affected traders operating within the national territory and provided that they affect in the same manner, in law and in fact, the marketing of domestic products and of those from other Member States.[237]

The facts of the case concerned French legislation prohibiting resale at a loss. Keck and Mithouard were prosecuted under this legislation for selling in their respective supermarkets certain items at a loss. In their defence, they raised the defence that the French law was contrary to Article 30 since it had a potential negative effect on trade. Applying the new ruling (set out above) to the facts, the ECJ decided that a prohibition on resale at a loss was a selling arrangement which affected all traders operating within the national territory and therefore fell entirely outside the scope of Article 30.

ECJ and national case-law subsequent to, and applying, this new departure by the ECJ is discussed in detail in the following chapter. For the present discussion, it may be noted that the essential tenet to the case law as laid down in *Keck* is a distinction between 'rules that lay down

---

[235] The instances in which the national courts explicitly state that the indistinctly applicable nature of a national measure excludes the application of Art. 30 are too numerous to cite comprehensively. As examples, see before the French courts: *Perron*, n. 69 above & *Rxxxx*, *Cour de Cassation*, ch. crim., 14 May 1996, Arrêt no. 2334 (transcr. available on Lexis); before the Dutch courts in *Autohandel- en sloperij J. R. BV*, n. 196 above and before the English courts in *Hodgkinson* v. *Nottingham City Council*, [1993] 3 CMLR 503.

[236] Cases C–267 & 268/91, n. 89 above.   [237] Paras. 15 & 16 of judgt.

requirements to be met by goods' on the one hand and 'selling arrangements' on the other. *Cassis de Dijon* remains of application to the former type of rule, while the new *Keck* approach applies only to the latter. In other words, if an indistinctly applicable national measure may be brought within the category of 'selling arrangements', it will fall outside Article 30 EC altogether provided that the measure in question applies 'to all affected traders operating within the national territory and provided that they affect in the same manner, in law and in fact, the marketing of domestic products and of those from other Member States'. It appears, therefore, that the ECJ has, departing from its *Dassonville/Cassis de Dijon* approach, introduced a discrimination requirement for the application of Article 30 to indistinctly applicable national measures that fall within the category of 'selling arrangements'.

(i) Requirements that goods be sold by qualified persons

National provisions requiring that certain goods be sold exclusively by retailers holding particular qualifications have been challenged as being in breach of Article 30 EC. One such example was provided by French legislation[238] which granted pharmacists the exclusive right to sell medical products. In a series of cases before the French courts, certain supermarkets were prosecuted for selling medical products contrary to this French legislation. These retailers raised a defence based on Article 30, claiming essentially that if the products could be marketed in other Member States as cosmetics, restricting channels of distribution for the products in France by limiting their sale through pharmacies affected trade between Member States within the meaning of the *Dassonville* formula. The French national courts accorded this defence a mixed reception. On the one hand, the Paris *Cour d'appel* in *Laboratoires Searle SA* v. *Laboratoires SARPP*[239] quoted the wording of the *Dassonville* formula and noted that the products in question were not restricted to sale by pharmacists in other Member States, and concluded that 'the existence of this monopoly, contrary to the free movement of goods, is manifestly of such a nature as to restrict (*restreindre*) importation'. By contrast, the *Cour de Cassation* in *Ministère public* v. *Norbert Desolière*[240] held that the French legislation in question 'was not of such a nature as to be a barrier to the free movement of pharmaceuticals between Member States'.[241] The matter was subsequently referred to the

---

[238] Art. L. 512 of the *Code de santé publique* (Public Health Act).

[239] *Cour d'appel* Paris, 1re ch. A, 16 Dec. 1987, Gaz. Pal. 1988, I Jur. 245.

[240] *Cour de Cassation*, ch. crim., 18 Oct. 1988, Bull. Cass. Crim. 1988, no. 352 p. 945; Gaz. Pal. 1989, I Jur. 683 (with note by Mauro); JCP 1988, IV 404 (summary); Dalloz 1988, IR 284 (summary).

[241] The *Cour de Cassation* went on to hold that the measures were, in any event, justified for the protection of public health under Art. 36 EC. See discussion of this aspect of this judgt in Ch. 7, sect. 4 (B).

ECJ by the *Tribunal de grande instance* of Nice in *Delattre*[242] and by the *Cour d'appel* of Aix-en-Provence in *Ministère public* v. *Jean Monteil et Daniel Samanni*.[243] In both these cases, the ECJ held that the French legislation was capable of breaching Article 30, since

a monopoly granted to dispensing pharmacists in respect of the marketing of medicinal or other products is capable, in so far as it restricts sales to certain channels, of affecting the possibilities of marketing imported products and may accordingly constitute a measure having an effect equivalent to a quantitative restriction on imports within the meaning of Article 30 of the Treaty.[244]

French national court decisions handed down *after* these ECJ judgments correctly assumed that Article 30 was breached by the legislation and proceeded directly to the question of justification under Article 36 EC.[245] The only somewhat peculiar decision after the ECJ judgment was that of the *Cour de Cassation* in *Nauleau*[246] where an appeal was dismissed simply by stating that 'the barrier to imports is in principle and, in the absence of proof to the contrary by the defendant, is justified with respect to medical products'.[247] It is submitted that the fact that the barrier to imports 'is in principle' should have been irrelevant as the ECJ had held (as is set out above) that the crucial aspect was that sales to certain channels were restricted.[248]

An analogous set of cases with respect to national requirements that goods be sold by qualified persons has arisen with respect to national monopolies accorded to opticians for the sale of reading spectacles and contact lenses. The issue arose before the English courts in *SA Magnavision NV* v. *General Optical Council* (No. 1).[249] In that case, Magnavision, a Belgian company, marketed spectacles in the UK through a chain of concessions in British department stores where customers simply tested their own sight using a test-card and then selected an appropriate pair of spectacles without a prescription and without the supervision of an optician. Magnavision was prosecuted for selling spectacles without an optician or

---

[242] *TGI* Nice, 12 Dec. 1988.

[243] *Cour d'appel* Aix-en-Provence, 7e ch. corr., 7 Nov. 1988.

[244] Case C–369/88 *Delattre* [1991] ECR I–1487 at para. 51 & Case C–60/89 *Ministère public* v. *Jean Monteil et Daniel Samanni* [1991] ECR I–1547 at para. 38.

[245] See *Bocquin, Cour de Cassation*, ch. crim., 14 Oct. 1992, Bull. Cass. Crim. 1992, no. 326 p. 899; *Conseil National de l'Ordre des Pharmaciens* v. *Ruth, Cour de Cassation*, ch. crim., 25 May 1994, Bull. Cass. Crim. 1994, no. 202 p. 468; Dalloz 1994, IR 185 (summary); [1995] 1 CMLR 718 and *Kxxxx and Mxxxx, Cour de Cassation*, ch. crim., 3 Nov. 1994, Pourvoi no. 92-86.577, (transcr. available on Lexis).

[246] *Cour de Cassation*, ch. crim., 10 Mar. 1993, Bull. Cass. Crim. 1993, no. 108 p. 261.

[247] In the original French: '*l'entrave apportée aux importations est en principe et sauf preuve contraire à la charge du prevenu, justifiée en ce qui concerne les medicaments.*'

[248] The conclusion of the *Cour de Cassation* in *Nauleau* that the measure was justified is also inadequate and is discussed further at p. 265.

[249] [1987] 1 CMLR 887.

prescription in breach of Section 21 of the Opticians Act 1958 according to which spectacles could not be sold in Britain except under the supervision of a doctor or optician or on production of an optician's prescription. The firm was convicted by Cardiff Magistrates' Court and appealed by way of case stated to the Divisional Court, arguing that the United Kingdom legislation breached Article 30 EC in that it limited channels of distribution which, although indistinctly applicable, was capable of actually or potentially affecting imports of spectacles into the United Kingdom from other Member States. This alleged breach of Article 30 was rejected by MacPherson J in the Queen's Bench Division of the English High Court. In a very poor application of Article 30, the High Court excluded the application of Article 30. The High Court set out the *Dassonville* formula, but then proceeded to distinguish the application of that formula on the facts.[250] Given that the ECJ has repeated the precise wording of the *Dassonville* formula in a multitude of subsequent cases, the attempt to limit the formula to the facts of that case is, with respect, ludicrous. Even more surprising is the statement that:

It is true that the *Cassis de Dijon* case shows that national measures can infringe Article 30 even though they apply to both imported and domestic products, subject to justification by reference to the mandatory requirement under examination . . . But *Cassis de Dijon* involved effectively a direct ban upon the sale of the low alcohol beverage and thus upon its import to Germany. So that the measures were plainly discriminatory and protectionist in their effect.[251]

The discussion of the *Cassis de Dijon* case above[252] suffices to show that the facts of that case involved neither a direct ban and nor were the measures discriminatory. As has been noted, the ECJ was faced in *Cassis de Dijon* with a non-discriminatory rule which applied to all fruit liqueurs marketed in Germany, without making any distinction according to origin; a liqueur lawfully produced and marketed in France was excluded from the German market, not because of specific German legislation prohibiting the marketing of French Cassis in Germany, but simply because the rules in Germany differed from the rules in France. The exclusion of the application of Article 30 by the English High Court was thus considerably wide of the mark.[253] This is confirmed by a subsequent decision of the ECJ on a reference from the French *Cour de Cassation* in *Laboratoire de protèses oculaires (LPO)* v. *Union nationale des syndicats d'opticiens de France*.[254] That case

---

[250] Ibid. at 891.   [251] Ibid. at 892.   [252] pp. 53–4.

[253] The application of Art. 30 in *Magnavision* is also critically examined at pp. 96–9 with regard to the High Court's failure to recognize that a 'potential' effect on trade is sufficient for Art. 30 to bite and at p. 426 with regard to its failure to make an Art. 177 reference to the ECJ.

[254] *Cour de Cassation*, ch. comm., 2 June 1992, Bull. Cass. Civ. 1992, IV no. 216 p. 151; Dalloz 1993, IR 185; Case C–271/92 [1993] ECR I–2899.

concerned French legislation virtually identical to the English legislation at issue in *Magnavision*, which conferred upon qualified opticians the sole right to sell contact lenses. The ECJ held that

[T]he French legislation at issue in the main proceedings applies without distinction to domestic and imported products and has no direct effect on imports. However, as that legislation prohibits certain forms of marketing, it must be borne in mind that the Court has held that national legislation which grants to members of a specific profession the exclusive right to distribute certain products is capable, in so far as it restricts sales to certain channels, of affecting the possibilities of marketing imported products and may accordingly constitute a measure having an effect equivalent to a quantitative restriction on imports within the meaning of Article 30 of the Treaty . . . It follows that legislation of the kind at issue in the main proceedings, which reserves to specialized agents the sale of contact lenses and related products, is capable of affecting intra-Community trade.[255]

Although the ECJ went on to hold that the French legislation was nevertheless justified under Article 36 on the grounds of public health, the acceptance that the national requirement breached Article 30 in the first place, demonstrates that the complete rejection of the application of Article 30 by the English High Court in *Magnavision* was, at that time at least, far from certain. For the sake of completeness, it may be noted that the *Cour de Cassation* had no problem when it came to implementing the judgment of the ECJ in *Laboratoire de protèses oculaires (LPO)* v. *Union nationale des syndicats d'opticiens de France* in accepting that the French legislation infringed Article 30 but was nevertheless justified under Article 36.[256]

Following the judgment of the ECJ in *Keck and Mithouard*,[257] national rules requiring that goods be sold only by qualified persons would now almost certainly be considered to be 'selling arrangements' and accordingly fall outside the scope of Article 30 altogether.[258]

(ii) Restrictions on advertising and promotion

The ECJ's judgment in *Keck and Mithouard* has similarly had a significant impact on previous case law governing national restrictions on advertising and promotion. Before *Keck*, the ECJ consistently took the view that

---

[255] [1993] ECR I–2899 at paras. 6–8.

[256] *Cour de Cassation*, ch. comm., 4 Jan. 1994, Bull. Cass. Civ. 1994, IV no. 2 p. 1, Dalloz 1994, IR 26, [1994] ECC 457. See also *LPO* v. *Syndicat des Opticiens Français Independents*, *Cour de Cassation*, ch. sociale, 14 Nov. 1995, transcr. 93-17.485, which concerned the subsequent award of damages and *Syndicat des Opticiens Français Independents* and *Ministre delegue à la santé* v. *Dreher*, *Conseil d'Etat*, 23 Oct. 1995 (transcr.; 150.212).

[257] n. 89 above.

[258] See esp. Case C–391/92 *Commission* v. *Hellenic Republic* [1995] ECR I–1621 (concerning national legislation requiring processed milk for infants to be sold exclusively through pharmacists' shops) and discussion of post-*Keck and Mithouard* case law in Ch. 3, sect. 3.

indistinctly applicable national measures which restricted certain methods of advertising breached Article 30 and were subject to justification under either the rule of reason (usually under the head of consumer protection) or Article 36. The ECJ reasoned that 'legislation which restricts or prohibits certain forms of advertising and certain means of sales promotion may, although it does not directly affect trade, be such as to restrict the volume of trade because it affects marketing opportunities'.[259] For example, in *Aragonesa* v. *Departamento de Sanidad*,[260] the ECJ held that Spanish legislation which prohibited the advertising in certain places of beverages having an alcoholic strength of more than 23 per cent constituted a hindrance to imports from other Member States contrary to Article 30 (but justified for the protection of public health under Article 36).

The most striking feature of the application by national courts of this pre-*Keck* case law is the frequency with which these courts excluded the application of Article 30 on the facts of individual cases. In practice, this usually involved a finding by the national court that, on the facts of an individual case, the volume of trade was not restricted because marketing opportunities were not in any way affected. Thus for example, the *Arrondissementsrechtbank* Amsterdam in *L'Oréal SA* v. *Stichting Reclamecode*,[261] upheld the decision of the *CvB* of the *SNRC*[262] that the Code on Misleading Advertising (*Nederlandse Code voor het Reclamewezen*) had been breached by the advertising by L'Oréal of its 'Plenitude' skin-care product. The *Arrondissementsrechtbank* rejected the argument that L'Oréal was thereby prevented from using an advertising slogan in the Netherlands which it was able to use in other Member States since it had been shown on the facts that the advertising for 'Plenitude' in other Member States used a different slogan and that in any event, in each language area L'Oréal used a different packaging such that 'the possible importance of a uniform slogan is of very little practical importance'. On similar facts before the *RCC* in *Ferrero BV* v. *STER*[263] it was similarly held that it had not, on the facts, been shown that the same television advertising campaign as that at issue in that case had been used in other Member States.[264]

---

[259] Case C–362/88 *GB-Inno-Bm* v. *Confédération du Commerce Luxembourgoise* [1990] ECR I–667, [1991] 2 CMLR 801 at para. 7. See also Case 286/81 *Oosthoek's Uitgeversmaatschappij* [1982] ECR 4547, [1983] 3 CMLR 428 & Case C–126/91 *Schutzverband gegen Unwesen in der Wirtschaft* v. *Yves Rocher* [1993] ECR I–2361.

[260] Cases C–1 & 176/90 [1991] ECR I–4151, [1994] 1 CMLR 887.   [261] n. 133 above.

[262] See discussion in sect. 4 (B) concerning the status of this body in Dutch law and the question as to whether its actions could be considered to have been 'enacted by Member States'.

[263] n. 128 above.

[264] See also *L'Oréal Nederland BV*, n. 122 above, where it was held that the television advertising that was found to be misleading in that case did not, on the facts, affect marketing opportunities since the advertising slogan used in France (the only other Member State where the product had been advertised on television) was not, in any event, the same as that in the Netherlands.

The German courts have occasionally also taken a similar line excluding the application of Article 30 on the facts. In for example, *Re a cosmetics advertising slogan*,[265] the *Oberlandesgericht* Munich rejected the argument that prohibiting misleading advertising (under section 3 of the German Unfair Competition Act (*Gesetz gegen den unlauteren Wettbewerb (UWG)*) of certain Yves Rocher cosmetics would breach Article 30 on the grounds that the defendant had failed to show 'that such advertising would be permitted abroad'.[266] It thus seems that the effect of the wide view of Article 30 adopted by the ECJ before *Keck* (according to which national advertising restrictions which may affect marketing opportunities would fall within the scope of Article 30), was somewhat blunted in the national courts by their finding that marketing opportunities were not really affected on the facts of individual cases.

The French courts have also had occasion to reject the application of Article 30 on the facts in similar circumstances. In *Syndicat de l'Armagnac et des vins du Gers*[267] the *Conseil d'Etat* held that the schedule of conditions of a television channel could prohibit the advertisement of alcoholic drinks with an alcoholic content exceeding 9 per cent as long as this prohibition was applicable in the same way to national products as it was to imports from Member States of the EC. The *Conseil d'Etat* took care to explain that there was absolutely no evidence to prove that the degree of alcohol chosen would be to the advantage of national products *vis-à-vis* imports and thus held that Article 30 was not infringed. While the assumption by the *Conseil d'Etat* in this judgment that indistinctly applicable measures may not breach Article 30 is open to criticism,[268] it is interesting to note within the context of the present discussion, that this is yet another instance of a national court denying the application of Article 30 on the facts.

As was noted above, the goal posts in this area have been substantially shifted by the judgment of the ECJ in *Keck and Mithouard*. ECJ judgments subsequent to that judgment appear to make clear that indistinctly applicable national restrictions on advertising are to be regarded as 'selling arrangements' and, subject to the provisos set out in *Keck*,[269] will now fall

---

[265] *OLG* München, 17 Sept. 1992, [1994] 3 CMLR 41.

[266] Ibid. at 50. It may be noted that the *OLG* Munich did, in the alternative, go on to find that if it was nevertheless concluded that Art. 30 was breached, the national restriction would be justified for consumer-protection reasons under the rule of reason. For similar instances before the Belgian courts, see a judgt of the President of the Comm. Mechelen, 18 Mar. 1991, Jaarboek Handelspraktijken/Annuaires Pratiques du Commerce 1991, 70 (with note by Straetmans) and *Cubic* v. *APT Data Services*, Comm. Bruxelles, 4 Sept. 1992, noted by Wytink, 'The Application of Community law in Belgium: 1986–1992' at 1002.

[267] *Conseil d'Etat*, 17 Dec. 1986, AJDA 1987, 125; CDE 1989, 418 (summary); Rev. franç. dr. admin. 1987, 25 (noted by Azibert and De Boisdeffre AJDA 1987, 80).

[268] See discussion on this point at pp. 54–5.

[269] See p. 55.

entirely outside the scope of Article 30.[270] Given this, it is surprising that
in the judgment of the *Arrondissementsrechtbank* Amsterdam in *L'Oréal SA*
v. *Stichting Reclamecode*[271] (discussed above) no mention was made of the
Keck judgment in spite of the fact that this judgment was delivered little
under a year after *Keck*. The same is true of a decision of the French *Cour
de Cassation* in *Bowes*[272] where the *Keck* judgment (which had been handed
down six months earlier) was neither mentioned nor applied. The *Bowes*
case concerned the controversial *Loi Evin* in France,[273] Article L. 18 of
which provides that *any* advertisement of alcoholic drinks is limited to
going *no further* than mentioning 'the alcoholic strength, the origin, the
name and the composition of the product, the identity and address of
the producer, agents and stockists and, with the minimum elaboration, the
arrangements for sale and directions for consumption of the product'.
That Article of the French legislation goes on to add that 'information
regarding the region of production/soil (*terroir de production*) and awards
obtained' may also be mentioned. In other words, the advertising of alcoholic drinks in France will only be lawful if it limits itself to those characteristics mentioned in L. 18.

The defendants in this case were distributors for J&B whisky in France
and were prosecuted for an advertisement placed in a magazine spanning
several pages of night views of various capital cities with a gap in the sky
showing part of the label of a bottle of J&B whisky. On the last page of the
magazine there was the full label of the bottle with a gap showing a sky at
night. The defendants were convicted by the *Cour d'appel* of Paris of a
breach of Article L. 18 of the *Loi Evin*. It was held that the advertisement in
question went beyond the Article L. 18 limitations, which allow only a
simple reference to 'arrangements for sale' and 'directions for consumption'. The *Cour de Cassation* upheld the conviction and simply repeated the
operative part of the *Cour d'appel*'s judgment. The latter court was, however, more cryptic with respect to the arguments about the free movement
of goods. It had been argued that by allowing mention in advertisements
of *terroir de production* (the region of production/soil), Article L. 18
favoured advertising of wine products as against other alcoholic drinks
and thus constituted arbitrary discrimination. The *Cour de Cassation* disagreed and held that 'the word "region" used in Article L. 18 is not specific

---

[270] See Case C–292/92 *Hünermund* v. *Landesapothekerkammer Baden-Württemberg* [1993]
ECR I–6787 & Case C–412/93 *Leclerc-Siplec* v. *TF1 Publicité* [1995] ECR I–179.

[271] n. 133 above.

[272] *Cour de Cassation*, ch. crim., 18 May 1994, Bull. Cass. Crim. 1994, no. 190 p. 434; Dalloz
1994, IR 184–5 (summary); [1995] 1 CMLR 455.

[273] Loi No. 91-32, 10 Jan. 1991, JORF 12 Jan. 1991; JCP 1991, III 64484 amending the *Code
Débits Boissons* (Sale of Beverages Code). See Decocq, 'Le Nouvelles restrictions à la publicité
en faveur des boissons alcooliques' & Grelon, 'La Publicité sur le territoire français des
Boisssons Alcooliques: Les incertitudes actuelles de la Loi Evin'.

to wine products and also relates to other alcoholic beverages, whether French or foreign'. Furthermore, the *Cour de Cassation* went on to hold that 'the restrictions imposed by French law on advertising for alcoholic beverages affected national products as well as products imported from other Member States of the Community, with no distinction as to origin, and are therefore not discriminatory measures'.[274] It would thus appear that the *Cour de Cassation* was holding that Article 30 was not breached by the French legislation. However, without further explanation, the *Cour* went on to discuss the question of the protection of public health under Article 36 and the proportionality issue.[275] Thus, on the one hand the *Cour de Cassation* seems to have excluded the application of Article 30 on the basis that it was indistinctly applicable[276] while on the other hand, without making clear that this is in the alternative, it held that the measure was justified under Article 36. These observations aside, what is rather surprising in the context of the present discussion is that the *Cour de Cassation* neither cited nor applied the *Keck and Mithouard* judgment which had been handed down by the ECJ six months prior to the *Cour de Cassation*'s judgment. Indeed, as has been explained above, if the *Cour de Cassation* wished to exclude the application of Article 30, the correct grounds available at the time of the judgment would have been to conclude that indistinctly applicable national measures restricting advertising are to be considered as 'selling arrangements' and thus outside the scope of Article 30 altogether. Indeed it has subsequently been held by the ECJ in *Leclerc-Siplec* v. *TF1 Publicité*[277] that the provisions of the *Loi Evin* fall within the definition of 'selling arrangements'. It is submitted that, at the very least, the *Cour de Cassation* should, as a court of last resort, have considered the possibility of referring the question to the ECJ under the Article 177 EC preliminary-rulings procedure.[278]

This apparent failure to perceive the application of the *Keck* judgment by the *Cour de Cassation* in *Bowes* may be contrasted with a judgment of the Supreme French Administrative Court, the *Conseil d'Etat*, in *Société Tour*

---

[274] See also to similar effect, *ANPA* v. *Brasseries Heineken, TGI* Paris, 1re. ch., 3 Nov. 1993 (noted Revue européenne de droit de la consommation 1994, 72).

[275] See discussion of this aspect of the judgt at p. 277.

[276] See also the recent judgments of the Criminal Division of the *Cour de Cassation* in *Boulet, Cour de Cassation*, ch. crim., 2 Apr. 1997, pourvoi no. 95-82.191 (transcr. available on Lexis) & *Decaux* v. *Société RPMU, Cour de Cassation*, ch. crim., 10 Apr. 1997, pourvoi no. R 96-83.152 (transcr. available on Lexis), where certain restrictions on advertising were held not to breach Art. 30 explicitly because they were indistinctly applicable. For sharp criticism of the national courts for incorrectly assuming that indistinctly applicable national measures do not breach Art. 30, see pp. 54–5.

[277] Case C–412/93 [1995] ECR I–179.

[278] The *Cour de Cassation* did not even consider making a reference to the ECJ under Art. 177(3) EC, although the grounds of appeal explicitly included a reference to the necessity for such a reference.

Pol.[279] In that case, the relevance of the *Keck* judgment to certain French restrictions on the advertising of health products was recognized and the *Conseil d'Etat* held that such a restriction did not, after the *Keck* judgment, breach Article 30. This judgment of the *Conseil d'Etat* is discussed in depth in the following chapter in the context of the application of the *Keck* ruling in national courts.[280]

(iii) Restrictions regulating the time and place where goods may be sold

The construal of national restrictions regulating the time and place where goods may be sold as indistinctly applicable measures capable of breaching Article 30 has been one of the most sensitive and confusion-ridden areas of the ECJ's case law on Article 30. For example, the ECJ has been faced with the compatibility with Article 30 of national regulations governing shop-opening hours,[281] doorstep selling[282] and the licensing of sex shops.[283] In short, the problem has been that the ECJ has failed to sail a steady course. The confused and contradictory ECJ case law is discussed in depth in the following chapter, as is the national court case law attempting, with great difficulty, to follow in the ECJ's wake. As will be seen, the national courts have encountered considerable difficulties in applying the confused ECJ case law. These difficulties have centred principally on the insufficient guidance which the ECJ has offered the national courts as to the relevance of a *potential* effect on trade (see discussion in Chapter 3) and the adjacent question of whether the 'restrictions' may nevertheless be justified (see discussion in Chapter 6).

In general, apart from certain difficulties in discerning an 'actual or potential effect on trade', the national courts have shown themselves willing in cases concerning national restrictions on the time and place where goods may be sold to find a breach of Article 30 and to proceed to the question of justification. Where there has been a difficulty, it has usually stemmed from the common assumption by the national courts that indistinctly applicable measures do not breach Article 30.[284] Thus, in the first reported Sunday-trading case in the United Kingdom, the English High

---

[279] CE, 7 July 1995, Rec. Lebon 1995, 287.   [280] See Ch. 3, sect. 3 (B).

[281] See Case C–145/88, n. 102 above (referred to the ECJ by Cwmbran Magistrates' Court and implemented by that court [1990] 3 CMLR 455).

[282] Case 382/87 *Roger Buet et SARL Education Business Services* v. *Ministère public* [1989] ECR 1235 (referred to the ECJ by the *Cour d'appel* Paris, 9e ch. corr. B, 27 Nov. 1987, [1988] 3 CMLR 426).

[283] Case C–23/89 *Quietlynn Ltd and Richards* v. *Southend-on-Sea BC* [1990] ECR I–3059; [1990] 3 CMLR 55 (referred to ECJ by Chelmsford Crown Court); Case C–350/89 *Sheptonhurst Ltd* v. *Newham LBC* [1991] ECR I–2387; [1991] 3 CMLR 463 (referred to the ECJ by the Queen's Bench Division of the High Court). See also the decision of the Court of Appeal in *Portsmouth CC* v. *Richards & Quietlynn Ltd* [1989] 1 CMLR 673.

[284] See discussion of this point at pp. 54–5.

Court granted an injunction to restrain the opening of a market on a Sunday and dismissed the Article 30 defence, since

To make a good defence based on Article 30 . . . the defendants must show that any particular prohibitions to which they object are provisions which in practice put imported products at a disadvantage compared to domestic products capable of being regarded as acceptable substitutes for them.[285]

A suggestion that non-discriminatory national rules on shop-opening hours may not breach Article 30 was also voiced by the *Cour d'appel* of Montpelier in *Gérard Leib* v. *Ministère public* which commented that 'the closing on Sundays prevents the sale of all furniture, even if of French origin' and so the French legislation could not be considered to be 'an anti-competitive or protectionist measure'.[286] Similarly, in *Falck*, the *Cour de Cassation* held that French legislation requiring that temporary shops (*vente au deballage*) receive prior authorization from local authorities did not breach Article 30 since 'it was not shown, nor even alleged, that the [goods] sold . . . were submitted to conditions of sale more rigorous than those applying to national products'.[287] Finally in *SA British Motors Wright* v. *SCP Boscher, Studer et Fromentin et Nado GmbH*, the *Cour d'appel* of Paris held that French legislation which prohibited the sale of second-hand goods by auction unless the vendor had been registered for at least two years in the local business register, was not incompatible with Article 30 since the measure applied without discrimination with respect to the origin of the goods for sale in that case.[288] That this was an incorrect conclusion was confirmed by the subsequent judgment of the ECJ on a referral on appeal by the *Cour de Cassation*.[289] The ECJ held that in spite of the fact that the measure applied without distinction to the sale of domestic and imported products, it was nevertheless 'liable to impede the free movement of goods, since its effect is to require the owner of the goods either to use the services of a trader operating at the place of the sale or to refrain from selling the goods by public auction'.[290] The above cases demonstrate that in cases concerning national restrictions on the time and place where goods may be sold, the national courts have been particularly apt to

[285] *Wychavon District Council* v. *Midland Enterprises (Special Event) Ltd* [1988] 1 CMLR 397 at 405. See also *London Borough of Waltham Forest* v. *Scott Markets Ltd* [1988] 3 CMLR 773 and discussion of the Sunday-trading cases in Ch. 6, sect. 4 (E).

[286] *Cour d'appel* Montpellier, 3e ch. corr., 5 Nov. 1990, Gaz. Pal. 1991, I Jur. 253 (with note by Roubach).

[287] *Cour de Cassation*, ch. crim., 25 Oct. 1993, Bull. Cass. Crim. 1993, no. 309 p. 776. The *Cour de Cassation* went on, however, to find that the national measure was in any event justified for the protection of consumers. See further discussion of this aspect of the judgt at p. 189.

[288] *Cour d'appel* Paris, 1re ch. A, 5 Nov. 1988, Dalloz 1988, IR 296 (summary); Gaz. Pal. 1989, I Jur. 159 (with note by Marchi).

[289] *Cour de Cassation*, ch. comm., 3 July 1990, Bull. Cass. Civ. 1990, IV no. 198 p. 137; JCP 1990, IV 332 (summary).

[290] Case C–239/90 [1991] ECR I–2023, [1994] 3 CMLR 410 at paras 16 & 17.

assume that indistinctly applicable measures do not breach Article 30. Prior to the ECJ judgment in *Keck and Mithouard*, this was an incorrect assumption for the national courts to have made.[291] Following the *Keck* judgment, of course, national restrictions on the time and place where goods may be sold are considered to be 'selling arrangements' and, as such, now fall outside the ambit of Article 30 so long as they apply to all traders operating within the national market.[292]

(iv) Restrictions as to the presentation of goods

The judgment of the ECJ in *Cassis de Dijon* makes clear that indistinctly applicable national measures concerning the presentation of goods will breach Article 30. A well-known ECJ decision illustrating this concerned a Belgian requirement that margarine be marketed in Belgium in cubic (rather than circular) packaging so as to allow consumers to distinguish margarine from butter. The ECJ held that although indistinctly applicable, the Belgian requirement on the presentation of margarine breached Article 30 since

it is of such a nature as to render the marketing of [the imported] products more difficult or more expensive either by barring them from certain channels of distribution or owing to the additional costs brought about by the necessity to package the products in question in special packs which comply with the requirements in force on the market of their destination.[293]

The national courts have encountered little difficulty in construing national requirements on the presentation of goods as breaching Article 30 and subject to justification. Thus, for example, in *Openbaar Ministerie v. R.-Bakkerijen BV*,[294] the *Rechtbank* Arnhem held that Article 3 of the Dutch Decision Concerning Bread (*Broodbesluit*) requiring that the nature and composition of bread be clear from the name of the bread alone, was a hindrance to the importation of bread (*in casu 'roggebrood'* lawfully marketed in Germany) subject to justification.[295]

Regrettably, application by national courts of this point has not been completely problem-free. The reasoning of the national courts has often been far from clear. In *Smanor SA v. Syndicat national des fabricants de*

---

[291] See discussion at pp. 54–5 on this point.

[292] See esp. Cases C–69 and 258/93 *Punto Casa v. Sindicato del Commune di Capena* [1994] ECR I–2355, Cases C–401 & 402/92 *Tankstation 't Heukske vof and J. B. E. Boermans* [1994] ECR I–2199; Cases C–418–421/93 & 460–464/93 & 9–15/94 & 23–24/94 & 332/94 *Semeraro Casa Uno Srl* [1996] ECR I–2975 & Case C–387/93 *Criminal proceedings against Giorgio Domigo Banchero* [1995] ECR I–4663.

[293] Case 261/81 *Walter Rau v. De Smedt* [1982] ECR 3961, [1983] 2 CMLR 496 at para. 13.

[294] *Arrondissementsrechtbank* Arnhem, 6 Apr. 1981, NJ 1981, 388.

[295] For other straightforward examples, see *De Alternatieve Konsumentenbond v. Mars BV*, RCC, 15 June 1993, IER 1993, 38; BIE 1995, 22 and *Campin, Cour de Cassation*, ch. crim., 9 Nov. 1987, Bull. Cass. Crim. 1987, no. 394 p. 1038.

produits surgelés et congelés,[296] Smanor applied to have French legislation (the effect of which was to prohibit Smanor from using the designation 'yoghurt' for the sale of deep-frozen yoghurt in France)[297] annulled on the basis that it breached Article 30. The argument was that the product in question could be presented in other Member States as deep-frozen yoghurt and thus that the restriction in the French legislation on the use of the term yoghurt was a hindrance to trade. The *Conseil d'Etat* dismissed the Article 30 argument since

the sole object of the provisions, which do not in themselves entail any quantitative restriction on importation, is to restrict the denomination 'yoghurt' in the interests of consumers to certain products presenting certain characteristics and they cannot be regarded as having an effect equivalent to such restrictions.

The reasoning of the *Conseil d'Etat* is, with respect, extremely confused.[298] In particular, there is no reference to anything resembling the *Dassonville* formula, and nor is it clear whether the *Conseil* was holding that the measure was justified under the rule of reason. It is only by reading the conclusions of *Commissaire du Gouvernement* Lasserre to the *Conseil d'Etat*, that it emerges that what it appears to have meant was that the French measure was justified under the rule of reason and, as such, did not breach Article 30. The status and effect of the rule of reason is discussed elsewhere in this work,[299] but in the context of the present discussion, it suffices to note that before the rule of reason applies, a breach of Article 30 must first be established. This is confirmed by the subsequent judgment of the ECJ in *SA Smanor* on a separate reference from the *Tribunal commercial* of L'Aigle,[300] where the ECJ cited the *Dassonville* formula and held that although the French legislation on the presentation of the product 'does not absolutely preclude the importation into the Member State concerned of products originating in other Member States . . . it may none the less make their marketing more difficult and thus impede, at least indirectly, trade between Member States'.[301] Thus, a

[296] *Conseil d'Etat*, 19 Nov. 1986, Rec. Lebon 1986, 259, JCP 1987, II 20822; AJDA 1986, 714; RTDE 1988, 117; CDE 1989, 418.

[297] Art. 11, Law of 5 Aug. 1905 as amended by Law of 10 Jan. 1978 and Decree No. 82-184 of 22 Feb. 1982, JORF 25 Feb. 1982, 676.

[298] For criticisms of this judgment see Azibert and De Boisdeffre AJDA 1986, 681; Constantinesco, Simon and Soler-Couteaux, RTDE 1988, 113–17. The Fourth Report to the European Parliament on Commission Monitoring of the Application of Community Law [1987] OJ C338 commented that the *Conseil d'Etat* 'interpreted and applied Community law in a manner which, at the very least, raises questions in view of the established case law of the Court of Justice concerning Art. 30'. Even more virulent was the Sixth Report [1989] OJ C330/I (includes appendix, 'The Attitude of National Supreme Courts to Community Law') which described the *Conseil d'Etat*'s judgt as a 'serious breach of the principle of uniformity of judicial decisions'.

[299] See Ch. 6.   [300] *Trib. Comm.* L'Aigle, 21 Sept. 1987.

[301] Case 298/87 [1988] ECR 4489 at para. 12.

national requirement restricting the presentation of deep-frozen yoghurt in France, was controversially misconstrued by the French *Conseil d'Etat* by its conclusion that Article 30 was not breached.[302]

An equally serious misapplication of Article 30 was carried out by the Dutch *RCC* and its *College van Beroep* in *Dommelsch NA België*.[303] That case concerned the importation into the Netherlands of beer with an alcohol content of 0.5 per cent from Belgium. However, the effect of the Dutch Beer Regulation (*Nederlandse Bierverordening*) was to restrict the presentation of beer with an alcohol content of less than 0.6 per cent by prohibiting such beer from being labelled *alcoholvrij* (alcohol-free) and requiring it to be presented as *alcoholarm* (low alcohol). The problem was that Belgian legislation provided that beer with an alcohol content of less than 1 per cent could nevertheless be labelled alcohol-free (*alcoholvrij*). Thus the practical effect of the Dutch requirement was that the beer had to be relabelled for the Dutch market. Confronted with the argument that this would breach Article 30, the *RCC* simply denied the application of that Article. It was held that the provisions of the *Bierverordening* 'do not have the characteristics of a quantitative restriction on imports or a measure having equivalent effect under Article 30 EEC Treaty' and that the Dutch provisions do not form either a direct or indirect or potential restriction on the import of Dommelsch beer, which is not in any way any less well treated than national products so that there was no 'factual disadvantage' for the imported product.[304] On appeal, the *CvB* explicitly left open the question of whether Article 30 was breached and decided the matter on the basis that the Belgian legislation did not comply with a decision of the Committee of Ministers of the Benelux on 5 October 1982, concerning the labelling and presentation of beer. It is submitted that contrary to these rulings, there was, on the facts of this case, a clear breach of Article 30 (subject to justification). It is submitted that this is a classic *Cassis de Dijon*-type case: a product lawfully marketed in Belgium was excluded from the Dutch market because the Dutch requirements on the presentation of the product were different to the Belgian ones. According to this well-established case law, such rules will be contrary to Article 30 and thus require justification (probably for the protection of consumers[305]). It is

---

[302] The misconstrual is all the more serious since, when the ECJ's judgment in the separate reference (n. 301 above) came back before the *Tribunal commercial* of L'Aigle for implementation, Smanor had gone into receivership. It seems very likely that the misconstrual by the *Conseil d'Etat* in this decision had a role to play in pushing Smanor out of business. It may also be noted that the owners of SA Smanor were subsequently unsuccessful in an attempt to obtain legal redress: see judgment of the *Cour de Cassation*, ch. crim., 25 June 1996, Arrêt No. 2889, transcr. available on Lexis.

[303] *RCC*, 10 Apr. 1991 & *CvB*, 28 Oct. 1991, both reported at *RCC* 1991, no. 663 p. 79.

[304] See also *Crodino*, *RCC* 30 Dec. 1988 & *CvB*, 23 May 1989, both reported at *RCC* 1989, no. 6054 p. 96.

[305] See discussion of this in Ch. 6, sect. 3.

thus somewhat surprising that the *RCC* stated that the Dutch provisions did not have the characteristics of a quantitative restriction or a measure of equivalent effect without stating what those characteristics were. The reference to the fact that the Dutch measure was indistinctly applicable and that there was no 'factual disadvantage' for imports would seem to be irrelevant as the very essence of the *Cassis de Dijon* approach is that indistinctly applicable measures are capable of breaching Article 30.[306]

Finally, it may be noted that the *Keck and Mithouard* judgment does not affect the long-standing position in ECJ case law that indistinctly applicable national measures concerning the presentation of products which restrict trade between Member States will breach Article 30 and require justification.[307]

(v) Language requirements

As is clear from the above section concerning restrictions on the presentation of products, it follows by virtue of the same logic that language requirements for the marketing of products will also breach Article 30. Just as set out in the previous section, the ECJ reasons that although language requirements 'do not wholly preclude the importation into the Member State concerned of products originating in other Member States or in free circulation in those States it may none the less make their marketing more difficult' by making it necessary to alter the label for the imported products lawfully marketed in the exporting Member State.[308] More emphatically, the ECJ has held that 'the obligation exclusively to use the language of the linguistic region constitutes a measure having equivalent effect to a quantitative restriction on imports, prohibited by Article 30 of the Treaty'.[309]

Before the national courts, the fact that language requirements are capable of breaching Article 30 has not caused undue difficulties. The breach of Article 30 is rarely contested and the national courts correctly tend to concentrate on the question of whether the measures can nevertheless be justified under the 'rule of reason'.[310] Thus, in the implementation of the ECJ's *Fietje* judgment,[311] the Dutch *Economische Politierechter* in the

---

[306] See discussion of this point at pp. 54–5.

[307] See para. 15 of *Keck and Mithouard*, cited at page 55. This has been confirmed in subsequent ECJ rulings such as in Case C–315/92 *Verband Sozialer Wettbewerb* v. *Clinique Laboratories SNC* [1994] ECR I–317; Case C–470/93 *Verein gegen Unwesen in Handel und Gewerbe* v. *Mars GmbH* [1995] ECR I–1923 & Case C–368/95 *Vereinigte Familiapress Zeitungsverlags- und vertriebs* v. *Heinrich Bauer Verlag* [1997] ECR I–3689.

[308] See Case 27/80 *Fietje* [1980] ECR 3839 at para. 10.

[309] Case C–369/89 *ASBL Piageme* v. *BVBA Peeters* [1991] ECR I–2971 at para. 16. The ECJ has handed down a second judgment in this case in Case C–85/94 [1995] ECR I–2955, but this second case was limited to an interpretation of Directive 79/112 [1979] OJ L33/1 and explicitly left the application of Art. 30 to one side.

[310] See discussion in Ch. 6.   [311] n. 308 above.

Arrondissementsrechtbank Assen assumed, following the ECJ's judgment, that Article 30 was breached and only really discussed the question of justification at any length.[312] The Belgian courts have equally assumed that Article 30 is in principle breached by national language requirements and have concentrated on the question of justification.[313]

The issue of language requirements has also arisen before the French courts, but their compatibility with Article 30 has yet to be directly challenged before those courts. This may be considered surprising given the far-reaching nature of French legislation in this field. Indeed, the issue of language is a contemporary issue in France, especially in the wake of the so-called *Loi Toubon*[314] concerning the use of the French language. Under this legislation, use of the French language is compulsory in all commercial transactions, audio-visual programming, education, and advertising. The compatibility of this legislation with Article 30 is questionable but has not yet come under challenge before the courts.[315] The predecessor of the *Loi Toubon*, *Loi 75-1349*,[316] similarly provided that the French language was obligatory for the offering, presentation, advertising, and conditions of guarantee of goods or services. The compatibility of this earlier legislation with Article 30 was pleaded before the French *Cour de Cassation* in *Association générale des usagers de la langue français (AGULF) et Ministère public v. Daniel Jambon et Sociéte France Quick*,[317] which concerned the prosecution of the director of a branch of the 'Quick' restaurant chain for selling food and drink with English rather than French names contrary to the French legislation.[318] The *Cour de Cassation* deftly side-stepped the Article 30 argument by holding that the products in question were produced, sold, and consumed in France, and that since there was no import or export involved, the Treaty's rules on the free movement of goods were

---

[312] *Ec. Politierechter* in the *Arrondissementsrechtbank* Assen, 23 Feb. 1981 (transcr. available from court). See discussion of this aspect of the judgment at p. 194.

[313] Prior to the decision of the ECJ in Case C–369/89 (n. 309 above), see the judgment of the *Correctionele Rechtbank* Mechelen, 28 Sept. 1987, *Journal des Tribunaux* 1988, 48 concerning labelling of Coca-Cola and noted in (1978) 3 ELRev. 72 at 74. Subsequent to Case C–369/89, see Comm. Leuven, 17 Dec. 1991, AR 43.056 and 43.437 & Comm. Bruxelles, 24 Sept. 1990, Jaarboek Handelspraktijken/Annuaire Pratique du Commerce 1990, 466 (with note by Wytinck).

[314] Named after Mr Jacques Toubon, the former French Secretary of Cultural Affairs; Loi No. 94-665, 4 Aug. 1994, JORF 5 Aug. 1994 at 11392.

[315] See Albers and Swaak, 'The Trouble with Toubon: Language Requirements for Slogans and Messages in the Light of Art. 30 EC'; Bigot, 'Publicité et usage de la langue française: Réflexions sur la loi du 4 août 1994' & McCarthy and Mercer, 'Language as a Barrier to Trade: The Loi Toubon'. See also Faberon, 'La protection juridique de la langue française' (1997) Revue du droit public et de la science politique en France et à l'etranger 323.

[316] Law of 31 Dec. 1975, JORF 4 Jan. 1976 at 189.

[317] *Cour de Cassation*, ch. crim., 25 Apr. 1989, Bull. Cass. Crim. 1989, no. 167 p. 431; Gaz. Pal. 1989, II Som. p. 472; RTDComm. 1990, 87.

[318] The products in question included 'Giant', 'Fishburger', 'Cheeseburger' and 'Sandwichs'.

not applicable. The question was put more squarely in a subsequent case before the *Cour de Cassation*, concerning a prosecution for the importation of certain beverages from Belgium which had not been re-labelled into the French language as required by *Loi 75-1349*. In this case however, the *Cour de Cassation* implicitly accepted that there was a breach of Article 30 by holding that

Whilst Article 30 of the Treaty of Rome prohibits measures having equivalent effect to quantitative restrictions, the European Court of Justice has already in the similar Case 120/78 of February 1979 namely *Rewe-Zentral* [*Cassis de Dijon*] decided that national regulations remain legal in derogation to Article 30 of the Treaty of Rome if they are necessary in order to satisfy mandatory requirements for the protection of consumers and the fairness of commercial transactions.[319]

Whilst the finding in this case that the *Cassis de Dijon* mandatory requirement is satisfied, without any discussion of the proportionality and alternative means principles, is open to criticism,[320] what is interesting in the context of the present discussion is that the *Cour de Cassation* implicitly accepted that Article 30 was breached in the first place.

Following the judgment of the ECJ in *Keck and Mithouard*, there is the possibility that these language requirements in French legislation, insofar as they apply to advertising, may be considered to be 'selling arrangements' within the terms of that ruling.[321] However, the moment that the application of the language requirements result in practice in the re-packaging or a modification in the get-up of a product for sale on the French market, it is submitted that this would be a 'product requirement' and will be contrary to Article 30. It seems that the French legislation in its present form (the *Loi Toubon*) is rarely enforced and is principally of 'symbolic' value.[322] Indeed, if it was more frequently enforced, it might be expected, given the discussion above, that the compatibility of the legislation with Article 30 would be seriously challenged.

(vi) Product requirements

National product requirements, that is, requirements as to the composition of products, will clearly breach Article 30. Thus, national requirements restricting the ingredients for certain foodstuffs or setting out technical requirements that must be met by products will, even if they apply equally to national products, fall foul of Article 30. Such was the case in *Cassis de Dijon* (discussed above) and such has been confirmed by a multitude of ECJ authorities.[323] Since national requirements as to the

---

[319] *Campin, Cour de Cassation*, ch. crim., 9 Nov. 1987, Bull. Cass. Crim. 1987, no. 394 p. 1038.
[320] See discussion at p. 190.   [321] See discussion of this point in sect. 5 (B) (*ii*).
[322] This is a point made by Bigot, n. 315 above.
[323] Amongst these authorities, see Case 53/80 *Officier van Justitie* v. *Koninklijke Kaasfabriek Eyssen* [1981] ECR 409, [1982] 2 CMLR 20; Case 130/80 *Kelderman* [1981] ECR 527; Case 94/82

composition of products have an obvious impact on the access to the market of goods imported from other Member States, national courts have had little difficulty in finding a breach of Article 30 in such cases. Indeed, since such national requirements will often be justified for the protection of public health, the national courts frequently glide over the Article 30 breach (which is assumed) and proceed directly to the question of whether the measure may be justified on those grounds provided for in Article 36. In *Openbaar Ministerie* v. *Miro BV*, which concerned the importation of *Jenever* (Geneva) with an alcohol content of 30 per cent from Belgium into the Netherlands contrary to the Dutch Regulation of the appellation of *Jenever* (*Verordening Benaming van Jenever*), Article 1(4) of which provided for a minimum alcohol content of 35 per cent for that drink, the Dutch national court did not hesitate to find a breach of Article 30. The *Gerechtshof* Arnhem established that the Dutch legislation 'made the marketing of the product in the Netherlands more difficult and onerous because it was necessary to change the label and abandon the traditional appellation'.[324] Thus, in its referring judgment to the ECJ, the *Gerechtshof* established the breach of Article 30 as a matter of fact and the questions referred to the ECJ concerned only the issue of justification under the rule of reason.[325]

National measures concerning product requirements which have been held by the national courts to breach Article 30 include: the Dutch Milk Order (*Melkbesluit*) regulating the amount of active bacteria which may be present in sterilized products;[326] the Dutch Food and Drugs Law (*Warenwet*) on the addition of vitamins to food and beverages for human consumption;[327] the Dutch Cheese Decision (*Kaasbesluit*) regulating the amount of sorbic acid in cheese;[328] the French *Code des Usages de la Charcuterie et de la Salaison* (Code of Practice for the Delicatessen and Salted Meat Trade) regulating the *taux de humidité du produit dégraissé* (water content of fat-reduced products) of imported salami;[329] the French Public

---

De Kikvorsch [1983] ECR 947, [1984] 2 CMLR 323, & Case 407/85 *Drei Glocken* v. *USL* [1988] ECR 4233.

[324] *Gerechtshof* Arnhem, 18 June 1984, CDE 1989, 403.

[325] Case 182/84 [1985] ECR 3731.

[326] *CMC Melkunie, Hoge Raad (Strafkamer)*, 10 May 1983, NJ 1983, 671, CDE 1989, 401 & *Hoge Raad (Strafkamer)*, 13 Nov. 1984, NJ 1985, 338; SEW 1985, 227 (with note by Mulder).

[327] *Officier van Justitie* v. *Sandoz BV, Economische Politierechter Arrondissementsrechtbank* 's-Hertogenbosch, 31 Oct. 1983, NJ 1984, 178; *Sandoz BV* v. *Minister van Welzijn, Volksgezondheid en Cultuur, Raad van State (Afd. Rechtspraak)*, 28 July 1983, AB 1984, 383 (with note by Slot) and *Raad van State (Afd. Rechtspraak)*, 14 Nov. 1988, SEW 1990, 93 (with note by Mortelmans); & *Openbaar Ministerie* v. *Richardson Vicks BV, Hoge Raad (Strafkamer)*, 14 June 1994, NJB-katern 1994, 448 nr.182; transcr. 96.869 E.

[328] *Gerdabel Nederland BV* v. *Openbaar Ministerie*, Gerechtshof Amsterdam, 2 Feb. 1978, SEW 1978, 430.

[329] *Roger Ruchat* v. *Ministère public, TGI* Créteil, 11e ch., 5 May 1987, La Semaine Juridique—éd. entreprise 1987, II 15041 (with note by Anstett-Gardea and Schmidt).

Health Code (*Code de Santé Publique*) restricting the treatment of onions with maleic hydrazide[330] and the Food and Household Products Act (of 15 August 1974) restricting the type of fats that may be contained in sausages.[331]

The national courts have occasionally displayed a degree of confusion by, on the one hand, holding that an obvious product requirement does not breach Article 30 but then, on the other hand, going on to find that it is justified. For example, in *Floch*, the French *Cour de Cassation* held that the *Code des Usages de la Charcuterie et de la Salaison* regulating the *taux de humidité du produit dégraissé* of salami imported from Italy 'does not set up a discriminatory regime . . . All products marketed in France are subject to rules which are applicable without distinction according to nationality'.[332] Notwithstanding the point that the non-discriminatory nature of a product requirement does not exclude the application of Article 30,[333] the *Cour de Cassation* went on to find that the French requirement was justified under the rule of reason.[334] Similarly in *Aboobakar*, concerning the importation of a soft drink containing eritrosine from Spain into Portugal where eritrosine was prohibited, the Portuguese *Tribunal de Relação* of Lisbon held that the Portuguese legislation did not breach Article 30 because it applied in a non-discriminatory way but also, rather inexplicably, went on to hold that the protection of health provided for in Article 36 justified the exclusion.[335] Alves Viera has noted that this judgment is confused as the national requirement either does not breach Article 30 or alternatively, it breaches that Article but is justified under Article 36; it cannot, in the absence of the national court explicitly stating that it is deciding in the alternative, do both.[336]

It was noted above that since national product requirements have an obvious impact on the access to the market of goods imported from other Member States, the majority of national courts have experienced little difficulty in finding a breach of Article 30 in such cases. In a series of cases before the English courts however, the breach of Article 30 of certain product requirements for the licensing of taxis has by no means been 'obvious'

---

[330] *René Malagutti* v. *Ministère, Cour de Cassation*, ch. crim., 8 Jan. 1985, Bull. Cass. Crim. 1985, no. 15 p. 38–41; Dalloz 1985, Jur. 586 (with note by Fourgoux); CDE 1989, 403.
[331] *Re Dietary Sausages*, Case 3 C 33.89, *Bundesverwaltungsgericht*, 23 Jan. 1992, [1993] 3 CMLR 118.
[332] *Cour de Cassation*, ch. crim., 2 Feb. 1994, Bull. Cass. Crim. 1994, no. 51 p. 103.
[333] See discussion of this point at pp. 54–5.
[334] See discussion of this aspect of the ruling at pp. 190–1.
[335] Portuguese *Tribunal de Relação* of Lisbon, 19 Apr. 1989, Colectâna de jurisprudencia 1989, Vol II p. 165.
[336] Alves Viera, 'The Application of Community law by Portuguese Courts' at 349. For a similar instance before the Belgian courts, see *Blesgen* v. *Belgium, Tribunal correctionel* Verviers, 21 Dec. 1977, JT 1978, 379; ELD 1979, 108 and noted by Herbert (1979) 4 ELRev. 396 at 397.

to the English national courts. These cases involved the power granted to
any district council in the United Kingdom by Section 47(1) of the Local
Government (Miscellaneous Provisions) Act 1976 to attach to the grant of
taxi licences such conditions as 'it may consider reasonably necessary'.
Section 47(2) of this Act further provides that the local council may require
taxis to be 'of such design or appearance or bear such distinguishing
marks as shall clearly identify' them as taxis. On the basis of these provisions, several local councils adopted a policy requiring licensed taxis to
be of the traditional London 'Black Cab' design (known as the FX4).
Subsequently, following letters addressed to these local councils from the
Home Office stating that this requirement may breach Article 30, the local
councils amended these policies by framing the policy in terms of technical specifications (i.e. the size of doors, the shape of the vehicle, the turn-
ing circle, the hinging of the boot lid) which only the FX4 met. There were
only two manufacturers which produced cars which met these specifications ('Metrocab' and 'Fairway') and they were both British.

The policies of the local councils were challenged several times before
the English courts by way of judicial review proceedings. It was argued
that the technical specifications for taxis contained in these policies
amounted to product requirements which restricted access to the market
for licensed taxi vehicles manufactured in other Member States since in
order to get access, these manufacturers would be put to the considerable
expense of developing a vehicle which meets these specifications. In none
of the cases before the English courts was the Article 30 argument successful. Furthermore, the reasoning of these courts in rejecting the Article
30 argument left much to be desired. For example, in *Hodgkinson* v.
Nottingham City Council,[337] the application of Article 30 was excluded by
Nottingham Crown Court on the basis, *inter alia*, that 'there was no intention on the part of the Council to regulate trade within the Community'.[338]
In spite of the fact that the ECJ in *Keck and Mithouard* held that the selling
arrangements at issue in that case did not have the 'purpose' of regulating
trade between Member States,[339] it is submitted that the absence of that
'purpose' remains irrelevant with respect to national product requirements. As Gormley has commented, 'if intention to regulate trade between
Member States were to be a criterion in deciding whether a measure was
capable of affecting trade between Member States it would have been
impossible to condemn, for example, the German *Reinheitsgebot* provisions
relating to beer'.[340] Perhaps more serious is the fact that the English courts
seemed to be persuaded that the non-discriminatory nature of the require-

---

[337] n. 235 above.   [338] Ibid. at 509.

[339] *Keck and Mithouard*, Cases C–267 & 268/91, n. 89 above at para. 12.

[340] Gormley, 'Reasoning Renounced? The Remarkable Judgment of *Keck and Mithouard*' at
66. The *Reinheitsgebot* case is Case 178/84, n. 234 above.

ments, which meant that it was possible for manufacturers in other Member States to comply with these requirements, precluded the application of Article 30. This was evident in *R. v. Metropolitan Borough Council of Wirral, ex. p. The Wirral Licensed Taxi Owners Association* where Glidewell J remarked that 'the requirements . . . are not met by standard production of saloon cars and are met by the metropolitan type cabs, though it is now open of course to any continental manufacturer, if he so chooses, to make a vehicle which combines that description'.[341]

Similarly, Harrison J in *R. v. Doncaster Metropolitan Borough Council, ex. p. Kelly* held that the Article 30 argument had 'no substance' since

the terms of the policy do not refer to any specific vehicle manufactured in this country, but rather to black London-style purpose-built Hackney carriages with wheelchair facilities. This does not restrict, in any way, the place where such a vehicle is manufactured. It is open to any manufacturer in a Member State to manufacture such a vehicle and for it to be imported into this country.[342]

Finally, the Court of Appeal in *R. v. Luton Borough Council, ex. p. Mirza* similarly held that 'these policies are not discriminatory policies and do not place other manufacturers outside the United Kingdom at a disadvantage . . . Any manufacturer throughout the European Community can comply with those requirements'.[343] The underlying thread implicit in all these arguments is that Article 30 cannot be breached since the taxi requirements are indistinctly applicable and allow manufacturers in other Member States to comply with the product requirements. Apart from the fact that these judgments fail to recognize that indistinctly applicable measures are also capable of breaching Article 30,[344] they also, with respect, seem to miss the point. As was noted above, the technical specifications for taxis contained in these policies amounted to product requirements which, it is submitted, may more properly be held to breach Article 30 since they restricted access to the market for licensed taxi vehicles manufactured in other Member States because, in order to get access, these manufacturers would be put to the considerable expense of developing a vehicle which meets these specifications.

There is thus cause for concern at the English courts' consistent refusal to construe the local taxi regulations as a breach of Article 30 which requires justification either under the rule of reason or Article 36.[345] Indeed, this issue is clearly a sensitive one which is evidenced by the Commission's equally consistent refusal to take action on this matter.[346] If

---

[341] [1983] 3 CMLR 150 at 159.

[342] Unrep. judgt of the High Court, 20 Oct. 1994 (transcr. available on Lexis).

[343] Unrep. judgt 2 Feb. 1995 (transcr. available on Lexis).

[344] See discussion of this point at pp. 54–5.

[345] See discussion of possible justifications in Chs. 6 & 7.

[346] Art. 169 infringement proceedings against the UK were begun in 1984 (*lettre de mise en demeure* was sent in Dec. 1984) but were closed in Apr. 1985.

Article 30 does indeed apply, these cases underline the extent of intervention that the free movement of goods involves in national regulation of
economic life. It is submitted that the application of Article 30 to such
national product requirements should be upheld.

Finally, it may be noted that the application of Article 30 to indistinctly
applicable national product requirements is explicitly unaffected by the
Keck and Mithouard departure.[347] For this reason, it is surprising that the
English Courts have also applied the *Keck* ruling to exclude the application
of Article 30 to the local taxi requirements discussed above. These developments will however be discussed in the following chapter.[348]

(vii) Price-fixing

The relationship between national price-fixing measures and Article 30
does not fit easily into the mainstream ECJ case law interpreting that
Article of the Treaty. By price-fixing, one is referring to national measures
setting minimum or maximum prices, or setting fixed profit margins for
the retail sale of goods. Such price-fixing is a widely used means of economic regulation and forms an integral part of the economic policies of the
Member States. Since the original Treaty provisions (see in particular
Articles 103 and 104 EEC) left Member States latitude to take economic
policy measures, Oliver is right to point out that 'it would have been rash
indeed [for the ECJ] to have held that all price controls automatically constitute measures of equivalent effect'.[349] The approach of the ECJ has
essentially been to require discrimination against imports before national
price-fixing measures will be held to breach Article 30. The ECJ first developed this approach with respect to maximum prices set by national
authorities. In *Tasca*, it held that

Although a maximum price applicable without distinction to domestic and
imported products does not in itself constitute a measure having an effect equivalent to a quantitative restriction, it may have such an effect, however, when it is
fixed at a level such that the sale of imported products becomes, if not impossible,
more difficult than that of domestic products. A maximum price, in any event insofar as it applies to imported products, constitutes therefore a measure having an
effect equivalent to a quantitative restriction, especially when it is fixed at such a
low level that, having regard to the general situation of imported products compared with that of domestic products, dealers wishing to import the products in
question into the Member State concerned can do so only at a loss.[350]

Similarly, with respect to minimum prices fixed by national authorities,
the ECJ has held that such prices will breach Article 30 where

---

[347] See para. 15 of that judgment and cases cited at n. 307 above.
[348] See Ch. 3, sect. 3 (B).   [349] Oliver, n. 71 above, 162.
[350] Case 65/75 [1976] ECR 291, [1977] 2 CMLR 183 at para. 13.

a minimum price fixed at a specific amount which, although applicable without distinction to domestic and imported products, is capable of having an adverse effect on the marketing of the latter in so far as it prevents their lower cost price from being reflected in the retail selling price.[351]

Finally, with respect to fixed profit margins, the ECJ has held that a minimum profit margin set at a specific amount by national authorities, and not being set as a percentage of the cost price, is 'incapable of producing an adverse effect on imported products' as long as they apply to domestic as well as imported products.[352] It may also at this stage be added that following the ECJ judgment in *Keck and Mithouard*, price-fixing measures will now almost certainly be subsumed under the category of 'selling arrangements' and thus remain, in the absence of discrimination, outside the scope of Article 30.[353]

In sum then, the ECJ has, in the case of price-fixing measures, diverged from its usual interpretation of Article 30 by requiring that before it is breached, there must be discrimination against imports, or at least the price fixed must be set at a level such that the sale of imported products becomes, if not impossible, more difficult than that of domestic products. It is for this reason that price-fixing is difficult to fit within the distinction created by the ECJ, and adopted in this chapter, between directly and indirectly applicable measures. Price-fixing measures may be indistinctly applicable (i.e. indirectly applicable) but will only be considered to breach Article 30 if they have the effect of a distinctly applicable (i.e. directly applicable) measure. Although price-fixing measures do thus not fit snugly within the ECJ's (and this chapter's) scheme, the national case law on price-fixing will nevertheless be dealt with in this section.

It will be noted that the case law of the ECJ with respect to price-fixing (set out above) gives the Member States much greater freedom of action than it does with respect to other types of indirectly applicable national measures. One would not expect, therefore, that the national courts would encounter many serious difficulties in applying this case law. Broadly speaking, the experience of the national courts has not borne this out. For example, the issue of fixed profit margins arose before the Dutch *CBB* in *Koninklijke Nederlandse Maatschappij ter bevordering der Pharmacie (KNMP)* v. *Centraal Orgaan Tarieven Gezondheidszorg (COTG)*,[354] which concerned a challenge to the then Law on the Price of Pharmaceuticals (*Wet tarieven*

---

[351] Case 82/77, n. 77 above at para. 18.

[352] Ibid. at para. 17.

[353] See Case C–63/94 *Groupement national des négociants en pommes de terre de Belgique* v. *ITM Belgium* [1995] ECR I–2467.

[354] Pres. *CBB*, 31 Dec. 1987, AB 1988, 237. See also *Koninklijke Maatschappij ter Bevordering der Pharmacie* v. *Centraal Orgaan Tarieven Gezondheidszorg, CBB*, 10 Apr. 1990, AB-Kort 1990, no. 539 (summary).

gezondheitszorg).[355] The latter legislation restructured the system of tariffs chargeable by pharmacists in such a way that every prescription dispensed, irrespective of the cost price of the pharmaceutical, had to have a fixed supplement added to the price. This replaced the previous system under which the supplement was calculated for each product as a percentage of the cost price of that product. It was argued that the new system breached Article 30 since it discouraged cheaper imports because the fixed supplement applied irrespective of the cost price of the product. The *CBB* rejected this argument on the grounds that it lacked factual foundation. The Dutch court pointed out that, if anything, the new system would favour cheaper imports since, under the previous system, the greater the cost price, the greater the supplement pocketed by the pharmacist. Under the new provisions, however, the supplement was fixed at the same level for all products, irrespective of the cost price. This judgment of the *CBB* undoubtedly reaches the correct result according to ECJ case law. It is only a pity that the Dutch court based its rejection of the Article 30 argument on factual findings rather than by relying on the legal grounds set out by the ECJ in, for example, *Van Tiggele*,[356] where, as we have seen, the ECJ explicitly held that a minimum profit margin set at a specific amount by national authorities, and not being set as a percentage of the cost price, is 'incapable of producing an adverse effect on imported products' as long as they apply to domestic as well as imported products.[357]

The reasoning of the French *Conseil d'Etat* in two cases concerning fixed profit margins has also been rather incomplete. In *SA Des Laboratoires Merck Sharp Dohme Chibret*[358] and *Lacombe*[359] certain French pharmacies challenged Article L. 162–38 of the French *Code de la securité sociale* which allowed the Ministers of Economics, of Health, and of Social Security to fix the profit margins for the sale of certain medical products on the ground, *inter alia*, that this provision breached Article 30 EC. In both cases, the *Conseil d'Etat* rejected the Article 30 argument. In the *Laboratoires Merck* case, the *Conseil d'Etat* simply held that there was 'nothing in the file demonstrating that the lowering of the price of Zocor [the product at issue in that case] was of such a nature as to cause quantitative restrictions on

---

[355] It may be noted that a new *Wet Geneesmiddelenprijzen* (Medicine Prices Act) has recently entered into force in the Netherlands which sets a fixed price for pharmaceuticals sold in the Netherlands calculated on the basis of the average price at which the pharmaceutical is sold in the UK, Belgium, France, & Germany. For a discussion of the compatibility of this new legislation with Art. 30, see Mok, TVVS 1995, 305. The *Rechtbank* 's-Gravenhage has held in interim proceedings that the new legislation is not incompatible with EC law: *OPG Groothandel* v. *Minister van Volksgezondheid, Welzijn en Sport*, Pres. *Rechtbank* 's-Granvenhage, 19 July 1996, KG 1996, 279.

[356] n. 77 above. For other ECJ authorities to a similar effect concerning fixed profit margins, see Case 78/82 *Commission* v. *Italy* [1983] ECR 1955 & Case 116/84 *Roelstraete* [1985] ECR 1705, [1986] 3 CMLR 562.

[357] Ibid. at para. 17.   [358] n. 72 above.   [359] n. 73 above.

importation or exportation of products'. In *Lacombe*, the *Conseil d'Etat* equally briefly dismissed the argument by holding that the *arrêté* under challenge in that case 'did not have the effect of reducing the quantities of imported medical products'. In the absence of fuller reasoning by the *Conseil d'Etat*, it is difficult to second-guess the *ratio* of these brief judgments. It is submitted that, even allowing for the brevity that is customary in decisions of the *Conseil d'Etat*, the perfunctory dismissal of the EC law arguments in these cases was too brief by any standards.[360] It appears that the *Conseil d'Etat* rejected the Article 30 argument on the basis that the national measures did not affect the quantity of imports and could not therefore constitute quantitative restrictions.[361] Again, as in the *Koninlijke Nederlandse Maatschappij ter bevordering der Pharmacie* case,[362] it seems that the national court reached the correct result (so long as the profit margins fixed in the French legislation were not simply set as a percentage of the cost price) but fails to cloak this conclusion in terms echoing the reasoning of the ECJ in cases with respect to fixed profit margins.[363]

National case law in application of the ECJ case law on minimum price-fixing has equally been rather unsatisfactory. This is demonstrated by a series of cases before the Dutch courts which concerned minimum prices set for the retail sale of bread in the Netherlands. Article 2 of the *Verordening Broodprijzen* (Bread Prices Order)[364] prohibited the sale of bread produced in the Netherlands below a fixed minimum price. In fixing that minimum price, the President of the *Produktschap voor Granen, Zaden en Peulvruchten* (The Cereal, Seed, and Pulse Board) had to take into account the total production costs of well-organized and efficiently operated producers of bread together with the total distribution costs of well-organized and efficiently operated distributors. Litigation before the Dutch courts concerning these provisions took place both before the criminal (criminal proceedings were brought against certain supermarkets for selling bread at below the minimum price) and civil courts (proceedings were instituted by competitors of such supermarkets, seeking an injunction to prevent the sale of bread in breach of the provisions). Almost without exception, the supermarkets concerned argued as a defence before the Dutch courts that the Dutch provisions setting a minimum price for bread

---

[360] See discussion of the influence on the application of EC law by national courts of the style of judgments according to national legal traditions at p. 254.

[361] See discussion of this aspect of the judgt at pp. 18–19.

[362] n. 354 above. For cases concerning the fixing of pharmaceutical prices before the Greek courts, see Dioikitiko Protodikeio Athinon, Tmima 1, 19 Sept. 1986, Epitheorisis Dikaiou Koinonikis Asfaliseos 1987, 97 and Dioikitiko Protodikeio Athinon, Tmima 1, 7 Dec. 1987, Armenopoulos 1990, 1154, Elliniki Epitheorisi Evropaikou Dikaiou 1991, 279. See also Ioannou, 'Recent Developments in the Application of Community law in Greece'.

[363] See ECJ judgts cited at n. 356 above.

[364] Adopted on 2 Sept. 1976 by the *Produktschap voor Granen, Zaden en Peulvruchten*.

breached Article 30 of the EC Treaty, since the fixed minimum price, although applicable without distinction to domestic and imported bread, was capable of having an adverse effect on the marketing of imported bread in so far as it prevented the lower cost price of that bread from being reflected in the retail selling price. This defence was rejected out of hand by the President of the *Arrondissementsrechtbank* Amsterdam which simply held that 'for the time being, it has not been established that the minimum bread price requirements are measures having equivalent effect to quantitative restrictions which are prohibited by Article 30 EEC'.[365] Rather perplexingly, the Amsterdam court furnished no reasons as to why it thought that this was the case.

A more detailed analysis was carried out by the *Economische Politierechter* Almelo in *Openbaar Ministerie* v. *Supermarket N. N. te Enschede*.[366] That judgment was handed down after the ECJ's judgment in *Tasca*[367] concerning maximum price-fixing, but before the *Van Tiggele*[368] judgment which concerned minimum prices. The *Economische Politierechter* cited the *Tasca* judgment and held that although that judgment concerned maximum price-fixing, it was clear that the ECJ's ruling in that case applied equally in the present case concerning minimum price-fixing.[369] Thus, the *Economische Politierechter* held that minimum price-fixing was not as such a measure having equivalent effect contrary to Article 30 unless, in an individual case, the fixed price made import, if not impossible, at least more difficult. Applying this to the facts, the *Economische Politierechter* held that the minimum price fixed for bread did not make import of *standaardbrood* (standard bread) more difficult. In reaching this conclusion, the *Economische Politierechter* made four findings of fact: (i) that it was established that Dutch *standaardbrood* was not manufactured in any other Member State; (ii) that should a producer in another Member State wish to manufacture Dutch *standaardbrood*, it would have to prepare the bread specifically to Dutch tastes as to composition and would, in order to meet the requirements of freshness, have to have special provision for quick transport to the Netherlands; (iii) that it was established that import of *standaardbrood* does not take place and was unlikely to do so in the future; and finally (iv) that should such import take place, the minimum price for

---

[365] *Dirk van den Broek Supermarkten BV* v. *Leendert Arie Vente*, Pres. *Arrondissementsrechtbank* Amsterdam, 2 June 1977, NJ 1980, 401.

[366] *Ec. Politierechter* Almelo, 6 Sept. 1977, SEW 1978, 157 (with note by Mok). Noted also by Kellermann, Grondman and Tromm, 'Implementation of Community Law in the Netherlands' at 407 & 409 and Kellermann, 'The Netherlands in Face of its Community Obligations' at 327.

[367] n. 350 above.   [368] n. 77 above.

[369] The *Economische Politierechteer* held that the fact that the *Tasca* judgt should also apply in the case of minimum price-fixing was so clear that there was no need to refer questions to that effect to the ECJ under the Art. 177 EC preliminary-rulings procedure.

bread (based on well-organized and efficiently operated producers) was set at such a low level that any imports could definitely not be sold at a lower price. The *Economische Politierechter* concluded from these findings of fact that 'there is thus no possibility that actual or potential imports of the bread in question is made impossible or more difficult than the marketing of Dutch products as a result of the Order'.

This judgment of the *Economische Politierechter* Almelo in *Openbaar Ministerie* v. *Supermarket N. N. te Enschede* has been criticised by Mok.[370] While Mok agrees that the extension of the ECJ's *Tasca* ruling to minimum price-fixing was correct, Mok questions whether it was, at the time of the judgment, correct for a national court to make such an extension especially given that the reference in *Van Tiggele* was, at that time, still pending before the ECJ.[371] Furthermore, Mok comprehensively criticizes the four findings of fact made by the *Economische Politierechter*. In particular, Mok doubts that such findings of fact are, according to Dutch rules on evidence,[372] credible. For example, to find that Dutch *standaardbrood* was not manufactured in any other Member State would be difficult to prove and it would furthermore be difficult to exclude the possibility that the minimum price for bread in the Netherlands was the very reason why such bread was not imported from other Member States. Further, Mok doubts that the point about freshness and transportation made by the *Economische Politierechter* was of any substance, given modern methods of preservation and transport. These criticisms are undoubtedly justified. What the *Economische Politierechter* in effect reasoned was that the importation of bread from other Member States would be so difficult and costly that the fact that there is a minimum price in the Netherlands was irrelevant. As Mok points out, this reasoning is flawed since, not only is this impossible to prove, but also because it does not recognize the possibility that the reason why there was at that time no importation of bread from other Member States was because the fixed minimum price was such that producers of bread in other Member States could no longer exploit their competitive price advantage. It is submitted that it would have been better for the *Economische Politierechter* to have either referred the matter to the ECJ itself, or to at least have waited for the ECJ's judgment in *Van Tiggele* which was pending. Had it done so, it would have been able to apply the simple test enunciated by the ECJ in that case that a minimum price will breach Article 30 where it prevents the lower cost price of imports from being reflected in the retail selling price.[373]

---

[370] n. 366 above.
[371] The *Van Tiggele* case was referred to the ECJ by the *Gerechtshof* Amsterdam (*economische kamer*) on 30 June 1977.
[372] See esp. Art. 339(2) *Wetboek van Strafvordering* (Code of Criminal Procedure).
[373] n. 351 above.

In 1982, the *Verordening Broodprijzen* was amended to provide for a separate regime for imported bread. Under the amendment, Dutch-produced bread was still subject to Article 2 of that Order while a new Article 2(A) was added to apply to imported bread. The effect of the amendment was that bread produced in the Netherlands was subject to a minimum price which was calculated on the basis of efficient production *and* distribution costs, while imported bread, on the other hand, had to be sold at at least the cost price plus a fixed margin based on efficient distribution costs. In criminal proceedings against Edah BV for selling bread at below the minimum price, it was argued that the Dutch provisions were restrictive of importation of bread from other Member States and thus contrary to Article 30. In particular, it was argued that in cases where the production costs of both Dutch-produced bread and bread imported from another Member State were higher than that taken into consideration by the *Produktschap* (production costs of well-organized and efficiently operated producers of bread) in setting the minimum price, the Dutch produced bread could still be retailed at the minimum price while the imported bread would have to be sold at the sum of the higher production cost *plus* the added fixed margin. In such a case, imported bread could only be sold at a higher price than bread produced in the Netherlands, even though the cost price of both was the same. As such, it was argued that imports were treated less favourably than domestic products contrary to Article 30. This argument was rejected by the *Arrondissementsrechtbank* 's-Hertogenbosch.[374] It seems that that court was unconvinced by the hypothesis set out above since, if the cost price of the bread produced in the Netherlands was higher than that taken into account by the *Produktschap* in setting the minimum price, the Dutch retailer would have to sell that bread at an extremely low margin if it was indeed to sell the bread at the minimum price. On this point, the *Arrondissementsrechtbank* held that

the decision of a retailer to accept a lower margin than that calculated for an efficient and well-organized distributor, as a result of which it is likely that the retailer makes a loss on the product in question, does not lead to a disturbance on the EEC market caused by Articles 2 and 2(A) of the Order.

It is not clear what the *Arrondissementsrechtbank* meant by 'a disturbance on the EEC market' or indeed what relevance this has in an analysis of a breach of Article 30. The *Arrondissementsrechtbank* went on to hold that it had not been shown that the minimum price had been set at such a *low* level that the import of bread from other Member States was made more

---

[374] *Officier van Justitie* v. *Edah BV, Arrondissementsrechtbank* 's-Hertogenbosch (Ec. Raadkamer), 5 Feb. 1985, NJ 1985, 308.

difficult. This too, is confused since the correct issue is surely whether the minimum price is set at such a *high* level that cheaper imports from other Member States are unable to exploit their competitive advantage. Finally, the judgment of the *Arrondissementsrechtbank* in this case is misguided since it fails to recognize that the Dutch provisions were in fact discriminatory in effect. As was noted above, a different regime applied to the pricing of bread depending on whether the bread was produced in the Netherlands or imported from other Member States. As a result, the Dutch provisions were not applicable to national and imported products alike and the ECJ case law on price-fixing should therefore have been excluded. Indeed, this was confirmed by the ECJ in its subsequent judgment on a reference from the Dutch courts in a case again involving Edah BV. In the latter case, the ECJ held that although there was a presumption that price-fixing applying to imports and domestic products alike did not constitute a measure of equivalent effect, such was not the case here since the Dutch provisions related to different rules for domestic and imported products 'laid down by different instruments adopted at different times and differing in substantive content'.[375]

The response of the Dutch courts to the argument that Dutch provisions on the minimum price for bread were contrary to Article 30 was thus far from satisfactory. This response ranged from rejecting the application of Article 30 without giving any further reasons[376] to the making of findings of fact, for example that imports could not in any event be cheaper than Dutch-produced bread, which were, with respect, unsustainable.[377] Finally, we have seen that a separate and less favourable price-fixing regime applicable only to imports was equally held to be outside the reach of Article 30 on the rather perplexing ground that they did not cause a 'disturbance on the EEC market'.[378] In none of these cases was there a satisfactory application of the ECJ case law on price-fixing.

It was noted in the discussion above that the ECJ case law on price-fixing applies only when the fixed price applies equally to imports as it does to domestic products. This was confirmed by the ECJ's judgment in *Cullet* v. *Leclerc*[379] where the ECJ held that a minimum price for petrol sold in France which was fixed on the basis of *national* ex-refinery prices alone was contrary to Article 30 because it deprived importers of their competitive price advantage. Prior to the latter judgment of the ECJ, there were a series of cases before the French courts in which the validity of the French

[375] Cases 80 & 159/85 *Nederlandse Bakkerij Stichting* v. *Edah BV* [1988] ECR 3359, [1988] 2 CMLR 113 at para. 12.

[376] See *Dirk van den Broek Supermarkten BV* v. *Leendert Arie Vente*, n. 365 above.

[377] See *Openbaar Ministerie* v. *Supermarket N. N. te Enschede*, n. 366 above.

[378] See *Officier van Justitie* v. *Edah BV*, n. 374 above.

[379] Case 231/83 [1985] ECR 305, [1985] 2 CMLR 524.

legislation was contested.[380] The response of the French national courts faced with the compatibility of the French legislation with Article 30 was mixed. Some courts immediately recognized that there was a breach of Article 30 since the effect of the legislation was that the competitive advantage of imported petrol would be 'neutralized'.[381] Other courts, on the other hand, simply issued injunctions to prevent sale of petrol at below the fixed price either because of the commercial damage that was being caused to competitors,[382] or because a judge in summary proceedings (*juge des référés*) was incompetent to decide the issue.[383] The problems encountered in this series of French cases arose principally as a result of the special competence of the *juge des référés* in French law, and will therefore be discussed in detail elsewhere in this work.[384]

A similar series of cases before the French courts concerned resale price maintenance for books. In *Leclerc* v. *Au Blé Vert*[385] the ECJ interpreted Article 30 in the context of French legislation[386] and held that in so far as the French legislation created for imported books separate regulations from those applicable to books published in France, such legislation infringed Article 30. As in the petrol-pricing cases discussed above, the response of the French national courts when faced with the compatibility of the French legislation with Article 30 prior to the ECJ judgment was mixed. A particularly poor application was carried out by the *Cour d'appel* of Versailles in *SA Argendis (Centre Leclerc) et Société ACDELEC* v. *Union syndicale des libraires de France et Syndicat des librairies professionnels de Paris et de la région parisienne* which held that 'resale price maintenance which makes no distinction between national and imported products normally has purely internal effects'.[387] The *Cour d'appel* clearly failed to recognize that the French legislation did in fact make a distinction between imported

---

[380] The French legislation was contained in Ordinance 45-1483 of 30 June 1945 and Orders 82.10 A, 82.11 A, 82.12 A, & 83.13 A of 29 Apr. 1982.

[381] See, e.g., *Sté Maignam* v. *Sté Vitry-Distribution, Cour d'appel* Paris, 1re ch. A, 4 July 1984, Dalloz 1985, IR 273 (with note by Gavalda and Lucas De Leyssac) and noted at Gaz. Pal. 1984, III Doct. 48; *Hypermarché Continent* v. *Chambre syndicale nationale du commerce et de la réparation automobile (CSNCRA), Cour d'appel* Paris 1re ch.A, 4 July 1984, Gaz. Pal. 1984, II Jur. 658 (with note by Fourgoux); *SARL Dige-NCO* v. *SA Cora, TGI* Pontoise (*Référés*), 22 Feb. 1984, Gaz. Pal. 1984, I Jur. 296 and *SA Neudis (Centre Leclerc)* v. *SARL Mottet (Shell français), Cour d'appel* Lyon, 1re ch., 4 Oct. 1984, [1985] 1 CMLR 247.

[382] See, e.g., *SA Gueret distribution (Centre Leclerc)* v. *Maryan Martin, Cour d'appel* Limoges, 1re ch. civ., 20 Oct. 1983; *SA Montgeron Distribution (Centre Leclerc)* v. *SA Garage Picot, Cour d'appel* Paris, 14e ch. C, 29 Mar. 1984, Gaz. Pal. 1984, II Som. 120 (summary) and *Claudine Dumoussaud* v. *Syndicat des artisans mécaniciens de l'automobile du Lot, Cour d'appel* Agen, 1re ch., 28 Nov. 1984.

[383] See *Sodialfo—Rennes Ouest*, n. 25 above, *SA Allouette Distribution*, n. 25 above & *SARL Bianchi* v. *SA Sarredis, Cour d'appel* Metz, ch. civ., 7 Feb. 1984.

[384] See Ch. 10, sect. 2 (A).   [385] Case 229/83, n. 149 above.

[386] Loi No. 81-766, 10 Aug. 1981, JORF, 11 Aug. 1981, relative au prix du livre (Book Prices Act).

[387] *Cour d'appel* Versailles, 1re ch. I, 30 May 1984, [1986] ECC 197 at 202.

and national products.[388] As with the French petrol-pricing cases, however, the problems encountered before the French courts in the series of cases concerning retail price maintenance for books arose principally as a result of the special competence of the *juge des référés* in French law, and will therefore be discussed in detail elsewhere in this work.[389]

6 CONCLUSIONS

In any legal system, it will always be possible to identify individual judgments of courts which are 'incorrect'. Such judgments might be 'incorrect' for a number of reasons: because the reasoning is fundamentally flawed, because a certain text or precedent is clearly misconstrued or simply because the judgment is subsequently overturned or clarified on appeal. The Community legal system is no exception to this. Consequently, it is to be expected that some of the judgments of national courts applying Article 30 of the EC Treaty will, according to these terms, be considered 'incorrect'. In drawing conclusions as to the national courts' application of Article 30 therefore, care will be taken to concentrate on those areas where a problem may be identified in their application of that Article.

The first point which emerges from the discussion in this chapter is that the national courts do not, perhaps understandably, seem to share the ECJ's emphasis on the need to interpret Article 30, as a basic freedom under the Treaty, as broadly as possible. While the national courts show no signs of dismissing the fundamental importance of the provisions on the free movement of goods, they are nevertheless very much more sober in their approach. For the national courts, Article 30 is a complex and at times technical legal provision which requires workmanlike application rather than expressions of expansive principle.

One of the central questions which the study of national case law gives rise, is the extent to which the approach of the ECJ *itself* should be adapted to take into account problems of application of its case law in national courts. The discussion in this chapter allows several such suggestions to be made. For example, with respect to quantitative restrictions, it was noted that the ECJ has not always maintained a rigorous distinction between 'quantitative restrictions' and 'measures having equivalent effect' in its Article 30 case law. This is usually of little consequence since both types of measure are in any event prohibited by Article 30. However, it was noted that the loose distinction between these two terms can lead to abuse before

---

[388] Fortunately, this judgment was overturned on appeal by the *Cour de Cassation*, ch. com., 18 Feb. 1986, CDE 1989, 411 (summary) which was handed down after the ECJ judgment in *Leclerc* v. *'Au Blé Vert'*.

[389] See Ch. 10, sect. 2 (A).

national courts which have, on occasion, analysed national measures as quantitative restrictions to the exclusion of measures having equivalent effect.[390] A more tightly defined concept of quantitative restrictions can only reduce the possibility of such abuse. Similarly, the reference to 'trading rules' in the *Dassonville* formula of measures having equivalent effect has been rather liberally interpreted by the ECJ in subsequent cases. It was also noted that the term 'trading rules' has often been neglected and even omitted by the ECJ in subsequent judgments. The experience of national courts in applying Article 30 suggests that the ECJ should either abandon the reference to 'trading rules' altogether or at least define the meaning of the term more tightly. The reason for this is that the loose application of this term by the ECJ has opened up the possibility for abuse by the national courts. Thus, we have seen national courts, for example, excluding the application of Article 30 to national Sunday-trading legislation on the grounds that it does not constitute a 'trading rule' within the *Dassonville* formula.[391] Such abuse could be avoided if the ECJ clarified the reference to 'trading rules'. Finally, the issue of whether Article 30 can impose obligations on individuals has never been conclusively settled by the ECJ. The reference to rules 'enacted by Member States' in the *Dassonville* formula strongly suggest that they cannot. The discussion of the case law of the judicial body the *SNRC* in particular (as to the application of Article 30 to advertising rules of self-regulation) demonstrates that more clarity from the ECJ would be desirable. Furthermore, national case law has also called into question whether, if Article 30 applies only to State measures, the ECJ's case law defining the State for the purpose of the vertical direct effect of Directives applies *mutatis muntandis* to Article 30 analyses.[392]

A further question to which the study of national case law gives rise is the question of whether the application of Article 30 by the national courts allows one to have confidence that the system is functioning satisfactorily. As was noted above, in any system of the administration of justice, it is inevitable that there will be certain court decisions which, for whatever reason, may be considered 'incorrect'. The analysis in this chapter indeed reveals that the national courts have handed down some very questionable judgments in application of Article 30 which would have benefited from an Article 177 reference to the ECJ.[393] More serious are the unsatis-

---

[390] See discussion of the judgts in *SA Des Laboratoires Merck Sharp Dohme Chibret*, n. 72 above; *Lacombe*, n. 73 above & *Esge* v. *Alpha Trading*, n. 78 above.

[391] See discussion of *W. H. Smith Do It All and Payless DIY Ltd* v. *Peterborough City Council*, n. 100 above and other judgts of national courts discussed in that section.

[392] See esp. discussion of *R. v. Chief Constable of Sussex, ex p. International Trader's Ferry*, n. 114 above & *R. v. Coventry City Council, ex p. Phoenix Aviation*, n. 116 above.

[393] See, e.g. the discussion of the national-court judgments in *Re Labelling of Dutch Poultry*, n. 213 above; *SA Magnavision NV* v. *General Optical Council* (No. 1), n. 249 above; *Dommelsch*

factory applications handed down by courts against whose decisions there is no further judicial remedy within the national legal system which still refrain from making a reference to the ECJ.[394] Most serious of all are the few cases where the national court does not apply Article 30 correctly even after a preliminary ruling of the ECJ.[395] Finally, the analysis in this chapter has also revealed examples of national courts within a Member State coming to different conclusions as to the breach of Article 30 of the same piece of national legislation.[396]

Certain areas may be singled out as being particularly problematic before the national courts. For example, the national courts have not always adhered to the ECJ's attempts to delineate the relationship between Article 30 and other Articles of the Treaty. In particular, the instances where the national courts mix various provisions, with the result that the provisions on the free movement of goods are used to justify breaches of other Treaty Articles, is particularly worrying.[397] Furthermore, there are still judgments in national courts which analyse national charges for inspections under Article 30 rather than Articles 12 or 95.[398] In the context of national price-fixing measures, it has been shown how the response of the Dutch courts to the argument that Dutch provisions on the minimum pricing of bread were contrary to Article 30 was far from satisfactory. This response ranged from rejecting the application of Article 30 without giving any further reasons[399] to the making of findings of fact, for example that imports could not in any event be cheaper than Dutch produced bread, which were, with respect, unsustainable.[400] Finally, we have seen that a separate and less favourable price-fixing regime applicable only to imports was equally held to be outside the reach of Article 30 on the rather perplexing ground that they did not cause a 'disturbance on the EEC market'.[401] In none of these cases was there a satisfactory application of the ECJ case law on price-fixing.

België, n. 303 above; and the cases concerning technical requirements for taxis in the UK, n. 337 above.

[394] See, e.g., discussion of the judgments of national court in *Syndicat national des importateurs français en produits laitiers et avicoles et Decker et Cie*, n. 159 above; *Smanor SA* v. *Syndicat national des fabricants de produits surgelés et congelés*, n. 296 above & *Openbaar Ministerie* v. *Autohandel- en sloperij J. R. BV*, n. 195 above.

[395] See, e.g. discussion of the judgt of the *Cour de Cassation* in *Nauleau*, n. 246 above.

[396] See *Laboratoires Searle SA* v. *Laboratoires SARPP*, n. 239 above & *Ministère public* v. *Norbert Desolière*, n. 240 above.

[397] See, e.g. discussion of *Geniteau*, n. 23 above & *Fromagerie Bel—La vache qui rit* v. *SA Entremont*, n. 24 above.

[398] See, e.g. discussion of *Holland Champignon*, n. 39 above; *Zuid Vleeshandel*, n. 38 above & *Jandet*, n. 40 above.

[399] See *Dirk van den Broek Supermarkten BV* v. *Leendert Arie Vente*, n. 365 above.

[400] See *Openbaar Miniterie* v. *Supermarket N. N. te Enschede*, n. 366 above.

[401] See *Officier van Justitie* v. *Edah BV*, n. 374 above.

On the other hand, however, it would be unfair to paint a picture of rampant misapplication. The analysis in this chapter does not support such a conclusion. The vast majority of cases applied Article 30 in a confident and competent way.[402] The sections in this chapter discussing national case law on import inspections, language, and product requirements and national restrictions as to the presentation of goods in particular, all provide excellent illustrations of applications of Article 30 by those courts. Indeed, it has been commented several times that in straightforward cases, national courts frequently glide over the Article 30 breach (which is assumed) and proceed directly to the question of whether the measure may be justified. Furthermore, it should not be forgotten that many of those judgments which were questionable were either corrected on appeal or subsequently referred to the ECJ.[403]

Prior to the ECJ departure in *Keck*, the single most striking 'error' which the national courts made in applying Article 30 was to assume, contrary to the *Cassis de Dijon* case law, that a national measure which applies equally to national products and to imports, is not capable of breaching Article 30. Time after time, national courts expressly stated that the indistinctly applicable nature of a particular national measure precluded the application of Article 30. This view was expressed by the national courts primarily, though by no means exclusively, in cases concerning national restrictions on the time and place where goods may be sold and national rules restricting the advertising and promotion of products. The judgment of the ECJ in *Keck* has, to some extent, legitimated these 'errors' of the national courts, by holding that certain categories of national measures do not breach Article 30 *unless* they are distinctly applicable. The impact of that judgment is the subject of the following chapter.

[402] In this respect, see, e.g., discussion of the judgments of national courts in *Syndicat national du commerce de la chaussure* v. *Ministère du commerce extérieur et Ministre de l'industrie et de la recherche*, n. 164 above; *Ministre de l'économie, des finances et du budget* v. *Société Lefebvre*, n. 168 above; *R.* v. *Secretary of State for Social Security, ex. p. Bomore Medical Supplies Ltd*, n. 192 above; *Ex p. Bell Lines*, n. 205 above; *Nederlandse Melkhandelaren Organisatie* v. *Konmar BV*, n. 211 above; *Openbaar Ministerie* v. *R.-Bakkerijen BV*, n. 294 above.

[403] See, e.g. *SA British Motors Wright* v. *SCP Boscher, Studer et Fromentin et Nado GmbH*, n. 289 above; *R.* v. *Henn and Darby*, n. 61 above; *Esge* v. *Alpha Trading*, n. 81 above & *W. H. Smith Do It All and Payless DIY Ltd* v. *Peterborough City Council*, n. 103 above.

3

Actually or potentially hindering intra-Community trade

1 INTRODUCTION

This final limb of the *Dassonville*[1] definition of measures having equivalent effect, namely that intra-Community trade be 'actually or potentially' hindered, has been the focus of great attention. It is the acceptance in this definition that even a *potential* effect on trade would be sufficient to bring Article 30 EC into play that has ensured an extremely broad scope for the application of Article 30 EC. Unfortunately, it has also ensured that the ECJ has encountered serious difficulties in maintaining a satisfactory and consistent body of case law. The striking breadth of the *Dassonville* definition inevitably led to a need to locate the outer margins of the scope of Article 30 EC. This problem of the demarcation line at the fringes of Article 30 EC has been the area of significant academic comment[2] and important recent case law of the Court in its now infamous *Keck and Mithouard*[3] judgment attempting to clarify and modify its earlier case law. The trend of these recent developments has been to narrow the scope of Article 30 EC in limited but nevertheless important respects.

The discussion in this section of the application of these principles by national courts will necessarily be divided into two sections: the application of the case law prevailing *before* the *Keck and Mithouard* judgment of 24 November 1993 and the application by national courts *subsequent to* that judgment. As was suggested above, it is widely accepted that the case law of the ECJ on this part of the *Dassonville* formula prior to *Keck and Mithouard* was in a state of considerable confusion. The amazing turnaround of the ECJ in its judgment in *Keck and Mithouard* may be seen, therefore, as an explicit attempt to 're-examine and clarify its case law on this matter'.[4] The analysis which follows of national case law prior to *Keck*

---

[1] Case 8/74 *Procureur du Roi* v. *Dassonville* [1974] ECR 837, [1974] 2 CMLR 436.

[2] See, e.g., White, 'In Search of the Limits to Article 30 of the EEC Treaty'; Gormley, 'Actually or Potentially, Directly or Indirectly? Obstacles to the Free Movement of Goods'; Mortelmans, 'Article 30 of the EEC Treaty and Legislation Relating to Marketing Circumstances: Time to Consider a New Definition?'; Steiner, 'Drawing the Line: Uses and Abuses of Article 30'; Chalmers, 'Free Movement of Goods Within the European Community: An Unhealthy Addiction to Scotch Whisky'; Wils, 'The Search for the Rule in Article 30 EEC: Much Ado About Nothing'.

[3] Cases C–267 & 268/91 *Keck and Mithouard* [1993] ECR I–6097, [1995] 1 CMLR 101.

[4] Para. 14 of judgt in *Keck and Mithouard*, n. 3 above.

and Mithouard thus affords interesting avenues of discussion as to whether the *Keck and Mithouard* volte-face was either necessary or desirable. One such question is whether the national courts were experiencing sufficiently serious difficulties in locating the outer margins of Article 30 EC to merit a drastic change of heart on the part of the ECJ, even at the risk of upsetting well-established case law. Finally, national case law applying the *Keck and Mithouard* judgment will also be discussed and evaluated in this chapter.

2 APPLICATION OF THE CASE-LAW PREVAILING BEFORE THE *KECK AND MITHOUARD* JUDGMENT OF 24 NOVEMBER 1993

In order to discuss national case law prior to the *Keck and Mithouard* judgment, the case law of the ECJ prevailing before that judgment requires brief explanation. In theory, the requirement in the *Dassonville* definition of measures having equivalent effect that intra-Community trade be 'actually or potentially' hindered is entirely sensible. It has long been established and accepted that Article 30 EC encompasses an *effects* doctrine. The form or purpose of the national measure has, quite rightly, been considered to be irrelevant in establishing a breach of Article 30 EC.[5] Furthermore, although a finding that a particular national measure discriminates against imported goods 'may be sufficient, even conclusive, to bring a measure within Article 30 EC, it is not a necessary precondition for Article 30 EC to apply'.[6] Indeed, Gormley has written:

The judgment of the Court in Case 8/74 *Dassonville* made it plain that it was not necessary to show that a measure was discriminatory, it was merely necessary to show that it was capable of hindering, actually or potentially, directly or indirectly trade between Member States.[7]

Accordingly, any national rule that can be linked, even potentially, to an effect on trade is caught by Article 30 EC and is therefore unlawful, subject to justification either under Article 36 EC or under the rule of reason. This broad interpretation of the scope of Article 30 EC has undoubtedly made a vital contribution to the elimination of barriers to trade and consequently to achieving a truly integrated single market.

---

[5] See, e.g., Case 59/82 *Schutzverband gegen Unwesen in der Wirtschaft* v. *Weinvertriebs* [1981] ECR 1217.

[6] Adv. Gen. Slynn in Joined Cases 60 & 61/84 *Cinéthèque SA* v. *Fédération nationale des cinémas français* [1985] ECR 2605 at 2609. It should nevertheless be repeated that the discriminatory nature of a measure precludes a Member State's reliance on the *Cassis de Dijon* rule of reason to justify trading restrictions in breach of Art. 30 EC. Discriminatory restrictions can only be justified under the exhaustive heads of justification provided for in Art. 36 EC. See further discussion of this point at p. 177.

[7] Gormley, *Prohibiting Restrictions on Trade Within the EEC*, 262.

One would expect that from the national courts' perspective, discerning an actual or potential effect on trade, and therefore a breach of Article 30 EC, would be a relatively 'user-friendly' test.[8] Indeed, in a straightforward case, this is undoubtedly so. A good example is the judgment of the English High Court in *Ex p. Bell Lines*.[9] Until 1983, the only milk imported into the UK was from Ireland, shipped into the two Irish Sea ports of Fleetwood and Newport. In 1983 however, following the judgment of the ECJ in *Commission* v. *United Kingdom* (Re UHT Milk),[10] all imports were banned unless they came in through seventeen designated UK ports, none of which was either Fleetwood or Newport or indeed any port convenient to Ireland. On an application by the shippers and exporters of Irish UHT milk and cream for a declaration that Fleetwood and Newport should be included as designated ports of entry, the High Court had no difficulty in finding a restriction on inter-State trade contrary to Article 30 and therefore granted the declaration sought. In such a case, the 'actual or potential effect on trade' was clear. The practical effect of the UK system of designated ports was to require sea-borne imports from Ireland to travel out of the sea in which their natural ports are situated and round the coast to another sea in order to reach the nearest designated port, thereby incurring uncompetitive extra costs. Accordingly, the effect on trade (which at the time of the case was only potential as, on the facts, no damage had yet been suffered by the shippers[11]) was easy for the national court to discern.

It must be noted that, in the vast majority of applications of Articles 30 to 36 EC by national courts, discerning an 'actual or potential' effect on trade has been a 'non-issue'. In cases involving distinctly applicable measures in particular,[12] once the national court has either identified or rejected the existence in national regulations of a preference or advantage for domestic products, the 'actual or potential' effect on trade for the purposes of Article 30 is correspondingly either assumed or rejected and is not usually discussed in any detail, if at all. This is not to say that there have not been considerable problems in certain cases in national courts in applying the 'actual or potential' effect on trade test. In an important minority of cases, particularly those involving indistinctly applicable

---

[8] This is especially the case when one compares this test to the difficult and sophisticated economic analysis of commercial agreements and practices (in the market context in which they occur) required of national courts in discerning a breach of Art. 85(1) EC. See Whish, 'The Enforcement of EC Competition Law in the Domestic Courts of Member States'.

[9] *R.* v. *Minister of Agriculture, Fisheries and Food, ex p. Bell Lines Ltd and An Bord Bainne Co-operative Ltd (The Irish Dairy Board)* [1984] 2 CMLR 502.

[10] Case 124/81 [1983] ECR 203, [1983] 2 CMLR 1.

[11] n. 9 above at 514.

[12] I.e., national measures that only apply to imports. Often also referred to as directly applicable measures. See further discussion in Ch 2, Sect. 5 (A).

measures,[13] the significance of a minimal effect on trade has been a cause for concern. Two essential problems may be identified. Firstly, the confused and often irreconcilable case law of the ECJ on this point has undoubtedly caused concern and confusion in national courts, to the point of introducing a damaging lack of legal certainty. Secondly, the fact that a *potential* effect on the *volume* of imports was in principle enough for Article 30 EC to bite, led to concern in the national courts in cases where no apparent *hindrance* to inter-State trade could be discerned.

(A) A limit of common sense for Article 30?

The national courts have on occasion given firm indications as to what they consider to be within the bounds of common sense as to the scope of Article 30. In *Gillingham Borough Council* v. *Medway (Chatham) Dock Co*[14] the English High Court considered an action brought by Gillingham Borough Council for a declaration that passage of heavy goods vehicles to and from a port between 7 pm and 7 am constituted a public nuisance. Medway Dock Co raised the argument to the effect that if the declaration were to be granted (with the practical effect that delivery to and from the port during those hours would be prohibited), there would be an 'actual or potential' effect on trade contrary to Article 30. Buckley J held, *obiter dictum*, that such an injunction would 'not be designed to govern the patterns of trade between Member States' and that Article 30 would not apply. He added that he would be 'surprised and disappointed' if the ECJ did not reach the same result. We see here a clear expression by a national court of what it considers to be the 'common-sense' limits of Article 30. Similarly, prior to the *Torfaen* judgment concerning United Kingdom Sunday trading legislation,[15] the English national courts were sceptical about the application of Article 30 to the Shops Act 1950. In *Charles Robertson (Developments) Ltd* v. *Caradon DC*[16] Judge Sir Jonathan Clarke in Bodmin Crown Court referred the question of the compatibility of the Shops Act 1950 with Article 30 to the ECJ, while nevertheless himself taking the common-sense view that a reading of Article 30 would not seem, on the ordinary meaning of the words in that Article, to catch these measures:

[A]t first reading of that Article [Article 30] and of the relevant provisions of the 1950 Act, I see no justification for believing that the terms of the Act are properly described either as a quantitative restriction on imports or having equivalent effect.[17]

---

[13] I.e., national measures that apply to national products as well as imports. Often also referred to as indirectly applicable measures or equally applicable measures.

[14] [1992] 3 All ER 923; [1992] 4 J. Environ. Law 251–71 (with note by Crawford).

[15] Case C–145/88 *Torfaen B.C.* v. *B & Q* [1989] ECR 3851.

[16] [1988] 1 CMLR 293.   [17] Ibid. at 295.

Similarly, in *Payless DIY Ltd* v. *Peterborough City Council, W. H. Smith Do-It-All Ltd* v. *Same*, Peterborough Crown Court held (also pre-*Torfaen*) that

since the purpose of Article 30 was to promote unfettered free trade within the European Community it was not intended to override national regulatory provisions of Member States which are not enacted to regulate trade or specifically aimed at imports from Member States.[18]

The English national courts thus assumed pre-*Torfaen* that Article 30, on a common-sense view, would not apply to national legislation governing shop-opening hours. This view was shared by Advocate General Leijten of the Dutch *Hoge Raad* who, in a pre-*Torfaen* case concerning the Dutch *Winkelsluitingswet* (Shop Hours Act), suggested that measures that apply equally to both imports and national products should not fall under the prohibition in Article 30, unless a Member State misuses the competence it has in principle to regulate domestic trade, making import either impossible, or more difficult or costly than national produce.[19] Similarly, the *Tribunal de grande instance* of Paris in its judgment referring questions to the ECJ in *Cinéthèque* stated that

There does not seem to be an obvious incompatibility between the national legislation imposing a temporal gradation of different modes of broadcast of cinematographic works without discriminating with respect to nationality and the principle of free movement of artistic works and goods set out in the Treaty of Rome.[20]

The above examples illustrate that there was a clear expectation in the national courts that Article 30 would not apply in cases where no *hindrance* to inter-State trade could be discerned. The views and expectations of national courts are not as irrelevant as they may at first seem. It has already been noted that the spirit of judicial co-operation is the cornerstone of the Community's judicial structure. The ECJ, and the development of EC law in general, relies heavily on the co-operation of the national courts. The views of these courts should not therefore be cast aside without careful consideration. Indeed, once the supremacy and direct effect of EC law has been accepted by the national courts, the next step is for them to apply the substantive rules of EC law in a confident and accurate manner. References to the ECJ should, in the long term, be the exception rather than the rule. The status of national courts as the

[18] Judgt 30 Nov. 1988, summarized on appeal (post-*Torfaen*) to the QBD in judgt of 4 June 1990 [1990] 2 CMLR 577; [1991] 1 QB 304; [1990] 3 WLR 1131; [1991] 4 All ER 193.

[19] *Officier van Justitie* v. *Makro Zelfbedieningsgroothandel Nuth CV, Hoge Raad* (Strafkamer), 4 Nov. 1986, NJ 1987, 384 (with note by Van Veen); SEW 1990, 674 (with note by AM); (1988) ELDig. 14; (1989) CDE 481.

[20] *TGI* Paris, 1re Ch. I, 15 Feb. 1984, Rev. juris. comm. 1984, 265–7 (with note by De Montblanc); Gaz. Pal. 1984, Som. II 352. See also Servan-Schreiber, 'EEC law in French Courts 1980–1984' at 169 & Guyot-Sionnest, 'Un vide juridique. Le problème des vidéo-cassettes'.

'Community Courts' with 'primary responsibility for applying Article 30'[21] means that it is desirable that national courts may be relied upon to weed out those cases in which the integrationist merit is negligible.

National courts do, in general, form an effective filter to weed out most such cases. The English High Court in *R.* v. *Birmingham City Council, ex p. Wesson*[22] rejected the argument that road-works in front of a shop restricted imports. The Dutch *CBB* in *Cyanamid Benelux* v. *Minister van Landbouw en Visserij*[23] refused to accept that authorization under certain conditions for experiments to develop certain animal medicines constituted a restriction on trade in such animals. The English Court of Appeal in *R.* v. *Southwark Crown Court, ex p. Watts*[24] held that a regulation of a local authority requiring a market trader to attend his stall personally in no way constituted a 'clog on the free movement of goods'. It is submitted that national courts should have the capacity to weed out such cases. From the point of view of the healthy development of Community law, it is indeed desirable that only in cases where there is a genuine issue concerning the free movement of goods should the ECJ be called upon to rule on the matter.

The French *Cour de Cassation* has in two cases rejected arguments based on Article 30 in the context of French legislation requiring that temporary shops (*vente au deballage*) obtain prior authorization from local authorities before opening.[25] The aim of the legislation was to protect sedentary (permanent) retailers. In both cases, the *Cour de Cassation* upheld the convictions of the managers of two temporary premises for opening without the prior authorization. The *Cour de Cassation* held that it was argued in vain that the authorization requirement was a measure having equivalent effect to a quantitative restriction. The Article 30 defence was rejected since 'it was not shown, nor even alleged . . . that they were submitted to conditions of sale more rigorous than those applying to national products'. It is possible to criticize these judgments for assuming that the non-discriminatory nature of the French requirement had the result that Article 30 could not be breached. On the other hand, the 'actual or potential' effect on trade was surely negligible and there was clearly no hindrance to the access of goods from other Member States. It would be difficult to argue that by requiring temporary shops to have a licence from a local authority, one was depriving goods from another Member State a rapid and effective means of entering the French market. It is submitted that on the facts of

---

[21] Adv. Gen. Jacobs in Case C–412/93 *Leclerc Siplec* v. *TF1 Publicité* [1995] ECR I–179 at 194.
[22] [1992] 3 CMLR 377.
[23] Pres. *CBB*, 28 Jan. 1988, SEW 1987, 791 (with note by Mortelmans).
[24] [1992] 1 CMLR 446; [1992] PL 155.
[25] Law of 30 Dec. 1906 & Decree of 26 Nov. 1962. *Couat, Cour de Cassation*, ch. crim., 10 July 1990, Bull. Cass. Crim. 1990, no. 279 p. 705 and *Falck, Cour de Cassation*, ch. crim., 25 Oct. 1993, Bull. Cass. Crim. 1993, no. 309 p. 776.

cases such as these, it is right and proper that the national court rejected the free-movement-of-goods argument without troubling the ECJ. The integrationist merit at stake was simply too small.[26]

The conclusion is that national courts do, quite rightly, have the expectation that Article 30 should have some limit of common sense. Since it is the national courts that are charged with the day-to-day application of Article 30, it is important that such expectations are not ignored by the ECJ in the development of its case law on Article 30. A limit of common sense for Article 30 which conforms to the expectations of the national courts is imperative for another reason: in the interests of its work-load and the importance of the Community, the ECJ must be able to rely on the national courts to weed out those cases where the integrationist merit is very small, allowing it to concentrate on those issues of most significance for the maintenance of an effective internal market. Such an imperative assumes that there is a clear body of ECJ case law for the national courts to apply, so that the latter can perform their task as the ordinary Community courts effectively. It is to the absence of such clear ECJ case law that we now turn.

(B) Confused ECJ case law

The background of difficult and inconsistent ECJ case law must be briefly outlined.[27] Such inconsistency is demonstrated in a case such as *Blesgen*[28] on the one hand, where the ECJ held that a legislative provision in Belgium prohibiting the sale of strong spirits for consumption on the premises in all places open to the public 'has in fact no connection with the importation of the products and for that reason is not of such a nature as to impede trade between Member States'.[29] On the other hand, however, in *Oosthoek*,[30] the ECJ held that Dutch legislation restricting the offer of free gifts with encyclopaedias *was* capable of affecting sales of imported goods because it affected marketing opportunities for the imported products.[31] In not explaining why the measures in *Blesgen* could not be

---

[26] It may be noted that after the *Keck and Mithouard* judgment, national rules such as those at issue in these two cases would almost certainly be held to be 'selling arrangements' and therefore outside the scope of Art. 30 altogether. See discussion at sect. 3 (B) as to whether this is a more satisfactory approach from the point of view of legal certainty in the national courts.

[27] For a more detailed discussion of this case law see Oliver, *Free Movement of Goods in the European Community*, 96 & discussion in the literature cited in n. 2 above.

[28] Case 75/81 [1982] ECR 1211, [1983] 1 CMLR 431.

[29] Para. 9 of judgt. In a similar vein see also Case C–23/89 *Quietlynn* v. *Southend B.C.* [1990] ECR I–3059; Case 148/85 *Forest* [1986] ECR 3448; Case C–69/88 *Krantz* [1990] ECR I–583 & Case C–93/92 *CMC Motorradcenter* v. *Pelin* [1993] ECR I–5009.

[30] Case 286/81 *Oosthoek Uitgeversmaatschappij BV* [1982] ECR 4575, [1983] 3 CMLR 428.

[31] Para. 15 of judgt. For judgments to the same effect see, Case 362/88 *GB-INNO* v. *CCL* [1990] ECR I–667; Case 382/87 *Buet* v. *Ministère Public* [1989] ECR 1235; Case C–369/88

considered to have an 'actual or potential' effect on inter-State trade while those in *Oosthoek* could, these inconsistent lines of authority reduced legal certainty to nil. The difficulties were exacerbated by the fact that, in accepting that a potential or very slight connection with intra-Community trade was sufficient to bring Article 30 EC into play, the ECJ was increasingly being faced with adjudicating on national laws concerned with the place or time or manner of marketing products and not with rules affecting access to markets. The pinnacle was reached when the ECJ accepted that national laws concerning shop-opening hours on Sundays were 'actually or potentially' capable of affecting trade between Member States since, by being forced to close on a Sunday, retailers suffered a reduction in their total sales—which would include a reduction in the volume of imports from other Member States.[32] By holding that such national rules governing socio-economic life, which neither affected market access for products nor isolated the market of one Member State from the rest of the common market, as 'actually or potentially' capable of hindering intra-Community trade, the ECJ opened up its case law to abuse by traders. Consequently, all manner of national regulations were referred to the ECJ for a decision as to their compatibility with the provisions on the free movement of goods. This reached the point of becoming a burden to the ECJ as it was then obliged to deal with the question of whether or not the measures could nevertheless be justified. Such questions involved evaluations which, because of their subjectivity, proved fiendishly difficult to apply in practice. The latter problems need not concern us at this juncture.[33] What concerns us in this section is how the national courts reacted to and applied the inconsistent case law of the ECJ regarding the question of whether there is an 'actual or potential' effect on trade sufficient to bring Article 30 EC into play.

One of the most striking cases involving this issue in the English courts was the *Magnavision* litigation.[34] SA Magnavision NV, a Belgian company, marketed spectacles in the United Kingdom. It did so through a chain of concessions in British department stores where customers simply tested their own sight using a test-card and then selected an appropriate pair of spectacles without a prescription and without the supervision of an optician. SA Magnavision NV was prosecuted for selling spectacles without

---

Delattre [1991] ECR I–1487; Cases C–1/90 & C–176/90 *Aragonesa de Publicidad Exterior SA* v. *DSSC* [1991] ECR I–4151 & Case C–126/91 *Schutzverband gegen Unwesen in der Wirtschaft* v. *Yves Rocher* [1993] ECR I–2361.

[32] See Case C–145/88 n. 15 above and Case C–169/91 *Stoke-on-Trent* v. *B & Q* [1992] ECR I–6635. For comment see, Arnull 'What Shall We Do on Sunday?'; Barnard 'Sunday Trading: A Drama in Five Acts' & Jarvis 'The Sunday Trading Episode: In Defence of the Euro-Defence'.

[33] See discussion in Ch. 6, Sect. 4.

[34] *SA Magnavision NV* v. *General Optical Council* (No. 1) [1987] 1 CMLR 887.

an optician or prescription in breach of Section 21 of the Opticians Act 1958 according to which spectacles could not be sold in Britain except under the supervision of a doctor or optician or on production of an optician's prescription.[35] The firm was convicted by Cardiff Magistrates' Court and appealed by way of case stated to the Divisional Court, arguing that the United Kingdom legislation breached Article 30 EC in that it limited channels of distribution which was capable of 'actually or potentially' affecting imports of spectacles into the UK from other Member States. This alleged breach of Article 30 was rejected by MacPherson J in the Queen's Bench Division of the English High Court. In a judgment littered with inaccurate applications of the ECJ's Article 30 case law,[36] MacPherson J held that

> [T]he cases show that before Article 30 will bite there must be proved to exist some particular restrictive effect upon imports. If this were not so then any sales restriction (such as a requirement that guns can only be sold by licensed dealers, or that alcohol may only be sold by holders of Justices' licences) could similarly involve breach of Article 30.[37]

He went on to state that 'Before Article 30 could catch the 1958 Act restrictions it would have to be established that the measures did truly affect the Belgian imports adversely. It is not enough simply to prove that sales are affected, since otherwise all such measures could be caught.'[38]

Applying this interpretation of Article 30 to the facts, it was held that the Magistrates were entitled to conclude that Article 30 'did not bite at all in this case'.[39] In the above statements, it is clear that the national court assumed that a 'restrictive effect' adversely affecting imports was required before Article 30 could apply. In holding that 'it is not enough simply to prove that sales are affected', it is clear that the national court was influenced by a fear that the application of Article 30 would become unduly wide. Nevertheless, this seems to go against the literal interpretation of the *Dassonville* formula by the ECJ in some cases according to which even a *potential* effect on trade is enough to bring a measure within Article 30 and equally, seems to go against the explicit rejection by the ECJ of a *de minimis* principle for Article 30.[40]

---

[35] It may be noted that this provision was subsequently amended by the Health and Medicines Act 1988, s. 13.

[36] Such inaccuracies included, in particular, quoting the *Dassonville* formula followed by an attempt to limit that case to its facts (see n. 34 above at 891), which seems questionable given the verbatim repetition of the *Dassonville* formula by the ECJ in countless subsequent cases. Equally puzzling is that the measures at issue in Case 120/78 *Rewe* v. *Bundesmonopolverwaltung für Branntwein* ('Cassis de Dijon') [1979] ECR 649, [1979] 3 CMLR 494 were distinguished as 'plainly discriminatory and protectionist in their effect' (see n. 34 above at 892). This is, with respect, certainly incorrect as it is clear that indistinctly applicable measures were involved in that case. See discussion of these points at pp. 57–8.

[37] n. 34 above at 892.   [38] Ibid. at 893.   [39] Ibid. at 894.

[40] See discussion in sect. (C) on the question of *de minimis* in national courts' interpretation of Art. 30.

What is interesting in this case however, is the way in which the national court reached this conclusion. The High Court in *Magnavision* relied heavily on the ECJ's judgment in *Blesgen*.[41] That judgment was used as authority for the proposition that 'if there is no true connection between the restriction and the importation of the product then Article 30 has no effect'[42] because such measures are not of such a nature as to impede trade between Member States. MacPherson J went on to admit that the ECJ's judgment in *Oosthoek*[43] 'appears to be out of line with the other cases' but simply dismissed that judgment by saying 'it is not in my judgment helpful further to analyse that case in all the circumstances'.[44] It seems clear therefore that the ECJ's contradictory case law did have an adverse influence. The national court was able to rely on *Blesgen* without convincingly being able to reject the cases on the other side of the fence (such as *Oosthoek*). It is a sad reflection on the contradictory state of the ECJ's case law that a national court was able to rely on one strand of interpretation in *Blesgen*, dismissing the authorities going the other way, as 'out of line' when most commentators regard the *Blesgen* line of authority as the odd one out.[45]

It is submitted that while the English High Court in *Magnavision* may certainly be criticized for having refused to accept that a potential effect on trade, however small, may bring Article 30 into play, the confused ECJ case law is ultimately to blame for having provided the 'tools' for divergent decisions before national courts. Following the judgment of the ECJ in *Torfaen*,[46] Mustill LJ remarked that the reasoning of the High Court in *Magnavision* could no longer survive.[47] Indeed, the subsequent decision of the ECJ in *Laboratoire de Prothèses Oculaires* v. *Union Nationale de Syndicats d'Opticiens de France*[48] that French legislation which conferred upon qualified opticians the sole right to sell contact lenses was capable of affecting trade between Member States, thereby constituting a breach of Article 30 (but nevertheless justified on public-health grounds under Article 36), suggests that the High Court's conclusion in *Magnavision* that 'this is not an Article 30 case at all'[49] was, at that time, far from a foregone conclu-

---

[41] Case 75/81, n. 28 above. [42] n. 34 above at 893.
[43] Case 286/81, n. 30 above. [44] n. 34 above at 893.
[45] See Gormley, n. 7 above, 70 who explains the *Blesgen* case on the basis of American case law on police powers; and Oliver, n. 27 above, 94.
[46] n. 32 above. [47] *Payless* and *Do-It-All Ltd* n. 18 above.
[48] Case C–271/92 [1993] ECR I–2899. This case was referred to the ECJ by the French *Cour de Cassation*, ch. comm., 2 June 1992, Bull. Cass. Civ., 1992, IV no. 216 p. 151; Dalloz, 1993, IR 185, and implemented *Cour de Cassation*, ch. comm., 4 Jan. 1994, Bull. Cass. Civ., 1994, IV no. 2 p. 1; Dalloz, 1994, IR 26; [1994] ECC 457. See also the French judgments on this issue: *Cour de Cassation*, ch. sociale, 14 Nov. 1995 (transcr. 93-17.485) & *Conseil d'Etat*, 23 Oct. 1995 (transcr. 150.212).
[49] [1987] 1 CMLR 887 at 894.

sion.[50] It may at this stage be noted that following the *Keck and Mithouard*[51] case, national rules such as those at issue in *Magnavision* would now almost certainly be considered to be 'selling arrangements' and accordingly outside the scope of Article 30 altogether.[52]

Another English case in which the contradictory ECJ case law proved to be a problem was *London Borough of Waltham Forest* v. *Scott Markets Ltd.*[53] This case was one of the early English Sunday-trading cases concerning the Shops Act 1950. The Borough of Waltham Forest applied for an interim injunction to close the defendant's Sunday market in the Lea Valley Trading Estate in London. The Chancery Division of the High Court, in giving a preliminary view pending full trial, held that the defendant's arguments that the ban on Sunday opening infringed Article 30 were not persuasive. As in *Magnavision*, it was again the ECJ's judgment in *Blesgen*[54] which was relied upon most heavily by the national court to reach this conclusion. Rather worryingly, the High Court suggested that the effect of *Blesgen* was that discrimination was required to found a breach of Article 30.[55] The High Court admitted that the ECJ's judgment in *Cinéthèque SA* v. *Fédération nationale des cinémas français*[56] casts doubt upon this conclusion but held that 'the *Blesgen* case would, I think, apply unless any wider standard of interpretation has been introduced by the *Cinéthèque* case. In my view it has not been so introduced'.[57]

Here again, therefore, we see inconsistent ECJ judgments being played off against each other. The conclusion is that, far from being treated as the odd one out, the *Blesgen* case was taken by the national courts to be the norm. The other cases, which suggested an extremely broad interpretation of Article 30 in allowing any effect on trade, however small, to bring Article 30 into play (such as *Oosthoek* and *Cinéthèque*), were treated as the odd ones out.

A final case before the English High Court which may be used to illustrate the problem national courts had following the ECJ's difficult and inconsistent case law arose in *R.* v. *Birmingham City Council, ex p. Wesson.*[58] This case concerned judicial review proceedings of the highway authority's decision to carry out road improvement works in order to increase

---

[50] The subsequent decision of the English High Court in *SA Magnavision NV* v. *General Optical Council* (No. 2) [1987] 2 CMLR 262 that the matter was *acte clair* and that an Art. 177 preliminary ruling was not necessary without having the question examined by a court of final instance is examined in Ch. 11, sect. 4.

[51] Case C–267 & 268/91, n. 3 above.

[52] See esp. Case C–391/92 *Commission* v. *Hellenic Republic* [1995] ECR I–1621 (concerning national legislation requiring processed milk for infants to be sold exclusively through pharmacists' shops) and discussion of post-*Keck and Mithouard* case law in sect. 3 (A).

[53] [1988] 3 CMLR 773.   [54] Case 75/81, n. 28 above.

[55] See discussion of this point at pp. 54–5.

[56] Joined Cases 60 & 61/84, n. 6 above.

[57] n. 53 above at 783 (per Robert Wright QC).   [58] n. 22 above.

the protection of pedestrians outside Mr Wesson's shop (an off-licence). Mr Wesson raised (amongst others) the remarkably bold argument that the road improvements in question restricted access to his shop for delivery vehicles with the result that his turnover would drop, thereby reducing his throughput of items imported from other Member States which would result in an 'actual or potential' effect on trade in breach of Article 30. The Queen's Bench Division of the High Court rejected this argument as 'hopeless'.[59] Rose J held that

[T]he mere fact that the measure may lead to a reduction in imports to the United Kingdom is not, having regard to the decision of the European Court in *Quietlynn Ltd* v. *Southend BC* itself sufficient to lead to the assumption that Article 30 applies to the measure.[60]

The High Court thus based its conclusion on the ECJ's judgment in *Quietlynn*.[61] This is a perfectly feasible analysis of that judgment. The ECJ had indeed held in that case (citing its judgments in *Blesgen*[62] and *Oebel*[63]) that national provisions prohibiting the sale of lawful sex articles from unlicensed sex establishments had 'in fact no connection with intra-Community trade, since the products covered by the 1982 Act may be marketed through licensed sex establishments and other channels . . . Moreover, those provisions are not intended to regulate trade in goods within the Community and they are therefore not of such a nature as to impede trade between Member States'.[64] The High Court's reliance on this reasoning in *Ex p. Wesson* was thus perfectly defensible. Unfortunately, given the ECJ's inconsistent case law, the High Court again had difficulty in distinguishing the ECJ judgments going the other way. The High Court distinguished the *Torfaen, Dassonville, Ex p. Association of Pharmaceutical Importers*[65] and *Cinéthèque* cases on the basis that 'each was concerned with a discriminatory measure or, in the case of the *Torfaen* case, manifestly, on the face of it, with a trade measure'.[66] It is respectfully submitted that none of the cases cited by the High Court involved discriminatory measures. In all those cases, the national measures in question applied equally to national and imported products. It is submitted therefore that while the High Court was perfectly reasonable in its interpretation and application of the *Quietlynn* judgment, the distinguishing of the ECJ authorities going the other way was unsatisfactory. Ultimately the *Quietlynn* judgment was difficult to square with a judgment like *Torfaen* and since the two lines of

---

[59] Ibid. at 383.   [60] Ibid.   [61] Case C–23/89, n. 29 above.
[62] Case 75/81, n. 28 above.
[63] Case 155/80 *Summary proceedings against Oebel* [1981] ECR 1993.
[64] Para. 11 of judgt in *Quietlynn*, n. 29 above.
[65] Cases 266 & 267/87 *R.* v. *The Royal Pharmaceutical Society of Great Britain, ex p. Association of Pharmaceutical Importers* [1989] ECR 1295.
[66] n. 22 above at 383.

cases were irreconcilable, the conclusion is inevitably that the inconsistent case law of the ECJ itself was ultimately at fault.

The irreconcilable case law of the ECJ has also been a point of contention before Dutch courts. The most notable instance concerned a judgment of the *Hoge Raad* regarding the compatibility of the Dutch Shop Opening Hours Act 1951 (*Winkelsluitingswet*) with Article 30.[67] Makro was prosecuted for opening on a Wednesday evening after 6 pm (selling groceries) contrary to that Act and raised the Article 30 defence. The defence was identical to that raised in the English Sunday-trading cases, except in this case, the proximity of the defendant shop (situated in Nuth) to the German border was an additional feature. In short, Makro argued that if it had to be closed after 6 pm, it would be in a less favourable position than the self-service wholesalers in the German border region of Metro Aken which would, or could, lead to a lowering of its turnover and thereby to a lowering of purchasing by the appellant of provisions from the Netherlands and from other countries of the Community, and thus of import. The *Hoge Raad* dismissed this argument. Firstly, the *Hoge Raad* held that the question of whether Makro was in a less favourable position was a judgment of a factual nature which it, as a court of cassation, could not reopen.[68] Secondly, however, the *Hoge Raad* went on to hold that Article 30 did not stand in the way of national legislation such as the *Winkelsluitingswet*. The *Hoge Raad* reached this conclusion by relying heavily on the judgment of the ECJ in *Oebel*[69] and held that

[T]he Act in question comprises a collection of provisions in which the hours which a retail shop is prohibited from being open to the public are regulated. When, in the framework of social economic policy, the *Winkelsluitingswet* 1951 regulates the sale and delivery of products in shops to the retail customer, but does not apply to other trade other than retail trade, it cannot be said that this law actually or potentially affects intra-Community trade contrary to Article 30.

The extent to which the above relies on the ECJ's reasoning in *Oebel* is apparent. The *Oebel* case concerned German restrictions on night-work in bakeries and also the transport of bakers' goods before a certain hour. On this point the ECJ had held in *Oebel*:

If such rules are confined to transport for delivery to individual consumers and retail outlets only, without affecting transport and delivery to warehouses or intermediaries, they cannot have the effect of restricting imports or exports between

---

[67] *Officier van Justitie* v. *Makro Zelfbedieningsgroothandel Nuth CV*, HR 4 Nov. 1986, NJ 1987, 384 (with note by Van Veen); SEW 1990, 674 (with note by AM); (1988) ELDig. 14; (1989) CDE 481.

[68] The judgment of the ECJ in Cases C–430 and 431/93 *Van Schijndel* [1995] ECR I–4705 would appear to confirm that the *Hoge Raad* was correct on this point.

[69] n. 63 above.

Member States. In this case, indeed, trade within the Community remains possible at all times, subject to the single exception that delivery to consumers and retailers is restricted to the same extent for all producers wherever they are established. Under these circumstances, such rules are not contrary to Articles 30 and 34 of the Treaty.[70]

In the light of the above, the *Hoge Raad* would appear to have been justified in relying on *Oebel*. National legislation on shop-opening hours at the retail level does not affect transport and delivery to warehouses or intermediaries and, following *Oebel*, 'trade within the Community remains possible at all times'. While this might be a correct application of the *Oebel* judgment, it leaves far too many questions unanswered. For example, it ignores the ground of appeal before the *Hoge Raad* explicitly pleading that a lowering of turnover would be enough for Article 30 to apply. The *Hoge Raad* might have been correct to state that trade at the wholesale level remained possible at all times, but it does not address the argument (which the ECJ subsequently accepted in *Torfaen*) that if Makro was closed, its turnover would be reduced, thereby reducing wholesale trade and leading to a potential effect on inter-State trade. In this light, it seems that an Article 177 reference would have been desirable especially since the subsequent references from French and English courts on this point suggest that it was not equally clear to jurisdictions in other Member States.[71] This is not to say that the *Hoge Raad* was wrong—the argument that national shop-opening hours breached Article 30 was always stretching the *Dassonville* formula to the limit—it is simply to underline the fact that the ECJ's case law on this point was inconsistent. As the above discussion demonstrates, this was far from satisfactory for the national courts.

The practical effect of the inconsistent ECJ case law was to tie the hands of the national courts. It has already been noted in the national court judgments discussed above that reliance on one line of ECJ authority did not allow the national courts to satisfactorily distinguish the authorities going the other way. Thus in *R. v. Birmingham City Council, ex p. Wesson*,[72] the spurious argument that road-improvement works outside a shop were capable of 'actually or potentially' affecting intra-Community trade could only be rejected by relying on *Quietlynn* without being able to satisfactorily distinguish that case from either *Torfaen* or *Cinéthèque*. This puts the national court in an intolerably difficult position. ECJ case law simply did

---

[70] n. 63 above at para. 20.

[71] It will be remembered that one of the conditions which the ECJ laid down for the application of the *acte clair* doctrine in Case 283/81 *CILFIT* v. *Italian Ministry of Health* [1982] ECR 3415 was that the national court or tribunal must be convinced that the matter is equally obvious to the courts of the other Member States.

[72] n. 22 above.

not permit the national court to authoritatively and convincingly reject the tenuous arguments based on Article 30 raised by the traders.

The difficult position into which the case law put the national courts is clearly demonstrated by a judgment of the Chancery Division of the English High Court in *South Pembrokeshire District Council* v. *Wendy Fair Markets Ltd.*[73] On the facts of the case, South Pembrokeshire District Council, a Welsh municipal council, held an ancient (fourteenth-century) monopoly right to hold a market in the small Welsh town of Tenby within an area of almost seven miles of its centre. Wendy Fair Markets Ltd, a commercial operator, threatened to hold its own market in two fields, respectively one and two miles from the centre, and so within the monopoly area. The Chancery Division of the High Court granted an interim injunction pending full trial to prevent Wendy Fair Markets from holding the market, but held that there *was* a triable issue on the Article 30 point raised by Wendy Fair Markets. The argument was, clearly borrowing the Sunday-trading argument, that if the Market could not be held, there would be an 'actual or potential' effect on trade between Member States as some of the articles sold at the market would have originated from other Member States.[74] Wendy Fair Markets were able to present evidence from economists showing that a slight effect on trade could not be ruled out if the market were not permitted to take place. Jacob J in the Chancery Division explicitly stated that he was unable to decide the point because EC law was so confused on the matter. Equally, however, he added that he could not rule out the possibility that Article 30 could be infringed. This was not for want of trying on the part of the Chancery Division. In a long judgment, Jacob J discussed the relevant ECJ authorities comprehensively[75] and concluded:

I confess I find some of the decisions as to whether a measure is outside Article 30 altogether or within it but justified by mandatory requirements perplexing. I am not alone. For instance the learned authors of Halsbury describe the court in *Oebel* and *Blesgen* as 'less than convincing in its approach',[76] and suggest the cases can be justified under the mandatory requirement exception. That may be so, but I have to deal with what the court itself has said. Prof. Arnull goes so far as to say (in an article with the enticing title 'Anyone for Tripe?'[77]) that: 'it is widely acknowledged that the Court's case law on Article 30 is in disarray'.[78]

---

[73] [1994] 1 CMLR 213.

[74] On the facts, evidence was adduced that some such products included Irish cheese, a gadget called the 'Gourmet V Slicer', and a car polish called 'Mer' (the last two both imported from Germany).

[75] The following ECJ judgments were discussed in detail by Jacob J: *Dassonville*, Case 8/74, n. 1 above; *Blesgen*, Case 75/81, n. 28 above; *Oebel*, Case 155/80, n. 63 above; *Quietlynn*, Case C–23/89, n. 29 above; *Krantz*, Case C–69/88, n. 29 above; & Case 177/82 *Van de Haar* [1984] ECR 1797; [1983] 1 CMLR 510.

[76] *Halsbury's Laws of England*, vol. 52, para. 12.82, n. 12.

[77] (1993) 18 ELRev. 314 at 321.   [78] n. 73 above at 222.

This statement demonstrates the damaging effect of the confused ECJ case law in national courts in practice. Interestingly, Jacob J went on to comment rather prophetically in *Wendy Fair Markets* that 'It may well be that in due course the Court of Justice would be willing to elaborate on *Dassonville* and *Cassis de Dijon* further, in particular in relation to trading rules which are essentially non-discriminatory'.[79]

Only eight days after Jacob J delivered this judgment, the ECJ did just that in its *Keck and Mithouard* judgment.[80] In that judgment, the ECJ finally attempted to 're-examine and clarify its case law on this matter'.[81] Given the discussion in this section of the problems encountered in national courts applying the pre-*Keck* case law, such a re-examination could not have come sooner.[82]

(C) Article 30 and *de minimis*

The fact that a *potential* effect on the *volume* of imports is enough for Article 30 to bite, following the *Dassonville* formula, has led to concern in national courts in cases where no *hindrance* to inter-State trade can be discerned. It will be remembered that the ECJ has hitherto always rejected any role for a *de minimis* principle for Article 30. Indeed, in *Van de Haar*[83] the ECJ held that

> If a national measure is capable of hindering imports it must be regarded as a measure having equivalent effect to a quantitative restriction, even though the hindrance is slight and even though it is possible for imported products to be marketed in other ways.[84]

This clear rejection of a *de minimis* doctrine for Article 30 remains good law. However, the strength of the rejection by the ECJ has implicitly been 'watered down' by some of the inconsistent judgments discussed in the previous section. Furthermore, the ECJ appears to have introduced a *de minimis* test by the back door in its *Stoke-on-Trent* v. *B & Q*[85] judgment where it held that in appraising the proportionality of national rules under the rule of reason it must be considered whether the restrictive effects on intra-Community trade are 'direct, indirect or purely speculative and whether those effects do not impede the marketing of imported products more than the marketing of national products'.[86] Nevertheless, the ECJ's formal position remains unchanged and it is submitted that the *Keck and Mithouard* judgment in no way introduces a *de minimis* test into Article 30.

---

[79] [1994] 1 CMLR 213.
[80] Cases C–267 & 268/91, n. 3 above.
[81] Para. 14 of judgt.
[82] For a discussion of post-*Keck* case law in national courts, see sect. 3.
[83] Case 177/82, n. 75 above.
[84] Para. 13 of judgt. See also Case 16/83 *Criminal proceedings against Prantl* [1984] ECR 1299, [1985] 2 CMLR 238.
[85] Case C–169/91, n. 32 above.
[86] Para. 15 of judgt.

Indeed, the ECJ has, for the time being, ignored the suggestion advanced by Advocate General Jacobs in *Leclerc Siplec* v. *TF1 Publicité*[87] that a *de minimis* test should replace the *Keck and Mithouard* approach for equally applicable measures.[88]

The national courts have not always heeded the clear rejection by the ECJ of a *de minimis* doctrine for Article 30. For example, in *Openbaar Ministerie* v. *J. G. C. van Schaik*[89] the *Rechtbank* Arnhem was faced with the compatibility of the Dutch Road Traffic Law with the provisions of Community law. On the facts of the case, van Schaik was prosecuted for driving along the A12 in the Netherlands in a car without a valid Netherlands *APK* (*Algemene Periodieke Keuring*: vehicle roadworthiness test certificate) certificate contrary to Article 9a(1)(d) of the *Wegenverkeerswet* (*WVW*: Road Traffic Act). With respect to the provisions concerning the free movement of goods, van Schaik argued that the *APK* regulations might have the effect that car owners may not avail themselves of the perhaps cheaper services of garage businesses in other Member States, and of the possibility of obtaining the requisite spare parts there, because it is practical to have maintenance and repairs carried out in a garage in which the periodic vehicle roadworthiness test is carried out as part and parcel of a repair or a service. The *Rechtbank* Arnhem accepted that there may be a potential effect on trade because of the practical reasons in having a service together with an *APK* test, but nevertheless rejected the argument based on Article 30 because 'that effect, which manifests itself exclusively in the vicinity of the southern and eastern borders of the Netherlands, is only on a limited scale'. This statement clearly flies directly in the face of the clear statement of the ECJ in paragraph 13 of its judgment in *Van de Haar* (set out above). It may be noted that the point was subsequently appealed to the *Hoge Raad* which made a reference to the ECJ.[90] In its judgment, the ECJ refused to deal with the free-movement-of-goods point referred to it, as the supply of goods (spare parts, oil etc.) during servicing in another Member State was held to be 'incidental to the provision of services' and thus the ECJ dealt with the matter exclusively on the basis of the freedom to provide services.[91] While it is true that the

---

[87] 'If the principle is that all undertakings should have unfettered access to the whole of the Community market, then the appropriate test in my view is whether there is a substantial restriction on that access', Case C–412/93, n. 21 above at 194–5.

[88] For a discussion of whether the absence of *de minimis* also applies to Art. 34 EC and exports, see discussion in Ch. 4, sect. 3.

[89] *Rechtbank* Arnhem, 21 Jan. 1992, NJ, 1993 368.

[90] *Hoge Raad* (*Strafkamer*), 16 Feb. 1993, NJ 1993, 368 (with note by ter Kuile); Verkeersrecht 1993, no. 120, p. 290.

[91] Case C–55/93 [1994] ECR I–4837, citing Case C–275/92 *Her Majesty's Customs and Excise* v. *Schindler* [1994] ECR I–1039. The judgment was implemented by the *Hoge Raad* on 6 Dec. 1994, NJ 1995, 210, NJB Bijl. 1995, 186 where it was held that Art. 9a *WVW* was not contrary to EC law and the conviction of van Schaik was accordingly upheld.

services were the main activity in *van Schaik* and that the ECJ was merely being realistic as to the economic realities involved in that case, it is submitted that it is regrettable that the ECJ passed over the Article 30 point. This is particularly the case when one considers that the *Hoge Raad* had, in its referring judgment, found as a matter of fact that there was a potential (albeit on a small scale in border regions) effect on trade. It would thus have been desirable for the ECJ to have addressed the Article 30 point regarding *de minimis* and the 'actual or potential' effect on trade. Thus, while the *Rechtbank* Arnhem had held Article 30 inapplicable as the effect on trade was 'only on a limited scale', the ECJ did so on the basis that the effect on trade was merely 'incidental to the provision of services'.

The explicit rejection of a *de minimis* doctrine by the ECJ has not always been heeded by the English courts either. In *Hodgkinson* v. *Nottingham City Council*,[92] the argument that Nottingham City Council's newly introduced policy requiring licensed taxis to be of the type approved by the London Carriage Office (i.e. the London 'black cab') and wheelchair-accessible breached Article 30, was rejected by Nottingham Crown Court. One of the reasons adduced by the court to reach this conclusion was that 'the outcome of the policy on intra-Community trade is of no sensible or practical effect' and 'minuscule'.[93] Again, this seems to fly in the face of the ECJ's explicit rejection of a *de minimis* doctrine for Article 30. Once the Court in *Hodgkinson* had admitted there was an effect on trade, the fact that it was 'minuscule' or of 'no sensible or practical effect' should have been irrelevant considerations on a strict application of ECJ case law.

Difficulties in dealing with *de minimis* and an 'actual or potential' effect on trade may also be identified in certain judgments of the Dutch courts. A particularly good example is to be found in a decision of the *Rechtbank* 's-Hertogenbosch in *Officier van Justitie* v. *Edah BV*.[94] This case concerned Article 2 of the Dutch *Verordening Broodprijzen* setting a minimum price for bread produced in the Netherlands. This minimum price was set by the President of the *Produktschap voor granen, zaden en peulvruchten* (Cereal, Seed, and Pulse Board) based on the total production costs of well-organized and efficiently operated bakers and the total distribution costs of well-organized and efficiently operated distributors. Imported bread, on the other hand, was subject to Article 2(A) of the *Verordening Broodprijzen* which sets a minimum price for the sale of this bread based on the sum of the purchase price and a margin equal to the total distribution costs of a well-organized and efficiently operated distributor. In other words, bread produced in the Netherlands was subject to a minimum price (set taking into consideration reasonable production and distribu-

---

[92] [1993] 3 CMLR 503.   [93] Ibid. at 509.
[94] *Rechtbank* 's-Hertogenbosch (*Ec. Raadkamer*), 5 Feb. 1985, NJ 1985, 308.

tion costs), while imported bread had to be sold for at least the cost price of the bread plus a margin (set taking into consideration reasonable distribution costs). In criminal proceedings against Edah BV for selling bread below the minimum price, Edah BV raised the defence that the legislation breached Article 30. Edah argued that the Netherlands legislation could work in a restrictive way in a case in which both Netherlands-produced and imported bread had production costs higher than those taken into consideration by the *Produktschap* in setting the minimum price under Article 2 of the *Verordening*. The effect of the legislation was, it was argued, that bread produced in the Netherlands could in such a case still be sold by retailers at the set minimum price, while imported bread would have to be sold at the higher production cost price *plus* the added fixed margin which would be higher than the fixed minimum price for which the Netherlands-produced bread could be sold. The *Rechtbank*'s-Hertogenbosch rejected this argument holding that

the decision of a company to accept a lower margin than that calculated for an efficient and well-organized company, through which it is likely that the company makes a loss on the product in question does not lead to a *disturbance on the EEC market*, caused by Article 2 and 2(A) of the *Verordening*.[95]

Whether the *Rechtbank*'s reference to a 'disturbance on the EEC market' (*'EEG marktverstorting'*) should be read as meaning an 'actual or potential effect on inter-State trade' is unclear. It is submitted that the two are not the same: the requirement of a 'disturbance' sets a higher threshold than the requirement of a simple 'effect'. That the *Rechtbank* was misguided is confirmed by the subsequent judgment of the ECJ in this case, where the ECJ held that the Dutch legislation did have the effect that 'in certain cases imported bread must be sold at a price higher than the minimum price applicable to domestically produced bread' and that such provisions therefore 'are capable of hindering trade between Member States and are therefore contrary to Article 30 of the EEC Treaty'.[96] The requirement that there be a 'disturbance on the EEC market' set out by the *Rechtbank*'s-Hertogenbosch thus ignored the absence of a *de minimis* principle for Article 30.

---

[95] Ibid., emphasis added.

[96] Para. 13 of ECJ judgment in Cases 80 & 159/85 [1986] ECR 3359. It may be noted that the usual case law on minimum prices was not applicable in this case since the legislation applicable to imports and domestic bread respectively was not the same (para. 11 of ECJ judgt). Furthermore, it may also be noted that the ECJ also held that the restriction on imports was removed by the subsequent amendments introduced by a Regulation dated 7 Mar. 1985 and providing that the prohibition applicable to imported bread was no longer applicable to bread sold at a price equal to or higher than the minimum price applicable to Netherlands-produced bread. This finding by the ECJ, contrary to the submissions by the Commission in that case, has been questioned: see Akÿuerek-Kievits, SEW 1987, 516; Mortelmans, Tijdschift voor consumentenrecht 1987, 40 and Mok, SEW 1978, 157.

An equally unsatisfactory rejection on the facts of an 'actual or potential' effect on trade is to be found in the *SORECOP* v. *Techni* case before the French courts.[97] Techni had refused to pay a fee laid down by Section 31–44 of the Copyright (Amendment) Act 1985[98] on blank audio-tapes. Under the French law, a fee was charged on the sale in France of blank cassettes in order to compensate for the loss of revenue to holders of copyright in sound recordings when such recordings are copied on to blank cassettes. Techni argued that the French provisions were contrary to Article 30 because the amount of the fee was larger than that set in other Member States and thus that the French fee acted as a barrier to the free movement of goods. The Paris *Cour d'appel* held that 'it is not established that these rights may be considered to be quantitative restrictions on importation and that the difference in the level of fees in other States may *really and sufficiently* affect intra-Community trade'.[99]

It is not clear what the *Cour d'appel* considered to 'really and sufficiently' affect inter-State trade. Again, as in the decision of the *Rechtbank* in *Edah*,[100] the threshold of a 'real and sufficient' effect on trade seems to be higher than an 'actual or potential' effect. This is all the more serious as this issue was never properly addressed in subsequent judgments before the French courts in the same case. Thus, when the case went back before the *Tribunal de grande instance* of Paris, it was merely held that 'the plaintiffs have not proved that this system, or at least the rate applicable, affects trade in the Community'.[101] Before the *Cour de Cassation*, where one of the grounds of appeal was explicitly based upon the argument that the courts below had failed to evaluate statistics to determine whether the measure had the result of reducing the importation of blank tapes, the *Cour de Cassation* simply rejected this ground stating that the *Cour d'appel* below had found that it was not established that Community trade was affected.[102] In the absence of more explicit and elaborate reasoning in the judgments of French courts, it is impossible to assess whether the effect on inter-State

---

[97] *Société pour la rémuneration de la copie privée sonore (SORECOP) et Société pour la rémuneration de la copie privée audiovisuelle (Copie France)* v. *Techni import professionnel (TIP) SA, Cour d'appel* Paris, 1re ch. A, 12 Dec. 1988, RIDA 1989, no. 141 p. 266.

[98] Law of 3 July 1985 [1986] 2 CLE F87 (French text); [1987] 1 CLE 1 (English text).

[99] n. 97 above, emphasis added. In the original French: '*Il n'est nullement établi que ses droits soient assimables à des restrctions quantitatives à l'impotation et que la différence entre leur montant et le coût des mesures équivalentes adoptées dans les autres pays soit réelle et suffisante pour affecter les échanges intra-communautaires*'.

[100] n. 94 above.

[101] *TGI* Paris, 17 Jan. 1990, [1991] ECC 317; RIDA 1990, no. 144 p. 231. Noted by Kerever, RIDA 1990, no. 144 p. 143–4.

[102] *Cour de Cassation*, ch. comm., 4 Jan. 1994, Bull. Cass. Civ. 1994, IV no. 3 p. 3; Dalloz 1994, IR 54. It seems surprising that this case was not analysed in any of the French courts on the basis of Art. 95 EC prohibiting discriminatory internal taxation since it was a pecuniary 'fee' which the legislation in question introduced. It was, however, analysed on the basis of Art. 36 and the protection of industrial and commercial property; see discussion at pp. 330–1.

trade was sufficiently examined. On the face of the judgments themselves, the rejection of Article 30 because of the absence of 'real and sufficient' effect on trade, without specifying what this meant, does not seem to be in keeping with the rejection by the ECJ of a *de minimis* principle for Article 30 or the simple requirement set down in *Dassonville* that trade only has to be actually or potentially affected for Article 30 to bite.

The explicit rejection of a *de minimis* doctrine for Article 30 by the ECJ does occasionally put the national courts in an awkward position. This is most evident in those cases where the alleged potential effect on trade is very small indeed. In both the *Ex p. Wesson* and *Wendy Fair Markets* cases discussed above, the *de minimis* point was mentioned by the English High Court and, on the facts of those cases, the effect on trade could only be described as minuscule (the effect on trade caused by roadworks outside a shop and restricting the holding of a market in a small Welsh town respectively). In *Magnavision*, it was held that 'before Article 30 will bite there must be proved to exist some particular restrictive effect on imports'.[103] Similarly, in *Wychavon District Council* v. *Midland Enterprises (Special Event) Ltd*[104] the Chancery Division of the English High Court held that

The [ECJ] has also consistently held that legislative measures applicable to domestic products and imported products alike do not in themselves constitute measures having an effect equivalent to a quantitative restriction on imports, but that they may have such an effect if, in practice, they put imported products at a disadvantage compared to identical domestic products.[105]

Finally, in *R. v. Southwark Crown Court, ex. p. Watts*,[106] the English Divisional Court held that national regulations requiring a market licensee to put in a personal attendance at his stall does not constitute 'a clog on the free movement of goods'. All these cases suggest that, from the national courts' point of view, a finding of an 'actual or potential' effect on the volume of inter-State trade will not always be sufficient to found a breach of Article 30. They will also look for a 'restrictive effect', a 'disadvantage' or a 'clog': in other words, in certain circumstances, a *hindrance* will also be necessary.

Does the above discussion suggest that, from the national courts' perspective, the introduction by the ECJ of a *de minimis* principle for Article 30 would be desirable? The strongest argument against a *de minimis* test for Article 30 is that it would be difficult to apply in practice.[107] Oliver points out that identifying criteria for the application of *de minimis* would be a

---

[103] n. 34 above.   [104] [1988] 1 CMLR 397; [1988] RTDE 620; [1989] CDE 419.
[105] [1988] 1 CMLR 397 at 404.
[106] *The Independent*, 9 Jan. 1991; CO/1637/38 (transcr. available on Lexis).
[107] See, e.g., Adv. Gen. Tesauro in para. 21 of his Opinion in Case C–292/92 *Hünermund* v. *Landesapothekerkammer Baden-Württemburg* [1993] ECR I–6787.

difficult task: 'are they to be purely statistical, does the market have to be defined and, if so, how?'.[108] Gormley has concluded that 'a *de minimis* criterion in Article 30 is unworkable and the Court should continue to avoid it'.[109] However, for national courts saddled with the actual application of Article 30 in individual cases, the awkward position into which they are put by the absence of a *de minimis* principle for Article 30 should, it is submitted, be addressed by the ECJ. As was noted above, the ECJ has to be vigilant to avoid any adverse consequences for judicial co-operation upon which the entire Community judicial structure is based. While Advocate General Jacobs, in his conclusions to the ECJ in *Leclerc Siplec* v. *TF1 Publicité*[110] advocated a full blown *de minimis* test, it is submitted that it would be more instructive to refrain from using the *de minimis* terminology in the field of the free movement of goods.[111] As the national-court cases discussed above demonstrate, measures that cause no direct or substantial *hindrance* to access to the market of a Member State are difficult for national courts to assess. In practice, this has led them to either ignore the ECJ rejection of a *de minimis* principle, or apply such a test *de facto*. In this respect, it may be said that the national courts are, to a certain extent, already applying a *de minimis* test to Article 30. Arguably therefore, it is the ECJ that has got some catching up to do.[112]

(D) Proof of an actual or potential effect on trade

The finding of an 'actual or potential' effect on trade is a question of fact. As such, it is primarily a matter for the national court to assess on the facts of individual cases. It was noted above that one would expect that, from the national courts' perspective, this would constitute a relatively 'user-friendly' test.[113] In the majority of cases, this factual finding will indeed be clear. However, in an important minority of cases, the factual question of

---

[108] Oliver, n. 27 above, 109–10.   [109] 'Two years after *Keck*' at 882.

[110] Case C–412/93, n. 21 above.

[111] While *de minimis* is helpful in competition law, where it can be given precise shape by reference to turnover figures, the same cannot be applied in analyses of the four freedoms.

[112] It might be that the ECJ has already started this process. In a string of recent cases, the ECJ has dismissed Art. 30 arguments referred to it by national courts simply by holding that the restrictions imposed on the free movement of goods between Member States of the national legislation in question were 'too uncertain and indirect for the obligation which they impose to be regarded as being capable of hindering trade between Member States'. See Joined Cases C–140–142/94 *Dip sPa* v. *Comune di Bassano del Grappa* [1995] ECR I–3257, para. 29; Case C–134/94 *Esso Espagnola SA* v. *Comunidad Autonoma de Canarias* [1995] ECR I–4223, para. 24; Case C–96/94 *Centro Servizi Spediporto* v. *Spedizioni Marittima del Golfo* [1995] ECR I–2883, para. 41 & Case C–379/92 *Criminal proceedings against Matteo Peralta* [1994] ECR I–3453, para. 24. None of these cases has yet been referred to or relied upon in a national-court judgment covered by this work.

[113] n. 8 above.

whether intra-Community trade is affected comprises an extremely difficult factual assessment.

These difficult assessments of fact manifested themselves most clearly in the Sunday-trading episode in England and Wales, but also in cases concerning shop-opening hours in both France and the Netherlands.[114] In the first reported English Sunday trading case, *Wychavon District Council v. Midland Enterprises (Special Event) Ltd,*[115] the defendants were prosecuted for organizing a market on Sundays at Tilesford Park in Worcester contrary to the Shops Act 1950. With respect to the Article 30 defence, Millett J in the Chancery Division of the High Court held that there was no factual evidence of either a disadvantage to imported products or of any effect on inter-State trade. The defendants had argued that imports were disadvantaged by Schedule 5 to the Shops Act which, it was argued, favoured fresh produce over pre-packaged produce. One example advanced was that fresh milk could be sold on a Sunday whilst canned milk could not. On this argument, Millett J was able to find that, as a matter of fact, this was not shown since on the evidence adduced, there had been no fresh produce sold at the market but only 'fancy goods, jewellery, crockery, shoes, clothing and the like'. Furthermore, as a matter of fact, Millett J was unhappy with the correlation between fresh produce and domestic produce on the one hand, and pre-packaged produce and imported products on the other.[116] On the question of whether there was, on the facts, an actual or potential effect on trade, Millett J held

It is for the national court to investigate the facts and to decide whether the statute is capable of having any adverse effect on the volume of imported goods. Whatever the answer the European Court may give to the interpretation of Article 30, there is no evidence before me to hold that any of the provisions of the Shops Act have such an effect.[117]

Thus, the High Court concluded that the defence based on Article 30 should be dismissed. A similar finding of fact was made by the Paris *Cour d'appel* in *SA Virgin Megastores* v. *Fédération des Services CFDT,*[118] concerning the opening of a branch of the Virgin Megastore on the Champs Elysées in Paris on Sundays from midday to midnight contrary to L. 221–2–5 of the *Code du travail*. In this judgment, handed down after the ECJ's judgment in *Torfaen*, the *Cour d'appel* held that

---

[114] See detailed discussion of the national legislation on shop-opening hours in Ch. 6, sect. 4.

[115] n. 104 above.

[116] [1988] 1 CMLR 397 at 406. It may be noted with a certain amount of amusement that Millett J reached this conclusion based on the 'evidence of my own eyes' since, he remarked, 'despite a popular belief to the contrary, judges do go out and about in the world. They accompany their wives.' (at 406).

[117] Ibid. at 407.

[118] *Cour d'appel* Paris, 1re ch. A, 19 Dec. 1990, Gaz. Pal. 1991, I Jur. 249; Dalloz 1991, IR 76.

neither the peculiarities of the French audio-visual market, nor the extension of choice offered by Virgin Stores and the cultural dimension that they claim to be a part of their commercial activity, nor the surveys of their customers and the conclusions that they draw therefrom regarding the preferences of consumers provide proof that the closure of their shop on a Sunday specifically affects the sale of products imported from other countries of the Community.

The *Cour d'appel* appears to have confused issues relevant to the proportionality of the French legislation with the actual effect on trade itself. Most commentators are agreed that, while the judgment of the ECJ in *Torfaen* was far from clear, the ECJ may be taken to have held in that judgment that Article 30 was breached, but that the Sunday trading legislation could be justified under the rule of reason subject to the application of the proportionality principle by the national court.[119] It is true that the *Torfaen* judgment did not alter the possibility for a national court to find that, on the facts of an individual case, there is no effect on trade between Member States. The conclusions of Advocate General Delafaye to the *Cour d'appel* in *Virgin Megastores*,[120] make it clear that this is indeed what the *Cour d'appel* seems to have held. Delafaye concluded that the effect of the *Torfaen* judgment was to find that Sunday closing could have a restrictive effect on trade and that the *Cour d'appel* should confine itself to determining whether or not this effect was excessive. However, in applying this (correct) summary of the *Torfaen* judgment, Delafaye drew on findings of fact which, it is submitted, are irrelevant to questions of whether the restrictive effects were excessive or not. For example, Delafaye drew on issues of fact in pointing out that this branch of the Virgin Megastore could open until midnight from Monday to Saturday, when customers could make their purchases. Advocate General Delafaye concluded that there was thus no compartmentalization of the French market or protectionism caused by the French legislation. Delafaye also pointed out that Virgin Megastores had only a 6 per cent market share as compared with other retailers of audio-visual goods such as FNAC (25 per cent market share) and supermarkets in general (42 per cent market share). Relying on this, Delafaye concluded that by opening on a Sunday, Virgin Megastores would gain a competitive advantage over those retailers which did close on a Sunday as required by the law. It is submitted that these issues of fact are irrelevant in ascertaining whether the restrictive effects on trade exceed 'the effects intrinsic to trade rules'.[121] It seems therefore that the Paris *Cour d'appel*, which followed Delafaye's conclusions, hid behind the ambiguities in *Torfaen* (which, admittedly, were there for the taking) to

---

[119] See, e.g., Gormley (1990) 27 CMLRev 141. See further discussion of the justifications based on the rule of reason in Ch. 6.

[120] Gaz. Pal. 1991, I Jur. 250–2.

[121] Para. 15 of *Torfaen*, Case C–145/88, n. 15 above.

conclude that on the facts, there was no proof that 'the closure of their shop on a Sunday specifically affects the sale of products imported from other countries of the Community'. Just as the English High Court had done in the *Wychavon* case,[122] the Paris *Cour d'appel* thus held that the national legislation affecting shop opening hours did not, on the facts, have any 'actual or potential' effect on trade. While such a finding of fact by a national court is entirely within their competence, it may be questioned whether it was correct, post-*Torfaen*, to conclude that the market share of Virgin Megastores and the fact that it could open until midnight for the rest of the week, inevitably led to the conclusion that there was no effect on trade between Member States.

A finding of fact that there *was* an 'actual or potential' effect on trade was, by contrast, found by the *Tribunal de Police de Narbonne* in *Ministère public* v. *Duhoux*.[123] In this case, it was found, as a matter of fact, that half of the sales of the shop in question (Conforama) were achieved on a Sunday and that the goods sold were almost entirely imported from other Member States. This factual conclusion receives some support from Bandrac and Momège[124] who note that sales of furniture and electrical goods take place principally on Sundays. According to them, sales of something in the order of 30 per cent of furniture, 60 per cent of electrical goods, 35 per cent of colour televisions and 70 per cent of music recordings are imported from other Member States into France. They specifically cite the example of the Marseilles branch of the Virgin Megastore for which 50 per cent of its sales are imported from other Member States.[125] They conclude that the prohibition of Sunday opening thus produces a 'compartmentalization of undeniable vigour in certain sectors'.[126]

That the finding of fact that shop-opening hours legislation 'actually or potentially' affects intra-Community trade can be a difficult matter in individual cases, is demonstrated by the decision of Northampton Crown Court in *Wellingborough Borough Council* v. *Payless D.I.Y. Ltd* and *Kettering Borough Council* v. *W. H. Smith Do-It-All Ltd*.[127] In those cases, Allen J held that he was, on the facts, unable to find a reduction of imports. He considered evidence adduced by a ceramic tiles supplier to Texas Homecare do-it-yourself shop stating that if that shop was closed on a Sunday, he *might* have to 'reassess his stocks' from other Member States. Echoing the conclusions of Delafaye to the Paris *Cour d'appel* in *Virgin Megastores*[128] this was, according to Allen J, not enough to demonstrate, as a matter of fact, that imports were potentially hindered:

---

[122] n. 104 above.
[123] *Trib. police* Narbonne, 22 Jan. 1990, D094/2 4/5 May 1990; noted by Bandrac & Momège, Gaz. Pal. 1990, III Doct. p. 552–7 and Roubach, Gaz. Pal 1991, I Jur. 254.
[124] Bandrac & Momège, 'La Fermeture Dominicale et le Droit Communautaire'.
[125] Ibid. in footnote 25 of the article. [126] Ibid. at 555–6.
[127] [1990] 1 CMLR 773. [128] n. 120 above.

Concentrating on the affairs of one company gives no significant view of the effect or potential effect on imports of this measure. If someone wants ceramic tiles and cannot obtain them from Texas on Sunday he may not go to Texas on another day, but presumably he will go somewhere to buy his tiles possibly to a shop which complies with Section 47 [of the Shops Act 1950]. It would be wholly wrong for us to approach this matter on the basis of protecting other retail traders, but in considering whether closing a particular shop on a Sunday can affect imports one has to bear in mind the reality of the situation, namely that customers will, on the whole, go elsewhere and at other times for the same goods. One cannot jump from the fact that a particular business is losing trade to a conclusion that imports may be affected.[129]

These very interesting observations indicate how, from an economic point of view, an analysis of an effect on inter-State trade may be extremely delicate in practice. It will be recalled that Cwmbran Magistrates' Court,[130] in its questions referred to the ECJ in *Torfaen*, assumed as a matter of fact that there had been a reduction in the volume of imports from other Member States. References from other English courts made similar findings of fact. For example in *Charles Robertson (Developments) Ltd* v. *Caradon DC*[131] Bodmin Crown Court held that the shops prosecuted for opening on a Sunday in that case

sell a substantial quantity of goods on a Sunday—it being perhaps one of the busiest, if not the busiest, trading day of the week—and if they were not free to sell goods of that kind on a Sunday *it would necessarily reduce their import of goods* from other EEC countries. *We accept that as fact* and, indeed, it is not in dispute. If they sold less, as indeed they would if not able to trade on a Sunday, they would import fewer goods from EEC countries.[132]

The consequence of such factual assumptions was that the ECJ in *Torfaen* was 'forced' to accept that Article 30 was breached by the Sunday trading legislation. In cases subsequent to *Torfaen*, the majority of French and English national courts assumed Article 30 was breached and thus concentrated on the issue of justification.[133] It is submitted that the effect on

---

[129] n. 127 above at 777. It may be noted that Allen J, in an excellent judgment, went on in the alternative to consider whether the legislation was justified if it was nevertheless found that there was an effect on inter-State trade and thus a breach of Art. 30.

[130] Unreported judgt, 25 Apr. 1988.   [131] n. 16 above.

[132] Ibid. at 294, emphasis added. While this judgment referred questions to the ECJ pursuant to Art. 177 EC, the reference was never in fact received by the registry of the ECJ. The reference was in all likelihood withdrawn by the parties once it was clear that the reference in *Torfaen* was already pending. For other referals from English courts on this point which were also withdrawn pending *Torfaen*, see *Suffolk Coastal D.C.* v. *Notcutts Garden Centres*, referred by Woodbridge Magistrates' Court and withdrawn on 10 May 1990 (C–118/88); *Wakefield Metropolitan D.C.* v. *B & Q*, referred by Wakefield Magistrates' Court and withdrawn on 17 Jan. 1990 (C–166/88); *Torfaen B.C.* v. *Texas Homecare Ltd*, referred by Cwmbran Magistrates' Court and withdrawn on 21 Feb. 1990 (C–291/88); *Leonard Lindsay for Mansfield D.C.* v. *Payless DIY*, referred by Mansfield Magistrates' Court and withdrawn on 17 Jan. 1990

trade resulting from Member States' legislation affecting shop-opening hours was, as a matter of fact, ill-considered by the national courts referring questions to the ECJ and by the ECJ itself. Indeed, from an economic point of view, things were not so simple. Apart from the points raised by Delafaye in his conclusions to the Paris *Cour d'appel* in *Virgin Megastores*[134] and Allen J in *Wellingborough Borough Council* v. *Payless D.I.Y. Ltd*[135] discussed above, the United Kingdom, in its submissions to the ECJ in *Stoke-on-Trent City Council* v. *B & Q*[136] pointed out further difficulties with this analysis. It is clear from the Report for the Hearing in that case that the United Kingdom had questioned the utility of the factual estimates advanced by B & Q as to the effect upon imports which would take place in the absence of the UK legislation. For example, the UK pointed out that B & Q's calculations were drawn from a time when their shops were open on Sundays whilst many of their competitors were closed, thus distorting the true figures. Furthermore, it is not clear how to take into consideration the fact that extra money, which would be spent on additional Sunday purchases, would be available for spending on other imported goods. In sum, the factual difficulties in making reliable estimates as to potential effects on trade were much more subtle than both the ECJ in its Sunday trading judgments and the national courts which referred the questions to them, let on. It is perhaps a blessing that the ECJ in *Torfaen* was obliged to assume a reduction in imports and therefore a breach of Article 30. If it had not, and the breach of Article 30 depended on fine factual distinctions relying on economic evidence varying from shop to shop and from sector to sector, the relatively few divergent decisions on this point might have been far greater. This would have aggravated the difficulties of the

---

(C–134/88) and *Derry C.C.* v. *Hampden Homecare plc* referred by Londonderry Magistrates' Court and withdrawn on 17 Sept. 1991 (C–232/88).

[133] In English courts, see, e.g., *Shrewsbury and Atcham B.C.* v. *B & Q* [1990] 3 CMLR 535; *Stoke-on-Trent City Council* v. *B & Q, Norwich City Council* v. *B & Q* [1991] 4 All ER 221; [1990] 3 CMLR 31; [1991] 2 WLR 42 (per Hoffmann J); *Stoke-on-Trent City Council* v. *Toys 'R' Us Ltd*, (per Brown-Wilkinson VC) and *Payless* and *Do-It-All Ltd*, n. 18 above. In the French courts, see *Sté Boulanger Frères, Ikea e.a.* v. *Fédération nationale du négoce et de l'artisanat, Cour d'appel* Lyon, Ch. des Urgences, 12 Mar. 1990, noted by Bandrac & Momège, Gaz. Pal. 1990, III Doctr. p. 552–7; *Syncomen et Société Conforama* v. *Préfet du Rhône*, Trib. admin. Lyon, 1re ch., 4 Oct. 1990, Rev. jurisp. social 1991, 506 (summary); *Conseil d'Etat*, Section du Contentieux, 7 Dec. 1992, Rec. Lebon 1992, 692 (summary) and *Gérard Leib* v. *Ministère public, Cour d'appel* Montpellier, 3e ch. corr. 5 Nov. 1990, Gaz. Pal. 1991, I Jur. 253 (with note by Roubach). Rather strangely, the *Cour de Cassation*, ch. crim. held that the ECJ's decision in Case C–312/89 *Union départmentale des syndicats CGT de l'Aisne* v. *SIDEF Conforama* [1991] ECR I–997 that the French legislation was proportionate and justified meant that the ECJ decided there was no effect on inter-State trade which equally precluded the application of Art. 85: *The Republic* v. *Teil, Cour de Cassation*, ch. crim., 31 Mar. 1992, Bull. Cass. Crim. 1992, no. 133 p. 349; [1993] 1 CMLR 593. It is submitted that there is no basis for drawing such a comparison between the effect on inter-State trade required for Art. 30 and Art. 85 respectively.

[134] n. 120 above.   [135] n. 127 above.   [136] n. 32 above.

national courts, which were experiencing enough problems in applying the proportionality principle to justifications for the legislation.[137]

It seems therefore that proof of an actual or potential effect on trade can, in certain cases, involve difficult assessments of fact for the national court. The Sunday trading cases provide one such example of this difficulty. Irrespective of ECJ case law on the scope of Article 30, it is always open to a national court to find that, on the facts of an individual case, there is no effect on trade between Member States. The discussion above illustrates that the fact that the turnover of an individual retailer is reduced does not, on an economic analysis, necessarily lead to an adverse effect on imports. The influence of the market share of individual retailers in a particular sector on such findings of fact is equally unclear. Furthermore, to what extent should the national court take into account the percentage of the total turnover of a retailer made up of imported goods? Proof of an actual or potential effect on trade involves a complicated economic analysis by the national court. One should thus be careful to ensure that the seemingly straightforward factual test of whether intra-Community trade is 'actually or potentially' affected does not mask the factual difficulties encountered by the national courts in a minority of cases in practice.

(E) Incorrect applications of the ' "actual or potential" effect on trade' test

The story of national case law concerning that part of the *Dassonville* formula which refers to the 'actual or potential' effect on trade is not simply a story of difficulties encountered by the national courts. As has been pointed out above, in the vast majority of national court applications of Articles 30 to 36 EC, discerning an 'actual or potential' effect on trade has been a 'non-issue'.[138] There are however a handful of rather worrying misapplications of this part of the *Dassonville* formula by the national courts.

One such misapplication is contained in the judgment of the Queen's Bench Division of the English High Court in *R. v. Pharmaceutical Society of Great Britain and Secretary of State for Social Services, ex p. Association of Pharmaceutical Importers*.[139] That case concerned rules of a pharmacists' professional body in the United Kingdom which required pharmacists to supply the products specified in doctors' prescriptions so that where a doctor prescribed a product by its trade-mark ('brand') name, only the product bearing that name could be supplied by the pharmacist. The Association of Pharmaceutical Importers (API) contended that the rule infringed Article 30. The High Court rejected this argument holding that

---

[137] See discussion of this point in Ch. 6, sect. 4 (D) & (E).
[138] See text at n. 12 above.   [139] [1987] 2 CMLR 504.

whilst the effect of the measures sought to be challenged is no doubt to depress the level of intra-Community movement of parallel imports, it is in our judgment only designed to ensure that the customer gets what he specifies. Its adverse effect is in truth attributable not to any violation of Article 30 but rather to doctors failing to prescribe parallel imports.[140]

It is submitted that this is a clear misapplication of ECJ case law in that the acceptance by the High Court that there was a reduction in intra-Community trade should have been enough for it to have concluded that Article 30 was breached and for it to proceed to the question of possible justification. Fortunately, on appeal to the Court of Appeal, Kerr LJ stated 'with the greatest respect for the reasoning of the Divisional Court' that its view was 'quite untenable'[141] and referred the case to the ECJ which confirmed that it could not 'exclude the possibility that, in the particular circumstances of the case, the said rule is capable of hindering intra-Community trade'.[142]

While the misapplication in *Ex p. API* was corrected on appeal after a reference to the ECJ, such was not the case in a less fortunate decision of the Chancery Division of the High Court in *Extrude Hone Corporation's Patent*.[143] The latter case concerned the Patents Act 1977 under which a compulsory licence could be granted against a patentee's wishes if a patentee met the demand for his invention in the United Kingdom by importation from a third country (including an EC Member State). The effect of this legislation was, of course, to encourage the holder of a patent who wanted to maintain exclusivity, to locate production in the UK, thereby amounting to a clear preference of UK manufacture over manufacture in other Member States. The Superintending Examiner of Patents (Patents Office) granted a compulsory licence on the basis of this legislation and firmly rejected the Article 30 point raised by the patentee holding that 'I do not accept that the possibility that the licence would result in fewer machines being imported makes it a measure having the effect of a quantitative restriction'.[144]

Whitford J, sitting in the Chancery Division of the High Court, similarly dismissed the appeal stating that, 'The fact that imports are reduced does not mean that they are restricted. It cannot, on anything other than a gross misuse of language, be said to restrict imports'.[145]

It is submitted that both the above statements are clear misapplications of the clear definition of measures having equivalent effect as set out in the *Dassonville* formula that an 'actual or potential' effect on intra-Community trade is sufficient to found a breach of Article 30. In exactly the same way as by the Queen's Bench Division in *Ex p. API*, a reduction in imports was

---

[140] Ibid. at 513 (per May LJ).
[142] n. 65 above at para. 19.
[144] [1981] 3 CMLR 379 at 398.

[141] [1987] 3 CMLR 951 at 965.
[143] [1981] 3 CMLR 379. Noted (1982) ELRev. 241.
[145] Ibid. at 404.

accepted by the national court and yet a breach of Article 30 was denied. Unlike in *Ex p. API*, however, the decision of the Chancery Division in *Extrude Hone* was not corrected on appeal. That this case constitutes a serious misapplication of Article 30 is confirmed by a decision of the ECJ ten years later in infringement proceedings initiated by the Commission under Article 169 EC holding that this very provision of the Patents Act 1977 infringed Article 30.[146] The fact that the matter was incorrectly decided by the English courts in *Extrude Hone Corporation's Patent* without seeking an Article 177 reference from the ECJ must thus be seen as a missed opportunity in the 'dual vigilance' system of policing national legislation contrary to the EC Treaty.

3 APPLICATION OF POST-*KECK AND MITHOUARD* CASE LAW

(A) *Keck* and the scope of Article 30

It was in response to the background of confused case law (discussed above) that the ECJ, in the landmark decision of *Keck and Mithouard*,[147] overturned its previous case law 'in view of the increasing tendency of traders to invoke Article 30 of the Treaty as a means of challenging any rules whose effect is to limit their commercial freedom even where such rules are not aimed at products from other Member States'[148] and held that

[C]ontrary to what has previously been decided, the application to products from other Member States of national provisions restricting or prohibiting certain selling arrangements is not such as to hinder directly or indirectly, actually or potentially, trade between Member States within the meaning of the *Dassonville* judgment, provided that those provisions apply to all affected traders operating within the national territory and provided that they affect in the same manner, in law and in fact, the marketing of domestic products and of those from other Member States.[149]

The facts of the case concerned French legislation prohibiting resale at a loss. Keck and Mithouard were prosecuted under this legislation for selling in their respective supermarkets certain items at a loss. In their defence, they raised the defence that the French law was contrary to Article 30 since it had a potential negative effect on trade. Applying the new ruling (set out above) to the facts, the ECJ decided that a prohibition on resale at a loss was a selling arrangement which affected all traders operating within the national territory and therefore fell outside the scope of Article 30 altogether.

---

[146] Case C–30/90 *Commission* v. *United Kingdom* [1992] ECR I–829; [1992] 2 CMLR 709. Noted by Gormley (1993) 18 ELRev. 66.

[147] n. 3 above.   [148] Para. 14 of judgt.   [149] Para. 16 of judgt.

This somersault by the Court has, needless to say, caused a considerable stir and provoked much comment and criticism.[150] One author has called the judgment 'inexplicable', 'impudent', and the 'wrong answer to the right question'.[151] The principal grudge with this judgment is the paucity of the legal reasoning. For example, to explain, as the ECJ does in paragraph 14 of its judgment, that it has been led to modify its case law 'in view of the increasing tendency of traders to invoke Article 30' is remarkably audacious since, it was the poor and inconsistent case law of the ECJ itself which caused and even invited this 'increasing tendency'. Bold traders challenging national legislation as incompatible with EC law have always been the darlings of the ECJ. While the Court once praised 'the vigilance of individuals concerned to protect their rights'[152] it now censures them. More importantly, for a judgment which explicitly claims to be clarifying previous case law, it is surprising that one is left in the dark as to which cases the Court intended to overrule. What is to be understood as falling within this new category of 'selling arrangements' (*modalités de vente*)? Would a national rule like that in *Oosthoek*,[153] restricting the offer of free gifts with encyclopaedias now be within the category of selling arrangements, and therefore outside the ambit of Article 30? Most serious, however, is that the Court has now introduced a rule-based test which robs the previous approach of its dynamism. Under *Keck*, if a measure is within the category of selling arrangements, it falls outside the scope of Article 30. Under the pre-*Keck* case law, such measures would breach Article 30 but have to be justified. When deciding whether a measure is justified, the Court was able to unearth genuine disguised restrictions and to take into account the stage of integration of markets that had been reached. This is no longer possible with the formalistic rule-based *Keck* approach. Indeed, Weatherill has commented that the *Keck* judgment 'created the risk that, at national level or even in Luxembourg, the internal market baby might be thrown out with the bathwater of general regulation of commercial freedom'.[154]

From a practical perspective, however, the departure in *Keck* may receive a more positive evaluation. A rule-based approach is better for legal certainty. Moreover, the ECJ, in what was clearly a policy judgment,

---

[150] See Mattera, 'De l'arrêt *Dassonville* à l'arrêt *Keck*: l'obscure clarté d'une jurisprudence riche en principes novateurs et en contradictions'; Gormley, 'Reasoning Renounced? The Remarkable Judgment of *Keck and Mithouard*' and 'Two Years After *Keck*'; Weatherill, 'After *Keck*: Some Thoughts on How to Clarify the Clarification'; Reich, 'The "Nov. Revolution" of the European Court of Justice: *Keck*, *Meng* and *Audi* Revisited; Chalmers, 'Repackaging the Internal Market—The Ramifications of the *Keck* Judgment'; Ross, '*Keck*—Grasping the Wrong Nettle' (Wiley, 1996); Stuyck, (1994) CDE 435; Roth, (1994) 31 CMLRev. 845; Mortelmans, (1994) SEW 115 & 236.

[151] Mattera, n. 150 above.

[152] Case 26/62 *Van Gend en Loos* [1963] ECR 1, [1963] CMLR 105.

[153] Case 268/81, n. 30 above.   [154] 'After *Keck*', n. 150 above at 885.

may be commended for finally addressing the inconsistencies in its case law. An amazing volte-face it might be, but for a court not bound by precedent in the common-law sense, such amazement should be qualified.[155] The new departure may also be seen as a reflection of the maturity of the common market. In the 1980s the broad *Dassonville* emphasis was born of the desire to use the provisions on free movement of goods as an active tool to integrate and merge markets into regulatory uniformity. The state of integration of markets has now reached the stage where the role of Article 30 may arguably be limited to securing and maintaining access to markets for goods, thereby realizing the economies of scale possible in an internal market. Finally, the *Keck* approach, by leaving to national law the arrangements as to the time, place, and manner in which goods may by marketed, is consistent with the move towards subsidiarity in the Community.[156]

The impact and importance of the *Keck* judgment should not be overstated. This view has been borne out by subsequent case law. In a pragmatic if somewhat mechanical way, the ECJ has applied the *Keck* ruling on a case-by-case basis. Thus, it has decided that Article 30 does not apply to a rule of professional conduct which prohibits pharmacists from advertising outside their pharmacy para-pharmaceutical products which they are authorized to sell;[157] that it does not apply to national legislation on the closure of shops;[158] that it does not apply to national legislation prohibiting the broadcasting on television of advertisements for the distribution sector;[159] that it does not apply to national legislation requiring processed milk for infants to be sold only through pharmacists' shops;[160] that it does not apply to national legislation which prohibits sale with an extremely small profit margin,[161] and finally, that Article 30 does not apply to

---

[155] For an even more spectacular reversal, see the overruling of Case 192/73 *Van Zuylen* v. *Hag* (Hag I) [1974] ECR 731 in Case C–10/89 *CNL-Sucal* v. *Hag* (Hag II) [1990] ECR I–3711.

[156] The application of the principle of subsidiarity, as enshrined in Art. 3b EC, to the free-movement-of-goods field is unclear. What is meant here is that the *Keck* development is consistent with the political move (the so-called 'Spirit of Edinburgh' after the Edinburgh European Council in Dec. 1992, see Bull. EC 12-1992) towards letting objectives be undertaken by the Member States unless they can be better achieved at Community level. It may also be noted that Chapter 9 of the Treaty of Amsterdam adds a protocol to the EC Treaty on the application of the principles of subsidiarity and proportionality.

[157] Case C–292/92, n. 107 above.

[158] Cases C–69 and 258/93 *Punto Casa SpA* v. *Sindaco del Comune di Capena* [1994] ECR I–2355; Cases C–401 & 402/92 *Tankstation 't Heukske and J. B. E. Boermans* v. *Openbaar Ministere* [1994] ECR I–2199 & Joined Cases C–418–421/93, C–460–462/93, C–464/93, C–9–11/94, C–14–15/94, C–23–24/94 & C–332/94 *Semeraro Casa Uno Srl* [1996] ECR I–2975.

[159] Case C–412/93, n. 21 above. See also Joined Cases C–34–36/95 *Konsument-ombudsmannen* v. *De Agostini (Svenska) Förlag AB* [1997] ECR I–3843 at paras. 39–47.

[160] Case C–391/92 *Commission* v. *Greece* [1995] ECR I–1621.

[161] Case C–63/94 *Groupement national des négotiants en pommes de terre de Belgique* v. *ITM Belgium SA and Vocarex SA* [1995] ECR I–2467.

national legislation which reserves the retail sale of manufactured tobacco products to authorized distributors.[162] In each of these cases, the Court has reaffirmed the *Dassonville* formula but stated that national provisions restricting or prohibiting certain selling arrangements no longer fall under the *Dassonville* formula so long as they apply to and affect all traders in that national territory. In subsequent cases, therefore, the ECJ has shown itself willing to apply the *Keck* ruling on a pragmatic case-by-case basis.[163]

That the impact and importance of the *Keck* judgment should not be overstated is also demonstrated by an analysis of the measures that have been found, in cases subsequent to *Keck*, to remain *within* the scope of Article 30. A close analysis demonstrates that the *Dassonville* formula stands proud as good law in the majority of cases concerning national laws regulating the composition and presentation of products. In *Verband Sozialer Wettbewerb* v. *Clinique*,[164] the application of German legislation precluding the marketing of a cosmetic product under the name 'Clinique' in Germany, in spite of the fact that the same product was freely marketed under that name in other Member States, was at issue. In its judgment, the Court reiterated its previous case law under which national rules setting down requirements as to designation, form, size, weight, composition, presentation, labelling, and packaging, even if applied without distinction to all products, fell within the ambit of Article 30. Such case law, the ECJ held, was unaffected by the ruling in *Keck*. On the facts of the case, the Court found that intra-Community trade was indeed impeded because 'the undertaking in question is obliged in that Member State alone to market its products under a different name and to bear additional packaging and advertising costs'.[165] Similarly, in *Commission* v. *Germany* (Re Expiry Dates),[166] it was held that the national legislation which restricts to two a year (30 June and 31 December) the expiry dates which may be shown on

---

[162] Case C–387/93 *Criminal proceedings against Giorgio Domingo Banchero* [1995] ECR I–4663.

[163] It is also possible to discern a trend in post-*Keck* ECJ case law concerning the other Treaty freedoms in which the ECJ has adopted a less 'formalistic' approach to setting the limits to the basic freedoms. With respect to the freedom to provide services (Art. 59 EC), see Case C–384/93 *Alpine Investments* v. *Minister van Financiën* [1995] ECR I–1141 at paras. 33–38 and with respect to the free movement of workers (Art. 48 EC), see Case C–415/93 *Union Royale Belge des des Sociétés de Football Association ASBL* [1995] ECR I–4921 at para. 103 f. See also Weatherill, n. 150 above. However, the ECJ has yet to transfer that less formalistic approach to the free movement of goods and has refused to do so in Joined Cases C–418–421/93, C–460–462/93, C–464/93, C–9–11/94, C–14–15/94, C–23–24/94 & C–332/94 *Semeraro Casa Uno Srl* [1996] ECR I–2975. However, in Joined Cases C–34–36/95, n. 159 above at paras. 39–47, the ECJ adopted a less formalistic approach to the application of the second proviso in *Keck* in that it recognized the possibility that a ban on television advertising aimed at children less than 12 years old might not 'affect in the same way, in fact and in law, the marketing of national products and of products from other Member States'. The ECJ left the latter assessment to the national court.

[164] Case C–315/92 [1994] ECR I–317.

[165] Para. 19 of judgt.

[166] Case C–317/92 [1994] ECR I–2039.

the packaging of medical products is a measure relating to the conditions to be satisfied by products and is likely therefore to affect intra-Community trade in so far as it may reduce the period of marketing of imported products, and involve additional costs in altering packaging.[167] Finally, in *Mars GmbH*,[168] national legislation which would require re-packaging and additional advertising costs for products lawfully marketed in other Member States was equally held to be incompatible with Article 30.[169] The conclusion must therefore undoubtedly be that the practical application of *Keck* is limited. Subsequent case law of the Court has shown that, although it will steadfastly stand by its departure in *Keck*, national laws regulating the composition and presentation of goods, or prescribing technical standards will still need to be tested against the *Dassonville* formula.

(B) Application of *Keck* before the national courts

The most explicit application by a national court of the *Keck* case law was carried out by the French *Conseil d'Etat* in *Société Tour Pol*.[170] The latter case concerned Article L. 552 of the *Code de la santé publique*, under which any form of advertising of products which claimed to have effects on health or physical effects could be prohibited by the Minister of Health if it could not successfully be established that the products in question actually did possess those claimed properties. The provision also required the Minister of Health to take advice from an independent commission after having heard the submissions of the manufacturer, importer or distributor of the products. By an *arrête* of 9 April 1987 the Minister of Health made such a prohibition under the French legislation for the advertising by Société Tour Pol of three products.[171] On the points of French law, the *Conseil d'Etat* held that there were no procedural irregularities and that Tour Pol had correctly been given the opportunity to present its observations but had failed to produce scientific evidence supporting the mental and physical effects claimed in the advertisements. The Minister had not therefore committed '*une erreur manifeste d'appreciation*'. With respect to the argu-

---

[167] Para. 12 of judgt. See also Case C–320/93 *Lucien Ortscheit* v. *Eurin-Pharm* [1994] ECR I–5243.

[168] Case C–470/93 *Verein gegen Unwesen in Handel und Gewerbe Koeln* v. *Mars GmbH* [1995] ECR I–1923.

[169] See also to similar effect, Case C–368/95 *Vereinigte Familiapress Zeitungsverlags- und vertriebs* v. *Heinrich Bauer Verlag* [1997] ECR I-3689.

[170] *Conseil d'Etat*, 7 July 1995, Rec. Lebon 1995, 287.

[171] The products involved were 'Body-Choc' and 'Zero–3', the advertising of which claimed that these products could promote a loss of weight of 26kg. in 3 months and 'Pak-Heat', the advertising of which claimed that this product could cure a variety of medical complaints in 10–15 hrs.

ment that the French legislation (and the *arrête* based upon it) were contrary to Article 30 EC, the *Conseil d'Etat* held that

Article L. 552 . . . applies in the same way irrespective of whether the objects, devices, or methods in question were of national origin or imported; thus, decisions taken on the basis of this Article do not form an obstacle to the sale of the products in question and they are not susceptible to being a barrier to trade between Member States of the European Community and to constitute a measure having equivalent effect to a quantitative restriction on importation prohibited by Article 30 of the EC Treaty according to the interpretation of that Article by the Court of Justice of the European Communities in its judgment of 24 November 1993 in C–267 and 268/91 [*Keck and Mithouard*]; and thus the argument that Article 30 of the Treaty is breached must be rejected.

This is a characteristically brief judgment by the *Conseil d'Etat* rejecting the application of Article 30 on the basis of the *Keck* reasoning. Indeed, the *Conseil d'Etat's* reasoning may be criticized for being far too brief. For example, there is no mention in the judgment of 'selling arrangements', nor any explanation as to why the French legislation in this case fell within that category. In the absence of clear reasoning, it may be assumed that the *Conseil d'Etat* fully accepted the submissions of its *Commissaire du gouvernement*. In his conclusions to the *Conseil d'Etat*, *Commissaire du gouvernement* Abraham described the situation with respect to EC law as 'delicate' but stated that:[172]

This ground of appeal must certainly be rejected, but the question is according to what reasoning. That which you will adopt will not be the same as that which you would have had to hold if you had decided this appeal before 24 November 1993, the date of the important judgment of the Court of Justice of the European Communities in *Keck and Mithouard* (C–267 & 268/91).[173]

Commissaire du gouvernement Abraham concluded that if the case were to be decided according to ECJ case law prior to *Keck*, the French legislation would have to be considered to be a measure having equivalent effect to a quantitative restriction under Article 30 since the ECJ's reasoning, as it then was, led to the conclusion that

[P]rohibiting a selling arrangement or restricting advertising necessarily reduces the possibilities of marketing imported products, thus, even if the reduction also applies to national products, this constitutes a reduction, even if it be only potential, in the volume of intra-Community trade.[174]

After having noted that the ECJ had held in paragraph 14 of its judgment in *Keck* that 'in view of the increasing tendency of traders to invoke Article

---

[172] The conclusions of *Commissaire du Gouvernement* Abraham to the *Conseil d'Etat* in this case were not reported; a transcript of the conclusions is however available from the Publications Office of the *Conseil d'Etat*.

[173] Transcr., p. 4.   [174] Ibid.

30' it was convinced that it had to reconsider its case law, Abraham outlined the new approach in *Keck and Mithouard*. The learned *Commissaire du gouvernement* then briefly discussed the ECJ's judgments in *Hünermund*,[175] *Leclerc Siplec*[176] and *Lucien Ortscheit*[177] and concluded that following *Keck*, the French legislation did not constitute a measure having equivalent effect contrary to Article 30, and that it was thus not necessary to consider whether the legislation was justified on grounds of consumer protection or public health 'which would probably have justified the restrictions on advertising that would result'.

It is submitted that even though the conclusions of the *Commissaire du gouvernement* were more elaborate than the reasoning of the *Conseil d'Etat*, they nevertheless fall short of full and satisfactory reasoning. Again, we see no discussion of why the said provisions constitute 'selling arrangements'. The fact that the ECJ had dealt with similar legislation concerning advertising in *Leclerc Siplec* was not addressed in any detail by Abraham. Nevertheless, the conclusion that the French legislation falls under the *Keck* jurisprudence seems unassailable given the ECJ's application of that jurisprudence in subsequent cases. National legislation concerning advertising seems clearly to fall within the definition of 'selling arrangements' following the conclusion of the ECJ in *Hünermund* that a prohibition on pharmacists from advertising outside their pharmacy falls outside Article 30 subject to the two provisos set out in *Keck*. Furthermore, the conclusion of the ECJ in *Leclerc Siplec*,[178] that French legislation prohibiting the broadcasting of advertisements for the distribution sector by television broadcasters was a selling arrangement 'since it prohibits a particular form of promotion (televised advertising) of a particular method of marketing products (distribution)'[179] would seem equally to apply here irrespective of the warnings advanced by Advocate General Jacobs to the ECJ in his conclusions in that case as to the considerable importance of advertising as a means for traders to penetrate new markets.[180] It seems, therefore, that the judgment of the *Conseil d'Etat* in *Tour Pol* was a perfectly defensible, if brief, application of the *Keck and Mithouard* jurisprudence.

More recently, the *Cour d'appel* of Versailles has again applied the *Keck and Mithouard* case law in a case concerning similar facts. In *Sogramo Carrefour* v. *Chambre syndicale des pharmaciens et Union profesionalle de la pharmacie*,[181] French legislation[182] which granted pharmacists the exclusive right to sell medical products was at issue. Sogramo Carrefour was

---

[175] Case C–292/92, n. 107 above.
[176] Case C–412/93, n. 21 above.
[177] Case C–320/93, n. 167 above.
[178] Case C–412/93, n. 21 above.
[179] Ibid., para. 22 of judgt.
[180] Case C–412/93, n. 21 above.
[181] *Cour d'appel* Versailles, 22 Jan. 1996, Gaz. Pal. 1996, II Som. pp. 32–3 (summary); La Semaine Juridique, éd. entreprise, 1996 PAN. 175 (summary); Les petites affiches, 1996, no. 34 p. 4–7 (transcr. available on Lexis).
[182] *Code de santé publique* Art. L. 512.

convicted under this legislation for selling products containing Vitamin C products in the absence of a qualified pharmacist. The *Cour d'appel* of Versailles recalled that the ECJ had previously held that this very French legislation was capable of breaching Article 30 but could be justified for the protection of public health under Article 36 subject to an application of the proportionality test.[183] However, the *Cour d'appel* referred to the ECJ's judgments in *Keck and Mithouard* and *Commission* v. *Greece* (Re Processed Millk for Infants)[184] and set out the ECJ's ruling in those cases to conclude that it was no longer necessary to examine whether the monopoly given to pharmacists for the sale of Vitamin C in France was proportionate and justified for the protection of health in Article 36, since the French legislation fell within the category of 'selling arrangements', applied in the same way to imports as to domestic products and was therefore outside the scope of Article 30 altogether.[185] Again, as in the *Conseil d'Etat*'s judgment in *Tour Pol*, the judgment of the *Cour d'appel* of Versailles in this case constituted a perfectly defensible application of the *Keck and Mithouard* jurisprudence.

A much less defensible application of the *Keck* jurisprudence was carried out by the English Courts in *R.* v. *Luton Borough Council, ex p. Mirza*. That case concerned local taxi regulations.[186] It will be recalled that Section 47(1) of the Local Government (Miscellaneous Provisions) Act 1976 provided that 'a District Council may attach to the grant of a licence of a hackney carriage under the Act of 1847 such conditions as the District Council may consider reasonably necessary'. Mirza initiated judicial review proceedings of the refusal by Luton Borough Council to grant him a licence as, according to Luton's policy, taxis had to be of the same type and design as hackney carriages licensed to apply for hire in London or a saloon car which could carry at least one wheelchair-bound disabled person. One of the arguments raised by Counsel for Mirza was that these regulations infringed Article 30. In the Queen's Bench Division of the High Court, Brooke J cited the English authorities of *R.* v. *Metropolitan Borough Council*

---

[183] Case C–369/88, n. 31 above & Case C–60/89 *Ministère public* v. *Jean Monteil et Daniel Samanni* [1991] ECR I–1547. See further discussion of the breach of Art. 30 at p. 57 and the application of the public-health justification by the French courts at pp. 263–5.

[184] Case C–391/92, n. 160 above.

[185] This judgment of the *Cour d'appel* of Versailles may be contrasted with judgments of the Criminal Division of the *Cour de Cassation* in *Rxxxx*, *Cour de Cassation*, ch. crim., 24 Jan. 1996, Arrêt no. 506 (transcr. available on Lexis) & *Levionnais*, *Cour de Cassation*, ch. crim., 9 July 1996, Bull. Cass. Crim. 1996, 288 where, with respect to the same French legislation, the *Cour de Cassation* upheld judgments of *Cours d'appel* applying the proportionality test to the public-health justification set out by the ECJ in Case C–369/88, n. 31 above & Case C–60/89, n. 183 above, for disinfectant solutions while making no reference to the *Keck and Mithouard* ruling. See also, *Brugdorf et Continent*, *Cour de Cassation*, ch. crim., 30 Oct. 1996, Arrêt no. 4708 (transcr. available on Lexis); Dalloz, 1997, IR 47 (summary); JCP 1997 IV, 66 (summary).

[186] See discussion of *Hodgkinson* v. *Nottingham City Council*, n. 92 above & discussion of the UK taxi cases at pp. 73–6.

of Wirral, ex p. The Wirral Licensed Taxi Owners Association,[187] *R.* v. *Doncaster Metropolitan Borough Council, ex p. Kelly*[188] and *R.* v. *Birmingham City Council, ex p. Wesson*[189] and proceeded to summarize fully the approach of the ECJ in *Keck and Mithouard* as repeated in *Tankstation 't Heukske* v. *Boermans.*[190] These authorities led Brooke J to conclude that he was 'completely satisfied that the present jurisprudence of the Court makes it quite clear that a provision, such as that laid down by Luton Borough Council, does not offend Article 30'.[191] What is, with respect, so unsatisfactory with this judgment is that the High Court drew explicitly on the *Keck* case law to reach this conclusion.

On appeal to the Court of Appeal, the judgment of the High Court that Article 30 was not breached was upheld.[192] Again, the *Keck* case law was used to reach this conclusion. After quoting the relevant paragraph from *Keck*, Leggatt LJ held that

The policies of the two Councils with which this Court is concerned are not intended to regulate, and do not regulate, trade in goods within the Community. The policies apply to all traders in the United Kingdom; they affect the marketing of domestic products in the same way as those from other Member States; there is no restriction on importation; and manufacturers in the United Kingdom and in other EEC countries have to fulfil the same conditions in order to produce a vehicle which fulfils the Council's requirements.

This judgment confirms all the worst fears expressed by commentators concerning the *Keck* judgment. It is, with the greatest respect, submitted that the national regulations at issue in this case could not, and should not, have been considered to be 'selling arrangements' within the *Keck* case law. Regulations setting down type and design requirements for licensed taxis are 'product requirements' *par excellence*. Commentators are, without exception, agreed that the ECJ in *Keck* made a clear distinction between 'rules that lay down requirements to be met by goods' in paragraph 15 of that judgment and 'selling arrangements' in paragraph 16: the former are still within the scope of the Article 30 prohibition while the latter are not.[193] The question of whether local taxi regulations in the United Kingdom breached Article 30 is discussed elsewhere in this work.[194] What is of interest in the context of the discussion in this section is the fact that the *Ex p. Mirza* judgments of the English High Court and Court of Appeal dismissed the Article 30 argument, relying unjustifiably on the *Keck* case law. It was always the danger inherent in the *Keck* departure that the national courts would abuse that judgment to reject arguments based on

---

[187] [1983] 3 CMLR 150.   [188] Not reported.   [189] n. 22 above.
[190] Cases C–401 & 402/92, n. 158 above.
[191] Unreported judgt of 4 Nov. 1994 (transcr. available on Lexis).
[192] Unreported judgt of 2 Feb. 1995 (transcr. available on Lexis).
[193] See e.g. Oliver, n. 27 above, 101.   [194] See pp. 73–6.

Article 30. That this is a serious concern is demonstrated by this case as it is by no means certain that, if the measure fell within Article 30, it would be justified under either the rule of reason or the grounds set out in Article 36 EC.[195] This judgment thus serves to illustrate the manifest dangers of the *Keck* approach before the national courts.

The *Keck* case law can only be approved of if it is satisfactorily applied by the national courts. In order for them to do so, it is essential that the national courts give full reasons for their applications of *Keck*. In particular, it is submitted that it is desirable that the national court should explain why the national regulation in question may be considered to be a 'selling arrangement' and furthermore, it should rigorously apply the two provisos set down by the ECJ, namely that the national provisions 'apply to all affected traders operating within the national territory' and 'that they affect in the same manner, in law and in fact, the marketing of domestic products and of those from other Member States'.[196] It is submitted that the latter proviso deserves particularly sharp application in individual cases as its application could arguably mitigate the adverse effects of the *Keck* approach.[197] In cases, for example, where an importer argues that the fact that he is deprived of a selling method available in his own country has the result that he is not, *in fact*, affected to the same extent by the measure as the domestic producer, a rigorous application of this second proviso may mean that the measures that were at issue in *Buet*[198] and *GB-INNO* v. *CCL*[199] may still be caught by Article 30.

Regrettably, the first signs are that the national courts will refrain from applying the two provisos rigorously. For example, the judgment of the ECJ in *Tankstation 't Heukske* v. *Boermans*[200] was implemented by the *Hof*'s-Hertogenbosch in an extremely brief fashion. It will be recalled that, in that case, the ECJ applied its *Keck* case law to the Dutch *Winkelsluitingswet* (Shop Hours Act) and held that the opening by the defendant of a shop attached to a petrol station in breach of those provisions could not, after *Keck*, be challenged under Article 30. In the implementing judgment, the *Hof*'s-Hertogenbosch did not even refer to the ECJ judgment nor even to

---

[195] See esp. Gormley (1983) 8 ELRev 141 who argues that the national regulations constituted arbitrary discrimination and were thus not capable of justification. See also Gormley, n. 109 above at 883, where he likens the spreading of local authority conditions of fitness for taxis to an 'infection'.

[196] Cases C–267 & 268/91, *Keck*, n. 3 above, para. 16.

[197] There are, however, signs in the ECJ's judgment in Joined Cases C–418–421/93, C–460–462/93, C–464/93, C–9–11/94, C–14–15/94, C–23–24/94 & C–332/94, n. 163 above that the 2 provisos set out in *Keck* will not be rigorously applied. See paras. 18–24 of that judgt. However, more recently in Joined Cases C–34–36/95, n. 159 above at paras. 39–47, the ECJ adopted a more rigorous approach to the application of the second proviso in *Keck*; see discussion in n. 163 above.

[198] Case 382/87, n. 31 above.

[199] Case 362/88, n. 31 above.   [200] Cases C–401 & 402/92, n. 158 above.

EC law and simply upheld the conviction of the defendant.[201] While admittedly the ECJ had clearly stated in its judgment in *'t Heukske* that 'Article 30 of the Treaty is to be interpreted as not applying to national rules concerning the closing of shops', it did go on to add 'which apply to all traders operating within the national territory and which affect in the same manner, in law and in fact, the marketing of domestic products and of products from other Member States'.[202] It is not here contended that the prohibition of selling certain articles at a shop attached to a petrol station does not, in fact, affect to the same extent the marketing of domestic products and of products from other Member States. Nevertheless, the fact that the Dutch national court in applying the judgment did not even mention EC law, let alone apply the provisos, is not an encouraging indication for a thorough application of the provisos contained in the *Keck* case law by the national courts.

The final national case in which the *Keck* case law arose was a decision of the English Court of Appeal in *Stedman* v. *Hogg Robinson Travel*.[203] Stedman was an assistant manager at a branch of Hogg Robinson Travel Agents which was situated inside a branch of the supermarket ASDA which opened on a Sunday. Stedman refused to work on a Sunday and was duly dismissed. Under United Kingdom law, she had no right to unfair dismissal protection because she had not been working for two years as required by the Employment Protection (Consolidation) Act 1978. Stedman attempted to challenge the dismissal on the basis of a far-fetched EC law argument. It was argued that Sunday-trading legislation was within the scope of EC law as is demonstrated by the ECJ's Article 30 case law, and that once within the scope of EC law, fundamental rights and the European Convention on Human Rights, which form an integral part of EC law, require that an individual cannot be forced to work on a Sunday. Not surprisingly, the Court of Appeal rejected this argument as 'quite unarguable'.[204] In so doing, the Court of Appeal cited the ECJ's judgment in *Punto Casa SpA* v. *Sindaco del Comune di Capena*[205] in which the ECJ had held (on the same day as its judgment in *Tankstation 't Heukske*[206]) that national Sunday-trading legislation fell completely outside the scope of Article 30 following *Keck*. Hoffmann LJ held that

The European Court has told us that Article 30 does not apply and there is no other basis that I can see upon which Sunday trading could come within the scope of European law at all. It also seems to me extraordinary to rely upon an Article of the

---

[201] *Hof* 's-Hertogenbosch, 3 Jan. 1995, transcr.
[202] Cases C–401 & 402/92, n. 158 above, para. 15 of judgt.
[203] Unreported judgt of 27 Oct. 1994 (transcr.available on Lexis).
[204] Unreported judgt of 27 Oct. 1994 (transcr. available on Lexis).
[205] Cases C–69/93 and C–258/93, n. 158 above.
[206] Cases C–401 & 402/92, n. 158 above.

Treaty, namely Article 30, which, if it has any effect at all, is directed to striking down the restriction on Sunday trading, in order to create a European right which requires that there should be restrictions on Sunday trading.

What is interesting in this judgment is the assumption that the consequence of a finding that a measure falls outside the scope of Article 30 according to the *Keck* case law, is that Sunday trading is excluded from the scope of Community law altogether. This raises the important issue of whether a narrowing of Article 30 inevitably brings with it a narrowing of Community competences. The Court of Appeal's reasoning suggests that it took the view that this was indeed the case. This view, if pushed to its logical conclusion, would mean that if the scope of Article 30 is narrowed, then so too is that of Article 100a EC and thus the competence of the Community to legislate for the establishment and functioning of the internal market. Thus, although the *Keck* case law only arose indirectly in this case, and the Court of Appeal was entirely correct to reject what was an extremely far-fetched argument, there are some interesting currents underlying the decision. If the Court of Appeal is right, and if it is therefore the case that the narrowing of Article 30 by the ECJ in *Keck* brings with it a narrowing of the competences of the Community, then the consequences of the *Keck* judgment may be more far-reaching than was at first perceived.[207]

4 CONCLUSIONS

Until recently, the ECJ had always advocated an extremely broad scope for Article 30 EC. The striking breadth of the *Dassonville* formula has undoubtedly made a vital contribution to the elimination of barriers to trade and consequently to achieving a truly integrated single market. The strength of the *Dassonville* approach is that it lays down a straightforward test for the national courts to apply: any national rule that can be linked, even potentially, to an effect on trade is caught by Article 30 and subject to justification.

The experience of national courts in applying this approach, however, gives rise to cautionary warnings. The discussion of national case law in this section clearly illustrates that the national courts have the expectation that Article 30 should have some limit of common sense. An unduly wide interpretation of Article 30 does not always conform to those expectations in the practical 'day-to-day' application of Article 30. This is important for

---

[207] See discussion by Steyger, 'Nogmals het *Keck*-arrest: De nieuwe onduidelijkheid in de toepassing van artikel 30 EG-verdrag' & Mortelmans, 'De interne markt en het facettenbeleid na het *Keck*-arrest: national beleid, vrij verkeer of harmonisatie'.

two reasons. Firstly, the healthy development of EC law relies heavily on the co-operation of the national courts and thus the views of these courts should not be cast aside without careful consideration. Secondly, in view of the work load of the ECJ, it is desirable that the national courts be equipped with the 'tools' to weed out those cases where the integrationist merit is negligible.

The requisite 'tool' to satisfy the two latter points is a clear body of case law on the scope of Article 30 for the national courts to apply. Before the *Keck* judgment, such 'tools' were indeed missing. National case law demonstrates that the practical effect of the inconsistent ECJ case law was to tie the hands of the national courts. This led to the damaging position in which legal certainty was reduced to nil and to the intolerably difficult position in which reliance on one line of ECJ authority did not allow the national courts to satisfactorily distinguish the authorities pointing in the opposite direction.

A further difficulty arose from the fact that even a *potential* effect on the volume of imports was enough for Article 30 to bite. In the absence of a *de minimis* principle for Article 30, this led to concern in the national courts in cases where no hindrance to inter-State trade could be discerned. Some national courts have solved this problem by effectively ignoring the ECJ's rejection of a *de minimis* test. Others have done so implicitly by requiring a 'restrictive effect', a 'disadvantage' or a 'clog' on the free movement of goods before they will find a breach of Article 30. The time thus seems ripe for the ECJ to reconsider its position in light of the fact that the national courts are *de facto* applying a *de minimis* test by requiring a hindrance before Article 30 will be held to apply.

The *Keck and Mithouard* judgment does, of course, represent an important reconsideration by the ECJ of its case law. Irrespective of one's views on that judgment, it must be conceded that the experience of national courts applying *Keck* to date does not inspire confidence. It has been seen how in *Ex p. Mirza*,[208] the *Keck* approach was abused to reach the result that Article 30 did not apply to technical requirements for taxis. In other national court judgments applying *Keck*, the application has been brief with little or no discussion of whether and why the measures in question were 'selling arrangements'. Furthermore, the two provisos set down in *Keck* have also not been applied as rigorously as is desirable.

The application by the *Conseil d'Etat* of the *Keck* judgment in *Société Tour Pol*[209] merits further comment. It will be recalled that that case concerned a challenge to an *arrête* restricting the advertising of certain products, the properties of which could not be substantiated by scientific evidence.[210] It was noted that the judgment of the *Conseil d'Etat* contained a perfectly

---

[208] nn. 191 & 192 above.   [209] n. 170 above.   [210] n. 171 above.

defensible, if brief, application of the *Keck and Mithouard* jurisprudence.[211] What is interesting, however, is that *Commissaire du gouvernement* Abraham in his conclusions also found that the *Keck* case law applied, but added that even if the measure fell within Article 30 it would 'probably' have been justified on grounds of consumer protection or public health. Herein lies the rub. The dynamism of the pre-*Keck* approach meant that such measures would breach Article 30 but have to be justified. When the national court proceeded to decide whether a measure was justified, the possibility to unearth genuine disguised restrictions on a case-by-case basis was left open. Under *Keck*, all such measures fall outside the scope of Article 30 altogether. On the facts of *Tour Pol*, it seems that the prohibition of the advertising of the products in question[212] would indeed be justified for consumer protection reasons under the rule of reason. The point is that the *Keck* case law robs the previous approach of its dynamism. If an *arrête* was issued on the basis of the French legislation prohibiting the advertising of a product for which the risks to health or to consumer protection were so small that a prohibition was disproportionate, the national court would be able to scrutinize the measure and, if the restriction led to arbitrary discrimination in an individual case, the *arrête* could be set aside.[213] After *Keck* on the other hand, any such analysis is precluded since such a measure would fall entirely outside the scope of Article 30.

From the point of view of legal certainty however, the rule-based approach in *Keck* is an improvement. Although the judgment in *Keck* may rightly be criticized for not making clear which of its previous case law it was overruling, the ECJ has, in cases subsequent to *Keck*, somewhat clarified the scope of that ruling by applying the *Keck* departure on a pragmatic case-by-case basis. Perhaps the biggest advantage of the *Keck* approach from the national courts' point of view is that they can now avoid the difficult questions of justification which, because of their subjectivity, have proved to be so difficult to apply in practice.[214] These 'benefits' have, however, yet to filter through to the national courts. The judgments of national courts applying *Keck* to date confirm more the dangers than the advantages of that ruling. It remains to be seen whether the national courts will reap the benefits of a more consistent case law on the limits of Article 30 in the future.

The two crucial questions, identified at the outset, are firstly whether the national courts were, pre-*Keck*, experiencing sufficiently serious

---

[211] See text at n. 180 above.   [212] See n. 170 above.

[213] This point is all the more important on the facts of the *Sogramo Carrefour* case (n. 181 above) since the necessity and proportionality of restricting the sale of Vitamin C to pharmacists for reasons of public health seems more doubtful.

[214] See discussion of the application of justifications for restrictions to the provisions concerning the free movement of goods in Chs. 6 & 7.

difficulties in locating the outer margins of Article 30 to merit the drastic volte-face by the ECJ in *Keck*, and secondly, whether the national courts' experience in applying *Keck* has been a positive one. With respect to the first question, it is submitted that the answer is a resounding yes. The discussion of the national case law above illustrates the intolerable position into which the inconsistent ECJ case law put national courts. That something had to be done to clarify the outer limits of Article 30 seems unchallengeable. As to the second question, it must be stated that the experience of national courts in applying *Keck* to date gives rise to caution. It is perhaps telling that the benefits in legal certainty have yet to filter through, whereas the dangers of abuse of *Keck* have, on the other hand, already raised their ugly head.

4

Article 34 EC and exports

1 INTRODUCTION

Article 34 EC is very much the black sheep of the free-movement-of-goods herd. While the wording of the first part of that Article[1] is identical to the wording of Article 30 EC concerning import restrictions, the ECJ has always taken a less rigorous attitude towards restrictions on exports than it has towards restrictions on imports. In the case of national export restrictions, the ECJ has held that discrimination is a necessary element in concluding that a particular measure is a measure having equivalent effect to an export restriction. This is in contrast to the *Dassonville* interpretation of Article 30 under which, as we have seen, discrimination is not a prerequisite for the application of that Article. This interpretation of Article 34 was first set out by the ECJ in *Groenveld* v. *Produktschap voor Vee en Vlees*.[2] That case concerned Dutch legislation banning the possession of horsemeat by manufacturers of meat products which was designed to safeguard exports of such products to such countries which prohibit the sale of horseflesh. The ECJ held that the Dutch legislation was non-discriminatory and did not breach Article 34 since

[T]hat provision concerns national measures which have as their specific object or effect the restriction of patterns of exports and thereby the establishment of a difference of treatment between the domestic trade of a Member State and its export trade in such a way as to provide a particular advantage for national production or for the domestic market of the State in question at the expense of the production or of the trade of other Member States.[3]

In other words, the national measures must be clearly discriminatory before they will be held to breach Article 34.[4]

Although it was at first thought that the *Groenveld* judgment would prove to be an exceptional judgment handed down by a Chamber of the ECJ, the interpretation of Article 34 in that judgment has proved to be durable. The ECJ has applied and repeated the operative part of the

---

[1] Art. 34 EC provides: 'Quantitative restrictions on exports, and all measures having equivalent effect, shall be prohibited between Member States.'

[2] Case 15/79 [1979] ECR 3409; [1981] 1 CMLR 207.　　　　　[3] Ibid. at para. 7.

[4] See, e.g., Case 53/76 *Bouhelier* [1977] ECR 197, [1977] 1 CMLR 436; Case C–47/90 *Etablissments Delhaize Frères and Compagnie Le Lion SA* v. *Promalvin SA and Age Bodegas Unidas SA* [1992] ECR I–3669; Case C–426/92 *Germany* v. *Deutsches Milch-Kontor GmbH* [1994] ECR I–2757.

Groenveld judgment (set out above) in a series of subsequent cases, although it has dropped the last part of that formula, namely that the advantage be 'at the expense of the production or of the trade of other Member States'.[5] The principles underpinning the divergence of interpretation by the ECJ to Articles 30 and 34 are not entirely clear. After all, the *Dassonville*[6] formula does not refer only to imports but to measures having equivalent effect to quantitative restrictions in general. Gormley has argued that the correct explanation of the ECJ's attitude is that it was 'strongly influenced by the American case law with its clear distinction between measures which only incidentally affect inter-State trade and measures which are clearly designed to affect it'.[7] Whatever the origin of the approach, one of the earliest rationales to have been extrapolated from the Article 34 case law was provided by VerLoren van Themaat who emphasized the completely different situations involved in Article 30 and 34 respectively.[8] More recently, the ECJ's approach has been explained by pointing out that Article 30 rightly applies to non-discriminatory national measures because they may impose a 'dual burden' on the importer who will have to satisfy the relevant rules in his own State and also the State of import. In a case such as *Groenveld*, by contrast, the 'goods for the domestic market and goods for export were subject to the same rule and, at that stage in the production process, to no other'.[9] Ultimately however, the reason for the ECJ's interpretation of Article 34 may be a more mundane one: the assumption that Member States are unlikely to wish to impede exports. If the latter is the case, Article 34 will not be required to police non-discriminatory national rules actually or potentially affecting exports.

It is surprising that the principles underlying the divergence of approach by the ECJ to interpreting Articles 30 and 34 should still be unclear. As a matter of principle, the divergence between Article 30 and 34 according to the ECJ's current case law is 'a matter for some regret and does little to assist a coherent interpretation of the concept of measures capable of hindering intra-Community trade'.[10] Advocate General

---

[5] See esp. Case 155/80 *Oebel* [1981] ECR 1993; Cases 141–143/81 *Holdijk* [1982] ECR 1299, [1983] 2 CMLR 635; Case 172/82 *Syndicat national des fabricants raffineurs d'huile de graissage* v. *Groupement d'interêt economique (GIE) Inter-Huiles* [1983] ECR 555, [1983] 3 CMLR 485; Case 237/82 *Jongeneel Kaas* v. *Netherlands* [1984] ECR 43, [1985] 2 CMLR 53; Case 15/83 *Denkavit Nederland* v. *Hoofdproduktschap voor Akkerbouwprodukten* [1984] ECR 2171; Case 251/83 *Haug-Adrion* v. *Frankfurter Versicherungs-AG* [1984] ECR 4277, [1985] 3 CMLR 266; Case 98/86 *Ministère Public* v. *Mathot* [1987] ECR 809, [1988] 1 CMLR 411; C–302/88 *Hennen Olie BV* v. *Stichting Interim Centraal Orgaan Voorraadvorming Aardolieprodukten and Staat der Nederlanden* [1990]; ECR I–4625; & C–47/90 *Delhaize* v. *Promalvin*, n. 4 above.

[6] Case 8/74 *Procureur du Roi* v. *Dassonville* [1974] ECR 837, [1974] 2 CMLR 436 at para. 5.

[7] Gormley, *Prohibiting Restrictions on Trade Within the EEC*, 107.

[8] 'De artikelen 30–36 van het EEG-Verdrag' (1980) *R.M. Themis* 378.

[9] Weatherill and Beaumont, *EC Law*, 530.

[10] Gormley, n. 7 above, 96. See also Mattera, *Le marché unique européen—Ses règles, son fonctionnement*, 516.

Capotorti issued a warning in his conclusions to the ECJ in *Oebel*[11] that 'the abandonment of a single concept of what constitutes measures having an effect equivalent to quantitative restrictions is likely to give rise to confusion'.[12] Indeed, it is difficult to disagree with the conclusion of Oliver that 'as regards measures of equivalent effect under Article 34 the basic principles do not yet appear to have been fully worked out'.[13]

From the point of view of the application of Article 34 by national courts, the essential question thus seems to be whether Article 34 is sufficiently clear in practice. Have the dangers alluded to in the literature surfaced before the national courts? Does the apparent absence of clear explanation for the divergence in interpretation of Articles 30 and 34 cause undue problems for the national courts? Apart from these questions, this section will also address the question of Article 34 and the *de minimis* principle, the protection of the environment, and finally Article 34 and common organizations of the market.

2 IS ARTICLE 34 SUFFICIENTLY CLEAR IN PRACTICE?

The first observation arising from national court application of Article 34 is that that Article is all too often overlooked by the national court. In cases concerning purely national measures not concerning imports from other Member States, the only foothold in the provisions in the Treaty concerning the free movement of goods is Article 34. National courts often fail to recognize this. In *R. v. Secretary of State for Health, ex p. United States Tobacco International*[14] a manufacturer of oral snuff in Scotland challenged a decision of the Secretary of State for Health which banned the production of oral snuff.[15] Taylor LJ in the Queen's Bench Division of the High Court simply held that Article 36 EC justified the ban for reasons of the protection of public health. The High Court did not make clear which provision it considered to have been breached in the first place. Since US Tobacco International was manufacturing the oral snuff in Scotland and was thus not importing into the United Kingdom, it may be assumed that Article 34 (rather than Article 30) was considered to have been breached. However, it is difficult to see how this could possibly be the case. The ban on oral snuff applied irrespective of whether the snuff was destined for export or the home market and thus, according to the *Groenveld* case law, would not seem to breach Article 34. A similar example of national courts neglecting to apply Article 34 is to be found in the decision of the President of the

---

[11] Case 155/80, n. 5 above. [12] Case 155/80 [1981] ECR 1993 at 2016.
[13] Oliver, *Free Movement of Goods in the European Community*, 179.
[14] [1992] 1 QB 353; [1992] 1 All ER 212.
[15] Oral Snuff (Safety) Regulations 1989, which came into force on 13 Mar. 1990.

Afdeling Bestuursrechtspraak of the Dutch *Raad van State* in *Conté Nederland* v. *VROM*.[16] Conté Nederland was fined for having infringed Article 2(1) of the *Cadmiumbesluit Wet Milieugevaarlijke stoffen* (Cadmium Order Environmentally Dangerous Substances Act)[17] and appealed, arguing *inter alia* that the fine breached the provisions of the EC Treaty concerning the free movement of goods. An interesting aspect of this case was that a notification by the Netherlands to the Commission for exemption from Directive 91/338[18] under Article 100a(4) EC was pending.[19] It was held that 'in waiting for the decision of the Commission on the application by the Netherlands government under Article 100a(4) EC, the President is for the time being of the opinion that it is not unlikely that the legislation in question is justified for the necessity of protecting public health and the environment'. In this very brief summary judgment, it seems that the President of the *Raad van State* assumed that Article 34 had been infringed. As in *Ex p. United States Tobacco International*,[20] the facts of this case concerned a Dutch company manufacturing and producing in the Netherlands and not importing from other Member States. It is again difficult to see how a breach of Article 34 could be established in this case. The ban in the Dutch legislation on certain levels of cadmium applied irrespective of whether the product was destined for export or the home market and thus, again according to the *Groenveld* case law, would not seem to breach Article 34. These cases thus demonstrate the extent to which national courts fail to recognize and explain the application of Article 34.

Even in cases where the national court explicitly recognizes the application of Article 34, there is evidence that, in the early days at least, the *Groenveld* case law had not filtered through into the national courts and was not being applied. Such was the case in the English case *Potato Marketing Board* v. *Drysdale*[21] concerning the Potato Marketing Scheme in the United Kingdom. Essentially, this case concerned the suit of registered potato producers for payment of a potato farming levy due under the Potato Marketing Scheme. The defence was raised that the Scheme was unlawful as it was contrary, *inter alia*, to Article 34. It was argued that the Scheme, taken as a whole, had an inherent bias against exports in that the provisions for price support, the quota system, and the levy on producers were capable of having the effect of discouraging exports. In the Court of Appeal, Balcombe LJ cited the ECJ's judgment in *Oebel*[22] which repeated

---

[16] 19 Oct. 1994, SEW 1995, 444 (with note by Mortelmans). [17] Stb. 1990, nr. 538.
[18] Council Directive of 18 June 1991, amending for the 10th time Directive 76/769 on the approximation of the laws and administrative provisions of the Member States relating to restrictions on the marketing and use of certain dangerous substances and preparations: [1991] OJ L186.
[19] For a discussion of this aspect of this case, see in Ch. 9, sect. 4.
[20] n. 14 above. [21] [1986] 3 CMLR 331. [22] Case 155/80, n. 5 above.

the *Groenveld* formula under which, as has been shown, Article 34 only concerns national measures which have as their specific object or effect the restriction of patterns of exports and thereby the establishment of a difference of treatment between the domestic trade of a Member State and its export trade. However, in applying this to the facts, Balcombe LJ held that there was no factual support to establish that the measures operated by the Board had a restrictive effect on exports: 'If one compares the situation as it is with the situation as it would be were there no such measures, we are quite unable to say, as a matter of necessary inference, that the absence of these measures would lead to an increase of exports'.[23]

It is submitted that this is not a correct application of the *Groenveld* case law to the facts. Following *Groenveld*, the correct approach would surely have been to look for a difference of treatment rather than for an increase in exports in the absence of the scheme in question. Such an approach had indeed been applied to identical facts by Oxford County Court in *Potato Marketing Board* v. *Robertsons*.[24] In that case, Clark J concluded that there was no element in the Scheme which had as its specific object or effect the restriction of patterns of exports.[25] It would seem therefore that the application of Article 34 by the Court of Appeal in *Drysdale*[26] was somewhat limited.

A similar failure to apply the *Groenveld* interpretation of Article 34 was evident in another decision of the English Court of Appeal in *British Leyland Motor Corporation* v. *T. I. Silencers Ltd*.[27] In that case, British Leyland sued T. I. Silencers for breach of copyright in drawings of motorcar assemblies by manufacturing and selling replacement parts for British Leyland vehicles based on these drawings. The Court of Appeal allowed the appeal from the decision of the Chancery Division of the High Court which had struck out the defences based on EC law as 'unarguable'.[28] What is of note is that the Court of Appeal reinstated the defences explicitly on the assumption that Article 34 would be breached since T. I. Silencers would be in a financially disadvantageous position *vis-à-vis* manufacturers in other Member States which did not have to pay such a royalty.[29] Again, the Court of Appeal made no reference to the *Groenveld* case law, which would have been pertinent in this case as the requirement in

---

[23] n. 21 above at 346.   [24] [1983] 1 CMLR 93.

[25] Ibid. at 125–6. It may be noted that Clark J went on to hold that even if he was wrong and there *was* a difference of treatment, his conclusion would remain unchanged as there was, on the facts, no actual or potential effect on exports within the meaning of the *Dassonville* formula. The judgment also dealt with the relationship between the Treaty provisions on the free movement of goods and those on State aid; see discussion on this point at p. 11.

[26] n. 21 above.

[27] [1981] 2 CMLR 75. Noted by Hicks (1981) EIPR 156.

[28] Judgments of Walton J on 11 July 1979 and 2 Apr. 1980 respectively: [1980] 1 CMLR 598 and [1980] 2 CMLR 332. Noted (1980) ELRev. 240.

[29] [1981] 2 CMLR 75 at 83.

English law to pay the copyright royalties applied irrespective of whether the product was destined for the domestic market or for export. These relatively early cases therefore demonstrate that the *Groenveld* case law did not receive immediate application by the English Court of Appeal.

The *Groenveld* case law had equally failed to filter into certain cases before the French courts. A good example is provided by the *Smanor* case concerning the production and sale of deep-frozen yoghurt in France. On an application by Smanor to have French legislation (the effect of which was to prohibit Smanor from using the designation 'yoghurt')[30] annulled, the *Conseil d'Etat* held that 'the contested provisions of the decree apply only to products sold on the French market and do not therefore have any connection with the exportation of yoghurts and frozen fermented milk'.[31] Although this is an improvement on the opinion of *Commissaire de gouvernement* Lassere in that case, who did not even mention Article 34, it is submitted that it would have been preferable for the *Conseil d'Etat* to have come to the same conclusion but on the basis that the national measures did not have as their specific object or effect the restriction of patterns of exports and thereby the establishment of a difference of treatment between domestic and export trade, rather than simply asserting that the provisions had no connection with export.[32]

It is in two cases before the English courts, however, in which the difficulties involved in the application of the *Groenveld* case law are most vividly exposed. Both cases involved the export of live animals to other Member States, and in both cases the application of Article 34 proved to be surprisingly unclear. Firstly, in *R. v. Minister of Agriculture, Fisheries and Food, ex p. Roberts*,[33] the Queen's Bench Division of the High Court was faced with an application for judicial review of a decision of the Minister of Agriculture not to refuse to grant export licences for the export of live lambs to France.[34] The objection to export was based on animal-rights

---

[30] Art. 11 of Law of 5 Aug. 1905 as amended by Law of 10 Jan. 1978 and Decree No. 82–184 of 22 Feb. 1982, JORF 25 Feb. 1982, p. 676.

[31] *Smanor SA* v. *Syndicat national des fabricants de produits surgelés et congelés*, *Conseil d'Etat*, 19 Nov. 1986, Rec. Lebon 1986, 259; JCP 1987, II 20822; AJDA 1986, 714; RTDE 1988, 117; CDE 1989, 418. Noted by Azibert, De Boisdeffre, AJDA 1986, 681; Constantinesco, Simon, Soler-Couteaux, RTDE 1988, 113–17 and criticized in the Fourth Report to the European Parliament on Commission Monitoring of the Application of Community Law [1987] OJ C338 and the Sixth Report [1989] OJ C330/1 (includes appendix, 'The attitude of national supreme courts to Community law').

[32] This judgment of the *Conseil d'Etat* may also be criticized for its reasoning with respect to Art. 30; see discussion on this point at pp.66–8. See also the subsequent judgment of the ECJ in Case 298/87 *SA Smanor* [1988] ECR 4489 on a subsequent reference by the *Trib. comm.* L'Aigle of 21 Sept. 1987. For a similar rejection of the application of Art. 34 on incorrect reasoning, see *Sté Les Films du Diamant* v. *FNCF*, Cour d'appel Paris 1re Ch. A., 19 June 1985, Dalloz 1986, IR 243 (with note by Hassler). [33] [1991] 1 CMLR 555.

[34] The decision of the Minister of Agriculture, Fisheries and Food was based on the Animal Health Act 1981, ss. 37(2) & 39, and the Export of Animals (Protection) Order 1981, Art. 3.

grounds[35] following a number of horrifying incidents in France in which farmers had violently mistreated lambs which had been imported from Britain and were being transported to destinations in France.[36] The applicants sought a declaration that the Minister of Agriculture was wrong in law to have stated in the decision that refusal of export licences was likely to be contrary to Community law. On the question of whether Article 34 would indeed have precluded the refusal of export licences, the High Court cited the relevant authorities of *Holdijk*, *Oebel* and *Groenveld*,[37] and noted that although 'construction of [Article 34] by the English courts would undoubtedly lead to the conclusion that measures to prevent free movement of goods in the EEC such as exports were not allowed', the ECJ had diverged from its interpretation of Article 30 in Article 34: 'Thus, identical words in the two Articles have received different interpretation'.[38] In applying the Article 34 case law, the High Court was decidedly unclear:

> It is argued that though restrictions on *production* may now be governed by the *Groenveld* type of cases, there is no clear authority regarding *sales*. In *Oebel* itself, in regard to the night delivery of bread, there was a restriction on sale: the Court applied the same test for Article 30 and Article 34. There is in the judgment of what has come to be known as the *Cassis de Dijon* case ([1979] ECR 649) support for the view that restrictions on sale may be contrary to Article 34, even though they apply in the same way to exports and to goods put on the national market.
>
> Bans sought to be imposed without reference to whether these were goods for export or goods for the national market are contrary to the fundamental freedom of movement of goods in the Community and in particular contrary to the literal interpretation of Article 34. Whether the European Court ever intended that the *Groenveld* formula should apply to the instant case is decidedly unclear.[39]

It is, with respect, very difficult to fathom the reasoning of the High Court in this passage. It begins by attempting to draw a distinction in the Article 34 case law between restrictions on *production* and on *sales* with the *Groenveld* formula applying only to the former. But the High Court then cites *Oebel* as a case concerning *sales* in which the ECJ applied the same test to Articles 30 and 34 respectively. We have seen that this is simply not true.[40] In *Oebel*, the ECJ applied its *Groenveld* formula to Article 34, even contrary to the conclusions of its Advocate General. Furthermore, it is difficult, again with respect, to see where the support in the *Cassis de Dijon* judgment is for the contention that Article 34 covers restrictions even

---

[35] Roberts was representing the Royal Society for the Prevention of Cruelty to Animals (RSPCA).

[36] The incidents included putting lambs out on poisoned grass, burning them alive and slaughtering them outside an abattoir.

[37] nn. 2 & 5 above.

[38] [1991] 1 CMLR 555 at 581 (per Popplewell J). See discussion of this divergence in text at n. 6 above.

[39] Ibid. at 582.   [40] Case 155/80, *Oebel*, n. 5.

though they apply in the same way to exports and to goods put on the national market. Ultimately, the passage quoted above demonstrates that the ECJ interpretation of Article 34 in *Groenveld* was unclear for the High Court. On what it termed a 'literal interpretation' of Article 34, it seemed that that Article was breached, but the impact of the *Groenveld* formula was 'decidedly unclear' to the High Court.

It is submitted that the correct approach on the facts of the case would have been to hold that, if the Minister had refused export licences, such a move would constitute a ban on the export of live sheep to France, which is a distinctly applicable measure contrary to Article 34 EC (subject to justification under Article 36). In other words, the measure applies to exports alone, and the correct interpretation of the ECJ case law in such a case is that the basic principle expounded in *Dassonville* applies without qualification. That this is the correct interpretation on the facts seems to have been confirmed by the recent judgment of the ECJ in *R. v. Ministry of Agriculture, Fisheries and Food, ex p. Hedley Lomas*.[41] That case involved an instance when the Minister of Agriculture, Fisheries and Food actually went ahead and systematically refused to issue licences for the export to Spain of live animals for slaughter.[42] In the proceedings before the ECJ, the Ministry did not deny that the refusal to issue the export licences constituted a quantitative restriction on exports contrary to Article 34 EC. This was implicitly accepted by the ECJ which proceeded to examine whether the ban could nevertheless be justified under the applicable Directives or Article 36 EC.[43] The point is that the correct interpretation for the English High Court to have taken in *Ex p. Roberts* seems to be that if the Minister had refused export licences for sheep to France, there would be a clear breach of Article 34 which could only have been saved by evaluation under Article 36. Instead, as we have seen, the High Court tangled itself up in the confusion of the application of the *Groenveld* case law.[44]

---

[41] Case C–5/94 [1996] ECR I–2553.

[42] The grounds for the refusal were that the treatment of the animals in Spanish slaughterhouses was contrary to Directive 74/577 on stunning of animals before slaughter: [1974] OJ L316/10.

[43] See para. 12 of the ECJ judgment.

[44] Ultimately, however, it may be noted that the decision of the High Court refusing the declaration sought by the applicants in *Ex p. Roberts* did not turn on the Art. 34 point. The High Court, quite rightly, held that even if the Minister had taken the wrong view of Art. 34, so that he was not inhibited from imposing a total ban, the result would have nevertheless been the same, since the High Court held that the decision not to refuse export licences was perfectly reasonable under English law. In other words, the fact that the Minister *could* have refused export licences without breaching Art. 34 did not mean that he *had* to issue such a refusal. After all, the fact that refusal of export licences might breach Art. 34 was only one of the reasons given by the Minister in declining to refuse export licences. See also, to the same effect, the earlier judgment of the High Court of 20 Sept. 1990 involving the same parties; transcr.: Marten Walsh Cherer (per MacPherson J).

The second English case in which the difficulties in the application of the *Groenveld* case law were equally vividly exposed was *R.* v. *Coventry City Council, ex p. Phoenix Aviation and others.*[45] The facts again concerned the export of live animals for slaughter in other Member States. This case, however, concerned the more recent protests in the United Kingdom against the export of live calves to other Member States for rearing in veal crates, a practice banned in the UK since 1990. There were three applications for judicial review of decisions of various public authorities which had the effect of banning the export of live calves.[46] The High Court held that under the applicable English law, the public authorities had no discretion to refuse exports of live animals for slaughter,[47] and thus there was no need to discuss the EC law points raised in any detail. Importantly however, Simon Brown LJ in the High Court went on to identify the central questions of EC law that arose, which he described as 'difficult questions, very far from *acte clair*, and questions which we would have regarded as appropriate for reference to the Court of Justice of the European Communities had these challenges turned upon them'. One of the points identified concerned the question of whether Article 34 was breached by the decisions of the public authorities. Simon Brown LJ set out the difficulty concerning the question of a breach of Article 34 thus:

[I]s the test of such breach that set out in the line of cases represented by *P. B. Groenveld* v. *Produktschap voor Vee en Vlees, Summary proceedings against Oebel, Criminal proceedings against Holdijk* and *Commission* v. *Belgium* (in which event the respondents powerfully contend that they are not in breach because their measures provide no particular advantage for national production or for the domestic market at the expense of the production or trade of another Member State), or is the test to be applied rather that enshrined in *Procureur de la République* v. *Bouhelier, Jongeneel Kaas* v. *State of Netherlands* and *R.* v. *Ministry of Agriculture, Fisheries and Food, ex p. Jaderow*—essentially the *Dassonville* test applicable under Article 30 in which case these measures probably breach it. [Counsel for the applicants] contend that the *Dassonville* approach applies because these bans are 'distinctly applicable' measures, i.e. ones affecting exports only. The contrary argument is that distinctly applicable measures or not, the *Groenveld* test applies and that in any

---

[45] [1995] 3 All ER 37.

[46] The relevant decisions were that of Coventry City Council suspending flights from their airport, Dover Harbour Board suspending cross-Channel services carrying live animals and Associated British Ports refusing to suspend the export of live calves. See Elworthy, 'Crated Calves and Crazed Cows: Live Animals and Free Movement of Goods' in Holder (ed.), *The Impact of EC Environmental Law in the United Kingdom*, (Wiley, 1997) at 303.

[47] Air Navigation Order 1989, art. 78(3)2; Harbours, Docks and Piers Clauses Act 1847, s. 333; & Harbours Act 1964, s. 404 respectively. The High Court held that under the respective statutory regimes there was no general discretion to distinguish between different lawful trades and no defence of necessity. Furthermore, the High Court added that even if there was a discretion, the Rule of Law did not allow public authorities to respond to unlawful protest and threats from pressure groups by surrendering to their dictates.

event the measures are properly to be regarded as only indistinctly applicable, i.e. as affecting internal transits also.

Two points of confusion concerning the correct interpretation of Article 34 are exposed by this statement. Firstly, the question of when the *Groenveld* as opposed to the *Bouhelier*[48] case law should apply. This is a crucial point of confusion since, as Simon Brown LJ points out, the concrete finding of a breach of Article 34 is different depending on which case law is applicable. The central question is whether the *Groenveld* formula applies as a global interpretation of Article 34 or whether it only applies to indistinctly applicable measures. If the latter is the case, the further question is whether it is simply the *Dassonville* formula which applies to distinctly applicable measures restricting exports. It is submitted that the correct interpretation is that *Groenveld* only applies to indistinctly applicable measures and that the *Dassonville* formula does apply to distinctly applicable measures restricting exports. Nevertheless, the fact that the High Court raised this as a point of 'difficulty' suggests that the ECJ case law on the extent of application of the *Groenveld* case law was not sufficiently clear for the national courts. The second point of confusion concerns the application of the *Groenveld* formula itself. It will be remembered that the ECJ in *Groenveld* held that Article 34 applied only to national measures establishing a 'difference of treatment between the domestic trade of a Member State and its export trade'. In the context of export bans on the export of live animals, is it open for a public authority refusing such export, to argue that internal transits are also affected? In other words, the High Court was unsure as to whether such a public authority could successfully argue that there is no difference in treatment since similar restrictions could be placed on domestic trade should similar objections based on animal-rights grounds present themselves. It is submitted that EC law would require that such an argument should be rejected. The measures that had been taken had in fact the effect of banning exports and only exports. Indeed, in a judgment of the Queen's Bench Division of the High Court three months later in *R.* v. *Chief Constable of Sussex, ex p. International Trader's Ferry*,[49] a prima facie breach of Article 34 was found on similar facts. In that case, the Chief Constable of Sussex issued decisions to the effect that the local police had insufficient resources to provide effective police support for more than two days a week for lorries containing live animals, destined for export via the port of Shoreham. Lorry movements, and thus exports, were banned on other days. The argument that there was no difference in treatment, since the Chief Constable would have taken a similar attitude had there been a problem caused by animal-rights demonstrators protesting against

---

[48] Case 53/76, n. 4.   [49] [1995] 3 CMLR 485.

the carriage of livestock within the UK, was rejected by Balcombe LJ in the following terms:

The fact that, in certain hypothetical circumstances which have not yet occurred, and may never occur, the Chief Constable would have applied similar restrictions to livestock being transported within the United Kingdom is neither here nor there: the only measure which he has in fact applied is to goods destined solely for export.[50]

It is submitted that this is the correct view. A ban on export is surely sufficient to satisfy the 'difference in treatment' part of the *Groenveld* test. Nevertheless, the uncertainty raised by Simon Brown LJ in *Ex p. Phoenix Aviation* demonstrates that such a view was not self-evident to the national courts in applying the *Groenveld* interpretation of Article 34.

It will furthermore be remembered that the second part of the *Groenveld* formula goes on to provide that the national measure must apply in such a way as to 'provide a particular advantage for national production or for the domestic market of the State in question at the expense of the production or of the trade of other Member States'. Applying this to the facts of *Ex p. Phoenix Aviation*, the High Court mentioned that the difficulty was that the public authorities had 'powerfully contended' that the export bans did *not* provide a particular advantage for national production. If anything, the export ban was a disadvantage to national production as it led to a decrease in sales. Indeed, it is difficult to see how an export restriction could *ever* favour national production. For this reason, Oliver has described this limb of the *Groenveld* formula as 'superfluous'.[51] It seems therefore, that the High Court in *Ex p. Phoenix Aviation* put its finger very firmly on one of the major difficulties in applying the *Groenveld* formula in practice. Fortunately, as we have seen, the High Court was able to hold that under English law the public authorities had no discretion to refuse export of live animals, and thus the challenges did not turn on the Article 34 point.[52] Nevertheless, the points raised by the High Court in that case demonstrate that the application of the *Groenveld* interpretation of Article 34 is not unreservedly clear in all cases in practice.

In summary then, it seems that the *Groenveld* interpretation of Article 34 has not been particularly well applied by the national courts in practice. Part of the 'blame' for this must lie with the national courts. We have seen

---

[50] Ibid. at 497.

[51] Oliver, n. 13 above, 121. The only circumstance in which Oliver conceives that an export restriction may favour national production is if the export restriction related only to raw materials or component parts giving an advantage to national finished products. Furthermore, there are conceivably instances when an export restriction may favour national interests such as when a product is scarce in a period of serious difficulties regarding balance of payments. However, in such a case, it would be the national interest, rather than national production itself, which would be favoured.

[52] n. 47 above.

that the *Groenveld* approach has all too often been neglected by the national courts, as they failed to recognize and explain the application of Article 34.[53] Furthermore, even if the application of Article 34 was recognized, there is evidence that the *Groenveld* formula had not filtered down into the reasoning of the national courts.[54] However, only part of the 'blame' for the Article 34 difficulties can be laid at the door of the national courts. The warnings in the literature that a divergent interpretation of Article 30 and 34 respectively was likely to cause confusion seems, to a certain extent, to have been borne out. We have seen the English High Court commenting in *Ex p. Roberts*[55] that 'identical words in the two Articles have received different interpretation' and that a 'literal' interpretation under English rules of construction of Article 34 conflicts with the *Groenveld* interpretation of that Article by the ECJ.[56]

The experience of the national courts suggests that the ECJ case law is in need of clarification. The application of *Groenveld* to export bans, and thus distinctly applicable measures, is unclear. If it is the case that *Groenveld* does not apply in the latter case, the second question is which interpretation does apply? Is it then simply the *Dassonville* formula that applies; namely that all national measures that hinder directly or indirectly actually or potentially intra-Community trade will breach Article 34? Finally, the national courts have occasionally been tangled in confusion in the application of the requirement in the *Groenveld* formula that the national measure must 'provide a particular advantage for national production'. As was noted above, it is difficult to conceive of instances when an export restriction will *ever* benefit national production.[57] This part of the *Groenveld* formula is indeed unclear in practice and seems rather illogical in principle.

Fortunately, the difficulties in applying the *Groenveld* interpretation of Article 34 have not, in any of the cases discussed, led to any serious misapplication in practice. In most of the cases, it is clear that there was no real danger of export trade being affected and, in the cases in which such a danger was present, the Article 34 point was not decisive and the problems discussed were purely *obiter dicta*. It may be hoped that if the case had turned on the Article 34 points, the national courts would have made a reference to the ECJ under Article 177 EC. It is then the ECJ itself which would be confronted with the difficulties in its *Groenveld* case law. It is submitted that the latter is desirable for the coherent and uniform development of EC law.

---

[53] See *Ex p. United States Tobacco*, n. 14 above and *Conté Nederland* v. *VROM*, n. 16 above.
[54] See *Drysdale*, n. 21 above; *T. I. Silencers*, n. 27 above and *Smanor*, n. 31 above.
[55] n. 33 above.   [56] n. 38 above.   [57] n. 51 above.

3 ARTICLE 34 AND *DE MINIMIS*

The ECJ has consistently rejected the role of a *de minimis* principle for Article 30.[58] It has never had occasion, however, to explicitly hold that a *de minimis* doctrine has no place with respect to either export restrictions or Article 34 EC. It has been argued that the *Groenveld* interpretation of Article 34 was itself an application of *de minimis*.[59] This argument has however received little support.[60]

The issue of Article 34 and *de minimis* arose indirectly before the Dutch *CBB* in *Cyanamid Benelux SA NV* v. *Minister van Landbouw en Visserij*.[61] Cyanamid Benelux was developing animal medicines in the Netherlands and was experimenting with bovine somatotropine (BST) to increase milk production by cows. Cyanamid had registered these experiments as required by the *Diergeneesmiddelenwet* (Animal Medicines Act) of 1 May 1986 and a *Regeling* (Regulation) of 28 January 1987 based on this Act.[62] The tests had been cleared by the Dutch authorities subject to certain conditions. Cyanamid claimed that these conditions were so limiting that in practice they prevented the tests being carried out at all. It argued, *inter alia*, that the Dutch legislation constituted a trade restriction contrary to the free movement of goods since trade in milk and beef from BST-treated cows was potentially prevented. The *CBB*, in an extremely brief interim judgment, doubted the existence of a trade restriction but suggested that it would nevertheless be justified under Article 36 EC for the protection of public health. Mortelmans has criticized this judgment for its lack of reasoning, which is indeed regrettable considering that the *CBB* is a court against whose decisions there is no appeal.[63] Mortelmans is correct to point out that the inter-State trade element was tiny in this case and that it is an unfortunate omission on the part of the Court not to have addressed the *de minimis* point as, if anything, it was exports and therefore Article 34 which was at issue. The question as to whether the rejection of *de minimis* applies equally to Article 34 cases thus remains unresolved. In the absence of reasoning by the *CBB* in this case, the views of the Dutch courts are also unclear.

4 PROTECTION OF THE ENVIRONMENT AND ARTICLE 34

The protection of the environment is not one of the grounds of justification for breaches of the free movement of goods provided for in Article 36 EC.

---

[58] See discussion in Ch. 3, sect. 2 (C).
[59] See Everling (1982) EuR 301.
[60] See, e.g., Gormley, n. 7 above, 109.
[61] Pres. *CBB* 28 Jan. 1988, SEW 1987, 791 (with note by Mortelmans).
[62] Stcrt. 20.
[63] n. 61 above.

Nevertheless, the ECJ has accepted that the protection of the environment might be considered a mandatory requirement within the 'rule of reason'.[64] A condition for the application of the rule of reason is that the national measure be indistinctly applicable.[65] It has already been noted that Article 34 EC, according to the *Groenveld* formula, applies only to national measures that discriminate against exports (i.e. distinctly applicable measures). This would thus seem to exclude the application of the rule of reason to Article 34. Consequently, the possibility of advancing a justification based on the protection of the environment for a breach of Article 34 thus seems to be excluded.[66] The only justification provided for in Article 36 that might conceivably be invoked in the protection of the environment field, is the protection of the health and life of humans. Nevertheless, it is clear that the ECJ regards environmental justifications as falling under the rule of reason rather than Article 36. If this were not the case, the ECJ would not, in the *Walloon Waste Case*,[67] have embarked upon such tortuous reasoning to conclude that the measure at issue in that case was indistinctly applicable and thus eligible for the justification of environmental protection under the rule of reason.[68] There is thus a loophole in the ECJ case law. As this case law stands at present, environmental concerns may never, technically, justify a breach of Article 34 by means of an export ban. This is illogical and regrettable and yet another reason why the *Groenveld* interpretation of Article 34 may be subject to criticism.[69] Indeed, the present case law makes it arguable that any provision of a

[64] See Case 302/86 *Commission* v. *Denmark* [1988] ECR 4607. See further discussion of the rule of reason in Ch. 6. For an application of the 'protection of the environment' justification under the rule of reason before national courts, see the judgment of the Belgian Court of Arbitration of 2 Feb. 1995 in Case 8/95, *Journal des tribunaux*, 1995, 474 concerning a system of refunds on the return of used batteries, and the judgment of the *Austrian Verfassungsgericht* (Constitutional Court) of 12 Dec. 1995, Case V 136/94–10 concerning a ban on the marketing of mineral water other than in glass bottles.

[65] See, e.g., Case 788/79 *Gilli and Andres* [1980] ECR 2071, [1981] 1 CMLR 146; Case 113/80 *Commission* v. *Ireland* (Irish Souvenirs) [1981] ECR 1625, [1982] 1 CMLR 706 and Case 207/83 *Commission* v. *United Kingdom* (Mandatory Origin-marking) [1985] ECR 1202, [1985] 2 CMLR 259.

[66] See Oliver, n. 13 above, 122.

[67] Case C–2/90 *Commission* v. *Belgium* [1992] ECR I–4431, [1993] 1 CMLR 365.

[68] It is of interest to note that the French *Conseil d'Etat* (*Section du contentieux*) in *Freymuth*, 15 Apr. 1996 (transcr. available on Lexis), has held that a ban on the import of waste into France under certain circumstances was capable of being justified for the protection of the environment under the rule of reason since such a national measure, even though it distinguished according to the place of origin of the waste, was non-discriminatory 'given the special nature of waste'. The *Conseil d'Etat* cited no ECJ authority to support this conclusion, but it may be assumed that it had the *Walloon Waste* case in mind.

[69] See discussion of this problem in Jans, *Europees Milieurecht in Nederland*, 252 and discussion by the same author in annotation of *GS van Nederland*, Pres. *Raad van State* (*Afd. Rechtspraak*), 14 July 1989 in M & R 1990, 428 where he seems to assume that the protection of the environment might justify an export ban. See also annotation by Jans of *Wubben* v. *VROM*, *Raad van State* (*Afd. Bestuursrechtspraak*), 3 Aug. 1995, M & R 1996, 21.

Directive that provides for the possibility for a Member State to impose an export ban in specific circumstances according to criteria based on environmental protection, does not comply with the Treaty's rules on the free movement of goods. On the other hand, now that the environment is an explicit and well-developed policy of the Community provided for in Article 130r EC, it might be that the ECJ would uphold such provisions in a Directive.[70]

The loophole described above has not explicitly surfaced in any of the national judgments considered in this work.[71] Nevertheless, it has lurked in the background in a series of cases before the Dutch *Raad van State* (*Afdeling Geschillen van Bestuur*) regarding decisions issued by the Ministry of the Environment (*Volkshuisvesting, Ruimtelijke Ordening en Milieubeheer* (*VROM*)) refusing permission for the export of hazardous waste from the Netherlands to other Member States. The decisions were issued on the basis of Article 16b(1) of *Wet Chemische Afvalstoffen* (*WCA*: Law on Chemical Waste) and the challenges were based primarily on the argument that this provision was contrary to Directive 84/631[72] on the supervision and control within the European Community of the trans-frontier shipment of hazardous waste. However, it was also argued that the policy underlying the Dutch legislation, namely that waste created in the Netherlands should be treated in the Netherlands unless there are no suitable facilities for doing so, was contrary to Article 34 EC. In the judgments of the *Raad van State*, the Article 34 EC point seems to have been lost.[73]

---

[70] In Case C–422/92 *Commission* v. *Germany* [1995] ECR I–1097, the ECJ did effectively uphold such a provision in Directive 84/631 [1984] OJ L326/31 since it was in conformity with the principle in Art. 130r(2) EC that environmental damage should as a priority be rectified at source. The Dutch *Raad van State* (*Afd. Bestuursrechtspraak*) has referred questions to the ECJ asking whether national provisions, according to which permission to export dangerous waste will only be given if disposal abroad is of a higher standard, is compatible with Art. 34 EC and capable of justification: *Chemische Afvalstoffen Dusseldorp* v. *Minister van Volksvesting, Ruimtelijke Ordening en Milieubeheer, Raad van State* (*Afd. Bestuursrechtspraak*), 23 Apr. 1996, AB 1996, 306.

[71] It should be noted, however, that in *Bakker Barendrecht Export* v. *Kwaliteitscontrole-Bureau voor Groenten en Fruit*, 3 July 1990, KG 1990, 249; SEW 1991, 203, the President of the *Arrondissementsrechtbank* Haarlem held that the refusal by the *Kwaliteitscontrolebureau voor Groenten en Fruit* (*KCB*: Quality Control Office for Vegetables and Fruit) to issue a certificate for the export of strawberries infringed Art. 34 and would not be justified under the rule of reason as 'necessary for the protection of consumers or the fairness of commercial transactions'. Mortelmans SEW 1991, 203 has pointed out that this is not, strictly speaking, correct as the refusal was a distinctly applicable measure which would therefore preclude the application of the rule of reason. See further discussion of the substance of this judgment in text at n. 84 below.

[72] [1984] OJ L326/31 as amended by Directive 86/279 [1986] OJ L181/13. Both Directives were repealed with effect from 6 May 1994 by Reg. 259/93 of 12 Feb. 1993 on the supervision and control of shipments of waste within, into and out of the European Community ([1993] OJ L30/1).

[73] See *GMU Nederland BV* v. *Minister van Volksvesting, Ruimtelijke Ordening en Milieubeheer*, Pres. *Raad van State* (*Afd. Geschillen van Bestuur*), 11 Dec. 1989, KG 1990, 72;

Although the question of whether the *VROM*'s decisions were compatible
with Article 34 EC had been raised in the pleadings, none of the judgments
dealt with the argument. Instead, the *Raad van State* dealt exclusively with
the question of whether the Dutch legislation was compatible with the
Directive and neglected to deal with the question of whether the Directive
itself complied with the primary Treaty rules contained in Article 34. It is
submitted that it would have been desirable for the *Afdeling Geschillen van
Bestuur* to have remembered that even the rules in Community secondary
legislation are subject to the EC Treaty rules on the free movement of
goods.[74] Indeed, the ECJ has shown itself willing to test Community
Directives against the vicissitudes of the Treaty's rules on the free movement of goods in its judgment in *ADBHU*,[75] where the ECJ held that
Directive 75/439[76] was compatible with the Treaty provisions on free
movement of goods. It is submitted that it is regrettable that the *Raad van
State* neglected to deal with the Article 34 arguments, since it would then
have had to have dealt with the application of the rule of reason (the
mandatory requirement to protect the environment) to Article 34.

In a further judgment of the *Raad van State*, the problem of the application of environmental justifications to breaches of Article 34 again lurked
in the background. In *Wubben* v. *VROM*,[77] the *Raad van State* applied the
judgment of the ECJ in *Inter-Huiles*[78] to find a breach of Article 34 by the
Dutch legislation at issue in that case (again, the *WCA*). Significantly however, the *Raad van State* went on to remark that 'the Court furthermore
holds that none of the grounds of justification provided for in Article 36 of
the EEC Treaty are applicable here'.[79] One may speculate as to whether, by
only mentioning Article 36, the *Raad van State* was implicitly assuming

M & R 1990, 423 (with note by Addink and Jans); *Raad van State* (*Afd. Geschillen van Bestuur*),
6 Sept. 1990, AB 1991, 12 (with note by Drupsteen); M & R 1991, 37 (with note by Jans);
RegelMaat 1991, 70 (with note by Drexhage); *Ecoservice Nederland* v. *VROM*, Pres. *Raad van
State* (*Afd. Geschillen van Bestuur*), 16 Aug. 1990, KG 1990, 324; *Eldim BV* v. *VROM*, Pres. *Raad
van State* (*Afd. Geschillen van Bestuur*), 14 Jan. 1992, AB 1992, 455 (with note by Drusteen); M
& R 1992, 486 (with note by Addink); *Raad van State* (*Afd. Geschillen van Bestuur*), 17 Feb. 1993,
AB 1993, 424 (with note by Drusteen); M & R 1993, 303 (with note by Addink); SEW 1993, 618
(with note by Jans); *Edelchemie Panheel BV* v. *VROM*, *Raad van State* (*Afd. Bestuursrechtspraak*),
20 Jan. 1994, M & R 1994, 60 (with note by Jans). See more generally, Jans, 'Het beginsel van
voorkeur voor binnenlandse afvalwerking' (1990) NJB 694.

[74] See Case C–47/90 n. 4 above at para. 26 & Case C–315/92 *Verband Sozialer Wettbewerb
EV* v. *Clinique Laboratories SNC and Estée Lauder Cosmetics GmbH* [1994] ECR I–317.

[75] Case 240/83 *Procureur de la République* v. *Association de defense des Bruleurs d'Huiles
Usagées (ADBHU)* [1985] ECR 531.

[76] On the disposal of waste oils: [1975] OJ L194/23.

[77] *Raad van State* (*Afd. Bestuursrechtspraak*), 3 Aug. 1995, AB 1996, 27; M & R 1996/2 No. 21
(with note by Jans). Noted also in Addink et al. (eds.), *Europese milieurechtspraak, 104 nationale
uitspraken met Europees milieurechterlijke aspecten*, 136–8 and 220.

[78] Case 172/82 *Syndicat national des fabricants raffineurs d'huiles de graissage* v. *Groupement
d'interêt économique (GIE) Inter-Huiles* [1983] ECR 555, [1983] 3 CMLR 485.

[79] n. 77 above.

that the justifications opened up by the rule of reason (including the protection of the environment) were not applicable here to justify a breach of Article 34. It is indeed remarkable that, in such a recent judgment, the possibilities of justification under the rule of reason were not mentioned by the *Raad van State*.[80] The question as to whether (and how) the loophole in the ECJ's case law with respect to environmental justifications for breaches of Article 34 may be closed thus remains unresolved both in ECJ and national case law.

5 ARTICLE 34 AND COMMON ORGANIZATIONS OF THE MARKET

In fields covered by the common organization of the agricultural market, the ECJ has, by way of exception to the restrictive *Groenveld* interpretation of Article 34, accorded a much broader interpretation to Article 34 which is more akin to the *Dassonville* formula.[81] If there is a common organization of the market, 'the principle of free movement applies in the widest form'.[82] The approach of the ECJ is to hold that:

Article 30 and 34 of the Treaty dealing with the abolition of quantitative restrictions on imports and exports and all measures having equivalent effect form an integral part of the common organizations of the markets in the agricultural sectors. As far as trade within the Community is concerned, the common organizations of the markets are therefore based on freedom of commercial transactions and are incompatible with any national legislation capable of hindering intra-Community trade.[83]

---

[80] See also *Heijmans Milieutechniek* v. *GS van Noord-Brabant, Raad van State (Afd. Bestuursrechtspraak)*, 25 July 1996, AB 1996, 425 (with note by ChB); M & R 1996/12, 134 and *Heidemij Realisatie* v. *Gedeputeerde Staten van Noord-Brabant, Raad van State (Afd. Bestuursrechtspraak)*, 25 July 1996, Jurisprudentie bestuursrecht 1996, 189 (with note by Claes) where it was held in the context of a restriction to the export of waste (and thus a breach of Art. 34 EC) that: 'Given that the protection of the environment is not as such mentioned as a ground of justification in Art. 36 of the Treaty . . . the Court is of judgment that [the national provision] cannot be justified under this Article'. Again, the *Raad van State* seems to have assumed that the justification for the protection of the environment under the rule of reason cannot apply to justify a breach of Art. 34 EC. It is submitted that it would have been more satisfactory for the *Raad van State* (a court from which there is no further appeal) to have directed a preliminary reference on this question to the ECJ pursuant to Art. 177 EC. See further discussion of these cases in Ch. 5, sect. 4.

[81] See Case 190/73 *Officier van Justitie* v. *Van Haaster* [1974] ECR 1123; Case 111/76 *Officier van Justitie* v. *Van der Hazel* [1977] ECR 901; Case 83/78 *Pigs Marketing Board* v. *Redmond* [1978] ECR 2347; Case 177/78 *Pigs and Bacon Commission* v. *McCarren* [1979] ECR 2161; Case 94/79 *Vriend* [1980] ECR 327; Case 29/82 *F. Van Luipen en Zoon BV* [1983] ECR 151 & Case 237/82 *Jongeneel Kaas* v. *Netherlands State* [1984] ECR 43, [1985] 2 CMLR 53.

[82] Barents, *The Agricultural Law of the EC* (Kluwer, 1994), 83–4. See also Gormley, n. 7 above, 111–21.

[83] Case 29/82 *Van Luipen*, n. 81 above at para. 8.

Thus, if there is a common organization of the market, Article 34 will be held to be integral to that common market, and will be given the broader *Dassonville* interpretation under which any trading rule hindering directly or indirectly, actually or potentially, intra-Community trade will be prohibited.

The case law of the ECJ in this field has, on the whole, been faithfully implemented by the national courts which have not encountered any serious difficulties. The crucial question is for the national court to identify whether there is a common organization of the market. Thus, in *Bakker Barendrecht Export* v. *Kwaliteitscontrole-Bureau voor Groenten en Fruit*,[84] the Rechtbank Haarlem had no problem in deciding that the existence of the common organization[85] of the market in fruit and vegetables[85] had the result that Article 34 had to be interpreted broadly. The case concerned the refusal by the *KCB* to issue a certificate for the export of strawberries. Bakker had concluded a contract with Marks & Spencer in the United Kingdom for the delivery of Dutch strawberries in the summer of 1990, a period during which a huge quantity of strawberries is consumed. According to the contract, Marks & Spencer stipulated that the strawberries be delivered in 375g. packs. The *KCB* refused the export certificate for strawberries in the 375g. packs since Article 5.2.2.2. of Regulation *Produktschap Groenten en Fruit* (PGF: Vegetable and Fruit Board) 1977 required strawberries to be packed in 250g., 500g., or 1000g. packs. Bakker challenged this refusal, and the *Rechtbank* Haarlem cited the ECJ's judgment in *Van Luipen*[86] and held that according to that judgment, Articles 30 to 34 formed an integral part of the common organizations of the markets which were based on the freedom of competition and trade and that it is 'contrary to this goal when the export to another Member State of a consignment of strawberries which satisfy Community quality standards are hindered on the sole ground that these strawberries must be packaged according to Article 5.2.2.2. in a different way. The regulation in Article 5.2.2.2. is thus a restriction on the export of strawberries of Dutch origin and is thus contrary to Article 34 of the EEC Treaty and Regulation 1035/72'. In *Holland Champignon BV*,[87] on the other hand, the Dutch *Hoge Raad* held that there was, on the facts of that case, no common organization of the market. In that case, Holland Champignon BV was prosecuted under Article 2(2) of Regulation *PGF* 1981 on canned vegetables and the *Warenwet* (Food and Drugs Act) for selling canned mushrooms containing the preservative benzine acid which was prohibited by this legislation. Holland Champignon BV raised the defence that this was contrary to

---

[84] Pres. *Arrondissementsrechtbank* Haarlem, 3 July 1990, KG 1990, 249; SEW 1991, 203 (with note by Mortelmans).

[85] Reg. 1035/72 [1972] OJ Spec. Ed. (II) 437 and Reg. 2638/69 [1969] OJ Spec. Ed. (II) 611.

[86] n. 81 above.   [87] *Hoge Raad* (*Strafkamer*), 11 Jan. 1994, NJ 1994, 409, SEW 1995, 138.

Article 34 as the canned mushrooms were destined for export to Germany. The *Hoge Raad* rejected this defence by holding that Regulation 426/86 of 24 February 1986, although based on Articles 42 and 43 EC, introduced no Community quality standards for mushroom preservation and thus that there was no common organization of the market. By reading the opinion of Advocate General Fokkens, it is clear that the *Hoge Raad* agreed with its Advocate General that in the absence of a common organization of the market, the *Groenveld* interpretation of Article 34 applied and since the Dutch legislation in question applied equally to canned mushrooms destined for the national market and to those destined for export, there was no difference of treatment and thus Article 34 did not apply.

The crucial question is thus for the national court to discern correctly whether or not there is a common organization of the market. There is every reason to agree on the one hand with the *Rechtbank* Haarlem that there was in *Bakker Barendrecht* a common organization of the market and, on the other hand, with the *Hoge Raad* in *Holland Champignon BV* that there was not such a common organization in that case. The same is true of the judgments of the English courts in *Potato Marketing Board* v. *Robertsons*[88] and *Potato Marketing Board* v. *Drysdale*,[89] which were discussed in section 2 above. It will be recalled that in those cases, the *Groenveld* interpretation of Article 34 was applied.[90] Again, however, that interpretation was applied only after the national court had established that there was no common organization of the potato market.[91]

There are however a handful of cases in which the national courts have omitted to look for the existence of a common organization of the market. In *Holland Champignon BV* v. *Produktschap voor Groenten en Fruit*,[92] the *CBB*, in an extremely brief judgment, implicitly referred to the *Groenveld* case law without any discussion as to whether the national legislation at issue in that case[93] fell under the common organization of the market in fruit and vegetables, and thus whether the broader interpretation of Article 34 should have been applied. Equally, in *Cyanamid Benelux SA NV* v. *Minister van Landbouw en Visserij*[94] the *CBB* again failed to discuss whether the common organization of the market in milk[95] had the result that the broader interpretation of Article 34 according to the *Van Luipen* case law should have been applied.[96] Mortelmans has been critical of these

---

[88] n. 24 above. [89] n. 21 above.

[90] See discussion above as to the correctness of the application of the *Groenveld* formula in these cases.

[91] See specifically [1986] 3 CMLR 331 at 345–6.

[92] Judgt 10 Apr. 1987, SEW 1988, 486 (with note by Mortelmans).

[93] *Produktschap Groenten en Fruit* 1971 on canned vegetables providing for a quality check on canned mushrooms.

[94] n. 61 above. [95] Reg. 804/68: [1968] OJ L148.

[96] Case 29/82, n. 81 above.

omissions in the judgments of the *CBB*.[97] He is correct to point out that such omissions are even more objectionable when one considers that the *CBB* is a court against whose decisions there is no appeal within the Dutch legal system. Nevertheless, despite these isolated examples of the Dutch *CBB* judgments, the overall picture is that the national courts have had few problems in identifying a common organization of the market, and thus whether the broad interpretation of Article 34 applies.

6 CONCLUSIONS

The interpretation given by the ECJ of Article 34 is rather eccentric. We have seen how the ECJ has diverged in its interpretation of Articles 30 and 34 respectively. The doctrinal underpinnings of such a divergence of interpretation of identically worded Treaty Articles remains unexplained. Furthermore, the divergence of interpretation is not applied consistently. In cases where there are common organizations of the market, for example, the restrictive interpretation is abandoned. The interpretation of Article 34 by the ECJ, which requires discrimination before that Article will be applicable, finds itself on very thin theoretical ice when faced with the application of the rule of reason and the environmental protection justification in particular. Faced with this doctrinally difficult and at times illogical ECJ case law interpreting Article 34, the national courts could almost be forgiven for expressing confusion. The national court experience in applying Article 34 has ranged from failing to recognize the Article 34 point at all to not applying the *Groenveld* formula since its application is 'decidedly unclear'.[98]

Ultimately, comparatively few Article 34 cases have arisen before the national courts. The majority of the cases that have come before national courts have not turned on the Article 34 point and could be decided on other grounds. The ECJ has thus not yet been forced to confront some of the doctrinal difficulties which underlie its case law. The discussion in this chapter of the difficulties which have lurked in the national case law to date suggests that the ECJ will sooner or later be called upon to explain and re-examine its approach to Article 34 and exports.

[97] See annotations by Mortelmans of these judgments in SEW 1988, 486 & SEW 1989, 791.
[98] *R. v. Minister of Agriculture, Fisheries and Food, ex p. Roberts*, n. 39 above.

5

Reverse discrimination and purely national measures

1 INTRODUCTION

It has been shown how the ECJ has interpreted Article 34 to conclude that only discriminatory national provisions are prohibited by that Article.[1] Thus, national measures which apply to all goods, irrespective of their destination, do not breach Article 34 even if they impede the ability of national goods to penetrate the markets of other Member States. The logical corollary of this approach is that it should not be possible for Article 30 to be invoked to challenge discrimination by a Member State against its own nationals (so-called 'reverse discrimination'). Thus, while a non-discriminatory national restriction on sale may be challenged by an importer (for example, because it has the effect of reducing the volume of imports in breach of Article 30 and cannot be justified under either the 'rule of reason' or Article 36) the same should not be the case for a national producer and potential exporter since, if it would be possible for the national producer to invoke Article 30 in such circumstances, the ECJ's interpretation of Article 34 would be rendered nugatory. The ECJ has been alive to this potential conflict and has maintained the coherence of its case law by holding that neither the provisions concerning the free movement of goods[2] nor the other EC Treaty freedoms[3] prohibit reverse

[1] See Ch. 4.
[2] See, e.g., Case 286/81 *Oosthoek's Uitgeversmaatschappij* [1982] ECR 4575, [1983] 3 CMLR 428; Case 314–316/81 & 83/82 *Ministère public and CNDCA* v. *Alex Waterkeyn* [1982] ECR 4337; Case 229/83 *Leclerc* v. *Au Blé Vert* [1985] ECR 1, [1985] 2 CMLR 286; Cases 80 & 159/85 *Nederlandse Bakkerij* v. *Edah* [1986] ECR 3359, [1988] 2 CMLR 113 at para. 23; Case 355/85 *Draincourt* v. *Cognet* [1986] ECR 3231, [1987] 2 CMLR 942; Case 98/86 *Ministère Public* v. *Mathot* [1987] ECR 809; Case 160/86 *Ministère public* v. *Verbrugge* [1987] ECR 1783, [1989] 2 CMLR 51; Case 168/86 *Rousseau* [1987] ECR 995.
[3] With respect to the free movement of workers (Art. 48): Case 175/78 *R.* v. *Saunders* [1979] ECR 1129; Cases 35 & 36/82 *Morson and Jhanjan* v. *Netherlands* [1982] ECR 3723, [1983] 2 CMLR 221; Case 180/83 *Moser* v. *Land Baden-Wurttemburg* [1984] ECR 2539, [1984] 3 CMLR 720; Cases C–54 & 91/88 and C–14/89 *Niño* [1990] ECR I–3537, [1992] 1 CMLR 83; Cases C–330–331/90 *López Brea and Hidalgo Palacios* [1992] ECR I–323 at para. 7; Case C–332/90 *Steen* v. *Deutsche Bundespost* [1992] ECR I–341 at para. 9; Case C–133/93 *Steen* v. *Deutsche Bundespost* [1994] ECR I–2715; Case C–299/95 *Kremzow* v. *Austria* [1997] ECR I–2629 at para. 16 & Cases C–64–65/96 *Land Nordrhein-Westfalen* v. *Uecker* [1997] ECR I–3171 at para. 16. With respect to the freedom to provide services (Art. 59): Case 52/79 *Procureur du Roi* v. *Debauve* [1980] ECR 833 at para. 9; Case C–41/90 *Höfner and Elser* v. *Macrotron* [1991] ECR I–1979 at para. 37; Case C–60/91 *Batista Morais* v. *Ministerio Public* [1992] ECR I–2085; Case C–70/95

discrimination. In such cases therefore, an importer is treated more favourably under EC law than the domestic producer (and potential exporter).

It is submitted that the refusal by the ECJ to prohibit purely national measures and reverse discrimination is far from satisfactory. It is true that such an approach is necessary in order to maintain the logic of the current interpretation of Article 34. Additionally, it is also true that the ECJ's refusal to prohibit reverse discrimination is explicable on the basis that purely national measures, applying only to domestic goods put on the national market, are not concerned with either imports or exports and therefore not concerned with either Article 30 or Article 34.[4] Nevertheless, the ECJ's refusal to prohibit purely national measures and reverse discrimination accepts an inequality which is anathema to a genuine internal market. This point has recently been recognized by the ECJ itself when it held in the context of charges having equivalent effect to customs duties (Article 9 EC *et seq*.) that

Since the very principle of a customs union covers all trade in goods, as provided by Article 9 of the Treaty, it requires the free movement of goods generally, as opposed to inter-State trade alone, to be ensured within the union.[5]

There are indeed indications that the issue of reverse discrimination is, incrementally, being reconsidered by the ECJ.[6] In an important recent

Sodemare SA and others v. *Regione Lombardia* [1997] ECR I–3395 at para. 38. With respect to the freedom of establishment (Art. 52): Case 44/84 *Hurd* v. *Jones* [1986] ECR 29; Case 20/87 *Ministère Public* v. *Gauchard* [1987] ECR 4879, [1989] 2 CMLR 489; Cases C–29–35/94 *Aubertin and others* [1995] ECR I–301 at para. 9. With respect to discriminatory internal taxation (Art. 95): Case 86/78 *Peureux* v. *Directeur des Services Fiscaux* [1979] ECR 897.

[4] Oliver, *Free Movement of Goods in the European Community*, 124. It may also be noted that, in practical terms, it is unlikely that Member States will wish to maintain national provisions which put national producers at a competitive disadvantage. However, a conceivable exception might arise when a Member State perceives that there is advantage to be gained from the maintenance of certain national provisions for national producers even though they cannot be applied to imports. See, e.g., German Government's decision after the ECJ's judgment in Case 178/84 *Commission* v. *Germany* [1987] ECR 1217, [1988] 1 CMLR 813 to maintain the application of the laws on beer purity (*Reinheitsgebot*) to German beer producers even though they could no longer be applied to beer imported from other Member States.

[5] Case C–363/93 *Lancry* v. *Direction Générale des Douanes* [1994] ECR I–3957 at para. 29. See also confirmation of this judgment in Case C–485–486/93 *Maria Simitzi* v. *Dimos Kos* [1995] ECR I–2655 & Case C–45/94 *Cámara de Comercio, Industria y Navegación de Ceuta* v. *Ayuntamiento de Ceuta* [1995] ECR I–4385. However, in the field of the free movement of workers, the ECJ has recently held that 'citizenship of the Union, established by Art. 8 of the EC Treaty, is not intended to extend the scope *ratione materiae* of the Treaty also to internal situations which have no link with Community law': Cases C–64–65/96 *Land Nordrhein-Westfalen* v. *Uecker*, n. 3 above at para. 23.

[6] With respect to the free movement of workers, see Case C–415/93 *Union Royale Belge des Sociétés de Football Association ASBL* v. *Bosman* [1995] ECR I–4921 which concerned a restriction on the exercise of the right to move to work in another Member State. See also Case C–370/90 *R.* v. *IAT and Surinder Singh, ex p. Secretary of State for the Home Department* [1992] ECR I–4265. With respect to the freedom to provide services, see Case C–384/93 *Alpine*

judgment (*Pistre*), the Fifth Chamber of the ECJ seems to have softened the refusal to prohibit reverse discrimination by holding, in a case concerning facts which were confined to the territory of one Member State (*in casu* France), that

whilst the application of a national measure having no actual link to the importa- tion of goods does not fall within the ambit of Article 30 of the Treaty (judgment in Case 286/81 *Oosthoek's Uitgeversmaatschappij* [1982] ECR 4575, paragraph 9), Article 30 cannot be considered inapplicable simply because all the facts of a spe- cific case before the national court are confined to a single Member State.[7]

It is unclear as to exactly how this recent judgment will affect previous ECJ case law. The rationale of the *Pistre* judgment appears to be that national measures which facilitate the marketing of domestic goods to the detri- ment of imported goods are capable of having effects on the free move- ment of goods between Member States contrary to Article 30 and thus that both importers and domestic producers should be permitted to challenge such measures.[8] What is unclear is whether Article 30 would equally be held to apply to a case whose facts are confined to a single Member State where the national measure at issue makes no distinction between imports and exports or even facilitates the marketing of imports to the detriment of domestic goods. If Article 30 could be invoked in the latter case, the ECJ's approach to reverse discrimination, and by implication its interpre- tation of Article 34 EC, would be fundamentally shifted. If, on the other hand, the implication of the *Pistre* judgment is that it will only be possible

Investments v. *Minister van Financiën* [1995] ECR I–1141, which concerned a restriction on the provision of services in another Member State. See discussion of this point by Weatherill, 'After *Keck*: Some Thoughts on How to Clarify the Clarification' at 901. With respect to Art. 177 jurisdiction and 'internal situations', see Case C–28/95 *Leur-Bloem* v. *Inspecteur der Belastingdienst* [1997] ECR I–4161. It should, however, be noted that the ECJ has recently reaf- firmed that Arts. 48, 52 & 59 do not apply to a situation 'which is confined in all respects within a single Member State': Case C–134/95 *USSL* v. *INAIL* [1997] ECR I–195 at paras. 19–23.

[7] Cases C–321–324/94 *Pistre, Barthes, Milhau and Oberti* [1997] ECR I–2343, [1997] 2 CMLR 565 at para. 44.

[8] Ibid. at para. 45. The facts of *Pistre* concerned French legislation governing the use of the description 'mountain' in relation to agricultural products and foodstuffs. The legislation in question discriminated against imports since it reserved use of the description 'mountain' to products manufactured on national territory. Thus, the legislation in question was prima facie discriminatory against imports. However, there was no discrimination on the actual facts of the case since the prosecutions for breach of the French legislation were against French nationals, concerning French products which had been marketed on French territory. Thus, while it is formally true that the French legislation facilitated the marketing of domes- tic goods by allowing such goods the possibility (if the conditions in the legislation were met) of using the description 'mountain', it is also true that by allowing the national producer the possibility to invoke Art. 30 in such circumstances, one is in effect according a national pro- ducer the same right to challenge the French legislation as an importer. As a result, chal- lenges to national measures by a domestic producer which have hitherto been precluded by the ECJ's interpretation of Art. 34 EC might now be successful under Art. 30.

to invoke Article 30 to a factual circumstance where there is no actual link with importation if it can be shown that the national measure at issue facilitates the marketing of domestic goods to the detriment of imported goods, the impact of *Pistre* on current case law will be more limited in scope. Nevertheless, the *Pistre* judgment is of great significance in that the ECJ explicitly accepted, for the first time, that Article 30 could be invoked in a case involving facts which were confined to a single Member State.[9] This is to be welcomed as a positive step towards achieving a genuine internal market.

Even before the *Pistre* judgment, however, the ECJ had occasionally overlooked the reality that the facts of individual cases were confined, in all respects, within a single Member State. For example, in *SA Smanor*[10] the French Government had argued before the ECJ that the facts of that case involved a purely national situation since it concerned the application of a French law to a French company manufacturing and marketing deep-frozen yoghurt on French territory. In its judgment, the ECJ simply noted that deep-frozen yoghurts were lawfully marketed in other Member States and that it could not be ruled out that such products could be imported into France and that in any event 'it is for the national courts, within the system established by Article 177 of the Treaty, to weigh the relevance of the questions which they refer to the Court, in the light of the facts of the cases before them'.[11] The ECJ thus went on to rule on the compatibility of the French legislation with the provisions concerning the free movement of goods.[12]

The national courts have also occasionally overlooked the reality that the facts of cases before them have been confined in all respects within a single Member State.[13] However, these courts have also often applied the ECJ's case law in this field to conclude *inter alia* that purely national measures fall outside the scope of Article 30. For example, in *Daniel Jambon et*

---

[9] After the *Pistre* judgment, it is questionable whether the ECJ judgments in, for example, Cases 314–316/81 & 83/82 *Waterkeyn*, n. 2 above & Case 355/85 *Draincourt*, n. 2 above still represent good law.

[10] Case 298/87 [1988] ECR 4489.

[11] Ibid. at para. 9. It may also be noted that there was also no indication in the infamous judgment in Cases C–267–268/91 *Keck and Mithouard* [1993] ECR I–6097, [1995] 1 CMLR 101 that the actual products involved were on the facts imported from other Member States. See Gormley, (1996) 19 Fordham Int. LJ 866 at 867 and (1994) EBLR 63 at 66. See further discussion of the *Keck* judgment in Ch. 3.

[12] For a discussion of the application of the *Smanor* case before the French courts, see Ch. 2, sect. 5 (B) (*iv*).

[13] See, e.g., *R. v. Secretary of State for Health ex. p. United States Tobacco International Inc* [1992] 1 All ER 212, [1992] 1 QB 353 (QBD); *British Leyland Motor Corporation v. T. I. Silencers* [1980] 1 CMLR 598 (ChD); [1980] 2 CMLR 332 (ChD); [1981] 2 CMLR 75 (CA); *Löwenbräu München v. Grunhalle Lager International Ltd* [1974] 1 CMLR 1 (ChD); *Conté Nederland BV v. Minister van VROM*, Pres. Raad van State (*Afd. Bestuursrechtspraak*), 19 Oct. 1994, SEW 1995, 444.

Société France Quick[14] the French *Cour de Cassation* held that the goods at issue on the facts of that case (food and drink sold in a fast-food restaurant) were produced and consumed in France and that there was therefore no barrier to intra-Community trade contrary to Article 30.[15] It is interesting to note that in *Nederlandse Bakkerij Stichting* v. *Edah BV* the President of the *Arrondissementsrechtbank* Almelo[16] implemented the ECJ's judgment in that case concerning the compatibility of Dutch legislation on the minimum price for bread by holding that there was no breach of Article 30 'because it cannot be seen why the entire regulation should not be binding now that the present facts concern . . . breaches by national bread and not foreign bread'. If only the national court had made this factual finding *before* it referred the questions to the ECJ, the ECJ would have been spared the need to deliver what was a complex judgment.[17]

ECJ case law concerning reverse discrimination has caused a certain amount of confusion before the national courts in general, and the French courts in particular. Three groups of cases before these courts may be identified: cases concerning French legislation restricting the advertising of alcoholic beverages, cases concerning French legislation on resale price maintenance for books and national legislation governing the disposal of waste. Each of these groups of cases will be examined in turn.

---

[14] *Association générale des usagers de la langue français (AGULF) et Ministère public* v. *Daniel Jambon et Sociéte France Quick, Cour de Cassation*, ch. crim., 25 Apr. 1989, Bull. Cass. Crim. 1989, no. 167 p. 431. This case, which concerned French legislation on the use of the French language, is discussed further in Ch. 2, sect. 5 (B) (*iii*).

[15] Before the French courts see also *Falck, Cour de Cassation*, ch. crim., 25 Oct. 1993, Bull. Cass. Crim. 1993, no. 309 p. 776; *Sté Les Films du Diamant* v. *Fédération nationale des cinémas français (FNCF), Cour d'appel*, 1re ch. A, 19 June 1985, noted by Hassler, Dalloz 1986, IR p. 243–244; *Bouyer, Cour de Cassation*, ch. crim. R, 2 Feb. 1994, Bull. Cass. Crim. 1994, no. 48 p. 95; JCP 1994, IV 137; *Société Yves Saint Laurent Parfums* v. *Institute Nationale des Appelations d'origine, Cour d'appel* Paris, 15 Dec. 1993, [1994] ECC 385; Dalloz 1994, Jur. 145; JCP 1994, II 22229; Gaz. Pal. 1994, Jur. 55. Before the Dutch courts, see e.g. *Eco fles, RCC*, 3 Nov. 1993, RCC 1994, 60 and *Chanel SA* v. *Maxis BV, Gerechtshof* Amsterdam, 28 Feb. 1991, BIE 1992, 36.

[16] Pres. *Arrondissementsrechtbank* Almelo, 11 Mar. 1987; transcr.

[17] Cases 80 & 159/85 [1986] ECR 3359. See other judgments before the Dutch courts concerning this legislation on the minimum price for bread in *Openbaar Ministerie* v. *Supermarket N. N. te Enschede, Economische Politierechter* Almelo, 6 Sept. 1977, SEW 1978, 157 (with note by Mok); *Dirk van den Broek Supermarkten BV* v. *Openbaar Ministerie, Gerechtshof* Amsterdam, 27 Apr. 1978, NJ 1979, 281 (noted by Tromm (1981) 6 ELRev. 312 at 315) and *Dirk van den Broek Supermarkten BV* v. *Leendert Arie Vente*, Pres. *Arrondissementsrechtbank* Amsterdam, 2 June 1977 & 4 Jan. 1978, NJ 1980, 401 and discussion of these cases in Ch. 2, sect. 5 (B) (*vii*).

2 FRENCH LEGISLATION RESTRICTING THE ADVERTISING OF ALCOHOLIC BEVERAGES

In *Commission* v. *France*[18] the ECJ held that certain French legislation[19] infringed Article 30 EC by subjecting advertising in respect of alcoholic beverages to discriminatory rules. In particular, the ECJ held that whilst distilled spirits typical of national produce (such as rums and spirits obtained from distillation of wines, ciders, or fruits) enjoyed completely unrestricted advertising, similar products which were mainly imported (notably grain spirits such as whisky and *Jenever*) could not be advertised at all.[20] The ECJ proceeded to hold that the legislation in question could not be justified under Article 36 EC. The terms of this ECJ judgment were thus simple enough. However, the application of this judgment by the French courts gave rise to confusion.

On the one hand, some courts decided that the effect of the ECJ judgment was that the French provisions were inapplicable only as against imported products, but that they were fully applicable as against French products which had been neither imported nor exported. An example of such a decision is that of the *Cour d'appel* of Paris in *Rossi di Montalera*[21] which held that 'The provisions of the Treaty of Rome only have the aim of ensuring equality of treatment between competing products from other Member States. Community law cannot therefore substitute national law to decide a situation that only calls upon the latter.' The Paris *Cour d'appel* proceeded to point out that the ECJ had 'expressly' limited its judgment in *Commission* v. *France* to apply to the 'importation of products from other Member States' and thus that 'the condemnation pronounced by this High Jurisdiction does not prevent the application of the French Code on the Retail sale of Alcoholic Drinks when the consequences apply exclusively to a French product, produced and sold on national territory'. The *Cour d'appel* held that since the products at issue in the case before it were produced in France and had never been exported, the French legislation continued to apply to them and that their advertising was rightfully restricted. In short, the *Cour d'appel* held that the case concerned a purely national situation and that the ECJ's judgment interpreting Article 30 did not therefore apply.

Other French courts, on the other hand, drew other consequences from the ECJ's judgment in *Commission* v. *France*.[22] These courts held that the

[18] Case 152/78 [1980] ECR 2299, [1981] 2 CMLR 743.
[19] Arts. L. 17 and L. 18 of the *Code des Débits de Boissons et des Mesures contre l'Alcoolisme* (Code on the retail sale of beverages and on measures against alcoholism).
[20] Case 152/78, n. 18 above at para. 13 of ECJ judgt.
[21] *Ministère public et CNDCA* v. *Théo Rossi di Montalera, Cour d'appel* Paris, 13e ch. corr. B, 26 Mar. 1981, Gaz. Pal. 1981, I Jur. 681 (noted by Bouzat, RTDComm. 1983, 136).
[22] Case 152/78, n. 18 above.

effect of the ECJ's judgment in that case was that the French legislation on the advertising of alcoholic beverages was contrary to Article 30 in its entirety and thus that it was unenforceable even against alcoholic beverages produced in France. The underlying reasoning in this line of cases was based upon the supremacy of Community law as accepted by Article 55 of the French Constitution. Thus, for example, the *Cour d'appel* of Versailles in *Rossi di Montalera*[23] held that

France agreed to a limitation of its sovereignty and the institution of Community law directly applicable in each Member State. As a result, the body of the Community's own law is integrated into the legal systems of the Member States and takes a position at the top of the hierarchy of sources of law in each of them. The national judge is bound to recognize the primacy of Community law and is competent to ensure that it is respected in the face of any conflicting national law, without the need to distinguish between laws which come into effect before or after the entry into force of the Treaty of Rome.[24]

The *Cour d'appel* of Versailles continued:

[E]ven though the Court of Justice of the European Communities gave as the grounds of its judgment of 10 July 1980 the need to eliminate French rules which result in a restriction of imports into France of alcoholic drinks produced in other countries of the EEC, that does not prejudice the overall effect of the condemnation, which can therefore be relied on by any individual brought before a French criminal judge on the basis of sections L.17 and L.21 of the Code on the retail sale of beverages, *even if the advertising in question relates to a beverage manufactured in France.*[25]

Similarly, the *Tribunal de grande instance* of Evry held in *Gerard Seul* that '[t]here is no point in examining whether the advertising considered to be illegal was carried out for imported or non-imported drinks from a Member State of the EEC, since the [ECJ] plainly considered and judged that it was the French regulation itself, and specifically Article L. 17 serving as the base for the present action, which was contrary to the EEC Treaty'.[26] It appears, therefore, that the central reason adduced by these courts for applying the ECJ's judgment in *Commission* v. *France*[27] to a purely internal situation was the supremacy of Community law. A further reason was, however, offered by the *Cour d'appel* of Grenoble in *Bernard*

---

[23] *Ministère public* v. *Théo Rossi di Montalera, Cour d'appel* Versailles, 7e ch., 27 Apr. 1981, [1984] 1 CMLR 489, RTDE 1981, 305 (noted by Jeantet (1983) CDE 304).

[24] [1984] 1 CMLR 489 at 504.   [25] Ibid. Emphasis added.

[26] *Gerard Seul* v. *CNDCA, TGI* Evry, 23 Feb. 1981, Gaz. Pal. 1981, I Jur. 315. See also *Ministère public* v. *Bernard Cuel, Henri Rioult de Neuville et Michel Geerons, Cour d'appel* Rouen, ch. corr., 10 July 1979, Gaz. Pal. 1980, II Som. 271 (summary) and *Cour d'appel* Rouen, ch. corr., 2 Apr. 1981, cited in Gaz. Pal. 1981, I Jur. 685.

[27] n. 18 above.

Cambournac,[28] where it also held that the French legislation was, following the ECJ's judgment, inapplicable even against French nationals selling and advertising alcoholic drinks manufactured in France, since

[I]t would be artificial to maintain that in the absence of trade between Member States, Community law cannot override national law, with the latter remaining applicable to nationals of a Member State on its territory. Indeed, Article 3(f) of the Treaty provides: 'the Community shall have as its task . . . the institution of a system ensuring that competition in the common market is not distorted'. In prohibiting or restricting the advertisement of certain drinks, Article L. 17 interferes with the freedom of competition. The free movement of nationals of Member States is very important to the Community, notably on French territory which attracts 10 per cent of world tourism. A company which is an exporter finds itself, through enforcement of provisions prohibiting or restraining advertisements, in an unfavourable competitive position in the foreign market.

Although the reasoning in this passage is not entirely clear, it seems that the *Cour d'appel* of Grenoble felt that reverse discrimination should be prohibited and that the ECJ's judgment should apply to a purely internal situation on the grounds that competition in the common market would otherwise be distorted.[29] Clearly, the Court was persuaded that to allow reverse discrimination would be contrary to the principle of undistorted competition in a common market. In the meantime, the *Tribunal de grande instance* of Paris took a different line and referred questions to the ECJ pursuant to Article 177 asking for clarification of the effect of the ECJ's judgment in *Commission* v. *France*.[30] The ECJ answered these questions in its judgment in *Waterkeyn* in a most unhelpful manner.[31] The ECJ read the French Court's question literally and held that its earlier judgment in *Commission* v. *France* was limited to holding that the French legislation was contrary to Article 30 only insofar as it applied to imports, and that

The only inference which must be drawn from the judgment to which the preliminary question refers is therefore that, as far as advertising is concerned, the French Republic must treat alcoholic products originating in other Member States in the same way as competing national products.[32]

The ECJ thus answered the national court's question at face value by explaining the scope of its previous ruling, but was silent as to whether Community law more generally also prohibited the application of the French regulations to national products; in other words, whether

---

[28] *Bernard Cambournac* v. *Union départementale des associations familiales des Alpes-de-Haute-Provence et CNDCA, Cour d'appel* Grenoble, ch. corr., 24 Apr. 1981, Gaz. Pal. 1981, I Jur. 684; RTD Comm. 1982, 136 (with note by Bouzat); Dalloz 1983, IR 228.

[29] Art. 3(f) EEC to which the *Cour d'Appel* of Grenoble makes reference is now renumbered as Art. 3(g) EC.

[30] Case 152/78, n. 18 above.   [31] Cases 314–316/81 & 83/82 n. 2 above.

[32] Ibid. at para. 12.

Community law prohibited reverse discrimination. Although Oliver has argued that it is clear from the wording of the judgment in *Waterkeyn* that the ECJ was not merely explaining the terms of its earlier judgment but was holding that Article 30 did not prohibit reverse discrimination,[33] the subsequent application of this judgment by the French courts illustrates that this was not clear to the national courts and that the answer provided by the ECJ was *'évidente mais incomplète à l'attente des juridictions nationales'*.[34]

Given the failure of the ECJ in *Waterkeyn* to elaborate explicitly on its position with respect to reverse discrimination, the French *Cour de Cassation* took the matter into its own hands and held that the French legislation could no longer be applied to nationally-produced goods and, in effect, that Community law prohibited reverse discrimination. In *Bernard Cambournac* and *Rossi di Montalera* the *Cour de Cassation* held that

according to Article 30 of the EEC Treaty, all measures having equivalent effect to quantitative restrictions on imports are prohibited between Member States. In addition, Article 7 of the Treaty prohibits discrimination on grounds of nationality. Finally, it may be inferred from Article 3(f) that these rules must be implemented in such a way that trade throughout the whole territory of the Community in products originating from Member States is not distorted as a result, *even if the products are of national origin*.[35]

The *Cour de Cassation* thus effectively held that reverse discrimination was prohibited by Community law. Importantly, it is clear from the above passage that the *Cour de Cassation* reached this conclusion by interpreting Community law; *in casu* the combined effect of Article 30, Article 7 EEC (now Article 6 EC), and Article 3(f) (now Article 3(g) EC). The *Cour de Cassation* in *Bernard Cambournac* remitted the case to the *Cour d'appel* of Lyon which acquitted the defendant on the facts of the case since it held that if the restriction on advertising of Pastis 51 was applied in that case, it would result in a 'not only discriminatory but also shocking' restriction on trade, as foreign products such as gin and whisky (which it ruled had comparable characteristics) could be advertised freely.[36] Indeed, the *Cour d'appel* of Lyon explicitly mentioned in its judgment that since the ECJ's judgment in *Commission* v. *France*,[37] French newspapers had been replete

---

[33] n. 4 above, 125.   [34] Isaac, RTDE 1983, 470 at 480.

[35] Emphasis added. *Bernard Cambournac* v. *Union départementale des associations familiales des Alpes-de-Haute-Provence et CNDCA, Cour de Cassation*, ch. crim., 16 June 1983, [1984] 2 CMLR 556; JCP 1983, II 20044 (with note by Decocq); La Semaine Juridique—éd. entreprise 1983, II 14118; Dalloz Jur. 1984, 43 (with note by Ryziger) and *Ministère public* v. *Théo Rossi di Montalera, Cour de Cassation*, ch. crim., 16 June 1983, RTDE 1983, 468 (with note by Isaac). Noted by Jeantet (1983) CDE 521.

[36] *Bernard Cambournac* v. *Union départementale des associations familiales des Alpes-de-Haute-Provence et CNDCA, Cour d'appel* Lyon, 4e ch. corr., 22 June 1984, Gaz. Pal. 1984, I Jur. 665.

[37] n. 18 above.

with whisky, gin and vodka advertisements while advertisements of Pastis produced in France were prohibited. It may be noted that the *Cour d'appel* of Lyon also based its conclusion that reverse discrimination was prohibited by referring to the provisions of Community law itself. For example, the *Cour d'appel* of Lyon held that the discrimination which would arise if the advertising of Pastis was restricted was particularly 'shocking' because it would be contrary to the aims of the Community as set out in Article 2 of the EEC Treaty.[38] In other words, the assumption was that if reverse discrimination was to be permitted, this would be contrary to the very essence of the common market. In much the same way, the ECJ's judgment in *Waterkeyn* was subsequently implemented by the *Cour d'appel* of Paris which gave judgment in *Waterkeyn* after the *Cour de Cassation*'s judgments in *Bernard Cambournac* and *Rossi di Montalera*.[39] The *Cour d'appel* of Paris followed the interpretation of the *Cour de Cassation* and held that since imports of Italian beverages at issue in that case could advertise freely, similar French products must also enjoy such freedom in order to avoid causing a distortion in competition contrary to the objectives of the EC Treaty. The *Cour d'appel* of Paris also added that such a difference in treatment would be contrary to the principle of the equality of all in front of the criminal law. In other words, both French and Community law were invoked to conclude that reverse discrimination was prohibited.

The conclusion by the French courts in these cases, that reverse discrimination was prohibited, has been widely criticized by commentators.[40] At the most basic level, it was most surprising that the *Cour de Cassation* in its judgments in *Bernard Cambournac* and *Rossi di Montalera* did not even mention or refer to the ECJ's judgment in *Waterkeyn* which the ECJ had handed down only six months earlier. More significant is the conclusion reached by these courts that reverse discrimination was prohibited by Community law. It is true that it was only after these judgments that clear ECJ authority emerged unequivocally holding that Community law does not prohibit reverse discrimination in cases involving Article 30.[41] However, this only serves to underline the fact that the issue was not *acte*

---

[38] The *Cour d'appel* Lyon had recourse to the wording in Art. 2 EC which provided that 'The Community shall have as its task, by establishing a common market and progressively approximating the economic policies of Member States to promote throughout the Community a harmonious development of economic activities, a continuous and balanced expansion, an increase in stability, an accelerated raising of the standards of living and closer relations between the States belonging to it'. It may be noted that this Article has now been amended by Art. G(3) EU.

[39] *Cour d'appel* Paris, 13e ch. corr., 20 Nov. 1984, Dalloz 1985, IR 276.

[40] See the commentaries cited in n. 35 above. An exception is a note by Ryziger, Dalloz 1984, Jur. 44 who describes the *Cour de Cassation*'s judgments in *Bernard Cambournac* and *Rossi di Montalera* as 'ingenious' decisions 'in complete conformity with Community law'.

[41] See ECJ judgts cited at n. 2 above.

clair and that the omission of the *Cour de Cassation* to even consider making a reference to the ECJ pursuant to Article 177 constituted a 'flagrant'[42] breach of Article 177(3) EC. In fact, what ECJ case law there was at that time suggested that Community law did not prohibit reverse discrimination.[43] A clear indication had been given by the ECJ in *Peureux*[44] where, in the context of discriminatory internal taxation under Article 95 EC, it had held that

Although Article 95 prohibits any Member State from imposing internal taxation on products imported from other Member States in excess of that on national products, it does not prohibit the imposition on national products of internal taxation in excess of that on imported products. Disparities of this kind do not come within the scope of Article 95.[45]

In fact, the *Cour de Cassation* had itself reached this very same conclusion in a judgment on exactly the same facts before the ECJ had handed down its judgment in *Peureux*. In *Claude Peureux et Direction générale des impôts*, the *Cour de Cassation* had refused to stay proceedings until the ECJ had given judgment in *Peureux* and held that Community law was not applicable since the facts before it did not concern trade between Member States.[46] Additionally, the *Conseil d'Etat* had also taken the same line with respect to Article 7 EEC (now Article 6 EC) by holding that

[I]t is obvious that this provision has got no other aim but to eliminate discrimination against nationals of other Member States and that would in no circumstances limit the powers with which the national authorities are invested with respect to their own nationals.[47]

In the light of these ECJ and French court judgments holding, albeit with respect to other Articles of the EC Treaty, that Community law does not prohibit reverse discrimination, it is all the more surprising that the *Cour de Cassation* in *Bernard Cambournac* and *Rossi di Montalera* concluded that reverse discrimination was prohibited without seeking a reference from

---

[42] Isaac, n. 34 above at 482. In fact, Isaac notes that the *Cour de Cassation* did not even precede its analysis with the words 'It is clear that . . .' (*'Il résulte clairement . . .'*) to indicate that it thought the question was *acte clair*, if indeed that is what it was doing.

[43] In the context of the free movement of goods the ECJ had already held in Case 286/81 *Oosthoek*, n. 2 above that 'the application of the Netherlands legislation to the sale in the Netherlands of encyclopedias produced in that country is in no way linked to the importation or exportation of goods and does not therefore fall within the scope of Articles 30 and 34 of the EEC Treaty' at para. 9. In the context of the free movement of workers, the ECJ's refusal to prohibit reverse discrimination was already rather well developed; see ECJ judgts in Case 175/78 *R. v. Saunders* and Cases 35 & 36/82 *Morson and Jhanjan v. Netherlands* n. 3 above.

[44] Case 86/78 *Peureux v. Directeur des Services Fiscaux* [1979] ECR 897.

[45] Ibid. at paras. 32–33.

[46] *Claude Peureux et Direction générale des impôts*, Cour de Cassation, ch. crim., 20 Oct. 1977, Gaz. Pal. 1978, I Jur. 223; RTDE 1978, 319 (with note by Didier); Bull. Cass. Crim. 1977, 805.

[47] *Syndicat national des spiritueux consommés à l'eau*, Conseil d'Etat, Assemblée, 27 July 1979, Rec. Lebon 1979, 335; AJDA 1979, 36. Noted by Drago, RDP 1980, 214.

the ECJ pursuant to Article 177. Had the *Cour de Cassation* reached this conclusion on the basis of French law alone, the matter would be unobjectionable.[48] However, the passages extracted from the judgments set out above clearly show that the conclusion that reverse discrimination was prohibited was based explicitly on the combined effect of Articles 30, 7, and 3(f) EEC, and thus on Community rather than French law.

The importance of this series of cases before the French courts should not be underestimated and is noted by Isaac who states that '[i]ts practical importance is really quite considerable as . . . it included the destabilization of the entirety of a very sophisticated Act, which since 1979 at least has not been applied'.[49] Criticism of those French courts which held, on the basis of Community law that reverse discrimination was prohibited, is well-founded. The matter was certainly not *acte clair* and subsequent ECJ case law makes perfectly clear that the conclusion that reverse discrimination is prohibited under Community law is, according to the ECJ at least, incorrect. However, it must be stated that the ECJ had itself been most unhelpful in its judgment in *Waterkeyn* where it answered the question referred to it literally rather than providing the national court with a definitive answer to the question of reverse discrimination and Article 30 which the national court clearly required. Furthermore, the reasoning adopted by the French courts is not, from the perspective of Community law, wholly untenable. On the contrary, it has been argued that the refusal of the ECJ to prohibit reverse discrimination is far from satisfactory.[50] Indeed, as has already been stated, the ECJ's approach to reverse discrimination accepts an inequality which is illogical in a genuine internal market and after the recent judgment of the ECJ in *Pistre*,[51] it is unclear whether the ECJ would maintain this line. In the final analysis, however, it is the ECJ's interpretation at the time which is, of course, decisive and the views of the French courts in these cases, although illuminating, were clearly incorrect. A further reference to the ECJ under Article 177 was undoubtedly indispensable.

---

[48]   e.g., Jeantet, n. 23 above at 317 approves of the *Cour de Cassation*'s judgment had it been based on the principle under French law that 'the law must be the same for all' (*la loi doit être la même pour tous*). See also Decocq, n. 35 above, who rather unconvincingly re-rationalizes the *Cour de Cassation*'s reasoning to conclude that the *Cour de Cassation* must have intended to base its reasoning on French law alone. Note also the judgment of the *Cour d'appel* Paris, 20 Nov. 1984, n. 39 above, which had added that to allow reverse discrimination would be contrary, not only to Community law, but also to the principle under French law of the equality of all in front of the criminal law.

[49]   n. 34 above at 470.   [50]   See discussion at p. 154.   [51]   n. 7 above.

3 FRENCH LEGISLATION CONCERNING RESALE PRICE MAINTENANCE FOR BOOKS

The question of reverse discrimination has also arisen in a series of cases before the French courts concerning resale price maintenance for books for which a judgment of the ECJ is again the starting point.[52] In *Leclerc* v. *Au Blé Vert*[53] the ECJ interpreted Article 30 in the context of French legislation (the Book Prices Act 1981: generally referred to as the *'loi Lang'*), which required retailers to sell books at the price set by their publishers allowing for a maximum discount of no more than 5 per cent of that price. However, while books which had been published in France had their price fixed by the French publisher, imported books were subject to the price set by the main importer of the book. The ECJ held that insofar as the French legislation created for imported books regulations which were separate from those applicable to books published in France, such legislation infringed Article 30 and was not justified under Article 36.

Of particular interest in the context of the present discussion is that the ECJ held in *Leclerc* v. *Au Blé Vert* that the system applicable to books published in France infringed Article 30 in that it 'treats unfavourably the sale on the market of re-imported books to the extent that it deprives the importer of such a book of the opportunity to pass on in the retail price any benefit deriving from a more favourable price obtained in the Member State of exportation'.[54] However, the ECJ went on to add that 'this conclusion does not apply to cases where the objective facts show that the books in question have been exported solely for the purposes of re-importation in an attempt to circumvent legislation of the kind in the present case'.[55] Thus, the implicit message in this judgment is that the *loi Lang* was of continued application to books published in France which had never left French territory. It is only in so far as the *loi Lang* applied to books published in France which had first been exported to another Member State

---

[52] For a discussion of these cases before the French courts, see Grelon, 'La *"loi Lang"* sur le prix du livre et la discrimination à rebours'; Le Tallec, 'Le soubassement juridique des affaires Leclerc carburants et Leclerc livres' JCP 1986, I 3231; Racine, 'Les sanctions pénales aux infractions à la législation relative au prix du livre' Revue de science criminelle et de droit pénal comparé 1985, 783 and Delvolvé, 'Légalités des réglementations nationale des prix et responsabilité des Etat-membres et des entreprises au regard du droit communautaire de la concurrence' Gaz. Pal. 1985, Doctr. 473.

[53] Case 229/83, n. 2 above. See also, to exactly the same effect, Case 95/84 *Ministère public* v. *Alain Darras et Dominique Tostain* [1986] ECR 2253.

[54] Case 229/83, *Leclerc*, n. 2 above at para. 26.

[55] Ibid. at para. 27. It may be noted that there is some debate as to whether this ECJ proviso is based on an 'abuse of rights' doctrine, or whether it may more correctly be explained on the basis that such 'imports' were in commercial reality purely internal transactions. See Oliver (1986) 23 CMLRev 325 at 327 & n. 4 above, 127, and Wyatt & Dashwood, *European Community Law*, 232. It is submitted that the ECJ's proviso in this case may appropriately be likened to the equitable maxim: 'he who comes to equity must come with clean hands'.

and which were re-imported into France that it infringed Article 30. In this way, it is submitted that the ECJ was implicitly countenancing reverse discrimination against books published in France which had never been exported or books which had been exported to another Member State but only as a ruse to attempt to benefit from the provisions on the free movement of goods.[56] Indeed, this is the way in which the overwhelming majority of French courts applied the ECJ's judgment. In a series of judgments, the French courts held that the *loi Lang* continued to apply to books published and remaining in France.[57] That this was the correct interpretation was subsequently confirmed by the ECJ in *Draincourt* v. *Cognet*,[58] where it was held that Article 30 did not prohibit reverse discrimination since

[T]he purpose of that provision is to eliminate obstacles to the importation of goods and not to ensure that goods of national origin always enjoy the same treatment as imported or reimported goods . . . A difference in treatment between goods which is not capable of restricting imports or of prejudicing the marketing of imported or re-imported goods does not fall within the prohibition contained in Article 30.[59]

In the wake of this clear ECJ judgment holding that Article 30 does not prohibit reverse discrimination, the French courts were able to conclude in a straightforward fashion that the *loi Lang*[60] continued to apply to books which had been published in France and which had not been exported and re-imported.[61]

[56] The proviso in this case has been applied by the French courts in *Editions Gallimard SA* v. *FNAC SA, Cour d'appel* Paris, 1re ch. A, 24 Apr. 1985, [1986] ECC 59; Gaz. Pal. 1985, I Jur. 337 where the existence of an artificially created international circuit to avoid *loi Lang* was identified. See also before the German courts, the *Reimport* case, *OLG* Karlsruhe, 28 Sept. 1988, 6U 145/88 [1989] ZLR 480 (noted by Tegeder (1994) 19 ELRev. 86), where it was held that beer which had been produced in Germany, exported to France and reimported by a wholesaler into Germany and which did not meet the characteristics required by German law (para. 10(3) *Biersteuersgesetz*) benefited from Art. 30 unless it was shown that it was exported in order to be reimported for which there was held to be no evidence on the facts.

[57] See, e.g., *FFSL* v. *SA Nanterre distribution (NANDIS) (Centre Leclerc), Tribunal de commerce* Nanterre (*Référés*), 5 Feb. 1985, Gaz. Pal. 1985, I Jur. 183; *Association des centres distributeurs Edouard Leclerc* v. *Syndicat des librairies de Loire Océan, Cour de Cassation*, ch. comm., 15 May 1985, Dalloz 1986, Jur. 159 (with note by Goyet); Bull. Cass. Civ. 1985, IV 133; CDE 1989, 405 (summary) and *SA Dammarie distribution (Centre Leclerc)* v. *FFSL, Cour d'appel* Paris, 1re ch. A, 10 Feb. 1988, Dalloz 1988, IR 81.

[58] Case 355/85, n. 2 above.

[59] Ibid. at para. 10. See also to precisely the same effect Case 168/86 *Rousseau* and Case 160/86 *Verbrugge*, both n. 2 above. It may be noted that after the ECJ's recent judgment in *Pistre*, n. 7 above, it is questionable whether the ECJ would be able to maintain this line of reasoning.

[60] As amended by Law 85–500 of 13 May 1985.

[61] See, e.g., *SA Carrefour Sogara* v. *Association Libairies présentes en Aquitaine et SARL La machine à lire, Cour de Cassation*, ch. comm., 7 Feb. 1989, Bull. Cass. Civ. 1989, IV no. 48 p. 31; *Superouest, Cour de Cassation*, ch. comm., 10 May 1988, Bull. Cass. Civ. 1988, IV no. 153 p. 107; *SA Carrefour* v. *SARL Edilic-librairie chroniques, Cour de Cassation* Paris, 1re ch. A, 11 Apr.

There were only a handful of judgments before the French courts which went in the other direction. For example, the *Tribunal de grande instance* of Bordeaux held that the effect of the ECJ's judgment in *Leclerc* v. *Au Blé Vert*[62] was that the *loi Lang* was no longer applicable, even against books published and remaining in France.[63] The Bordeaux court held that '[t]he Court of Justice of the European Communities did not hold that the law of 10 August 1981 was in conformity with Community law with the exception of certain provisions concerning imported books' and that the ECJ had explicitly rejected the justifications invoked by the French Government. Consequently the *Tribunal de grande instance* of Bordeaux concluded that the *loi Lang* was no longer enforceable, even in a case involving only domestically-produced books. This somewhat 'surprising'[64] judgment may at least be excused for having been delivered before the clear ECJ judgment in *Draincourt* v. *Cognet*.[65] The same cannot unfortunately be said for the judgment of the *Tribunal d'instance* of Bressuire which was charged with implementing the judgment of the ECJ in *Draincourt* v. *Cognet* which it had itself referred to the ECJ.[66] The *Tribunal d'instance* of Bressuire noted the ECJ's judgment but held that 'to the extent that the solution given by the ECJ in its judgment of 23 October 1986 causes a distortion to competition, the French law cannot be applied since it causes an obstacle to the application of the Community rules on competition which need to be upheld in conformity with Article 3(f) of the Treaty of Rome on all Community territory'. Thus the *Tribunal* held that if the *loi Lang* could not be applied to imported books, it could equally not be applied in a case involving only books published and remaining in France. This amounted to a direct challenge to the authority of the ECJ's judgment

1988, Dalloz 1988, IR 126 and *Union syndicale des libraires de France et Association 'Librairies présentes'* v. *Sté Disanto et SA Levallois distribution (Centre Leclerc)*, *Cour de Cassation*, ch. comm., 5 May 1987, Bull. Cass. Civ. 1987, 83. On the other hand, the French courts have refused to apply the *loi Lang* in cases concerning books published in and imported from other Member States: see e.g. *SA des marchés et usines Auchan* v. *Jean-Pierre Rudin*, *Cour de Cassation*, ch. comm., 5 May 1987, [1989] ECC 101; RIDA 1987, no. 134 199; Bull. Cass. Civ. 1987, IV 84.

[62] Case 229/83, n. 2 above.

[63] *Association 'Librairies présentes en Aquitaine' et SARL 'La machine à lire'* v. *SA Carrefour Sogara*, TGI Bordeaux (*Référés*), 4 Apr. 1985, Gaz. Pal. 1985, I Jur. 340 (with note by Mauro).

[64] Errera, 'French Courts and Art. 177 of the Treaty of Rome'. On the other hand, Mauro, n. 63 above, explains that this judgment is less surprising in the context of the particular position of the *juge des référés* under French law according to which it is arguable that a *juge des référés* does not have the competence to apply only part of an Act. See also *Syndicat national de l'édition* v. *SA Rocadis (Centre Leclerc)*, TGI Poitiers (*Référés*), 17 Apr. 1987, RTDE 1987, 555 and noted by Grelon, RTDE 1987, 405 at 407 where the issue of the competence of the *juge des référés* was also discussed. See further discussion of the position of the *juge des référés* under French law in Ch. 10, sect. 2 (A).

[65] n. 2 above.

[66] Referring judgt of *Tribunal d'instance* Bressuire, 11 Oct. 1985. Judgt applying ECJ judgt in Case 355/85 *Draincourt* v. *Cognet* by *Tribunal d'instance* Bressuire, 10 Apr. 1987, RTDE 1987, 553.

in *Draincourt* v. *Cognet*. As we have seen, the ECJ was extremely clear in that judgment (set out above) in holding that reverse discrimination was not prohibited by Article 30. For the *Tribunal d'instance* of Bressuire to wheel out arguments based on Article 3(f) EEC goes directly contrary to the judgment of the ECJ which the *Tribunal d'instance* of Bressuire had itself sought by means of Article 177. Grelon has correctly pointed out that there is nothing to stop the national court applying French national law to prohibit reverse discrimination on the basis of the principle of equality.[67] However, the Bressuire court did no such thing here since its reasoning was based exclusively on grounds of Community law (Article 3(f) EEC).

Fortunately, the case was appealed through the French courts up to the *Cour de Cassation* which put the matter on a correct footing by holding that since the facts concerned books which had been published in France and which had never been exported, the *loi Lang* was still applicable and furthermore that the law was contrary to neither Article 85 nor Article 86 EC.[68]

In sum, the majority of the judgments of the French courts in these cases held that reverse discrimination was not prohibited by Article 30 and therefore that the *loi Lang* was still enforceable against books published and remaining in France. This position is in contrast to the majority of the earlier judgments in the alcohol advertising cases, discussed in the previous section, where Community law was used to conclude that reverse discrimination was prohibited. However, the French courts were at least assisted in the book-pricing cases by the clear ECJ ruling in *Draincourt* v. *Cognet* compared to the more cryptic *Waterkeyn* judgment in the alcohol advertising cases. It is interesting to note that the 'rebel' cases in this section again reached the conclusion that Community law prohibited reverse discrimination on the grounds that any other solution would lead to a distortion of competition contrary to Article 3(f) EEC. The ECJ's position with respect to reverse discrimination has thus not gone unchallenged before the national courts.[69]

4 NATIONAL LEGISLATION CONCERNING THE DISPOSAL OF WASTE

The issue of purely national measures has also arisen in the context of national legislation concerning the disposal of waste. The question here

---

[67] Grelon, above n. 52 at 412.

[68] *Cour de Cassation*, ch. crim., 19 Dec. 1988, [1990] ECC 85; Bull. Cass. Crim. 1988, 1153. Noted by Bouloc, RTDComm. 1989, 706. The compatibility of the *loi Lang* with Arts. 85 & 86 had been confirmed by the ECJ itself in *Au Blé Vert* and subsequently in Case 254/87 *Syndicat des Libraries de Normandie* v. *L'Aigle Distribution* [1988] ECR 4457.

[69] It may also be noted that the ECJ itself seems to have called into question the correctness of its approach in the recent *Pistre* judgment. See discussion of this judgment at n. 7 above.

was not so much one of reverse discrimination against national installations for the disposal of waste, as one of the effect of ECJ judgments on the continued application of national legislation to such national installations. The difficulties which arose before the national courts have their origin in ECJ judgments which held that French legislation implementing Directive 75/439[70] on the disposal of waste oils established an implicit prohibition on the export of waste to other Member States contrary to that Directive and to Article 34 EC.[71] In subsequent cases before the French courts, installations were prosecuted for being in possession of and recycling waste oils without the licence required by the French legislation. As a defence, these installations argued that according to the ECJ judgments,[72] the implementation of the Directive into French law was unlawful. The problem was that according to the ECJ judgments it was not the system of dividing French territory into zones and the licensing system as such which was contrary to EC law, but rather the fact that the French legislation provided no exemption for resale to collectors with a licence in other Member States. The question before the national courts, therefore, was whether the ECJ judgments provided the defendant companies with a defence. Was the French licensing system *as a whole* contrary to the Directive and Article 34, or was the effect of the ECJ judgments that the French licensing system was contrary to the Directive and Article 34 EC only in so far as exports were concerned? In other words, what is the effect of ECJ judgments on the continued application of the national legislation to purely national installations?

In the French courts, the answer to this question was not entirely self-evident. On the one hand, the *Cour d'appel* of Amiens in *SA Boudoux*[73] held that 'the system of approval which gives a French undertaking in a *département* the monopoly of collection of waste oils cannot be justified by the interests provided for in Article 36 of the Treaty of Rome and the system is thus contrary to the provisions of Article 34 of the same Treaty'. On the other hand, this decision was overturned on appeal by the *Cour de Cassation* which held that 'it follows from the Directive and from judgments of the European Court of Justice, that the only limit on legislation of the Member States is the prohibition of any measure restricting Community trade'.[74] The *Cour de Cassation* rejected the defences by stating

---

[70] [1975] OJ L194/23.

[71] See the ECJ judgments in Case 172/82 *Syndicat national des fabricants raffineurs d'huiles de graissage* v. *Groupement d'interêt économique (GIE) Inter-Huiles* [1983] ECR 555, [1983] 3 CMLR 485; Case 173/83 *Commission* v. *France* [1985] ECR 491; Case 240/83 *Procureur de la République* v. *Association de defense des Bruleurs d'Huiles Usagées (ADBHU)* [1985] ECR 531.

[72] i.e. those in n. 71 above.   [73] *Cour d'appel* Amiens, ch. corr., 30 Jan. 1989.

[74] *Cour de Cassation*, ch. crim., 7 Nov. 1990, Bull. Cass. Crim. 1990, no. 371 p. 939. See also *Renaudier*, *Cour de Cassation*, ch. crim., 21 June 1990, Bull. Cass. Crim 1990, no. 251 p. 651 and *Marie Paule*, *Cour de Cassation*, ch. crim., 6 Mar. 1992, Bull. Cass. Crim. 1992, no. 102 p. 257 where the *Cour de Cassation* took the same approach concerning amended French legislation.

that the licensing system was not as such contrary to the Directive or Article 34 and thus could still be enforced against national installations operating without a licence within national territory. These judgments of the *Cour de Cassation* thus simply held that the licensing system introduced by the French legislation was in conformity with the Directive, although other parts of the implementing legislation containing an implicit ban on export were not. In other words, the whole of the French legislation was not inapplicable after the ECJ rulings.

Similar difficulties were encountered by the Dutch courts.[75] On the one hand, in *Heijmans Milieutechniek* v. *GS van Noord-Brabant*, both the *Rechtbank* Den Bosch[76] and the President of the *Afdeling Bestuursrechtspraak* of the *Raad van State*[77] held that in a case where there was on the facts no connection with inter-State trade, Article 34 could not be breached. This case concerned a rejection by the Provincial Executive of the Province of Noord-Brabant of an application for an exemption under Article 9 of the Noord-Brabant Industrial Waste Regulation (*Verordening bedrijfsafvalstoffen*) 1992 for the transport of sludge residues from the province of Noord-Brabant to Noord-Holland. The terms of Article 9 of the Noord-Brabant Industrial Waste Regulation were broad enough to prohibit, not only the transportation of industrial waste to other provinces, but also such transportation to other Member States. However, since there was no connection with inter-State trade on the facts of this case, both the *Rechtbank* Den Bosch and the President of the *Raad van State* held that the compatibility of the decision with Article 34 EC was not at issue and that the latter Article was not therefore breached. At full trial, the same division of the *Raad van State* came to precisely the opposite view.[78] In this case it was held that since Article 9 of the Noord-Brabant Industrial Waste Regulation 1992 was applicable not only to exports to other provinces in the Netherlands, but also to exports to other Member States, that Article infringed Article 34 EC and could not therefore be enforced. Similarly, in *Wubben* v. *VROM*,[79] the *Raad van State* effectively reached the same conclusion in a different case concerning similar facts. In that case, Wubben appealed against a refusal

---

[75] See generally, Drupsteen, 'Grensoverschrijdend vervoer van afval' M & R 1997, 129.

[76] *Rechtbank* Den Bosch, 29 Nov. 1994, AWB 94/3338 BELEI and AWB 94/4545 VEROR. See Leefmans and Veltkamp, 'Nationale en provinciale zelfvoorziening' NTER 1995, 84 and Jans, 'Dutch Idiosyncracies and the Direct Effect of EC Law' (1996/1) LIEI 93.

[77] Pres. *Raad van State* (*Afd. Bestuursrechtspraak*), 6 Apr. 1995, AB 1996, 28 (with note by ChB).

[78] *Heijmans Milieutechniek* v. *GS van Noord-Brabant, Raad van State* (*Afd. Bestuursrechtspraak*), 25 July 1996, AB 1996, 425 (with note by ChB); M & R 1996/12, 134. See also *Heidemij Realisatie* v. *Gedeputeerde Staten van Noord-Brabant, Raad van State* (*Afd. Bestuursrechtspraak*), 25 July 1996, Jurisprudentie bestuursrecht 1996, 189 (with note by Claes).

[79] *Raad van State* (*Afd. Bestuursrechtspraak*), 3 Aug. 1995, AB 1996, 27; M & R 1996/2 no. 21 (with note by Jans) and noted in Addink et al (Eds.), *Europese milieurechtspraak, 104 nationale uitspraken met Europees milieurechterlijke aspecten*, 136–138 and 220.

to issue a licence for the collection of chemical waste. Under Article 21 of the *Wet Chemische Afvalstoffen* (*WCA*: Law on Chemical Waste), the collection of chemical waste without a licence was prohibited.[80] Wubben held a licence in Zeeland and Noord-Brabant and wanted to expand operations to Zuid-Holland where he applied for, and was refused, a licence. The grounds for the refusal were that Wubben did not have a disposal installation in Zuid-Holland and, according to the Province's 'action programme', only companies with disposal installations in Zuid-Holland would be granted a licence. The *Raad van State* annulled the refusal and held that the policy was contrary to Article 34 following the ECJ's judgment in *Inter-Huiles*.[81] The *Raad van State* held that the free movement of goods rules precluded Member States from organizing the collection of waste in its territory in such a way that export to recognized disposal companies in other Member States was prohibited. This was held to be the case here, since the granting of licences was dependent on the possession of an installation in the Netherlands, which was in practice an export ban contrary to Article 34. At first sight, this judgment appears to be a straightforward application of the ECJ's judgment in *Inter-Huiles*. On closer inspection, it is interesting to note that Wubben was a Dutch company with disposal installations in the Netherlands and not in other Member States. The *Raad van State* did not comment on this factual circumstance. It appears therefore that the *Raad van State*, in contrast to the French *Cour de Cassation* in *SA Boudoux*, took a much broader interpretation of the ECJ judgment in *Inter-Huiles*. As a result, the approach of the *Rechtbank* Den Bosch and the President of the *Raad van State* in *Heijmans Milieutechniek* was 'diametrically opposed'[82] to that of the *Afdeling Bestuursrechtspraak* of the *Raad van State* at full trial in *Heidemij* and *Wubben v. VROM*.[83]

---

[80] The granting of such licences was governed by the Nota *Vergunningenbeleid Chemische afvalstoffen* (licence policy for chemical waste), the Nota of *Toelichting op het Besluit inzameling chemische afvalstoffen* (Explanation of the Order on the Collection of Chemical Waste) and the Notitie *Chemische afvalstoffen uit olie- en/of slibafscheiders* (Chemical Waste from Oil and/or Silt Separators) of Sept. 1989.

[81] Case 172/82, n. 71 above.   [82] Jans, n. 76 above at 96.

[83] It should be noted that the *Raad van State*'s approach in the latter two cases amounted effectively to an application of the doctrine in Dutch law of '*onsplitsbare wilsverklaring*' (a doctrine according to which the intention of the legislature is deemed to be indivisible) although this was not made explicit in the judgments themselves. See Jans, 'Onsplitsbare wilsverklaringen en interne situaties; een Europeesrechtelijke confrontatie' in Vucsan, (ed.), *De Awb-mens: boeman of underdog?: Opstellen aangeboden aan Leo Damen* (Ars Aequi Libri, 1996) at 71. It is equally of interest to note that the *Raad van State* has recently taken a more restrictive approach to provincial regulations which restrict export of waste within the Netherlands but which explicitly do not apply to the export of waste to other Member States: *BFI Afvalverwerkingstechnieken v. GS van Noord-Holland*, Pres. *Raad van State* (*Afd. Bestuursrechtspraak*), 14 Oct. 1996, KG 1997, 24; M & R 1997/4, 46 (with note by Jans). In this case, it was held that the measure in question (*in casu*: the *Provinciale Milieuverordening Noord-Holland*) had no connection with export and thus that there was no possible breach of Art. 34 EC.

Of interest in the context of the present discussion is also the judgment of the *Gerechtshof* Arnhem in the analogous case of *Openbaar Ministerie* v. *Nertsvoederfabriek Nederland BV*. In that case, Nertsvoederfabriek was prosecuted under Article 5 of the *Destructiewet* (Law on the destruction of animal carcasses and offal) of 21 February 1957[84] for operating without a licence a plant intended for rendering offal innocuous by processing it into useful products suitable for incorporation in animal foodstuffs. On raising the defence that the Dutch legislation breached Article 34, the *Gerechtshof* Arnhem referred this point to the ECJ.[85] The questions referred by the national court were broad and asked the ECJ not only whether the requirement in the *Destructiewet* to have a licence was contrary to Article 34, but also whether the requirement in that legislation that all producers of such offal must dispose of it only to approved rendering plants was also contrary to that Article. The ECJ held that Article 34 was breached 'to the extent to which the national rules, by imposing an obligation on producers to deliver poultry offal to their local authority, involve by implication a prohibition of exports'.[86] The ECJ went on to hold that such a breach was not justified for the protection of health and life of humans provided for in Article 36.[87] What is of interest in the context of the present discussion, is the application of this judgment on its return before the *Gerechtshof* Arnhem. Back before the national court, Nertsvoederfabriek BV argued that the effect of the ECJ judgment was that the Dutch legislation was 'as a whole' contrary to Article 34 and that the ECJ decided this on the basis of the legislation 'in its totality'. It was thus argued that the consequence of the ECJ ruling was that the legislation was inapplicable and that the criminal indictment should be set aside. The *Gerechtshof* Arnhem rejected this argument and held that there was, on the facts, no connection with import from or export to other Member States and thus, 'any possible incompatibility of the *Destructiewet* with Articles 30, 34 and 36 of the EEC Treaty does not affect the validity of the provisions of Article 5 of the *Destructiewet*'.[88] The long and short of it is that the Arnhem court held that the ECJ did not hold that the licensing system under the *Destructiewet* as was such contrary to Article 34, but only that the requirement for producers to deliver poultry offal to their local authority (which involved, by implication, a prohibition of exports) was contrary to that Article. Given that Nertsvoederfabriek was only prosecuted for not having a licence, the ECJ judgment did not affect the validity of such a national requirement

---

[84] Stb. 1957/84, p. 155.　　　　[85] *Gerechtshof* Arnhem, 27 Mar. 1986.
[86] Case 118/86 [1987] ECR 3883 at para. 11.　　　　[87] Ibid. at paras. 12–17.
[88] *Gerechtshof* Arnhem, 1 Feb. 1988; transcr. available from court. See also, *Riho Veenendaal BV* v. *Minister van Landbouw en Visserij*, Pres. Raad van State (*Afd. Rechtspraak*), 13 Nov. 1985, A.B. 1987, 417 (with note by Slot) and *Godeschalk en Postma* v. *Minister van WVC*, Pres. Raad van State (*Afd. Rechtspraak*), 3 Jan. 1985, SEW 1985, 531 (with note by Slot).

and the conviction was upheld.[89] Thus, in much the same way as the French *Cour de Cassation* in the waste oils cases, but in contrast to the position of the *Raad van State* in *Heidemij,*[90] *Heijmans*[91] and *Wubben* v. *VROM,*[92] the *Gerechtshof* Arnhem held that the effect of the ECJ judgment was not that the *whole* of the national legislation was inapplicable. The licensing system itself was not contrary to Article 34 (and was thus of undiminished application) and it was only the implied prohibition on export to plants in other Member States which contravened that Article.

5 CONCLUSIONS

The application of the ECJ's approach to reverse discrimination and purely national measures has given rise to considerable difficulties before the national courts. In particular, the national courts have had difficulty in ascertaining whether national legislation, which has been found by the ECJ to infringe Articles 30 or 34, is still applicable to purely internal undertakings operating within that national territory. This is particularly difficult for national courts following an ECJ judgment given pursuant to infringement proceedings under Article 169 EC. The very nature of the latter proceedings ensure that the ECJ's judgment has a more 'global' impact on the validity of national legislation as compared to judgments given pursuant to the Article 177 EC preliminary-rulings procedure. Clearly, there are important differences between ECJ judgments rendered under Article 177 and those under Article 169. Firstly, Article 177 has at its heart a co-operation with the national courts while Article 169 concerns specific national laws which are brought before the ECJ for a decision as to their compatibility with EC law. Secondly, by their very nature, preliminary rulings under Article 177 are given in the abstract and the national court, in line with the co-operative nature of the procedure, is left to apply the ruling to the facts. Thirdly, in Article 177 proceedings the interpretation of EC law itself is at issue while in Article 169 judgments, the compatibility with EC law of a particular national law is at issue. As a result, when a Member State's legislation is held in Article 169 proceedings to be contrary to Articles 30 or 36, if the Member State in question does not amend its legislation quickly to comply with Community law, the national courts have difficulty in ascertaining what the remaining effect of the national

---

[89] It seems therefore that the reference by the *Gerechtshof* Arnhem to the ECJ was entirely superfluous. This was also the case with respect to the implementation of the ECJ's judgment in Cases 80 & 159/85 *Nederlandse Bakkerij Stichting* v. *Edah BV* by the Pres. *Arrondissementsrechtbank* Almelo, 11 Mar. 1987, where it also seems that, since only domestic products were involved, the reference to the ECJ was unnecessary. See discussion of this point at n. 16 above.

[90] n. 78 above.   [91] n. 78 above.   [92] n. 79 above.

legislation should be for purely internal undertakings operating within that national territory. The cases discussed in this chapter show that the line between purely national measures and measures which have a nexus with either import or export is a difficult one to draw in practice. This difficulty becomes even more apparent as national markets integrate further into a mature internal market.

A second difficulty which the national courts have encountered concerns the explicit refusal by the ECJ to prohibit reverse discrimination. One would perhaps have expected to find that the national courts had embraced this refusal on the part of the ECJ to interfere with the internal affairs of a Member State with little resistance. However, it should not be forgotten that it is the national courts which have to deal with the injustices that reverse discrimination can cause in practice. For example, why should a French retailer be allowed to sell *Tintin* cartoon albums imported from Belgium at a more competitive price than *Lucky Luke* cartoon albums published in France?[93] Why should it be possible to advertise whisky imported from Scotland but not pastis produced in France? Faced with the prospect of such inequalities, the French courts have often concluded, sometimes explicitly contrary to ECJ judgments, that to allow such a distortion of competition would be illogical in a genuine common market and have drawn primarily on Article 3(f) EEC (now Article 3(g) EC) to support this conclusion. Such open challenges by the national courts cannot be condoned, especially when they are handed down by a national court against which there is no appeal and without referring preliminary questions to the ECJ under Article 177(3) EC.[94] Nevertheless, these challenges serve to highlight a problem. It remains to be seen whether the ECJ's recent judgment in the *Pistre* case[95] signifies a far-reaching change of approach in ECJ case law on reverse discrimination and purely national measures. In the light of the difficulties which have been encountered by the national courts applying the current case law, it may be hoped that it does.

[93] This example is drawn from Racine, n. 52 above at 787–8.
[94] See esp. the much criticized judgts of the *Cour de Cassation* in *Bernard Cambournac* and *Rossi di Montalera*, both n. 35 above.
[95] n. 7 above.

6

The rule of reason

1 INTRODUCTION

There are two possible sources of justification for restrictions to the free movement of goods; one Treaty-based, and the other a creation in the case law of the ECJ. Firstly, Article 36 of the Treaty enumerates certain specific grounds of justification. These will be discussed in the following chapter. A second possibility for justifying restrictions to the free movement of goods was opened up by the ECJ in its *Cassis de Dijon*[1] judgment where it introduced in full its 'rule of reason' approach, holding that in the absence of common rules set down at Community level

Obstacles to movement within the Community resulting from disparities between the national laws relating to the marketing of the products in question *must be accepted in so far as those provisions may be recognized as being necessary in order to satisfy mandatory requirements* relating in particular to the effectiveness of fiscal supervision, the protection of public health, the fairness of commercial transactions and the defence of the consumer.[2]

Thus, once a trader has established that an import restriction contained in a national law or regulation has breached the Article 30 prohibition, Member States may claim, in addition to the possible justifications set out in Article 36, that the restriction is 'necessary in order to satisfy mandatory requirements' and that it is therefore outside the scope of Article 30.[3] The *Cassis de Dijon* case was thus a double-edged sword: on the one hand, the

---

[1] Case 120/78 *Rewe* v. *Bundesmonopolverwaltung für Branntwein* [1979] ECR 649, [1979] 3 CMLR 494.

[2] Para. 8 of *Cassis de Dijon*, n. 1 above; emphasis added. It may be noted that the 'rule of reason' approach was present in ECJ case law interpreting Art. 30 prior to the *Cassis de Dijon* judgment. For example, in Case 8/74 *Procureur du Roi* v. *Dassonville* [1974] ECR 837, [1974] 2 CMLR 436 the ECJ referred to national measures to prevent unfair practices being subject to the condition that they be 'reasonable' (para. 6 of judgt). Nevertheless, the *Cassis de Dijon* judgment constituted the first detailed establishment of the rule of reason approach.

[3] It may be noted that there is academic debate as to whether the rule of reason 'mandatory requirements' are really a justification for restrictions to the free movement of goods. Strictly speaking, if a measure restrictive of trade is 'justified' as a mandatory requirement under the *Cassis de Dijon* doctrine, the Art. 30 prohibition is not breached at all. By contrast, if a measure is justified under one of the grounds in Art. 36, it is assumed that Art. 30 or Art. 34 has been breached but that the measure is nevertheless justified. However, in practice if not in theory, the *Cassis de Dijon* rule of reason may be treated as a second possibility of justification additional to Art. 36 of the Treaty. For further discussion see Gormley, *Prohibiting Restrictions on Trade Within the EEC*, 51–7 and Weatherill & Beaumont, *EC Law*, 500–7.

ECJ succeeded in that judgment in re-invigorating the common market by setting up a presumption on free trade by holding that '[t]here is . . . no valid reason why, provided that they have been lawfully produced and marketed in one of the Member States, alcoholic beverages should not be introduced into any other Member State'.[4] On the other hand, the ECJ also opened up the possibility for Member States to justify restrictions to the free movement of goods in addition to those grounds mentioned in Article 36. The latter approach has become commonly known as the 'rule of reason' and will be referred to as such in the discussion which follows.

Because of the fundamental importance of the principle of the free movement of goods, the Treaty rules governing this freedom have been strictly enforced by the ECJ. As has already been noted, a common theme running throughout the ECJ's interpretation of the provisions concerning the free movement of goods is that the prohibition contained in Article 30, as a basic freedom under the Treaty, must be interpreted as broadly as possible. Correspondingly, the exceptions and justifications have been strictly construed and are thus of a narrow scope. As a result, the ECJ has interpreted the rule of reason justifications narrowly. Thus, the purpose of the mandatory requirements of the rule of reason should be understood as merely allowing national provisions to derogate from the principle of free movement of goods in individual cases. The ECJ has pursued a narrow interpretation of the *Cassis de Dijon* mandatory requirements by subjecting justifications advanced by Member States on the basis of the rule of reason to a rigorous application of the 'proportionality' test. The proportionality test is applied in two stages. Firstly it involves a *necessity test*. What is being asked in this limb of the test is whether the same objective could be obtained by other means which are less of a hindrance to trade. Secondly, a *balancing test* is applied which adds the further question of whether the restrictive effects on free movement of goods are out of proportion to their purpose. It is thus not sufficient for a Member State to merely point to one of the grounds of justification to justify a trade restriction. A Member State also has to demonstrate that the measure in question is appropriate and necessary to achieve the objective recognized by Community law. Since the proportionality test is a strict one, this is often an important limitation to the ability of Member States to justify restrictions under the rule of reason.[5]

An important feature of the rule-of-reason mandatory requirements is that the list of possible heads of justification is not an exhaustive one.[6] This

---

[4] Para. 14 of judgt.

[5] See the detailed discussion of the proportionality principle in the section on shop-opening hours at pp. 202–27.

[6] This may be contrasted with the grounds of justification which are listed in Art. 36 which the ECJ has refused to extend. See, e.g., Case 113/80 *Commission* v. *Ireland* ('Souvenirs') [1981] ECR 1625, [1982] 1 CMLR 706.

was evident from the use of the words 'in particular' by the ECJ when it enumerated examples of possible mandatory requirements in the *Cassis de Dijon* judgment itself,[7] and has been confirmed in subsequent judgments where the ECJ has gradually expanded the list of mandatory requirements which it has recognized. The mandatory requirements which have been accepted by the ECJ include: the protection of the working environment,[8] environmental protection,[9] the protection of national socio-cultural characteristics,[10] the protection of cultural expression,[11] the protection of the consumer[12] and the protection of the plurality of the press.[13]

Finally, it will be recalled that Article 30 prohibits measures which directly affect imports as well as those whose effects are indirect.[14] Although it would appear that the distinction between directly and indirectly applicable measures is unimportant, since both are capable of falling under Article 30, the distinction between the two remains pertinent since justification of a restriction under the *Cassis de Dijon* rule of reason is only possible if the measure in question is indirectly applicable; i.e. if it applies to both imports and domestic products alike.[15] For example, in *Leclerc* v. *Au Blé Vert*[16] the ECJ rejected the possibility for the French State to advance a justification on the grounds of 'the protection of consumer interests' and 'the protection of artistic creation and cultural diversity in the field of books' since these grounds were not listed in Article 36 and the rule of reason was held to be inapplicable because the French legislation at issue applied only to imported books.[17] In practice, an indirectly applicable measure may thus be justified either under one of the grounds in Article 36 or under one of the non-exhaustively listed mandatory requirements. In some cases, such as the protection of public health (which is both

---

[7] See para. 8 of the *Cassis de Dijon* judgt set out at n. 2 above.

[8] Case 155/80 *Oebel* [1981] ECR 1993, [1983] 1 CMLR 390.

[9] Case 302/86 *Commission* v. *Denmark* [1988] ECR 4607, [1989] 1 CMLR 619.

[10] Case 145/88 *Torfaen BC* v. *B & Q* [1989] ECR 3851, [1990] 1 CMLR 337. Noted by Gormley (1990) 27 CMLRev. 141.

[11] Case 60 & 61/84 *Cinéthèque* v. *Fédération Nationale de Cinemas Françaises* [1985] ECR 2605, [1986] 1 CMLR 365.

[12] See, e.g., Case 382/87 *Buet* v. *Ministère Public* [1989] ECR 1235.

[13] Case C–368/95 *Vereinigte Familiapress Zeitungsverlags- und vertriebs* v. *Heinrich Bauer Verlag* [1997] ECR I–3689.

[14] See discussion in Ch. 2, sect. 5.

[15] See, e.g., Case 788/79 *Gilli & Andres* [1980] ECR 2071, [1981] 1 CMLR 146; Case 113/80 *Commission* v. *Ireland* [1982] ECR 1625, [1982] 1 CMLR 706; Case 207/83 *Commission* v. *United Kingdom* (Origin-Marking) [1985] ECR 1201, [1985] 2 CMLR 259 & Cases C–321–324/94 *Pistre, Barthes, Milhau and Oberti* [1997] ECR I–2343, [1997] 2 CMLR 565 at para. 52. This was explicitly followed by the English Court of Appeal in *R.* v. *Secretary of State for Social Security, ex. p. Bomore Medical Supplies Ltd* [1986] 1 CMLR 228 which held that the discriminatory nature of an NHS scheme (under which chemists were reimbursed for the supply of medicines) precluded recourse to the rule of reason justifications. See further discussion of this judgment at p. 44.

[16] Case 229/83 [1985] ECR 1, [1985] 2 CMLR 286.

[17] Ibid. at para. 30.

a mandatory requirement and listed in Article 36), it will not matter
whether one draws on Article 36 or the rule of reason to justify an indirectly applicable national measure. However, in other cases, such as consumer or environmental protection (grounds of justification under the rule
of reason only), it will be necessary for the measures in question to be indirectly applicable if these grounds of justification are to be relied upon.[18]

The application of the rule of reason in practice may be illustrated by a
discussion of the *Cassis de Dijon* case itself. The facts of *Cassis de Dijon* concerned German legislation which precluded the sale of any spirits of the
category into which the fruit liqueur Cassis fell, if the alcohol content was
below 25 per cent. The problem was that the alcohol content of the Cassis
de Dijon in question, which had been lawfully produced and marketed in
France, was between 15 and 20 per cent. Importers of the Cassis from
France initiated proceedings in Germany since their application to the
Bundesmonopolverwaltung (Federal Monopoly Administration for Spirits)
for authorization to market the drink in Germany had been refused. The
ECJ was thus faced with a non-discriminatory national rule which applied
to all fruit liqueurs marketed in Germany, without making any distinction
according to origin.[19] Faced with the question of whether the German
legislation was compatible with Article 30, the ECJ replied that given that
the product had been lawfully produced and marketed in France, that provision was indeed breached. With respect to the justification of the
German legislation under the rule of reason, the ECJ considered the protection of public health and consumer protection. With respect to public
health, it had been argued by the German Government that the German
legislation was necessary to prevent the proliferation of alcoholic beverages with a low alcohol content since such products might more easily
induce a tolerance towards alcohol than more highly alcoholic beverages.
This justification was rejected as 'not decisive' by the ECJ which noted that
'the consumer can obtain on the market an extremely wide range of
weakly or moderately alcoholic products and furthermore a large proportion of alcoholic beverages with a high alcohol content freely sold on the

---

[18] This can lead to arbitrary results as there seems to be no good reason in logic why distinctly applicable measures may not be justified for, say, consumer or environmental protection simply because such concerns were less important at the time of the drafting of Art. 36
of the Treaty of Rome. Consequently, the ECJ has, on occasion, been driven to tortuous reasoning to maintain the formal authority of its approach: see Case C–2/90 *Commission* v.
Belgium (Walloon Waste) [1992] ECR I–4431, [1993] 1 CMLR 365. See also discussion by
Oliver, *Free Movement of Goods in the European Community*, 110–14.

[19] It is a matter of considerable dismay that before the English High Court, MacPherson J
in *SA Magnavision NV* v. *General Optical Council* (No. 1) [1987] 1 CMLR 887 at 892 referred to
the *Cassis de Dijon* case as one involving a direct ban upon the sale of a low-alcohol beverage
'so that the measures were plainly discriminatory and protectionist in their effect'. This is,
with respect, incorrect as the German legislation at issue in *Cassis de Dijon* was undoubtedly
indistinctly applicable.

German market is generally consumed in a diluted form'.[20] With respect to consumer protection, the German Government had argued that since alcohol constitutes by far the most expensive constituent of beverages by reason of the high rate of tax to which it is subject, consumers need protection against the lowering of the alcohol content of beverages specifically in order to secure a competitive advantage. This the ECJ also rejected since there were alternate means of protecting the consumer because 'it is a simple matter to ensure that suitable information is conveyed to the purchaser by requiring the display of an indication of origin and of alcohol content on the packaging of products'.[21]

The approach of the ECJ in *Cassis de Dijon* gives rise to three comments. Firstly, it will be evident that the ECJ applied the proportionality test extremely rigorously. This is in line with the restrictive interpretation of justifications for breaches of fundamental freedoms under the EC Treaty which has already been noted. Secondly, it should be noted that whilst the rule-of-reason approach may be credited for enhancing consumer choice, it has also given rise to the anxiety that it will push Member States towards increasing deregulation of their markets. This deregulatory flavour is evident in *Cassis de Dijon* itself, which had the effect of imposing a common standard within the Community set at the level of the lowest alcohol content permitted in any of the Member States.[22] Thirdly, it will be noted that the appreciation and application of the rule of reason is a delicate matter in practice. The system set up by this approach walks an extremely fine line. This is further illustrated by noting, for example, that in *Duphar*[23] the ECJ took the view that a limit placed on expenditure on medical products by the Dutch health service did not breach Article 30 (provided that they were non-discriminatory) whereas Advocate General Mancini had opined in that case that the Dutch measures breached Article 30 but were justified. In *Ex p. Association of Pharmaceutical Importers*,[24] on the other hand, the ECJ held that the measures at issue in that case breached Article 30 but were justified for the protection of public health, whereas Advocate General Darmon had opined in that case that the measures fell outside of Article 30 altogether.[25] The latter case is all the more interesting since the English Court of Appeal, which had referred the case to the ECJ, had expressed the

---

[20] Para. 11 of judgt. [21] Para. 13 of judgt.

[22] See further discussion in Reich, 'Protection of Diffuse Interests in the EEC and the Perspective of Progressively Establishing an Internal Market' and McGee & Weatherill, 'The Evolution of the Single Market—Harmonisation or Liberalisation?'.

[23] Case 238/82 *Duphar BV and others* v. *Netherlands State* [1984] ECR 523, [1985] 1 CMLR 256.

[24] Case 266 & 267/87 *R.* v. *Pharmaceutical Society of Great Britain and Secretary of State for Social Services, ex. p. Association of Pharmaceutical Importers* [1989] ECR 1295, [1989] 2 CMLR 751.

[25] See discussion by Weatherill, (1990) 53 MLR 699.

view that the measures at issue in that case were capable of breaching Article 30 and were *not* capable of justification.[26] The edifice is thus very delicate because the consequence of an uncertain national court finding that a particular measure falls outside the scope of Article 30 is that the rule of reason does not get applied at all. In some such cases, if the national court had concluded that Article 30 had been infringed, it would have been extremely difficult to justify the measures under the rule of reason.[27]

The application of the rule of reason in practice thus comprises a complex and finely balanced exercise. This is all the more so given the extent of intervention that the free movement of goods involves in national regulation of economic life. There are several important theoretical issues underlying the application of the rule of reason which go to the very core of the division of powers between the Community and its Member States. It is for this reason that the national court application of the rule of reason is of great practical interest in assessing the success of the administration of justice in the Community's legal order.

National case law applying the rule of reason for the protection of cultural expression, the protection of the consumer, the fairness of commercial transactions, and the protection of national socio-cultural characteristics will be discussed in turn in the remainder of this chapter.

2 THE PROTECTION OF CULTURAL EXPRESSION

The ECJ has never expressly recognized the protection of cultural expression as a mandatory requirement under the rule of reason. As has already been noted, in *Leclerc* v. *Au Blé Vert*[28] the ECJ rejected the possibility of advancing a justification on the grounds of 'the protection of artistic creation and cultural diversity in the field of books' since these grounds were not listed in Article 36 and the rule of reason was not applicable in that case because the French legislation at issue was distinctly applicable.[29]

---

[26] [1987] 3 CMLR 951, [1989] RTDE 716.

[27] See e.g. the cases before the English courts concerning technical requirements for taxis in *R.* v. *Metropolitan Borough Council of Wirral, ex. p. The Wirral Licensed Taxi Owners Association* [1983] 3 CMLR 150; *Hodgkinson* v. *Nottingham City Council* [1993] 3 CMLR 503 and *R.* v. *Luton Borough Council, ex. p. Mirza* (transcr.: John Larking) which held on rather uncertain grounds (see discussion at pp. 73–6) that Art. 30 was not breached. Had a breach of Art. 30 been found, Gormley (1983) ELRev. 141 has argued that it would have been very difficult to justify the national provisions in question under the rule of reason. Before the Dutch courts, see *Dommelsch NA België, CvB* of the RCC, 28 Oct. 1991, *RCC* 1991, nr. 663 p. 79 and '*Crodino*', *CvB* of the *RCC*, 23 May 1989, *RCC* 1989, nr. 6054 p. 96 where an uncertain finding that a measure did not breach Art. 30 would equally have been difficult to justify under the rule of reason.

[28] Case 229/83, n. 16 above.

[29] Ibid. at para. 30. In a judgment of the *Cour d'appel* of Versailles handed down by that court before the ECJ's judgment in *Leclerc* v. *Au Blé Vert*, it had been held that 'books have a peculiar character which justifies the making of special conditions . . . and any anti-competitive

There is the implicit suggestion in this judgment that, had the French legislation been indistinctly applicable, there would have been the possibility of invoking 'the protection of artistic creation and cultural diversity in the field of books' as a mandatory requirement under the rule of reason. The ECJ now appears to have recognized 'the protection of cultural expression' as a mandatory requirement under the rule of reason in its judgment in *Cinéthèque* v. *Fédération Nationale de Cinemas Françaises*.[30] That case concerned French legislation providing that within one year of the authorization to show a film in cinemas in France, no video-cassettes of that film could be sold or hired for private showing.[31] The ECJ held that the French legislation was contrary to Article 30 since 'such a system may create barriers to intra-Community trade in video-cassettes because of the disparities between the systems operated in the different Member States'.[32] The ECJ then suggested that the French legislation was capable of justification but was extremely vague as to where the justification for the breach of Article 30 originated. It seems fair to assume, however, that the ECJ held that a justification would lie under the rule of reason for the protection of cultural expression.

French courts were confronted with the compatibility of the above French legislation before the ECJ judgment in *Cinéthèque*. Their response to the EC law argument was far from confident. For example, in *Thorn-EMI Video France* v. *Fédération nationale des cinémas français*,[33] the *Cour d'Appel* of Paris held that the EC-law argument was not a serious one since the French legislation had been enacted for the purpose of the general interest and was applicable to national as well as imported products. Other French courts faced with this question prior to the ECJ's judgment in *Cinéthèque* dealt only with the position of a judge in interim proceedings (*juge des référés*) faced with EC law and did not really enter into the substance of the case.[34] Thus, for example, the *Tribunal de grande instance* of Paris held in interim proceedings that no 'obvious incompatibility exists' between the French legislation and EC law and that 'in waiting for the decision of the Community Court, seized of a preliminary ruling on the

measures . . . are taken for the public benefit and take precedence over the need for the free movement of goods': *SA Argendis (Centre Leclerc) et Société ACDELEC* v. *Union syndicale des libraires de France et Syndicat des librairies professionnels de Paris et de la région parisienne, Cour d'appel* Versailles, 1re ch. I, 30 May 1984, [1986] ECC 197. This approach is untenable following the ECJ's judgment in *Leclerc* v. *Au Blé Vert*.

[30] Case 60 & 61/84, n. 11 above.

[31] Art. 89 of Law no. 82-652 of 29 July 1982 on audio-visual communication and Decree 83-4 of 4 Jan. 1983. See Chevallier, 'Le statut de la communication audiovissuelle' AJDA 1982, 555 and Romi, 'L'organisation économique du cinéma: changement et continuté' RDP 1984, 1633.

[32] Cases 60 & 61/84, n. 11 above at para. 22.

[33] *Cour d'appel* Paris, 27 Nov. 1984, noted in Servan-Schreiber, 'EEC law in French Courts 1980–1984' at 169.

[34] See discussion of this aspect of these cases in Ch. 10, sect. 2 (A).

compatibility of the internal law with the Community law, and in the absence of a suspensory effect of this preliminary procedure, the rules of national law are applicable'.[35]

The ECJ judgment in *Cinéthèque* was very finely balanced and was, with respect, far from clearly reasoned. It has already been noted that the ECJ was surprisingly vague in its judgment as to the head of justification to which it was alluding. As in the *Torfaen* judgment with respect to Sunday-trading legislation,[36] the lack of clarity in this judgment reveals the sensitivity of the national legislation in question. How does one begin to justify national legislation for the protection of cultural expression? The alleged aim of the legislation was to protect the French film industry. However, it is also true that the legislation was highly beneficial to cinema owners. On the other hand, the retailers of video-cassettes which ignored the French legislation were able to pose as the champions of deregulation and commercial freedom against *dirigiste* and unduly restrictive legislation. At the heart of the matter was the question of who deserved more protection: the owners of cinemas or the owners of film copyright? In short, the legislation rested upon finely balanced political issues and raised fundamental questions of commercial freedom and the role of the State.[37] The ECJ may thus almost be excused for having been reluctant to enter into this battlefield.

Not only did the ECJ fail to specify clearly which head of justification it was referring to in *Cinéthèque*, it was also equivocal as to whether it was itself holding that the French legislation was justified and, more importantly, proportionate. The ECJ held that

[A] prohibition of exploitation laid down by such a system is not compatible with the principle of the free movement of goods provided for in the Treaty unless any obstacle to intra-Community trade thereby created does not exceed that which is necessary in order to ensure the attainment of the objective in view and unless that objective is justified with regard to Community law.[38]

The ECJ proceeded immediately to add that 'It must be conceded that a national system which, in order to encourage the creation of cinematographic works irrespective of their origin, gives priority, for a limited initial period, to the distribution of such works through the cinema, is so justified.'[39] At first sight it appears that the ECJ itself held that the French legislation was justified. However, a closer reading suggests that it is possible to argue that it was only the *objective* which the ECJ held to be

---

[35] *Fédération nationale des cinémas français (FNCF)* v. *Société Editions René Château Vidéo TGI* Paris (*Référés*), 9 Apr. 1985, in Hassler, Dalloz 1986, IR 243 at 243.

[36] n. 114 below.

[37] See Guyot-Sionnest, 'Un vide juridique. Le problème des vidéo-cassettes' and De Montblanc, Revue de jurisprudence commerciale 1984, 267.

[38] Cases 60 & 61/84, n. 11 above at para. 22.   [39] Ibid. at para. 23.

'justified with regard to Community law'. It could be argued that the question of whether the obstacle 'exceeds that which is necessary in order to ensure the attainment of the objective' remained open for the national court to apply. These ambiguities should however be offset against the fact that the 'tone' of the ECJ's judgment was very much to decide that the French rules were justified.[40]

If the ambiguities in the ECJ's judgment outlined above were real, they were certainly not apparent to the French courts charged with applying the ECJ judgment. The *Cour de Cassation* in *Thorn-EMI Video France* v. *Fédération nationale des cinémas français*[41] did not even mention the ECJ ruling and simply held that the French legislation was justified and compatible with EC law without discussing whether the legislation 'exceeds that which is necessary in order to ensure the attainment of the objective'.[42] Similarly, in *Editions Proserpine SARL* v. *Fédération nationale des cinémas français (FNCF)*[43] the *Cour de Cassation* at least cited the ECJ judgment, but again very briefly rejected the EC-law arguments following the ECJ's *Cinéthèque* judgment without any discussion of the nature of the justification.[44]

The application of the provisions concerning the free movement of goods by the French courts both before and after the ECJ's judgment in *Cinéthèque* was thus far from satisfactory. The French legislation was based on finely balanced political questions and both the French courts and the ECJ seemed reluctant to interfere with the choice made by the French legislature. While the position was admittedly delicate, these cases hardly represent an example of coherent application of the rule of reason.

3 CONSUMER PROTECTION AND THE FAIRNESS OF COMMERCIAL TRANSACTIONS

Consumer protection is one of the most important and frequently invoked mandatory requirements in the rule of reason. Its importance is underlined by the fact that there is no equivalent head of justification provided for in Article 36 and the acceptance by the ECJ of this interest as a

[40] It may be noted that Adv. Gen. Slynn had taken the view that since the French legislation was indistinctly applicable and not protectionist it fell outside the scope of Art. 30.

[41] *Cour de Cassation*, 1re ch. civ., 22 Apr. 1986, Bull. Cass. Civ. 1986, I no. 96 p. 96.

[42] It is submitted that this would involve an application of the proportionality test. See discussion of this with respect to the *Torfaen* judgment below.

[43] *Cour de Cassation*, 1re ch. civ., 17 Feb. 1987, Bull. Cass. Civ. 1987, I 42; Gaz. Pal. 1987, Som. II 101 (summary); JCP 1987, IV 138 (summary).

[44] See also *Sté Les Films du Diamant* v. *Fédération nationale des cinémas français (FNCF)*, *Cour d'appel* Paris, 1re ch. A, 19 June 1985, noted by Hassler, Dalloz 1986, IR pp. 243–4 and *Société Argos Films* v. *Société Lido Musique*, *Cour d'appel* Paris, 4e ch., 20 Mar. 1990, [1991] ECC 268; RIDA 1990, no. 146 279 (with note by Kéréver); Dalloz 1990, Som. 354–5.

mandatory requirement is thus a significant supplement to Article 36. While the ECJ has shown itself willing to hear arguments based on consumer protection, such arguments are always subjected to a rigorous application of the proportionality test.[45] In practice, the application of the proportionality test will often turn on the first limb of that test, namely the necessity and alternative means tests. In the field of consumer protection, the ECJ has placed great emphasis on the consumer as an 'information-seeker' and it has thus repeatedly held that *labelling* is a sufficient alternative means of protecting the consumer which is less restrictive of intra-Community trade.[46] Howells and Wilhelmsson have commented that

The emphasis on labelling and information in many of the negative harmonisation cases (in which substantive regulation was outlawed in favour of information provisions) clearly presupposes a consumer who really makes efforts to read the information on labels and make use of other information offered. The consumer image of the [ECJ] does not seem to be of the hasty and relatively uncritical consumer who just throws a fast glance at advertisements and other written materials, but rather the [ECJ] supposes a critical and attentive consumer who makes use of all the information offered.[47]

Furthermore, the ECJ has also always taken the view that consumer preference for domestic products may not be invoked by Member States to exclude access to the market of unfamiliar imported products.[48] This is based on the rationale that Member States must not be permitted to crystallize the habits of consumers, who should be the beneficiaries of the increased choice offered by the single market while the possibility for them to select the familiar domestic product remains open.

The ECJ has not always respected the strict interpretation of the Article 177 preliminary-rulings procedure and has on occasion gone beyond pure interpretations of the Treaty to deciding, as a matter of fact, whether certain national provisions restrictive of intra-Community trade may be justified for the protection of consumers.[49] The inevitable consequence of this

[45] See discussion in Weatherill, 'The Role of the Informed Consumer in European Community Law and Policy' (1994) 2 Consum. LJ 49.

[46] See, e.g., the *Cassis de Dijon* case itself, Case 120/78, n. 1 above; Case 788/79, n. 15 above; Case 261/81 *Walter Rau* v. *de Smedt*, [1982] ECR 3961, [1983] 2 CMLR 496 and Case 407/85 *Drei Glocken* v. *USL Centro-Sud* [1988] ECR 4233.

[47] Howells and Wilhelmsson, 'EC Consumer Law' in Howells (ed.), *European Business Law*, (Dartmouth, 1996), 297.

[48] See, e.g., Case 94/82 *De Kikvorsch Groothandel* [1983] ECR 947, [1984] 2 CMLR 323 at para. 8 and Case 178/84 *Commission* v. *Germany* (*Reinheitsgebot*) [1987] ECR 1227, [1988] 1 CMLR 780 at para. 32.

[49] In Case 286/81 *Oosthoek's Uitgeversmaatschappij BV* [1982] ECR 4575 and Case 382/87 *Buet* v. *Ministère Public*, n. 12 above the ECJ accepted the consumer-protection justifications advanced in those cases. On the other hand, in Case 362/88 *GB-INNO* v. *CCL* [1990] ECR I–667; Case C–126/91 *Schutzverband gegen Unwesen in der Wirtschaft* v. *Yves Rocher* [1993] ECR I–2361 & Case C–135/92 *Verband Sozialer Wettbewerb* v. *Estée Lauder* [1994] ECR I–317 the ECJ rejected the consumer-protection defences advanced.

is that the ECJ is gradually developing a Community-wide concept of 'reasonably circumspect consumers'[50] at the expense of existing national conceptions.[51]

Applications of the ECJ's interpretation of the consumer protection mandatory requirement by national courts can be very effective. For example, the *Gerechtshof* Den Haag in *Bijou Brigitte Modische Accessoires AG* v. *Waarborg Platina, Goud en Zilver NV*[52] applied the ECJ's judgment in *Robertson*[53] where the ECJ had held that Member States cannot require a fresh hallmark to be affixed to gold and silver products imported from other Member States in which they have been lawfully marketed and hallmarked in accordance with legislation of that State, where the information provided by that hallmark is 'equivalent to those provided by the hallmarks prescribed by the Member State of importation and intelligible to consumers of that State'.[54] The ECJ had in that judgment added that '[i]t is for the national court to make the findings of fact needed for the purposes of determining whether or not such equivalence exists'.[55] The *Gerechtshof* Den Haag, which was faced with the prosecution of a German company for selling gold and silver imported into the Netherlands from Germany without the hallmark required by the Dutch *Waarborgwet* 1986,[56] summarized the ECJ judgment in *Robertson* and then dealt with certain arguments advanced by the Dutch Government as to why there was no equivalence guaranteed by the German hallmark such that the protection of consumers justified the restriction on marketing in the Netherlands. On the one hand, the *Gerechtshof* rejected as irrelevant the objection that the German legislation did not make a hallmark stamp compulsory since the facts of the case

---

[50] Case C–470/93 *Verein gegen Unwesen* v. *Mars GmbH* [1995] ECR I–1923 at para. 24. However, the ECJ will only do so if it has sufficient documents before it to carry out substantive applications to the facts: see for example, Case C–313/94 *Fratelli Graffione SNC* v. *Ditta Fransa* [1996] ECR I–6039, [1997] 1 CMLR 925 at para. 25.

[51] It is also interesting to note that there are signs that the emerging Community-wide concept of consumer protection is also influencing purely domestic-law cases concerning consumer protection where it appears that the ECJ approach to consumer protection (and the emphasis on labelling as an alternative means) was applied to a case not concerning Art. 30: *Re Dietary Sausages* Case 3 C 33.89, *Bundesverwaltingsgericht*, 23 Jan. 1992, [1993] 3 CMLR 118. For other cases concerning the consumer-protection justification under the rule of reason before German courts, see *OLG* Frankfurt, 14 May 1981, GRUR 1982, 58 (noted by Roth (1991) 28 CMLRev. 137 at 158); *OLG* Cologne, 20 Nov. 1981, GRUR 1983, 71; LG Aachen, 31 Oct. 1984, RiW 1985, 139 (noted by Roth (1991) 28 CMLRev. 137 at 157); *OLG* Köln, 30 Nov. 1984, GRUR 1986, 323; *OLG* Hamburg, 3 Sept. 1987, GRUR 1988, 66; *OLG* Köln, 29 Apr. 1988, GRUR 1989, 694; [1990] 2 CMLR 104 (noted by Roth (1991) 28 CMLRev. 137 at 158); BGH, 26 Jan. 1989, BB 1989, 722. Equally, before the Belgian courts, see Pres. Comm. Mechelen, 18 Mar. 1991, Jaarboek Handelspraktijken/Annuaire Pratique du Commerce 1991, 70 (with note by Straetmans) and *Cubic* v. *APT Data Services* Comm. Bruxelles, 4 Sept. 1992. Both cases are noted by Wytinck (1993) 30 CMLRev. 981 at 1002.

[52] *Gerechtshof* 's-Gravenhage, 17 Mar. 1992, NJ 1993, 213.

[53] Case 220/81 [1982] ECR 2349, [1983] 1 CMLR 556.

[54] Ibid. at para. 12 of judgt.   [55] Ibid. at para. 13 of judgt.

[56] The Netherlands Law on guaranteed standards for precious metals, Stb. 38/1987.

concerned gold and silver which *had* been hallmarked in Germany. On the other hand, the *Gerechtshof* accepted that since there was no preliminary check by the Government or the independent body which affixes the hall-mark in Germany, and since there were technical differences in that the German provisions allowed larger differences between the stated fineness and the actual fineness than the Dutch provisions, the German hallmark did not provide equivalent protection to Dutch consumers.[57] The justifica-tion of the protection of consumers was equally confidently applied by the *RCC* in *Alternatieve Konsumentenbond* v. *Mars BV*,[58] which concerned a claim that the import of 'Bounty' chocolate bars from Germany with the *'Der Grüne Punkt'* logo[59] would mislead Dutch consumers into thinking that the product had environmentally friendly properties. The *RCC* held that such a restriction would constitute a breach of Article 30 which would not be justified on the grounds of the protection of consumers since the packaging was labelled in several languages and the logo only formed part of the German labelling, which was aimed at the German, and not the Dutch, consumer.[60] Labelling was not held to be sufficient to protect con-sumers by the *CBB* in *Hema BV* v. *Minister van Verkeer en Waterstaat*[61] which concerned the importation into the Netherlands of the 'Kingtel' telephone, which did not comply with the technical requirements as set out in Article 29 of the *Wet op de Telecommunicatievoorzieningen*.[62] The *CBB* held that it was not certain whether Article 30 EC applied to the case since

[57] The judgment of the *Gerechtshof* Den Haag has been confirmed by the ECJ in Case C–293/93 *Houtwipper* v. *Openbaar Ministerie* [1994] ECR I–4249. In contrast to the *Robertson* case (n. 53 above), where the ECJ left the application to the facts to the national court, the ECJ in *Houtwipper* decided the merits of the consumer-protection justification on the facts of the case. In the light of the fact that the *Gerechtshof* Den Haag in *Bijou Brigitte* applied the *Robertson* judgment extremely confidently to the facts, it may be questioned whether it was necessary for the ECJ in *Houtwipper* to have made the findings of fact which it could, and arguably should, have left to the national court.

[58] *RCC*, 15 June 1993, IER 1993, 38; BIE 1995, 22.

[59] Which in Germany, signifies to consumers that the packaging may be recycled—Duales Systeem Deutschland (DSD) sells this logo in return for collecting and recycling the packag-ing material.

[60] The confident application of the *RCC* is somewhat marred by the reference in the judg-ment to 'the protection of the consumer as meant by Art. 36 of the EEC Treaty'. Consumer protection is, of course, a mandatory requirement under the rule of reason and is not men-tioned in Art. 36. For confident applications of the consumer-protection justification before the German courts with respect to national provisions prohibiting misleading advertising or labelling, see *Re 'Hellebrekers' Advocaat*, Case 6U 42/90, *OLG* Cologne, 11 Jan. 1991, [1993] 2 CMLR 61; *Re 'Grand Marnier' Liqueur* Case 6U 97/90, *OLG* Frankfurt-am-Main, 19 Sept. 1991, [1993] 2 CMLR 123 and *Re a Cosmetics Advertising Slogan* Case 6 U 2417/91, *OLG* Munchen, 17 Sept. 1992, [1994] 3 CMLR 41.

[61] *CBB*, 30 Jan. 1991, SEW 1991, 489 (with note by Mortelmans), Ars Aequis 1991, 8.

[62] Dutch law on telecommunication facilities (Stb. 1988/520) implementing Directive 88/301 [1988] OJ L131/73. These technical requirements should have been notified to the Commission under Directive 89/189 [1983] OJ L109/8. See discussion of this aspect of the judgment at p. 363.

it was unclear whether the telephones in question had met the requirements of having been 'put into circulation in another Member State'. Nevertheless the *CBB* held that the Dutch provisions were justified for the protection of consumers under the rule of reason. The *CBB* embarked upon an excellent and in-depth application of the rule of reason and concluded that the consumer could not have been equally protected by providing information by means of labelling as to the points at which the Dutch requirements were not met by the 'Kingtel' telephone. Such technical knowledge was held to be beyond that which could be expected of the average consumer and the *CBB* also rejected the argument that consumers could be assumed to be aware as a result of the low price of the telephone that it was a low-quality product. The *CBB* held that the technical requirements were not only necessary for the protection of the consumer buying the telephone, but for the protection of all users of the telephone network and that the low price was irrelevant. The requirements for the protection of consumers were clearly overwhelming and the detailed analysis of the *CBB* has much to commend it.[63]

The commendable national case law needs, however, to be balanced against several examples of less than satisfactory applications of the justification by the consumer-protection rule of reason by these courts. Without drawing any firm conclusions at this stage, it will be noted that it is predominantly in judgments of the French courts that one finds examples of insufficiently reasoned applications of this justification for restrictions to the free movement of goods. A telling example is provided by the judgment of the *Conseil d'Etat* in *Smanor SA* v. *Syndicat national des fabricants de produits surgelés et congelés*[64] which concerned an application by Smanor to have French legislation (the effect of which was to prohibit Smanor from using the designation 'yoghurt' for the sale of deep-frozen yoghurt in France)[65] annulled on the basis that it infringed Article 30. The argument was that the product in question could be presented in other Member States as deep-frozen yoghurt and thus that the restriction in the French legislation on the use of the term yoghurt was a hindrance to trade. The *Conseil d'Etat* dismissed the Article 30 argument, since

---

[63] Mortelmans, n. 61 above, also commends the *CBB* for settling this case without troubling the ECJ with an Art. 177 reference. The breach of Art. 30 was unclear, but a reference to the ECJ on that point was not necessary for settling the case since even if that Article was breached, it would be justified for the protection of consumers under the rule of reason. Mortelmans observes that the *CBB* refrained from making a reference to the ECJ not because the Art. 30 point was *acte clair* nor because it was *acte éclairé* but because it was *acte neutre*.

[64] *Conseil d'Etat*, 19 Nov. 1986, Rec. Lebon 1986, 259, JCP 1987, II 20822; AJDA 1986, 714; RTDE 1988, 117; CDE 1989, 418.

[65] Art. 11 of Law of 5 Aug. 1905 as amended by Law of 10 Jan. 1978 and Decree no. 82-184 of 22 Feb. 1982, JORF 25 Feb. 1982, p. 676.

the sole object of the provisions, which do not in themselves entail any quantitative restriction on importation, is to restrict the denomination 'yoghurt' *in the interests of consumers* to certain products presenting certain characteristics and they cannot be regarded as having an effect equivalent to such restrictions.[66]

The reasoning of the *Conseil d'Etat* is, with respect, extremely confused.[67] In particular, it is not clear whether the *Conseil d'Etat* was holding that the measure was justified 'in the interests of consumers' under the rule of reason. It is only by reading the conclusions of *Commissaire du Gouvernement* Lasserre to the *Conseil d'Etat* in this case, that it can be seen that it seems that what the *Conseil d'Etat* meant was that the French measure was justified under the rule of reason and, as such, did not breach Article 30. Not only is this judgment of the *Conseil d'Etat* woefully insufficiently reasoned, it is also probably wrong. This appears to follow from the subsequent judgment of the ECJ in *SA Smanor* on a separate reference from the *Tribunal commercial* of L'Aigle,[68] where the ECJ held that Article 30 was breached and 'appears to be disproportionate in relation to the objective of consumer protection'.[69] The ECJ noted that 'information may however be given effectively, without forbidding the use of the name "yoghurt", by requiring adequate labelling with the compulsory inclusion of the description "deep-frozen", to show clearly the particular treatment which the products in question have undergone'.[70] Furthermore, the ECJ drew on evidence drawn up by the Food and Agriculture Organization (FAO) in the *Codex Alimentarius* and the World Health Organization (WHO) to conclude that the characteristic feature of a product marketed as 'yoghurt' is the presence in abundant quantities of live lactic bacteria. Although the ECJ concluded that 'it is for the national court which has to decide on the merits of the case to determine . . . whether the extent to which deep-frozen yoghurt differs from the requirements of national rules relating to fresh yoghurt is such as to justify a different name',[71] it gave a strong hint that it was not so justified, stating that

[T]he prohibition by national rules of the use of the name 'yoghurt' for the sale of deep-frozen products appears to be disproportionate in relation to the objective of

---

[66] Emphasis added.

[67] For criticisms of this judgment see Azibert and De Boisdeffre AJDA 1986, 681; Constantinesco, Simon and Soler-Couteaux RTDE 1988, 113–17. The Fourth Report to the European Parliament on Commission Monitoring of the Application of Community Law [1987] OJ C338 commented that the *Conseil d'Etat* 'interpreted and applied Community law in a manner which, at the very least, raises questions in view of the established case law of the Court of Justice concerning Art. 30'. Even more emphatic was the Sixth Report [1989] OJ C330/1 (includes appendix, 'The Attitude of National Supreme Courts to Community Law') which described the *Conseil d'Etat*'s judgment as a 'serious breach of the principle of uniformity of judicial decisions'.

[68] *Trib. comm.* L'Aigle, 21 Sept. 1987.

[69] Case 298/87 [1988] ECR 4489 at para. 23.

[70] Ibid. at para. 19.   [71] Ibid. at para. 24.

consumer protection, when the characteristics of the deep-frozen products are not substantially different, particularly as regards the quantity of bacteria, from fresh products, and when appropriate labelling together with an indication of the date by which the product should be sold or consumed would suffice to give consumers proper information.[72]

This subsequent judgment of the ECJ strongly suggests that the *Conseil d'Etat*'s judgment was wrong in its conclusion that the French legislation was justified for consumer protection. At the very least, the ECJ judgment demonstrates that the analysis of the justification of the protection of consumers by the *Conseil d'Etat* was far too brief and superficial. These criticisms are all the more serious since, when the ECJ's judgment in the separate reference[73] came back before the *Tribunal commercial* of L'Aigle for implementation, Smanor had gone into receivership. It seems very likely that the misconstrual by the *Conseil d'Etat* in this decision had a role to play in pushing Smanor out of business.[74]

Similar examples of insufficient reasoning before the French courts are to be found in the judgment of the Criminal Division of the *Cour de Cassation* in *Falck*, where it was held that French legislation requiring that temporary shops (*vente au deballage*) receive prior authorization from local authorities did not breach Article 30 since 'it was not shown, nor even alleged, that the [goods] sold . . . were submitted to conditions of sale more rigorous than those applying to national products'[75] and that the French provisions had as their aim the protection of the consumer and the fairness of commercial transactions. This was the full extent of the *Cour de Cassation*'s application of the consumer-protection justification in this case.[76] Similarly, in *Campin*,[77] the *Cour de Cassation* upheld a conviction for marketing in France soft drinks imported from Belgium which infringed French legislation[78] in three respects: they were not re-labelled into the French language, they were labelled as 'limonade' while not presenting any of the characteristics of that drink, and they were labelled as '*jus de fruits*' even though they contained less than 12 per cent fruit (which was the threshold in the French legislation). The *Cour de Cassation* dismissed the Article 30 defence by holding that 'whilst Article 30 of the Treaty of

---

[72] Ibid. at para. 23.   [73] n. 68 above.

[74] It may also be noted that the owners of SA Smanor were subsequently unsuccessful in an attempt to obtain legal redress: see judgment of the *Cour de Cassation*, ch. crim., 25 June 1996, Arrêt no. 2889 (transcr. available on Lexis).

[75] *Cour de Cassation*, ch. crim., 25 Oct. 1993, Bull. Cass. Crim. 1993, no. 309 p. 776. See discussion of this aspect of the judgment at p. 65.

[76] See also *Couat*, *Cour de Cassation*, ch. crim., 10 July 1990, Bull. Cass. Crim. 1990, no. 279 p. 705 where the *Cour de Cassation* on similar facts held that there was no breach of Art. 30 and the possibility of justification for consumer protection was not even mentioned.

[77] *Cour de Cassation*, ch. crim., 9 Nov. 1987, Bull. Cass. Crim. 1987, no. 394 p. 1038.

[78] Art. 1 of Law 75–1349 of 31 Dec. 1975; Arts. 3, 4, & 8 of Decree of 7 Dec. 1984 and Art. 13 of Law of 1 Aug. 1905.

Rome prohibits measures having equivalent effect to quantitative restrictions, the ECJ has already in the similar Case 120/78 *Rewe-Zentral* (Cassis de Dijon) decided that national regulations remain lawful in derogation to Article 30 of the Treaty of Rome if necessary in order to satisfy mandatory requirements for the protection of consumers and the fairness of commercial transactions'.[79] The *Cour de Cassation* then stated that the lower court had correctly held that the French legislation was justified for the protection of the consumer. Again, this analysis falls short of a satisfactory application of the rule of reason which would at the very least require an application of the proportionality principle and consideration as to whether labelling would constitute an adequate alternative means of protecting the consumer. The *Cour de Cassation* appears to have been altogether too quick to allow the justification of protection of consumers under the rule of reason.

There is evidence to suggest that the lack of reasoning in applying the consumer-protection justification before the French courts is more prevalent in the higher French courts. This is to some extent born out by comparing the judgments on virtually identical facts of the *Tribunal de grande instance* of Créteil in *Roger Ruchat* v. *Ministère public*[80] with that of the Criminal Division of the *Cour de Cassation* in *Floch*.[81] Both cases concerned the importation of *charcuterie* into France from other Member States and their prosecution for having a '*taux de HPD*' (*Humidité du produit dégraissé*) greater than that permitted by the *Code des Usages de la Charcuterie et de la Salaison* (Code of Practice for the Delicatessen and Salted Meat Trade).[82] The defence that the French legislation breached Article 30 was raised in both cases, which *Les Services de la Répression des Fraudes* argued was justified in the interests of the protection of consumers. In *Ruchat*, the *Tribunal de grande instance* of Créteil held that

[I]t has not been shown that the increase in the *taux d'humidité* is of itself a breach of the protection of consumers. The salami in question is sold with a labelling which allows the consumer to inform himself of the origin of the product which he is buying. The salami conforms with Italian standards and it must be concluded that the sale in France of this product is permitted.

The Tribunal thus allowed the appeal, and although the Court did not cite any case law, it carried out the correct test required by the rule of reason, by referring to labelling being adequate together with mentioning that the

---

[79] See also *Biscuits Delacre* v. *Belin*, TGI Paris, 4 Dec. 1995 (transcr. available on Lexis) where the proportionality and alternative means tests were at least mentioned.

[80] *TGI* Créteil, 11e ch., 5 May 1987, *La Semaine Juridique*—éd. entreprise 1987, II 15041 (with note by Anstett-Gardea and Schmidt).

[81] *Cour de Cassation*, ch. crim., 2 Feb. 1994, Bull. Cass. Crim. 1994, no. 51 p. 103.

[82] *Ruchat* concerned the importation of salami from Italy and *Floch* concerned the importation of '*l'epaule de porc choix*' from Belgium.

salami was lawfully marketed in Italy. This may be contrasted with the judgment of the *Cour de Cassation* in *Floch* which first held that the French legislation did not breach Article 30, and then stated that 'the French regulation is necessary to satisfy mandatory requirements with a view to protecting the fairness of commercial transactions and the protection of consumers'.[83] The application of the rule of reason was elaborated on by the *Cour de Cassation* no further. It may very well be that the *Cour de Cassation* has a different perspective of consumer protection than that of the *Tribunal de grande instance*. It may also be that the products involved in the two cases were such that the French consumer needed more protection with respect to the levels of *HPD* in the *épaule de porc* in *Floch* than in the salami at issue in *Ruchat*. Nevertheless, the point is that the lack of reasoning in the *Cour de Cassation*'s judgment was such that it is impossible to know whether this was the case. While the *Tribunal de grande instance* of Créteil at least applied some semblance of the proportionality test required in any application of the rule of reason (concluding that labelling was sufficient alternative means), the *Cour de Cassation* leaves one totally in the dark as to why it considered that the import ban 'is necessary to satisfy mandatory requirements'. It is submitted that for an application of Community law to be satisfactory such an analysis on the face of the judgment by the national court is required.[84]

The balance of poor applications of the justification of protection of consumers in the rule of reason by the national courts gives rise to the question as to whether it would be desirable for the ECJ to be encouraged to decide the proportionality of consumer-protection justifications raised to the facts of the cases referred to it. It has already been noted that the ECJ has been somewhat erratic by deciding in some cases the proportionality of the consumer-protection justifications itself (and thus arguably overstepping its competence under Article 177 EC)[85] while leaving it to the national court in others.[86] When the ECJ decides the proportionality issue itself, the task of the national court in implementing the judgment is certainly made easier as it is very often left with little else to do than to 'rubber-stamp' the judgment of the ECJ. This was certainly the case in *Openbaar Ministerie* v. *Miro BV*,[87] where the ECJ clearly held that Dutch legislation prohibiting the use of the term *Jenever* for a drink imported and lawfully marketed in Belgium with an inferior alcohol content to that required by the Dutch legislation was not justified under the rule of

---

[83] n. 81 above.

[84] See discussion of the influence on the application of EC law by national courts of the style of judgments according to national legal traditions at p. 254.

[85] n. 49 above.

[86] See, e.g., Case C–313/94, n. 50 above, cf. Joined Cases C–34–36/95 *Konsumentombudsmannen* v. *De Agostini (Svenska) Förlag AB* [1997] ECR I–3843.

[87] Case 182/84 [1985] ECR 3731.

reason for the protection of consumers. The *Gerechtshof* Arnhem implemented the ECJ's judgment by simply referring to it and allowing the
appeal without any further comment.[88] Furthermore, if the ECJ itself
applies the consumer-protection justification to the facts, uniformity of
application in the national courts is ensured. In this way, the ECJ's judgment in *Kelderman BV*,[89] that the Dutch *Broodbesluit* (Regulation on Bread)
laying down levels of dry-matter in bread was not justified for consumer
protection since 'the provision of suitable information to consumers may
easily be ensured by appropriate means, such as requiring labelling showing, for example, the weight and specific composition of an imported
product'[90] was applied and even extended[91] in a further case before the
Arrondissementsrechtbank Arnhem in *Openbaar Ministerie* v. *R.-Bakkerijen
BV*.[92]

However, it is submitted that there are two reasons why the ECJ should
not be encouraged to itself apply the proportionality of justifications concerning the protection of consumers which are raised, to the facts of the
cases referred to it. Firstly, the ECJ has neither the fact-finding capacity of
the national courts nor the final word on the nuances of the national provisions involved. As a result, the ECJ's assessment of the facts often lacks
subtlety. An example is provided by the *Oosthoek* case[93] which concerned
Dutch legislation controlling the offer for sales-promotion purposes of
'free gifts' to buyers of encyclopaedias. The ECJ held that such legislation
was capable of breaching Article 30 but held that it was justified for the
protection of consumers since

It is undeniable that the offering of free gifts as a means of sales promotion may
mislead consumers as to the real prices of certain products and distort the conditions on which genuine competition is based. Legislation which restricts or even
prohibits such commercial practices for that reason is therefore capable of con-
tributing to consumer protection and fair trading.[94]

---

[88] *Gerechtshof* Arnhem, 28 Feb. 1986, NJ 1987, 67; CDE 1989, 411.
[89] Case 130/80 *Criminal Proceedings against Fabriek voor Hoogwaardige Voedingsprodukten
Kelderman BV* [1981] ECR 527. See more recent cases also concerning bread: Case C–17/93
Van der Veldt [1994] ECR I–3537 & Case C–358/95 *Morellato* v. *USL* [1997] ECR I–1431.
[90] Ibid. at para. 12.
[91] The *Kelderman* judgt was extended in the sense that the *Arrondissementsrechtbank*
Arnhem also held that Art. 3 of the *Broodbesluit*, which provided that the 'nature and composition' of the bread must be evident from the name of the bread, could equally not be justified for the protection of consumers. It was held that the *Officier van Justitie* (Public
Prosecutor) had not put forward any satisfactory reason as to why both the nature and the
composition had to be clear in the name of the bread (*in casu roggebrood*, lawfully marketed
and imported from Germany) and that it was not shown that labelling would not provide
sufficient protection to consumers.
[92] *Arrondissementsrechtbank* Arnhem, 6 Apr. 1981, NJ 1981, 388.
[93] n. 49 above.   [94] Para. 18 of judgt.

The *Gerechtshof* Amsterdam[95] had no difficulty in implementing this ECJ judgment and did so by stating that it 'adopts and takes as its own' the ECJ judgment and convicted the defendant. However there was a further appeal in this case to the *Hoge Raad*, arguing that the exception provided for in the Dutch legislation, which permitted a free gift to be offered provided that it is usually used or consumed at the same time as the main purchase,[96] was satisfied in this case.[97] The *Hoge Raad* dismissed the appeal and held that the strict interpretation of this exception, according to which the 'related consumption' must result from 'a connection of intrinsic usefulness between the gift and the goods sold', was not satisfied here.[98] It is submitted, therefore, that although the further appeal to the *Hoge Raad* in this case did not upset the ECJ's judgment, it seems that the ECJ decision that the justification of protection of consumers was satisfied on the facts made large assumptions as to the correct interpretation of the Dutch legislation, which was less settled than the ECJ assumed. It is submitted that had it left this question of fact entirely to the national court, the assessment of the consumer-protection justification could have been evaluated with a greater amount of subtlety, taking into consideration the full context of the national legislation.

The second reason why it is suggested that the ECJ should not be encouraged to decide the proportionality of consumer-protection justifications raised to the facts of the cases referred to it is that the national court is much better placed to carry out such an analysis in a dynamic fashion as opposed to the more generalized or 'broad-brush' approach to which the ECJ is limited. The dynamism of application by national courts is illustrated by the implementation by the French *Cour de Cassation* of the ECJ's judgment in *Wurmser*.[99] It will be recalled that the ECJ had held in that case that the verification of information on a product's composition supplied to consumers when the product is released for sale must allow the importer to rely on certificates issued by the authorities of the Member State of production, or by a laboratory approved by the said authorities for that purpose, or 'other attestations providing a like degree of assurance'. The ECJ added that '[i]t is for the national court to determine whether, having regard to all the circumstances of the case, the attestations provided by the importer are sufficient to establish that the latter has fulfilled his obligation to verify'.[100] In application of this judgment, the *Cour de Cassation* summarized the ECJ's judgment in detail and applied it to the facts holding that

---

[95] *Gerechtshof* Amsterdam, *Ec. kamer*, 11 Mar. 1983 (transcr.: Ec. 230750-81).
[96] This criterion is referred to in Dutch as *consumptieverwantschap* and may be described in English as 'related consumption'.
[97] *Hoge Raad*, 29 Nov. 1983, NJ 1984, 293 (with note by 't Hart).
[98] This strict interpretation is criticised by 't Hart, n. 97 above.
[99] Case 25/88 [1989] ECR 1105, [1991] 1 CMLR 173.　　　[100] Ibid. at para. 19.

'the documents of origin of the manufacturer himself, as well as his invoices and analyses carried out in his own laboratory' are not such as to constitute an 'attestation of like degree of assurance'.[101] The national court was able to apply the ECJ criteria to the facts in a dynamic fashion such that it could do so on a case-by-case basis. A similar excellent example of the dynamism of applications by national courts of the consumer-protection justification is provided by the implementation of the ECJ's *Fietje*[102] judgment by the *Economische Politierechter* in the *Arrondisse-mentsrechtbank* Assen. Again, it will be recalled that the ECJ had held that the application of Dutch provisions governing the obligation to use the word *'likeur'* for beverages defined in the *Likeurbesluit* (Decree on Liqueurs) could constitute a breach of Article 30 which would not be jus-tified for the protection of the consumer 'in so far as the details given on the original label supply the consumer with information on the nature of the product in question which is equivalent to that in the description pre-scribed by law. It is for the national court to make the findings of fact nec-essary in order to establish whether or not there is such equivalence.'[103] The implementation of this judgment was carried out most convincingly by the *Economische Politierechter* in the *Arrondissementsrechtbank* Assen.[104] That court summarized the ECJ's judgment in detail and proceeded to set out the relevant Dutch provisions[105] which it boiled down to two essential requirements: beverages had to be labelled as *'likeur'*[106] if firstly, the beverage included fruit juices and specifications of taste and aroma; and secondly, if the beverage had an alcohol content of more than 22 per cent. The *Arrondissementsrechtbank* then set out the original labelling which appeared on the beverage at issue in the case. The labelling read *'Berentzen Appel. Aus Apfel mit Weizenkom. 25 vol. %'* (Berentzen Appel. Made from apple and barley. 25% Vol). The *Arrondissementsrechtbank* then held that since both elements required by the Dutch provisions which it had already identified were satisfied by this labelling (i.e. the labelling made clear that the beverage included fruit juices and included specifications of taste and aroma and had an alcohol content of more than 22 per cent) 'the *Politie Rechter* is of judgment that the original label supplies the consumer with information on the nature of the product in question which is equivalent to that in the description prescribed by law'. Fietje was duly acquitted. This detailed application of the ECJ's judgment to the facts has much to

---

[101] *Cour de Cassation*, ch. crim., 17 Oct. 1991, Bull. Cass. Crim. 1991, no. 356 p. 888, Dalloz 1992, Jur. 208 (with note by Saintourens).

[102] Case 27/80 [1980] ECR 3839, [1981] 3 CMLR 722.				[103] Ibid. at para. 15.

[104] *Ec. Politierechter* in *Arrondissementsrechtbank* Assen, 23 Feb. 1981, transcript (parket-number 035332–9; Rolnumber 3179/79).

[105] Art. 1(1) *Likeurbesluit* of 11 Sept. 1953 (Stb. 466) which was enacted on the basis of Art. 14 of the *Warenwet* of 28 Dec. 1935 (Stb. 793).

[106] It was, incidentally, permissible to spell *'likeur'* as *'liqueur'*.

commend it and, it is submitted, is strong evidence that the ECJ should not be encouraged to itself apply the proportionality of justifications based on the protection of consumers raised, to the facts of the cases referred to it. The latter judgments illustrate the extent to which the national court is better placed to carry out the factual analysis in a dynamic fashion as opposed to the more generalized approach to which the ECJ is limited.

Finally, it may be noted that the ECJ has incorporated national unfair-competition laws within the concept of consumer protection. Thus, national provisions which fall within the definition of unfair-competition laws (e.g. passing off), and which breach Article 30, may nevertheless be justified for the protection of consumers under the rule of reason, subject to the usual proportionality test.[107] Before it was clear that the ECJ was to consider national unfair-competition laws within the concept of consumer protection under the rule of reason, the English courts seemed to assume that the tort of passing off fell within the meaning of 'industrial and commercial property' in Article 36.[108] Even after it was well established that this was not the case, it is somewhat surprising to find examples of cases before the Dutch courts in which it was held that certain Dutch provisions on unfair competition fell within the meaning of intellectual property rights provided for in Article 36.[109]

4 PROTECTION OF NATIONAL SOCIO-CULTURAL CHARACTERISTICS: NATIONAL LEGISLATION AFFECTING SHOP-OPENING HOURS

Since the judgment of the ECJ in *Keck and Mithouard*[110] limiting the broad scope of Article 30 in certain areas,[111] the ECJ has had the opportunity to confirm that shop-opening hours are within the category of

---

[107] See, e.g., the ECJ judgments in Case 58/80 *Dansk Supermarked* v. *Imerco* [1981] ECR 181, [1981] 3 CMLR 590; Case 6/81 *BV Industrie Diensten Groep* v. *Beele Handelsmaatschappij BV* [1982] ECR 707 and Case C–313/94, n. 50 above. For an application of these principles before the Belgian courts, see *Estée Lauder* v. *Spa*, Cour d'*Appel* Brussels, 31 Mar. 1983, Revue du droit commercial 1984, 124 (noted by Lenaerts and Sunaert (1989) 14 ELRev. 434 at 436).

[108] See, e.g. the judgments of Graham J in the Chancery Division of the English High Court in *Löwenbräu München* v. *Grunhalle Lager International Ltd* [1974] 1 CMLR 1 and *Maxims & Vaudable* v. *Joan Grace Dye* [1977] 2 CMLR 410; [1977] 1 WLR 1155.

[109] See, e.g., *Esge SA* v. *Alpha Trading BV en Wigo Gottlob Widman und Sohne GmbH*, Gerechtshof Amsterdam, 25 Sept. 1980, BIE 1982, 87 (with note by DWFV) (concerning '*slaafse nabootsing*' [precise imitation]); *Kierke Amsterdam BV* v. *EMI en CBS*, Arrondissementsrechtbank Haarlem, 8 Aug. 1989, Informatierecht/AMI 1990/10 p. 225–7 (with note by Cohen Jehoram) and *NVPI* v. *Bloemendaal*, Pres. Arrondissementsrechtbank Haarlem, 13 Oct. 1992, Informatierecht/AMI 1993, p. 72 (concerning '*onrechtmatige daad*' for copying sound recordings without permission. Since the action was not for breach of copyright, it is submitted that consumer protection in the rule of reason, rather than intellectual property rights in Art. 36, would appear to be the correct basis for any justification).

[110] Cases C–267 & 268/91 [1993] ECR I–6097.

[111] See detailed analysis of the *Keck* judgment in Ch. 3, sect. 3.

'selling arrangements' created by that judgment and are, subject to the provisos mentioned in *Keck*,[112] now outside the scope of Article 30 altogether.[113]

Prior to the *Keck* departure, however, the ECJ had held that national legislation affecting shop-opening hours was capable of breaching Article 30. In *Torfaen Borough Council* v. *B & Q*[114] the ECJ accepted the rather farfetched argument that United Kingdom legislation providing for the closure of shops on Sundays breached Article 30 since, by closing on a Sunday, retailers suffered a reduction in their total sales which would include a reduction in the volume of imports from other Member States. Once the breach of Article 30 was established, the question then was whether the legislation could nevertheless be justified under the rule of reason. The ECJ in *Torfaen* accepted that such national legislation prohibiting retailers from opening their premises on Sundays was in principle justified in order to protect 'national or regional socio-cultural characteristics'[115] so long as 'the restrictive effects on trade which may result therefrom do not exceed the effects intrinsic to rules of that kind'.[116] This formulation, which has been described as 'terse and unhelpful'[117] and 'delphic',[118] is to be understood as an expression of the proportionality principle. Thus, although the ECJ's approach in *Torfaen* was far from clear, it may be assumed that it held in that judgment that national legislation on the closure of shops was capable of breaching Article 30 but could in principle be justified under the rule of reason to protect the mandatory requirement of 'national or regional socio-cultural characteristics' subject to an application of the proportionality test. The ECJ in *Torfaen* refrained from itself applying the proportionality test to the facts and stated that '[t]he question of whether the effects of specific national rules do in fact remain within that limit is a question of fact to be determined by the national court'.[119] English and Welsh courts had great difficulty in applying this opaque test.[120] Subsequently, the waters were muddied further by the

---

[112] The national legislation must apply to all traders operating within the national territory and must affect in the same manner, in law and in fact, the marketing of domestic products and those from other Member States.

[113] See Cases C–69/93 & C–258/93 *Punto Casa SpA* v. *Sindaco del Comune di Capena* and *Promozioni Polivalenti Venete Soc. coop. arl (PPV)* v. *Sindaco del Comune di Torri di Quartesolo, Comune di Torri di Quartesolo* [1994] ECR I–2355, Cases C–401 & 402/92 *Tankstation 't Heukske VOF and J. B. E. Boermans* v. *Openbaar Ministerie* [1994] ECR I–2199 & Joined Cases C–418–421/93, C–460–462/93, C–464/93, C–9–11/94, C–14–15/94, C–23–24/94, & C–332/94 *Semeraro Casa Uno Srl* [1996] ECR I–2975.

[114] Case 145/88, n. 10 above.   [115] Para. 14 of judgt.

[116] Para. 15 of judgt.   [117] Arnull, 'What Shall We Do on Sunday?' at 112.

[118] Rawlings, 'The Euro-law Game: Some Deductions From a Saga' at 317.

[119] Para. 16 of judgt.

[120] The UK legislation in question applied only in England & Wales.

ECJ's rulings in *UDS* v. *Conforama*[121] and *Marchandise*[122] where it held that laws restricting the employment of staff on Sundays (French and Belgian respectively) did not, on the test it had enunciated in *Torfaen*, seem to create restrictive effects out of proportion to their aim. The ECJ simply said that '[i]t must further be stated that the restrictive effects on trade which may stem from such rules do not seem disproportionate to the aim pursued'.[123] This was, rather surprisingly, the full extent of the ECJ's application of the proportionality principle. On a second reference from the English courts, this time from the House of Lords, the ECJ finally held that the United Kingdom legislation was also justified and proportionate.[124] With respect to the application of the proportionality principle, the ECJ held

Appraising the proportionality of national rules which pursue a legitimate aim under Community law involves weighing the national interest in attaining that aim against the Community interest in ensuring the free movement of goods. In that regard, in order to verify that the restrictive effects on intra-Community trade of the rules at issue do not exceed what is necessary to achieve the aim in view, it must be considered whether those effects are direct, indirect or purely speculative and whether those effects do not impede the marketing of imported products more than the marketing of national products.

It was on the basis of these considerations that in its judgments in the *Conforama* and *Marchandise* cases the court ruled that the restrictive effects on trade of national rules prohibiting the employment of workers on Sundays in certain retailing activities were not excessive in relation to the aim pursued. For the same reasons, the court must make the same finding with regard to national rules prohibiting shops from opening on Sundays.[125]

This put an end to the saga which itself had done nothing for the reputation of the ECJ nor the Rule of Law. Litigation in English and Welsh courts during the period between the ECJ's judgment in *Torfaen Borough Council* v. *B & Q* and its decision in *Stoke-on-Trent*, a period of some three years, had been variously described as an abuse of the constitution[126] and 'a fragmentation of justice'.[127]

---

[121] Case C–312/89 *Union départmentale des syndicats CGT de l'Aisne* v. *SIDEF Conforama* [1991] ECR I–997.

[122] Case C–332/89 *Criminal proceedings against Marchandise* [1991] ECR I–1027.

[123] Para. 12 of Case C–312/89.

[124] See C–169/91 *Stoke-on-Trent City Council* v. *B & Q* [1992] ECR I–6635. Noted by Arnull (1993) 18 ELRev. 314. The precise reasoning of the ECJ in this case is not clear as it cited neither *Dassonville* nor the 'rule of reason'.

[125] Paras. 15 & 16 of judgt.

[126] Diamond (1993) Sol. Jo. 604. See also Jarvis, 'The Sunday Trading Episode: In Defence of the Euro-Defence'; Barnard, 'Sunday Trading: A Drama in Five Acts'; Diamond, 'Dishonourable Defences: The Use of Injunctions & the EEC Treaty—Case Study of the Shops Act 1950'.

[127] Gormley (1990) 27 CMLRev. 141.

At the heart of the problem of evaluating national legislation affecting shop-opening hours and the free movement of goods is the fact that such legislation is a highly charged political issue in all Member States.[128] Indeed, all Member States regulate, in some way, the opening of shops on Sundays.[129] Thus, the role played by EC law in obliging national courts to investigate the proportionality of such legislation is extremely sensitive. In general terms, liberalizing restrictions on the opening of shops on Sundays is supported by consumers and large stores seeking to increase their market share. Furthermore, liberal governments pursuing policies of deregulation argue that liberalizing shop-opening hours creates employment. On the other hand, such reform is opposed by small shopkeepers[130] and trade unions who fear a loss of market share and decreased worker-protection, as employers put pressure on shop assistants to work on a Sunday. Apart from Sweden, which has had no restrictions on Sunday opening for a decade, and the United Kingdom, which has had liberalized Sunday opening since 1994,[131] there is, in rather crude terms, a division between 'northern' and 'southern' Member States with respect to the underlying issues in the debate over Sunday opening. In 'northern' Member States, the issue is chiefly one of worker-protection backed by the power of the unions. Thus, recent incremental changes to German legislation on shop-opening hours (*Ladenschlussgesetz*) has left the ban on Sunday opening untouched largely due to the power of the unions. The same is true of Denmark which introduced new legislation in July 1995, extending opening hours during the week and on Saturdays but leaving Sunday untouched (except for grocery shops earning less than Dkr 12.5 million per year which can open 24 hours per day, seven days a week). Equally, an attempt in July 1995 to change Austria's rigid laws on shop-opening was foiled by a private-sector employees' union.

The debate in the 'southern' Member States on the other hand, is underpinned by the power of the small shopkeepers' lobby. Thus, for example, new legislation was introduced in Spain in 1994 to limit big stores to opening on a maximum of twelve Sundays and public holidays per year, largely as a result of pressure brought by small shopkeepers. In Italy, where cities and provinces set their own opening hours, a referendum to end restrictions on opening hours was defeated in June 1995, a tribute to

---

[128] See, e.g., 'Battle in store as more shops open their doors on a Sunday', *The European*, 26 Oct.–1 Nov. 1995.

[129] See, *Measures taken in the field of Commerce by the Member States of the European Community* (Official Publications, Luxembourg, 1985) and Askham, Burke & Ramsden, *EC Sunday Trading Rules*.

[130] Evidence suggests that the benefit for medium-sized shops in terms of increased turnover on a Sunday is negligible. Nevertheless, such shops generally favour liberalization to meet the demands of consumers and to retain market share.

[131] See discussion of the UK legislation at p. 200.

the power of the shopkeepers' lobby. Finally, in Portugal, Sunday opening was restricted to 6 hours for hypermarkets and other large stores in January 1995, again in response to lobbying by small shopkeepers. Indeed, the amendment of the legislation in Portugal provoked emotive national controversy which included the resignation of the Minister for the Economy (Mr Danial Bessa).[132]

National shop-opening legislation thus embodies a broad spectrum of political issues about which feelings run deep. On the one hand large stores pose as the champions of the consumers backed by governments welcoming the opportunity to defeat trade union objections. Such arguments are pitted against those of trade unions and small shopkeepers. The issues are not, however, only political. The views of traditionalists wishing to preserve the 'special nature of Sundays' for religious or cultural reasons must also be taken on board. Add also the objection that Sunday opening discriminates against women who, as predominately part-time workers, are disproportionately affected. For a little more spice, add also social concerns regarding the impact on family life and the welfare of city centres as large out-of-centre shopping hypermarkets develop at the expense of urban decay. Whatever the merits of these concerns may be, the point is that the application of the rule of reason by the national courts, according to which the proportionality of such national legislation has to be assessed, involves considerable intervention into national regulation of economic life. Such issues go to the core of the division of powers between the Community and its Member States as Hoffmann J (as he then was) has remarked:

The Member States of the Community differ widely in their histories, customs and social and cultural values. It was certainly not the object of the Community to introduce uniformity in all these matters.[133]

It will be clear that national legislation regulating shop-opening is a vexed issue in the national context and invariably reflects a compromise between the competing issues mentioned above. The analysis of national case law in this section will centre on the application of the rule of reason (as expressed by the ECJ in *Torfaen*) by the English, French, and Dutch courts. The applicable legislation in those Member States will thus be outlined in brief.

---

[132] Portugal has more small grocers per head than any other European country.
[133] *Stoke-on-Trent* v. *B & Q* [1991] 4 All ER 221 at 224.

(A) United Kingdom

Until recently, shop opening was regulated in England and Wales by the Shops Act 1950.[134] Section 47 of this Act provided that 'Every shop shall, save as otherwise provided by this Part of this Act, be closed for the serving of customers on Sunday.' Schedule 5 to the Act contained a list of items which could be sold on Sundays, such as intoxicating liquors, certain foodstuffs, tobacco, newspapers, and other products of everyday consumption. Much has been made of the anomalies that the exceptions in Schedule 5 contained. For example, gin but not tea; pornographic magazines but not bibles, and fresh milk but not canned milk could be sold. Under Section 71, local authorities are under a duty to enforce the Act. There were two ways in which they could do this. Firstly, they could institute criminal proceedings. Under Section 59 of the Act, trading on a Sunday was a criminal offence which was punishable by fine.[135] Secondly, local authorities had the power under Section 222 of the Local Government Act 1972 to apply for a civil injunction to prevent Sunday opening.

Sunday trading has always been a hot political potato in the United Kingdom. In 1985 Margaret Thatcher's Conservative Government introduced a bill for the total repeal of restrictions on Sunday trading in which, despite a three-line whip, Conservative MPs rebelled on a second reading to defeat the bill.[136] It is not without significance that this was the only major piece of Government legislation to have been defeated during Mrs Thatcher's term of office. The Shops Act 1950 has now been replaced by the Sunday Trading Act 1994, which entered into force on 26 August 1994. Under the new Act, Sunday opening by large shops is now lawful for up to six hours.[137]

(B) France

In general, French law recognizes in the Constitution the principle of the freedom of commerce and industry and hence there are no restrictions on shop-opening hours. However, French labour law protects employees by

---

[134] There was no comparable legislation in Scotland, where Sunday trading was deregulated.

[135] The applicable fine rose to a maximum of £2,500; little deterrence to large retailers for whom the opportunity of considerably boosting their profits on a Sunday far outweighed the burdens of this criminal sanction.

[136] See *Hansard*, HC, vol. 95 cols 584–702 (14 Apr. 1986).

[137] Under the new Act, shops of less than 280 sq. metres can open at any time on Sunday. Larger shops can open for a continuous 6-hour period between 10 am and 6 pm. This was in line with the proposals of the Shopping Hours Reform Council. For background on the options that were available to MPs see Cm. 2300, 'Reforming the Law on Sunday Trading: A Guide to the Options for Reform', July 1993. See also Maher, 'The New Sunday: Reregulating Sunday Trading' (1995) 58 MLR 72.

providing for a compulsory rest-day of twenty-four hours in each week and stipulates that the rest-days must, as a general rule, be taken on Sundays. This is provided for by the combination of Articles L. 221–2, L. 221–4 and L. 221–5 of the *Code du travail* (Employment Code).[138] In broad terms, there are three exceptions. Firstly, Article L. 221–9 provides for a waiver of the prohibition in a number of sectors exhaustively listed in that article. Such sectors include restaurants, hospitals, newspaper vendors, hotels, pharmacies, and flower shops. Secondly, Articles L. 221–5–1 and L. 221–10 provide for an exception to be made in the case of undertakings whose staff work in shifts. The application of this exception depends in principle on the conclusion of a collective labour agreement. Thirdly, Articles L. 221–6, L. 221–7 and L. 221–19 allow for temporary derogations to be granted on request to a local authority. Article L. 221–6 allows exceptions in favour of a business which can prove that it is detrimental to the public if it closes on Sundays. However, the consent of the local authority, the local chamber of commerce, syndicate of employers and trade unions is required. Decisions must be taken by a Mayor or *Préfet* and must state the legal basis upon which the decision is made. A decision may be challenged before the Administrative Courts by any person claiming to have an interest. Enforcement is, according to Article L. 221–17, carried out by actions brought by shop workers' unions, chambers of commerce, and employers' organizations requesting the *Préfet* to order that the shop closes. Alternatively, trade-union organizations may appear in criminal courts to obtain damages caused by the prejudice suffered as a result of Sunday opening.

The French legislation is long-standing and is entrenched in French social-economic traditions. Nevertheless, the status quo has increasingly come under attack by retailers unafraid to flout the laws.[139]

(C) The Netherlands

Shop opening hours are regulated in the Netherlands by the *Winkelsluitingswet* (Law on Shop Closing) of 23 June 1976.[140] Article 3(2) of the *Winkelsluitingswet* restricts shop-opening hours in the Netherlands in three ways: a maximum number of opening hours is laid down per week;

[138] The French legislation was somewhat relaxed in 1992. See R. 262-1-1 C.T., Decree of 6 Aug. 1992, JCP 1992 III 65559 and a Circular of 7 Oct. 1992, JCP III 65793.

[139] See, Prétot, 'Repos dominical et droit communautaire de la concurrence'; Bandrac & Momège, 'La Fermeture Dominicale et le Droit Communautaire'; Hennion-Moreau, 'La règle du repos dominical' Droit Social 1990, no. 5, p. 434. For a discussion of the compatibility of the French legislation with Community law by courts of summary jurisdiction in France (*juge des référés*), see Cavallini, *Le juge national du provisoire face au droit communautaire*, 177–206.

[140] For the content and origins of and recent amendments to the *Winkelsluitingswet*, see Mok, 'De winkeldeur op een kier' SEW 1993, 30.

there are earliest opening hours and latest closing hours depending on the day of the week, and compulsory Sunday closing. Despite those restrictions, the *Winkelsluitingswet* leaves shopkeepers a degree of freedom in so far as they can decide how to distribute the maximum number of opening hours per week over the periods during which the law allows shops to open. In order to prevent that freedom leading to non-compliance with the restrictions described above, Article 2(1)(a) of the *Winkelsluitingswet* requires shopkeepers to affix at each public entrance a certified notice setting out the opening hours.

Two decrees adopted pursuant to the *Winkelsluitingswet* set out derogations from the general rules. Firstly, the Decree of 14 December 1976[141] makes it possible to grant individual exemptions.[142] Secondly, Article 11 of the *Winkelsluitingswet* provides that exemptions from the prohibitions laid down in the Law may be granted by 'general administrative rules'. The Decree of 6 December 1977, which is a 'general administrative rule' within the meaning of the Law, grants such exemptions to, *inter alia*, museums, chemists, and shops selling newspapers and periodicals in, for example, stations, airports, petrol stations, or hospitals. In particular, Article 3(1) of the Decree of 6 December 1977, as amended by the Decree of 13 December 1988,[143] provides that petrol stations situated at the side of dual carriageways or motorways outside built-up areas and shops connected with them may be open night and day to sell certain articles 'for the road', such as petrol and tobacco products. In contrast, the general rules remain applicable to products which are not 'for the road': such products may be sold only within limited opening hours which have to be indicated at each public entrance to the shop. Outside the opening hours indicated, such products must be kept in a lockable cabinet.

(D) The proportionality principle

The principle of proportionality is one of the 'general principles of law' in the Community and applies throughout the whole sphere to which Community law applies.[144] As such, it is one of the basic principles of the emerging common law of Europe.[145] The application of the proportionality test in practice can often be a deceptively difficult task. The formulation

---

[141] Decree implementing Art. 10(3) of the *Winkelsluitingswet* 1976.

[142] Pursuant to that decree, municipalities may, e.g., grant individual exemptions to shops opening in the evening.

[143] Stb. 1988, p. 593.

[144] A version of the principle of proportionality is now provided for in Art. 3B, Treaty on European Union which provides: 'Any action by the Community shall not go beyond what is necessary to achieve the objectives of this Treaty'.

[145] For a full analysis of the proportionality principle see, Emiliou, *The Principle of Proportionality in European Law: A Comparative Study*, (Kluwer, 1996).

of the proportionality test in *Torfaen* seems to have its roots in Article 3 of Commission Directive 70/50[146] which states the formulation 'where the restrictive effect of such measures on the free movement of goods exceeds the effects intrinsic to trade rules'. That Article goes on to provide that '[t]his is the case, in particular, where—the restrictive effects on the free movement of goods are out of proportion to their purpose—the same objective can be attained by other means which are less of a hindrance to trade.' A more colloquial formulation was suggested by Lord Diplock as '[y]ou must not use a steam hammer to crack a nut, if a nutcracker would do.'[147]

Any application of the proportionality test must begin with an assessment of what the objective of the national measure is. Once the objective has been isolated, it is submitted that the proportionality test should then be applied in two stages.[148] Firstly a *necessity test* ('stage one'). What is asked in this limb of the test is whether the same objective could be obtained by other means which are less of a hindrance to trade. Secondly, a *balancing test* ('stage two'), which adds the further question of whether the restrictive effects on free movement of goods are out of proportion to their purpose. In the case law of the ECJ these two limbs have been clouded by such jargon as whether the measures are 'objectively necessary'[149] or whether they are 'relevant' or 'essential'[150] to achieve the purpose, or whether there are 'alternative means'[151] of reaching the same goal with less restrictive effects on trade. It is submitted that all these variations come down to the same two-limb test. Advocate General Van Gerven in his Opinion in *Stoke-on-Trent* v. *B & Q* has described this two-stage test thus:

First of all, it must be determined whether the national measure in question is *objectively necessary* in order to further the attainment of the objective pursued by it. That means that the measure must be *relevant* (effective), that is to say of such a nature as to afford effective protection of the public interest involved . . . and must be *essential* in order to attain the objective, which implies that the competent legislator does not have an equally effective alternative available to it which would have a *less restrictive* effect on the free movement of goods . . . Secondly, even if the national measure is effective and essential with regard to the objective pursued, it must be determined whether the restriction caused thereby to intra-Community trade is *in relation*, that is to say *proportionate*, to that objective.[152]

---

[146] [1970] OJ L13/29.   [147] *R* v. *Goldstein* [1983] 1 All ER 434 at 436 (HL).

[148] Cf. O'Neill, *Decisions of the ECJ and their Constitutional Implications*, 57 where he describes the proportionality principle as a 3-stage test.

[149] Case 238/82, n. 23 above.

[150] Case 45/87 *Commission* v. *Ireland* (Dundalk Water) [1988] ECR 4929, [1989] 1 CMLR 225; Case 27/80, n. 102 above.

[151] Case 261/81 *Walter Rau* v. *de Smedt* [1982] ECR 3961, [1983] 2 CMLR 496.

[152] Para. 30 of the Opinion. The emphases are those of the Advocate General. See a similar formulation by the learned Adv. Gen. in Case C–159/90 *SPUC* v. *Grogan* [1991] ECR I–4685 at para. 27 of the Opinion.

The difficulty with this two-stage test is that the relationship between the two limbs is unclear. For example, it is not difficult to imagine circumstances in which a particular national measure may be held essential and necessary to achieve the objective (thus satisfying stage one), but that the restrictive effect on trade between Member States is nevertheless so great that they are out of proportion to their purpose (thereby falling at stage two). For example, a national measure implemented for the protection of the environment may be necessary (for the attainment of the objective and enacted with the environmental objective in view where no less restrictive alternative for achieving that environmental goal was available) but may nevertheless be disproportionate since the restrictive effects on free movement of goods is out of proportion to their purpose. Alternatively, one could also imagine national measures for which the restrictive effect caused on inter-State trade is very small (thus satisfying stage two) but for which there is no necessity because there are alternative means of achieving the objective in question (thereby failing stage one). National legislation affecting the opening hours of shops is an example of the latter case. As we shall see, the problem with applying the proportionality test to such legislation is that a court is obliged to examine the necessity of national regulatory measures (under stage one) whose effect on trade is so small as to be proportionate under the second stage of the test.

(E) The application of the proportionality principle to national legislation affecting shop-opening hours

(i) Identifying the objective of the national legislation

As was noted above, any application of the proportionality test must begin with an assessment of what the objective of the national measure is. With respect to the applicable legislation in France, the French courts had no difficulty in identifying the objective of the provisions in the *Code du travail*[153] as being for the protection of workers. So much was obvious from the fact that it is French labour law on the protection of employees which provides for a compulsory rest-day of twenty-four hours in each week and stipulates that the rest-days must, as a general rule, be taken on Sundays. Thus in *SA Virgin Megastores* v. *Fédération des services CFDT*[154] the Paris *Cour d'Appel* held that the French legislation is the 'expression of a socio-political choice *to protect workers* by imposing a weekly rest adapted to national socio-cultural traditions'.[155]

[153] n. 138 above.
[154] *Cour d'appel* Paris, 1re ch. A, 19 Dec. 1990, Gaz. Pal. 1991, I Jur. 249 (with conclusions by Delafaye); Dalloz 1991, IR 76 (summary).
[155] Emphasis added. In the original French: '*l'expression d'un choix de politique sociale protectrice des salariés visant à imposer un repos hebdomadaire adapté aux particularités socioculturelles nationales*'.

Such clarity of objective was absent from the applicable legislation in England and Wales. The Shops Act 1950 was a rather eclectic, arbitrary and out-of-date piece of legislation for which the objectives were particularly difficult to locate. This was reflected in the national judgments applying the proportionality test to the Shops Act. The English and Welsh courts were divided between according the Shops Act a 'worker-protection' objective and a 'preservation of the special nature of Sunday' objective. On the one hand, in *London Borough of Waltham Forest* v. *Scott Markets Ltd*[156] it was held that 'the attainment of Sunday observance, whether for religious or recreational purposes, may be held to be the objective of the restrictions on Sunday trading in the Shops Act 1950'.[157] Similarly in *Torfaen Borough Council* v. *B & Q plc*[158] East Gwent Magistrates sitting at Cwmbran implemented the ECJ judgment in that case by explaining that '[w]e sought to establish the aims of s 47 but were not persuaded that there was any direct correlation between the effects of a rule and its objectives' but went on to hold that the aim of the Shops Act was 'to safeguard the special nature of the English and Welsh Sunday'.[159] Northampton Crown Court in *Wellingborough Borough Council* v. *Payless D.I.Y. Ltd, Kettering Borough Council* v. *W. H. Smith Do-It-All Ltd*[160] was even more forthright:

The objective of section 47 can be stated in a variety of ways, but it is wrong to say that it is unascertainable or to say that it has the limited objective of protecting shopworkers. The objective is the preservation of the special and traditional character of Sunday in England and Wales as a day for rest, relaxation, socialising and, for a significant part of the population, worship. It is a day when the pace of life is different from that on other days, a day on which most people appreciate being spared the business of other days. One part of the population entitled to benefit from the distinctiveness of Sundays is shopworkers; they can enjoy a day of rest on the same day as their relatives and friends and when weekend activities are available . . . The fact that some members of society do not agree with the objective, the fact that social habits change with the years are matters for Parliament to consider, but the objective of the present rule is clear.[161]

However, the existence of English judgments which identified a different objective for the Shops Act, namely the protection of shop workers, casts doubt upon the conclusion in this judgment of Northampton Crown Court that the 'objective of the present rule is clear'. For example, in *Shrewsbury and Atcham B.C.* v. *B & Q*[162] Northcote J, sitting in Shrewsbury Crown Court, concluded that 'the principal objective of s 47 was to protect

---

[156] [1988] 3 CMLR 773.

[157] Ibid. at 783. It may be noted that the High Court identified this objective of the Shops Act while the reference in *Torfaen* was still pending and thus was expressly only providing a 'preliminary view'.

[158] [1990] 3 CMLR 455.   [159] Ibid. at 456.   [160] [1990] 1 CMLR 773.

[161] Ibid. at 779 per Allen J.   [162] [1990] 3 CMLR 535.

employees who might not wish to work on Sundays'.[163] This conclusion
was reached by pointing out that the 1950 Shops Act had co-existed with
the Sunday Observance Act before the latter was repealed in 1969 and thus
that the contention that the Shops Act aimed to preserve 'the traditional
character of Sunday as a day of worship and rest' was untenable. This
view was shared by Hoffmann J sitting in the High Court in *Stoke-on-Trent*
v. *B & Q*,[164] where he held that the objective of the Shops Act was 'to
ensure that, so far as possible, shopkeepers and shop assistants did not
have to work on Sunday'.[165] Hoffmann J actually went on to add that
religious conviction or preserving the traditional quiet Sunday were 'incidental effects' which did not constitute the aims of the legislation.
Hoffmann J reached this conclusion by looking at Parliamentary history of
the Act and quoting Donovan J in the early judgment in *Waterman* v.
Wallasey where he held that '[t]he purpose of the Act is to protect shop
assistants'.[166] The application of the proportionality test to the applicable
English legislation thus got off to a poor start on account of the fact that the
Shops Act itself seemed to have no clear overriding objective which could
be agreed upon by all the courts. As we shall see this led to a divergence
of application within the national legal system.

(ii) Is the proportionality test unduly difficult to apply?

It will be recalled that once the objective of the national legislation has
been isolated, the national court is then required, in application of the proportionality principle, to examine first the necessity of the national measure (referred to above as stage one) and secondly to apply the balancing
test weighing the importance of the identified objective against the restriction to the free movement of goods (referred to above as stage two). The
practical application of both stages of the proportionality test give rise to
difficulties. Bandrac and Momège have argued that the application of
stage one is a rather arbitrary affair in the real social world.[167] They point
out that the application of the necessity limb requires the national court to
investigate, firstly whether another day could be substituted for a Sunday;
secondly whether the religious activities could not be exercised on another
day; and thirdly, whether the harmonious maintenance of family life is
promoted by Sunday closing at all. Bandrac and Momège conclude that
'[i]n the absence of a consensus with respect to these different points, the
judge may seriously doubt that the legislation being investigated passes

---

[163] Ibid. at 537.

[164] [1990] 3 CMLR 31, [1991] 4 All ER 221, [1991] 2 WLR 42.

[165] [1991] 4 All ER 221 at 232. See also Lord Goff in the House of Lords in *Kirklees Borough Council* v. *Wickes Building Supplies* [1992] 3 All ER 717 who also concluded that '[t]he aim of the legislation is to ensure that, so far as possible, shop keepers and shop assistants do not have to work on Sunday' (at 720).

[166] [1954] 2 All ER 187 at 188.   [167] Bandrac & Momège, n. 139 above at 552.

these'.[168] In the final analysis they note that 'Sunday closing seems to be a means of imposing or perpetuating long-lost traditions that the legislator believes to be desirable'.[169] The application of the 'stage two' test gives rise to equally serious difficulties expressed by Mustill LJ in *W. H. Smith Do-It-All Ltd* v. *Peterborough City Council*[170] thus:

How could . . . a desire to keep the Sabbath holy be measured against the free-trade economic premises of the common market? If this is what the *Cassis de Dijon* exception requires, it seems to me that the task would be difficult to the point of impossibility in any but the simplest case, where the balance is to be struck, not between two conflicting trade interests, but between the Community free trade interest on the one hand, and an intangible and elusive national moral, social or cultural norm on the other.[171]

In the light of these very real difficulties faced by the national courts in applying both stages of the proportionality test, the Opinion of Advocate General Van Gerven in *Stoke-on-Trent* v. *B & Q* appears rather optimistic when he states that the proportionality assessment 'implies an assessment which cannot be made solely on the basis of quantifiable data, but that does not mean that the assessment is impossible'.[172]

(iii) *The necessity test vs. the balancing test*

It has already been noted that once the objective of the legislation has been identified, the relationship between the two limbs of the two-stage test of proportionality is unclear. It is submitted that national legislation affecting the opening hours of shops clearly satisfies stage two of the test since the restrictive effect on inter-State trade caused by such legislation is sufficiently small so as not to be out of proportion to the objective. On the other hand, it is submitted that it is much less certain whether such legislation satisfies stage one of the proportionality test given that there are conceivable alternative means of achieving the same goal.[173] For example, assuming that the objective of the Shops Act was to ensure that shop workers had adequate time off, there are clearly other contractual means of achieving this same objective. Even if one supposes that the objective of the legislation was to ensure respect for the Christian Sabbath (or the traditional Sunday), the arbitrariness of the exceptions suggest that the ban cannot be

---

[168] Ibid. at 555. In the original French: '*En l'abesence, évidente, d'un consensus à propos de ces différents points, le juge peut sérieusement douter que l'adaptation recherchée par la mesure soumise à son examen passe infailliblement par celle-ci.*'

[169] Ibid. In the original French: '*la fermeture dominicale semble un moyen d'imposer ou de pérenisser des particularités disparues que le législateur croit souhaitables.*'

[170] [1990] 2 CMLR 577; [1991] 1 QB 304; [1990] 3 WLR 1131; [1991] 4 All ER 193.

[171] [1991] 4 All ER 193 at 210.　　　　　　　　　　　　[172] Para. 31 of the Opinion.

[173] It is interesting to note that the Commission, in its submissions to the ECJ in *Stoke-on-Trent* v. *B & Q*, had argued that if the ECJ should conclude that Art. 30 was breached, there would be difficulties in justifying the Shops Act in view of the alternative means available.

considered necessary.[174] If this analysis is correct, there is then a conceivable conflict between the two limbs of the proportionality test. Which limb of the test should predominate? It will be argued in the discussion of national court judgments applying the proportionality principle which follows, that when the emphasis is placed on the first stage of the test (the necessity and alternative means test), the national court has been more likely to reach the conclusion that the shop-opening legislation was disproportionate. It will also be shown that those judgments in which it was concluded that the shop-opening legislation was proportionate were able to do so only by giving precedence to the second stage of the proportionality test (the balance between the importance of the objective and the restriction to the free movement of goods).

The best known (and only reported) finding before the English courts that the Shops Act 1950 was disproportionate, was made by Shrewsbury Crown Court in *Shrewsbury and Atcham B.C.* v. *B & Q.*[175] In that case, Northcote J stated that the essential question was '[c]ould the objectives, namely employee protection with regard to Sunday employment, be achieved by other means which are less of a hindrance to trade?' He answered this question in the affirmative by explicitly suggesting four possible alternatives which would, in his view, provide equal employee protection with regard to Sunday employment with less of a restriction to intra-Community trade:

1. A contractual requirement that no employees should be required to work on Sundays against their will.
2. Extension of the 5th Schedule of the Act to include items the appellant desires to sell on Sundays. In passing we should say that the schedule is so obviously out of date, full of anomalies, that it would be impractical to justify in its present form.
3. Some limitation on the hours of opening for Sunday trading.
4. Licensing by local Authorities.[176]

---

[174] Arnull has argued that the arbitrariness of the exceptions had the result that the ban on Sunday trading was not necessary, since 'In the light of the exceptions to Section 47 of the Shops Act contained in the Fifth Schedule, it is difficult to discern any intelligible purpose behind the legislation. If it was not thought necessary to require pubs, restaurants, sweetshops and newsagents to close on Sundays, why should a prohibition on the sale of do-it-yourself and garden goods on Sundays have been considered necessary?' (n. 117 above). See also Gormley, 'Some Reflections on the Internal Market and Free Movement of Goods' at 15. The relevance of the arbitrary exceptions has been denied by Allen J in *Wellingborough* v. *Payless, Kettering* v. *Do-It-All Ltd* n. 158 above at 780 who pointed out that the exceptions, however illogical, did not alter the fact that the Shops Act provided for a general ban on Sunday shopping. Indeed it is true that even with the exceptions, however anomalous, the overall picture was still one of a ban on Sunday shopping in England & Wales. It may also be noted that the exceptions were not so much arbitrary as out of date since they were founded on practical considerations relevant to the 1950s: e.g., the fact that in 1950 there were fewer refrigerators made it reasonable to allow fresh produce to be sold on a Sunday but not tinned produce, which could be bought on any day of the week.

[175] n. 162 above.   [176] Ibid. at 538.

It will be clear that Northcote J in Shrewsbury Crown Court reached the conclusion that the Shops Act was disproportionate on a pure application of the necessity/alternate means (stage one) test of proportionality. Significantly, there was no mention of stage two and an analysis of whether the objective of the legislation was nevertheless proportionate to the extent of the restriction to trade. In other words, the finding of disproportionality was based on an application of the first stage of the proportionality test to the exclusion of the second.

This may be contrasted with the approach of the High Court in *London Borough of Waltham Forest* v. *Scott Markets Ltd*[177] which held that 'the attainment of Sunday observance, whether for religious or recreational purposes, may by held to be the objective of the restrictions on Sunday trading in the Shops Act 1950. In pursuit of that purpose domestic and imported goods are treated alike. The barrier to imports on the sketchy facts before me does not seem to be more than is necessary for enforcing compliance with the Act.'[178] Here, it will be noted that the High Court was only applying the second balancing test of the proportionality principle without addressing the necessity and alternative means issues. Similarly, in *Torfaen Borough Council* v. *B & Q*,[179] East Gwent Magistrates sitting at Cwmbran implemented the ECJ judgment by stating that:

We looked at the effects on intra-Community trade of the restrictions contained in s.47 and decided that, as a question of fact, these were not excessive in the context of the balance between the need to preserve the special nature of Sunday and such impact as there is upon that trade.[180]

Again, it is clear that the finding of proportionality was based exclusively on stage two of the proportionality test, avoiding any discussion of the necessity or alternative means questions.

A finding that the French legislation was justified and proportionate post-*Torfaen* was reached by the Paris *Cour d'Appel* in *SA Virgin Megastores* v. *Fédération des services CFDT*.[181] The Paris court cited and quoted the operative parts of the ECJ's *Torfaen* judgment and held that the UK legislation did not differ in substance from Article L. 221 of the *Code du travail* and thus that the *Torfaen* interpretation applied equally to the French legislation and that there was thus no need to make an Article 177 reference or to stay proceedings pending the ECJ's judgment in *Conforama*.[182] The *Cour d'Appel* held that 'it is up to the national legislator to abolish or reorientate the principle of Sunday rest based on the social and cultural traditions stemming back to Acts of 13 July 1906 and 23 December 1923' and that the French legislation was 'founded on objective criteria that are indistinctly applicable' and further that:

---

[177] n. 156 above.   [178] Ibid. at 783.   [179] n. 158 above.
[180] Ibid. at 456.   [181] n. 154 above.   [182] Case C–312/89, n. 121 above.

neither the peculiarities of the French audio-visual market, nor the extension of choice offered by Virgin Stores and the cultural dimension that they claim to be a part of their commercial activity, nor the surveys of their customers and the conclusions that they draw therefrom regarding the preferences of consumers *provide proof that the closure of their shop on a Sunday specifically affects the sale of products imported from other countries of the Community*. Consequently, it does not appear, on the facts submitted to the Court, that the prohibition on Sunday opening resulting from the application of social legislation exceed the effects intrinsic to rules of that kind.[183]

A close reading of this judgment of the Paris *Cour d'Appel* reveals that the conclusion that the prohibition on Sunday opening does not 'exceed the effects intrinsic to rules of that kind' followed directly from the finding that there was no 'proof that the closure of their shop on a Sunday specifically affects the sale of products imported from other countries of the Community'. It is of considerable interest that the *Cour d'Appel* did not address the issues of proportionality or alternative means (i.e. stage one of the proportionality test). It seems therefore that this is a further case in which the second limb of the proportionality test was applied to the exclusion of the first.

In neither the *Torfaen* nor the subsequent *Conforama* and *Marchandise* judgments did the ECJ give any detailed guidance as to how the proportionality principle should be applied in practice. While in *Conforama* and *Marchandise* the ECJ did indeed hold that the French and Belgian legislation were proportionate, it gave absolutely no indication as to its reasoning in reaching this conclusion. In the subsequent judgment of the ECJ in *Stoke-on-Trent* v. *B & Q*,[184] the ECJ did, however, give some indication as to why the national legislation was to be considered as proportionate. In this judgment the ECJ held that:

Appraising the proportionality of national rules which pursue a legitimate aim under Community law involves weighing the national interest in attaining that aim against the Community interest in ensuring the free movement of goods. In that regard, in order to verify that the restrictive effects on intra-Community trade of the rules at issue do not exceed what is necessary to achieve the aim in view, it must be considered whether those effects are direct, indirect or purely speculative and whether those effects do not impede the marketing of imported products more than the marketing of national products.[185]

It seems therefore that the ECJ itself in *Stoke-on-Trent* applied the proportionality test such that the stage two test took precedence. The extent of the effect on trade seems to be the crucial feature in the application of the proportionality test, at least in so far as the ECJ interpretation of the rule of

---

[183] Gaz. Pal. 1991, I Jur. 249 at 252.   [184] Case C–169/91, n. 124 above.
[185] Ibid. at para. 15 of judgt. Emphasis added.

reason and legislation on shop-opening hours is concerned. The ECJ's analysis in *Stoke-on-Trent* v. *B & Q* is notable for the absence of any examination of the necessity of the national legislation or a search for alternative means less restrictive of trade.[186] This conclusion lends support to the argument[187] in which it was noted that when the emphasis is placed on the first stage of the test (the necessity and alternative means test), the national court has been more likely to reach the conclusion that the shop-opening legislation was disproportionate. When, on the other hand, the national courts, as the ECJ subsequently did in *Stoke-on-Trent* v. *B & Q*, give precedence to the second stage of the proportionality test (the balance between the importance of the objective and the restriction to the free movement of goods), the conclusion that the shop-opening legislation was proportionate may more readily be reached.

The national court application of the proportionality test by national courts in these cases has illustrated that there is a tension between the two stages of application of that test. For the moment at least, the ECJ seems to have accorded a dominant role for the stage two test according to which the 'direct, indirect or purely speculative' nature of the trade restriction is a crucial element. The national court judgments demonstrate that only by giving dominance to the second balancing limb of the proportionality test is it possible to easily conclude that national shop-opening legislation is proportionate. Seen in this light, it is not surprising that the ECJ also followed this approach in its subsequent judgment in *Stoke-on-Trent*.

(iv) The application of the proportionality principle before the French courts

After the *Torfaen* judgment, the French courts came down almost uniformly in favour of the proportionality of the French legislation. There was only one divergent decision handed down by the *Tribunal de Police* of Narbonne in *Ministère public* v. *André Duhoux*[188] which held that the French legislation was not justified post-*Torfaen* since the prosecution had brought no evidence as to the 'justified objective' which was in any event disproportionate. This case was clearly the exception[189] and all the

---

[186] It is difficult to see why the ECJ seems to suggest in this judgment that the question of whether the national measure is discriminatory is relevant to the application of the proportionality test in the rule of reason, when the discriminatory nature of the measure would have precluded the application of the rule of reason in the first place. Given that the application of the proportionality principle by the ECJ in *Stoke-on-Trent* v. *B & Q* was somewhat idiosyncratic, it is strange that the ECJ has cited this test subsequently as settled authority for the application of the proportionality principle: Case C–323/93 *Société Civile Agricole de Centre d'insemination de La Crespelle* [1994] ECR I–5077 at para. 36.

[187] See discussion at pp. 203–4.

[188] *Trib. police* Narbonne, 22 Jan. 1990, D094/2 4/5 May 1990.

[189] That it was the exception is underlined by Roubach, Gaz. Pal. 1991, I Jur 254 who comments on the amount of media attention which this case received. See also Bandrac & Momège, n. 139 above.

remaining reported judgments concluded that the French legislation did not infringe the provisions concerning free movement of goods. There was thus stability in the French courts in the wake of *Torfaen* as the French *Code du travail* was uniformly applied. There was certainly none of the disunity or fragmentation of justice which characterized the application of the *Torfaen* judgment in the English and Welsh courts. Since the compatibility of the French legislation with the provisions concerning free movement of goods was subsequently confirmed by the ECJ in *Conforama*,[190] it would, at first sight, seem that the French courts should be commended for having avoided the pitfalls and difficulties encountered by their common-law brethren across the Channel. Unfortunately, a closer look at the (lack of) reasoning in the French judgments in these cases yields a different conclusion. In every judgment of the French courts post-*Torfaen* but pre-*Conforama*, neither the *Torfaen* judgment nor any semblance of a proportionality test was applied.

After *Torfaen*, the leading judgment was handed down by the *Cour de Cassation* in *Joëlle Lenel*.[191] In this case, the *Cour de Cassation* upheld a conviction of a shop manager for opening on Sunday, without even citing the *Torfaen* judgment. The *Cour de Cassation* only mentioned that it was 'argued in vain' that the lower court should have stayed proceedings until after the ECJ's judgment in *Conforama* which was then pending without elucidating as to why it thought that this was the case. On the substance, the *Cour de Cassation* simply held that

[T]he provisions of Article L. 221–5 of the *Code du travail*, adopted in the interests of workers imposing the obligation to give them a weekly rest on a Sunday, do not have as their object the regulation of trade between Member States of the European Community and are not incompatible with the provisions of the Treaty which prohibit quantitative restrictions on imports as well as measures having equivalent effect.

That this constitutes an inadequate application of the free-movement-of-goods provisions after *Torfaen* is manifestly the case. Not only is it brief, but there is also a complete absence of any reasoning. As such the *ratio* of the *Cour de Cassation* is unclear. Did it hold that Article 30 was not breached at all? If so, is this because it considered that that Article was not breached or was it holding that the rule of reason applied to bring the national measure outside the scope of Article 30? If the latter is the case, there is then an absence of reasoning as to why the 'restrictive effects were not beyond those intrinsic to trade rules of that kind'. The influence of this

---

[190] Case C–312/89, n. 121 above.
[191] *Cour de Cassation*, ch. crim., 20 Nov. 1990, Bull. Cass. Crim. 1990, no. 392 p. 989; JCP 1991, IV 75 (summary); Gaz. Pal. 1991, no. 160162 p. 7 (summary); Rev. juris. social 1991, 22 (summary).

judgment on further challenges to the French legislation before French courts should not be underestimated. As a result, the Article 30 defence was in effect closed off before the French courts.[192] This only serves to make the inadequate reasoning all the more unsatisfactory.

The poor reasoning set out above was repeated by the *Cour de Cassation* in two subsequent judgments where the *Torfaen* criteria were again neither cited nor applied. The *Cour de Cassation* simply held that Articles 30 to 36 were not infringed because Article L. 221–5 'concerns only the resting of employees and does not comprise any prohibition on the exercise of commercial activities on Sundays'.[193] It is submitted that this is clearly inaccurate as the ECJ subsequently confirmed in *Conforama* that '[n]ational legislation which prohibits the employment of staff on Sundays . . . is not designed to control trade. None the less, it may entail restrictive effects on the free movement of goods.'[194] The fact that the French legislation regulated employee working-times rather than shop-opening times proper was thus irrelevant. The *effect* of the French legislation was to prevent shops opening on Sundays.

Regrettably, the lower French courts' application of the rule of reason post-*Torfaen* was no more satisfactory. For example, the *Cour d'Appel* of Angers in *Cuuf et Cie* v. *Syndicat de la nouveauté*[195] at least cited and set out the ECJ's formulation in *Torfaen* that Article 30 does not apply to national Sunday-trading legislation 'where the effects on Community trade which may result therefrom do not exceed the effects intrinsic to rules of that kind' and simply added, 'which, in this case, Cuuf cannot claim'.[196] The *Cour d'Appel* of Angers provided no reasons as to why this was the case. The conclusion is undoubtedly that the French courts simply did not, post-*Torfaen*, carry out a satisfactory application of the proportionality test.[197]

---

[192] This is illustrated by the fact that the Dalloz version of the *Code du travail* provides an annotation of the relevant Articles of the *Code* and refers to this decision of the *Cour de Cassation* as authority for the fact that Art. L221-5 'was not contrary to the Treaty of Rome'. It is likely that this would have had the effect of dampening the enthusiasm of zealous *advocats* seeking to challenge the provisions.

[193] *Michel Balavoine* v. *Ministère public, Cour de Cassation*, ch. crim., 9 Oct. 1990, Rev. juris. social 1990, 643 (summary) and *Roger Gilardi* v. *Ministère public, Cour de Cassation*, ch. crim., 8 Jan. 1991, Rev. juris. social 1991, 174 (summary). [194] n. 121 above at para. 8 of judgt.

[195] *Cour d'appel* Angers, 16 Jan. 1991, Gaz. Pal. 1991, I Jur. 352 (with note by Roubach).

[196] In the original French: '*ce que, en l'espèce, ne peut prétendre la société Cuuf*'. See also to similar effect *Fédération des Services CFDT* v. *SA Virgin Megastores*, TGI Paris, 3 Jan. 1992, Europe 1992 Act. no. 166 p. 9 (summary).

[197] See also the strange judgment in *Syncomen et Société Conforama* v. *Préfet du Rhône, Trib. admin.* Lyon, 1re ch., 4 Oct. 1990, Rev. juris. sociale 1991, 506 (summary) where it was rather alarmingly suggested that the breach of Art. 30 by the French legislation was justified under Art. 117 EC which provides that: 'Member States agree upon the need to promote improved working conditions and an improved standard of living for workers, so as to make possible their harmonization while the improvement is being maintained'. Art. 117 EC, which falls under the chapter in the Treaty on social policy, does not have direct effect and cannot be invoked as a justification for restrictions to the free movement of goods.

(v) *The application of the proportionality principle before the English and Welsh courts: the doctrine of Parliamentary sovereignty*[198]

English and Welsh courts are wedded to the doctrine of Parliamentary sovereignty. It is still regarded as the corner-stone of the constitution. The fundamental tenet of this doctrine is that 'Parliament has the right to make or unmake any law whatever; and further, that no person or body is recognized by the law of England as having a right to override or set aside the legislation of Parliament.'[199] This constitutional principle has been limited dramatically by Section 2(1) of the European Communities Act 1972. It would seem to have been, at least so far as Community law is concerned, almost reduced to vanishing point by the House of Lords in the *Factortame* litigation[200] which makes clear that the doctrine of implied repeal has no application to the 1972 Act nor to directly enforceable Community rights taking effect thereunder.

The judgments of the English courts after *Torfaen* expressed serious reservations about applying the Community law proportionality principle in the light of the doctrine of Parliamentary supremacy. The reason why this doctrine obstructed the application of the proportionality principle with regard to the Shops Act in English courts is made plain from the opening words of Hoffmann J's judgment in the Chancery Division in *Stoke-on-Trent*:[201] 'Who is to decide whether shops should be allowed to open on Sundays? Is it to be Parliament or this court?' The division of powers between the legislature and judiciary was the learned judge's principal concern:

In my judgment it is not my function to carry out the balancing exercise or to form my own view on whether the legislative objective could be achieved by other means. These questions involve compromises between competing interests, which in a democratic society must be resolved by the legislature. The duty of the court is only to inquire whether the compromise adopted by the United Kingdom Parliament, so far as it affects Community trade, is one which a reasonable legislature could have reached. The function of the court is to review the acts of the legislature but not to substitute its own policies or values.

This is not an abdication of judicial responsibility. The primacy of the democratic process is far more important than the question of whether our Sunday trading laws could or could not be improved.[202]

These concerns were echoed by Mustill LJ in the Queen's Bench Division of the High Court in *W. H. Smith Do-It-All Ltd* v. *Peterborough City*

---

[198] The discussion in this section draws on the author's article in (1995) 44 ICLQ 451.

[199] Dicey, *Law of the Constitution* (10th edn., 1959) p. xviii.

[200] [1991] 1 AC 603, [1990] 3 WLR 818. For the constitutional implications of these cases, see Craig, 'Supremacy of the United Kingdom Parliament after Factortame' (1991) 11 YEL 221.

[201] n. 164 above.   [202] [1991] 4 All ER 221 at 235.

Council, Payless DIY Ltd v. *Peterborough City Council*[203] who equally robustly stated that 'According to the doctrine of separation of powers, as understood in the United Kingdom, the legislative acts of the Queen in Parliament are impregnable . . . If Parliament speaks, the courts must obey.'[204] The same concerns were expressed in a less dogmatic manner by Allen J in *Wellingborough Borough Council* v. *Payless D.I.Y. Ltd, Kettering Borough Council* v. *W. H. Smith Do-It-All Ltd*[205] who stated that '[w]e accept that the courts cannot simply follow the choice made by Parliament as to specific national rules, but must enquire as to whether or not the effects are limited to those intrinsic to rules of that kind'.[206] Nevertheless, Allen J added in his concluding paragraph that

The national courts are not called upon to make political and economic choices regarding working and non-working hours. These matters are for the national legislature. Parliament is the proper and only forum for discussion of the desirability of retaining a rule such as Section 47.[207]

As a result of these concerns, Hoffmann J in *Stoke-on-Trent*[208] came to the conclusion that the proportionality requirement was met because the compromise adopted by the United Kingdom Parliament in the form of the Shops Act 1950 was one which a 'reasonable' legislature could have reached. It is not the intention here to discuss in any detail the future of the doctrine of Parliamentary sovereignty in the United Kingdom;[209] suffice it to point out that the application of the proportionality test

does not mean that the national court is called upon to substitute its own policies for those of the legislature. The national court is simply required to decide whether the option chosen by the legislature is lawful. If it concludes that it is unlawful, the task of finding an alternative way of protecting the interests in question is one for the legislature.[210]

The refusal of Hoffmann J to carry out this test may therefore be seen as a denial of the duty incumbent upon the English courts under Community law. Any application of a reasonableness test is not the same as the proportionality test. In other comparable contexts, the English courts have shown themselves willing to accept that, unlike in an application of *Wednesbury* reasonableness,[211] the proportionality test in Article 36 EC requires the court to examine, not whether a Minister's decision was

---

[203] n. 170 above. [204] [1991] 4 All ER 193 at 196. [205] n. 160 above.
[206] Ibid. at 778. [207] Ibid. at 780. [208] n. 164 above.
[209] See Craig, n. 200 above. On the proportionality principle in English administrative law, see Boyron, 'Proportionality in English Administrative Law: A Faulty Transition' (1992) 12 OJLS 237 and *R.* v. *Secretary of State for the Home Department, ex. p. Brind* [1991] 2 WLR 588. See also O'Neill, n. 148 above, 91–6.
[210] Arnull, n. 117 above at 120.
[211] See *Wednesbury Corporation* v. *Minister of Housing and Local Government* [1966] 2 QB 75, [1965] 1 All ER 186.

unreasonable, but rather whether it was correct. Indeed, as Vaughan and Randolph comment, 'the principle of administrative reasonableness in the *Wednesbury* rules is not applicable in Community law cases: the question is whether the decision under review is correct or not'.[212] In other words, unlike reasonableness, the proportionality principle requires the national court to examine the substance of the measure.[213] Advocate General Van Gerven in *Stoke-on-Trent* v. *B & Q* criticized the approach of Hoffmann J stating that in his view 'the national court may not automatically accept the view of the national legislature or limit itself to deciding whether the national legislature, in the light of the proportionality requirement, could reasonably have adopted the legislative provisions in question'.[214] In support of this view Van Gerven pointed to the ECJ's judgment in *Miro*[215] where the ECJ expressly rejected an argument that it was for the national legislature to assess the need for a prohibition on the use of the term *Jenever* and that the national courts were bound to follow that assessment.[216]

It seems therefore that the application of the proportionality principle was not correctly carried out by the High Court which clung to the doctrine of Parliamentary sovereignty when in fact the doctrine need not have obscured the application of the proportionality principle in this case, and allowing it to do so was a denial of the full supremacy of Community law. It is submitted that the real reason why their Lordships were apprehensive was because they had little practical experience applying this principle.[217] The Sunday-trading cases were the first occasion when the English courts were confronted head on with the proportionality principle. Regrettably,

---

[212] Vaughan and Randolph, 'The Interface between Community Law and National Law: The United Kingdom Experience' at 225. See discussion of the proportionality principle with respect to Art. 36 at pp. 267–9.

[213] It is interesting to note that in Case C–304/90 *Reading Borough Council* v. *Payless DIY* [1992] ECR I–6493, which was handed down by the ECJ on the same day as its *Stoke-on-Trent* judgment, Reading and Sonning Magistrates' Court had specifically asked in the questions referred whether the proportionality principle was the same as that of reasonableness. The ECJ merely referred to the *Stoke-on-Trent* judgment and held the Shops Act proportionate without addressing the question directly. In asking this question, the Magistrates' Court was implicitly challenging the correctness of Hoffmann J's approach in *Stoke-on-Trent* and Rawlings has commented that '[t]his is a good illustration of the way in which the existence of Art. 177 procedure alters the balance of forces between superior and inferior courts inside a national system' n. 118 above at 321.

[214] Case C–169/91, n. 124 above at para. 27 of the Opinion.

[215] Case 182/84 [1985] ECR 3731.

[216] The English courts' interpretation of proportionality as a test of reasonableness was not discussed by the ECJ in its judgment in *Stoke-on-Trent*. When the House of Lords implemented the judgment ([1993] 2 All ER 297) Lord Goff refused to be drawn on the matter as the ECJ had not discussed it.

[217] This lack of experience is largely due to the fact that, as Mustill LJ remarked in *W. H. Smith Do It All Ltd* v. *Peterborough CC, Payless DIY Ltd* v. *Peterborough CC* [1991] 4 All ER 193 at 196 'The United Kingdom has no constitutional courts in the same sense as in other countries'. To this extent, Community law requires the UK to develop such courts.

the ECJ had given them little guidance in *Torfaen* as to how the test should be applied in practice. Perhaps the ECJ took it for granted that the national court would be competent to carry out the balancing exercise without further elucidation. Thus, although some of the responsibility for the unease with which the proportionality principle entered the English legal system must lie with the ECJ, such unease may also be seen merely as a teething problem occurring whilst a new and unfamiliar principle entered English legal analysis. Community law has been particularly dynamic in its influencing of national legal analysis. In much the same way as the English courts have had to embrace a teleological interpretation (as opposed to the literal statutory interpretation with which they are accustomed) when interpreting Community legislation,[218] the 'incoming tide'[219] of Community law requires them to shift from applying the 'reasonableness' test to applying the proportionality test when interpreting Community law.[220] Seen in this light, the courts will have learnt from the experience gained during the Sunday-trading litigation and, when they are next called upon to engage the principle of proportionality, it is to be hoped that they will embrace it with greater confidence.

(vi) Proportionality as a question of fact

Is the application of the proportionality principle a question of law or of fact? It appears that the ECJ is clearly of the view that it is a question of fact since it explicitly held in *Torfaen* that '[t]he question whether the effects of specific national rules do in fact remain within that limit is a question of fact to be determined by the national court'.[221] If one assumes that it is a

---

[218] With respect to teleological interpretation, the words of Lord Diplock in the House of Lords in *R. v. Henn and Darby* [1979] 2 CMLR 495 are worthy of recall: 'The European Court in contrast to English courts, applies teleological rather than historical methods to the interpretation of the Treaties and other Community legislation. It seeks to give effect to what it conceives to be the spirit rather than the letter of the Treaties; sometimes, indeed, to an English judge, it may seem to the exclusion of the letter. It views the Communities as living and expanding organisms and the interpretation of the provisions of the treaties as changing to match their growth.' Such an embracing of the proportionality principle is similarly required by the English courts.

[219] *Bulmer v. Bollinger* [1974] 3 WLR 202, [1974] 2 All ER 1226 per Lord Denning who described the impact of Community law on English law as 'like an incoming tide. It flows into the estuaries and up to the rivers'.

[220] For other examples of the 'indirect' influence of Community law, see *Woolwich Equitable Building Society v. Inland Revenue Commissioners* [1993] AC 70 (per Lord Goff) and *M. v. Home Office* [1993] 3 All ER 537 (per Lord Woolf). See discussion by O'Neill, n. 148 above, 84–7 and Bingham, 'There is a World Elsewhere: The Changing Perspectives of English law' (1992) 41 ICLQ 513. On the limits of the 'indirect' influence of Community law see *R. v. Ministry of Agriculture, Fisheries and Food, ex p. First City Trading* [1997] 1 CMLR 250, [1997] EuLR 195.

[221] Case 145/88 n. 10 above at para. 16 of judgt. For a contrary view, see Bandrac & Momège, n. 139 above, who argue that the application of proportionality is a question of law not fact. Since the ECJ itself decided that the UK legislation was proportionate in *Stoke-on-Trent*, O'Neill has argued, n. 148 above, 66 that '[p]roportionality becomes, then, a test of

question of fact, the question which then arises is what the standard of proof is and upon whose shoulders the burden of proof lies. With respect to the standard to proof, East Gwent Magistrates sitting at Cwmbran in *Torfaen Borough Council* v. *B & Q*[222] held that the standard was the 'normal one of being satisfied so that we are sure'.[223] The question of the burden of proof is, however, more vexed. One would assume that, by analogy with the Article 36 justifications, where the ECJ has held that a national authority relying on Article 36 bears the burden of proving that measures are justified under that provision,[224] the same would apply to the justifications based on the rule of reason.[225] Indeed this is supported by the system of ECJ judgments applying the rule of reason and general acceptance that this is the case is underlined by the fact that it has never been challenged. Thus, although there is no direct ECJ authority to this effect, it is submitted that the burden of proof should be upon the Member State to prove that restrictions on shop-opening hours are proportionate to the objective of protecting 'national or regional socio-cultural characteristics'.

In *Torfaen Borough Council* v. *B & Q*[226] East Gwent Magistrates sitting at Cwmbran found it unnecessary to decide the point concerning the burden of proof but in *Shrewsbury and Atcham B.C.* v. *B & Q*,[227] Shrewsbury Crown Court held that the burden of proof lay on the Council using the analogy of a criminal case where the defence of 'self-defence' is raised. The French courts, on the other hand, have come down very strongly in favour of placing the burden of proof upon the retailers' shoulders.[228] This was suggested in the judgment of the *Cour d'Appel* of Lyon in *Sté Boulanger Frères, Ikea* v. *Fédération nationale du négoce et de l'artisanat*[229] which held post-*Torfaen* that a conviction of a retailer under the French legislation for having opened on a Sunday should be upheld since the defendant had not 'produced the evidence as to disproportionality such that there was a doubt not overcome by the defendant'. Clearly, the *Cour d'Appel* seems to have assumed that the burden of proof to demonstrate disproportionality rested with the retailer rather than with the French authorities to demonstrate that the legislation was proportionate. In much the same way, the *Cour d'Appel* of Montpellier in *Gérard Leib* v. *Ministère public*[230] repeated the

general principle rather than one the result of which might vary with different findings of fact made by individual courts in particular cases or with the application by them of different national views or tests of proportionality'.

[222] Case 145/88, n. 10 above.　　　　　　[223] Ibid. at 456.
[224] See discussion at p. 232.　　　　　　[225] See Oliver, n. 18 above, 181.
[226] Case 145/88, n. 10 above.　　　　　　[227] n. 162 above.
[228] See discussion of this point from the perspective of judgments given in summary proceedings in France (*juge des référés*) in Cavallini, n. 139 above, 204.
[229] *Cour d'appel* Lyon, Ch. des Urgences, 12 Mar. 1990, noted in Bandrac & Momège, n. 139 above at 552–7.
[230] *Cour d'appel* Montpellier, 3e ch. corr., 5 Nov. 1990, Gaz. Pal. 1991, I Jur. 253 (with note by Roubach).

operative passages of the *Torfaen* judgment and held that 'in the present case, it has not been established that the intrinsic effects have been exceeded' and added that 'the closing on Sundays prevents the sale of all furniture, even if of French origin', and so the French measure could not be considered to be 'an anti-competitive or protectionist measure'. Again, it is notable that the *Cour d'Appel* held that it had not been proved that the French legislation was disproportionate rather than putting the burden upon the French authorities to prove that it was proportionate. Finally, we have already seen that the *Cour d'Appel* of Angers in *Cuuf et Cie* v. *Syndicat de la nouveauté*[231] repeated the formulation of the ECJ in *Torfaen* that Article 30 does not apply to national Sunday trading legislation 'where the effects on Community trade which may result therefrom do not exceed the effects intrinsic to rules of that kind, *which, in this case, Cuuf cannot claim*'.[232] Again, the clear suggestion is that the burden of proof is on the retailers rather than on the French authorities.

It is submitted that the better view would have been for the national courts to have held that the burden of proof lay on the national authorities. This is because it is the retailers who had successfully alleged the breach by the national legislation of Article 30 and it should, it is submitted, then be up to the national authorities to demonstrate that the national legislation was nevertheless justified and proportionate under the rule of reason. This would be consistent with the ECJ's approach with respect to Article 36 and is in line with the narrow interpretation of derogations to fundamental Treaty freedoms.

(vii) A real problem of fragmentation of justice in application of the proportionality principle?

Assuming that the application of the proportionality principle is a question of fact, there is clearly the latent danger that the assessment of the facts, and therefore the proportionality of a particular piece of national legislation, will vary from national court to national court and from Member State to Member State. The problem is that the first decision of a national court with respect to the proportionality of the measure will not bind other national courts. This is the case even in the precedent system of the common law since questions of fact are for the appreciation of the court in each individual case. Furthermore, it should be noted that Article 30 does not operate to strike down national measures as such, but rather to preclude reliance upon them to the detriment of individual rights protected by Community law. Consequently the proportionality issue has to be approached on a case-by-case basis by the national courts.

---

[231] n. 195. [232] Emphasis added.

A solution to this dilemma was suggested by Hoffmann J in *Stoke-on-Trent* v. *B & Q*[233] who decided that the High Court could decide the proportionality issue by 'judicial notice'. 'Judicial notice' was defined by Hoffmann[234] as including 'matters of a public nature such as history, social customs and public opinion, which may be culled from works of reference'.[235] Importantly, judicial notice produces uniformity of decision on matters of fact since in matters decided on judicial notice, the normal rules of judicial precedent come into play. Hoffmann J held that '[i]t follows that if the court is satisfied on the basis of judicial notice that the requirements of proportionality have been met, there is no need for the prosecution to adduce oral or documentary evidence' thereby obviating the need for 'a troupe of experts'[236] to tour the country. It seems that this approach was followed by other English courts. Sir Nicholas Browne-Wilkinson VC threw his support behind the conclusion of Hoffmann J that the Shops Act did meet the proportionality requirement in the unreported decision in *Stoke-on-Trent* v. *Toys 'R' Us Ltd*.[237] Indeed, the Vice-Chancellor stated that courts of first instance should consider it 'a definitive judgment'. It seems that they did. In his speech in the House of Lords in *Kirklees BC* v. *Wickes Building Supplies Ltd*,[238] Lord Goff stated that Hoffmann J's decision 'has been regarded as definitive, by judges of first instance, as to the application of the *Torfaen* principle in this country'.[239] An example of this relative 'stability' may be seen in the decision of the Chancery Division of the High Court, in *Coventry City Council* v. *Woolworths plc*.[240] The decision in this case was handed down after Hoffmann J's decision in *Stoke-on-Trent*, with the appeal to the House of Lords by the 'leap-frog' procedure pending. It was stated that 'it has been the consistent practice of the judges of this Division, pending a decision in such appeal, to proceed upon the assumption that the earlier decision is correct'.[241] The commonly held impression that the ECJ's ruling in *Torfaen* led to divergent decisions in the English courts seems, therefore, to be more illusory than real. The picture was in fact, at least so far as the application of the proportionality principle is concerned, a very much more stabile one.

Indeed, in England, Wales, and France, the vast majority of courts concluded that the national legislation was proportionate. In France the only reported decision which went the other way was that of the *Tribunal de Police* of Narbonne in *Ministère public* v. *André Duhoux*.[242] In the United Kingdom there was also only one reported case following *Torfaen* in which

---

[233] Case 169/91, n. 124 above.
[234] Citing *Cross on Evidence* (Butterworths, 5th edn., 1979), 160.
[235] [1991] 4 All ER 221 at 231.					[236] Ibid.
[237] Judgt 18 Oct. 1990.
[238] [1992] 2 CMLR 765, [1993] AC 227, [1992] 3 WLR 170, [1992] 3 All ER 717.
[239] [1992] 3 All ER 717 at 730.				[240] [1991] 2 CMLR 3.					[241] Ibid. at 4.
[242] n. 188 above.

it was concluded that the Shops Act was disproportionate.[243] It seems therefore that the often-stated view that the application of the proportionality principle caused a 'fragmentation of justice' should not be overstated. It remains the case that the application of the proportionality principle by both the United Kingdom and the French courts was extremely poor. As we have seen, the English courts refused to apply the proportionality test, replacing it with one of reasonableness as a result of perceived difficulties with the doctrine of Parliamentary sovereignty. The French courts, on the other hand, simply did not apply a full and reasoned proportionality test after the *Torfaen* judgment of the ECJ. Nevertheless, the situation, in so far as the application of the proportionality principle was concerned, was very much more stabile in the sense that the national courts overwhelmingly held the national legislation affecting the opening hours of shops was justified and proportionate.

(viii) The origin of the 'chaos' before the English courts: the availability of injunctions to enforce the Shops Act

The conclusion in the previous section that the application of the proportionality principle by the English courts was very much more stable than has often been claimed is not to deny the fact that there was very real chaos in England and Wales as some local authorities attempted to enforce the Shops Act while others turned a blind eye. However, it is the contention here that it was the difficulties under English law with respect to the availability of injunctions to enforce the Act, rather than the application of the proportionality principle, which was principally responsible for the chaos.[244]

As has already been noted, the enforcement of Section 47 of the Shops Act by the criminal sanction was ineffective as a deterrent.[245] Much more effective, therefore, was the possibility of a civil injunction to restrain retailers.[246] The problem was that the House of Lords had held in 1974, in *Hoffmann-La Roche* v. *Secretary of State for Trade & Industry*,[247] that the

---

[243] *Shrewsbury & Atcham B.C.* v. *B & Q*, n. 162 above. Even in that judgment, it is somewhat ironic to see the *Torfaen* judgment being described as 'commendably brief' [1990] 3 CMLR 535 at 537. It seems that the national judge in that case had little sympathy for the Shops Act which was described as a piece of legislation which was 'unclear, seldom observed, out of date with present day mores and can find little or no support from members of the public' (at 539). The only other case known to the present writer in which this conclusion was reached was the decision of a stipendiary magistrate at Pendle (unreported, but referred to by Hoffmann J in *Stoke-on-Trent* n. 164 at 237) who identified the objective of the Shops Act as being to protect Sunday leisure activities and concluded that since many people regarded Sunday shopping in do-it-yourself and garden centres as a leisure activity, a ban on such shopping was disproportionate.

[244] This view is fully argued by the author, n. 126 above, 460–3.   [245] n. 135 above.

[246] Under Local Government Act 1972, s. 222.

[247] [1974] 2 All ER 1128, [1975] AC 295.

Crown could not be required to give cross-undertakings in damages when enforcing an Act of Parliament by injunction. When the Article 30 EC defence surfaced, this became crucial because retailers were understandably concerned that, should the Shops Act be found contrary to Article 30 EC, they should have a right to damages from the local authorities for the period during which they were restrained from opening by injunction. The retailers argued, therefore, that if the English courts were to grant injunctions to restrain them from opening on Sundays, the local authorities should give cross-undertakings in damages. The implications of this were significant. Such an undertaking on behalf of the local authorities was clearly too onerous given their restricted budgets. In short, if they were required to give cross-undertakings, the Shops Act would in practice become unenforceable. It is here that the origins of the chaos in the Sunday-trading cases lay. This is made clear from the progress of the litigation in *Kirklees MBC* v. *Wickes Building Supplies Ltd.* In the Chancery Division of the High Court,[248] Mervyn Davies J allowed an injunction without requiring cross-undertakings in damages from Kirklees Metropolitan Borough Council (distinguishing *Hoffmann-La Roche* v. *Secretary of State for Trade & Industry*[249]). The Court of Appeal[250] allowed the appeal, holding that cross-undertakings were required under both English and Community law. Finally, the House of Lords[251] lifted the appeal and reinstated the decision of the Chancery Division. Lord Goff in the House of Lords in *Kirklees* indicated that 'as many as 100 injunctions were granted . . . following the approach of Mervyn Davies J'.[252] These were likewise discharged after the decision of the Court of Appeal. Presumably, after the decision of the House of Lords in *Kirklees*, these injunctions were again reinstated. The sheer volume of injunctions that were granted and then withdrawn around the country made a mockery of the enforcement of the Shops Act. It is here, therefore, rather than in the application of the admittedly obscure *Torfaen* ruling, that the origins of the chaos lay. It would seem that the real reason why the Sunday-trading cases became a 'saga' is not only because of difficulties in the application of the proportionality principle, but primarily because it was not clear whether local authorities could enforce the Shops Act through civil injunctions, without the millstone of cross-undertakings in damages around their necks. This lack of clear guidance, as is demonstrated by the progress of the *Kirklees* litigation, effectively put the Shops Act into suspension. The farce of 100 injunctions being granted and then withdrawn severely dented the credibility of the Rule of Law and gave the whole episode its flavour of 'drama'.[253] Given the confusion over the availability of injunc-

---

[248] [1990] 1 WLR 1237.
[250] [1991] 4 All ER 240, [1991] 3 CMLR 82.
[252] [1992] 3 All ER 717 at 722.

[249] n. 247 above.
[251] n. 238 above.
[253] Barnard, n. 126 above.

tions, there was a great disincentive for local authorities to enforce the law, and even the Attorney-General refused to intervene.[254] There was concern about the maintenance of the integrity of the national legal system as the Shops Act was put into 'suspended animation'.[255] The very Rule of Law was perceived to be under threat. Even the then Home Secretary, Mr Kenneth Clarke, was forced to admit that 'nobody knows what the law is, so no law at all is being applied'.[256] This complacency was seen by pressure groups such as the 'Keep Sunday Special Campaign' as the Government allowing deregulation of Sunday trading through the back door when they had failed to introduce it by democratic means.[257]

(ix) Is it desirable for the ECJ to decide the proportionality issue itself?

It has been noted that while the ECJ in *Torfaen* had left the question of proportionality to the national court to apply, in its subsequent *Conforama*,[258] *Marchandise*[259] and *Stoke-on-Trent*[260] judgments, the ECJ decided the proportionality issue itself. In the light of the experience of national courts post-*Torfaen*, should the ECJ be encouraged to decide the proportionality question in individual cases?

A finding of proportionality carried out by the ECJ certainly facilitates easy application by the national courts. Thus, after the *Conforama* judgment, the French courts were able to cite that ECJ judgment and conclude that the French legislation was justified because it pursued an objective justified with respect to Community law and that the restrictive effects on trade that could follow were not excessive with respect to the objective pursued.[261]

There are, however, serious dangers involved when the ECJ decides to settle the proportionality issue itself rather than leaving it to the national court.[262] One of these dangers is that the ECJ's finding with respect to pro-

---

[254] *Hansard*, HC, vol. 199, col. 913 (27 Nov. 1991).

[255] Per Pill J in *R. v. HM Attorney-General, ex. p. Edey*, Judgt 13 Jan. 1992 (transcr.: Marten Walsh Cherer).

[256] *Hansard*, HC, Vol. 212, col. 557 (22 Oct. 1992). [257] See n. 136 above.

[258] n. 121 above. [259] n. 122 above. [260] n. 124 above.

[261] See, e.g., *Syncomen et Société Conforama* v. *Préfet du Rhône, Conseil d'Etat*, Section du Contentieux, 7 Dec. 1992, Rec. Lebon 1992, 692 (summary) (full transcr. available on Lexis); *Chaussures André, 'La Halle aux Chaussures', Cour de Cassation*, ch. soc., 11 Oct. 1994, Bull. Cass. Civ. 1994, V no. 268 p. 181; JCP 1994, IV 2477; Rev. juris. social 1994, no. 1271; *Union départmentale des syndicats C.F.D.T. du Puy-de-Dôme, Conseil d'Etat*, 20 Oct. 1993, Rec. Lebon 1993, 295. Nevertheless, one would expect that the least that the national court could do would be to cite the *Conforama* judgment. The *Cour de Cassation* did not do so in *Bontron, Cour de Cassation*, ch. crim., 18 July 1991, Bull. Cass. Crim. 1991, no. 301 p. 758 which was the first *Cour de Cassation* judgment after *Conforama* where the *Cour de Cassation* simply held that the French legislation was 'not incompatible with the provisions of Art. 30 of the Treaty of Rome which prohibits quantitative restrictions and measures having equivalent effect'. See also *Teil, Cour de Cassation*, ch. crim., 31 Mar. 1992, [1993] 1 CMLR 593; Bull.Cass.Crim 1992, no. 133 p. 349 where the *Conforama* judgment was again not cited.

[262] See further discussion of this question in the context of proportionality and Art. 36 in Ch. 7, sect. 4 (C).

portionality will necessarily be of a generalized nature. As such, the dynamic application of the proportionality principle by the national courts on a case-by-case basis is precluded. This is all the more difficult when a finding of proportionality by the ECJ with respect to the legislation of one Member State is followed by a national court in another Member State. Such was the case before the Dutch courts in *Nederlandse Organisatie van Tijdschiften Uitgevers* v. *Staat der Nederlanden*.[263] In that case, the *Rechtbank* of Den Haag cited the ECJ's *Conforama* judgment and held that 'the regulation of shop-closing times in the present state of Community law is in principle a matter for the Member States' and held that there were no 'specific circumstances' why Article 30 should apply in that case. It had been argued before the *Rechtbank* Den Haag that the Dutch provisions,[264] which listed newspapers, but not magazines, on the list of goods 'typically connected with road transport' and thus capable of being sold in petrol stations, was disproportionate because such magazines could be sold in airport and railway stations. It was furthermore argued that the distinction between newspapers and magazines was arbitrary. Faced with this argument, it would have been possible for the Dutch court to have concluded that the provisions were proportionate since newspapers needed to be read on the day of publication whereas magazines can be bought during the rest of the week. However, the Dutch court engaged in no such discussion of the proportionality of the provisions and merely relied on the *Conforama* authority of the ECJ. It may be questioned whether the Dutch court was correct to have applied the *Conforama* judgment in the context of Dutch legislation. The impact of the ECJ itself having applied the proportionality test to the facts in *Conforama* is that the national courts will tend thereafter to follow that finding without carrying out a full investigation in individual cases. While the application of the *Conforama* judgment to the Dutch *Winkelsluitingswet*[265] had the benefit of legal certainty, there is the danger that the ECJ application of the proportionality principle to the facts of individual cases will have the effect of closing off the application in national courts of the proportionality test on a case-by-case basis, thereby discarding the strength of the broad scope of Article 30 coupled with the application of the rule of reason. If the ECJ wished to close

---

[263] Pres. *Arrondissementsrechtbank*'s-Gravenhage, 21 Oct. 1991, [1993–1] Mediaforum Bijlage [5] p. B18.

[264] See discussion of the Dutch legislation in sect. 4 (C).

[265] The compatibility of the *Winkelsluitingswet* with Art. 30 was also dealt with by the *Hoge Raad* in *Officier van Justitie* v. *Makro Zelfbedieningsgroothandel Nuth CV*, Hoge Raad, Strafkamer, 4 Nov. 1986, NJ 1987, 384 (with note by Van Veen); SEW 1990, 674 (with note by AM); (1988) European Law Digest 14; (1989) CDE 481–2. The *Hoge Raad* held in that case that Art. 30 was not even breached by the Dutch legislation (see discussion of this aspect of the judgment at p. 101) and thus the rule of reason and the proportionality of the *Winkelsluitingswet* was not dealt with in the judgment.

off the invocation of Article 30 to challenge national legislation affecting shop-opening hours in a general fashion, it is more honest for it to do so, as it now has,[266] by reducing the scope of Article 30. It does little for the integrity of the rule of reason for the ECJ to apply the proportionality principle in a 'blanket' fashion applicable in all circumstances.

(x) Summary

National legislation affecting the opening hours of shops has long been a target for attack by large retailers with a deep pocket willing to take all legal measures possible to challenge restrictions to their ability to open their outlets in order to extract maximum profit.[267] This point is underlined by the fact that even after the Article 30 defence had become a dead letter, the retailers pursued other avenues to challenge the legislation. Thus, it was subsequently argued that the enforcement of the legislation requiring the shops to close on a Sunday breached the Equal Treatment Directive 76/207[268] since it was argued that the great majority of those who work in retail establishments on Sundays were women and that by forcing a retail outlet to close on a Sunday, a far greater number of women than men would lose their jobs. This argument was struck out before the English courts in *Chisholm and Others* v. *Kirklees Metropolitan Council*[269] as not breaching the principle of equal treatment which would in any event be 'objectively justified'.[270] The French courts have also had the opportunity to reject such challenges to the French legislation.[271] The retailers then brought a number of further proceedings before the English courts. In *R.* v. *Kirklees MBC ex. p. Tesco Stores Ltd*[272] the Divisional Court rejected a claim that Kirklees Metropolitan Borough Council was not discharging its duties under Section 71 of the Shops Act by adopting a discriminatory enforcement policy which involved prosecuting a group of large retailers rather than small traders. The English court held that it was legitimate for the Council to take into consideration the scarcity of its resources and the many other statutory duties it had to enforce when deciding to prosecute. In *R.* v. *Lincoln City Council ex. p. Wickes Building Suppliers Ltd*[273] the Queen's Bench Division of the High Court rejected the application that the policy of Lincoln City Council of laying informations of breaches of

---

[266] Cases C–401 & 402/92, n. 113 above. See other cases cited at n. 113.

[267] See, e.g. *Stoke-on-Trent* v. *B & Q* [1984] AC 754, [1984] 2 WLR 929, [1984] 2 All ER 332 in which the Sunday trading legislation was challenged before the English courts long before the EC law arguments were 'conceived'.

[268] [1976] OJ L39/40.   [269] [1994] 3 CMLR 340.

[270] It may be noted that the challenge by the employees in this case was supported by their employers (B & Q).

[271] See *Baggio, Cour de Cassation*, ch. crim., 10 Jan. 1995, Rev. juris. social 1995, no. 387; *Cuny, Cour de Cassation*, ch. crim., 10 Jan. 1995, Rev. juris. social 1995, no. 388 and *Gilardi, Cour de Cassation*, ch. crim., 9 Mar. 1994, Rev. juris. social 1994, no. 557.

[272] The Times, 26 Oct. 1993.   [273] The Times, 6 Aug. 1993.

Section 47 of the Shops Act allowing them to 'stack up' each weekly breach without bringing their informations and consequent summonses to trial was oppressive and an abuse of process. The court held that this was a reasonable exercise of discretion by the local authority.[274] The actions of the retailers thus constituted a concerted campaign which succeeded at times in 'snarling up' the legal system and discouraging all but the most conscientious of local authorities from enforcing the law. The ultimate success of their campaign was the repeal of the Shops Act and its replacement by the Sunday Trading Act 1994 which liberalized Sunday opening for the entire United Kingdom.

The Sunday-trading episode seemed to bring out the worst in all the parties concerned. On the one hand, the ECJ's judgments were extremely unhelpful as it was willing in *Torfaen* to accept an extremely broad scope for Article 30 without bearing the consequences of that approach, by giving the national courts guidance as to the application of the proportionality principle. Subsequently in *Conforama* the ECJ provided absolutely no reasoning as to why the French legislation was to be considered proportionate. The English courts' performance was also less than satisfactory since they refused to apply the proportionality test by replacing it with a test of reasonableness. The French courts were equally poor as they simply did not apply the proportionality test to the facts of the cases before them. Finally, the concerted assault on the courts by 'repeat players' may be considered an abuse of the legal system as they exposed the inadequacies of an out-of-date piece of legislation.[275]

The shop-opening hours 'episode' thus created, especially in the United Kingdom, much sound and fury. The centre-point of the action was the application of the proportionality principle. The national court application discussed in this section highlights five points of particular significance. Firstly, the national case law demonstrates the difficulties in locating the 'objective' of national legislation which often represents a compromise between several highly charged political and social interests. Secondly, the discussion shows that the application of the proportionality principle can be extremely difficult in practice as the free-trade economic premises of the single market have to be balanced against worker-protection or a desire to ensure respect for the Christian Sabbath (or the 'traditional Sunday'). Thirdly, there is a conflict between the two limbs of the proportionality test and judgments of national courts demonstrate that only by giving dominance to the second, balancing limb of the proportionality test

---

[274] See also *R. v. Tunbridge Wells and Cranbrook Magistrates' Court, ex. p. Comet Group plc; R. v. Coventry Magistrates, ex. p. Woolworths plc*, (QB 16 July 1993) (transcr.: John Larking), and the rather far-fetched counter attack in *Stedman v. Hogg Robinson Travel Ltd* (CA 27 Oct. 1994) (transcr.: John Larking).

[275] See Rawlings, n. 118 above.

is it possible to easily conclude that national shop-opening legislation is proportionate. Fourthly, if the application of the proportionality principle is to be regarded as a question of fact, who should bear the burden of proving its proportionality or otherwise? Fifthly, again if the application of the proportionality principle is to be regarded as a question of fact, should it be possible for the first decision of a national court with respect to the proportionality of the measure to be capable of binding other national courts (for example, by deciding the question on 'judicial notice')?

In response to these points, three comments or tentative solutions may, and to a certain extent have, been offered. Firstly, it is imperative that the ECJ should be clearer in its guidance to the national courts as to how they should interpret and apply the proportionality principle in individual cases.[276] In particular, it could, as it did in *Stoke-on-Trent* v. *B & Q*, indicate to the national court which limb of the proportionality test should be given precedence. Secondly, the national courts need to grow in their maturity in applying Community law. In particular, the French courts need to reason their interpretations of the proportionality principle more clearly and the English courts need to develop in their familiarity with the proportionality principle setting aside or adapting the doctrine of Parliamentary sovereignty. Thirdly, the ECJ has now, in *Keck and Mithouard*,[277] finally addressed the inconsistencies in its Article 30 case law by holding that national legislation affecting the opening hours of shops fall outside the scope of Article 30. The far-fetched analysis of shop-opening hours as restricting inter-State trade may now be put to one side. Given that the ECJ had eventually reached the position in which it made quite clear that it would consider any national legislation affecting shop-opening hours as proportionate to socio-cultural objectives, irrespective of the detail or nature of the national legislation, it is submitted that it is more intellectually honest to hold, as the ECJ now has, that such legislation falls outside the scope of Article 30 in the first place.

5 CONCLUSIONS

The discussion in this chapter underlines the extent to which the application of the rule of reason in practice comprises a complex and finely balanced exercise. This is all the more so given the extent of intervention that the free movement of goods involves in national regulation of economic life. There are several important theoretical issues underlying its application which go to the very core of the division of powers between the

[276] Although it is in no way suggested that the ECJ should be encouraged to apply the proportionality test to the facts of individual cases itself.

[277] n. 110 above.

Community and its Member States. The kind of national legislation to which the rule of reason applies tends to be highly sensitive in its nature, often reflecting a broad spectrum of political issues about which feelings run deep. The application of the rule of reason almost always requires national courts to adjudicate on challenges launched by large commercial undertakings claiming that certain national legislation, which of itself comprises a political compromise, is not proportionate to that legislation's objective. Consequently, large commercial enterprises are able to pose as the champions of free trade and the defenders of consumer interests fighting against over-regulated markets. It is for such cases that the rule of reason is frequently called up as a reluctant conscript. As a result, the role played by EC law obliging national courts to investigate the proportionality of such legislation is extremely sensitive.

The discussion of applications by national courts of the ECJ's interpretation of the rule of reason demonstrates how effective the application of EC law by national courts can be. There is nothing more conducive to the establishment of a single market than when courts within a Member State conclude that certain national provisions are restrictive of trade and are not objectively justified to protect mandatory requirements such as, for example, the protection of consumers. In this way, national provisions which are restrictive of trade can be evaluated by a Member States' own courts on a case-by-case basis.

At the heart of national-court application of the rule of reason is the application of the proportionality test. The application of this test is not an easy one and often puts national courts into difficult and sensitive positions. Consequently, the application of the proportionality principle has undoubtedly presented the national courts with difficulties. The discussion has shown that national courts have encountered difficulties in locating the 'objective' of national legislation which often represents a compromise between several highly charged political and social interests. Furthermore, the two-stage application of the proportionality test often gives rise to a conflict between the two limbs of the test. In particular, it has been shown that a conflict arises in cases concerning national measures for which the restrictive effect on inter-State trade is very small (thus satisfying the balancing-test limb of the proportionality test) but for which there is no necessity because there are alternative means of achieving the objective in question (thereby failing the necessity test). As has been shown, the problem with applying the proportionality test to such legislation is that a national court is obliged to examine the necessity of national regulatory measures whose effect on trade is so small as to be proportionate under the 'balancing' stage of the test. National court judgments demonstrate that it is frequently only by giving dominance to the balancing limb of the proportionality test that it is possible to easily conclude that national 'socio-cultural' legislation is proportionate. Since the application of this test is rather subjective in practice, the discussion has also, not surprisingly, given rise to examples of disunity of application of the principle within a Member State. It should also be added that the discussion has also revealed that the application of the proportionality principle by the national courts (and the French courts in particular) has often been far from satisfactory. The reasoning in such judgments is frequently insufficient and the national courts have been all too quick to conclude that national provisions are justified under the rule of reason.

The balance of poor applications of the rule of reason by the national courts gives rise to the question as to whether it would be desirable for the ECJ to be encouraged to decide the proportionality of justifications raised to the facts of the cases referred to it. It has been noted that the ECJ has been somewhat erratic by deciding in some cases the proportionality of rule-of-reason justifications itself (and thus arguably overstepping its competence under Article 177 EC) while leaving it to the national court in others. When the ECJ decides the proportionality issue itself, the task of the national court in implementing the judgment is certainly made easier as it is very often left with little else to do than to 'rubber-stamp' the judgment of the ECJ. Furthermore, if the ECJ itself applies the rule-of-reason justification to the facts, uniformity of application in the national courts in ensured. However, it is submitted that the discussion of the experience of national courts in applying the rule of reason exposes serious dangers in cases in which the ECJ steps in to decide the proportionality issue itself rather than leaving it to the national court. One of these dangers is that the ECJ's finding with respect to proportionality is necessarily of a generalized nature. As such, the dynamic application of the proportionality principle by the national courts on a case-by-case basis is precluded. This is all the more difficult when a finding of proportionality by the ECJ with respect to the legislation of one Member State is followed by a national court in another Member State. Further, the ECJ has neither the fact-finding capacity of the national courts nor the final word on the nuances of the national provisions involved. As a result, the ECJ's assessment of the facts often lacks subtlety. The experience of national courts also demonstrates that the national court is undoubtedly much better placed to carry out an analysis of the facts in a dynamic fashion as opposed to the more generalized or broad-brush approach to which the ECJ is limited. The conclusion is thus very firmly that the ECJ should not be encouraged to decide the proportionality justifications raised to the facts of the cases referred to it.

Given that it is the application of the proportionality principle that gives rise to the greatest difficulties before the national courts, it is imperative that the ECJ should be clearer in its guidance to the national courts as to how they should interpret and apply the proportionality principle in individual cases. It is submitted that the ECJ could do this, not by applying the proportionality test to the facts itself, but by indicating to the national court which limb of the proportionality test should be given precedence. Additionally, the national courts need to grow in their maturity in applying Community law. In particular, the French courts need to give reasons for their interpretations of the proportionality principle more clearly and the English courts need to develop their familiarity with the proportionality principle, setting aside or adapting the doctrine of Parliamentary sovereignty.

7

Article 36 Grounds of Justification

1 INTRODUCTION

The EC Treaty provides for certain grounds which Member States may
rely upon to justify infringements to the provisions concerning free movement of goods. Article 36 EC provides:

The provisions of Articles 30 to 34 shall not preclude prohibitions or restrictions on
imports, exports or goods in transit justified on grounds of public morality, public
policy or public security; the protection of health and life of humans, animals or
plants; the protection of national treasures possessing artistic, historic or archaeological value; or the protection of industrial and commercial property. Such prohibitions or restrictions shall not, however, constitute a means of arbitrary
discrimination or a disguised restriction on trade between Member States.

It will be noted that Article 36 is made up of two sentences. The first sentence lists the heads of justification which the Member States may invoke.
These heads of justification represent an exhaustive list, which the ECJ has
not been willing to extend,[1] of all the possible grounds of justification
available under Article 36. Each head of justification listed in the first sentence of Article 36 will be discussed in this chapter except for the 'protection of industrial and commercial property' which is dealt with in the
following chapter on intellectual property rights.

Because of the fundamental importance of the principle of the free
movement of goods, the Treaty rules governing this freedom have been
strictly enforced by the ECJ. A common theme running throughout the
ECJ's interpretation of the provisions on free movement of goods is thus
that the prohibition contained in Article 30, as a basic freedom under the
Treaty, must be interpreted as broadly as possible. Correspondingly, the
exceptions and justifications have been strictly construed and are thus of a
narrow scope. As a result, the ECJ has interpreted Article 36 narrowly.[2]
The narrow interpretation of Article 36 may also be explained by a wish to
avoid the danger that the Article 36 justifications may develop into a
'catch-all' for Member States to justify serious restrictions to the free movement of goods. In this respect, the ECJ has held that the purpose of Article

---

[1] See, Case 113/80 *Commission v. Ireland* (Souvenirs) [1981] ECR 1625.

[2] See, e.g., Case 7/68 *Commission v. Italy* [1968] ECR 423, [1969] CMLR 1; Case 13/68 *Salgoil*
v. *Italian Ministry for Foreign Trade* [1968] ECR 453, [1969] CMLR 181, & Case 46/76 *Bauhuis*
v. *Netherlands* [1977] ECR 5.

36 EC is merely to allow national legislation to derogate from the principle of free movement of goods on an individual basis. Thus, Article 36 is not to be understood as reserving certain matters to the exclusive jurisdiction of the Member States.[3]

Perhaps most importantly, the ECJ has refused to accept economic-based justifications under Article 36. In other words, a Member State cannot be allowed to avoid the effects of measures provided for in the Treaty by pleading economic difficulties caused by the elimination of barriers to intra-Community trade.[4] Finally, the ECJ has held that the burden of proving that an infringement of the rules on the free movement of goods is justified lies with the Member State wishing to rely on Article 36.[5]

The second sentence of Article 36 sets out the second hurdle which the Member State must clear in order to justify a measure under Article 36 successfully. Thus, once a Member State has demonstrated that the national restriction in principle falls under one of the heads of justification provided for in the first sentence of Article 36, it must then proceed to show that the restriction does not constitute an 'arbitrary discrimination' or a 'disguised restriction' on trade between Member States according to the second sentence of that Article. In practice, the second sentence of Article 36 has been applied by the ECJ as the familiar 'proportionality' and 'alternative means' tests.[6]

Application by national courts of the Article 36 justifications is of particular interest. In many respects, the granting of justifications under Article 36 is at the sharp end of national-court application of EC law. The granting of such justifications is the point at which the Community system entrusts the greatest amount of responsibility to the national courts. Indeed, the fact that the ECJ has held that Article 36 has direct effect,[7] and thus that national courts are competent to grant and apply the justifications provided for in that Article, puts remarkable responsibility and trust in the national courts' ability to apply those justifications correctly. This may be contrasted with the position under the Treaty's competition rules. In that context, it will be noted that Article 9(1) of Regulation 17/62[8] provides that the European Commission has the 'sole power' to grant an exemption from the prohibition of anti-competitive agreements contained

---

[3] Case 153/78 *Commission* v. *Germany* [1979] ECR 2555.

[4] See Case 95/81 *Commission* v. *Italy* [1982] ECR 2187; C–324/93 *R.* v. *Secretary of State for the Home Department, ex p. Evans Medical Ltd* [1995] ECR I-563; C–265/95 *Commission* v. *France* [1977] ECR 1–nyr (judgt 9 Dec. 1997) at para. 62, cf. Case 72/83 *Campus Oil* v. *Minister for Industry and Energy* [1984] ECR 2727.

[5] See, e.g., Case 251/78 *Denkavit Futtermittel* v. *Minister of Agriculture* [1979] ECR 3369, [1980] 3 CMLR 513 & Case 227/82 *Leendert van Bennekom* [1983] ECR 3883, [1985] 2 CMLR 692.

[6] See discussion of the proportionality principle at p. 202.

[7] See, e.g., Case 74/76 *Ianelli and Volpi* v. *Meroni* [1977] ECR 557.

[8] [1962] OJ Spec. Ed. 204/62 at 87.

in Article 85(1) EC provided for in Article 85(3) EC. Thus, a national court may not *itself* carry out and apply the assessment under Article 85(3).[9] This causes serious legal complications for the national courts in the application of Article 85.[10] However, the system adopted in the application of Articles 30 to 36, under which the national courts *can* grant justifications, also gives rise to legal complications of an equally serious nature: the ability of national courts to admit justifications for restrictions to the free movement of goods opens up a potential for legal disunity as a result of different legal traditions in different Member States. If the application of Community law is not to be fragmented, it is imperative that the national courts may be trusted to apply, in a consistent way, the derogations to the provisions concerning the free movement of goods which are provided for in Article 36. The heads of justification provided for in Article 36 are particularly susceptible to divergent interpretations in different Member States. For example, the courts of one Member State may have a considerably wider definition of the concept of 'public policy' than the courts of another. Thus, in the discussion of national case law applying Article 36 which follows, special attention will be devoted to the extent to which such divergences have actually emerged. In light of the latter discussion, the question of whether it would be desirable for the ECJ to develop clearer definitions of the concepts mentioned in Article 36 will also be addressed. Is the experience of the national courts' application of Article 36 such that a Community-wide definition of, for example, 'public morality' would be desirable in the interests of consistent legal application throughout the Community? Are national courts respecting the ECJ's clear intention to keep the Article 36 justifications as narrow as possible? Do some national courts afford Article 36 justifications more easily than others? Are the courts of some Member States more rigorous in applying the proportionality principle (contained implicitly in the second sentence of Article 36) than others?

---

[9] However, a national court may of course rely on an existing Commission decision granting exemption under Art. 85(3).

[10] See, e.g., Whish, 'The Enforcement of EC Competition Law in Member States' Courts'; Van Bael, 'The Role of the National Courts'; Weatherill & Beaumont, *EC Law*, 789–805. See also the judgt of the CFI in T–24/90 *Automec Srl* v. *Commission* (Automec II) [1992] ECR II–2223, [1992] 5 CMLR 431 & the ECJ in C–234/89 *Stergios Delimitis* v. *Henninger Brau* [1991] ECR I–935 & Commission Notice on co-operation between national courts and the Commission in applying Articles 85 and 86, [1993] OJ C39/6, [1993] 4 CMLR 12. Before the English courts, see *MTV Europe* v. *BMG Record (UK)* [1997] 1 CMLR 867, [1997] EuLR 100 and *Iberian (UK)* v. *BPB Industries* [1996] 2 CMLR 601, [1997] EuLR 1. Before the Dutch courts, see *Vierkant Beheer, Hoge Raad,* 22 Dec. 1995, NJ 1997, 118 and *Free Record Shop,* Pres. *Rechtbank* Amsterdam, 1 Feb. 1996, SEW 1996, 149 (with note by Biesheuvel & Duk). Before the Irish courts, see *HB Ice Cream* v. *Masterfoods* [1993] 11 ILRM 145 (Irish High Court). The position with respect to the Treaty's competition rules is further complicated by the parallel competence of national competition authorities. See 'Preliminary draft Commission notice on co-operation between national competition authorities and the Commission in handling cases falling within the scope of Articles 85 or 86 of the EC Treaty' [1996] OJ C262/5.

It will be clear that the answers to all these questions are of extreme importance for the consistent application of EC law throughout the Community. It is with these issues in mind that we may proceed with the discussion of the national court application of Article 36. The national courts' application of each head of justification provided for in Article 36 will be dealt with in turn.

2 PUBLIC MORALITY

The question of public morality in the context of Article 36 has arisen before the ECJ in two cases concerning the import of 'indecent' goods into the United Kingdom.[11] The approach of the ECJ with respect to this head to justification in Article 36 has been to hold that 'in principle, it is for each Member State to determine in accordance with its own scale of values . . . the requirements of public morality in its territory'[12] subject to the proviso that there is no lawful trade in the articles being denied access to the market, in the Member State in question.[13] In *Henn and Darby*,[14] the ECJ found that, on the facts of that case, there was 'on a comprehensive view' no lawful trade within the United Kingdom of the goods at issue in that case, and thus that the restriction on importation was justified under Article 36. In *Conegate*[15] by contrast, the ECJ found that the goods in question could be manufactured freely in the United Kingdom and could be marketed there subject only to certain limited restrictions. Accordingly, the ECJ held that there was a lawful trade in the United Kingdom, and thus that the ban on import could not be justified under Article 36. In sum then, it seems that the ECJ's approach is to allow Member States to choose the standard of public morality that they wish to protect for the purposes of Article 36, but to subject their reliance on the latter Article to whether or not there is a lawful trade in the goods in question within that Member State.

Before proceeding to a full critique of the consequences for the application by national courts of the ECJ's approach outlined above, the view taken by the English Court of Appeal in *Henn and Darby*[16] (before the reference to the ECJ by the House of Lords) requires brief attention. In application of Article 36, the Court of Appeal hesitated as to whether the word 'justified' in Article 36 meant 'necessary' and concluded that it would 'give

---

[11] Case 34/79 *R* v. *Henn and Darby* [1979] ECR 3795 & Case 121/85 *Conegate* v. *HM Customs and Excise Commissioners* [1986] ECR 1007.

[12] Case 34/79, n. 11 above, at para. 15 & Case 121/85, n. 11 above, at para. 14.

[13] The requirement that there be 'no lawful trade' of the goods within the Member State is an application of the second sentence of Art. 36.

[14] Case 34/79, n. 11 above.   [15] Case 121/85, n. 11 above.

[16] [1978] 1 WLR 1031; [1978] 3 All ER 1190; [1978] 2 CMLR 688. For a discussion of the definition of 'quantitative restrictions' by the CA in this case see Ch. 2, sect. 2.

effect to the plain English words of this version of the Treaty'[17] and held that '[W]hen one comes to look at Article 36 its plain purpose is to preserve prohibitions, which in turn have the plain purpose of supporting public morality. We cannot see how prohibition on the introduction of obscene literature can be other than a prohibition justified on the grounds of public morality and public policy.'[18]

It is submitted that given that there was at that time no ECJ authority on the scope of the 'public morality' justification under Article 36, the Court of Appeal was too quick to conclude that the ban was justified under Article 36. In particular, there is absolutely no sign that the Court of Appeal took into consideration the well-established principle emphasized by the ECJ that the fact that Article 36 permitted derogation from the fundamental principle of the free movement of goods meant that that Article must be narrowly construed.[19] Furthermore, the Court of Appeal may be criticized for not having proceeded to look at the second sentence of Article 36 and the question of whether the import ban was a proportionate means of achieving the objective. This too, was a well-established principle in ECJ case law at the time of the Court of Appeal's judgment.[20] Finally, in the light of the above comments, the Court of Appeal may be criticized for having refused to refer questions to the ECJ. This is particularly surprising since, as Gravells has pointed out,[21] the Court of Appeal had recently made a reference to the ECJ in *R.* v. *Thompson, Johnson and Woodiwiss*[22] in a case concerning the 'public policy' head of justification in Article 36.

Fortunately, on appeal before the House of Lords, a reference was made to the ECJ in *Henn and Darby*.[23] The judgments of the ECJ in both *Henn and Darby* and *Conegate* have been outlined above. Since the ECJ effectively answered the questions before the national courts, neither national court encountered any difficulty in implementing the ECJ judgments. Thus, in *Henn and Darby*, the House of Lords simply recited the questions it had referred, quoted the answers provided by the ECJ and upheld the

---

[17] [1978] 2 CMLR 688 at 691. This reference to 'the plain English words' is subject to serious criticism since the ECJ had long established that none of the official language versions of the Treaty is definitive: see, e.g., Case 19/67 *Sociale Verzekeringsbank* v. *Van der Vecht* [1967] ECR 345, [1968] CMLR 151 & Case 29/69 *Stauder* v. *City of Ulm, Sozialamt* [1969] ECR 419, [1970] CMLR 112. The latter point has been further underlined by the ECJ in Case 283/81 *CILFIT* v. *Italian Ministry of Health* [1982] ECR 3415 at 3430, [1983] 1 CMLR 472.

[18] [1978] 2 CMLR 688 at 692 (per Widgery LCJ).

[19] See ECJ judgts cited at n. 2 above.

[20] See, e.g., Case 29/72 *Marimex* v. *Italian Finance Administration* [1972] ECR 1309, [1973] CMLR 486.

[21] Gravells (1978) 3 ELRev. 442.

[22] [1980] 2 All ER 102; [1978] 1 CMLR 390. For a full discussion of this judgt see pp. 244–5.

[23] [1980] 2 All ER 166; [1979] 2 CMLR 495.

convictions of the defendants.[24] Similarly, in *Conegate*, the Queen's Bench Division of the High Court simply quoted the answers provided by the ECJ and, since both parties were in agreement that the defendants should, following the ECJ judgment, be acquitted, the High Court accordingly acquitted Conegate. It may be noted that the national courts' task was facilitated in both cases by the fact that the ECJ had overstepped its competence in Article 177 proceedings by applying its interpretation to the facts of the case rather than leaving this task to the national court. Formally speaking, the duty of the ECJ under Article 177 is to interpret the relevant Community law referred to it and not to apply its interpretation to the facts. In *Costa* v. *ENEL*[25] the ECJ emphasized that Article 177 'gives the Court no jurisdiction either to apply the Treaty to a specific case or to decide upon the validity of a provision of domestic law in relation to the Treaty, as it would be possible for it to do under Article 169'.[26] However, as Collins has remarked, 'the distinction between interpretation of Community law and ruling on the validity of national law is as elusive as the distinction between interpretation and application'.[27] As a result, the English courts in *Henn and Darby* and *Conegate* had little to do except mechanically apply the answer provided by the ECJ.

The ease with which the English courts were able to implement the ECJ's judgments in these two cases is, however, extremely deceptive since they mask serious difficulties underlying the approach of the ECJ in both of these cases. The judgment of the ECJ in *Henn and Darby* in particular, has been widely criticized.[28] As was set out above, the crux of what the ECJ held in that case was that there was 'no lawful trade' in the articles being denied access to the market in the United Kingdom. This factual assessment has been described as 'factually incorrect'[29] and 'undoubtedly wrong'.[30] This is a conclusion with which it is difficult to disagree. The legislative regime in the United Kingdom applicable to indecent and obscene goods was different depending on whether the goods were produced in the United Kingdom or imported. There were essentially two differences. Firstly, there was a difference in applicable criteria: the sale of goods in the United Kingdom was subject to Section 1 of the Obscene Publications Act 1959 which prohibited only those goods which tend to 'deprave and cor-

---

[24] [1980] 2 WLR 597 + 633; [1981] 1 AC 850 + 902; [1980] 2 All ER 166 + 194; [1980] 2 CMLR 229.

[25] Case 6/64 [1964] ECR 585 at 592.

[26] See also Case 13/61 *De Geus* v. *Bosch* [1962] ECR 45, [1962] CMLR 1.

[27] Collins, *European Community Law in the United Kingdom*, 167.

[28] See, Catchpole & Barav (1980/1) LIEI 1; Weiler (1981) 44 MLR 91; Gormley, *Prohibiting Restrictions on Trade Within the EEC*, 126; & Oliver, *Free Movement of Goods in the European Community*, 196.

[29] Oliver, n. 28 above, 196.   [30] Gormley, n. 28 above, 128.

rupt',[31] whereas imported goods were subject to Section 42 of the Customs Consolidation Act 1876 which prohibited those goods which were 'indecent or obscene'.[32] In practice, therefore, it is clear that the criteria applicable to imports are stricter: the import of 'indecent and obscene' goods is prohibited while only the sale of obscene goods is prohibited in the UK but indecent material may nevertheless be sold. As McFarlane has pointed out, 'the advantage enjoyed by Customs and Excise is that indecency as a concept catches a much wider range of articles than obscenity'[33] since the notion of indecency is far less rigorous than obscenity. Furthermore, McFarlane goes on to point out that it is not merely the importer who is subject to Section 42 of the Customs Consolidation Act 1876. Once the importation has taken place, anyone who has been knowingly concerned in carrying, removing, depositing, harbouring, keeping, concealing, or in any manner dealing with the goods would be open to prosecution under this section. This would extend to subsequent dealing inland, so long as an importation had at some stage taken place. In practice, therefore, 'those investigating material alleged to be pornographic would look for evidence of importation so that they could avoid the sterner test of the Obscene Publications Act 1959, and bring in Customs and Excise if necessary'.[34]

The second important difference between goods sold in the United Kingdom and those imported is that goods sold in the United Kingdom had the possibility of relying on section 4(1) of the Obscene Publications Acts 1959 which excepted from the provisions of the Act obscene articles when their obscenity was 'justified as being for the public good on the ground that it is in the interests of science, literature, art or learning, or of other objects of general concern'. No equivalent justification was available for imports under the Customs Consolidation Act 1876.

With these two differences between import and sale in the UK in mind, the conclusion of the ECJ in *Henn and Darby* that 'on a comprehensive view . . . there is no lawful trade in such goods in the United Kingdom' does indeed seem to be factually incorrect. Thus, it is not only the fact that the ECJ entered into a factual assessment but also the factual assessment itself, which is open to criticism. It would have been preferable had the ECJ simply held that in principle, it is for each Member State to determine in

---

[31] Obscene Publications Act, s. 1 reads: 'For the purposes of this Act an article shall be deemed to be obscene if its effect . . . is, taken as a whole, such as to tend to deprave and corrupt . . .'.

[32] Customs Consolidation Act 1876, s. 42 provides for a prohibition on 'Indecent or obscene prints, paintings, photographs, books, cards, lithographic or other gravings, or any other indecent or obscene materials'. Under this section, it is sufficient that the articles should offend against recognized standards of propriety without necessarily having the tendency to deprave and corrupt. The offence is created by Customs and Excise Act 1952, s. 304 and the goods liable to forfeiture under Customs and Excise (Management) Act 1979, s. 49(1)(b).

[33] McFarlane, 'Indecency and Obscenity: The View from Europe' at 50.   [34] Ibid.

accordance with its own scale of values the requirements of public morality in its territory subject to the proviso that there is no lawful trade in the articles being denied access to the market, in the Member State in question. The question of whether on the facts there was a lawful trade in the articles in the UK should, it is submitted, have been left to the national court. Instead, the ECJ took a broad-brush approach and effectively held that the entire United Kingdom legislation in question was justified under Article 36.

The effect of the broad-brush approach by the ECJ in *Henn and Darby* and *Conegate* was damaging and a recipe for disaster before the national courts. Regrettably, these fears have been borne out. In a test case concerning the import of certain books into the United Kingdom which were seized by Customs and Excise as being obscene articles the importation of which was prohibited under Section 42 of the Customs Consolidation Act 1876, the specific point was raised as to whether or not the applicants were entitled to call evidence and make submissions as to whether the publication of the books was for the public good within the meaning of Section 4 of the Obscene Publications Act 1959. In *R.* v. *Bow Street Magistrates' Court and Martin Dubbey, ex. p. Noncyp Ltd*, both the English High Court[35] and the Court of Appeal[36] rejected the application and held that such a rejection was, following the judgment of the ECJ in *Henn and Darby*, justified under Article 36. Before both courts, the applicants argued that it was impossible to decide whether there is 'no lawful trade' in the books in question in the UK unless the section 4 evidence has been admitted. In the High Court, Woolf LJ on the one hand accepted that a more extensive restriction on goods which are imported than that which is imposed on articles manufactured in England and Wales would not accord with the general intent of the EC Treaty, but went on to hold 'However, I do not consider that European law has as yet developed that far. To hold that it has involves a complete departure from and the virtual overruling of the decision in *Henn and Darby*.[37]

With utmost respect, this is all the more reason for the High Court to have made a reference to the ECJ. In *Wünsche Handelgesellschaft GmbH* v. *Germany*[38] the ECJ expressly stated that it was open to a national court to re-refer questions which had been the subject of earlier references when new facts might lead the ECJ to giving a different answer.[39] What is even more disappointing is that Woolf LJ admits that the result he reaches 'could lead in theory to illogical results'[40] and he expresses the hope that in a case where there has already been a failed prosecution in respect of

---

[35] [1988] 3 WLR 827, [1988] 3 CMLR 84.
[36] [1989] 3 WLR 467, [1990] 1 QB 123, [1989] 1 CMLR 634.
[37] [1988] 3 CMLR 84 at 91.   [38] Case 345/82 [1984] ECR 1995.
[39] See also Cases 28–30/62 *Da Costa* [1963] ECR 31, [1963] CMLR 224 & Case 28/67 *Molkerei-Zentrale* [1968] ECR 143, [1968] CMLR 187.
[40] [1988] 3 CMLR 84 at 92.

the same books under the Obscene Publications Act 1959 in the UK, the Commissioners of Customs and Excise would allow importation since it would be 'an abuse of their discretion' if they did not. This is, again with respect, all well and good, but ignores the point that in most cases it is extremely unlikely that there will be a failed prosecution in the UK with respect to the same books. The subsequent judgment of the Court of Appeal is equally puzzling. In his judgment in the Court of Appeal, Croom-Johnson LJ himself points out that not only do domestic products benefit from the section 4 possibility of exemption, but also the definition of what is obscene within the Obscene Publications Act 1959 has a narrower meaning than under the Customs Consolidation Act 1876. Nevertheless, the ECJ's judgment in *Henn and Darby* was again relied on as 'clear authority' for the proposition that the UK legislation was justified.

The dangers alluded to above were further confirmed by the more recent judgment of the English High Court in *R. v. Uxbridge Justices, ex. p. Webb*.[41] This case again concerned the importation into the United Kingdom of certain videos which were seized by Customs as being prohibited under section 42 of the Customs Consolidation Act 1876. Glidewell LJ in the High Court dealt with the EC law argument in a single paragraph by simply rejecting the Article 36 argument in the following terms:

This court held that this exception [Article 36] entitled the United Kingdom to continue to apply the prohibitions contained in the various Custom Acts on the importation of obscene material. In other words the decision of the Court of Appeal in *Noncyp* is conclusive against Mr Webb's argument in that respect.[42]

What is distinctly unsatisfactory with this judgment is that it allows a precedent within the national system to bind the decisions of further national courts as to the interpretation of EC law. As has been submitted above, the precedent itself provided an unsatisfactory interpretation of EC law. As a result, we see here developing the very real danger that EC law will not be correctly applied by the national courts. The High Court in *Ex p. Webb* did not even attempt to carry out the test required by EC law, but simply referred to another national judgment as conclusive authority on the matter. It is submitted that, at the very least, the High Court should have carried out an analysis according to which the prohibition on importation of obscene materials imposed by section 42 of the Customs Consolidation Act 1876 was permitted by Article 36 *in so far* as it related to the materials in which there was no lawful trade in the United Kingdom. There is simply no discussion to this effect in *Ex p. Webb* with the result that the tests enunciated by the ECJ in *Henn and Darby* and *Conegate* have been reduced to vanishing point before the English courts.

---

[41] [1994] 2 CMLR 288.
[42] Ibid. at 291. See also *Wright v. Customs and Excise*, The Times, 23 Feb. 1998.

There are several lessons to be learnt from this episode before the UK courts. Firstly, the discussion in this section confirms that the criticisms of the ECJ's approach in *Henn and Darby* for going too far (in the context of an Article 177 reference) into the facts of the case, were justified. The appreciation of the facts by the ECJ was flawed. Such appreciations of fact are better left to the national court which is better placed to decide such questions. The seeds for trouble were thus sown by the ECJ itself.

The interpretation of the *Henn and Darby* judgment by the English courts in subsequent cases was, on a literal interpretation of that judgment, perfectly defensible. After all, the ECJ in *Henn and Darby* clearly had the possibility of the section 4 of the Obscene Publications Act 1959 exemption in mind when it said in paragraph 19 of its judgment that:

In these questions the House of Lords takes account of the appellants' submissions based upon certain differences between, on the one hand, the prohibition on importing the goods in question, which is absolute, and, on the other, the laws in force in the various constituent parts of the United Kingdom, which appear to be less strict in the sense that . . . even if [possession in obscene articles] is generally forbidden, *trade in such articles is subject to certain exceptions, notably those in favour of articles having scientific, literary, artistic, or educational interest.*[43]

Furthermore, the English courts cannot be blamed for simply following the explicit finding of the ECJ in paragraph 21 of its judgment that:

A prohibition on imports which *may in certain respects be more strict than some of the laws applied within the United Kingdom* cannot therefore be regarded as amounting to a measure designed to give indirect protection to some national product or aimed at creating arbitrary discrimination.[44]

On the other hand, the English courts are not completely blameless. While they followed the ECJ judgments to the letter, it could also be said that they followed the *Henn* ruling too literally. In any event, it is submitted that a further reference to the ECJ should have been made in either *Ex p. Noncyp* or *Ex p. Webb*. As was noted above, there is no impediment to a national court referring the same question to the ECJ again. In fact, it was arguable that the facts were substantially different from either the *Henn and Darby* or the *Conegate* case. In *Henn and Darby*, the nature of the materials that had been seized in that case was such that their 'indecency' could be confirmed on virtually any view.[45] In fact as Woolf LJ in *Ex p. Noncyp* remarked, the defendants in *Henn and Darby* 'not surprisingly having regard to the contents of the books and films, did not seek to rely upon sec-

---

[43] Emphasis added.   [44] Emphasis added.
[45] The case concerned films and magazines which included a number of scenes of violence and aberrant sexual behaviour including scenes of child abuse and intercourse between human beings and animals.

tion 4 of the Obscene Publications Act 1959'.[46] Thus it could be argued that the *Henn and Darby* judgment be limited to the facts of that case, in view of the materials at issue. The materials in *Ex p. Noncyp* and *Ex p. Webb* were of such a different nature that the possibility of the Section 4 exception could not so obviously be excluded.[47] Indeed, this is given support by the opinion of Advocate General Warner in *Henn and Darby* where he stated that:

Perhaps the most glaring disparity lies in the fact that, although an obscene book may be lawfully on sale in English bookshops, for instance because its publication is judged to be for the public good on the ground of its scientific value or literary merit, the identical book published in another Member State may not be imported into England. That undoubtedly constitutes discrimination. In a case that was concerned with such a book, it might not be easy to decide whether the discrimination was 'arbitrary' or was 'justified'. From the description we have been given in the Agreed Statement of Facts of the films and magazines with which this case is concerned, it seems improbable that the House of Lords will be confronted here with such a difficult question. It seems more probable that those films and magazines belong to a category of articles that the laws of the United Kingdom treat in much the same way whether they be home-produced or foreign.[48]

If it is arguable that the *Henn and Darby* judgment can be limited to its facts, it is also arguable that the *Conegate* case could be distinguished. In *Conegate* the manufacture and marketing of the articles at issue in that case (inflatable rubber dolls) in the United Kingdom was *lawful* subject to restrictions, while in *Ex p. Noncyp* and *Ex p. Webb* the manufacture and marketing of the materials was *unlawful* in the United Kingdom unless exempted under section 4 of the Obscene Publications Act 1959. It is thus arguable that both ECJ authorities were distinguishable and that a fresh reference from the English courts was required. This is underlined by the fact that the *Ex p. Noncyp* case was an explicit 'test case' which had been set up in co-operation with Customs and Excise. The refusal of the Court of Appeal in that case to make a reference to the ECJ may, in this light, be regarded as an abuse of Article 36.

The decision of the High Court in *Ex p. Webb* is also subject to serious criticism. It may be considered distinctly unsatisfactory that a precedent within the national system was held to bind the decisions of further

---

[46] [1988] 3 CMLR 84 at 88.

[47] *Ex p. Noncyp* concerned 6 books bearing the titles *Men in Erotic Art*; *Men Loving Men*; *Men Loving Themselves*; *My Brother Myself*; *Roman Conquests*; & *Below the Belt* and were imported by the applicants who owned and ran a bookshop called 'Gay's the Word' in London. *Ex p. Webb* concerned 6 videos containing explicit representations of homosexual activity which were seized in the personal baggage of the applicant and which he intended to view privately in connection with his work for a campaigning organization, the National Campaign for the Reform of the Obscene Publications Acts.

[48] Case 34/79, n. 11 above, at 3828.

national courts as to the interpretation of EC law. As has been submitted above, the precedent itself provided an unsatisfactory interpretation of EC law. As a result, we see here developing the very real danger that EC law will not be correctly applied by the national courts. The whole point of Article 36 is that it must be applied by the national courts on a case-by-case basis. As was noted above, Article 36 has the purpose of allowing national measures to derogate from the principle of the free movement of goods on an individual basis, and is not to be interpreted as 'reserving' certain matters to the exclusive jurisdiction of the Member States.[49] On the other hand, it was the ECJ itself which paved the way for this divergence by its statement in *Henn and Darby* that 'it cannot be disputed that the statutory provisions applied by the United Kingdom in regard to the importation of articles having an indecent or obscene character come within the powers *reserved* to the Member States by the first sentence of Article 36'.[50]

The discussion above demonstrates the weakness that is latent in the Article 177 procedure on preliminary rulings. At source, the ECJ delivered a judgment which had questionable factual foundations. It is submitted that it should have left the findings of fact to the national courts and certainly should not have framed its findings in such a broad-brush manner. On the other hand, the national courts should be careful to refrain from following judgments of the ECJ too literally. In these cases, the English Courts followed *Henn and Darby* literally when a purposive interpretation of Article 36 makes a nonsense of the result. The weakness of the Article 177 system is that the national court could, in such circumstances, refuse its discretion to make a reference. Poor ECJ judgments were taken advantage of by the national courts. However, the problem with Article 177 is that, should the national court refuse to make a reference, the ECJ has no opportunity to reconsider its previous judgment.

It should, for the sake of completeness, be mentioned that in *McAfee* v. *Smyth and Quigley*,[51] the Belfast Recorder's Court held that a ban on the importation of CB radios into the United Kingdom from the Republic of Ireland constituted a breach of Article 30 which was nevertheless justified under Article 36 for the protection of 'public security'. The possibility that the ban could be justified under the head of 'public morality' was also considered and put to one side because 'whilst it is possible that the prohibition might be justified on this ground, I do not consider that the incidence of soliciting by prostitutes or their procurers is to any great extent increased by the existence of Citizens' Band radios'.[52] This judgment will be discussed further below in the section on public security.

---

[49] n. 3 above.
[51] [1981] 1 CMLR 410.

[50] Para. 15 of judgt. Emphasis added.
[52] Ibid. at 417.

3 PUBLIC POLICY AND PUBLIC SECURITY

The justifications in Article 36 of both public policy and public security have been extremely narrowly construed by the ECJ. Only rarely has the Court been willing to accept a justification under one of these heads. This is not surprising since these two concepts are notoriously vague and there would be a very real danger that Article 36 would develop into a 'catch-all' for Member States to justify serious restrictions to the free movement of goods if the ECJ did not attach a narrow interpretation to their scope.

(A) Public policy and public security and economic considerations

One of the central dangers with these two heads of justification has always been that Member States would attempt to invoke them to justify measures taken for economic purposes to relieve short-term economic difficulties. This would be undesirable since it would drive a coach and horses through Articles 30 and 34 and would give Member States unilateral power to bypass those provisions by pleading economic difficulties. As has already been noted, the ECJ has always refused to accept economic-based justifications under Article 36.[53] It appeared that the ECJ had, however, opened the door to such justifications in *Campus Oil* v. *Minister for Industry and Energy*.[54] In that case, the ECJ held that the maintenance of essential oil supplies was covered by the 'public security' head of justification since the exceptional importance of petroleum products as an energy source in the modern economy is 'of fundamental importance for a country's existence' because not only a state's economy but 'above all its institutions, its essential public services and the survival of its inhabitants' depend upon it.[55] To ensure that Member States did not get the impression that economic justifications were thus permitted, the ECJ went on in *Campus Oil* to stress the special nature of that case. It recalled that Article 36 refers exclusively to matters of a non-economic nature but held that:

[I]n the light of the seriousness of the consequences that an interruption in supplies of petroleum products may have for a country's existence, the aim of ensuring a minimum supply of petroleum products at all times is to be regarded as *transcending purely economic considerations* and thus as capable of constituting an objective covered by the concept of public security.[56]

---

[53] n. 4 above.   [54] Case 72/83, n. 4 above.   [55] Ibid. at para. 34.
[56] Ibid. at para. 35. Emphasis added. The ECJ has also had occasion to reject the public-security justification on similar facts in Case 347/88 *Commission* v. *Greece* [1990] ECR I–4747 since Greece had 'not shown that if the State's rights with regard to the importation and marketing of petroleum products were not maintained in force, the public-sector refineries would be unable to dispose of their products on the market at competitive prices and thereby ensure their continued operation' (para. 49 of judgt).

Given that the ECJ has always gone out of its way to stress that Article 36 does not cover economic matters, it is surprising to find decisions of national courts which nevertheless admit certain restrictions explicitly on economic grounds. The most blatant example is to be found in the judgment of Gower QC sitting in Maidstone Crown Court at Canterbury in *R. v. Thompson, Johnson and Woodiwiss*.[57] This case concerned the prosecution of three British nationals for being knowingly involved in a fraudulent evasion of the prohibition on importation of gold coins into the United Kingdom and on the export from the United Kingdom of silver alloy coins minted before 1947.[58] One of the issues in this case was whether the gold or the coins fell under the Treaty provisions on goods or those on capital.[59] On the assumption that they fell under the Treaty provisions on goods, Gower QC held that the breach of either Article 30 or 34 was nevertheless justified under the head of public policy in Article 36. While this may not in itself be considered objectionable, the fact that Gower QC went on to expressly rule that Article 36 covered economic considerations is. Gower QC reasoned that 'in a Treaty which . . . is about economic relationships, certain provisions which are specifically inserted to deal with economic problems, that (*sic*) public policy must include economic considerations'.[60] In deciding that it was 'self-evident that the public policy of a Member State justifies it in imposing restrictions of the kind here', Gower QC seemed oblivious to ECJ case law which had long established that purely economic justifications were not permissible under Article 36.[61] Given the traditional suspicion with which English law has always regarded public policy, it is surprising that Gower QC was not more cautious in reaching this conclusion.[62] On appeal before the Court of Appeal, a reference was made to the ECJ.[63] It is of interest to note that the ECJ, in its judgment, agreed that preventing the export of silver coins (which were no longer

[57] [1978] 1 CMLR 226.

[58] The importation of gold coins into the UK was prohibited by the Import of Goods (Control) Order 1954, SI 1954/23 and the export of the coins was prohibited by the Export of Goods (Control) Order 1970, SI 1970/1288.

[59] See discussion of this aspect of the case in Ch. 2, sect. 1 A.

[60] n. 57 above at 240.

[61] See Case 7/61 *Commission* v. *Italy* [1961] ECR 317, [1962] CMLR 39. Furthermore, in the context of Art. 48(3) EC Adv. Gen. Warner had also reiterated that a State cannot invoke the notion of public policy to embrace any domestic social or economic issue about which it may feel concerned: Case 30/77 *R.* v. *Bouchereau* [1977] ECR 1999 at 2025. Furthermore, Art. 2(2) of Directive 64/221 on the co-ordination of special measures concerning the movement and residence of foreign nationals which are justified on grounds of public policy, public security or public health [1964] OJ Spec Ed 850/64, 117 provides that 'such grounds shall not be invoked to service economic ends'.

[62] The familiar English law analogy of public policy as an 'unruly horse' as a reason for the Court to be wary of mounting the beast was indeed alluded to by Adv. Gen. Slynn in Case 72/83, n. 4 above at 2767.

[63] [1978] 1 CMLR 390, [1980] 2 All ER 102.

legal tender) was justified under public policy in Article 36 'because it stems from the need to protect the right to mint coinage which is traditionally regarded as involving the fundamental interests of the State'.[64] It is interesting to note that the ECJ reached its decision, not on the basis of economic considerations, but purely on grounds of fundamental interest, namely the right to mint and protect the integrity of coinage which remains the property of the state. As Oliver has noted, 'the protection of a property right is a very different matter from the protection of the economy as a whole'.[65]

The possibility that 'public policy' in Article 36 covers economic measures has also been explicitly suggested by the French courts. It was argued in a series of cases before those courts that legislation concerning the compatibility of French legislation imposing minimum retail prices for petrol was justified under Article 36 for reasons of public policy. The *Tribunal de Grande Instance* of Le Mans in *SARL Haincourt* v. *SARL M.P. (Leclerc Service) et SA des marchés et usines Auchan*[66] held that the restrictions were permitted under Article 36 for reasons of public policy (*ordre public*).[67] The Tribunal held that the petrol market was particularly sensitive to the economy and that all governments must be able to regulate its sale to prevent the drastic lowering of petrol prices and the potentially serious consequences for the economy. Furthermore, the *Tribunal* noted that small-scale distributors assured local distribution over greater geographical spread and thus the lowering of prices would put at risk the economic interests of the country. This decision has been criticised by Gavalda and Lucas De Leyssac[68] for its broad interpretation of *ordre public* in Article 36. Gavalda and Lucas De Leyssac note that other '*plus circonspectes*' French courts had referred the matter to the ECJ for a preliminary ruling on the matter. In the subsequent judgment of the ECJ on a reference from other French courts in *Cullet* v. *Centre Leclerc*,[69] the ECJ dealt briefly with (and rejected) the public policy justification. In considering the justification of public policy (*ordre public*), the ECJ dealt exclusively with questions concerning the danger of public unrest and did not even mention the possibility of other economic justifications.[70] This silence on the part of the ECJ may be taken as an implicit rejection that the economic considerations,

[64] Case 7/78 [1978] ECR 2247 at para. 34.

[65] Oliver, n. 28 above, 199. It may, for the sake of completeness, be noted that the implementation of the ECJ judgt caused no difficulties back before the CA and that, in fact, the applicants had voluntarily withdrawn their appeal: [1980] 2 All ER 102 at 137.

[66] *TGI* Le Mans, 11 July 1983, Gaz. Pal. 1984, II Som. 121, Dalloz 1985, IR 273.

[67] On the different connotations attached to the French *ordre public* and the English *public policy*, see discussion in the following section.

[68] Dalloz 1985, IR 273.   [69] Case 231/83 [1985] ECR 305, [1985] 2 CMLR 524.

[70] The question of whether the danger of public unrest or violence may be justified under Art. 36 for reasons of public policy, is discussed in the following section.

which had influenced the *Tribunal* in Le Mans in *SARL Haincourt*, were relevant under Article 36.

(B) Public policy and civil unrest

As will be clear from the foregoing analysis, the ECJ envisages that 'public policy' may, in certain circumstances, cover public unrest. The French term *ordre public* would thus seem to translate better into English as 'public law and order' rather than the term 'public policy' which is found in the English version of the Treaty. As has already been noted, the ECJ in *Cullet v. Centre Leclerc*,[71] was faced with the argument that the abolition of the French minimum petrol-price legislation would risk causing social unrest involving violence and that the maintenance of the legislation would thus be justified for reasons of both public policy and public security. This the ECJ rejected on the facts of that case, since 'the French Government has not shown that it would be unable, using the means at its disposal, to deal with the consequences which an amendment of the rules in question . . . would have upon public order and security'.[72]

The ECJ thus clearly left open the possibility that, if it could be shown that a Member State did not have the means available to deal with such unrest, a justification under the heads of public policy and security might be well founded. It has been pointed out that the ECJ diverged on this point from the Opinion of Advocate General VerLoren van Themaat in this case.[73] The learned Advocate General had rejected the French Government's argument in principle, on the grounds that it would be unacceptable if the possibility of civil disturbances could be used by a Member State to jeopardize the attainment of the free movement of goods.[74]

The question of civil disturbances and Article 36 has arisen before the French courts in the context of the so-called *guerre du vin*: following the poor vintage of 1973–4 which resulted in the sale at a loss of this wine, wine growers in the south of France began protesting vehemently against cheap Italian wine imports. In 1975 the French Government responded to this by taking protective measures, first suspending, then taxing wines of Italian origin. In 1976, the French Government withdrew the tax following

---

[71] n. 69 above.

[72] n. 69 at para. 33. See more recently to the same effect, Case C–265/95, *Commission v. France*, n. 4 above at paras. 56–7.

[73] For a full discussion of the differences between the Advocate General's Opinion and the judgment of the ECJ see Weatherill & Beaumont, n. 10 above 460–2.

[74] See also the Opinion of Adv. Gen. Léger in Case C–1/96 *R. v. Ministry of Agriculture, Fisheries and Foods, ex p. Royal Society for the Prevention of Cruelty to Animals and Compassion in World Farming*, delivered 15 July 1997, at para. 111.

the threat of legal action by the Commission[75] but the expressions of *colère* by French wine-farmers continued unabashed. Against this background, a number of local measures were undertaken to placate the farmers, amongst them an order of 17 March 1975 by the *Préfet* of Hérault forbidding all tankers, no matter what their nationality and wherever they came from, entry into the port of Sète. Les Fils d'Henri Ramel, a French company which owned Italian wine carried on a tanker which was prevented from entering the port, claimed that the administrative measure was contrary to Article 30 EC and thus sought damages. In a much criticized judgment,[76] the *Conseil d'Etat* held that the *Préfet*'s order could be justified under Article 36 EC. While the *Conseil d'Etat* referred to the 'clear requirements' of Article 36, it did not specify which head of Article 36 it was referring to nor did it discuss the question of proportionality or alternative means. Since the opinion of *Commissaire du Gouvernement* Genevois concluded that the import restriction at the port of Sète could be justified under the head of protection of public policy (*ordre public*) in Article 36, it may be assumed that it was also this head which the *Conseil d'Etat* had in mind.

The conclusion by the *Conseil d'Etat* in this judgment is highly contestable. There is absolutely no reasoning in the *Conseil d'Etat*'s judgment as to why it is clear that Article 36 applies. The conclusion of *Commissaire du Gouvernement* Genevois that it is clear that Article 36 applies 'taking into account the guidance given in the case law of the Court of Justice'[77] is questionable since there was at that time no ECJ case law on the scope of the public-policy exception in Article 36. Although the *Conseil d'Etat* never mentioned the possibility of directing an Article 177 reference to the ECJ, it clearly alluded to the fact that it thought the matter was *acte clair*. Since this judgment was delivered before the ECJ's *CILFIT*[78] judgment, where the ECJ formally accepted the doctrine of *acte clair* subject to strict conditions, this judgment of the *Conseil d'Etat* was remarkably bold. It is respectfully submitted that the absence at that time of any ECJ authority as to the scope of public policy in Article 36 makes the wide interpretation of that term by the highest French administrative court in this case, an abuse of Article 177(3).[79] Such criticism is supported by the subsequent judgment of the ECJ in Article 169 proceedings brought by the Commission against France for infringing Article 30 by subjecting Italian wine at the frontier to

---

[75] The tax was withdrawn by a Decree of 31 Mar. 1976, JORF 1 Apr. p. 1972. In Cases 80 and 91/77 *Les Fils de Henri Ramel* [1978] ECR 927 the ECJ held that an importer of wines from Italy was entitled to have reimbursed the money paid in taxes before the French Government withdrew the tax.

[76] *SARL Les fils de Henri Ramel* v. *Ministre de l'interieur et Préfet de l'Hérault, Conseil d'Etat*, 7 Dec. 1979, Rec. Lebon 1979, 456; Dalloz 1980, Jur. 303; JCP 1981, II 19500 (with note by Pacteau); noted by Audeoud, Berlin & Manin (1982) 19 CMLRev. 289 at 295.

[77] Dalloz 1980, Jur. 303 at 305.   [78] Case 283/81 n. 17 above.

[79] See Pacteau JCP 1981, II 19500.

delays considerably longer than necessary.[80] In that case, the French
Government sought to argue that its measures were adopted to protect the
health of consumers which the ECJ rejected since the measures were disproportionate. What is of particular interest is that although the ECJ's
judgment records 'violent demonstrations . . . among the wine-growers in
the *midi* in France',[81] the public-order defence under Article 36 was plainly
not even thought worth advancing. Furthermore, we have seen that in
Cullet v. *Centre Leclerc*,[82] where the public-policy point was raised, the correct test would have been for the *Conseil d'Etat* to examine whether the
French Government had the means available to deal with the disturbances
of public order that were alleged. In sum, the *Conseil d'Etat's* dealing with
Article 36 in *SARL Les fils de Henri Ramel* v. *Ministre de l'interieur et Préfet de
l'Hérault* was most unsatisfactory.[83]

The issue of civil disturbances and Article 36 has also arisen before the
English courts in the context of protests in the United Kingdom against the
export of live calves to other Member States for rearing in veal crates, a
practice banned in the United Kingdom since 1990. The question of
whether public policy in Article 36 includes civil disturbances was
addressed *obiter dictum* by the High Court in *R.* v. *Coventry City Council, ex
p. Phoenix Aviation.*[84] The High Court held that under the applicable
English law, the public authorities had no discretion to refuse exports of
live animals for slaughter,[85] and thus there was no need to discuss the
points of EC law raised in any detail. Importantly, however, Simon Brown
LJ in the High Court went on to identify the central questions of EC law
that arose. With respect to public policy, the High Court quoted the ECJ's
statement (set out above) in *Cullet* v. *Centre Leclerc*,[86] and explicitly rejected
that the implication of the ECJ's judgment in that case was that, had the
French Government been able to produce evidence that it was unable to
'deal with the consequences', the public-policy defence would stand. The
High Court cited academic comment[87] and Advocate General VerLoren
van Themaat's Opinion (also set out above) and concluded that the correct

---

[80] Case 42/82 *Commission* v. *France* [1983] ECR 1013, [1984] 1 CMLR 160.
[81] See paras. 7 & 15 of judgt.   [82] n. 69 above.
[83] It may be noted that the *Conseil d'Etat* nevertheless held the French State liable to pay
Ramel damages on the basis of no-fault (*sans faute*) liability since the damage was not a risk
that Ramel knowingly undertook and '*présentent un caractère de specialité qui justifie leur réparation par l'Etat*'. Ramel thus got its compensation irrespective of the poor *Conseil d'Etat* reasoning on the Art. 36 point. This aspect of the judgment is discussed at pp. 398–9.
[84] [1995] 3 All ER 37.
[85] Air Navigation Order 1989, art. 78(3)2; Harbours, Docks and Piers Clauses Act 1847, s.
333; Harbours Act 1964, s. 404 respectively. The High Court held that under the respective
statutory regimes there was no general discretion to distinguish between different lawful
trades and no defence of necessity. Furthermore, the High Court added that even if there was
a discretion, the rule of law did not allow public authorities to respond to unlawful protest
and threats from pressure groups by surrendering to their dictates.
[86] n. 69 above.   [87] Wyatt and Dashwood, *European Community Law*, 229.

interpretation of the ECJ's judgment in *Cullet* v. *Centre Leclerc* is that the ECJ rejected the public-policy argument summarily. This judgment may be contrasted with the decision of the High Court only three months later in *R.* v. *Chief Constable of Sussex, ex p. International Trader's Ferry*.[88] In that case, the Chief Constable of Sussex had issued decisions to the effect that the local police had insufficient resources to provide effective police support for lorries containing live animals destined for export via the port of Shoreham for more than two days a week. Lorry movements, and thus exports, were banned on other days. In contrast to the *obiter dicta* of Simon Brown LJ in *Ex p. Phoenix Aviation*, Balcombe LJ in *Ex p. International Trader's Ferry* held that the correct principle to be derived from the ECJ's judgment in *Cullet* v. *Centre Leclerc* is that national authorities cannot 'rely on the effect of civil disturbances as affording a public policy defence under Article 36, provided that the resources are available to deal with such disturbances, and the cost of doing so is not disproportionate'.[89] Applying this to the facts of the case, Balcombe LJ held that the Chief Constable had 'not even started to fulfil' the burden of proof that his resources were inadequate since he had not yet made any application for further financial support from central government. Balcombe LJ added that had an unsuccessful application already been made, there might have been a case for an Article 177 reference to the ECJ, but that since no such application had taken place, such a reference was unnecessary in that case.

The judgment of the High Court in *Ex p. International Trader's Ferry* was subsequently overturned by the Court of Appeal.[90] It seems that the central reason why the Court of Appeal took a different view was that, unlike the High Court, the Court of Appeal held that nothing could turn on the failure of the Chief Constable to make an approach to the Home Office for financial assistance 'when it was abundantly clear that such an approach would not have met with a favourable response'.[91] After discarding the relevance of the resources issue, the Court of Appeal proceeded to find that the limitation on days of export from the port of Shoreham was justified for public policy under Article 36 and was also proportionate.[92] In this respect, the Court of Appeal held that the Chief Constable had a duty to use his available resources to police as effectively as he could in the area for which he was responsible and that 'If . . . that was his aim when he made the decisions which are now being criticised then . . . it must be an aim countenanced by Article 36, because proper policing is obviously public policy'.[93] It is, with respect, submitted that this finding is subject to sharp

---

[88] [1995] 3 CMLR 485.   [89] Ibid. at 499.
[90] [1997] 2 All ER 65, [1997] 2 CMLR 164.   [91] [1997] 2 All ER 65 at 80.
[92] See further discussion of the application of the proportionality principle by the Court of Appeal in this case, at n. 185 below.
[93] [1997] 2 All ER 65 at 80.

criticism. It is highly unlikely that such a statement is in conformity with ECJ case law emphasizing the narrow interpretation of Article 36 given that that Article provides for an exception to the fundamental principle of the free movement of goods in the EC Treaty.[94] The suggestion that 'proper policing is obviously public policy' is objectionable since it gives Member States far too much unilateral scope to invoke Article 36. Indeed, in *Prantl*[95] the ECJ explicitly rejected the argument advanced by the German Government in that case that any national rule supported by criminal sanctions should be considered justified for reasons of public policy within the meaning of Article 36. By the same token, it is submitted that the argument that any measure taken within the scope of 'proper policing' under national law falls within the meaning of public policy in Article 36 should equally have been rejected. The approach of the High Court in its interpretation of public policy in Article 36 is thus to be preferred to that of the Court of Appeal. Nevertheless, the scope of 'public policy' under Article 36 in such circumstances is in need of clarification by the ECJ and it is, in this sense, also regrettable that the Court of Appeal did not even consider directing a reference to the ECJ on this matter pursuant to Article 177 EC.

(C) Public policy and public security and the second sentence of Article 36

Even if a national measure may be brought within the public-policy or public-security heads of justification, the next step, following the second sentence of Article 36, is for the national court to investigate whether the measure taken was proportionate and necessary. In practice this involves investigating whether there were alternative means available to the Member State to reach the same goal with less restriction on intra-Community trade. This is demonstrated by the ECJ's analysis in *SA British Motors Wright* v. *SCP Boscher, Studer et Fromentin et Nado GmbH*[96] where the ECJ held that French legislation which prohibited the sale of second-hand cars by auction unless the vendor had been registered for at least two years in the local business register infringed Article 30 and was not justified for reasons of public policy because 'the goal purportedly pursued, namely prevention of the sale of stolen cars, may be attained by appropriate control measures, such as checking the chassis number'.[97] Thus, any justification must also satisfy the proportionality and alternative means tests.

---

[94] See discussion of this point at n. 2 above.
[95] Case 16/83 [1984] ECR 1299, [1985] 2 CMLR 238.
[96] Case 239/90 [1991] ECR I–2023; [1994] 3 CMLR 410.
[97] Ibid. at para. 23.

It will be obvious that it is vital that national courts apply the proportionality and alternative means tests faithfully and rigorously according to the strict interpretation adopted by the ECJ. An excellent example illustrating the different approaches by the national courts in applying them is provided by national legislation controlling the possession and use of Citizens Band radios. Such radios are controlled under United Kingdom,[98] Dutch[99] and French legislation.[100] In all three Member States, the issue arose before the respective national courts as to whether an import ban or licensing system for CB radios which breached Article 30 was nevertheless justified under Article 36 for the protection of public policy and public security. The potential danger which the national legislation in question was aiming to prevent was the effect which CB radios have on a whole variety of electronic devices.[101] The treatment of the Article 36 justification by each jurisdiction is revealing.

Firstly, before the United Kingdom's courts, the issue arose in two reported cases. In *R. v. Goldstein*, the English Court of Appeal carried out a full and lengthy analysis of the justification of public security.[102] It cited several ECJ authorities on the question of the proportionality and necessity of justifications and analysed in great detail the evidence of expert witness as to the dangers of CB radios. These considerations led the Court of Appeal to the conclusion that 'the suggestion that everybody from aircraft manufacturers or manufacturers of aircraft avionics, the fire service and the police and army should alter their frequencies to cater for the situation is, to our mind, quite extraordinary and untenable'. Given that CB radios are practically impossible to trace, the Court of Appeal added that 'it seems to us that the judge was absolutely correct in coming to the conclusion that nothing short of a ban on import would have any effect on the use of these articles'.[103] This judgment was upheld on appeal before the House of Lords[104] where Lord Diplock enunciated his well-known reformulation of the proportionality test as 'you must not use a steam hammer to crack a nut if a nutcracker will do'.[105] Applying this to the case in hand, Lord Diplock concluded, again after an exhaustive analysis of the evidence, that the suggestion that important services should change their frequency

---

[98] Wireless Telegraphy Act 1967, s. 7 & Radiotelephonic Transmitters (Control of Manufacture and Importation) Order 1968, SI 1968/61, Art. 3.

[99] Article 3quater *Telegraaf- en Telefoonwet* (Telegraph and Telephone Law) 1904.

[100] Article R. 242-4 of the *Code de la Route* (Highway Code).

[101] CB radios have the potential to affect aircraft instrument-landing systems, hospital bleep-paging systems and fire and police service communication wavelengths. In the context of the situation in Northern Ireland, it was also relevant that CB radios could be used by terrorists to detonate remote-control explosive devices.

[102] [1982] 1 WLR 804; [1982] 3 All ER 53; [1982] 2 CMLR 181.

[103] [1982] 3 All ER 53 at 60.

[104] [1983] 1 CMLR 244; [1983] 1 All ER 434; [1983] 1 WLR 151.

[105] [1983] 1 CMLR 244 at 247.

'would indeed be using a steam hammer to crack a nut'. The importation of CB radios also arose before Belfast Recorder's Court in *McAfee* v. *Smyth and Quigley*.[106] That Court also concluded that the prohibition on the importation of Citizens' Band radios was justified on grounds of public security since they are of 'the greatest assistance to terrorists and are often used by them'.[107] In applying the second sentence in Article 36, the Court was 'absolutely satisfied that the prohibition was not imposed for the purpose of fostering any UK industry, but was genuinely imposed for the reasons given'.[108] The Belfast Court also considered whether the evidence of interference with emergency services justified the prohibition on the ground of public policy in Article 36. After having consulted the French, German, and Italian versions of this term in the Treaty, the Belfast Court held that the concept of public policy was a difficult one and that, although a justification under this head was 'probable', the Court relied exclusively on the public-security head. The United Kingdom Court judgments discussed in this section can thus be highly commended for having carried out a full and comprehensive application of the public-security and public-policy heads of justification in Article 36 and the proportionality test in the second sentence of that Article in particular.

The detailed approach of the UK courts may be contrasted with the approach of the Dutch courts in an analogous case. In *Criminal Proceedings against Eric Leonard P.* the defendant was prosecuted for not having a licence for a CB radio mounted in a car in the Netherlands as required by Dutch legislation.[109] The *Gerechtshof* Arnhem held that:

It cannot be seen how the provisions of the Telegraaf- en Telefoonwet 1904 can be quantitative restrictions or a measure having equivalent effect within Article 30 EEC with respect to the devices in question. The grounds of Article 36 of this Treaty gives the Netherlands the competence to limit the free movement of goods for reasons of the protection of public security—the Dutch legislator has made the possession of the radio devices subject to a permit with a view to the protection of public security.[110]

On appeal before the *Hoge Raad*, the Dutch Supreme Court simply quoted the judgment of the *Gerechtshof* Arnhem and added that 'the court has correctly dismissed the appeal. More detailed reasoning was not required'.[111] It is, with the greatest respect, submitted that this is an inadequate application of public security in Article 36. Both Dutch courts appear far too quick to conclude that firstly the ban falls within the head and secondly, that it is proportionate and not subject to alternative means. For example, it is only by reading the opinion of Advocate General

---

[106] n. 51 above. [107] Ibid. at 416. [108] Ibid. at 417.
[109] n. 99 above. [110] *Gerechtshof* Arnhem, 9 Apr. 1985.
[111] *Hoge Raad (Strafkamer)*, 2 Dec. 1986, NJ 1987, 538.

Remmelink that it appears that the *Hoge Raad* had the possible interference of CB radios with air-traffic radios and police radios in mind. Furthermore, there is absolutely no reference to the second sentence of Article 36. Such a reference would have been pertinent as it appears that there *were* alternative means of achieving the same goal. Between the judgment of the *Gerechtshof* Arnhem and the appeal to the *Hoge Raad*, new provisions came into force in the Netherlands concerning CB radios.[112] Under the new provisions, non-residents of the Netherlands could enter the Netherlands with their CB radios provided that in the Member State of their origin the possession of the CB radio was lawful and that the CB radios in question possessed certain type-specifications. The *Hoge Raad* refused to apply the new provisions since, as a court of cassation, it could not assess the facts found by the *Gerechtshof*. Nevertheless, it is submitted that the very fact that there was new legislation which clearly modified the previous ban is strong evidence that there *were* indeed alternative means of achieving the same objectives as to public security. The lack of application of a strict interpretation of Article 36 and its second sentence in particular by the Dutch courts is thus open to criticism.

Finally, the ban on certain radio devices which interfered with the functioning of instruments for the detection of traffic offences also arose before the French courts. In *Roland Perron* v. *Ministère public*,[113] the *Cour de Cassation* held that the applicable French legislation[114] applied to national products as well as imports and was within the *ordre public* exception provided for in Article 36 and did not constitute arbitrary discrimination or a disguised restriction on trade. This was the full extent of the *Cour de Cassation*'s dealing with the compatibility of the French legislation with the provisions concerning free movement of goods. It appears that the *Cour de Cassation* was too quick to allow a justification under Article 36 without providing full reasons or strictly applying the second sentence of that Article.

It is not suggested that the national legislation restricting the use and import of CB radios could not be justified under Article 36. Indeed, it would clearly not be proportionate to require the emergency services and air-traffic control devices to move to a different frequency simply to allow the use of CB radios by individuals. Indeed, in *De Peijper*, the ECJ recognized that national measures may not 'come within the exceptions specified in Article 36 of the Treaty unless it is clearly proved that any other

---

[112] *Regeling vrijstelling citizenband-apparatuur niet-ingezetenen* (Regulation Exempting Citizens' Band Apparatus for Non-residents), Stcrt 1985, 178.

[113] *Cour de Cassation*, ch. crim., 17 Feb. 1988, Bull. Cass. Crim. 1988, 207; Gaz. Pal. 1988, I Jur. 848; Dr. et pr. du com. int. 1988, 792 (summary); JCP 1988, IV 154 (summary); Dalloz 1988, IR 98 (summary). Noted by Berr, La Semaine Juridique—éd. entreprise 1989, II 15556.

[114] n. 100 above.

rules or practice would obviously be beyond the means which can reasonably be expected of an administration operating in a normal manner'.[115] However, a comparison between the British, French, and Dutch courts' application of the justification of public security in Article 36 reveals that only the UK courts are carrying out the full analysis which the ECJ case law clearly envisages. The Dutch and French courts are far too ready to allow the justification without furnishing any reasons as to why the strict interpretation of the ECJ is satisfied. Clearly, the common-law system, with its emphasis on long and fully reasoned judgments, goes some way towards explaining the comparatively full approach of the UK judgments discussed above. However, it is submitted that the civil law's approach of briefer judgments can only go so far in 'excusing' the lack of fully reasoned judgments before the Dutch and French courts. As has already been noted in other parts of this work, the absence of clear and elaborate reasoning in the judgments of the French and Dutch courts in applying the provisions concerning the free movement of goods needs special attention. A national measure cannot satisfactorily be upheld by a national court as justified under Article 36 in a single line without further elaboration. It has been pointed out that criticism of insufficient reasoning on the part of national courts must be qualified by a care to appreciate the context of the national legal system. For example, the common-law expectation that judgments of courts of law should give reasons and discuss the law in great detail cannot be applied *mutatis mutandis* to civil law systems.[116] Nevertheless, the lack of motivation in some French judgments is unsatisfactory. Community law develops through case law. Particularly in the context of the Treaty freedoms, the law is to be located in ECJ case law rather than the Treaty provisions themselves. If it is true that the approach of EC law is in this respect akin to the common law, the national courts, in applying EC law, must develop an approach consistent with that ECJ approach.[117] In the context of public policy and public security, the ECJ approach suggests caution by the national courts. Indeed, it has been said that 'no Member State can feel confident of success when it puts forward public policy as a justification for hindering the free flow of goods between Member States'.[118] The judgments of the Dutch and French Courts regard-

---

[115] Case 104/75[1976] ECR 613 at 638, [1976] 2 CMLR 271.

[116] See generally, Ranieri, 'Styles judiciaires dans l'histoire européenne: modèles divergents ou traditions communes' in Jacob, *Le juge et le jugement dans les traditions juridiques européennes*, 181; Sauvel, 'Histoire du jugement motivé' RDP 1955, 5; Goutal, 'Characteristics of Judicial Style in France, Britain and the USA' (1976) 24 Amer. J Comp. Law 43, Gillis Wetter, *The Styles of Appellate Judicial Opinions: A Case Study in Comparative Law* (Sythoff, 1960) & Van Caenegem, *Judges, Legislators and Professors* (CUP, 1987).

[117] In much the same way, the English Courts, when interpreting EC law, have had to adopt a more purposive (rather than literal) approach. See *R. v. Henn and Darby* [1980] 2 CMLR 229 at 233 (HL) per Lord Diplock.

[118] Weatherill and Beaumont, n. 10 above, 462.

ing CB radios suggests that they are failing in their duty under the second sentence of Article 36 by not rigorously scrutinizing national measures as to their proportionality or necessity, as is clearly envisaged by the ECJ.[119]

The UK courts' application of the justification of public policy is not always exemplary. For example in *R. v. H.M. Treasury and The Bank of England, ex. p. Centro-Com srl*,[120] the implementation in the United Kingdom of Community Regulation 1432/92 (which was in itself the implementation of United Nations Security Council Resolution 757 of 30 May 1992 imposing sanctions on trade with Serbia and Montenegro) in the Serbia and Montenegro (United Nations Sanctions) Order 1992[121] was at issue. The UN Resolution and the Community Regulation prohibited exports to Serbia and Montenegro and payments for such exports from Serbian and Montenegran funds held in Member States, with the exception of exports (and related payments) of medicines or food notified to the United Nations Yugoslavia Sanctions Committee. This was implemented in the UK by freezing all Serbian bank accounts in the UK which could be unfrozen for payments relating to authorized exports of medicines provided that the export of the medicines was from the UK. Centro-Com Srl, an Italian company, had obtained authorization for such an export from Italy under the equivalent Italian legislation implementing the EEC Regulation and sought payment from the National Bank of Yugoslavia's bank account in the United Kingdom. Approval for this was refused by the Bank of England since the exportation had not been from the United Kingdom but rather from Italy. Centro-Com challenged this refusal before the English courts on the grounds, *inter alia*, that it breached Article 30 EC. The English High Court held that even if there was a breach of Article 30[122] the restriction was justified for the protection of public policy under Article 36 in order to prevent abuse or evasion of sanctions which had been imposed as a result of international concern. There is in this application an absence of discussion of whether the United Kingdom's policy constituted the least restrictive means of achieving the goal and whether the equal protection could have been afforded by co-operation with the Italian authorities. The application of Article 36 by the English High Court was in this respect unsatisfactory.[123]

---

[119] See also the judgt of the Trib. admin. Paris in *Garot et Société du Journal Le Point v. Etat (Ministre de l'interieur)*, 16 Mar. 1971, Rec. Lebon 1971, 857; RTDE 1971, 857, where it was held that a ban on the import of a magazine from Belgium into France covering the 1968 student riots in Paris was justified under public policy in Art. 36 with absolutely no discussion of proportionality and alternative means. A little more caution would, it is submitted, have been appropriate from the national court in such an early case.

[120] [1994] 1 CMLR 109.   [121] SI 1992/1302.

[122] The breach of Art. 30 was doubted. See discussion of this aspect of the judgment at pp. 21–3.

[123] The case was appealed to the Court of Appeal which made a reference to the ECJ (Court of Appeal (Civil Division), 27 May 1994, The Independent 3 June 1994 (transcr.: John

4 PROTECTION OF HEALTH AND LIFE OF HUMANS

The justification in Article 36 of greatest practical significance is that on the grounds of the protection of public health and life of humans. Clearly, the ECJ will only accept a justification under this head if the restriction to trade formed part of a 'seriously considered health policy'[124] rather than having been introduced for protectionist reasons. The onus rests on the national authorities to show, according to objective criteria, that there is indeed a serious risk to health.[125] The ECJ will not hesitate to scrutinize scientific evidence to assess the extent of the alleged danger to public health,[126] but in the event of equivocal scientific opinion, the Court will tend to conclude that the margin of discretion resides with the Member State.[127] Finally, the action taken on the basis of the protection of public health must have been proportionate to the danger posed[128] and the Court may require Member States to co-operate with the authorities of other Member States before simply banning goods on grounds of public health.[129]

The discussion in this section of national case law interpreting the Article 36 justification of public health will be centred upon the following themes. Firstly, decisions by national courts applying the duty on the part of the Member States to co-operate with the authorities of other Member States will be examined. This will be followed by a discussion of the application of the Article 36 justification of public health more generally. In particular, two problems with national-court application of this derogation to the free movement of goods will be isolated: firstly, those cases which suggest that the national courts are not respecting the narrow interpretation of Article 36 adopted by the ECJ; and secondly, those judgments demonstrating that the proportionality, necessity, and alternative means tests implicit in an application of the second sentence of Article 36 are not being satisfactorily applied. These issues will then lead to a discussion of whether it would be desirable for the ECJ to itself decide (wherever possible) the proportionality of a measure and the associated difficulties which arise when the ECJ embarks on fact-finding evaluations of scientific

Larking) but not on the free-movement-of-goods point since the CA concluded that there was no breach of Art. 30 in the first place. The ECJ handed down its judgment in this case in C–124/95 [1997] ECR I–81 where it held that the measures adopted by the UK were not compatible with the Common Commercial Policy as set out in Art. 113 EC.

124 Case 40/82 *Commission* v. *UK* (Newcastle Disease) [1982] ECR 2793, [1982] 3 CMLR 497.
125 Case 174/82 *Officier van Justitie* v. *Sandoz BV* [1983] ECR 2445 at para. 22.
126 Case 178/84 *Commission* v. *Germany* (*Reinheitsgebot*) [1987] ECR 1227.
127 Case 53/80 *Officier van Justitie* v. *Koninklijke Kaasfabriek Eyssen BV* [1981] ECR 409, [1982] 2 CMLR 20.
128 Case 42/82 *Commission* v. *France* (Table Wine) [1983] ECR 1013.
129 Case 124/81 *Commission* v. *United Kingdom* (UHT Milk) [1983] ECR 203, [1984] 1 CMLR 160.

evidence. These difficulties will then be balanced against the examples of extremely competent and dynamic applications of Article 36 justification of public health by the national courts leading to an evaluation of the competence of the national courts in this field as a whole.

(A) Equivalence and the duty on the part of Member States to co-operate with other Member States

One of the most important aspects of the interpretation by the ECJ of the Article 36 justification of public health is the duty placed on Member States to co-operate with the administrative authorities of other Member States to keep restrictions on the free movement of goods to a minimum. This may be seen as a manifestation of the second sentence of Article 36 since lack of co-operation may be regarded as arbitrary discrimination or a disguised restriction on trade. The classic ECJ authority on this point is *Frans-Nederlandse Maatschappij voor Biologische Producten BV*.[130] That case concerned the prosecution of a company for having imported and sold in the Netherlands a plant-protection product which, although lawfully marketed in France, had not received the requisite approval of the Dutch authorities.[131] The ECJ held that the Dutch approval requirement infringed Article 30 and with respect to Article 36 held that

Whilst a Member State is free to require a product of the type in question, which has already received approval in another Member State, to undergo a fresh procedure of examination and approval, the authorities of the Member States are nevertheless required to assist in bringing about a relaxation of the control existing in intra-Community trade. It follows that they are not entitled unnecessarily to require technical or chemical analyses or laboratory tests where those analyses and tests have already been carried out in another Member State and their results are available to those authorities, or may at their request be placed at their disposal.[132]

The application of these principles have a colourful history before the Dutch courts. In *Frans-Nederlandse Maatschappij voor Biologische Producten BV* itself, the case returned before the *Gerechtshof* Den Haag, which implemented the ECJ judgment by repeating the operative part of the ECJ judgment (set out above) and holding that, since the application for approval of the plant-protection product had been sent to the competent Dutch authority enclosing the results of the tests carried out by the French authorities, the defendant 'in these circumstances was correct to assume that the Dutch authorities' requirement of prior testing, which would be

---

[130] Case 272/80 [1981] ECR 3277.

[131] Art. 2, *Bestrijdingsmiddlenwet* (Law Relating to Plant-Protection Products).

[132] Case 272/80, n. 130 above at para. 14. This judgt has been confirmed in several ECJ judgts and most recently in Case C–293/94 *Brandsma* [1996] ECR I–3159.

very expensive, was contrary to the spirit of the EEC Treaty'.[133] The defendant was thus acquitted by the *Gerechtshof* Den Haag. This application of the ECJ judgment by the *Gerechtshof* Den Haag has been heavily criticised by Mulder, who pointed out that nothing in the ECJ approach suggested that it was no longer necessary for importers of plant-protection products to apply for prior authorization.[134] On the contrary, Mulder points out that the ECJ had held that prior approval was still permitted with the only reservation being that products which had been approved in another Member State could not be subjected to a full test going beyond verifying whether the tests already carried out were sufficient to satisfy public-health requirements. Thus, an application for prior authorization was still required since without such an application, the national control authority would not be able to examine whether the same analyses had already been undertaken in another Member State and thus whether supplementary testing was necessary. In the context of the judgment of the *Gerechtshof* Den Haag, Mulder argues that it was incorrect for the *Gerechtshof* to have held that since Frans-Nederlandse Maatschappij voor Biologische Producten had sent the French test results to the Dutch authorities, the Dutch approval requirement was *per se* unlawful. According to Mulder, a more correct application of the ECJ judgment would have been to examine the outcome of the Dutch authorities' examination. Only then would it be possible to see whether the Dutch authorities took the French authorization tests adequately into consideration.

Eight years later, in *Openbaar Ministerie* v. *Chemische Fabriek Brabant*, the Dutch *Hoge Raad* had the opportunity to accept Mulder's arguments. This case also involved a criminal prosecution for having sold an unapproved plant-protection product ('Acylon-P') contrary to the same Dutch legislation. Again, the defendant had imported the product from France where it had been tested and approved for sale. The *Hoge Raad* upheld the conviction of the defendant, since

at the time referred to in the indictment, the appellant company had not yet applied for any approval of the product in question, so that—since the approval procedure had not yet been begun—it also could not be held, in anticipation, that at that time that the authorities involved in the approval procedure were not complying with the obligation existing in law to operate in the context of that procedure in accordance with the judgment of the European Court of Justice . . . A mere expectation that the approval will appear *in concreto* to be contrary to EEC law cannot lead to discharge from prosecution.[135]

---

[133] *Gerechtshof*'s-Gravenhage, 6e kamer, 29 Oct. 1982, NJ 1983, 654.

[134] Mulder, SEW 1984, 99. See also Addink *et al.* (eds.), *Europese milieurechtspraak, 104 nationale uitspraken met Europees milieurechterlijke aspecten*, 109 & 167.

[135] *Hoge Raad (Strafkamer)*, 20 Nov. 1990, NJ 1991, 223; [1992] 1 CMLR 457; M & R 1992, 59; AB 1992, 13 (with note by Van der Burg); noted in Addink *et al.* (eds.), n. 134 above, 110 & 185. See also the much earlier judgt to similar effect in *Openbaar Ministerie* v. *HJB van D.*,

It is submitted that the approach of the *Hoge Raad* is entirely correct. It may be considered rather unsatisfactory that it should be necessary for an importer of a product lawfully marketed in another Member State to have to wait until the approval procedure in the importing Member State has come to an end before any damage suffered as a result of any lack of co-operation on the part of the authorities with those of other Member States is actionable before the national court. Nevertheless, this is the only logical solution given that the ECJ has held that according to Article 36, prior authorization requirements are not, as such, unlawful. In *Openbaar Ministerie* v. *Chemische Fabriek Brabant*, the defendant had sold the plant-protection product in the Netherlands without even applying for authorization. To argue that the Dutch authorities did not take into consideration the testing already carried out in France was therefore purely speculative.[136]

Although the Dutch courts have been strict in maintaining requirements for prior authorisation following the ECJ judgment in *Frans-Nederlandse Maatschappij voor Biologische Producten BV*, the duty laid down by the ECJ in that judgment to co-operate with the authorities of other Member States has been extremely broadly construed by the Dutch courts. This is particularly evident in a commendably expansive judgment of the *CBB* in *Chemische Fabriek Brabant J. W. Voorbraak BV* v. *Landbouw, Natuurbeheer en Visserij (Min.)*.[137] This case, which is commonly referred to as the *'even Parijs bellen'* ('just call Paris') case, concerned the refusal of the Ministry of Agriculture and Fisheries to authorize a plant-protection product which had already been authorized by the French authorities for marketing in France. Authorization in the Netherlands was refused on the grounds that the applicant had furnished insufficient information concerning the chemical make-up and safety of the product. The applicant argued that following the ECJ's judgment in *Frans-Nederlandse Maatschappij voor Biologische Producten BV*, the Dutch authorities should have procured the further information from the French authorities themselves. This was accepted by the *CBB* which examined the wording of the ECJ's judgment in its Dutch, French, and English language versions and concluded that

Gerechtshof Amsterdam, 25 May 1978, noted by Tromm, 'Case law 1978–1979' (1981) 6 ELRev. 312 at 315.

[136] For a case where the supposed authorization already granted in another Member State (*in casu* Germany) was rejected on the facts, see *W. Rottinghuis* v. *Minister Welzijn, Volksgezondheid en Cultuur*, CBB, 21 Dec. 1984 (transcr. obtained from *CBB*). See also *Upjohn NV* v. *Veterinaire Dienst 's-Gravenhage*, Pres. *Raad van State (Afd. Rechtspraak)*, 13 Oct. 1988, AB 1989, 200, KG 1988, 453.

[137] *CBB*, 13 Nov. 1992, AB 1993, 273 (with note by Van Veen); SEW 1994, 450 (with note by Temmink); Ars Aequis 1992, 68; M & R 1994, 46; UCB 1992, nr. 68; noted in Addink *et al.* (eds.), n. 134 above, 111 & 198.

[W]here the application for permission concerns import of a pesticide admitted in France, it may be demanded of the Dutch authorities that they request the French authorities for the results of technical or chemical analyses or of laboratory tests . . . Article 36 EEC cannot be called upon to justify a trading rule, for which the restrictive elements result from the desire to lessen the administrative load, unless the request . . . to the French authorities clearly goes beyond the boundaries of what may reasonably be expected.

Applying this to the facts, the *CBB* found that it could reasonably have been expected that the Dutch authorities would get the information from the competent French authorities and annulled the refusal. Although this *CBB* judgment puts an enormous load on the national administration to co-operate with their partner administrations in other Member States, it is submitted that it is a correct judgment. It is the logical extension of the fact that the burden of proof to satisfy an Article 36 justification rests upon the Member State that the responsibility for getting the French test results should also rest with the Member State. While this may be entirely proper in principle, there are foreseeable difficulties with this approach in practice. For example, what should happen if the French authorities take an unduly long time or indeed refuse to provide the information requested? Who should bear the cost of translating the information? In the event of a refusal, would the Dutch authorities then also be under a duty to take legal action to force the French authorities to pass on the information? Would national rules on confidentiality be capable of obstructing the obligation to co-operate? The duty to 'just call Paris' is thus not without practical difficulties. From the point of view of the free movement of goods, however, the judgment is to be welcomed. National ministries cannot be passive, but have to engage in an active policy to maximize the possibilities for the free movement of goods.

It is interesting to note that some of the difficulties outlined above actually arose before the English courts in *R* v. *Licensing Authority ex. p. Smith Kline and French Laboratories*. That case concerned the question of whether the Licensing Authority, when considering an application for a product licence for a pharmaceutical which had already been granted a licence, could refer to the dossier containing the confidential data which had been adduced to support the original application. The English High Court held that according to English law on confidentiality, the Licensing Authority was prevented from referring to the dossier.[138] The Court of Appeal, citing the ECJ judgments in both *Frans-Nederlandse Maatschappij voor Biologische Producten BV* and *De Peijper*,[139] allowed the appeal on the grounds that Articles 30 to 36 EC positively *required* the Licensing

---

[138] [1988] 2 CMLR 883.
[139] Case 272/80, n. 130 above and Case 104/75, n. 115 above respectively.

Authority to consult the dossier.[140] In yet a further appeal to the House of Lords, the judgment of the Court of Appeal was upheld, but exclusively on grounds of English law.[141] The House of Lords concluded that English law on confidentiality did not prevent the Licensing Authority from consulting the original dossier and thus that it was unnecessary to decide whether Article 36 also required such access. One cannot object to the reasoning of the House of Lords in this case.[142] The point of EC law did indeed become superfluous. Nevertheless, it does raise the interesting question as to whether the Court of Appeal had been correct in its assumption that even if English law on confidentiality precluded access to the original dossier, Article 36 would override the application of such a national rule.[143]

Returning to the Dutch courts, it may be noted that the expansive approach of the Dutch *CBB* in the *'even Parijs bellen'* ('just call Paris') case (discussed above) has been somewhat limited by a more recent judgment of that same court. In *Leo Pharmaceutical Products BV* v. *De staatssecretaris van Landbouw, Natuurbeheer en Visserij*,[144] the *CBB* was faced with an appeal against a refusal of the Ministry of Agriculture and Fisheries to grant an authorization to market a veterinary medicinal product.[145] The same medicine had already been authorized in the United Kingdom. The *CBB* interpreted Directive 81/851[146] and held that since the applicant had provided no information as to when and under which conditions the previous authorization had been granted in the United Kingdom, the appeal should be dismissed. The *CBB* held that EC law was 'far from having reached the point where Member States would be obliged to waive their national requirements if the applicant submits that the same veterinary medicinal product has already been registered in another Member State such that the registration must be granted or that the applicant has to submit less information'. It is surprising that the *CBB* reached this conclusion on the basis of Directive 81/851 alone. No mention is made of Articles 30 to 36 of the Treaty and the ECJ requirements in *Frans-Nederlandse*

---

[140] [1988] 3 CMLR 301, [1988] 3 WLR 896, [1989] 1 All ER 175.

[141] [1989] 2 CMLR 137, [1989] 2 WLR 397.

[142] Although, the Court of Appeal had refrained from making a reference to the ECJ on this point explicitly on the grounds that it would 'leave it to others to direct a reference if a reference be considered necessary' [1988] 3 CMLR 301 at 316.

[143] In the light of the ECJ's more recent judgt in Case C–201/94 *R.* v. *The Medicines Control Agency, ex p. Smith & Nephew Pharmaceuticals* [1996] ECR I–5819 it would appear that national rules of confidentiality would indeed have to be set aside when the proprietary medicinal products are the same (although not identical in all respects) in the sense that they have been manufactured according to the same formulation and using the same active ingredient.

[144] *CBB*, 14 Sept. 1994, AB 1995, 204.

[145] Under Art. 6(3), *Regeling registratie diergeneesmiddelen* (Regulation on the Registration of Animal Medicines).

[146] Council Directive of 28 Sept. 1981 on the approximation of the laws of the Member States relating to veterinary medicinal products [1981] OJ L317/1.

Maatschappij voor Biologische Producten BV[147] in particular. Whatever the correct interpretation of the Directive is, it is submitted that since even Directive provisions are subject to the primary Treaty rules, the *CBB*'s conclusion is at odds with its earlier judgment in the *'even Parijs bellen'* case where the onus was put on the national authority to procure the appropriate information as to the conditions under which the previous authorization had been granted in the other Member State.[148]

The discussion in this section shows that the application by the national courts of the duty on the part of the Member States to co-operate with the administrative authorities of other Member States has not been without its difficulties in practice.

(B) Cases which suggest that the national courts are not respecting the narrow interpretation of the Article 36 public-health justifications adopted by the ECJ

As has already been noted, it is simply essential that national courts apply the Article 36 derogations cautiously in view of the necessity for the uniform application of Community law which has been described by the ECJ as 'a fundamental requirement of the Community legal order'.[149] Unfortunately, there is a large body of national court case law in which the national courts have not shown the degree of caution which would have been desirable. These cases are too numerous to discuss individually, and it is only possible to mention a few here. Thus, by way of illustration, before the English courts in *Hodgkinson* v. *Nottingham City Council*,[150] it was held that technical specifications which must be met by vehicles in order to be licensed as taxis would, in the event that they breached Article 30,[151] be justified for the protection of health in Article 36. The national court did not discuss why this was so and furthermore why it would be a proportionate measure. It may be supposed that the court had the fact that the technical specifications allowed easy wheelchair access to the taxis in mind when it mentioned the protection of public health. However, since a normal saloon car (which did not meet the specifications laid down in the provisions in question) could be adapted for wheelchair access (albeit less comfortably), it is difficult to locate the element for the protection of public health in this case. In any event, the point is that there was simply no full application or discussion of Article 36 in the judgment. Similarly, before the Dutch courts in *Cyanamid Benelux SA NV* v. *Minister van*

---

[147] Case 272/80 n. 130 above.
[148] See Veltkamp in Addink *et al.* (eds.), n. 134 above, 112.
[149] Case C–143/88 & C–92/89 *Zuckerfabrik* [1991] ECR I–415 para. 26 & Cases C–46 & 48/93 *Brasserie du Pêcheur/Factortame* (No. 3) [1996] ECR I–1029, [1996] 1 CMLR 889 at para. 33.
[150] [1993] 3 CMLR 503.   [151] See discussion of this aspect of the case at pp. 73–6.

Landbouw en Visserij[152] it was held that a restriction on trade resulting from authorization requirements under certain conditions for experiments in developing certain animal medicines would 'find a justification in the importance in public health'. This was the full extent of the reasoning of the Dutch court which has been criticized by Mortelmans as being far too brief and neglecting to apply the principle of proportionality.[153] Finally, before the French courts in *René Malagutti* v. *Ministère public*,[154] the *Cour de Cassation* held that legislation banning the marketing of onions treated with maleic hydrazide was within the Article 36 public-health derogation. Although the *Cour de Cassation* mentioned that the French legislation 'does not hide any prohibited restriction in trade between Member States of the Community, and also that it affects national production as well as imported vegetables', it is of note that it ignored the specific ground of appeal which had argued that the complete prohibition that the French legislation undertook was more than was strictly necessary for the protection of public health. Indeed, in a subsequent judgment of the ECJ on this point (on a referral from another French court), the ECJ held that the ban was justified for the protection of public health in Article 36, but only after a detailed analysis of the proportionality of the measure.[155] For example, the ECJ took into consideration the variety between Member States of 'climatic conditions, the normal diet of the population and their state of health' and stated that the Member States must keep their requirements under regular review and allow for possibilities for exemption in special cases.[156] None of these considerations had been taken into account by the *Cour de Cassation* in its analysis of public health in Article 36 in *René Malagutti* v. *Ministère public*. That judgment was altogether too quick to conclude that the French measures were within the Article 36 derogation without embarking upon a proper investigation and application of Article 36.[157]

The national courts have also neglected to apply the proportionality, necessity, and alternative means tests implicit in the second sentence of Article 36 satisfactorily. This is graphically illustrated by a series of cases before the French courts in the wake of the ECJ judgments in *Delattre*[158]

---

[152] Pres. *CBB*, 28 Jan. 1988, SEW 1989, 791 (with note by Mortelmans). [153] Ibid.

[154] *Cour de Cassation*, ch. crim., 8 Jan. 1985, Bull. Cass. Crim. 1985, no. 15 p. 38, Dalloz 1985, Jur. 586; CDE 1989, 403.

[155] Case 54/85 *Ministère public* v. *Xavier Mirepoix* [1986] ECR 1067; [1987] 2 CMLR 44. See also the ECJ judgment in Case 94/83 *Officier van Justitie* v. *Albert Heijn* [1984] ECR 3263.

[156] Ibid. at paras. 13–17 of judgt.

[157] This *Cour de Cassation* judgment has been criticized by Fourgoux in Dalloz Jur. 1985, 587 and the neglect to make an Art. 177 reference to the ECJ was criticized in the Sixth Report to the European Parliament on Commission Monitoring of the Application of Community Law [1989] OJ C330/I (appendix on 'The Attitude of National Supreme Courts to Community Law').

[158] Case C–369/88 [1991] ECR I–1487.

and *Ministère public* v. *Monteil et Samanni*.[159] It will be recalled that those cases concerned Article L. 512 of the *Code de Santé Publique* which provided that medical products could only be sold through pharmacists. The ECJ held in those cases that such legislation breached Article 30 since it restricted sales to certain channels[160] subject to justification for the protection of public health under Article 36. On the latter point, the ECJ held that 'In the absence of harmonization of the rules on the distribution both of medicinal products and of "para-pharmaceutical" products, it is for the Member States to choose the level to which they wish to ensure the protection of public health.'[161] The ECJ then drew a distinction between 'medical products' and 'para-pharmaceutical' products. With respect to 'medical products', the ECJ held that

although *in principle* the Member States may reserve to pharmacists the right to make retail sales of products that fall within the Community definition of medicinal products and although, in those circumstances, their monopoly over those products *may be presumed* to constitute an appropriate way of protecting public health, *evidence to the contrary may be produced with respect to certain products whose use would not involve any serious danger to public health and whose inclusion within the pharmacists' monopoly would seem manifestly disproportionate*, that is to say contrary to the principles laid down by the Court for the interpretation of Articles 30 to 36 of the Treaty.[162]

With respect to 'para-pharmaceutical' products the ECJ held that

If pharmacists are granted a monopoly of other products, such as 'para-pharmaceutical' products, which may be of widely varying kinds, the need for such a monopoly in order to protect public health or the health of consumers must, regardless of how the products concerned are classified under national law, be established in each individual case, and those two aims *must not be attainable by measures less restrictive of intra-Community trade.*[163]

Crucially, the ECJ concluded by stating that 'it is for the national court to decide, *having regard to those criteria*, whether the action before it is well founded'.[164] In other words, the ECJ held that if the products were medicinal products, the restriction was in principle justified, subject to an application of the proportionality test. If the products were not medicinal products, the national court must establish in each individual case

---

[159] Case C–60/89 [1991] ECR I–1547.

[160] See discussion of this aspect of the judgment in Ch. 2, sect. 5 (B)(*i*) and note that after the ECJ's judgt in Cases C–267 & 268/91 *Keck and Mithouard* [1993] ECR I–6097, it is likely that such legislation will now be held to fall outside the scope of Art. 30 altogether. See discussion of the *Cour d'appel* of Versailles's judgment in *Sogramo Carrefour* v. *Chambre syndicale des pharmaciens et Union profesionalle de la pharmacie*, 22 Jan. 1996, Gaz. Pal. 1996, II Som. P. 32–3 (summary); La Semaine Juridique, éd. entreprise, 1996 PAN. 175 (summary) at pp. 124–5.

[161] *Delattre*, case C–369/88, n. 158 above at para. 53 of judgt.

[162] Ibid., para. 56. Emphasis added.   [163] Ibid., para. 57. Emphasis added.

[164] Ibid., para. 59. Emphasis added.

whether there were alternative means of achieving the public-health objective giving rise to less restriction on trade. The ECJ thus left these decisions to the national courts for application on a case-by-case basis.

The application of this ECJ judgment by the French courts was, with respect, far from satisfactory. In case after case, the French courts simply refused to apply a rigorous proportionality test and assumed that if the product could be classified as a medical product, it was justified.[165] Thus, in *Bocquin*,[166] which involved a product called 'Diascan' (a reactive bandage allowing one to test one's own level of glycerine; particularly useful to sufferers of diabetes), the *Cour de Cassation* did not even cite the ECJ judgments in *Delattre* and *Monteil et Samanni* and briefly held that the product was to be regarded as a medical product and upheld the conviction by the lower court. The *Cour de Cassation* held simply that the restriction was within Article 36 and therefore that there was *'aucune difficulté sérieuse'* and thus no Article 177 reference to the ECJ was necessary. It hardly needs pointing out that an application of the proportionality test which, as we have seen, the ECJ case law clearly requires, was entirely neglected by the *Cour de Cassation* in this judgment. In a further case, the *Cour de Cassation* cited the ECJ judgment in *Delattre* and simply stated that 'the barrier to imports is in principle and in the absence of proof to the contrary by the accused, is justified with respect to medicinal products'.[167] The *Cour de Cassation* gave absolutely no hint in its judgment as to why the restriction was justified with respect to medical products.[168] Even less satisfactory was the judgment of the *Cour de Cassation* in *Republic (Conseil National de l'Ordre des Pharmaciens)* v. *Ruth*.[169] That case concerned, *inter alia*, modified alcohol (70 per cent) which the *Cour de Cassation* noted was registered in the national pharmacopoeia under the heading 'alcohol for medical uses' and concluded that the lower court had correctly classified

[165] For an application of the public-health justification in Article 36 *before* the ECJ's judgts in *Delattre* & *Monteil et Samanni*, see *Ministère public* v. *Norbert Desolière, Cour d'appel* Colmar, ch. corr., 21 Sept. 1987, Gaz. Pal. I Jur. 1988, 58–9 & 285–6, *Cour de Cassation*, ch. crim., 18 Oct. 1988, Bull. Cass. Crim. 1988, no. 352 p. 945–7; Gaz. Pal. 1989, I Jur. 683 (with note by Mauro); JCP 1988, IV 404 (summary); Dalloz 1988, IR 284 (summary); *Laboratoires Searle SA* v. *Laboratoires SARPP, Cour d'appel* Paris, 1re ch. A, 16 Dec. 1987, Gaz. Pal. 1988, I Jur. 245. See also *André Jaud* v. *Ministère public, Cour de Cassation*, ch. crim., 24 Oct. 1989, Bull. Cass. Crim. 1989, no. 377 (Arrêt No. 2); *Conseil national de l'ordre des pharmaciens du Pas-de-Calais* v. *Francis Dubois, Cour de Cassation*, ch. crim., 19 Dec. 1989, Bull. Cass. Crim. 1989, no. 492; *Ministère public* v. *Abel Patraud, Cour de Cassation*, ch. crim., 19 Dec. 1989, Bull. Cass. Crim. 1989, no. 491; *François Bouquereau* v. *Conseil national de l'ordre des pharmaciens; Dominique Saclier* v. *Conseil national de l'ordre des pharmaciens, Cour d'appel* Paris, 11e Ch. A, 24 Sept. 1990 & 25 Sept. 1990 respectively, Dalloz 1990, IR 276 (summary).

[166] *Cour de Cassation*, ch. crim., 14 Oct. 1992, Bull. Cass. Crim. 1992, no. 326 p. 899.

[167] *Nauleau, Cour de Cassation*, ch. crim., 10 Mar. 1993, Bull. Cass. Crim. 1993, no. 108 p. 261.

[168] See also *Kxxxx and Mxxxx, Cour de Cassation*, ch. crim, 3 Nov. 1994, Pourvoi no. 92-86.577 (transcr. available on Lexis).

[169] *Cour de Cassation*, ch. crim., 25 May 1994, [1995] 1 CMLR 718; Dalloz 1994, IR 185 (summary).

the product as a medical product under L. 511 and L. 512 of the Public Health Code. However, the applicant had also argued that the lower court had failed to proceed in accordance with the ECJ judgment in *Delattre* to examine whether the risk was a serious one for public health and was not manifestly disproportionate. The *Cour de Cassation*, very inadequately, dismissed this ground of appeal stating that,

as modified alcohol of a strength of 70 per cent. is a medicinal product, the barrier created to the free movement of goods by the monopoly on selling it is justified, pursuant to Article 36 EEC, on grounds of the protection of public health of consumers. As matters stand, and as the legislation concerning the pharmacists' monopoly applies without distinction to national products and products imported from other Member States, the appeal court justified its decision without giving cause for the alleged complaint.

It will be evident that this hardly passes for a complete application of the proportionality test as set out by the ECJ in its case law.

The judgments discussed so far have constituted fairly blatant omissions on the part of the national courts to apply the Article 36 justifications on grounds of public health fully in line with the ECJ's strict approach. It is not however only the blatant omissions which are of concern. What is equally important is that national courts which purport to be applying the proportionality test implicit in the second sentence of Article 36, actually do so in a competent fashion. Here, too, the approach of the national courts has not been entirely satisfactory. One example to illustrate this point is provided by the implementation of the ECJ's judgment in *De Peijper*[170] by the *Kantongerecht* Rotterdam.[171] It will be recalled that the ECJ held in that case that Dutch legislation requiring importers of pharmaceutical products to supply certain information verified by the manufacturer of the products was capable of breaching Article 30 since the information required by the Dutch authorities was more readily obtainable by the authorized distributors of the drug in the Netherlands, thus restricting the possibility of parallel importing. With respect to the possibility that this could be justified under Article 36 for the protection of public health, the ECJ held that it was not justified under that head 'unless it is clearly proved that any other rules or practice would obviously be beyond the means which can reasonably be expected of an administration operating in a normal manner'.[172] The ECJ then went on to hint strongly that there were in that case alternative means of achieving the same level of protec-

---

[170] Case 104/75 n. 115 above.

[171] *Kantongerecht* Rotterdam, 6 Sept. 1976, NJ 1976, 549 (with note by Van Veen); [1977] 1 CMLR 321. Noted in Korte, Kellermann, Levelt-Overmars and Possen, *Primus Inter Pares: The European Court and National Courts* (1990 EUI Working Paper in Law no. 90/6), 14–15; & (1977) ELRev. 392 at 398.

[172] Case 104/75, n. 115 above.

tion, such as by making it compulsory for the official importer to pass on the relevant information.[173] When the case came back before the *Kantongerecht* Rotterdam, that court held:

> Naturally the Dutch legislator ought to have realised at the time when the alleged offences were committed that the said provisions had a discriminatory effect and ought to have found a way to counteract this injustice. It is not apparent anywhere that the Dutch legislator took any steps at that time, or endeavoured to find an adequate solution to remedy the situation now denounced by the Court of Justice.[174]

While the willingness of the Dutch court to set aside the Dutch provisions and to acquit Mr de Peijper may at first sight be commended, a closer look reveals that the ECJ's judgment was not fully implemented by the national court. The *Kantongerecht* Rotterdam seems to have assumed that there were alternative means open to the Dutch legislator (without expressing a view as to what these might be) but does not itself carry out the test set out by the ECJ as to whether these means were 'obviously beyond the means which can reasonably be expected of an administration operating in a normal manner'. It is submitted that the implementation of the ECJ judgment by the Dutch court was unsatisfactory in so far as the proportionality and alternative means tests implicit in the second sentence of Article 36 were not strictly applied.

The question of the proportionality of national measures for the protection of public health can indeed be difficult for national courts. The matter is made more complex for these courts since they also have to apply similar concepts of national law. The overlap between the proportionality requirements of Community and national law was evident in a case before the Dutch *Raad van State* in *De Bruin Auto's BV* v. *Minister van Verkeer en Waterstaat*,[175] where the date of registration by the Dutch authorities of a car imported from a dealer in Belgium was challenged. The date of registration of the car in the Netherlands which was set at 30 June 1991 by the Dutch authorities,[176] was unsatisfactory to the applicant for two reasons: firstly, because the registration document suggested that the car was already two years old when registered in 1993; and secondly, because the date set resulted in the car being due for a vehicle roadworthiness test sooner than would otherwise have been the case.[177] The *Raad van State* considered whether this might constitute a breach of Article 30 which was

---

[173] *Ibid.* at paras. 26–8 of judgt.   [174] n. 171 above.

[175] *Raad van State (Afd. Rechtspraak)*, 17 Dec. 1993, SEW 1994, 456 (with note by Temmink).

[176] 'Deel II' of the *Kentekenbewijs* (registration document) stated: '*Datum eerste toelating*: *300691, datum ambtelijk vastgesteld*'.

[177] In the challenge before the administrative courts, the *Minister van Verkeer en Waterstaat* raised the defence that it had not been demonstrated that the car in question had not already been used in the Netherlands or any other country since the documents (the sales receipt together with the declaration by the Belgian car dealer) emanated from neither the car manufacturer nor from the Belgian State.

nevertheless justified for the protection of public health under Article 36,[178] but was ultimately able to annul the decision on the basis of the Dutch law *motiveringsbeginsel* (principle of motivation). The *Raad van State* held that the Dutch authorities had supported their decision with insufficient reasoning and was contrary to the principle of competent administration (*het algemeen rechtsbewustzijn levend beginsel van behoorlijk bestuur*). The overlap between these principles of Dutch law and the EC law proportionality principle will be evident.[179] A similar overlap was revealed in the judgment of the English High Court in *R. v. Minister of Agriculture, Fisheries and Food ex. p. Bell Lines Ltd and An Bord Bainne Co-Operative Ltd* (*The Irish Dairy Board*).[180] In that case, Forbes J discussed the possible overlap between an application of the proportionality principle according to the second sentence of Article 36 and the English administrative law principle of *Wednesbury* reasonableness.[181] It was clear that *Wednesbury* reasonableness, under which it has to be shown that a Minister has acted in such a way that no minister properly directing himself could have acted, involves a much less stringent test than that required by the proportionality principle in EC law. The High Court, however, rejected the possibility that in a case involving Community law before an English court, *Wednesbury* reasonableness should apply to the exclusion of the EC law concept of proportionality implicit in Article 36.[182] The views of Forbes J in *Ex p. Bell Lines* have also received support in *R v. Minister of Agriculture, Fisheries and Food ex. p. Roberts*[183] where, in the context of the justification in Article 36 for the protection of animal life, Popplewell J held that according to the Community law proportionality test, the Court should not only look to see whether the Minister was reasonable to take his view of the law but the Court should rule whether the Minister was entitled to take that view even if it was reasonable for him to do so. In other words, it seems that the English courts have accepted that, unlike in an application of

---

[178] The *Raad van State* discussed the ECJ judgments in Case 50/85 *Schloh* [1986] ECR 1855 and Case 406/85 *Gofette and Gillard* [1987] ECR 2524. The question of registration dates of cars imported from other Member States was recently dealt with by the ECJ in Case C–240/95 *Schmit* [1996] ECR I–3179.

[179] See also before the Dutch courts the judgment in *Sky Radio* v. *Minister van Verkeer en Waterstaat*, CBB, 22 Mar. 1995, SEW 1995, julinummer and *Conté Nederland BV* v. *Minister van VROM*, Pres. *Raad van State* (*Afd. Bestuursrechtspraak*), 19 Oct. 1994, SEW 1995, 444 (with note by van de Gronden and Mortelmans). See also de Moor-van Vugt, *Maten en gewichten, het evenredigheidsbeginsel in Europees perspectief* (Schoordijk Instituut, 1995), 268.

[180] [1984] 2 CMLR 502.

[181] See *Wednesbury Corporation* v. *Ministry of Housing and Local Government* [1966] 2 QB 275 [1965] 1 All ER 186.

[182] n. 180 above at 511. See also the comments of Hoffmann J in *Stoke-on-Trent City Council* v. *B & Q* [1990] 3 CMLR 31. On the proportionality principle in English administrative law see Boyron, 'Proportionality in English Administrative Law: A Faulty Transition' (1992) OJLS 237 and *R. v. Secretary of State for the Home Department, ex p. Brind* [1991] 2 WLR 588.

[183] [1991] 1 CMLR 555.

Wednesbury reasonableness, the proportionality test in Article 36 requires the court to examine, not whether the Minister's decision was unreasonable, but rather whether it was correct.[184] Indeed, as Vaughan and Randolph comment, 'the principle of administrative reasonableness in the *Wednesbury* rules is not applicable in Community law cases: the question is whether the decision under review is correct or not'.[185] Thus, it is true that the application of a narrow definition of public health in Article 36 has not always been well respected by the national courts. However, it should be added that these difficulties have not been helped by the fact that the national court has to juggle both the Community concept of proportionality implicit in Article 36 *and* similar, but not identical, concepts in national law.

(C) Is it desirable for the ECJ to decide (wherever possible) the proportionality of a national measure?

If, as is suggested in the foregoing analysis, the national courts have encountered difficulties in applying the proportionality principle implicit in the second sentence of Article 36, the question which then arises is whether the ECJ should be encouraged to itself decide, in individual cases referred to it, the proportionality of a national measure under Community law. There are two problems with the ECJ adopting such an approach. Firstly, the Article 177 preliminary-rulings procedure does not give the ECJ competence to apply its judgments to the facts of the cases referred to it. The ECJ's competence is limited to questions of *interpretation of Community law* and the application of that interpretation to the facts of an individual case is a matter for the national court. The ECJ is thus formally unable to rule explicitly that a provision of national law is not compatible with EC law. Secondly, it is arguable that the ECJ is badly placed to decide, in an individual case, whether a national measure is proportionate to an aim compatible with Article 36.

---

[184] See, however, the judgment of Taylor LJ in *R.* v. *Secretary of State for Health, ex p. United States Tobacco International* [1992] 1 All ER 212, [1992] 1 QB 353 where he seems to have assumed that the 'irrationality' principle was akin to the proportionality principle.

[185] Vaughan and Randolph, 'The Interface between Community Law and National Law: The United Kingdom Experience' in Curtin & O'Keeffe (eds.) *Constitutional Adjudication in European Community and National Law*, 225. More recently however, in *R.* v. *Chief Constable of Sussex, ex p. International Trader's Ferry* [1997] 2 All ER 65 at 80, the CA has held that although the proportionality principle can in certain circumstances be a more exacting test than the *Wednesbury* irrationality principle, each test in practice yields the same result. The subsequent application of the proportionality principle by the Court of Appeal to the facts of the case is subject to criticism since it in effect applied a test of whether the alleged error was manifest or constituted a misuse of powers. It is respectfully submitted that this is not a correct application of the proportionality test as understood in ECJ case law.

The ECJ has circumvented the first objection outlined above by frequently holding that 'Although the Court has no jurisdiction in proceedings under Article 177 of the EEC Treaty to rule on the question whether provisions of national legislation are compatible with the Treaty, it may provide the national court with all such criteria for the interpretation of Community law which may enable it to answer that question.'[186] Recent ECJ case law suggests that the ECJ takes the view at present that if it has sufficient documents before it to enable it to assess the proportionality of a national measure, it will carry out the assessment itself.[187] However, such an approach has led the ECJ to engage in significant fact-finding missions. This has given rise to criticism. For example, Duk has criticized the ECJ's judgments in *Eyssen* and *Melkunie*[188] where the ECJ held that national provisions restricting the ingredients which may be contained in certain human foodstuffs were justified and proportionate measures for the protection of public health under Article 36.[189] Duk points out that the ECJ did more than interpret the Treaty in those cases, by in effect establishing the relevant facts which did not appear in the findings of the national court and by drawing on scientific evidence available from the Food and Agriculture Organization of the United Nations and from the World Health Organization. Duk argues that 'in most national proceedings such facts should be proven . . . and Article 177 proceedings do not provide for the guarantees normally accorded to the parties with regard to such judicial fact-finding'.[190] These criticisms are underlined by the fact that the ECJ's applications of the proportionality principle have been erratic in their comprehensiveness. Thus, while in *Aragonesa*[191] the ECJ devoted no less than fourteen paragraphs of its judgment to the question of whether certain Spanish restrictions on the advertising of alcoholic beverages could be justified as proportionate measures for the protection of public health under Article 36, in *Laboratoire de protèses oculaires* v. *Union nationale des syndicats d'opticiens de France*[192] only a single paragraph of the ECJ's judgment was addressed to the proportionality of French legislation which reserved the sale of contact lenses to traders holding the relevant

---

[186] Case 97/83 *CMC Melkunie* [1984] ECR 2367 at para. 7. See also Case 53/80 *Officier van Justitie* v. *Koninklijke Kaasfabriek Eyssen BV* [1981] ECR 409; Case 54/85, n. 155 above & Case 94/83, n. 155 above.

[187] See, e.g. Case C–169/91 *Stoke-on-Trent* v. *B & Q* [1992] ECR I–6635, [1993] 1 CMLR 426 at para. 14 & Case C–313/94 *Graffione and Fransa* [1996] ECR I–6039 at para. 25 where the ECJ held that it did not have sufficient information and left the proportionality analysis to the national court.

[188] Cases 53/80 and 97/83, n. 186 above.

[189] Duk, 'Some Remarks of a Dutch Advocate on the Preliminary Procedure of Article 177 EEC' in Schermers, Timmermans, Kellermann & Stewart Watson (eds.), *Article 177 EEC: Experiences and Problems*, 208.

[190] Ibid.   [191] Cases C–1 and 176/90 [1991] ECR I–4154.

[192] Case C–271/92 [1993] ECR I–2899.

professional qualifications.[193] Perhaps more serious is the fact that there is also reason to believe that the ECJ occasionally gets its findings of fact wrong. It is submitted that this was the case in its judgment in *R. v. Pharmaceutical Society of Great Britain and Secretary of State for Social Services ex. p. Association of Pharmaceutical Importers* where it held that the possibility of 'psychosomatic phenomena' in patients justified (on grounds of public health in Article 36) a restriction in the United Kingdom prohibiting pharmacists from substituting a generic product with identical therapeutic effect for a product specifically named in a doctor's prescription.[194] It seems certain that the ECJ was heavily influenced in reaching this conclusion by a report which the ECJ had asked the Commission to produce setting out the relevant rules governing the relations between doctors and pharmacists in other Member States. The report produced for the ECJ by the Commission showed that ten of the then twelve Member States had similar restrictions to those prevailing in the United Kingdom. It is submitted that such a finding of fact was given undue weight by the ECJ. This is suggested by the fact that the English Court of Appeal, in referring the judgment to the ECJ, had itself suggested that if Article 30 was infringed, it would be unlikely to be justified for the protection of public health in Article 36.[195] Indeed, the Court of Appeal had even given specific reasons as to why it thought that this was the case. These reasons included the fact that the doctor's freedom of choice with respect to therapeutic decisions remained unfettered under the restriction since the dispensing of generic equivalents by pharmacists did not override this freedom. Furthermore, the Court of Appeal noted that the doctor's discretion was already circumscribed by other applicable rules under which certain drugs could *only* be prescribed in their generic form. Given that the national court in its referring judgment cast explicit doubt on the factual proportionality of the national restriction, it is strange that the ECJ itself went against such factual findings and held that the restrictions were justified for the protection of public health under Article 36. Such fact-finding, it is submitted, is better left to the national court.

The foregoing discussion appears to suggest that the application of the Article 36 justification on the grounds of public health (and the second sentence of that Article in particular) by the national courts gives rise to two problems. On the one hand, there is evidence to suggest that the national courts' application of the proportionality of the public-health derogation in Article 36 is rather unsatisfactory. On the other hand, the ECJ has only limited competence in the context of Article 177 proceedings to engage in fact-finding to decide the proportionality issue itself. In any event it is

---

[193] Ibid. at para. 12.
[194] Case 266 & 267/87 [1989] ECR 1295; [1989] 2 CMLR 751 at para. 22.
[195] [1987] 3 CMLR 951.

questionable whether it is desirable for the ECJ to engage in the fact-finding analysis which an assessment of the proportionality of a national measure necessitates since the ECJ is ill-equipped to carry out such fact-finding in the absence of the normal procedural safeguards. These considerations suggest that the second sentence of Article 36 must, of necessity, be left to the national courts for application. It is therefore submitted that the deficiencies in the application of Article 36 by national courts should not be remedied by encouraging the ECJ to decide such matters. In the long term, the only satisfactory solution is for the national courts to improve their performance in conscientiously and rigorously carrying out their duty to analyse whether national restrictions on the free movement of goods may be held to be proportionate to the alleged objectives of the protection of public health advanced in individual cases.

(D) Examples of extremely competent and dynamic applications of the public-health justification in Article 36

The discussion of the unsatisfactory national case law applying the Article 36 justification on the grounds of public health must be balanced against the examples in such case law of extremely competent and dynamic applications of this derogation to the free movement of goods. If, as was concluded in the previous section, the national courts must, of necessity, be the competent forum to decide whether national restrictions on the free movement of goods may be held to be proportionate to the alleged objectives of the protection of public health advanced in individual cases, attention must be focused on those cases where the public-health justification was confidently decided. Happily, for every bad application of the public-health justification in the national courts, there is also an illustration of an extremely commendable application to counter-balance the analysis. Some of these illustrations will be discussed in this section.

The Dutch courts have provided some excellent applications of the public health justification in Article 36. In a relatively early judgment, the *Gerechtshof* Amsterdam showed itself willing to set aside Article 8(d) of the *Kaasbesluit* (Cheese Order) regulating the content of sorbic acid in cheese.[196] The Dutch court took into consideration a letter produced in evidence from a civil servant in the *Ministerie van Volksgezondheid en Milieuhygiëne* stating that sorbic acid at the level contained in the cheese (imported from France) in this case did not raise any dangers to public health. Furthermore, the Dutch court referred to the fact that the *Kaasbesluit* had not been amended since 1966 and was thus ripe for reconsideration. There were thus held to be no genuine public-health consider-

---

[196] *Gerdabel Nederland BV* v. *Openbaar Ministerie*, Gerechtshof Amsterdam, 2 Feb. 1978, SEW 1978, 430.

ations to justify the restriction to the free movement of goods. Equally, following the ECJ's judgment in *CMC Melkunie*[197] the Hoge Raad implemented the ECJ judgment fully by allowing the appeal against the decision of the *Gerechtshof* Amsterdam and sending the case back down before that court for re-consideration as to whether or not non-pathogenic microorganisms in milk caused a danger to the health of particularly sensitive consumers.[198]

One of the best illustrations of the effectiveness of the application by a national court of the justification on the grounds of public health is provided by the judgment of the *Hoge Raad* in *Jacques George Henri H.* v. *Openbaar Ministerie*.[199] That case provided an interesting sequel to the ECJ judgment in *de Peijper*.[200] It will be recalled that following the ECJ judgment in *de Peijper*, the Dutch provisions at issue in that case were amended to provide for a simplified procedure for the registration of pharmaceuticals by a parallel importer into the Netherlands.[201] Furthermore, these new provisions had been held to be compatible with Articles 30 to 36 EC by the ECJ in *Officier van Justitie* v. *Kortmann*.[202] In the present case, however, the *Hoge Raad* was faced with the parallel importation of pharmaceuticals, not by a parallel importer, but by a Dutch-registered pharmacist. The argument was advanced that the office of pharmacist itself was a sufficient guarantee that the health and lives of humans would be adequately protected. The *Hoge Raad* quoted the relevant ECJ authorities and held that the public-health justification in Article 36 could only apply if it could be shown that the national provisions were necessary and could not be achieved equally successfully by means less restrictive of intra-Community trade. Applying this to the facts of the present case, the *Hoge Raad* held that although the office of pharmacist was not in itself a sufficient guarantee, the aim of the new Dutch provisions was to identify the imported product and the lower court had not investigated whether that aim could have been achieved by other means such that the protection of public health was equally effectively protected. The *Hoge Raad* proceeded to state explicitly that the draftsmen of the new Dutch provisions had only envisaged the importation of pharmaceuticals by parallel importers and had not considered parallel importing by pharmacists.[203] The *Hoge Raad*

---

[197] Case 97/83 n. 186 above.

[198] *Hoge Raad (Strafkamer)*, 13 Nov. 1984, NJ 1985, 338, SEW 1985, 227 (with note by Mulder).

[199] *Hoge Raad (Strafkamer)*, 5 Nov. 1985, NJ 1986, 280 (with note by Van Veen), AB 1986, 309 (with note by FHvdB).

[200] n. 115 above.

[201] Art. 23, *Besluit Registratie Geneesmiddelen* (Order on the Registration of Medicines) of 8 Sept. 1977, Stbd. 1977, no. 537.

[202] Case 32/80 [1981] ECR 252; [1982] 3 CMLR 46.

[203] The *Hoge Raad* referred to a letter of 25 July 1978 in which the Chief Inspector of Public Health stated that the Dutch provisions made the assumption that pharmacists would not

thus allowed the appeal and referred the case back down to the *Arrondissementsrechtbank* Rotterdam. This is a very commendable judgment of the *Hoge Raad* which serves to highlight the potential effectiveness of the application by national courts of the second sentence of Article 36. The far-reaching analysis by the *Hoge Raad* of alternative means available to the Dutch authorities could not have been undertaken by the ECJ. It is particularly encouraging that the *Hoge Raad* ignored the Opinion of its Advocate General (Remmelink) in this case who had concluded that 'one should in principle assume that legislation is based on reasonable grounds and that the various interests have been considered against one another'. Contrary to this view, the *Hoge Raad* seems to have accepted that the very essence of granting national courts the competence to apply the Article 36 derogations is that they have the ability to investigate whether national provisions are 'based on reasonable grounds and that the various interests have been considered against one another'. In this way, the national courts play a vital role in unearthing arbitrary restrictions to the free movement of goods. The *Hoge Raad* carried out this role splendidly in this case.

The highest Dutch administrative court has also shown itself willing to carry out a full and rigorous application of the public-health justification in Article 36. Following the ECJ's judgment in *Officier van Justitie* v. *Sandoz BV*,[204] the *Raad van State* was faced with an appeal against a refusal by the Dutch Minister of Welfare, Health and Culture (*Minister van Welzijn, Volksgezondheid en Cultuur*) for authorization to market certain foods and drinks to which vitamins had been added.[205] Since the products had been imported from other Member States, the restriction on importation had to be justified for the protection of health in Article 36. The *Raad van State* held that in the present state of scientific research it was possible that the addition of vitamins to food could be damaging to human health and that labelling requirements were not sufficient to protect against the possibility of such damage. However, the ECJ had held that: 'Although in view of the present stage of harmonization of national laws at the Community level a wide discretion must be left to Member States, they must, in order to observe the principle of proportionality, authorize marketing when the addition of vitamins to foodstuffs meets a real need, especially a technical or nutritional one'.[206] With respect to this issue, the *Raad van State* held that the burden rested with the Member State to show that no such 'real need' existed. Applying this to the facts, the *Raad van State* held that the Dutch

parallel import and that if they did, the Department would consider amending the provisions further.

[204] Case 174/82 [1983] ECR 2445.

[205] *Sandoz BV* v. *Minister van Welzijn, Volksgezondheid en Cultuur, Raad van State (Afd. Rechtspraak)*, 14 Nov. 1988, SEW 1990, 93 (note by Mortelmans).

[206] Case 174/82, n. 204 above at para. 19 of judgt.

authorities had successfully shown that there was no real technical or nutritional need for the foodstuffs and that the argument raised by the applicants that there was a market for the goods did not satisfy the 'real need' criteria.[207] Although the *Raad van State* upheld on grounds of public health the refusal to authorize the marketing of certain foods and drinks to which vitamins had been added at the expense of the free movement of goods, the application of the derogation was rigorous and fully applied to the facts.[208] An in-depth analysis such as that carried out by the *Raad van State* in this case is fully in line with the interpretation by the ECJ of the public-health justification in Article 36.

The diligence of the *Raad van State* in the *Sandoz* case is matched by that of the *Gerechtshof* Den Haag in *Openbaar Ministerie* v. *Richardson Vicks BV*.[209] This case concerned 'Vicks Vitamin C Pastilles' which, by virtue of the fact that they had Vitamin C added to them, should have been the subject of an application for prior authorization to be marketed in the Netherlands. The *Gerechtshof* Den Haag engaged in a full analysis of Articles 30 to 36 and the relevant ECJ authorities on the public health justification in particular (including the *Sandoz* judgment[210]) and concluded that

The Court finds that the Netherlands Government no longer holds the view that it is necessary for effective health protection for foodstuffs with a low dose of Vitamin C added, such as the Vicks Vitamin C Pastilles in the present case, to maintain a system of prohibition unless prior permission has been granted. The Court finds that the Netherlands government plans, ahead of expected EEC harmonization, to implement a general Ministerial Order under which the marketing of these foodstuffs is liberalized as long as they comply with the labelling requirements contained in the Order. This follows from the Report of a meeting of the Commission for Public Health on 14 May 1992 with the Secretary of State for Health and Culture concerning the draft provisions (*Toestemmingregeling laaggedoseerde vitamine-preparaten* (*Warenwet*), Bijl. Hand. II, 1991–1992, 22300 XVI, nr. 131).

The *Gerechtshof* Den Haag then proceeded to conclude that since equally effective protection of health could be achieved by measures which are less restrictive of inter-State trade, it cannot be said that the present legislation is 'proportionate to the objective aimed at and thereby necessary

---

[207] Furthermore, the *Raad van State* rejected the argument that serious sportspersons had a real need for foodstuffs with added vitamins since it appeared, on the facts, that such a need was satisfied by using authorized multi-vitamin products on the market.

[208] It should, however, be noted that Mortelmans (n. 205 above) has criticized the *Raad van State* in this judgment for not having consulted international scientific research and relying exclusively on the research carried out in the Netherlands (by the *Voedingsraad* (Food Council)).

[209] *Gerechtshof* 's-Gravenhage, 12 Feb. 1993; quoted in the subsequent judgt of the *Hoge Raad* (14 June 1994), NJB-katern 1994, 448 nr. 182; transcr. 96.869 E, SEW 1995, 140 .

[210] Case 174/82, n. 204 above.

and as a consequence justified within the meaning of Article 36 EEC Treaty'. Again, this judgment must be highly commended. The effectiveness and dynamism of application by a national court of the Article 36 justification on the grounds of public health is fully exposed in this judgment of the *Gerechtshof* Den Haag.[211]

Three recent judgments handed down by the French *Cour de Cassation* also suggest that the public-health justification in Article 36 will be rigorously applied before the French courts. These cases concerned the importation into France of salad containing certain preservatives from Germany,[212] chocolates containing sorbic acid to preserve the crème fraiche in chocolates from Belgium[213] and cheese and cakes, also with preservatives in the form of sorbic acid, from Italy.[214] Such preservatives were prohibited under French legislation.[215] In all three judgments, handed down by the *Cour de Cassation* on the same date, it was held that the non-exhaustive harmonization in this field in the form of Directive 64/54[216] did not preclude Member States' recourse to Article 36 for reasons of public health provided that there was no arbitrary discrimination or any disguised restriction on trade. Applying this to the facts, the *Cour de Cassation* held that the lower courts had failed in these cases to examine scientific evidence carried out outside France (i.e. international research) with respect to the danger of the additives and had taken no account of the eating habits of the country. Furthermore, the *Cour de Cassation* held that the lower courts in these cases should have investigated whether there were exceptions which the importers could invoke to get a reasoned decision within a reasonable time. The *Cour de Cassation* thus sent the cases back to the lower courts for further consideration. Although the *Cour de Cassation* did not cite ECJ case law, it was clear that it was drawing heavily on ECJ judgments such as *Sandoz* and *Eyssen*.[217] The insistence on a full examination of international scientific research by the *Cour de Cassation*

---

[211] The judgment of the *Gerechtshof* Den Haag in *Richardson Vicks* may be contrasted with that of the President of the *CBB* in *Procter & Gamble Benelux BV* v. *Minister Volksgezondheid, Welzijn en Sport*, 2 Sept. 1994, KG 1994, 353 (concerning 'Punica Multivitamines' fruit juice) where the *CBB* held that the mere fact that the Minister had submitted draft legislation before an advice committee which would amend the present regime did not render the present legislation clearly inapplicable (*onmiskenbaar onverbindend*).

[212] *Kugelmann, Cour de Cassation*, ch. crim., 27 Feb. 1995, Bull. Cass. Crim. 1995, 83.

[213] *Crépin, Cour de Cassation*, ch. crim., 27 Feb. 1995, Bull. Cass. Crim. 1995, 83.

[214] *Bellon, Cour de Cassation*, ch. crim., 27 Feb. 1995, Bull. Cass. Crim. 1995, 83; Ed. du Juris-Classeur, Droit Pénal 1995, no. 147; Dalloz 1995, IR 117.

[215] Arts. 1 & 3 of Law of 1 Aug. 1905 (now Articles L. 213-1 and L. 213-3 of the *Code de la consommation*) and Art. 49 of the Law of 30 Mar. 1902 & Arts. 1 & 2 of Decree of 15 Apr. 1912.

[216] Council Directive of 5 Nov. 1963 on the approximation of the laws of the Member States concerning the preservatives authorized for use in foodstuffs intended for human consumption, [1963–64] OJ Spec. Ed. p. 99.

[217] Case 53/80, n. 186 above & n. 205 above.

may be commended as a rigorous application fully in line with the ECJ's interpretation of the public health justification in Article 36.

A similar example is provided by the decision of the French *Cour de Cassation* in *Bowes*[218] which concerned the controversial *Loi Evin* in France,[219] Article L. 18 of which set down limitations on the content of advertising of alcoholic drinks. The *Cour de Cassation* held that such legislation was justified for the protection of public health under Article 36 since 'advertising is a manifest inducement to consumption and a national law which limits advertisement will by this means fight against alcoholism which corresponds to the derogation for the protection of public health in Article 36'. The *Cour de Cassation* went on to add that the legislation was proportionate to the objective it pursued, namely to encourage moderation in consumption of alcoholic beverages and protection of the young. In so doing the *Cour de Cassation* noted that 'the contested French legislation does not entail a general prohibition on advertising such beverages, but regulates the content of advertising and the media for carrying it'. This case provides yet a further example of competent application of the public-health justification in Article 36.[220]

Finally, the Irish Courts have also shown a willingness to apply the public-health justification in a competent and dynamic fashion. In *United States Tobacco (Ireland)* v. *Ireland*[221] the Irish High Court held that a ban on the importation of oral smokeless chewing tobacco from the United Kingdom could be justified for the protection of public health in Article 36. Blayney J fully rehearsed the ECJ authorities in this field and held, after a full review of the facts and expert evidence, that the ban on import of smokeless chewing tobacco was justified, having regard to the available international research, for the protection of public health and that the ban did not offend the principle of proportionality since it was particularly suitable since the evidence established that a ban was more effective for health protection than the advertising and sale restrictions in place for other tobacco products already available in the Irish Republic. Again, this

---

[218] *Cour de Cassation*, ch. crim., 18 May 1994, Bull. Cass. Crim. 1994, no. 190 p. 434; [1995] 1 CMLR 455, Dalloz 1994, IR 184 (summary). See also *X . . . e.a.*, *Cour de Cassation*, ch. crim., 29 June 1994, transcr. available on Lexis).

[219] Loi No. 91-32 of 10 Jan. 1991, JORF 12 Jan. 1991; JCP 1991, III 64484 amending the *Code Débits Boissons* (Sale of Beverages Code). See Decocq, 'Le Nouvelles restrictions à la publicité en faveur des boissons alcooliques' & Grelon, 'La Publicité sur le territoire français des Boisssons Alcooliques: Les incertitudes actuelles de la Loi Evin'.

[220] In this context, it is interesting to note that the ECJ has recently held in Case C–189/95 *Allmänna Åklagaren* v. *Franzén* [1997] ECR I–5090 that the licensing system set up by the Swedish retail monopoly for the sale of alcohol in Sweden was not proportionate to the public health aim pursued by the system. However, the ECJ upheld the monopoly system as a whole which it analyzed exclusively under Article 37 EC.

[221] [1993] 1 Irish Rep. 241.

judgment is of note for its full and comprehensive application of the public health justification in Article 36.[222]

(E) Summary

In conclusion then, it seems that the problems with the application by national courts of the Article 36 justification on the grounds of public health must be balanced against the examples illustrating extremely competent and indeed, dynamic, applications of this important derogation to the free movement of goods. The latter cases demonstrate that the expectation of rigorous and faithful application by the national courts is not an unrealistic one. The view already expressed that it is the national courts, rather than the ECJ, which should have primary responsibility for scrutinizing the proportionality of individual public-health justifications is, in the light of these decisions, far from being untenable.

The potential dynamism of the application of the proportionality test by the national courts can also be taken a step further. If the national courts apply the second sentence of Article 36 rigorously, the pre-*Keck and Mithouard*[223] rationale, according to which Article 30 was given an extremely broad scope, is at its most effective. The broad scope of Article 30 ensured that several national restrictions were brought within Article 30 but had to be justified. The great benefit of this approach was that Article 36 could be applied by national courts on a case-by-case basis, weeding out genuine disguised restrictions to trade. These considerations have enormous relevance to the present discussion. The French legislation at issue in the *Delattre* case discussed above provides a telling example.[224] It is now almost certain that the legislation at issue in that case would now fall outside the scope of Article 30.[225] As a result, there is no longer any possibility of testing, in individual cases, whether the monopoly given to pharmacists by the French legislation is justified and proportionate under Article 36. Thus, the dynamism of the old approach is lost. This point is handsomely demonstrated by the decision of the *Cour d'Appel* of Colmar in *Hypermarché Cora* v. *Ministère public*.[226] The factual background to this case was identical to that in the *Delattre* case discussed above. The *Cour*

---

[222] This detailed and highly commendable application by the Irish High Court of Art. 36 may be contrasted with that of the English High Court in parallel proceedings in *Ex. p. United States Tobacco International* n. 184 above, where Taylor LJ held that the ban was justified for the protection of public health within the meaning of Art. 36 without providing any elaboration as to why this was the case.

[223] See discussion of this judgment in Ch. 3.   [224] See pp. 263–6.

[225] See esp. the judgment of the ECJ post-*Keck* in Case C–391/92 *Commission* v. *Greece* [1995] ECR I–1621. See also the recent decision of the French *Conseil d'Etat* in *Sté Tour Pol*, 7 July 1995, Rec. Lebon 1995 287.

[226] *Cour d'appel* Colmar, ch. corr., 23 Mar. 1988, Gaz. Pal. 1989, I Jur. 409.

d'Appel held that Article 30 was infringed subject to justification for the protection of public health under Article 36. With regard to the latter, the *Cour d'Appel* held (citing ECJ authorities) that to the extent that uncertainties persist in the present state of scientific research, it is up to Member States, in the absence of harmonization, to decide what level of protection of public health they wish to secure. However, the *Cour d'Appel* went on to state that it is up to national authorities to demonstrate in each case that their regulation is necessary to protect effectively the interests foreseen by Article 36 and notably that the product in question presents a serious risk to public health. Not only is this an excellent exposition of the correct analysis of the law, but the *Cour d'Appel* proceeded to apply it to the facts in an excellent fashion, by examining each product in turn to decide whether the sale through pharmacists alone was really necessary. Thus, on the one hand, the *Cour d'Appel* found that it was unnecessary to restrict the sale of *Vitamin C500* (a multivitamin) to sale through pharmacies. It had been argued that the pharmacist was necessary at the point of sale to protect children from doses of the product which can have a lightly exciting effect analogous to that of caffeine. The *Cour d'Appel* evaluated the factual evidence and found that there was no real danger.[227] This may be contrasted, on the other hand, with modified alcohol (70 per cent), for which the *Cour d'Appel* accepted that the restriction to sale by pharmacists was necessary as there was considerable evidence of dangers to the public if the product was not used correctly.[228] The dynamism of this approach will be evident. Each product is evaluated by the national court on a case-by-case basis to see whether it is really necessary to limit distribution through pharmacies given the restriction on trade between Member States. The weakness of the post-*Keck* rule-based approach is that such national legislation would now fall entirely outside the ambit of Article 30.

The potential of the old approach was therefore great. However, it should not be forgotten that the practical reality was far from glorious. We have already seen that the reality of the French courts' application of the proportionality test after the ECJ judgment in *Delattre* was most unsatisfactory. Seen in this light the previous approach, for all its dynamic potential, was a fool's paradise. The discussion in this section reveals that the national courts have some way to go before it can be said with confidence that they can be fully trusted to apply Article 36 and grant derogations from the fundamental right to the free movement of goods. This has to be balanced, however, against the cases where the national courts have applied the justification on the grounds of public health rigorously and

---

[227] The *Cour d'Appel* came to the same conclusion with respect to capsules containing powder from plants.

[228] The *Cour d'Appel* came to the same conclusion with respect to the inhalation of vegetable essence.

faithfully. While there is clearly room for improvement, the problems discussed in this section are not such as to warrant a radical change to the present system according to which it is the national courts, rather than the ECJ, which should have primary responsibility for scrutinizing the proportionality of individual public-health justifications.

5 PROTECTION OF ANIMALS AND PLANTS

The justification based on the protection of animals and plants and set out in Article 36 parallels that of the 'protection of health and life of humans' discussed in the previous section. Thus, the principles discussed in the previous section apply equally to this justification. In particular, a justification will only be accepted under this head if it forms part of a seriously considered policy for the protection of animals and plants rather than introduced for protectionist reasons. It is now clear that the protection of the health and life of animals in Article 36 covers animal welfare considerations.[229]

It has already been noted[230] that the second sentence of Article 36 is interpreted by the ECJ to conclude that the onus rests on the Member State relying on the justification in the first sentence of Article 36 (*in casu* action taken for the protection of animals and plants) was proportionate to the danger posed. However, just as with the public-health justifications discussed in the previous section, the national courts have not always carried out their application of the proportionality test satisfactorily. An example is provided by the implementation of the judgment of the ECJ in *Centre d'insemination de la Crespelle*[231] by the French *Cour de Cassation*. It will be recalled that the ECJ had held in that case that French legislation requiring economic operators who imported semen from other Member States to deliver it to an approved insemination or production centre, was justified for the protection of health and life of animals and humans. However, the ECJ had subjected this justification to an application of the proportionality test which it left to the national court, by stating that, 'The question whether the operation of the approved centres, so far as the conditions for storing semen are concerned, entails in practice discrimination against the imported product is one of fact which the national court must determine.[232]

---

[229] Case 141–143/81 *Holdijk* [1982] ECR 1299, [1983] 2 CMLR 635 concerning the minimum size of enclosures for fattening calves.
[230] n. 5 above.
[231] Case C–323/93 *Centre d'insemination de la Crespelle* v. *Cooperative d'elevage et d'insemination artificielle du departement de la Mayenne* [1994] ECR I–5077.
[232] Ibid. at para. 39 of judgt.

The *Cour de Cassation*, in implementing this judgment when it came back before it, carried out absolutely no such investigation of the facts.[233] The *Cour de Cassation* simply recited the operative part of the ECJ judgment in which the ECJ had stated that 'Articles 30 and 36 of the Treaty . . . must be interpreted as not precluding national rules that require economic operators who import semen from a Member State of the Community to deliver it to an approved insemination or production centre' and concluded that the argument based on Article 30 failed. No mention was made by the *Cour de Cassation* of the possibility that the conditions applied by individual centres for the storing of semen entailed discrimination against imports as the ECJ had clearly envisaged it should. Regrettably, therefore, it seems that the national court failed in this judgment to carry out a rigorous application of the proportionality test in line with the restrictive interpretation of Article 36 by the ECJ.

One of the most engaging problems which arises with respect to justifications for the protection of animals in Article 36 is the question of whether such justifications are capable of having extra-territorial application. Is a Member State entitled to rely on Article 36 in order to adopt measures for protecting animals against possible cruelty within the territory of another Member State? The answer to this question is elusive and has not yet been conclusively answered or addressed by the ECJ.[234]

On the one hand, there are compelling reasons to suppose that the protection of animals in Article 36 should be capable of extra-territorial application. Indeed, the very essence of this justification necessarily implies that cruelty to animals or infringements to animal welfare carried out in other Member States could justify an import or export ban. After all, a Member State is unlikely to ban the import or export of animals because of possible cruelty to those animals *within its own territory*. Thus, in order for this justification in Article 36 to have any practical meaning at all, it could be argued that it has to have application to measures applying *outside its territory*. There is some support in ECJ case law for the suggestion that Article 36 is capable of extra-territorial application. For example, in *Exportur*[235] the ECJ held that 'where the protection afforded by a State to names indicating regions or places in its territory is justified under Article 36 of the Treaty, that provision *does not preclude such protection from being extended to the territory of another Member State'*.[236]

---

[233] *Cour de Cassation*, ch. comm., 28 Nov. 1995 (transcr. 91-19.622 available on Lexis).

[234] See discussion by Mortelmans, 'Excepties bij non-tarifaire intracommunautaire belemmering: assimilatie in het nieuwe EG-Verdrag?' at 188–9. See, however, Case C–1/96 *R.* v. *Ministry of Agriculture, Fisheries and Foods, ex p. Royal Society for the Prevention of Cruelty to Animals and Compassion in World Farming*, pending.

[235] Case C–3/91 *Exportur* v. *Lor SA and Confiserie du Tech* [1992] ECR I–5529.

[236] Ibid. at para. 38 of judgt. Emphasis added. See also the Opinion of Adv. Gen. Jacobs in Case C–70/94 *Werner* v. *Germany* [1995] ECR I–3189 at para. 38 of Opinion. With respect to

Furthermore, it will be recalled that in *Inter-Huiles*[237] it had been argued before the ECJ that the French legislation in that case was justified for environmental protection since if the waste oils were not disposed of in France they might be exported to Belgium where they would cause environmental damage. The ECJ rejected this argument stating that '[c]learly, the environment is protected just as effectively when the oils are sold to an authorized disposal or regenerating undertaking of another Member State as when they are disposed of in the Member State of origin'.[238] Jans has pointed out that it is possible to argue that, following this statement by the ECJ, if it could be shown *a contrario* that the waste oils could not be sold to a satisfactory disposal undertaking in another Member State, export to that State could be prevented. However, as Jans himself points out, this is relatively weak authority for this proposition.[239]

Indeed, there are also strong arguments which would preclude any extra-territorial application for Article 36. Most commentators support the conclusions of Advocate General Trabucchi in *Dassonville* where he opined that 'States can derogate in the said manner [under Article 36] only for the purpose of the protection of their own interests and not for the protection of the interests of other Member States . . . Article 36 allows every State the right to protect exclusively its own national interests.'[240] There is also implicit support in *Nertsvoederfabriek Nederland BV*[241] where the ECJ held that 'it does not appear necessary [under Article 36] to prohibit the exportation of poultry offal, provided that the conditions relating to health laid down by these provisions are satisfied with respect to removal and transport *on national territory*'.[242] The implicit suggestion is that what happens outside national territory is of no concern to a Member State with respect to Article 36.[243] More recently, in *R. v. Ministry of Agriculture, Fisheries and Foods ex p. Hedley Lomas*[244] Advocate General Léger produced powerful arguments against the Article 36 justification based on the protection of animals having extra-territorial effect. In particular, the learned Advocate General was of the opinion that 'the principle of mutual confidence prohibits a Member State from adopting unilaterally a measure

the extra-territorial application of environmental justifications see Aland in Addink *et al.* (eds.), n. 134 above, 154.

[237] Case 172/82 *Syndicat national des fabricants raffineurs d'huiles de graissage e.a.* v. *Groupement d'intérêt économique (GIE) Inter-Huiles* [1983] ECR 555.

[238] Ibid. at para. 14 of judgt.   [239] Jans, *Europees Milieurecht in Nederland*, 255.

[240] Case 8/74 *Procureur du Roi* v. *Dassonville* [1974] ECR 837 at 860. See also the Opinion of Adv. Gen. Van Gerven in Case C–169/89 *Openbaar Ministerie* v. *Gourmetterie Van den Burg NV* [1990] ECR I–2143 at 2155. Oliver seems to assume that Art. 36 cannot have extra-territorial application: Oliver, n. 28 above, 186.

[241] Case 118/86 *Openbaar Ministerie* v. *Nertsvoederfabriek Nederland BV* [1987] ECR 3883.

[242] Ibid. at para. 16. Emphasis added.

[243] This point was made by Jans, n. 239 above at 255.

[244] Case C–5/94 [1996] ECR I–2553, [1996] 2 CMLR 391.

based on Article 36 for protecting animals within the territory of another Member State' and furthermore that 'only the Member State within whose territory the protective measure must be adopted is in a position to ensure that the measure is strictly necessary and to check that it is being complied with'.[245] There is some support in the ECJ's judgment in *Hedley Lomas* to suggest that Article 36 could not have extra-territorial application but, as it had in its judgment in *Gourmetterie Van den Burg*,[246] the ECJ based its reasoning in this case on the interpretation of a Directive[247] which it held to completely occupy the field to the exclusion of Article 36.[248] Given that there was a Directive applicable in the other Member State in *Hedley Lomas*, it was not difficult for the ECJ to conclude that 'a Member State may not unilaterally adopt, on its own authority, corrective or protective measures designed to obviate any breach by another Member State of rules of Community law'.[249] The point was that a possible *breach of Community law* by another Member State was being alleged in *Hedley Lomas*. Thus, the question as to whether a Member State would be entitled to rely on Article 36 in order to adopt measures for protecting animals against possible cruelty (*which is not contrary to EC law*) within the territory of another Member State, has not been conclusively answered by the ECJ and therefore remains an open point.

Given this uncertainty, it is perhaps not surprising that the national courts have displayed a degree of eclecticism on this issue. The question of the protection of animals in other Member States has arisen on several occasions before the Dutch courts. In *Openbaar Ministerie* v. *Gourmetterie Van den Burg NV*, the importation of a dead endangered bird (*lagopus lagopus scoticus*, commonly referred to as Red Grouse) from the United

---

[245] Para. 33 of Adv. Gen. Léger's Opinion. In para. 30, he also pertinently pointed out that: 'The onus was thus on the United Kingdom either to bring an action under Article 170 of the EC Treaty or to submit a complaint to the Commission in order for that institution, as guardian of the Treaties, to try to have the breach brought to an end and, if necessary, consider whether to institute infringement proceedings. The United Kingdom would then have been able, in infringement proceedings brought against Spain, to obtain authorization under Article 186 of the EC Treaty to suspend temporarily the issue of licences for the export of live animals to Spain'. See also the Opinion of Adv. Gen. Léger in Case C–1/96 n. 74 above, delivered on 15 July 1997 at paras. 86–91.

[246] Case C–169/89, n. 240 above.

[247] Council Directive 74/577 of 18 Nov. 1974 on stunning of animals before slaughter [1974] OJ L316/10.

[248] Case C–5/94, n. 244 above at paras. 18–19. See discussion of this point in Ch. 9, sect. 2. On the other hand, in Case C–149/94 *Criminal proceedings against Vergy* [1996] ECR I–299 at para. 18 the ECJ held that Directive 79/409 on the conservation of wild birds 'requires each Member State to ensure the protection of a species of bird naturally occurring in the wild state in the European territory of the Member States to which the Treaty applies, *even if the natural habitat of the species in question does not occur in the territory of the Member State concerned*' [1979] OJ L103/1 (emphasis added).

[249] Case C–5/94, n. 244 above at para. 20. See also Case C–14/96 *Denuit* [1997] ECR I–2785 at para. 35.

Kingdom for sale in the Netherlands contrary to Article 7 of the Dutch *Vogelwet* (Law on Birds) was at issue. The *Arrondissementsrechtbank* Den Haag held, *inter alia*, that this did not infringe Articles 30 to 36 'because the prohibition in Article 7 *Vogelwet* is not a measure that limits the importation of goods, but is a measure of protection of the bird population in Europe'.[250] On appeal before the *Hoge Raad*, the Dutch Supreme Court criticized this finding of the *Arrondissementsrechtbank* Den Haag and held that Article 7 *Vogelwet* was 'undoubtedly' (*onmiskenbaar*) a measure having equivalent effect to a quantitative restriction prohibited by Article 30 and that the only question was whether it could be justified under Article 36 for the protection of animals even though the animals in question were native to the United Kingdom and not in the Netherlands.[251] On this point, a reference was made by the *Hoge Raad* to the ECJ. However, as we have seen,[252] the ECJ did not address the Article 36 point since it concluded that Directive 79/409[253] 'regulated exhaustively the Member States' powers with regard to the conservation of wild birds',[254] which precluded recourse to Article 36.

In spite of the fact that the ECJ held in *Gourmetterie Van den Burg* that recourse to Article 36 was precluded when Directive 79/409 was of application, it is surprising that in a subsequent judgment of the French *Cour de Cassation* in *The State* v. *Vituret & Chambion*,[255] the possibility was mentioned that the protection of animals in Article 36 could apply to justify a ban on the sale in France of woodcock paté imported from Belgium contrary to a French Order of 20 December 1983. Although the *Cour de Cassation* also mentioned and applied the provisions of Directive 79/409,[256] it neither cited nor applied the ECJ's judgment in *Gourmetterie Van den Burg*. Furthermore, the *Cour de Cassation* did not even consider making an Article 177 reference to the ECJ. It is submitted that by applying Article 36 in circumstances contrary to the ECJ's express judgment in *Gourmetterie Van den Burg* without itself making a preliminary reference, the *Cour de Cassation* was in breach of its obligations in Article 177(3) EC.[257]

The Dutch courts have displayed a degree of confusion in their view of the question of whether the protection of animals set out in Article 36

[250] *Arrondissementsrechtbank* 's-Gravenhage, 25 Nov. 1987.
[251] *Hoge Raad*, 25 Apr. 1989, NJ 1989, 720, M & R 1989, 517; NJB 1990, 1322.
[252] Case C–169/89 n. 246 above.   [253] Council Directive 79/409, n. 248 above.
[254] Case C–169/89 n. 246 above at para. 9.
[255] *Cour de Cassation*, ch. crim., 2 Dec. 1992, [1995] 1 CMLR 185, Bull. Cass. Crim 1992, no. 401 p. 899.
[256] n. 248 above. It may be noted that woodcock was mentioned in Annex III of the Directive and thus that the Directive was of application.
[257] This is even more the case given that it is not clear why it was assumed that the protection of animals in Art. 36 was applicable when the preamble to Directive 79/409 refers only to environmental concerns and the common heritage of the Community and is silent on the protection of animals as such.

could apply extra-territorially. On the one hand, in the *Opgezette Buizerd* case,[258] the *Raad van State* held that a refusal under Dutch legislation for the protection of birds to grant a licence to import a stuffed buzzard (bird) from Germany into the Netherlands was 'without doubt (*buiten twijfel*) justified on the grounds of the protection of the life of animals as set out in Article 36 of the EEC Treaty'. The *Raad van State* was in this judgment, in effect, according an extra-territorial application to Article 36 because the buzzard was killed and stuffed in another Member State and not within the territory of the Netherlands. On the other hand, eight years later in *Van der Feesten* v. *Landbouw, Natuurbeheer en Visserij (Min.)*,[259] the same division of the *Raad van State* was confronted with an appeal against a refusal to licence the import into the Netherlands from Denmark two species of bird belonging to endangered species.[260] Neither bird was to be found in the wild in the Netherlands and it was common ground that the birds had been lawfully raised and marketed in Denmark and that, since neither species was mentioned in Annex III of Directive 79/409,[261] that Directive was not applicable.[262] The *Raad van State* held that 'although in light of the European Court of Justice's case law there is possible doubt (*mogelijke twijfel*) as to the defendant's defence in this case, we nevertheless assume that the defendants are entitled to refuse the licence applied for on the grounds mentioned in Article 36 EEC'. The *Raad van State* thus seems to have assumed in this case that the interests of the protection of birds captured in other Member States and imported into the Netherlands was capable of justifying restrictions to their importation. Again, the *Raad van State* was here implicitly according extra-territorial application to this ground of justification in Article 36. It is of extreme interest to note that the reason that the *Raad van State* felt obliged to make this decision in spite of there being 'possible doubt' and without making an Article 177 reference to the ECJ, was that 'making a preliminary reference to the [ECJ]—given that the applicant wishes to import the birds in question in the short term—offers, in the framework of that procedure, no result'. In other words, the delay which would be involved with an Article 177 reference would, on the facts of this case, have made the reference superfluous. If the importer could not import the birds in question at that time, the possibility that he could import the birds into the Netherlands eighteen months later would be of

---

[258] *Raad van State (Afd. Rechtspraak)* ARRS, 20 Mar. 1984, M & R 1985, 32 (with note by Jans). See also Addink *et al.* (eds.), n. 134 above, 150 & 167.

[259] Pres. *Raad van State (Afd. Rechtspraak)*, 14 Oct. 1992, M & R 1994, 13 (with note by Jans); AB 1994, 128. See also Addink *et al.* (eds.), n. 134 above, 152 & 197.

[260] The birds in question consisted of 50 pairs of *'haakbekken'* and 5 pairs of *'roodvoorhooftkanaries'*.

[261] n. 248 above.

[262] In contrast to the position in *Gourmetterie Van den Burg* Case C–169/89, n. 240 above.

no benefit.[263] We therefore see here a clear example of a case in which a national court refuses to make an Article 177 reference explicitly on the grounds that the length of time involved in such a reference would make the application of little purpose in practice.[264] The *Raad van State* thus decided to deal with the question itself and opted for an interpretation of the protection of animals justification in Article 36 giving that provision, in effect, extra-territorial application.[265] Leaving the Article 177 point to one side, it is submitted that it is commendable that the *Raad van State* recognized that there was possible room for doubt in the ECJ case law concerning the extra-territorial application of Article 36. This is particularly so given that it had, eight years earlier, in the *Opgezette Buizerd* case held that it was beyond doubt that Article 36 had such application. However, it is difficult to disagree with Jans, who observes that given that the burden of proof is on the Member State relying on Article 36 to satisfy that the restriction to the free movement of goods is justified, one would have thought that in the event of doubt, the national court should conclude that principles of free movement of goods should prevail.[266]

The question of the extra-territorial application of the Article 36 justification on the grounds of protection of animals has also arisen before the English Courts. In *R. v. Minister of Agriculture, Fisheries and Food ex. p. Roberts*,[267] the Queen's Bench Division of the High Court was faced with

---

[263] It is interesting to note that more recently in very similar circumstances, the President of the *Rechtbank* Zutphen came to the opposite conclusion. In *X. v. Minister van Landbouw, Natuurbeheer en Visserij*, Pres. *Rechtbank* Zutphen, 15 May 1996, KG 1996, 225, a licence to import certain species of duck into the Netherlands was refused. In interim proceedings, the Dutch court held that it was unable in such proceedings to reach a final view on whether the refusal could be considered proportionate and therefore justified for the protection of animals under Art. 36. However, unlike the *Raad van State* in *Van der Feesten*, the *Rechtbank* Zutphen held that given the doubt as to the application of Art. 36, the right of the applicant to continue in business meant that in the interim, he should be permitted to import as if he had the requisite licence. Although the doubt in the judgment of the *Rechtbank* Zutphen did not centre specifically upon the extra-territorial application of Art. 36, but rather the proportionality of the measure in question, it nevertheless remains interesting that, unlike the *Raad van State* in *Van der Feesten*, the *Rechtbank* Zutphen held that in the event of doubt, free movement of goods must prevail.

[264] See discussion of this point in Ch. 11, sect. 5.

[265] In a recent judgment, the *Raad van State* (*Afd. Bestuursrechtspraak*) has held in a case concerning very similar facts that, in the light of the ECJ's judgment in Case C–149/94, n. 247 above, Directive 79/409 did not apply to birds born and raised in captivity, and thus that the refusal by the Secretary of State for Agriculture to license importation of birds raised in such circumstances in Denmark was incorrectly reasoned: *Wilgers* v. *Staatssecretaris van Landbouw, Natuurbeheer en Visserij, Raad van State (Afd. Bestuursrechtspraak)*, 9 Dec. 1996, NJB 1997, 256. The issue of extra-territorial application of Art. 36 was thus neither raised nor dealt with by the *Raad van State*.

[266] Jans, M & R 1994, 24. Indeed this view has recently been taken by the President of the *Rechtbank* Zutphen in *X. v. Minister van Landbouw, Natuurbeheer en Visserij*, n. 263 above. The issue of extra-territorial application of justifications for restrictions to the free movement of goods has also arisen *obiter dicta* before the Dutch courts concerning the protection of the environment in *Ligtermoet Chemie BV* v. *Landbouw, Natuurbeheer en Visserij*, CBB, 24 Jan. 1992,

an application for judicial review of a decision of the Minister of Agriculture not to refuse to grant export licences for the export of live lambs to France.[268] The objection to export was based on animal rights' grounds[269] following a number of horrifying incidents in France in which farmers had violently mistreated lambs imported from Britain which were being transported to destinations in France. The applicants sought a declaration that the Minister of Agriculture was wrong in law to have stated in the decision that refusal of export licenses was likely to be contrary to Community law. The question of whether Article 34 was breached on those facts is discussed elsewhere in this work.[270] What is of interest in the context of the present discussion is that the High Court held that a ban on export would not be justified for the protection of animals under Article 36 and thus refused the declaration sought by the applicant. Popplewell J in the High Court considered that the Article 36 justification was not available since a ban could not be considered to be proportionate. The High Court reached this conclusion with respect to the proportionality of the measure since it noted that Article 4 of Directive 77/489 on the protection of animals during international transport[271] provided that Member States should 'take all necessary measures to avoid or reduce to a minimum the suffering of animals when strikes or other unforeseen circumstances in their territory impede application of this Directive'. Thus, concluded the High Court, a ban would have been disproportionate since the British authorities had complained to the French authorities which had a duty to comply with the Directive.[272] The High Court did not raise the issue of the

AB 1992, 253, M & R 1992, 247. In this case, the *CBB* implicitly expressed doubt that the protection of the environment on the territory of other Member States could justify a restriction on importation of a plant-protection product into the Netherlands.

[267] n. 183 above. It may be noted that there had been an earlier unsuccessful application for judicial review involving the same parties (QBD), 20 Sept. 1990, CO/1657/90, CO/1679/90 (Transcr.: Marten Walsh Cherer) (per Macpherson J). The Court of Appeal subsequently ordered that the renewed application for leave to apply for judicial review should be granted. It is this renewed application which is the subject of discussion here.

[268] The decision of the Minister of Agriculture, Fisheries and Food was based on the Animal Health Act 1981, ss. 37(2) & 39, & the Export of Animals (Protection) Order 1981, Art. 3.

[269] Roberts was representing the Royal Society for the Prevention of Cruelty to Animals.

[270] See discussion at pp. 138–40. It is however very odd that the High Court in this case discussed the Art. 36 justification *before* it examined whether Art. 34 was breached.

[271] [1977] OJ L200/10.

[272] It may be noted that the reasoning (but not the result) of the High Court in this case may be doubted following the recent judgment of the ECJ in *Ex p. Hedley Lomas* (Case C–5/94, n. 244 above) in which the analogous provisions of another animal welfare Directive (n. 247 above) were held to have completely occupied the field excluding recourse to Art. 36. The ECJ rejected the argument that the fact that the Directive did not lay down any Community procedure for monitoring compliance in the event of breach of the Directive's provisions affected this conclusion (see para. 19 of the judgment) and decided the case on the basis that 'a Member State may not unilaterally adopt, on its own authority, corrective or protective measures designed to obviate any breach by another Member State of rules of Community law' (para. 20).

extra-territorial application of Article 36. Nevertheless, it may be noted that the Article 36 justification was rejected on the basis of its disproportionality on the facts of the case, rather than because the extra-territorial application of Article was excluded in principle. The question of the extraterritorial application of the Article 36 justification on the basis of the protection of animals has thus not been conclusively settled before the English Courts.[273]

Thus, the single most important issue to which the national case law interpreting the Article 36 justification on the grounds of the protection of animals has given rise is the question of whether a Member State is entitled to rely on that justification to adopt measures for protecting animals against possible cruelty within the territory of another Member State. Although the ECJ has given certain indications in cases where there is a Community Directive completely occupying the field, the issue has not been directly settled by the ECJ. In particular, the position is uncertain in cases where there is no Directive and the alleged cruelty to animals in the other Member State is not prohibited by EC law. The national courts' response to this issue has ranged from finding that it is 'beyond doubt' that Article 36 may be a justification for protecting animals against possible cruelty within the territory of another Member State, to admitting 'possible doubt' as to the correct position and finally, to deciding the matter on proportionality grounds. The matter is thus ripe for further clarification and case law to guide the national courts.

6 PROTECTION OF NATIONAL TREASURES POSSESSING ARTISTIC, HISTORIC, OR ARCHAEOLOGICAL VALUE

There has been remarkably little ECJ case law interpreting this head of justification in Article 36. The only case before the ECJ in which this issue arose indirectly was in *Commission* v. *Italy*[274] which concerned a tax on the export of works of art from Italy. Although the ECJ held in that case that

---

[273] It is interesting to note that in the context of the freedom to receive services in another Member State under Art. 59 EC, the English High Court has held that such a restriction may be justified on grounds of public policy: *R* v. *Human Fertilisation and Embryology Authority, ex. p. Blood* [1996] 3 CMLR 921. The High Court dismissed an application for judicial review of the decision of the Human Fertilization and Embryology Authority refusing to permit the applicant to take sperm samples, which had been taken from her late husband, to another Member State for the purposes of artificial insemination. By so deciding the High Court was, in effect, according extra-territorial application to the public-policy exception. However, the fact that it amounted to extra-territorial application of that exception was not discussed in the judgt. An appeal in this case to the Court of Appeal was successful but was decided on other grounds: [1997] 2 All ER 687, [1997] 2 CMLR 591. See also *U.* v. *W. (Attorney-General Intervening)* [1997] 2 CMLR 431.

[274] Case 7/68, n. 2 above.

works of art are to be considered 'goods' within the meaning of the Treaty,[275] the ECJ held that the Italian tax fell to be considered under Articles 12 and 16 EC on customs duties and charges having equivalent effect rather than under Articles 30 to 36 EC. The ECJ did not therefore elucidate in that case on the scope of the Article 36 justification which thus remains rather uncertain.

Given that the precise meaning of the term 'national treasures' in Article 36 is unclear, it is a matter of considerable regret that the French *Conseil d'Etat*, in a case concerning the interpretation of Article 36, refused to make a reference to the ECJ on this point. In *Ministre de la culture* v. *Epoux Genty*[276] the *Conseil d'Etat* held that a refusal to grant export authorization for a Chinese earthenware jar was justified under Article 36 and that there was no need to make a reference to the ECJ pursuant to Article 177 EC. The export refusal in question was based on Article 1 of an Act of 23 June 1941, under which objects which were of 'national historical or artistic interest' (*un intérêt national d'histoire ou d'art*) required an authorization from the Secretary of State for Education before they could be exported from France.[277] Genty had inherited the Chinese jar (dating from the Yuan period (1279–1368)) and wished to sell it at auction. However, prior to the auction, the Director of Museums in France wrote a letter to the auctioneers stating that authorization to export the jar would be refused under the above legislation since it was of national historic and artistic value, and requested the auctioneers to announce this to potential bidders, which they duly did.[278] The jar was subsequently sold at auction, but at a price which was well beneath the market value. Genty applied for compensation on the ground, *inter alia*, that the letter and the law of 1941 was in breach of Article 34. The *Conseil d'Etat* held that neither was in breach of Article 34 or 36 'since it is clear that they authorize export restrictions justified, as in this case, by the protection of national treasures possessing artistic, historic, or archaeological value'.[279]

---

[275] The ECJ held that 'goods' include 'products which can be valued in money and which are capable, as such, of forming the subject of commercial transactions'.

[276] *Conseil d'Etat*, 7 Oct. 1987, Rec. Lebon 1987, 304; Dalloz 1988, Jur. 269 (with note by Laveissière); AJDA 1987, 768; Rev. fr. dr. admin. 1988, 861 (including conclusions of *Commissaire du Gouvernement* Van Ruymbeke).

[277] The law had been passed in Vichy France and was never replaced after the end of the Second World War. In this respect it was an out-of-date piece of legislation.

[278] Azibert & De Boisdeffre [1987] AJDA 720 explain that it was common practice for the Director of Museums to write such letters. The practice was developed to enhance and maintain France's position in the international art market by fostering confidence amongst dealers by making it known beforehand which items would be refused authorization for export.

[279] See also *Fxxxx, Cour de Cassation*, ch. crim., 14 Nov. 1996, Arrêt no. 4989 (transcr. available on Lexis) where the *Cour de Cassation* seems simply to have ignored the grounds of appeal based upon Arts. 34 & 36 EC in a case concerning the seizure at the Franco–Belgian border of works of art (*in casu*: paintings by Pissaro & Signac) which had not received the requisite export authorization.

This judgment has been heavily criticized in the literature. The principle complaint is that, in an area where there is next to no ECJ case law interpreting this head of justification in Article 36, the *Conseil d'Etat* should not, especially in such a brief fashion, declare that the export refusal was capable of justification under Article 36.[280] Furthermore, by holding that 'it is clear' (*il ressort clairement*) that Article 36 applies, the *Conseil d'Etat* was explicitly suggesting that the matter was *acte clair*. Given the uncertainties that remain as to the scope of this justification, this appears to be an unduly bold proposition. Azibert and De Boisdeffre point out that the wording of the French Act (*un intérêt national d'histoire ou d'art*) is wider than that of Article 36 (*trésor national*) and that the difference in wording should have prompted the *Conseil d'Etat* into making a reference.[281] Indeed, it is difficult to disagree with the conclusion of Azibert and De Boisdeffre that the *Conseil d'Etat*'s interpretation is unduly wide since it leads to the position that 'any object of historical or artistic interest that is on French territory, even for a very short time, becomes a French "national treasure" for the purposes of the Treaty'.[282] It is also of significant interest that the Commission in its Fifth Annual Report to the European Parliament on Commission Monitoring of the Application of Community Law[283] singles this judgment out for special criticism as 'another example of the undue application of the *acte clair* theory'. The Commission went on to substantiate this by stating that 'since the Court of Justice has in fact rarely had occasion to interpret this provision of the Treaty, the *Conseil d'Etat* should, as a court of last instance, have made a reference for a preliminary ruling'.

The *Genty* case before the *Conseil d'Etat* neatly illustrates the problem which Article 36 poses for the interpretation of national legislation by national courts. The essential question is whether, as the ECJ has held with respect to the 'public morality' derogation, it should be left to each Member State to define the concept of 'national treasures' or whether the ECJ should develop a Community-wide definition of that concept. It is submitted that the *Genty* case illustrates that a Community-wide definition is desirable. Voudouri has pointed out that the different language versions of Article 36 itself underlines the necessity for a cautious interpretation. Thus, the English, French, Danish, and Greek versions refer to concepts akin to 'national treasures', while the Italian, Spanish, and Portuguese ('*patrimonio nazionale*' or '*nacional*') and Dutch ('*national bezit*') versions are more akin to national patrimony.[284] It is suggested that national 'treasures' is stricter than the concept of national 'patrimony'.

---

[280] See Laveissière, Dalloz 1988, Jur. 270.

[281] n. 278 above.

[282] Ibid.

[283] [1987] OJ 1988 C310/44.

[284] Voudouri, 'Circulation et protection des biens culturels dans l'Europe sans frontières' at 486.

Indeed, it is submitted that it would be dangerous to leave the definition of a 'national treasure' to the national courts alone.

National legislation controlling the export of works of art varies widely from Member State to Member State. For example, in the United Kingdom, a national court would have to look to the Import, Export and Customs Powers (Defence) Act 1939 which would require a so-called application of the 'Waverley Criteria' which apply the following three tests:

1. Is the object so closely associated with our history and national life that its departure would be a misfortune?
2. Is the object of outstanding aesthetic importance?
3. Is the object of outstanding significance for the study of some particular branch of art, learning or history?

The Report of Sir Richard Scott's Inquiry into the Export of Defence Equipment to Iraq concluded that the powers based on the Import, Export and Customs Powers (Defence) Act 1939 'are based on wartime emergency legislation lacking provisions for Parliamentary supervision and control that would be expected and are requisite in a modern Parliamentary democracy' and that the Act is deficient in that it contains no indication of the purposes for which export control can legitimately be used.[285] There is thus room for argument both before an English court or the ECJ that the UK legislation is not proportionate.

Similarly, recent French legislation specifies two categories of article which constitute a national treasure:[286]

1. works to be found in public collections, property that has been classified and classified archives; and
2. any other article which is of major interest in the historical, artistic or archaeological fields.

As Polonsky and Canat point out, the second category in particular involves 'a certain subjectivity in determining what constitutes this "major" interest'.[287] Furthermore, since the effect of the French legislation is that an article classified as a national treasure is effectively blocked on French territory, questions of proportionality arise.

Problems thus remain with the definition of national treasures contained in Article 36. Some light has been shed on the matter by Council Directive 93/7 on the return of cultural objects unlawfully removed from the territory of a Member State[288] and Council Regulation 3911/92 on the

---

[285] Scott Report, para. K2.1, cited in Polonsky & Canat, 'The British and French Systems of Control of the Export of Works of Art' (1996) 45 ICLQ 557 at 564. Although the Scott Report did not extend specifically to controls on the export of works of art, it did nevertheless examine the power of the UK Government to impose controls on exports from the UK.

[286] Law of 31 Dec. 1992 Relating to Articles subjected to restrictions on circulation, Law no. 92-1477, JORF 5 Jan. 1993 p. 198. See Frier (1993) AJDA 264 and Voudouri, n. 284 above.

[287] n. 285 above at 583.   [288] [1993] OJ L74/74.

export of cultural goods outside the customs territory of the Community.[289] Directive 93/7 is of particular interest in this context as it contains an annex which defines non-exclusively the term 'cultural goods' by means of minimum age and financial thresholds. Although this annex may be of some use in defining 'national treasures', the preamble to the Directive explicitly states that 'the Annex to this Directive is . . . not intended to define objects which rank as "national treasures" within the meaning of the said Article 36'. Besides, many questions remain unanswered, not least the question as to whether Article 36 refers only to 'treasures' which were produced or created in a Member State of the Community.

Two comments emerge from the above discussion of application by national courts of this head of justification in Article 36, and the *Genty* judgment in particular. First, a Community-wide definition of 'national treasures' would clearly seem to be desirable, particularly in view of the divergences in national legislation and the views of commentators.[290] Such a definition should not be left to each Member State and each national court. Secondly, the *Genty* case provides yet another example of undue and hasty recourse to Article 36 by the national court. Since the latter judgment was handed down by a court of last resort, without making a reference to the ECJ, it constitutes, with utmost respect, an abuse of Article 36.

7 CONCLUSIONS

As was noted at the outset, national courts' application of Article 36 justifications is at the sharp end of their application of EC law. Indeed, the granting of such justifications is the point at which the Community system entrusts the greatest amount of responsibility to the national courts. It is therefore essential that they carry out this duty diligently.

The analysis of the national case law in this chapter has given rise to some examples where the potential for legal disunity has been exposed. For example, in the context of the public morality justification, we have seen the literal interpretation of ECJ authorities by the English courts developing into precedents misapplying EC law which are followed by other courts within the national legal system. Furthermore, the French

---

[289] [1992] OJ L395/1.

[290] See Pescatore, 'Le commerce de l'art et le marché commun' (1985) RTDE 456; Voudouri, n. 284 above; Mattera, 'La libre circulation des oeuvres d'art à l'intérieur de la Communauté et la protection des trésors nationaux ayant une valeur artistique, historique ou archéologique'; Margue, 'L'exportation des biens culturels dans le cadre du Grand Marché' (1993) RMUE 89; von Plehwe, 'European Union and the Free Movement of Cultural Goods' (1995) 20 ELRev 431; Polonsky and Canat, n. 287 above; Oliver, n. 28 above, 221–4, Biondi, 'The Merchant, the Thief and the Citizen: The Circulation of Works of Art Within the European Union'.

courts have, for example, accorded a different (and broader) meaning to 'public policy' than either the ECJ or other courts in other Member States. The question which arises at this point is whether this potential for disunity makes it desirable for the ECJ to develop definitions of the concepts provided for in Article 36 which would thus apply throughout the Community. The discussion in this chapter has demonstrated that in some of the categories mentioned in Article 36, a Community-wide definition is indeed essential. A Community-wide definition of 'national treasures' seems indispensable; however, in other fields, such a the protection of public health, it seems that the present approach of leaving the level of protection in the absence of harmonization, to the Member States (subject to the proportionality test) is a sensible one. It is evident that the latter view assumes a competent application of the proportionality test (contained implicitly in the second sentence of Article 36) by the national courts. In particular, since ECJ case law interpreting Article 36 clearly shows that the justifications mentioned in that Article are to be given a narrow scope, the application of the proportionality test becomes crucial. The single most important conclusion which emerges from the discussion in this chapter is that the application of the proportionality principle by the national courts is extremely erratic. All the heads of justification in Article 36 discussed in this chapter have given rise to examples before the national courts in which these courts have been far too quick in deciding that a particular national measure is justified. This is largely due to a neglect on the part of these courts to carry out a rigorous application of the proportionality principle. In some national courts, the application of this principle of Community law is complicated by the overlap with other similar, but not identical, concepts of national public law. The unsatisfactory application of the proportionality test by the national courts inevitably gives rise to the question of whether it would be desirable for the ECJ to itself decide the proportionality question in individual cases. The discussion in this chapter strongly suggests that the ECJ should refrain from adopting such an approach under the current system set up by Article 177 EC. Not only are their practical problems inherent in the ECJ engaging in fact-finding, but also there is the danger that the ECJ will make findings of fact which are either flawed (as in the public morality cases) or which are subsequently too literally applied by the national courts in later cases (as in the public-health cases in particular).

The application of Article 36 by the national courts has some way to go before it can be said with confidence that they are applying these justifications to the free movement of goods in a satisfactory fashion. In particular, it is submitted that these courts should be encouraged to further develop in their application of a rigorous proportionality test. Given the emerging maturity and familiarity of these courts in applying EC law, there seems to be little reason why these courts should not, subject to the reservations set out above, continue to be entrusted with the dynamic application of derogations to the free movement of goods in individual cases.

8

Intellectual Property Rights

1 INTRODUCTION

National intellectual property legislation, by its very nature, tends to contribute to a partitioning of the market along national lines. The very existence of such legislation inevitably restricts the free movement of goods and conflicts with the principle of market integration. At first sight, it would appear that the EC Treaty upholds the validity of national intellectual property rights. Article 36 EC provides for an exception to the principle of the free movement of goods for 'the protection of industrial and commercial property' and Article 222 EC provides that the EC Treaty 'shall in no way prejudice the rules in Member States governing the system of property ownership'. In the absence of harmonization,[1] it has fallen upon the ECJ to reconcile the conflict between the prohibition on any restrictions to the free movement of goods provided for in Articles 30 and 34 with the recognition in Articles 36 and 222 of national intellectual property rights. The ECJ has attempted to achieve such a reconciliation by drawing a distinction (originally in competition law cases)[2] between the 'existence' of intellectual property rights and the 'exercise' of them. It has held that the former is unaffected by the EC Treaty (in line with Article 222 EC) but that the latter may still fall within the EC Treaty's rules on the free movement of goods if 'exercised' in a way which unjustifiably restricts the single market. In this way, the ECJ has been able to apply Article 30 to cases involving intellectual property rights.

It should be noted that the approach adopted by the ECJ is not based on strong theoretical foundations.[3] The distinction between the 'existence' and 'exercise' of intellectual property rights amounts to little more than a

---

[1] Community harmonizing legislation in the field of intellectual property rights include: Council Directive 89/104 to approximate the laws of the Member States relating to trade marks [1989] OJ L40/1; Council Directive 91/250 on the legal protection of computer programs [1991] OJ L122/42; Council Directive 92/100 on rental right and lending right and on certain rights related to copyright in the field of intellectual property [1992] OJ L346/61; Council Directive 93/83 on the co-ordination of certain rules concerning copyright and rights related to copyright applicable to satellite broadcasting and cable retransmission [1993] OJ L248/15; Council Directive 93/98 harmonizing the term of protection of copyright and certain related rights [1993] OJ L290/9; and Council Regulation 40/94 on the Community trade mark [1994] OJ L11/1.

[2] See Cases 56 and 58/64 *Consten and Grundig* v. *Commission* [1966] ECR 299, [1966] CMLR 418 & Case 24/67 *Parke Davis* v. *Centrafarm* [1968] ECR 55, [1968] CMLR 47.

[3] See discussion in Rothnie, *Parallel Imports*, 374.

sleight of hand. For example, if it is indeed the 'exercise' of the intellectual property right which is at issue, this is at odds with the fact that Article 30 is addressed to measures 'enacted by Member States' and not to the actions of individuals.[4] If, however, one responds to this objection by pointing out that although it is true that the barrier to the free movement of goods only arises when an individual relies on the national intellectual property legislation, it is nevertheless that legislation itself, rather than the action of the individual, which should be identified as the measure having equivalent effect prohibited by Article 30, then one is back to the 'existence' of the intellectual property right itself rather than to its 'exercise'. Notwithstanding these theoretical difficulties, the ECJ has developed a commendable body of case law which has proved to be durable and flexible and based on practical and realistic tests for the national courts to apply.

In a nutshell, the ECJ's approach in intellectual property cases may be described as follows: once it has been established that reliance on a national intellectual property right prevents importation (and thus breaches Article 30), the ECJ proceeds to examine whether the intellectual property right in question falls within the definition of 'industrial and commercial property' provided for in Article 36, and if so, whether such reliance constitutes an 'arbitrary discrimination or a disguised restriction on trade' contrary to the second sentence in Article 36. In carrying out the latter examination, the ECJ identifies the 'specific subject-matter' or 'essential function' of the intellectual property right in question and analyses whether its 'exercise' in the given case is justified for the purpose of safeguarding rights which constitute the 'specific subject-matter' of that right. In particular, the ECJ will find that the 'exercise' of an intellectual property right is not necessitated by the 'specific subject-matter' of that right once the goods in question have been placed on the market in another Member State by the person who owns the intellectual property rights represented by the goods or with that person's 'consent'. In such a case, the intellectual property right is held to be 'exhausted' because the intellectual property right owner has been paid, or at least had the opportunity of being paid, in the other Member State for the rights embodied in the goods.

The above analysis is centred around three central concepts. First, the 'specific subject-matter' of a particular intellectual property right. The ECJ's definition of the specific subject-matter of patents, copyright and trade marks will be set out in the sections that follow. Secondly, the doctrine of 'exhaustion of rights'. The rationale of this doctrine is the principle that the intellectual property right owner must not be allowed to enjoy two bites of the same cherry. Thus, if the intellectual property right owner mar-

---

[4] See discussion of this point in Ch. 2, sect. 4.

kets his product in State A, where he holds an intellectual property right in the product, and a third party parallel imports that product into State B, where the same intellectual property right owner also holds an intellectual property right in the product, to allow such a party to rely on his right in State B to prevent importation would be to allow him two bites of the same cherry. The intellectual property right owner would, in effect, be able to enjoy the benefit of the right (whether that be in the form of royalties, the right to exclusively use an invention or the enjoyment of the reputation of a particular mark) in both State A and B with regard to the same product. In such a case, the ECJ holds that the intellectual property right owner has 'exhausted' his right in State A which precludes reliance on the equivalent right to stop importation into State B.[5]

Thirdly, there is the concept of 'consent'. This concept arises where the owner of an intellectual property right in State B wishes to prevent the importation of a product protected by the intellectual property right from State A, where he does not own the equivalent intellectual property right (either because no such right exists in State A or because no such right has yet been registered there). In such a case, the ECJ holds that if the intellectual property right holder has 'consented' to the marketing in State A he must therefore accept the consequences of this choice and he is therefore precluded from relying on the intellectual property right in State B to prevent importation.[6] The ECJ has set out this principle with respect to patents in *Merck* v. *Stephar*[7] in the following terms:

It is for the proprietor of the patent to decide, in the light of all the circumstances, under what conditions he will market his product, including the possibility of marketing it in a Member State where the law does not provide patent protection for the product in question. If he decides to do so he must then accept the consequences of his choice as regards the free movement of the product within the Common Market, which is a fundamental principle forming part of the legal and economic circumstances which must be taken into account by the proprietor of the patent in determining the manner in which his exclusive right will be exercised.[8]

This approach has recently been challenged by the English High Court in *Merck* v. *Primecrown*[9] which referred questions on similar facts to the ECJ suggesting that it reconsider or at least limit the scope of the 'consent' rule. In particular, the High Court wished to know whether a legal or ethical obligation to market in a Member State was capable of vitiating

[5] See, e.g., Case 15/74 *Centrafarm* v. *Sterling Drug* [1974] ECR 1147, [1974] 2 CMLR 480 & Case 16/74 *Centrafarm* v. *Winthrop* [1974] ECR 1183, [1974] 2 CMLR 480.

[6] See, e.g., Case 78/70 *Deutsche Grammophon* v. *Metro SB Grossmarkt GmbH* [1971] ECR 487, [1971] CMLR 631 and Cases 55 & 57/80 *Musik-Vertrieb Membran* v. *GEMA* [1981] ECR 147, [1981] 2 CMLR 44.

[7] Case 187/80 [1981] ECR 2063, [1981] 2 CMLR 463.

[8] Ibid. at para. 11 of judgt.   [9] [1996] 3 CMLR 724.

consent. Contrary to the opinion of Advocate General Fennelly,[10] the ECJ saw no reason to reconsider the underlying rationale of the 'consent' concept, except to concede that a genuine legal (but not ethical) obligation to market in a Member State does not amount to giving 'consent' to market the goods concerned.[11]

The volume of national case law concerning intellectual property rights and the free movement of goods is large. This is not surprising when one considers the huge commercial interests that are at stake in such cases involving the exclusive right to market goods in the Community's Member States. The principles governing this important area of EC law were only really fully worked out by the ECJ during the second half of the 1970s. As such the national courts may be forgiven for thinking prior to that that 'Articles 30 to 34 . . . are not, it is thought, on their wording *prima facie* apposite to cover measures such as the grant of an interlocutory injunction to protect patent rights'.[12] Indeed, the approach adopted by the ECJ in its case law was, at the time, unexpected. This is demonstrated by the progress of the litigation in the 1970s before the Dutch courts in *Ciba Geigy AG* v. *De Chemische Fabriek Brabant J. W. Voorbraak BV* where the Dutch courts failed to anticipate the developments in ECJ case law. The case concerned attempts by Ciba Geigy to rely on its patent in the Netherlands (for a preparation for slowing down plant growth) to prevent parallel importation by Voorbraak BV of the patented good from France where Ciba Geigy marketed the good in question under its equivalent French patent. In interim proceedings (*kort geding*) the President of the *Arrondissementsrechtbank* Breda referred to the territorial working of patent protection and held that Ciba Geigy could rely on Article 36 to prevent importation in breach of its Dutch patent.[13] However, in the interim, the ECJ delivered its seminal judgment in *Centrafarm* v. *Sterling Drug*[14] where, as has been discussed, it held that in such circumstances the patent right in France was 'exhausted' when Ciba Geigy first marketed the product there and thus that reliance on the patent held in the Netherlands to partition off the Dutch market was precluded. Following this ECJ judgment the *Arrondissementsrechtbank* Breda held at full trial that the interim judgment could no longer stand and duly lifted the injunction thereby allowing Voorbraak BV to resume import.[15] The matter was further complicated when Ciba Geigy's patent in France, though not in the Netherlands, subsequently expired. In two judgments, the *Gerechtshof*'s-

---

[10] Opinion of 6 June 1996.

[11] Cases C–267 & 268/95 [1996] ECR I–6285. See also Case 19/84 *Pharmon* v. *Hoechst* [1985] ECR 2281, [1985] 3 CMLR 775.

[12] ChDivision of English High Court in *Minnesota Mining* v. *Geerpres* [1973] 1 CMLR 259 at 264 (per Graham J).

[13] Pres. *Arrondissementsrechtbank* Breda (Kort Geding), 12 June 1973, transcr.

[14] Case 15/74, n. 5 above.   [15] *Arrondissementsrechtbank* Breda, 10 Feb. 1976, transcr.

Hertogenbosch held that after the expiry of the patent in France, there ceased to be parallel patents in both Member States and that consequently the *Centrafarm* v. *Sterling Drug* dicta ceased to apply. The *Gerechtshof* held that the territorial principle continued to apply for patents which were protected under national law when there is no parallel patent in the State of export.[16] Again, the ECJ subsequently had occasion in *Merck* v. *Stephar*[17] to hold that even if there is no parallel patent in the State of export, free movement of goods must prevail if the product was marketed in the exporting State with the owner's 'consent'. As a result of this development, the *Ciba Geigy* v. *Voorbraak BV* case was successfully appealed to the *Hoge Raad* which held that the judgment of the *Gerechtshof*'s-Hertogenbosch could no longer stand in the light of the ECJ's judgment in *Merck* v. *Stephar*.[18] The progress of the litigation in this case before the Dutch courts thus demonstrates the extent to which the development of the ECJ case law on intellectual property rights was unexpected by the national courts. However, although the national courts in this case failed to anticipate the ECJ judgments first in *Centrafarm* v. *Sterling Drug* and then in *Merck* v. *Stephar*, they certainly had little difficulty in giving them full effect on appeal. Indeed, the development of the ECJ approach to intellectual property rights and the free movement of goods throughout the 1970s was extremely bold, but also clear, thereby facilitating easy application by the national courts. The doctrine of 'exhaustion of rights' and the concept of 'consent' provide a simple test or rule of thumb for the national courts to apply. Consequently the ECJ case law, although based on shaky theoretical foundations, has proved durable by providing practical and realistic tests for the national courts to apply.

National case law adjudicating the validity of national intellectual property rights as against the free movement of goods will be discussed in the remainder of this chapter. National case law concerning patents, copyright and trade marks will be examined in turn and following that, special problems to which application by national courts has given rise will be identified. Amongst the latter problems which will be discussed in greater detail is the extent of intrusion that Article 36 should be permitted in defining the scope of national intellectual property rights, the meaning of 'consent', the question of whether one has to first sue for the intellectual property right infringement in the other Member State before one can prevent importation, questions dealing with the burden of proof, and finally the issue of importation from third countries.

---

[16] *Gerechtshof* 's-Hertogenbosch, 10 Apr. 1981 & 8 April 1983, RvdW 1984, 190, NJ 1985, 547.

[17] Case 187/80, n. 7 above.

[18] *Hoge Raad*, 16 Nov. 1984, NJ 1985, 547 (with notes by Heemskerk and Wichers Hoeth), BIE 1985, 30.

2 PATENTS

The ECJ has defined the specific subject-matter of patents as:

the guarantee that the patentee, to reward the creative effort of the inventor, has the exclusive right to use an invention with a view to manufacturing industrial products and putting them into circulation for the first time, either directly or by the grant of licences to third parties, as well as the right to oppose infringements.[19]

The application of the ECJ case law discussed above has presented very few difficulties in the national courts with respect to patents. The correct analysis seems to have filtered through to the national courts quickly and accurately. Thus in 1976 in *AGA Aktiebolag Zweden* v. *Indesit* the President of the *Arrondissementsrechtbank* Utrecht held that the exercise of a patent (in the production of a part of a television set) to enforce a temporary monopoly to recoup research expenses was within the specific subject-matter of patents. The Dutch court held that Article 36 could be relied upon to prevent the importation of television sets infringing this patent from other Member States unless an attempt was being made to partition markets within the Community by the patent holder or with his consent. Since such was not the case on the facts of this case, the restriction to the free movement of goods was held to be justified.[20]

'Licences of Right' under the Patents Act 1977

In the United Kingdom, the Patents Act 1977 (which entered into force on 1 June 1978) has been the subject of important litigation before both the English courts and the ECJ. In order to discuss this case law, it is necessary to first briefly describe the background to this legislation. The EC law difficulties that have arisen have resulted from the fact that the 1977 Act extended the period of validity of United Kingdom patents from sixteen to twenty years (in conformity with the provisions of the European Patent Convention). The 'trade-off' in the Act, contained in Schedule 1, was that a patent whose remaining period of validity on 1 June 1978 was greater than five years would be endorsed 'licenses of right' during the last four years of its period of validity. Section 46(3)(a) of the Act provided that where a patent had been endorsed 'licences of right', 'any person shall, at any time after the entry is made, be entitled as of right to a licence under the patent on such terms as may be settled by agreement or, in default of

---

[19] Case 15/74, n. 5 above at para. 9. See also Case 187/80, n. 7 above at para. 4.
[20] Pres. *Arrondissementsrechtbank* Utrecht, 9 Nov. 1976, BIE 1977, 55. For a similar case before the Dutch courts illustrating the quick and accurate application of ECJ case law in the field of patents, see *Utina Electowerk GmbH* v. *La Buvette SA*, Pres. *Arrondissementsrechtbank* Zwolle, 20 May 1977, BIE 1978, 62.

agreement, by the Comptroller on the application of the proprietor of the patent or the person requiring the licence'.[21]

The litigation concerning the free movement of goods centred on two provisions of the Patents Act 1977. Firstly, section 46(3)(c) provided that

If in proceedings for infringement of the patent (*otherwise than by the importation* of any article) the defendant or defender undertakes to take a licence on such terms, no injunction or interdict shall be granted against him and the amount (if any) recoverable against him by way of damages shall not exceed double the amount which should have been payable by him as a licensee if such a licence on those terms had been granted before the earliest infringement.[22]

This provision was challenged in *Allen & Hanburys Ltd* v. *Generics (UK) Ltd* which exercised all the higher English courts right up to the House of Lords, which eventually made a reference to the ECJ.[23] Allen & Hanburys manufactured the drug salbutamol, the patent for which they held in a number of European countries, but not in Italy because, at the time, patents were not available for drugs in Italy. Allen & Hanburys' UK patent had been granted under the Patents Act 1949 and would have expired sixteen years after the granting of the patent. However, under the Patents Act 1977, the terms were extended by four years during which period they were endorsed 'licences of right'. Generics wished to import into the UK salbutamol which had been manufactured in Italy without Allen & Hanburys' consent or licence. In August 1984, having failed to negotiate terms with Allen & Hanburys for a licence, Generics applied to the Comptroller of Patents under Section 46(3)(a) Patents Act 1977 to settle the terms of a 'licence of right' and they informed Allen & Hanburys that they intended to import the drug and would pay whatever royalty was eventually fixed by the Comptroller. Allen & Hanburys brought an action to protect their patent from infringement and applied for an injunction.

On the face of it, the case is not a difficult one with respect to the provisions of EC law on the free movement of goods. Allen & Hanburys held the patent in the United Kingdom and was attempting to stop the importation of goods from Italy, not connected to Allen & Hanburys nor produced in Italy with its consent, from breaching its United Kingdom patent. At first sight, it would seem that this factual circumstance is covered by the ECJ judgments in *Merck* v. *Stephar*[24] and *Centrafarm* v. *Sterling Drug*[25] and

---

[21] This section has been interpreted by the House of Lords in *Allen & Hanburys* v. *Generics* [1986] RPC 203 at 242 such that the Comptroller of Patents may exercise this discretion taking into account ss. 48 & 50 (set out below).

[22] Emphasis added.

[23] The passage of this litigation is an example, if ever there was one, of a case where early reference would have been far more satisfactory from the point of view of the saving of costs and time for the parties. It may be noted that by the time the ECJ finally handed down its judgment, the patent in question had expired and the judgment was thus of little purpose.

[24] Case 187/80, n. 7 above.   [25] Case 15/74, n. 5 above.

that the doctrine of 'exhaustion of rights' would not apply since there had been no such exhaustion in Italy by the intellectual property right holder and, since the products had not been marketed in Italy with his consent, the intellectual property right held in the United Kingdom could be relied on to preclude free movement. Appearances can, however, be deceptive. A closer reading of Section 46(3)(c) Patents Act 1977 (set out above) makes it plain that whilst the Comptroller of Patents, in proceedings for patent infringement, had the competence to impose terms prohibiting importation of the product covered by the patent, the same was not true of an undertaking which manufactured the product in the national territory which could be certain of obtaining a licence. This in effect meant that no injunction would be granted against an infringer who manufactured the product in the United Kingdom provided that he undertook to take a licence on the terms set by the Comptroller-General. Undertakings which infringed the patent by importing from other Member States, on the other hand, could be the subject of such an injunction. Furthermore, the amount of any damages which could be awarded against an infringer who manufactured the product in the United Kingdom could not exceed double the amount which would have been payable by him as licensee, whereas no such limit applied in the case of an undertaking which infringed the exclusive rights by means of importation.

The English courts took the view that Allen & Hanburys could rely on their patent to prevent importation. In the Chancery Division (Patents Court) of the High Court,[26] Falconer J seems to have been seduced by the fact that the ECJ authorities in *Centrafarm* v. *Sterling Drug* and *Merck* v. *Stephar* covered this factual situation in that the importation of the product was from a Member State where the product was not patentable and had not been manufactured by the patentee or with his licence or consent. Thus, Falconer J held that following *Merck* v. *Stephar*, the Comptroller was entitled to make an order preventing importation as this would be justifiable under Article 36 EC. As seductive as this may be, it is submitted that it is not correct. The essential mistake that Falconer J made was to assume that in the *Centrafarm* v. *Sterling Drug* and *Merck* v. *Stephar* cases the ECJ held '*the only limitation* to the exercise of patent rights in the EEC is exhaustion under the doctrine of exhaustion of rights'.[27] This suggestion is incorrect. There is nothing in the ECJ's judgments in *Merck* or *Centrafarm* to suggest this. Furthermore, Falconer J failed to recognize that Article 36 EC is made up of two sentences, the second of which prevents 'arbitrary discrimination' and 'disguised restrictions on trade'. This second sentence operates to catch measures which, although falling within one of the heads in the first sentence, encourage domestic manufacture. Under Section

26 [1985] 1 CMLR 619, [1985] FSR 229.
27 [1985] 1 CMLR 619 at 636. Emphasis added.

46(3)(c) Patents Act 1977, the patentee was confined to his remedy in damages for domestically produced goods whereas in the case of imported products, he could obtain an injunction. This difference in remedy amounted to a difference in treatment between products manufactured in the United Kingdom and those manufactured elsewhere in the Community. It is submitted therefore that Falconer J was seduced by the ECJ authorities which he implemented too literally and was blind to the discriminatory effect of the provisions.

The majority of the Court of Appeal went down the same road as Falconer J had in the Chancery Division.[28] May LJ concluded that 'the decided cases in the European Court show that the only limit on the protection given to patents by Article 36 is that arising out of what is described as the doctrine of the exhaustion of rights'.[29] He continued, '[i]n my opinion the issue and material facts in the instant case are in truth indistinguishable from those in *Centrafarm*.'[30] For the same reasons as are set out above, May LJ made the same errors in applying the Community provisions on free movement of goods as Falconer J had in the High Court. Slade LJ concurred with May LJ but produced other, equally incorrect, reasons for why there was no arbitrary discrimination contrary to Article 36. Apart from relying heavily on the exhaustion of rights doctrine, he placed emphasis on the fact that the reason that an injunction could be granted against imports was that, unlike the case of domestically produced goods, the importer was not likely to have any substantial assets in the United Kingdom. According to Slade LJ, persons who intend to exploit the patent in the United Kingdom without importing were *ex hypothesi* likely to have assets in the jurisdiction against which the patentee could proceed. Furthermore, Slade LJ opined that to constitute arbitrary discrimination, there must be a 'dominant motive' on the part of the legislator to give more favourable treatment to the products of their country than to those of other Member States. This led him to conclude that 'I see no reason to infer that the legislature, in reserving this special power to the Court by this particular subsection, had any intention of discriminating in favour of our national products'.[31] With due respect, it is submitted that this view is, as an interpretation of EC law, plainly wrong. Firstly, it is submitted that the fact that manufacturers do not have adequate assets in the United Kingdom should have been irrelevant. As the ECJ subsequently pointed out in its judgment when the case was referred to it by the House of Lords,

---

[28] [1986] 1 CMLR 101, [1986] RPC 203. It may be noted that although the Court of Appeal lifted the injuction imposed by Falconer J in the High Court (in line with its earlier judgment in *Beecham Group Plc* v. *Gist-Brocades NV* [1985] FSR 379), the majority nevertheless agreed with the lower court that the Comptroller of Patents could prevent imports which it held would be in conformity with Art. 36.

[29] [1986] 1 CMLR 101 at 115.   [30] Ibid. at 117.   [31] Ibid. at 129.

'such guarantees of payment can only be included among the terms fixed in the licensing agreement or, in default of an agreement, by the competent national authority'.[32] Secondly, Slade LJ's comment that the legislator had no intention of discriminating against imports is also fallacious as it is clear from the jurisprudence of the ECJ that it is the *effect* of the measures which is the crucial factor. In the present case, there was indeed such a discriminatory effect.

In an excellent dissenting judgment on the EC law points, Lloyd LJ clearly rejected the arguments of the other judges in the Court of Appeal that 'the *only* limitation on the exercise of patent rights in Community law is the exhaustion of those rights' (emphasis in original). Lloyd LJ continued: 'With all respect to the learned Judge, I doubt whether this is true; and I do not think it is established by the *Centrafarm* or *Merck* cases, or any other case to which we have been referred'.[33] On appeal before the House of Lords, Lord Diplock noted the dissenting opinion of Lloyd LJ on this point 'which itself goes some way towards showing that it was not *acte clair*' and referred the point to the ECJ.[34] The subsequent judgment of the ECJ[35] underlines the inadequate analyses provided by the English courts in this case. The ECJ confirmed that, contrary to what the High Court and the majority of the Court of Appeal had held, the United Kingdom was indeed precluded from allowing the issue of an injunction to prohibit the importation from another Member State of a product which infringed a patent endorsed 'licence of right' against an importer who had undertaken to take a licence on the terms prescribed by law, where no such injunction may be issued in the same circumstances against an infringer who manufactured the product in the United Kingdom. The ECJ went on to explicitly hold that this would constitute arbitrary discrimination prohibited by Article 36 and could not therefore be justified on grounds of the protection of industrial and commercial property and that this conclusion was not affected by the fact that the product in question was a pharmaceutical product imported from a Member State in which it is not patentable.[36]

---

[32] Case 434/85 [1988] ECR 1245, [1988] 1 CMLR 701 at para. 17 of judgt.

[33] n. 29 above at 136.

[34] [1986] 1 WLR 51 at 67. It was also held that imports from other EC Member States should not be allowed pending the ruling of the ECJ on the questions remitted to that court by the House of Lords: *Allen & Hanburys Ltd's (Salbutamol) Patent* [1987] RPC 327.

[35] Case 434/85, n. 32 above.

[36] It may be noted that the House of Lords had little difficulty in implementing the ECJ judgment: [1989] 2 CMLR 325, [1989] 1 WLR 414. As a more 'positive' footnote to the above cases, it is interesting to note the speed with which the ECJ's judgment in *Allen & Hanburys* v. *Generics* had an effect in the English courts. Ten days after the ECJ's judgment, the High Court in *EI du Pont de Nemours & Co* v. *Enka BV* (No. 2) [1988] RPC 497 set aside an existing injunction against patent infringement in the light of the ECJ's judgment. It is impressive to see an English court reacting so quickly and confidently to an ECJ judgment even before the referring court (the House of Lords) in *Allen & Hanburys* itself had implemented the ECJ's judgment.

The judgments of the English courts in *Allen & Hanburys Ltd* v. *Generics (UK) Ltd* were thus far from satisfactory as they accorded far too much importance to the doctrine of exhaustion of rights as the only principle applicable under Article 36 which blinded them to the clearly discriminatory elements in Section 46(3)(c) Patents Act 1977.

The second provision of the 1977 Patents Act which gave rise to litigation was Section 48(3) which provided that the Comptroller of Patents could grant compulsory licences under a patent:

(a) Where the patented invention is capable of being commercially worked in the United Kingdom, that it is not being so worked to the fullest extent that is reasonably practicable;

(b) where the patented invention is a product, that a demand for the product in the United Kingdom—

 . . . . (ii) *is being met to a substantial extent by importation.*

(c) where the patented invention is capable of being commercially worked in the United Kingdom, that it is being prevented or hindered from being so worked—

 (i) where the invention is a product, by the importation of the product

 . . .

(d) that by reason of the refusal of the proprietor of the patent to grant a licence on reasonable terms—

 (i) a market for the export of any patented product made in the United Kingdom is not being supplied, or

 . . .

 (iii) the establishment or development of commercial or industrial activities in the United Kingdom is unfairly prejudiced.[37]

The grant of a compulsory licence under this provision was contested before the English courts in *Extrude Hone* v. *Heathway Machine Sales*. This case concerned a patent relating to a method, apparatus, and material for abrading or honing surfaces. Heathway Machine Sales applied under Section 48(1) of the Patent Act 1977 for a compulsory licence of the patent relying on Section 48(3). Extrude Hone contested the applicability of Section 48(3) by arguing that it was contrary to Article 30 EC. In particular, Extrude Hone argued that if a compulsory licence was granted under Section 48(3), this would amount to a clear preference for United Kingdom manufacture over foreign manufacture. It was pointed out that the grant of a compulsory licence against the wishes of a patentee was a penalty, and that to penalize a patentee for meeting the demand for his invention in the United Kingdom by importation from an EC Member State was discrimination against that Member State and had an effect equivalent to that of a quantitative restriction on importation contrary to Article 30 EC. The English courts thought otherwise. Both the Superintending Examiner of

---

[37] Emphasis added.

Patents (Patent Office)[38] and the High Court (Chancery Division–Patents Court)[39] held that the United Kingdom legislation did not breach Article 30 even though they accepted that imports were reduced as a result of it. Whitford J in the High Court held that

The general scheme of the Treaty of Rome is well known. One of the main objects is to avoid prohibitions or restrictions on the development of economic activities. Another object is to encourage competition and to ensure so far as possible that competition in the Common Market countries is not distorted by restrictions other than those which are in specially excepted categories, as we find in Article 36. The grant of a compulsory licence is plainly not in terms a quantitative restriction. Nor is it, in my view, a measure having equivalent effect. It is, however, calculated to encourage competition and is entirely in accord with the general concept of the Treaty.[40]

It is submitted that it is beyond argument that Section 48(3) had an 'actual or potential effect' on trade between Member States and thus breached Article 30 EC.[41] Indeed, the provisions of the Patents Act were classic 'local grab' measures, since they encouraged the holder of a patent who wanted to maintain exclusivity to locate production in the United Kingdom, thereby stimulating investment and employment in the United Kingdom. For the purposes of the present discussion, it is submitted that it is equally clear that the English court erred in *Extrude Hone* v. *Heathway Machine Sales* by suggesting that the restriction caused by the Patents Act provisions were justified since the legislation was 'calculated to encourage competition and is entirely in accord with the general concept of the Treaty'. It is respectfully submitted that the High Court would have done better to stick more closely to the provisions in Article 36 rather than drawing on wider notions as to what it thought to be within the 'general scheme' of the EC Treaty. Indeed, just over ten years later, the ECJ had the opportunity to hold that these very provisions of the Patents Act 1977 breached Article 30 and with respect to Article 36 justification, the ECJ held that

[T]here is no reason relating to the specific subject-matter of the patent to justify the discrimination inherent in the contested provisions between exploiting the patent in the form of production on the national territory and exploiting it by importation from the territory of other Member States. Such discrimination is in fact motivated not by the specific requirements of industrial and commercial property but . . . by the national legislature's concern to encourage domestic production.[42]

---

[38] [1981] 3 CMLR 379, [1982] RPC 361.   [39] Ibid.

[40] [1981] 3 CMLR 379 at 404–5.

[41] Criticism of the breach of Art. 30 analysis by the English courts in this case is set out at p. 117. The fact that Art. 30 was infringed is confirmed by a judgment of the ECJ to this effect in Case C–30/90 *Commission* v. *United Kingdom* [1992] ECR I–829, [1992] 2 CMLR 709. Noted by Gormley (1993) 18 ELRev. 66.

[42] Ibid. at paras. 28 & 29.

The English judgments in *Extrude Hone* v. *Heathway Machine Sales* were thus clearly incorrect. It is therefore regrettable that no Article 177 reference was made to the ECJ. Indeed, the fact that the matter was incorrectly decided by the English courts in this case without seeking an Article 177 reference from the ECJ must thus be seen as a missed opportunity in the 'dual vigilance' system of policing national legislation contrary to the EC Treaty.

A sequel, of sorts, to the factual situation in *Extrude Hone* v. *Heathway Machine Sales* arose before the English courts in *Smith Kline and French Laboratories* v. *Generics*. In this case, Smith Kline and French (SKF) owned the patent for a pharmaceutical product 'Cimetidine' (marketed under the name 'Tagamet') which it exploited by manufacturing the raw material form in Ireland, making up the finished product in the United Kingdom. By virtue of the Patents Act 1977, SKF's patents for 'Cimetidine' in the United Kingdom were extended for a further four years during which period they were endorsed 'licences of right'. Generics applied for 'licences of right' to import Cimitidine into the United Kingdom from third countries (non-Member States). It was in this sense a sequel to the *Extrude Hone* case because, as we have seen, that case concerned imports from other Member States of the Community whilst the question under consideration in this case was whether, on the basis of those national provisions, the competent authorities could, for the purpose of refusing or granting the licensee of right for the authorization to import the product from *non-member countries*, take into account the Member State in which the proprietor of the patent manufactured the product. Both the Comptroller of Patents[43] and the Patents Court[44] granted the compulsory licence sought by Generics to import Cimitidine in raw material form (though not in finished-product form) from non-Member States on the grounds that demand for the raw materials of the patented product were being satisfied by SKF (the patent-holder) on the domestic market by imports from another Member State (Ireland). Fortunately the case was appealed to the English Court of Appeal[45] which referred questions to the ECJ. The ECJ came to a different interpretation of EC law to that of the lower English Courts in this case and held that Article 30 was indeed infringed by such legislation and was not justified for the protection of industrial and commercial property under Article 36 because it discriminated against production in other Member States.[46] It is a pity that the decision of the Comptroller of Patents and the Patents Court were never reported; the reasoning which these courts adopted in order to reach their

---

[43] Decision of the Comptroller of Patents, 13 Mar. 1988.
[44] Judgment of the Patents Court (per Falconer J), 2 Mar. 1989.
[45] [1990] 1 CMLR 416, [1990] RPC 203.
[46] Case C–191/90 [1992] ECR I–5335, [1993] 1 CMLR 89.

result is thus unknown. However, it is enough to point out that they both came to the wrong result as to EC law, and the progress of the litigation thus provides yet another warning of the dangers of national courts giving their interpretation of EC law without referral to the ECJ at an early stage.

The cases before the English courts dealing with the compatibility of the provisions of the Patents Act 1977 concerning 'licences of right' provide examples of poor applications of Article 36 with respect to discriminatory provisions in national patent legislation. In both *Allen & Hanburys Ltd* v. *Generics* and *Smith Kline and French Laboratories* v. *Generics* the Article 36 point was decided incorrectly by the lower English Courts before being referred to the ECJ for the correct interpretation of EC law. The judgment in *Extrude Hone* v. *Heathway Machine Sales*, on the other hand, represents a 'blacker' example, being a case in which the English courts decided the EC law point incorrectly without making a reference to the ECJ and without this misapplication being corrected on appeal.

3 COPYRIGHT

Although the ECJ applied the doctrine of exhaustion of rights to copyright as early as in its judgment in *Deutsche Grammophon*,[47] it was not until its judgment in *Musik-Vertrieb* v. *GEMA*[48] that it expressly ruled that copyright fell within the concept of 'industrial and commercial property' in Article 36. However, even in that case, the ECJ avoided promulgating an all-embracing definition of what the specific subject-matter of copyright comprises and has never done so to date. Although it may seem odd that the ECJ has been less forthright in defining the specific subject-matter of copyright, especially in comparison with its approach to other intellectual property rights, this reticence may nevertheless be explained by the fact that the label 'industrial and commercial property' ill fits national conceptions of copyright which emphasize more the 'artistic' or 'moral' rights attached to copyright protection. Furthermore, copyright is something of a special case given the variety of ways in which such rights may be exploited. For example, video-cassettes may, according to certain national copyright legislation, be exploited either by means of sale or by rental.[49] Equally, copyright in musical recordings may, according to the legislation of certain Member States, be exploited by their sale and by a supplemen-

---

[47] Case 78/70, n. 6 above.
[48] Cases 55 & 57/80, n. 6 above. See also C–337–95 *Parfums Christian Dior SA* v. *Evora BV* [1997] ECR I–nyr (judgment of 4 November 1997) at paras. 55–7.
[49] See Case 158/86 *Warner Bros* v. *Christiansen* [1988] ECR 2605, [1990] 3 CMLR 684.

tary royalty for their public performance (for example in a discothèque).[50] Films may be licensed for different Member States for the showing of the film in each State.[51] Given this variety, the prudence of the ECJ is therefore understandable and, in general terms, it is in any event clear that copyright is treated by the ECJ as conferring a monopoly to the right-holder for putting the copyrighted product into circulation for the first time, the right to grant licences in return for the payment of royalties and the right to oppose any infringements.

The application of the ECJ case law with respect to intellectual property rights has presented very few difficulties in the national courts in the context of copyright protection. It seems that the practical tests enunciated by the ECJ in this field have greatly facilitated accurate application by national courts. In most cases, the national courts are able to apply the exhaustion of rights and consent principles in a fairly straightforward fashion. For example, in *Société Argos Films* v. *Société Lido Musique*[52] the Paris *Cour d'Appel* held that the owner of the copyright in a video could not rely on that right to prevent importation of the video from the United Kingdom where it had been marketed through its exclusive distributor with its consent. The *Cour d'Appel* cited and discussed several ECJ authorities and held that:

Since the [Copyright Act 1957 (11 March 1957)] defines performance as the communication of the work to the public by any process whatever, particularly public exhibition or television broadcasting, and reproduction as putting the work into material form by any process enabling it to be communicated to the public indirectly, particularly mechanical recording, it appears that in the present case the video-cassettes incorporating the cinematographic work *Paris Texas* are products which permit such indirect communication to the public and that the right of reproduction attaching to them was exhausted when they were first marketed in a lawful manner in a Member State.[53]

The Paris *Cour d'Appel* was thus able to apply the ECJ case law in a competent and thorough fashion to conclude that the free movement of goods should prevail in such circumstances.[54] The national courts have equally encountered few difficulties in permitting restrictions to the free

---

[50] See Case 402/85 *Bassett* v. *SACEM* [1987] ECR 1747, [1987] 3 CMLR 173; Case 395/87 *Ministère Public* v. *Tournier* [1989] ECR 2321, [1991] 4 CMLR 248; Cases 110 & 241 & 242/88 *Lucazeau* v. *SACEM* [1989] ECR 2811.

[51] See Case 62/79 *Coditel* v. *Ciné Vog* [1980] ECR 833, [1981] 2 CMLR 362.

[52] *Cour d'appel* Paris, 4e ch., 20 Mar. 1990, [1991] ECC 268, RIDA 1990, no. 146 279, Dalloz Som. 1990, 354–5 (with note by Hassler). Noted by Françon, RTDComm. 1991, 46 & Kéréver, RIDA 1990, no. 146 p. 252.

[53] [1991] ECC 268 at 273.

[54] For a similarly straighforward application before the Dutch courts see *Bavaria Atelier GmbH* v. *BV Video Productions Robbesom, Arrondissementsrechtbank* Breda, 26 Feb. 1985, NJ 1985, 880 which concerned copyright in the video *Das Boot* marketed in Belgium with the consent of the Dutch copyright holder.

movement of goods which are justified for the purpose of safeguarding rights which constitute the specific subject-matter of copyright under Article 36. For example, in *Knoll International Gavina SpA* v. *Aliotta Diffusion*,[55] the French *Cour de Cassation* held that Knoll could rely on its design copyright (in an armchair model) in France to prevent importation of a chair from Italy in breach of the French copyright. The *Cour de Cassation* held, citing the ECJ's judgment in *GEMA*,[56] that Article 36 applied since Knoll had not authorized the production of the copy in Italy and therefore, that Knoll had not exhausted its rights. Similarly, before the Dutch courts, the President of the *Arrondissementsrechtbank* Breda held that reliance on a Dutch copyright in live recordings of the Rolling Stones, the Beatles and Led Zeppellin was permitted under Article 36 to prevent the importation of such recordings from Germany (where the copyright had expired) where they had been marketed without their licence or consent.[57] It also seems that the national courts have had little difficulty in applying the non-discrimination rule by holding that, as a matter of EC law, Italian furniture must be entitled to the same copyright protection as afforded to Dutch nationals.[58]

The national courts do not, however, have an unblemished record. There are a number of judgments in which the national courts have appeared to be ignorant of the correct principles governing the exercise of copyright under Article 36 EC. The litigation in *Régie nationale des usines Renault* v. *Roland Thévenoux, SpA Maxi-Car* provides a case in point. This case concerned a suit by Renault for infringement of its French design right in spare parts for cars under the Designs and Models Act 1909. The defendant was importing the spare parts from Italy where they were lawfully manufactured by a separate undertaking with no links to Renault. The *Tribunal de grande instance* of Roanne held that:

The argument based on Article 30 *et seq.* EEC relating to 'the elimination of quantitative restrictions between Member States' is irrelevant because those Articles relate to cross-border flows of goods but not to their production, especially where this is a fraud on the manufacturer's rights . . . The present action does not concern

---

[55] *Cour de Cassation*, ch. comm., 16 Jan. 1990, Bull. Cass. Civ. 1990, IV no. 14 p. 9; [1991] 2 CMLR 597; JCP 1990, IV 100; Dalloz 1990, IR 37 (summary). Noted by Roseren (1994) 31 CMLRev. 315 at 350.

[56] Cases 55 & 57/80, n. 6 above.

[57] *Nederlandse Vereniging van Producenten en importeurs van beeld- en geluidsdragers* v. *Wortelboer*, Pres. *Arrondissementsrechtbank* Breda, 29 Apr. 1992, BIE 1994, 118. See also *Curver BV* v. *Dubois SA*, Pres. *Arrondissementsrechtbank* Haarlem and *Gerechtshof* Amsterdam, 29 June 1979, 7 June 1978, BIE 1982, 31.

[58] *Giorgetti SpA* v. *Cantu Meubelen BV, Arrondissementsrechtbank* 's-Hertogenbosch, 11 Mar. 1994, [1995] 2 CMLR 136 directly and explicitly applying the ECJ's judgment in Cases C–92 & 326/92 *Phil Collins* v. *Imtrat Handelsgesellschaft* [1993] ECR I–5145, [1993] 3 CMLR 773.

the free movement of goods because the body components in question can be freely exported or re-imported if they do not constitute infringements of rights.[59]

This judgment shows little knowledge of the correct principles of interpretation of Article 36 in the field of intellectual property rights as there is a conspicuous absence of any mention of the doctrine of exhaustion of rights and of the principle of consent. While the result reached appears to be correct, the reasoning is inaccurate. Most noticeably, it is submitted that it is not correct to state, as the *Tribunal* did, that the principles on free movement of goods do not authorize the sale of spare parts which infringe rights. On the contrary, the principles on free movement of goods do authorize the sale of spare parts even if they infringe copyright if they are marketed in another Member State by the right-holder himself or with his consent. This case was appealed, first to the *Cour d'Appel* of Lyon,[60] and then to the *Cour de Cassation*[61] which allowed the appeal on other grounds and remitted the case to the *Cour d'Appel* of Dijon for final judgment.[62] Fortunately, the ECJ had by this stage handed down its judgment in *CICRA* v. *Renault*[63] where it had held that since the authority of the owner of a similar design-right in spare parts (in Italy) to oppose infringements of such a right by the import of such products without its consent in other Member States constituted the specific subject-matter of the exclusive right, Article 36 could be relied upon to stop importation in infringement of that right. The *Cour d'Appel* of Dijon was then able to draw upon this ECJ judgment to uphold the injunction. However, the seeming lack of awareness in this case of the principles of interpretation of Article 36 in the field of intellectual property rights by the *Tribunal de grande instance* of Roanne at first instance, was far from satisfactory.[64]

Copyright in television programme listings

Questions concerning the free movement of goods and copyright in television programme listings arose before the Dutch courts in the early 1980s. In a series of cases, the *Nederlandse Omroep Stichting* (*NOS*: Dutch Broadcasting Association) brought proceedings against a number of

---

[59] *TGI* Roanne, 29 Apr 1986, [1988] 3 CMLR 686; JCP 1987, II 20787; La Semaine Juridique—éd. entreprise 1986, II 14811 (with note by Bonet).

[60] *Cour d'appel* Lyon, 4e ch. corr., 27 May 1987, PIBD 1987, no. 421 II 431.

[61] *Cour de Cassation*, ch. crim., 29 Nov. 1988.

[62] *Cour d'appel* Dijon, ch. corr., 12 Jan. 1990, PIBD 1990, no. 478 III 342; Rev. int. prop. indus. art. 1990, no. 1 31–6.

[63] Case 53/87 [1988] ECR 6039. See also Case 238/87 *Volvo* v. *Veng* [1988] ECR 624.

[64] For a further example of a case before the French courts which displayed an equal lack of awareness of the principles governing the derogation for copyright under Art. 36, see *Swarovski et Cie* v. *SA Villeroy et Bosch et Noblesse Crystal*, *Cour d'appel* Paris, 4e ch., 6 Oct. 1988, PIBD 1989, no. 453 III 210.

weekly television magazines for breach of their copyright in television programme schedules which they held in the Netherlands. Almost uniformly, the magazines raised the defence that they had acquired these schedules in Belgium, and that in such circumstances, the free movement of goods prevailed over the exercise of the Dutch copyright. The majority of the Dutch courts correctly centred their analyses on Article 36 and addressed the question of whether the *NOS* had exhausted their copyright in Belgium or at least released the schedules there with their consent. The Dutch courts answered this question, which is clearly of a factual nature, to find almost unanimously that the *NOS* had *not* released the schedules in Belgium with their consent. In *Nederlandse Omroep Stichting* v. *Uitgeverij Independent Publishers BV* the President of the Arrondissementsrechtbank Amsterdam held that

[T]he principle of the free movement of goods and services cannot be upheld given that this principle cannot justify the actions of the defendant, who has conceded that he did not get permission from the Belgian weekly papers *Humo* and *TVekspres* to copy and publish in *Weekendkrant*. In these circumstances, it cannot be said that the exercise of copyright by the plaintiffs against the defendants is an arbitrary discrimination or a disguised restriction on trade between Member States within the meaning of Article 36 EEC.[65]

A judgment of the President of the *Arrondissementsrechtbank* Groningen provides the only reported instance where it was found that, as a matter of fact, the *NOS had* consented to the release of the copyrighted schedules in Belgium.[66] The *Arrondissementsrechtbank* Groningen held that

In these circumstances it must in our interim judgment be held that the rules on the free movement of goods in the EEC Treaty in Articles 30 and 36 do not allow the plaintiffs to rely on their copyright under Article 22 of the Broadcasting Law (*Omroepwet*) to prohibit use of the television listings. Thus, it must be stated that Article 22 of the *Omroepwet* goes beyond its proper boundaries and that the right in television listings provided for therein does not fall within the specific subject-matter of copyright, such that the protection of that right to television listings does not provide any justification for a limitation to the free movement of goods.

Apart from the question of consent, the other point which arose in these cases before the Dutch courts was whether the use of the copyrighted television listings in the Netherlands could be considered to be a 'separate publication' by the defendants. This was held to be the case by the

---

[65] Pres. *Arrondissementsrechtbank* Amsterdam, 3 June 1982, KG 1982, 98; EIPR 1982, 192. See also to similar effect *Nederlandse Omroep Stichting* v. *Uitgeverij De Vrijbuiter BV*, Pres. *Arrondissementsrechtbank* Breda, 27 Aug. 1982, KG 1982, 156 and *Nederlandse Omroep Stichting CS* v. *Nieuwsblad van het Noorden*, *Gerechtshof* Leeuwarden, 19 Jan. 1983, Auteursrecht/AMR 1983/2, p. 33.

[66] *Nederlandse Omroep Stichting* v. *Nieuwsblad van het Noorden*, Pres. *Arrondissementsrechtbank* Groningen, 22 Jan. 1982, Auteursrecht/AMR 1982/2, p. 33; (1982) 3 EIPR 192.

Gerechtshof Leeuwarden in *Nederlandse Omroep Stichting* v. *Nieuwsblad van het Noorden*,[67] which held that the publication of the television listings by the defendant in the Netherlands was a separate publication since the copyright legislation prohibited any publication without permission and that 'earlier publication does not exhaust the copyright'.[68]

These judgments of the Dutch courts dealing with the provisions concerning free movement of goods and the infringement of copyright in television listings display a high degree of competence. The conclusion reached by the majority of these courts that the *NOS* could successfully sue for copyright infringement relying on Article 36 seems perfectly reasonable given their findings of fact. Most importantly, the Dutch courts faithfully applied in these cases the principles developed by the ECJ in this field.[69]

4 TRADE MARKS

The ECJ has defined the specific subject-matter of trade marks in *Centrafarm* v. *Winthrop*[70] as

the guarantee that the owner of the trade mark has the exclusive right to use that trade mark, for the purpose of putting products protected by the trade mark into circulation for the first time, and is therefore intended to protect him against competitors wishing to take advantage of the status and reputation of the trade mark by selling products illegally bearing that trade mark.

In *Hoffman-La Roche* v. *Centrafarm*[71] the ECJ added that:

the essential function of the trade mark . . . is to guarantee the identity of origin of the trade marked product to the consumer or ultimate user, by enabling him without any possibility of confusion to distinguish that product from products which have another origin.

The vast majority of judgments by national courts dealing with the free movement of goods and trade-mark infringement have concerned cases in which the national court has been able to hold that Article 36 may be relied upon to prevent importation of a product protected by a trade mark from another Member State where the right had not been exhausted, either by the trade-mark holder having marketed the product in the other Member

---

[67] n. 65 above.   [68] See also *Uitgeverij De Vrijbuiter BV*, n. 65 above.
[69] It may be noted that the ECJ has more recently had the opportunity to address the question of copyright in television listings in Cases C–241 & 242/91P *RTE* v. *Commission* [1995] ECR I–743. However, that case dealt only with a refusal to supply television listings which was held to have prevented the emergence of a new product thereby constituting an abuse of dominant position contrary to Art. 86 EC.
[70] Case 16/74, n. 5 above.
[71] Case 102/77 [1978] ECR 1139, [1978] 3 CMLR 217 at para. 7 of judgt.

State himself or with his consent. The pattern which emerges from the judgments of national courts in such cases is that the application of the principles developed by the ECJ is being applied accurately and competently.[72] There are, however, inevitably exceptions to this relatively good record. For example, in *Société Céline* v. *SA Hermès*,[73] the *Cour d'Appel* of Paris held that the proceedings for trade-mark infringement in that case were 'exercised in conformity with French law . . . and are necessary to safeguard the specific subject-matter of intellectual property rights'. The French court also mentioned that the French trade-mark law gives the trade-mark owner a discretion to choose who to sue for infringement of its trade mark and that 'this does not amount to any discrimination on grounds of nationality nor to arbitrary discrimination'. However, the *Cour d'Appel* omitted to investigate or mention in its judgment whether the trade-mark rights had in fact been exhausted in the exporting Member State or whether the product had been marketed there with the trade-mark owner's consent.[74] This was, however, a fairly minor omission in a straightforward case and does not therefore, detract from the overall pattern of excellent application by the national courts.

(A) The Doctrine of Common Origin

Until the judgment of the ECJ in *CNL-Sucal* v. *Hag* (Hag II)[75] in 1990, the ECJ had maintained a doctrine of 'common origin' with respect to trade marks and the free movement of goods. Under this doctrine, where similar or identical trade marks having a common origin were separately owned in different Member States, the owner of one of the marks could not rely on it to prevent the importation of goods lawfully marketed under

[72] By way of examples, see esp.: *COGEAI* v. *Campinaire*, Cour de Cassation, ch. comm., 18 Jan. 1983, Bull. Cass. Civ. 1983, IV no. 17 p. 13; *SARL ISA France* v. *SA* Kores, *Cour d'appel* Paris, 4e ch. A, 16 July 1984, Gaz. Pal. 1986, II Som. 453 (summary); *Continent Hypermarché SA* v. *Prince Manufacturing*, *Cour d'appel* Paris 4e ch., 23 June 1988, PIBD 1989, no. 449 III 84; *SA Bourdillon* v. *Vivaldi sas di Mantone Torres Francesco et SA Daniel Ho*, TGI Paris, 3e ch., 12 Dec. 1983, La Propriété industrielle 1984, no. 347 III 135 and *Usines Samu Auchan* v. *SA Mobil Oil Française*, *Cour d'appel* Paris, 4e ch. A, 24 Nov. 1993, Gaz. Pal. 1994, Som. 371. For an example of a case in which the national court concluded that a trade mark could *not* be relied upon to prevent importation of a good falling under trade-mark protection since it had been marketed in the exporting Member State with the trade-mark holder's consent, see: *Saragan SA and Yamaha NV* v. *BV Bizerta Sport*, Pres. *Arrondissementsrechtbank* Haarlem, 12 Aug. 1983, BIE 1984, 74; NJ 1984, 217; KG 1983, 288.

[73] *Cour d'appel* Paris, 4e ch. B, 4 Mar. 1982, Gaz. Pal. 1982, II Som. 311; Annales de la propriété industrielle, artistique et littéraire 1983, 88.

[74] For examples of similar relatively straightforward judgments before the Dutch courts in which the reasoning is somewhat incomplete with respect to the exhaustion of rights and consent principles, see: *Droste BV* v. *Ickx BV*, Pres. *Arrondissementsrechtbank* Breda, 16 Dec. 1988, BIE 1989, 59 and *Emro, Import Export BV* v. *Rofa-Mavi*, Pres. *Arrondissementsrechtbank* Haarlem, 14 Feb. 1980, BIE 1980, 43.

[75] Case C–10/89 [1990] ECR I–3711, [1990] 3 CMLR 571.

the other mark.[76] Thus, trade marks having a 'common origin' which had since fallen into the hands of different owners in different Member States could not be relied upon to prevent importation. The doctrine of 'common origin' came in for much criticism,[77] and the ECJ has since explicitly over-ruled and abandoned its application.[78] Consequently, trade marks having a 'common origin' which have since fallen into different hands must now be analysed according to the familiar doctrine of consent.[79] The abandoning of the doctrine of 'common origin' is to be welcomed from the point of view of the greater respect accorded to the role of trade marks in the system of undistorted competition which the EC Treaty seeks to establish.[80] Nevertheless, the acceptance that voluntary assignment of trade marks can effectively lead to a partitioning of the market is far from satisfactory.

During the period before *HAG II*,[81] the national courts had to apply the 'common origin' doctrine. In most such cases, the national court was able to avoid its application by simply referring to it and holding that, on the facts, there was no 'common origin' of ownership in the trade marks at issue.[82] A more detailed analysis was required by the Chancery Division of the High Court (Northern Ireland) in *Tayto (NI) Ltd* v. *McKee*.[83] The facts of the latter case dated back to the 1950s when Murphy began manufacturing and selling potato crisps in the Irish Republic under the name 'Tayto'. In 1956, Murphy entered into an agreement with Tayto (NI) whereby Tayto (NI) would sell and manufacture 'Tayto' crisps in Northern Ireland under that name while each would retain territorial exclusivity for the Irish Republic and Northern Ireland respectively. In 1960, Tayto (NI) registered the trade mark 'Tayto' in the United Kingdom.

[76] Case 192/73 *Van Zuylen* v. *Hag* (Hag I) [1974] ECR 731, [1974] 2 CMLR 127.

[77] See, Kemp, 'The Erosion of Trade Mark Rights in Europe' (1974) 11 CMLRev. 360, Guy and Leigh, *The EEC and Intellectual Property*, 12.30 and Cornish, *Intellectual Property: Patents, Copyright, Trade Marks and Allied Rights* (Sweet & Maxwell, 2nd edn., 1989), 487.

[78] Case C–10/89, see Hag II, n. 75 above.

[79] Case C–9/93 *IHT* v. *Ideal Standard* [1994] ECR I–2789, [1994] 3 CMLR 857. Noted by Jarvis (1995) 20 ELRev. 195.

[80] The ECJ has, until recently, accorded less protection to national trade marks than it has to other intellectual property rights. The low point of the ECJ's respect for trade marks was probably reached when in Case 40/70 *Sirena* v. *Eda* [1971] ECR 69 the Court, in para. 7 of its judgment, remarked that 'a trade mark right is distinguishable in this context from other rights of industrial and commercial property, inasmuch as the interests protected by the latter are usually more important, and merit a higher protection, than the interests protected by an ordinary mark'.

[81] Case C–10/89, n. 75 above.

[82] e.g., before the Dutch courts see, *'Hij' Herenmode BV* v. *H.I.S. Sportswear*, Pres. Arrondissementsrechtbank Amsterdam, 25 July 1975 & Pres. *Gerechtshof* Amsterdam, 26 Feb. 1976, BIE 1977, 42 and before the French courts, see *SA Emballages plastiques* v. *Klarsichtpackung GmbH*, TGI Paris, 3e ch., 12 Nov. 1976, Annales de la propriété industrielle, artistique et littéraire 1977, 216; La Propriété industrielle 1977, no. 196 III 287–8. The 'common origin' doctrine was also applied by the German courts in *Re 'Klint' Trade Marks*, Bundesgerichtshof, Case I ZR 196/84, 6 Nov. 1986, [1988] 1 CMLR 340.

[83] [1991] 3 CMLR 269. Noted by Dawson (1990) 11 EIPR 428.

Over the years, the quality of the 'Tayto' crisps which Tayto (NI) and Murphy manufactured diverged. The crisps manufactured by Tayto (NI) were of a superior quality and enjoyed considerable goodwill in Northern Ireland. In time, Murphy registered the 'Tayto' trade mark in the Irish Republic. In 1985 a shopkeeper in Northern Ireland (McKee) obtained a supply of 'Tayto' crisps originating from Murphy in the Irish Republic and sold them in his shop knowingly passing them off as those of Tayto (NI). Tayto (NI) sued for trade-mark infringement. It was argued that since the 'Tayto' trade mark had a 'common origin', Tayto (NI) could not successfully sue for infringement as this would constitute a restriction to the free movement of goods which could not be justified under Article 36 following the ECJ's judgment in *HAG I*.[84] The High Court held that there was no 'common origin' on the facts of this case, firstly because, according to the High Court, 'common origin' required initial common ownership which was not the case here as the trade marks in the Irish Republic and the United Kingdom had never been owned by the same person. Secondly, the High Court held that there had, in this case, been no subdivision of the rights in the trade mark by legal assignment and thus held that the 'common origin' doctrine enunciated by the ECJ could be put to one side. Accordingly, the High Court held that an infringement of the United Kingdom trade mark had been established and granted the injunction to prevent import of 'Tayto' crisps from Ireland. This judgment has been criticized by Dawson, who argues that 'the limits of the common origin doctrine have yet to be fully worked out and the *Tayto* case raises more questions than it provides answers'.[85] It is true that there were undoubtedly links between Murphy and Tayto (NI) as is demonstrated by their agreement of 1956. On the other hand, it is also true to say that there was no initial common ownership of the two trade marks which were registered in two Member States independently of one another. For the High Court, this latter fact was held to be enough for it to rule the application of the 'common origin' doctrine out. While a reference to the ECJ pursuant to Article 177 would probably have been more desirable, it is submitted that the High Court's reasoning was perfectly defensible. In any event, as we have seen, the ECJ abandoned its 'common origin' doctrine only a year after the High Court's judgment in *Tayto (NI) Ltd* v. *McKee*.

(B) Repackaging products and trade-mark infringement

In order to allow parallel importers to take full advantage of the possibilities offered by the single market by successfully marketing products originating in other Member States, the ability to repackage products will

---

[84] Case 192/73, n. 76 above.   [85] n. 83 above, EIPR note at 430.

often be a prerequisite. However, national trade-mark legislation often forms a barrier to such a practice. As usual it has, in such circumstances, fallen upon the shoulders of the ECJ to reconcile the free movement of goods with the imperatives of national trade-mark protection. The ECJ achieved such a reconciliation in its judgment in *Hoffman-La Roche* v. *Centrafarm*[86] by holding that the proprietor of a trade mark right is justified (pursuant to the first sentence in Article 36) in preventing a product to which the trade mark has lawfully been applied in one Member State, from being marketed in another Member State, after it has been repackaged by a third party involving the affixing of the trade mark by that third party. However, the ECJ held that such a restriction would not be justified (pursuant to the second sentence in Article 36) where:

—It is established that the use of the trade-mark right by the proprietor, having regard to the marketing system which he has adopted, will contribute to the artificial partitioning of the markets between Member States;
—It is shown that the repackaging cannot adversely affect the original condition of the product;
—The proprietor of the mark receives prior notice of the marketing of the repackaged product; and
—It is stated on the new packaging by whom the product has been repackaged.

In the recent '*Paranova*' cases,[87] the ECJ has had the opportunity to clarify and expand upon these criteria which it had set out in *Hoffman-La Roche*. For example, the ECJ has expanded the third condition in *Hoffman-La Roche* to the extent that the parallel importer must, on demand, supply the trade-mark proprietor with a specimen of the repackaged product before the repackaged product is put on sale. The ECJ has also clarified the fourth condition set out above by stating that it is not necessary, when stating by whom the product has been repackaged, to indicate that the repackaging was carried out without the authorization of the trade-mark owner. Perhaps most importantly, the ECJ has added a further, fifth, condition to be satisfied, namely that

The presentation of the repackaged product is not such as to be liable to damage the reputation of the trade mark and of its owner; thus, the packaging must not be defective, of poor quality, or untidy.

---

[86] Case 102/77, n. 71 above. The *Hoffmann-La Roche* judgment was subsequently repeated and applied by the ECJ in Case 1/81 *Pfizer* v. *Eurim-Pharm* [1981] ECR 2913.
[87] See Joined Cases C–427, 429 and 436/93 *Bristol-Myers Squibb* v. *Paranova* [1996] ECR I–3457; Case C–232/94 *MPA Pharma* v. *Rhône-Poulenc Pharma* [1996] ECR I–3671 and Joined Cases C–71, 72 & 73/94 *Eurim-Pharm* v. *Beiersdorf* [1996] ECR I–3603. See also C–337–95, n. 48 above, where the ECJ held that a trade-mark owner could not prevent a retailer from using modes of advertising which were customary in that retailer's trade sector unless it is established that the use of the retailer's advertising 'seriously damages the reputation of the trade mark' (para. 46) and C–349/95 *F. Loendersloot* v. *George Ballantine & Son Ltd* [1997] ECR I–nyr (judgt 11 Nov. 1997) concerning the repackaging of alcoholic drinks.

Thus, so long as any would-be parallel importer abides by the five criteria set out by the ECJ in *Hoffman-La Roche* as expanded upon in the *'Paranova'* cases, the free movement of goods will be assured. Such assurances are however dependent upon competent application of these criteria by the national courts.

The application of the first condition set out by the ECJ in *Hoffman-La Roche* has been the subject of some difficulties before the national courts. In particular, the national courts have had difficulty in discerning the point at which it is possible to find 'artificial partitioning' of the markets between Member States and the extent to which it is necessary to demonstrate that the trade-mark owner deliberately sought to partition the markets between Member States. Such a difficulty arose before the Dutch courts in a trilogy of cases before the *Arrondissementsrechtbank* Rotterdam.[88] All three cases concerned parallel trade marks in pharmaceutical products held in the United Kingdom and the Netherlands, and the parallel import of the products after repackaging by a third party. The *Arrondissementsrechtbank* Rotterdam held that the repackaging constituted an infringement of the Dutch trade mark under section 13A(1)(i) of the Benelux Uniform Trade Mark Act and noted the ECJ judgment in *Hoffman-La Roche* which it summarized without explicitly laying out the four conditions set out by the ECJ. In fact, the Rotterdam court only really applied the first condition in *Hoffman-La Roche*, and examined whether the marketing system in each respective case contributed to the 'artificial partitioning' of the market between Member States. The *Arrondissements-rechtbank* Rotterdam then held that the repackaging 'obligation' in the cases before it arose, not from the artificial partitioning of the markets imputable to the marketing systems of the trade-mark owners, but rather from applicable Dutch legislation setting out labelling and packaging requirements.[89] Thus the court concluded that there was no artificial partitioning of the markets between Member States arising from the marketing system of the trade-mark holders and thus that reliance on Article 36 to preclude importation of the repackaged products was permitted. The judgment of the *Arrondissementsrechtbank* Rotterdam was upheld in an

---

[88] *The Boots Company Ltd* v. *Centrafarm BV*, *Arrondissementsrechtbank* Rotterdam, 29 Jan. 1979, [1979] 2 CMLR 497 (concerning the trade mark 'Brufen' for the generic drug 'ibruprofenum'); *Hoechst* v. *Centrafarm*, *Arrondissementsrechtbank* Rotterdam, 29 Jan. 1979, [1980] CMLR 650 (concerning the trade mark 'Lasix' for the generic drug 'furosemidum') and *Centrafarm BV* v. *Pfizer*, *Arrondissementsrechtbank* Rotterdam, 25 June 1979, NJ 1985, 300; BIE 1984, 49 (concerning the trade mark 'Vibramycin' for the generic drug 'doxycycline').

[89] The relevant Dutch legislation which was involved were two Royal Decrees of 8 Sept. 1977: *Besluit registratie geneesmiddelen*, Stb. 1977, no. 537 (Registration of Medicaments Decree) and *Besluit bereiding en aflevering van farmaceutische produkten*, Stb. 1977, no. 538 (Preparation and Marketing of Pharmaceutical Products Decree), sect. 34 of which provided for certain labelling, enclosed literature, and packaging requirements.

appeal in one of the three cases to the *Gerechtshof*'s-Gravenhage.[90] The latter court held that 'the lower court set as a requirement that there must be a connection between the exercise of the trade mark right by Pfizer and its marketing system' and that 'this was a correct criterion such that this ground of appeal is put forward in vain'. The *Gerechtshof* again noted that the repackaging requirement originated in the Dutch legislation and thus 'if Pfizer refuses to allow Centrafarm to affix the trade mark to the new packaging, it cannot be said that there exists a connection between this exercise of the trade mark and the marketing system of Pfizer'. It is submitted that this is a perfectly reasonable interpretation of the first condition as set down by the ECJ in *Hoffman-La Roche*. After all, the ECJ had itself stated in that judgment that the national court, in considering whether there was 'artificial partitioning' of the market, must have regard to the 'marketing system' which the trade-mark owner had adopted. The implication in the ECJ judgment is clearly that if the 'artificial partitioning' was due to factors other than the trade-mark owner's marketing system, the first condition would be satisfied. A similar interpretation of the first condition of *Hoffman-La Roche* was adopted by the Provincial Court of Appeal in Hamburg in *Re the 'Kerlone' Trade Mark*.[91] That case concerned the parallel import of pharmaceuticals (in the form of pills) from France into Germany for which there was a parallel trade mark in both Member States. The parallel importer was, in practice, forced to repackage the pills since they were distributed by the trade-mark owner in France in blister packs of twenty-eight (because of French legislation restricting a prescription to no more than one month's usage) and distributed in Germany in packs of fifty and 100 (following the prescription practice of German doctors pursuant to a joint recommendation of the associations of German chemists, of doctors, of statutory health insurance bodies and of the pharmaceutical industry). The *Oberlandesgericht* Hamburg held, again with respect to the first condition set out by the ECJ in *Hoffman-La Roche*, that 'the choice of differing package sizes for Germany and for France is not arbitrary; it is based on objective reasons' following French and German legislation and not the marketing system of the trade-mark owner. In particular, the *Oberlandesgericht* Hamburg held that

A partitioning of the market is to be regarded as 'artificial' if it does not arise from the state of competition and external influences legitimately affecting the participants in the market. In the case of a partitioning of the market which arises

---

[90] *Centrafarm BV* v. *Pfizer*, Gerechtshof 's-Gravenhage, 8 June 1983, NJ 1985, 300; BIE 1984, 49.
[91] Hanseatisches *OLG*, Hamburg, 25 Apr. 1991, [1993] 3 CMLR 190; Gewerblicher-Rechtsschutz und Urheberrecht, internationaler Teil 1992, 50; Wettbewerb in Recht und Praxis, 1992, 41.

'naturally' the exercise of the trade mark right does not objectively contribute to artificial partitioning of the market.[92]

Accordingly, the *Oberlandesgericht* held that, on the facts of this case, the partitioning of the market arose 'naturally' and thus that there was no 'artificial partitioning' of the market and thus the trade-mark owner could legitimately rely on Article 36 to stop the free movement of goods in such circumstances. This case was then appealed to the *Bundesgerichtshof* Vorlagebeschluß which referred questions on this point to the ECJ.[93] The ECJ's subsequent judgment constituted one of the *'Paranova'* judgments to which reference has already been made.[94] Contrary to what had been held by both the Dutch and German courts in the cases discussed, the ECJ held that 'artificial partitioning of the markets under the first condition does not imply that the importer must demonstrate that, by putting an identical product on the market in varying forms of packaging in different Member States, the trade-mark owner deliberately sought to partition the markets between Member States'.[95] Thus, the ECJ has held in the *'Paranova'* judgments that the first condition in *Hoffman-La Roche* is an objective one and that it is unnecessary to ascertain whether there had been a subjective intention on the part of the trade-mark owner to act unlawfully, it being sufficient that an artificial partitioning of the market within the Community occurs.

Thus, the applications by the national courts of the first condition set out by the ECJ in *Hoffman-La Roche* can no longer stand following this recent clarification of that condition by the ECJ in the *'Paranova'* judgments. However, as was noted above, the interpretation adopted by the national courts in these cases was perfectly defensible given the wording of the ECJ's judgment in *Hoffman-La Roche*, and it is submitted that it is the ECJ which has somewhat shifted its own position on this matter rather than any misapplication on the part of the national courts.

The second condition set out by the ECJ in *Hoffman-La Roche*, namely that the repackaging must not adversely affect the original condition of the product, has also been applied by the national courts. In *TDK* v. *Video Zuid Nederland BV*, the President of the *Arrondissementsrechtbank* Breda dealt with a suit for infringement of the 'TDK' trade mark in the Netherlands.[96] The defendant had bought large reels of unused blank TDK videotape (referred to as 'pancakes') in the United Kingdom which it had imported

---

[92] [1993] 3 CMLR 190 at 198. The *OLG* Hamburg cited Baumbach-Hefermehl, *Warenzeichenrecht* (12th edn.) to reach this conclusion.

[93] *Bundesgerichtshof* Vorlagebeschluß, 27 Jan. 1994, Europäische Zeitschrift für Wirtschaftsrecht 1994, 384; Europäische Wirtschafts- & Steuerrecht (EWS) 1994, 180; Gewerblicher-Rechtsschutz und Urheberrecht 1994, 374; Wettbewerb in Recht und Praxis, 1994, 237.

[94] Joined Cases C–71, 72 & 73/94, n. 87 above.   [95] Ibid. at para. 47 of judgt.

[96] Pres. *Arrondissementsrechtbank* Breda, 5 August 1991, BIE 1994, 39.

into the Netherlands and cut into appropriate lengths and installed into video-cassette cartridges for sale in the Netherlands. The defendant sold the blank videotapes in the Netherlands in boxes upon which it affixed the 'TDK' trade mark without the plaintiff's authorization. The *Arrondissementsrechtbank* Breda discussed Articles 30 to 36 and the ECJ's *Hoffman-La Roche* criteria in particular, and concluded that TDK could rely on its Dutch trade mark to prevent infringement in such circumstances. Apart from noting that TDK had not been notified of the repackaging as required by the *Hoffman-La Roche* criteria, the *Arrondissementsrechtbank* Breda held that 'the consumer, when he buys the cassette, cannot be sure that the original quality of the TDK tape is not affected let alone be sure that indeed it does contain TDK tape'. The *Arrondissementsrechtbank* Breda thus held, *inter alia*, that the second *Hoffman-La Roche* condition was not satisfied. It is submitted that this constitutes an effective application of the *Hoffman-La Roche* criteria by the Dutch court, which is indeed best placed to decide, as a matter of fact, whether the repackaging would adversely affect the original condition of the product.

The application of the *Hoffman-La Roche* criteria by the national courts in repackaging cases gives rise to two further comments. Firstly, there are unfortunate examples of judgments by national courts in which the *Hoffman-La Roche* criteria are 'abused' by the national court, which merely refer to the ECJ's *Hoffman-La Roche* judgment to conclude that Article 36 applies to justify the restriction, without making any attempt to apply the conditions rigorously to the facts.[97] Secondly, repackaging cases before the national courts have also given rise to the related question of whether the omission of manufacturers' 'identification numbers' by the parallel importer responsible for repackaging may be justified.[98] This question has recently been addressed by the ECJ on a reference from the Dutch courts.[99] The ECJ held that if manufacturers used 'identification numbers' in order to enable them to trace the route by which parallel importers got hold of their products, national intellectual property provisions could not be used to prevent the marketing of imports which had been repackaged so as to delete such numbers.[100] However, the ECJ added that Article 36 may be relied upon by manufacturers in order to prevent the omission by parallel

---

[97] See, e.g., *Empresa Cubana del Tabaco* v. *W. Pronk Import BV*, Pres. *Arrondissemnetsrechtbank* Breda, 17 Dec. 1991, BIE 1993, 77.

[98] See, e.g., *Chanel SA* v. *Maxis BV*, *Gerechtshof* Amsterdam, 28 Feb. 1991, BIE 1992, 36; *Schering AG* v. *Imex*, Pres. *Arrondissementsrechtbank* Middelburg, 15 Sept. 1992, KG 1992, 352 and *Merck* v. *Imex-Hulst*, Pres. *Arrondissementsrechtbank* Haarlem, 10 Aug. 1990, IER 1990, 71.

[99] C–349/95, *Loendersloot*, n. 87 above. The reference from the Dutch court is reported at *F. Loenderslot* v. *United Distillers*, *Hoge Raad*, 3 Nov. 1995, Nederlands juristenblad 1995, Bijl. 573.

[100] Case C–349/95, n. 87 above at para. 40.

importers of 'identification numbers' where such numbers had been affixed purely in order to facilitate effective recall of faulty products.[101]

(C) Confusingly similar trade marks

With respect to confusingly similar trade marks for similar products manufactured by independent parties, the ECJ has held that, provided there is a real risk of confusion that would justify the exclusion of a similar product, reliance on a trade mark would be justified under Article 36. In particular, the ECJ has left the decision as to whether in individual cases there is a real risk of confusion to the national court.[102] This approach has been criticized by Advocate General Jacobs in his opinion in *Hag II* where he argued that 'the concept of confusingly similar marks must inevitably vary from one Member State to another and this can lead to a certain lack of reciprocity and to distortions of trade'.[103] The ECJ has, however, maintained its approach in subsequent cases.[104] Before the national courts, the ECJ case law has been applied to find that in France, the trade mark 'Flotex' was confusingly similar to 'Filotex',[105] in the United Kingdom that 'Knoll' was confusingly similar to 'Knoll International',[106] and in the Netherlands that the trade mark 'Sanex' was confusingly similar to that of 'Sanicur'.[107]

Since 1 January 1993, the 'likelihood of confusion' between two trade marks is now a matter of Community law following the entering into force of the provisions of Articles 4 and 5 of the First Trade Mark Directive 89/104.[108] Article 4(1)(b) of the Directive refers to the 'likelihood of confusion . . . which includes the likelihood of association with the earlier trade mark'. The question which arises is whether the purely associative nature of two trade marks is sufficient to assume that a risk of confusion exists. This is a sensitive issue since there is a division between the concept of

---

[101] Case C–349/95, at para. 42. It is presumably on the 'protection of public health' head of justification (rather than intellectual property rights) in Art. 36 that this justification is based. See discussion of the 'protection of public health' justification in Art. 36 in Ch. 7 sect. 4.

[102] Case 119/75 *Terrapin* v. *Terranova* [1976] ECR 1039, [1976] 2 CMLR 482.

[103] Case C–10/89 n. 75 above at para. 36 of the Opinion.

[104] In Case C–317/91 *Deutsche Renault* v. *Audi*, [1993] ECR I–6227, [1995] 1 CMLR 461, the ECJ held that 'the adoption of criteria for a finding of risk of confusion forms part of the detailed rules for trade mark protection which . . . are a matter for national law . . . Community law does not therefore lay down any strict interpretative criterion of risk of confusion' (at paras. 32–3). See also Case C–9/93, n. 79 above.

[105] *SA Europe Décor* v. *SA Besnier Flotex; Société Tissages Filotex* v. *SA Bessnier Flotex, Cour de Cassation*, ch. comm., 16 Feb. 1977, Bull. Cass. Civ. 1977, IV 43; Annales de la propriété industrielle, artistique et littéraire 1979, 1; noted by Rideau (1977) 2 ELRev. 388 & (1978) 3 ELRev. 244.

[106] *Parker Knoll Plc* v. *Knoll Overseas Limited* [1985] FSR 349 (High Court).

[107] *Kortman Intradal BV* v. *Tranova BV*, Pres. *Arrondissementsrechtbank* Breda, 18 Jan. 1991, IER 1991, 15; BIE 1994, 102.

[108] [1989] OJ L40/1.

'confusion' in Benelux trade-mark law and the trade-mark law of the other Member States. Benelux trade-mark law accepts that not only confusion, but also association, may constitute an infringement of trade mark[109] whereas other Member States require confusion as to the origin of the products, and association alone will be insufficient to constitute an infringement. Clearly, the very *raison d'être* of Directive 89/104 is to harmonize the differing concepts prevailing in the Member States. It is therefore a matter of considerable dismay that national courts faced with the interpretation of Article 4(1)(b) of Directive 89/104 have been somewhat reluctant to refer questions to the ECJ pursuant to Article 177 EC. For example, in *Renault* v. *Reynolds Aluminium Holland BV*,[110] the *Gerechtshof* Arnhem has held that 'the Directive [89/104] does not aim by the term "likelihood of confusion" to introduce another criterion than the criterion "likelihood of association" as has been developed in the Benelux case law'. Without adducing any further reasoning, the *Gerechtshof* Arnhem simply stated that it would not refer questions to the ECJ under the Article 177 preliminary-rulings procedure. Conversely, the Chancery Division of the English High Court in *Wagamama* v. *City Centre Restaurants*[111] took a 'robustly independent line'[112] and concluded that Section 10 of the Trade Marks Act 1994, which implements Article 4(1)(b) of the Directive into English law, does not extend beyond 'classic' infringements (according to which there has to be confusion as to the source or origin of the goods) to also include the 'likelihood of association' where there was no possibility of misapprehension as to the origin of the particular goods. In reaching this conclusion, Laddie J rejected the relevance of evidence that under Benelux trade-mark law such 'likelihood of association' would constitute a breach of trade mark even where there is no confusion as to the source or origin of the goods. The High Court held that:

The purpose of the 1988 Directive was to ensure a measure of uniformity between the trade mark laws of Member States of the European Union. For that reason it is right that British courts should pay regard to decisions in the courts of other Member States on equivalent provisions in their law. However it is apparent from the expert evidence of Professor Gielen that the Benelux courts have simply assumed that the Directive made no alteration to their domestic law. . . In any event, the obligation of the English court is to decide what the proper construction

---

[109] See Art. 13A, Uniform Benelux Law on Trade Marks as interpreted by the Benelux Court of Justice in *Henri Jullien* v. *Verschueru Norbert* (Union/Union Soleure case), 20 May 1983, Jur. Benelux Court of Justice 1983, 36. See Furstner and Geuze, BIE 1988, 215.

[110] *Gerechtshof* Arnhem, 2 May 1995, BIE 1996, 73; IER 1995, 35.

[111] [1995] FSR 713. See Harris, 'UK Trademark Law: Are You Confused? The *Wagamama* Decision' (1995) 16 EIPR 601 and Prescott, 'Has the Benelux Trade Mark Law Been Written into the Directive?' (1997) 18 EIPR 99.

[112] Davis, 'First Principles or Old Principles?' (1996) Camb. LJ 441 at 443. See also *British Sugar* v. *James Robertson & Sons* [1996] FSR 281, [1996] RPC 281.

is. If that construction differs from that adopted in the Benelux countries, one, at least, is wrong. It would not be right for an English court to follow the route adopted by the courts of another Member State if it is firmly of a different view simply because the other court expressed a view first. The scope of European legislation is too important to be decided on a first past the post basis.

The High Court thus explicitly chose to reason from 'first principles' rather than take into consideration the position under the trade-mark law of other Member States which it acknowledged differed from the position under United Kingdom law. With due respect, it is a matter of considerable regret that the High Court did not even consider in its judgment the possibility of making a reference to the ECJ pursuant to Article 177 EC. This is all the more serious since Laddie J himself acknowledged that the divergence in the definition of 'confusingly similar' trade marks in the Benelux and the United Kingdom was 'regrettable since one of the main objectives of the 1988 Directive was to avoid differences in scope of trade mark rights which could lead to barriers to inter-state trade'. In these circumstances, the matter was surely crying out for early referral to the ECJ. Indeed, the scope of European legislation is 'too important to be decided on a first past the post basis' and, for this very reason, it is submitted that the English High Court should have referred the matter to the ECJ.

The *Gerechtshof* Arnhem in *Renault* v. *Reynolds Aluminium Holland BV* and the High Court in *Wagamama* may thus both be criticized for not having directed references to the ECJ on this issue. Fortunately, the meaning of 'confusion' in Article 4(1)(b) of Directive 89/104 has now been addressed by the ECJ on a reference to the ECJ by the German *Bundesgerichtshof*.[113] The ECJ has resolved the matter by rejecting the Benelux approach and has held that 'the criterion of "likelihood of confusion which includes the likelihood of association with the earlier mark" contained in Article 4(1)(b) of the Directive is to be interpreted as meaning that the mere association which the public might make between two trade marks as a result of their analogous semantic content is not in itself a sufficient

[113] Case C–251/95 *SABEL BV* v. *Puma AG, Rudolf Dassler Sport* [1977] ECR I–nyr (judgt 11 Nov. 1997). The reference to the ECJ is reported at BGH, 29 June 1995, Case no. I ZB 22/93; IER 1995, 212 (with note by Gielen).

ground for concluding that there is a likelihood of confusion within the meaning of that term'.[114] In other words, the ECJ has established that a 'likelihood of association' between two trade marks will not constitute a breach of trade mark unless there is also a 'likelihood of confusion' on the part of the public.

5 INDICATIONS OF SOURCE AND APPELLATIONS OF ORIGIN

Until recently, the ECJ has treated indications of source and appellations of origin as forming part of consumer protection under the rule of reason.[115] The ECJ has now unequivocally held that such rights fall within the meaning of 'industrial and commercial property' provided for in Article 36.[116] Appellations of origin operate to guarantee to the consumer that a particular product comes from a certain geographical area and possesses particular characteristics. As such, appellations of origin are akin to trade marks in that they function to protect the reputation of certain products. Nevertheless, there are important differences between the two, not least the fact that, unlike trade marks, appellations of origin cannot be exhausted or assigned.

The Paris *Cour d'Appel* has had occasion to hold that the *'appellation d'origine contrôlée'* for 'Champagne' justified any restriction to the free movement of goods which would result from an injunction to prevent the use of the name 'Champagne' by Yves Saint Laurent Parfums for a perfume.[117] In

---

[114] Case C–251/95, n. 113 above, at para. 26.

[115] See, e.g., Case 12/74 *Commission* v. *Germany* (Sekt and Prädikatssekt) [1975] ECR 181, [1975] 1 CMLR 340 and discussion of consumer protection and the rule of reason in Ch. 6, sect. 3.

[116] See Case C–47/90 *Delhaize* v. *Promalvin* [1992] ECR I–3669 and Case C–3/91 *Exportur* v. *LOR* [1992] ECR I–5529.

[117] *Société Yves Saint Laurent Parfums* v. *Institute Nationale des Appellations d'origine, Cour d'appel* Paris, 15 Dec. 1993, [1994] ECC 385; Dalloz 1994, Jur. 145 (with note by Tourneau); JCP 1994, II 22229 (with note by Pollaud-Dulian); Gaz. Pal. 1994, Jur 55. See notes by Lampre, 'Le champagne ou le parfum de la renommée', Dalloz 1994, Chr. 213 and Le Tarnec, 'Appellations d'origine et Marques: À propos de l'Affaire du parfum "Champagne" ', Gaz. Pal. 1994, Doctr. 176.

accordance with ECJ case law, the *Cour d'Appel* had specific recourse to 'industrial and commercial property' in Article 36 to reach this conclusion.

6 HOW INTRUSIVE SHOULD ARTICLE 36 BE?

One of the most vexing questions which arises with respect to national intellectual property rights and the free movement of goods is the extent to which Article 36 may be used to interfere with the actual scope of national intellectual property rights. On the one hand, as we have seen, the approach of the ECJ has been to itself identify the 'specific subject-matter' of the intellectual property right in question and to analyse whether its 'exercise' in a given case is justified for the purpose of safeguarding rights which constitute the 'specific subject-matter' of that right. In particular, the ECJ has held that any exercise will not be justified for the purpose of safeguarding rights which constitute the 'specific subject-matter' of that right if the goods have already been marketed in another Member State by the intellectual property right-owner himself or with his consent (the doctrine of 'exhaustion of rights'). As has already been discussed, the crux of this approach is that the ECJ *itself* identifies and defines what constitutes the specific subject-matter of particular intellectual property rights. Such an approach implicitly suggests that the specific subject-matter of intellectual property rights is a matter for EC rather than national law.

On the other hand, however, according to the ECJ's own distinction between the 'existence' and 'exercise' of intellectual property rights[118] the 'existence', and therefore the scope, of national intellectual property rights should remain untouched by Article 36 and the EC Treaty (in accordance with Article 222 EC). The ECJ has respected this position in a long line of case law. With respect to patents, the ECJ has held that 'since the existence of patent rights is at present a matter solely of national law, a Member State's patent legislation . . . is covered in principle by the derogations from Article 30 which are provided for in Article 36'.[119] Similarly, with respect to trade marks, the ECJ has held that 'in the present state of Community law and in the absence of Community standardization or harmonization of laws, the conditions and procedures for the protection of an intellectual property rights are a matter for national law'.[120] These words have been echoed by the ECJ in the field of copyright protection where it has stated that

[I]n the present state of Community law, which is characterised by a lack of harmonisation or approximation of legislation governing the protection of literary

---

[118] See discussion of this distinction at p. 295.
[119] Case 35/87 *Thetford* v. *Fiamma* [1988] ECR 3585 at para. 15.
[120] Case C–317/91, n. 104 above at para. 20.

and artistic property, it is for the national legislatures to determine the conditions and detailed rules for such protection. In so far as the disparity between national laws may give rise to restrictions on intra-Community trade in sound recordings, such restrictions are justified under Article 36 of the Treaty if they are the result of differences between the rules governing the period of the protection and this is inseparably linked to the very *existence* of the exclusive rights.[121]

Finally, with respect to designs and models for spare parts for cars, the ECJ has held that it was for 'the national legislature to determine which products qualify for protection' and that '[t]o prevent the application of the national legislation in such circumstances would therefore be tantamount to challenging the very *existence* of that right'.[122]

In all the above cases, the ECJ accepted that the scope of the intellectual property right at issue was a matter for national law subject only to the second sentence of Article 36. Thus, although the 'existence' of the right was not at issue, the ECJ was competent to nevertheless check that the grant of the intellectual property right did not give rise to an 'arbitrary discrimination' or a 'disguised restriction on trade'.[123]

In summary then, it appears that there is a conflict in the ECJ case law in that the ECJ adopts two distinct approaches. In some cases, the ECJ reasons that Article 36 only admits derogations from the fundamental principle of the free movement of goods to the extent to which such derogations are justified for the purpose of safeguarding rights which constitute the specific subject-matter of such property. Following this approach, the ECJ *itself* identifies which rights constitute the specific subject-matter of the intellectual property right. On the other hand, in other cases, the ECJ reasons that the scope and existence of national intellectual property rights, in the absence of Community harmonization, is a matter for national law subject only to the proviso that they do not constitute a means of arbitrary discrimination or a disguised restriction on trade between Member States under the second sentence of Article 36. The difference between these two approaches goes to the very heart of the question of how intrusive a role Article 36 should play in determining the scope of national intellectual property rights. In spite of a lack of clarity as to which of these two contrasting approaches will be applied by the ECJ, it is submitted that the choice of approach is not an arbitrary one. If one looks closely at all the cases in which the ECJ took the view that the scope of intellectual property rights was a matter for national law, it becomes clear that it only takes this

---

[121] Case 341/87 *EMI* v. *Patricia* [1989] ECR 79, [1989] 2 CMLR 413 at paras. 11–12. Emphasis added.

[122] Case 53/87 *Maxicar* v. *Renault* [1988] ECR 6039 at para. 11. Emphasis added. See also to similar effect concerning national design rights, Case Case 144/81 *Keurkoop* v. *Nancy Keane Gifts* [1982] ECR 2853, [1983] 2 CMLR 47.

[123] See, e.g. Case 35/87, n. 119 above at paras. 16–20 & Case 158/86 *Warner Bros* v. *Christiansen* [1988] ECR 2605, [1990] 3 CMLR 684 at para. 12.

view in cases when, as a matter of fact, the owner of the intellectual property right is attempting to prevent infringement of that right by imports from another Member State where that owner does not own an equivalent right and when the infringing imports are manufactured by a third party unconnected to the owner of the intellectual property right. In such cases, the ECJ holds that the scope of the intellectual property right is, in the absence of harmonization, a matter for national law subject only to the proviso that it does not constitute a means of arbitrary discrimination or a disguised restriction on trade between Member States under the second sentence of Article 36. This may be contrasted with cases which involve the importation of goods by a third party which are covered by an intellectual property right in both Member States owned by the same owner (in which case the 'exhaustion of rights' doctrine applies) or when the owner of the intellectual property right had himself marketed the goods in the other Member State where he held no intellectual property right (in which case the principle of 'consent' would apply). In the latter type of cases, the ECJ reasons that Article 36 only admits derogations from the fundamental principle of the free movement of goods to the extent to which such derogations are justified for the purpose of safeguarding rights which constitute the specific subject-matter of such property. As has been noted, following this approach, the ECJ *itself* identifies which rights constitute the specific subject-matter of the intellectual property right. It is therefore submitted that it can be deduced from ECJ case law that it is only in cases in which the owner of the intellectual property right is attempting to prevent infringement of that right by imports from another Member State where that owner *does not own an equivalent right* and when the infringing imports are manufactured by a *third party unconnected* to the owner of the intellectual property right that the ECJ holds that the scope and existence of national intellectual property rights, in the absence of Community harmonization, is a matter for national law.

In cases where the intellectual property right infringement is by import from another Member State where the owner of the intellectual property right does not own an equivalent right and when the infringing imports are manufactured by a third party unconnected to the owner, the national courts have, perhaps not surprisingly, come down very much in favour of finding that the national legislator remains free to decide upon the scope of intellectual property protection. For example, the Dutch courts have held that Article 36 does not affect the application of Dutch legislation providing for the non-retroactivity of patent annulments,[124] which had the result that, although a patent had already been annulled by a Dutch court, it could nevertheless be relied upon to prevent infringement (by importa-

---

[124] *Rijksoctrooiwet* (Patent Act), Art. 51(4).

tion or otherwise) until such time as that annulment entered into force.[125] Equally, the extension of Dutch patent protection to include a product which was 'directly produced by the [patented] action'[126] was held not to breach Article 36 as it was justified for the protection of rights that form part of the specific subject-matter of patent protection.[127] With respect to trade marks, the *Hoge Raad* has upheld a suit for infringement of a trade mark in circumstances in which the holder of the trade mark had not taken action to put an end to the infringement within five years.[128] Under Article 13A(1) of the Benelux Trade Mark Law there was no such five year rule as was the case in other Member States and indeed in Article 9 of the first trade mark Directive 89/104[129] which had not yet entered into force. The *Hoge Raad* simply rejected the Article 36 argument, which was fully explained in the opinion of Advocate General Koopmans, who correctly stated that it was clear from ECJ case law that in the absence of harmonization, it was up to national legislation to define the extent and duration of trade-mark protection and that it was thus perfectly compatible with Article 36 EC that the Benelux Trade Mark Law allowed suit for infringement even when the owner of the trade mark had taken no action within five years of the first infringement.[130]

The French courts have equally upheld the competence of the national legislator to decide upon the scope of intellectual property protection granted under it. For example, French copyright legislation[131] which allowed the owner of copyright in sound recordings to require prior authorization for the hiring out of sound recordings was held not to be in breach of the provisions on the free movement of goods. The *Cour d'Appel* of Pau in *Ministère public* v. *Jean Claude Vendome* held that any restriction to trade resulting from the French legislation did not 'exceed what is necessary to attain the objective of the Act, which is to encourage production as such'.[132] This conclusion was upheld on appeal to the *Cour de Cassation*,

---

[125] *Mecanorma-Polyvroom BV* v. *Letraset*, *Gerechtshof* 's-Gravenhage, 13 June 1979, NJ 1980, 358; *Akzo NV* v. *Du Pont de Nemours*, Pres. *Arrondissementsrechtbank* Arnhem, 1 Feb. 1985, KG 1985, 106; *Du Pont de Nemours* v. *Enka BV*, *Arrondissementsrechtbank* 's-Gravenhage, 10 Apr. 1981, BIE 1988, 70.

[126] Amendment introduced by the *Rijkswet* of 12 Jan. 1977 (Stb. 160).

[127] *Velcro Europe BV* v. *Ferd. van Damme*, *Gerechtshof* Arnhem, 12 Mar. 1979, NJ 1980, 277.

[128] *Compagnie Générale des établissements Michelin* v. *Michelen Besteck und Metallwaren-fabrikation Werner Michels*, *Hoge Raad*, 17 Dec. 1993, IER 1994, 4; NJ 1994, 573 (with note by Gielen); RvdW 1994, 6; BIE 1995, 64.

[129] Council Directive 89/104 to approximate the laws of the Member States relating to trade marks, n. 1 above.

[130] With respect to trade marks, see also *Moritz Thienelt Likörfabrik* v. *Bredasche Wijnhandel*, Pres. *Arrondissementsrechtbank* Breda, 15 Sept. 1977, BIE 1978, 18 which concerned reliance on a trade mark valid in the Netherlands for 'Kroatbeere' (berry liqueur) to prevent importation from Germany where it was no longer possible to register 'Kroatbeare' as a trade mark.

[131] Art. 21, Copyright (Amendment) Act of 3 July 1985 [1986] 2 CLE F87 and [1987] 1 CLE 1 (English text).

[132] *Cour d'appel* Pau, *Chambre des appels de police correctionnelle*, 29 Nov. 1989, [1991] ECC 57.

which added that 'the formulation and regulation of copyright are, pursuant to Article 222 EEC, the responsibility of Member States'.[133] The *Cour de Cassation* reiterated this conclusion in a judgment concerning the same French legislation by again holding that, even if there was a breach of Article 30, the provisions of the French legislation in question were 'inherent to the protection of copyright' in the sense of Article 36 and according to Article 222 EC, the regulation of copyright was a matter for Member States.[134] While the result reached by the French courts in these cases is undoubtedly correct, the reasoning was rather unsatisfactory. It is submitted that the French courts placed undue emphasis on Article 222. It should be remembered that although the ECJ has held in this type of case that the scope and existence of national intellectual property rights is a matter for national law in the absence of Community harmonization, the ECJ has also always proceeded to subject this conclusion to the proviso that they do not constitute a means of arbitrary discrimination or a disguised restriction on trade between Member States under the second sentence of Article 36. While there appears to be nothing arbitrary or discriminatory in the application of the French legislation in question, the judgments of the French courts would have inspired more confidence if they had, in these cases, explicitly applied the second sentence of Article 36 instead of relying purely on Article 222.

A similar case arose before the French courts in *SORECOP* v. *Techni import professionnel* which concerned a fee levied under French copyright legislation on the sale of blank audio- and video-cassettes in order to compensate copyright owners for loss of revenue arising from copying.[135] In response to the argument that such a fee breached Article 30, the *Cour d'Appel* of Paris held that even if that Article was breached, 'fees for private copying, to the extent that they are part of legislation for the protection of intellectual property, are in the sovereign domain of each Member State of the Community'.[136] In a second judgment in the same case, the Paris *Cour d'Appel* again held that 'a fee for private copying is within the specific subject-matter of copyright and must accordingly benefit from the exception contained in Article 36'.[137] The French legislation in question was perhaps

---

[133] *Cour de Cassation*, ch. crim., 13 Dec. 1990, Bull. Cass. Crim. 1990, no. 434; Dalloz 1991, IR 72; [1992] ECC 185.

[134] *Bouyer, Cour de Cassation*, ch. crim. R, 2 Feb. 1994, Bull. Cass. Crim. 1994, no. 48 p. 95; JCP 1994, IV 137. See also *Ministère public et Société civile des producteurs de phonogrammes (SCPP)* v. *V.*, *Trib. Corr.* Pau, 30 Mar. 1988, RIDA 1988, 113 (with note by Gaubiac).

[135] Arts. 31–44, Copyright (Amendment) Act of 3 July 1985, n. 131 above.

[136] *Cour d'appel* Paris, 1re ch. A, 12 Dec. 1988, RIDA 1989, no. 141 p. 266.

[137] *Cour d'appel* Paris, 1re ch., 8 Jan. 1991, RIDA 1991, no. 148 p. 142. On a further appeal to the *Cour de Cassation*, that court upheld the judgment of the Paris *Cour d'Appel* and simply mentioned that even if intra-Community trade was affected by the French legislation, the French provisions were within the specific subject-matter of copyright in Art. 36: *Cour de Cassation*, ch. comm., 4 Jan. 1994, Bull. Cass. Civ. 1994, IV no. 3 p. 3; Dalloz 1994, IR 54.

unusual in that it classified the fee as a 'copyright' fee in circumstances in which there is no commercial exploitation of copyright itself. However, the conclusion reached by these French courts seems unobjectionable: in the absence of harmonization, it is for national legislation to decide upon the scope of national intellectual property rights so long as they comply with the second sentence of Article 36.

The English courts have also approached this type of case by deciding that the extent of intellectual property protection was a matter for national law. This matter surfaced in several cases concerning copyright under United Kingdom law in the design of spare parts for cars. In such cases, the English courts tended to themselves define the specific subject-matter of such copyright. Thus, in *British Leyland Motor Corporation* v. *T. I. Silencers*, Walton J in the Chancery Division of the High Court held that specific subject-matter of the copyright in drawings of spare parts for motor vehicles was 'the right to prevent infringements of that copyright . . . and . . . as an alternative, to licence others to infringe that right'.[138] In another case before the Chancery Division, Foster J also defined the specific subject-matter of the same right as being 'to ensure that the skill and effort of the draughtsman are rewarded by the grant of an exclusive right to copy and make for sale three dimensional reproductions by the grant of licences and to prevent others from infringing that right'.[139] Both of these definitions of the specific subject-matter have been criticised by Arnull who has argued that

The specific subject-matter of artistic copyright has not yet been defined by the European Court and any definition offered by a domestic court can only confuse the issue. In particular, Walton J's definition does nothing to answer the crucial question of in what circumstances does Community law permit a copyright owner to exercise that right so as to prevent infringement of it.[140]

In a further commentary, the definition offered by the English courts in these cases has been criticized, since

[t]he right in question was that of the author of a drawing to protect against three-dimensional reproduction, based not on the drawing itself but on a previous three-dimensional reproduction. It is by no means certain that that right would be regarded by the Court of Justice as falling within the specific subject-matter of copyright; and the way to remove the uncertainty was by reference under Article 177.[141]

---

[138] [1980] 1 CMLR 598 at 603.

[139] *British Leyland Motor Corporation* v. *Armstrong Patents* [1982] 3 CMLR 603 at 605. With respect to the specific subject-matter of trade marks under English law see *Duracell International Inc* v. *Ever Ready Ltd* [1989] RPC 731 (High Court) and *Levi Strauss & Co.* v. *Tacchella* judgt of High Court of Justice (ChD), 29 Jan. 1982 (transcr. Martin Walsh Cherer).

[140] (1983) 8 ELRev. 365 at 372.

[141] Dashwood and Arnull, 'English Courts and Article 177 of the EEC Treaty' at 274.

It is, however, submitted that this objection to the national legislation, as interpreted by the national courts in its definition of the specific subject-matter of the copyright in spare parts for cars, is misplaced. While it is true that Walton J was putting it a little strongly in *T. I. Silencers* when he described the defences based on Community law as 'some of the most audacious allegations I have ever seen',[142] it is difficult to disagree with his analysis that the suit of infringers was the ordinary exercise of the specific subject-matter of the right and furthermore that there was no evidence of arbitrary discrimination. In a second judgment, in the same case, Walton J again dismissed the argument that the purely functional nature of the United Kingdom copyright in spare parts did not constitute 'industrial and commercial property', which was not recognized in all Member States, by adding that Article 222 EC provided that property rights were in no way to be prejudiced by the provisions of the EC Treaty.[143] Indeed, as Fox LJ observed in the English Court of Appeal in *Armstrong Patents*, 'in the absence of any specific assumption or provision in the Treaty of Rome (and there is none) one can only ascertain the rights which constitute the specific subject-matter of copyright by looking at national law'.[144] The latter point has now been clearly underlined by the ECJ in *Maxicar* v. *Renault* where it held in the context of similar Italian legislation granting design rights for spare parts in cars that

It must first be stated that . . . with respect to the protection of designs and models in the present state of Community law and in the absence of Community standardization or harmonization of laws the determination of the conditions and procedures under which such protection is granted is a matter for national rules. It is for the national legislature to determine which products qualify for protection, even if they form part of a unit already protected as such . . . To prevent the application of the national legislation in such circumstances would therefore be tantamount to challenging the very existence of that right.[145]

A similar scenario presented itself in the *Thetford Corporation* v. *Fiamma SpA* case before the English courts. That case concerned United Kingdom legislation which gave patent protection for an invention which had not been exploited for fifty years. On importation of a product which was covered by a patent granted under this legislation, it was argued that reliance on such a patent was not justified under Article 36 because it did not fall within the specific subject-matter of patent protection which required at least some element of novelty. This argument was struck out by the Chancery Division of the High Court, which held that 'The specific subject-matter of any industrial and commercial property rights is to be

---

[142] n. 138 above at 605.
[144] [1984] 3 CMLR 102 at 144.
[143] [1980] 2 CMLR 332.
[145] Case 53/87, n. 122 above at paras. 10–11.

determined by the domestic, that is to say the national law creating it'.[146] The High Court added that, 'As with any other industrial and commercial property right the mere absence of the patent protection in another Member State of the EEC has never been held to debar a patentee from injunctive relief against the importation of goods from that Member State into the State where his patent protection does not exist.'

Although the defence was reinstated on appeal by the Court of Appeal which referred the matter to the ECJ, the subsequent ECJ judgment confirmed the view which the High Court had expressed, namely that 'since the existence of patent rights is at present a matter solely of national law, a Member State's patent legislation . . . is covered in principle by the derogations from Article 30 which are provided for in Article 36'.[147]

The ECJ has thus given the Member States a remarkably wide discretion in this type of case with respect to national intellectual property legislation. It must be conceded that this approach is out of step with the ECJ's interpretation of the other heads of justification in Article 36 where it has been far readier to place limits upon the discretion of the Member States. Indeed, Oliver has commented that 'It is hard to overcome a sense of unease about these judgments which appear to concede to the Member States virtually unbridled powers to apply their own legislation, however unreasonable the result.'[148] It is indeed alarming to see the national courts referring to national intellectual property legislation as being within 'the sovereign domain of each Member State of the Community'.[149] However, it must also be conceded that there is no evidence which emerges from this analysis of the national courts' judgments to suggest that the application of the ECJ's approach leads to abuse. In none of the cases discussed in this section could it be said that undue or abusive restrictions to trade were being created. Intellectual property deserves special treatment by the ECJ given its indisputable commercial significance and, until such time as it is further harmonized through Community legislation, the application of non-discriminatory national legislation must, in the absence of exhaustion or consent, be maintained. This is not to say that there are no difficulties which emerge from the national court application of this approach. Indeed, it has been shown how certain national courts have placed too great an emphasis in these cases on Article 222 instead of explicitly applying the second sentence in Article 36. In *Yale Security Products Ltd* v. *Newman* the Chancery Division of the English High Court rejected the argument that copyright granted under United Kingdom legislation for

---

[146] High Court of Justice (ChD), judgt of 30 July 1985 (transcr. available on Lexis) (per Falconer J).

[147] Case 35/87, n. 119 above at para. 15.

[148] Oliver, *Free Movement of Goods in the European Community*, 260.

[149] *Techni import professionnel*, n. 136 above.

the design of 'key blanks' did not fall within the specific subject-matter of copyright by stating that 'the definition of the right concerned is a question of English law and that English law may be eccentric does not, as I understand the case, affect the matter'.[150] It is submitted that such a sweeping statement is pushing the Member State's discretion a little too far since it is clear that if the 'eccentricity' in the national legislation leads to arbitrary discrimination or a disguised restriction on trade, the matter would be very much affected, and would result in the national legislation being incompatible with Article 36. Furthermore, the seeming willingness of the English High Court to strike out so-called 'Euro-defences' based in Article 36 is undoubtedly a matter of concern.[151] However, as a general overview, it would not be true to say that the experience of the application by national courts of this point of the ECJ's case law has led to abuse or to arbitrary results. In view of the importance of intellectual property rights in fostering competition and innovation, this is indeed a happy conclusion.

7 DO YOU HAVE TO SUE FOR THE INTELLECTUAL PROPERTY RIGHT INFRINGEMENT IN THE OTHER MEMBER STATE?

A question which has never been explicitly raised or conclusively dealt with by the ECJ is whether it is necessary, in order to rely on an intellectual property right to prevent import from another Member State, to have sued for infringement of that right in the exporting Member State. In other words, is it possible to argue that the fact that proceedings for infringement have not been commenced in the exporting Member State has the consequence that one has, in such circumstances, implicitly consented to the marketing in the other Member State such that free movement of goods must prevail under the familiar ECJ case law?

---

[150] [1990] FSR 320. See also, *Biotrading & Finance OY* v. *Biohit Ltd*, judgment of the High Court of 28 Mar. 1995 (transcr. available on Lexis).

[151] It may be noted that in both *British Leyland Motor Corporation* v. *T. I. Silencers* [1981] 2 CMLR 75 and *Thetford Corporation* v. *Fiamma SpA* [1987] 3 CMLR 266 the Court of Appeal reinstated the defences based on Art. 36 after they had been struck out by the High Court under RSC Ord. 18 r. 19. In *T. I. Silencers*, the CA held that while the High Court's judgment with respect to Art. 222 was 'forceful and convincing' it went on to state that 'we have been warned, and on more than one occasion, of the danger of assuming too much knowledge of the way in which the European Court interprets the Treaty of Rome' ([1981] 2 CMLR 75 at 84). With respect to requests for leave to amend defences to include issues relating to Art. 36 and intellectual property rights, see *Hagen* v. *Fratelli D. & G. Moretti S.N.C.* [1980] 3 CMLR 253; [1980] FSR 517; *Windsurfing International Inc* v. *Tabur Marine Ltd*, judgt of High Court of Justice (Chancery Division—Patents Court) of 4 Mar. 1982 (transcript: Marten Walsh Cherer); *Levi Strauss & Co.* v. *Tacchella*, judgt of High Court of Justice (ChD) 29 Jan. 1982 (transcr.: Marten Walsh Cherer.

This question has arisen before the national courts. In *Firma Trioliet* v. *Maschinen- und Landmaschinenfabrik Husmann GmbH*, the *Gerechtshof* Leeuwarden was faced with the above argument with respect to the infringement of a patent in the Netherlands[152] through import from Germany. The defendant argued that because the plaintiff had known for over ten years that the product infringing the patent was being manufactured in Germany in breach of its German patent without bringing infringement proceedings in Germany, this amounted to consent and accordingly, that free movement of goods must prevail over the Dutch patent. The *Gerechtshof* Leeuwarden rejected this argument by stating that 'There is no reason to accept that the consent required can be given tacitly. It would be going too far to conclude without more . . . from the single fact that [the plaintiff] did not immediately take action against infringement of its patent by [the defendant] that consent was given.'[153] A similar line was taken by the President of the *Arrondissementsrechtbank* Roermond in *WAJ Berkers* v. *General Electro Music Industry SpA* where, on virtually identical facts, it was held that 'The only fact that [the plaintiff] (which according to him was the result of financial considerations) did not bring an action for infringement in Italy does not mean that he tacitly accepted production there.'[154] These judgments were taken a step further by the *Hoge Raad*, which has more recently held in a case in which infringement proceedings had been successfully initiated in the exporting Member State that the fact that the owner of the patent had agreed to postpone enforcement of that judgment in that Member State, did not amount to consent to the marketing of the patented good in that State such that free movement of goods under the ECJ's case law must prevail.[155]

An analogous question which has arisen before the French courts is whether an intellectual property right may be relied upon to prevent import of infringing goods from another Member State where an equivalent right was registrable in the exporting Member State but had never in fact been so registered. This question arose in *Société d'exploitation des Etablissements Colin Expansion* v. *Nakache*, which concerned an attempt to rely on copyright in a furniture design in France to prevent infringement of that right by importation from Italy of a good manufactured there by an independent third party. The copyright owner wishing to rely on his

---

[152] Under Art. 30 & 43, *Rijksoctrooiwet*.

[153] *Gerechtshof* Leeuwarden, 29 June 1983, BIE 1984, 55. For a judgment before the English courts in which this problem was raised, see *Letraset Ltd* v. *Limpet Tapes Ltd*, judgt of High Court of Justice (ChD) 14 Feb. 1985 (transcr. available on Lexis).

[154] Pres. *Arrondissementsrechtbank* Roermond, 3 Apr 1986, BIE 1983, 2. It may be noted that the President mistakenly referred in his judgt to Article 30 of the Brussels Convention instead of to that Article of the EEC Treaty (as it then was).

[155] *Boehringer GmbH* v. *Kirin Amgen Inc.*, *Hoge Raad*, 21 Apr. 1995, NJ 1996, 462, BIE 1995, 103.

copyright in France did not hold the equivalent copyright in Italy, not because such a right was not registrable in Italy, but simply because it had never registered the right there. The French courts held that the plaintiff could rely on its copyright in France to prevent importation in such circumstances.[156] Although the reasoning of these courts was precise and rigorous, it is of note that none of the French courts tackled the argument concerning the 'registrability' in Italy directly. This bypassing of the issue has been criticized by Burst and Kovar who argue that a reference to the ECJ pursuant to Article 177 would have been more satisfactory.[157] On the other hand, other commentators have fully approved of the solution adopted by the French courts as being in conformity with the spirit and the letter of Article 36 of the Treaty of Rome.[158]

It is perhaps true that it would have been desirable for one of these national courts to have referred this question to the ECJ for authoritative resolution of the matter. Nevertheless, it is submitted that the solution which all the national courts have adopted in these cases is correct and fully in line with the logic and spirit of the ECJ's interpretation of 'industrial and commercial property' in Article 36. It would be very surprising if the consent principle was to be interpreted so as to require an owner of an intellectual property right to sue for every infringement of that right in all corners of the Community before that right might be relied upon to prevent infringement in one Member State. Similarly, to hold that it was necessary to register a particular intellectual property right in every Member State which offers similar protection before one can rely on one's right in one Member State would equally appear to be unduly onerous. Thus, while the solution adopted by the national courts seems to be correct, these cases do nevertheless demonstrate that the simple formulation of the consent principle by the ECJ is often difficult to apply in practice.

---

[156] *TGI* Lyon, 6 July 1976, JCP 1978, II 18954; Annales de la propriété industrielle, artistique et littéraire 1978, 194. The case was then appealed to the *Cour d'appel* Lyon, 1re ch., 7 June 1977, JCP 1978, II 18954; Annales de la propriété industrielle, artistique et littéraire 1978, 199; Rev. crit. dr. int. priv. 1978, 561; La Propriété industrielle 1977, no. 201 III 405; and finally to the *Cour de Cassation*, ch. comm., 20 Feb. 1980, Bull. Cass. Civ. 1980, IV 68–9; JCP 1981, II 19619; Rev. crit. dr. int. priv. 1980, 779; La Propriété industrielle 1980, no. 201 III p. 111.

[157] Burst and Kovar JCP 1978 II 18954 and JCP 1981 II 19619. See also Chavanne and Azéma RTDE 1976, 520.

[158] Mollet-Vieville, Annales de la propriété industrielle, artistique et littéraire 1978 193. See also Françon, Rev. crit. dr. int. priv. 1978, 566 and Rev. crit. dr. int. priv. 1980, 781 and Audeoud, Berlin, Manin, 'The application of Community law in France: Review of French Court decisions from 1974 to 1981'.

8 THE BURDEN OF PROOF

With respect to the other heads of justification in Article 36,[159] the ECJ has held that the burden of proving that an infringement of the rules on free movement of goods is justified under one of those heads lies with the Member State wishing to rely on Article 36.[160] One would therefore expect that the same would apply to 'industrial and commercial property' and that, by analogy, the burden of proving that a restriction was justified would lie with the owner of the intellectual property right wishing to prevent the free movement of goods. The ECJ has never had the opportunity to explicitly hold that this is the case. It is at first sight surprising, therefore, to note that the national courts have taken the view that the reverse is the case; that is, that the burden of proof lies with the parallel importer being sued for the intellectual property infringement.

The burden of proof issue presented itself very neatly before the Dutch courts at an early stage. In *Ciba Geigy AG* v. *Luxan BV*,[161] the President of the *Arrondissementsrechtbank* Arnhem was faced with a suit for patent infringement in the Netherlands by import of a product falling under the patent (an agricultural chemical product) from another Member State. It was common ground that the patent owner in the Netherlands (Ciba Geigy) could not rely on that patent to prevent importation if the imported products had been marketed in the other Member State either by himself or with his consent. Ciba Geigy argued that it was for the importer (Luxan) to prove that the products in question had in fact been imported from another Member State and that they originated from Ciba Geigy or one of its licensees. The *Arrondissementsrechtbank* Arnhem accepted this argument and held that the party which claims that the product was put lawfully on the market bears the burden of proving that this is the case and that 'The present state of EEC law and the development of the case law of the Court of Justice do not, in our judgment, offer any support for the argument raised by Luxan that there is a reversal or a different division of the burden of proof to that which has applied hitherto.' Luxan had adduced as evidence a blank invoice and product packaging with serial numbers the authenticity of which Ciba Geigy denied. The *Arrondissementsrechtbank* Arnhem held that 'these materials do not provide satisfactory proof' and that the alleged origin was doubtful. The *Arrondissementsrechtbank* also rejected the argument that if Luxan had to adduce proof, Ciba Geigy would be able to use this information to ascertain which of its distributors in other Member States were selling to

---

[159] See Ch. 7.
[160] See, e.g., Case 251/78 *Denkavit Futtermittel* v. *Minister of Agriculture* [1979] ECR 3369, [1980] 3 CMLR 513 and Case 227/82 *Leendert van Bennekom* [1983] ECR 3883, [1985] 2 CMLR 692.

parallel importers, and thereby be able to amend its distribution network using this information to partition markets. The *Arrondissementsrechtbank* correctly stated that if such was indeed the case, this could be challenged as being contrary to Article 85 EC rather than under Articles 30 to 36 EC.

More recently, the President of the *Arrondissementsrechtbank* Breda in *Nederlandse Vereniging van Producenten en importeurs van beeld- en geluids-dragers* v. *Wortelboer* similarly suggested that it was up to the importer to show that the goods in question were marketed in the other Member State by the owner of the intellectual property right or with his consent.[162] In this case, which concerned copyright infringement of live music record-ings, the importer refused to disclose their supplier in the other Member State. The *Arrondissementsrechtbank* Breda held that if the recordings had been marketed in the other Member State by licence or consent of the Dutch copyright owner there would be no need for the importer to refuse to disclose its supplier in that Member State. In other words, the refusal to declare origin was itself taken by the Dutch court as evidence that these were illicit copies.

The English courts have taken a similar view in a case before the Chancery Division of the High Court concerning two different trade marks registered by the same owner for identical products in two Member States.[163] Trade marks for a herbicide known generically as 'fenox-apropethyl' were owned by Hoechst both in Belgium (where it had regis-tered the trade mark PUMA) and in the United Kingdom (where it had registered the trade mark CHEETAH). Hoechst sued the defendant for trade-mark infringement for having sold the product in the United Kingdom having imported it from Belgium and, although not repackaging the prod-uct itself, having used the CHEETAH trade mark on delivery notes and sub-sequent invoices. The High Court held that this was a breach of the United Kingdom trade mark and rejected defences based on Articles 30 to 36. The High Court reasoned that Hoechst had not first marketed the herbicide under the mark CHEETAH in any Member State and 'thus the rights of Hoechst in relation to the mark CHEETAH were not used by Hoechst on first marketing and have not been exhausted'. However, the defendant had further argued, relying on the ECJ's judgment in *Centrafarm* v. *American Home Products*,[164] that the registration of two different trade marks for dif-ferent Member States constituted arbitrary discrimination and was a dis-guised restriction on trade. In particular, the defendant relied on the latter ECJ authority in which the ECJ had held that reliance on a trade mark in

---

[161] Pres. *Arrondissementsrechtbank* Arnhem , 2 Mar. 1978 (transcr.).
[162] n. 57 above.   [163] *Hoechst UK Ltd* v. *Chemiculture* [1993] FSR 263.
[164] Case 3/78 [1978] ECR 1823.

similar circumstances[165] was in principle justified under the first sentence of Article 36 but would nevertheless breach the second sentence of that Article if the registration of different trade marks was 'part of system of marketing intended to partition the markets artificially' and that 'it is for the national court to settle in each particular case whether the proprietor has followed the practice of using different marks for the same product for the purpose of partitioning the markets'.[166] In carrying out this analysis, the High Court assumed that the defendant carried the burden of showing that the proprietor had in fact followed the practice of using different marks for the same product for the purpose of partitioning the markets. This is apparent in the High Court's rejection of the defendant's claim that the artificial partitioning of the market was demonstrated by the fact that the proprietor (Hoechst) sold the herbicide in Belgium at a much lower price. This the High Court rejected in the following terms:

But there may have been many reasons for this. The defendant may have bought up bankrupt stock or purchased cheaply at end-of-season sales. It has chosen to give no evidence as to the source of its product. In the absence of any evidence from it, the defendant fails to demonstrate an arguable defence in this respect.

Thus the assumption of the national courts has clearly been that the importer carries the burden of proof in such cases.[167] Although the position adopted by the national courts in these cases sits rather uneasily with the ECJ's interpretation of the other heads of justification in Article 36, it is submitted that the reversal of the burden of proof in such cases is justified by the special nature of ECJ case law on intellectual property rights. Unlike the other heads of justification in Article 36 'industrial and commercial property' has required the ECJ to develop a distinct approach, which it has done by introducing and applying the doctrine of exhaustion of rights and the principle of consent. Under these principles, it would be open to any defendant in infringement proceedings to argue that the infringing goods were imported from other Member States which had been marketed there by a licensee of the owner of the intellectual property right. If the defendant in such proceedings argues such a defence, it must surely also bear the burden of proving that this is the case. Indeed, it is submitted that it would be unduly onerous for the owner of the intellectual property right to have to prove, when suing for infringement, that the goods emanated from a third party. Surely it is more logical to hold, as the national courts

---

[165] The case concerned 2 trade marks owned by American Home Products for the pharmaceutical product known generically as 'oxazepamum': American Home Products had registered, for the same product, the trade mark SERENID in the United Kingdom and the trade mark SERESTA in the Netherlands.

[166] Case 3/78, n. 165 above, at para. 23.

[167] For an example to this effect before the French courts, see *TMR* v. *Soclaine, Cour d'appel* Paris, 25 Sept. 1996, no. 94/023319 (transcr. available on Lexis).

have in these cases, that the person making that allegation must also support his claim with evidence. Indeed, if the importer acquired the goods in another Member State legitimately, he has nothing to fear in disclosing the source. It is submitted that the national courts were entirely correct to reject the argument that the risk that the plaintiff would be able to use such information to partition markets in the future militated against such an approach. As the *Arrondissementsrechtbank* Arnhem pointed out in *Ciba Geigy* v. *Luxan*, such an objection could be met, should it in fact occur, under the Treaty's competition rules. Finally, intellectual property rights are a special case in the sense that, unlike under the other heads of justification in Article 36, it is individuals rather than Member States which in practice invoke Article 36. It should be remembered that the Member State is not a party to the proceedings for infringement before the national court. This is yet another reason why the usual burden of proof rules under Article 36 should not be decisive in intellectual property cases.

Thus, while the conclusion of the national courts in these cases can be fully approved of, it is nevertheless a pity that none of them thought it necessary to exercise their discretion to refer questions to the ECJ under Article 177. Given that they were departing from the rules on the burden of proof set down by the ECJ under other heads of justification in Article 36, such a course of action would indeed have been desirable.

9 IMPORTATION FROM THIRD COUNTRIES

The ECJ had the opportunity to emphasize in *EMI* v. *CBS*[168] that the Treaty did not prevent the owner of an intellectual property right (*in casu* a trade mark) in all the Member States of the Community from exercising that

[168] Case 51/75 [1976] ECR 811, [1976] 2 CMLR 235 (concerning imports from the USA into the UK); Case 86/75 [1976] ECR 871 (concerning imports from the USA into Denmark); Case 96/75 [1976] ECR 913 (concerning imports imports from the USA into Germany).

[169] Case 51/75, n. 168 above at para. 11.

[170] See, e.g., before the Dutch courts: *Beiersdorf AG* v. *Vomar Voordeelmarkt BV*, Pres. *Arrondissementsrechtbank* Haarlem, 28 Sept. 1990, BIE 1991, 98; *Riker Labroratories Inc.* v. *Arnhemse Pharmaceutische Onderneming 'Apharmo' BV*, Pres. *Arrondissementsrechtbank* 's-Gravenhage, 8 Dec. 1988, BIE 1989, 39. Before the English courts, see *Revlon Inc* v. *Cripps & Lee Ltd* [1980] FSR 85 (High Court) and *Smith Kline and French Labroratories Ltd* v. *Global Pharmaceuticals Ltd* [1986] RPC 394 (CA). Before the German courts, see *Levi Strauss* v. *Uli Knecht, Bundesgerichtshof*, 14 Dec. 1995, Case No. I ZR 210/93, GRUR 1996, 271. An analogous problem has arisen before the Dutch courts since Dutch trade-mark law used to accept world-wide exhaustion, whereas Art. 7 of Directive 89/104 (n. 1 above) provides only for exhaustion in another Member State. In 3 judgments before the Dutch courts, the world-wide exhaustion doctrine has been applied rather than interpreting the Dutch legislation in conformity to the Directive: see *Rigu Sound and Van Duyn* v. *Pink Floyd, Gerechtshof* Den Haag, 1 June 1995, IER 1995, 169; *Novell* v. *America Direct, Arrondissementsrechtbank* Den Haag, 7 July 1995, IER 1995, 172 and *The Polo/Lauren Company* v. *America Today Nederland*, Pres. *Arrondissementsrechtbank* Amsterdam, 26 Oct. 1995, IER 1996, 31. See criticism of these

right to prevent the importation of goods infringing the right coming from a third country. The ECJ reasoned in that judgment that the exercise of an intellectual property right in such circumstances could not be said to affect trade between Member States and thus could 'not in fact jeopardize the unity of the common market which Article 30 *et seq.* are intended to ensure'.[169] Since the *EMI* v. *CBS* judgment, the *dicta* of the ECJ in that case has been applied in a straightforward fashion on several occasions by the national courts.[170] A related question of a less straightforward nature concerns the application of the exhaustion doctrine in cases in which the proprietor of an intellectual property right in a Member State wishes to rely on that right to prevent import of the protected goods from another Member State into which it had been lawfully imported from a third country. In such a case, according to Articles 9(2) and 10(1) EC, so long as import formalities have been completed in the other Member State, the product in question should be able to benefit from the free movement of goods.[171] However, the *Oberlandesgericht* Hamburg has held in such circumstances that the consent given by the owner of the intellectual property right for the marketing of a protected product in the third country did not imply the necessary consent to market the product in one of the Member States of the Community as is required for the application of the exhaustion doctrine.[172] The English High Court has taken a similar view in a case concerning copyright. In *Chrysalis Records* v. *Goldberg*,[173] Chrysalis Records held the copyright in the United Kingdom for certain recordings[174] and a licensee manufactured the records in Canada. It was common ground that the direct import of records from Canada to the United Kingdom would be an infringement of Section 16(2) of the Copyright Act 1956. Goldberg, however, first marketed the records in the Netherlands[175] without the express consent of the copyright owner, although the copyright owner had never expressly forbidden the export of the records from Canada to the Netherlands. Goldberg then imported the records into the United Kingdom from the Netherlands. Chrysalis applied for an injunction to prevent these parallel imports on the basis that his

judgments by Swaak, 'Consistent Interpretation of National Law: Dutch Courts on the Wrong Track?' (1996) 2 European Public Law 219.

[171] See discussion of this point in Ch. 2, sect. 1(B).

[172] *OLG* Hamburg, 3 Sept. 1987, GRUR Int. 1988, 255. Noted by Roth (1991) 28 CMLRev. 137 at 161. See also to the same effect *BGH*, 28 Oct. 1987, GRUR 1988, 373.

[173] Transcr.: Marten Meredith. Noted by Guy and Newey (1982) 7 ELRev. 241; (1981) NLJ 989.

[174] *Autoamerican* (Blondie), *Parallel Lines* (Blondie), *Eat to the Beat* (Blondie), *The Wild, the Willing and the Innocent* (UFO), *Not the Nine O'clock News* (Various), *Super Trouper* (ABBA).

[175] The records could be imported into the Netherlands because their import and sale was not forbidden under Dutch law, despite the absence of a licence in the Netherlands, provided that they were genuine records and not pirate material manufactured by persons other than the rightful copyright owner or licensee.

copyright in the United Kingdom would otherwise be breached. Counsel for Goldberg argued however that the imports, being from the Netherlands, were protected by the overriding provisions of the EC Treaty relating to the free movement of goods. The High Court (per Price QC) undertook an excellent analysis of the relevant ECJ authorities and hesitated little in concluding that its discretion to grant an injunction should be exercised. The analysis of ECJ authorities led the High Court to the conclusion that in order for the defendants to raise a defence under the Treaty, they had to show that the records in question had been marketed in the Netherlands by or with the consent of the copyright owner. The contention by Goldberg that an absence of express prohibition to import the records from Canada into the Netherlands amounted to an act of positive consent was rejected by the High Court. It is submitted that this analysis, which has been adopted by other national courts,[176] is correct. It would be surprising if the ECJ was to interpret the consent principle so broadly as to accept that marketing a product through a licensee in a third country amounted to consent to marketing in another Member State of the Community. These cases before the national courts therefore provide yet another example of the difficulties which arise in the application of the consent principle in practice.

The ECJ has recently held in the context of trade-mark infringement that a national trade mark in a Member State may not be relied upon to prevent importation of the protected product from another Member State where the product in question had originally been manufactured in a non-member country and had been imported into the other Member State by the owner of the mark (or by another company in the same group) and the intellectual property rights in both Member States were owned by the same group.[177] This judgment does not however affect the two judgments of national courts discussed above, since in those cases the goods had not been imported from the third country into the other Member State by the owner of the intellectual property right.

---

[176] See, e.g. before the French courts: *Sté KIM et Cercle européen du livre* v. *Mouchard, Trib. corr.* Paris, 31e ch., 3 Dec. 1979, Gaz. Pal. 1980, I Jur 442 (with note by Marchi); RIDA 1980, no. 106 127; Rev. crit. dr. int. priv. 1982, 110. See also the judgt of the English High Court in *The Who Group* v. *Stage One Records* [1980] 2 CMLR 429. Noted by Hicks (1980) 1 EIPR 337 and Leigh & Fothergill (1980) 5 ELRev. 425.

[177] Case C–352/95 *Phytheron International SA* v. *Bourdon* [1997] ECR I–1729, [1997] 2 CMLR 199. The ECJ also laid down as conditions in this case that the product must have been lawfully acquired in the other Member State by an independent trader, that the product had not been processed, and that the packaging had not been changed.

10 CONCLUSIONS

It has been noted that the approach adopted by the ECJ in reconciling the free movement of goods with the existence of national intellectual property rights is not based on the strongest of theoretical foundations. Nevertheless, the ECJ has developed a commendable body of case law which has proved to be both durable and flexible. In particular, the doctrine of 'exhaustion of rights' and the concept of 'consent' provide a simple rule of thumb for the national courts to apply. Consequently the ECJ case law, although based on shaky theoretical foundations, has the merit of having provided the national courts with practical and realistic tests to apply when faced with a conflict between the free movement of goods and national intellectual property rights. The pattern which emerges from the judgments of national courts concerning intellectual property rights is that the application of the principles developed by the ECJ is being carried out in an accurate, straightforward and competent fashion.

Inevitably, the national courts do not have an unblemished record. There are, of course, a number of judgments in which the national courts have appeared to be ignorant of the correct principles governing the exercise of intellectual property rights under Article 36 EC. The cases before the English courts dealing with the compatibility of the provisions of the Patents Act 1977 on 'licences of right' provide examples of poor applications of Article 36 with respect to discriminatory provisions in national patent legislation. Similarly, the application of the ECJ's criteria for trademark infringement through repackaging has also not been without its problems in practice. For example, we have seen unfortunate examples of judgements by national courts in which the *Hoffman-La Roche* criteria are 'abused' by the national court, which merely refer to the ECJ's *Hoffman-La Roche* judgment to conclude that Article 36 applies to justify the restriction, without making any attempt to apply the conditions rigorously to the facts. Equally, the danger that 'confusingly similar' trade marks will be interpreted in divergent ways in different Member States has been exposed.

The discussion in this chapter has also revealed areas in which the national courts have dealt with questions which have never been raised before the ECJ. For example, the national courts have held that it is not necessary, in order to rely on an intellectual property right to prevent import from another Member State, to have sued for infringement of that right in the exporting Member State. Similarly, the national courts have held that the consent given by an owner of an intellectual property right for the marketing of a protected product in a third country does not imply the necessary consent to market the product in one of the Member States of the

Community as is required for the application of the exhaustion doctrine. Perhaps most striking of all, the national courts have concluded that the the parallel importer being sued for intellectual property infringement carries the burden of proving that the imported goods were acquired in the other Member State from the owner of the intellectual property right or with his consent. It is submitted that the solutions which all the national courts have adopted in these cases are defensible but nevertheless illustrate that the simple formulation of the consent principle by the ECJ is often more difficult to apply in practice.

In certain respects, the ECJ's case law reconciling the free movement of goods with intellectual property rights gives a remarkably wide discretion to national intellectual property legislation. As a general overview, it would not be true to say that the experience of the application by the ECJ's case law by national courts has led to abuse or arbitrary results. While it would occasionally have been preferable for the national courts to have sought confirmation of their reasoning by referring questions to the ECJ pursuant to Article 177 EC, they have, on the whole, applied the principles set out in the ECJ's existing case law faithfully and, at times, imaginatively. In view of the importance of intellectual property rights in fostering competition and innovation, and indeed in view of the large volume of intellectual property cases before the national courts, this is a happy conclusion.

9

Completion of the Internal Market and the Effect of Community Harmonization Legislation

1 INTRODUCTION

It has long been appreciated that a dynamic relationship exists between ECJ case law interpreting the fundamental freedoms provided for in the EC Treaty on the one hand, and Community harmonization legislation on the other. This dynamic relationship is characterized by the fact that these two tools of integration complement one another. On the one hand, ECJ case law constitutes 'negative' integration in the sense that it involves national provisions being held to be contrary to specific Articles of the EC Treaty in individual cases. On the other hand, Community harmonization legislation contributes towards 'positive' integration by introducing new standards at Community level which apply horizontally to promote free movement.[1]

The need for Community harmonization legislation was appreciated at the outset and found expression in Article 3(h) of the EC Treaty which provides that the activities of the Community shall include 'the approximation of the laws of Member States to the extent required for the functioning of the common market'. However, following a period of judicial activism during the 1970s, typified by the ECJ's judgments in *Dassonville*[2] and *Cassis de Dijon*,[3] a consensus emerged that the internal market could not be achieved by case law alone and that major legislative action was also required. This awareness manifested itself in a White Paper published by the Commission in 1985,[4] and the Single European Act (SEA) which amended the EEC Treaty to provide the legal machinery for the completion of the internal market by 31 December 1992.[5] Several legal methods

---

[1] See discussion in Weatherill & Beaumont, *EC Law*, 480–1 and Slot, 'Harmonisation' 379–82. See more generally Vignes, 'The Harmonisation of National Legislation and the EEC'; Curall, 'Some Aspects of the Relation between Articles 30–36 and Article 100 of the EEC Treaty With a Closer look at Optional Harmonisation'; and McMillan, 'La "certification", la reconnaissance mutuelle et le marché unique'.

[2] Case 8/74 *Procureur du Roi* v. *Dassonville* [1974] ECR 837.

[3] Case 120/78 *Rewe* v. *Bundesmonopolverwaltung für Branntwein* [1979] ECR 649.

[4] COM(85) 310 final. See generally, Bieber *et al.* (eds.), *1992: One European Market?: A Critical Analysis of the Commission's Internal Market Strategy.*

[5] The most important legal machinery introduced by the SEA is contained in Art. 7A & 100A EC and came into force in 1987. Art. 100A facilitates the task of completing the internal market by providing a legal base for internal market legislation under which the Council of

have been employed in Community harmonization legislation. For example, legislation has taken the form of complete or total harmonization, partial regulation and minimum regulation.[6] An important 'new approach' to technical harmonization and standards was launched in 1985 according to which legislative harmonization is limited to the adoption of essential safety requirements with which manufacturers may voluntarily comply in order to secure recognition in all Member States.[7] Harmonization legislation to complete the internal market is not, of course, value-free and there are several illuminating political underpinnings to such legislation.[8] This has been further emphasized by the emergence of the principle of subsidiarity both as a political instrument[9] but also through its inclusion in Article 3b EC.[10] The current emphasis in Community legislative activity is on consolidating the internal market by increased communication, access to justice and administrative co-operation.[11] This has led to an emphasis on simplifying and consolidating Community legislation in order to make it more transparent[12] and to the Single Market Action Plan to improve the functioning of the Single Market by 1 January 1999.[13]

Ministers may act by a qualified majority, whereas the original provision on harmonization—Art. 100—required unanimity within the Council. See further Glaesner, 'The Single European Act'; Jacqué, 'L'Acte Unique Européen' (1986) RTDE 575; Ehlerman, 'The Internal Market Following the SEA'; Pescatore, 'Some Critical Remarks on the "Single European Act"'; and Bermann, 'The Single European Act' (1989) Col. J. Transnat. L. 529.

[6] For a discussion of various harmonization methods which have been employed, see McGee & Weatherill, 'The Evolution of the Single Market—Harmonisation or Liberalisation' (1990) 53 MLR 578 at 582 and Slot, n. 1 above at 382.

[7] See Annex II of Council Resolution of 7 May 1985 setting out 'Guidelines for a New Approach to Technical Harmonisation and Standards' [1985] OJ C136/1. See also Pelkmans, 'The New Approach to Technical Harmonisation and Standardisation' (1987) 25 JCMS 249. For a classic example of a 'new approach' Directive, see Directive 88/378 on the approximation of the laws of the Member States concerning the safety of toys [1988] OJ L187/1.

[8] See, e.g. discussion by Weiler, 'The Transformation of Europe' (1991) 100 Yale LJ 2403 esp. at 2476.

[9] See the move in the so-called 'Spirit of Edinburgh' after the Edinburgh European Council in Dec. 1992, Bull. EC 12-1992 towards letting objectives be undertaken by the Member States unless they can be better achieved at Community level.

[10] Treaty of Amsterdam Chapter 9, adds a protocol to the EC Treaty on the application of the principles of subsidiarity and proportionality.

[11] See the influential Sutherland Report: 'The Internal Market After 1992—Meeting the Challenge' SEC(92) 2277 final. See also the follow-up to this Report in the Commission's Communication, 'Making the Most of the Internal Market: Strategic Programme' COM(93) 632 final and 'Follow-up to the Sutherland Report: Legislative consolidation to enhance the transparency of Community law in the area of the internal market' COM(93) 361 final.

[12] See Council Resolution on the quality of drafting of Community legislation [1993] OJ C166/1. See also the establishment of the high-level Molitor Group in 1994 to recommend areas of Community law that could be abolished in order to enhance the competitiveness of industry within the Community, COM(95) 288, and the launching in May 1996 of the SLIM pilot project (Simpler Legislation for the Single Market). It has been announced that in the second phase of SLIM, the Commission will present proposals concerning VAT, financial services, and external economic relations: Agence Europe, 16 Apr. 1997 at 10. See generally, Gormley, 'Consolidation, Codification and Improving the Quality of Community

Community harmonization legislation has important consequences for the ability of Member States to invoke justifications for restricting the free movement of goods. It has been noted that Article 36 EC provides for derogations to the free movement of goods to protect important and sensitive national interests.[14] However, Article 36 has only an interim role as harmonization legislation intervenes to remove the Article 36 justification by itself providing, in the form of a Community-wide rule, the protection mentioned in Article 36. In practical terms, this means that a Member State may not justify a measure by reference to Article 36 if a harmonized Community regime has exhaustively occupied the field.[15] Needless to say, if Community legislation does not cover the field exhaustively, recourse to Article 36 is still possible in those areas which are not comprehensively covered by the legislation.[16] The exclusion of recourse to Article 36 in the event of exhaustive Community harmonization legislation may be explained on the rationale that the very purpose of harmonization is to facilitate free circulation in the Community and thus any unilateral derogation by individual Member States must be excluded. In practice, it is most commonly recourse to the 'public-health' justification in Article 36 which is excluded by exhaustive Community legislation. Thus, if a Directive enacted under Article 100 or 100A EC provides for full harmonization of all the measures necessary for the protection of human health by placing the responsibility for public-health inspection of a product upon the Member State of export, the national authorities of the importing Member State will no longer be entitled to rely on Article 36 to subject the product to systematic inspection upon importation.

Legislation—The Community Customs Code' in Emiliou & O'Keeffe, *The European Union and World Trade Law: After the GATT Uruguay Round* (Wiley, 1996), 124; Kellerman in Curtin & Heukels (eds.), *Institutional Dynamics of European Integration, Essays in Honour of H. G. Schermers* (Martinus Nijhoff Publishers, 1994); and Barents (1994) MJ 101. See also, Bracke, *Voorwaarden Voor Goede EG-Wetgeving: Een Onderzoek naar de Kwaliteit van Europese Wetgeving* (Sdu Juridische & Fiscale Uitgeverij, 1996).

[13] See, *Action Plan for the Single Market, Communication of the Commission to the European Council, CSE* (97)1 final, 4 June 1997.

[14] See discussion of Art. 36 in Ch. 7.

[15] See Case 5/77 *Tedeschi* v. *Denkavit* [1977] ECR 1555, [1978] 1 CMLR 1 at para. 35; Case 251/78 *Denkavit Futtermittel* v. *Minister für Ernährung, Landwirtschaft und Forsten* [1979] ECR 3369, [1980] 3 CMLR 513 at para. 14; Case 227/82 *Van Bennekom* [1983] ECR 3883 at para. 35; Case 28/84 *Commission* v. *Germany* [1985] ECR 3097; Case 190/87 *Kreis Borken* v. *Moormann* [1988] ECR 4689, [1990] 1 CMLR 656; Case C–304/88 *Commission* v. *Belgium* [1990] ECR I–2801; Case C–128/89 *Commission* v. *Italy* [1990] ECR I–3239, [1991] 3 CMLR 720; Case C–169/89 *Gourmetterie Van den Burg NV* [1990] ECR I–2143 at para. 9; Case C–37/92 *Vanaker and Lesage* [1993] ECR I–4947 at para. 9; Case C–294/92 *Commission* v. *Italy* [1994] ECR I–4311; & Case C–323/93 *Centre d'Insémination de la Crespelle* v. *Coopérative de la Mayenne* [1994] ECR I–5077 at para. 31.

[16] See Case 4/75 *Rewe-Zentralfinanz* v. *Landwirtschaftskammer* [1975] ECR 843, [1977] 1 CMLR 599; Case 73/84 *Denkavit Futtermittel* v. *Land Nordrhein-Westfalen* [1985] ECR 1019; & Case 125/88 *Nijman* [1989] ECR 3533.

The necessary corollary to the ECJ's position set out above is that the regime set up by the harmonizing legislation should itself comply with the rigours of Articles 30 to 36 EC.[17] However, the ECJ has taken a softer line in examining the compatibility of Community legislation with Articles 30 to 36 EC than it has in examining such a compatibility of national legislation. For example, in *Denkavit Futtermittel* v. *Land Baden-Württemberg* the ECJ held in the context of a challenge to the compatibility of a Community Directive with Article 30 that 'the Community institutions must be recognized as enjoying a discretion in relation to the stages in which harmonization is to take place, having regard to the particular nature of the field subject to co-ordination'.[18] It appears that the ECJ takes the view that since the Community legislature acts in the general interest of the Community, it should enjoy greater freedom than that permitted for Member States under Article 30.[19] This position is perfectly defensible if one assumes that Community legislation which allows obstacles to the free movement of goods at national frontiers is always necessary to ensure the effective operation of the Community-wide system and always constitutes less of a hindrance to trade than the pre-existing system based on national controls. However, such a difference of treatment is somewhat anomalous in a genuine internal market.[20] Furthermore, the ECJ's approach has been rather erratic. For example, in *Bristol-Myers Squibb* v. *Paranova*,[21] the ECJ held that Article 7 of the First Council Directive to approximate the laws of the Member States relating to trade marks[22] 'comprehensively regulates the question of the exhaustion of trade mark rights for products traded in

[17] The ECJ has held that this is the case in Case C–47/90 *Delhaize* v. *Promalvin* [1992] ECR I–3669 at para. 26, Case C–315/92 *Verband Sozialer Wettbewerb* v. *Clinique* [1994] ECR I–317 at para. 12, Case C–51/93 *Meyhui* v. *Scholt Zweisel Glaswerke* [1994] ECR I–3879 at para. 11 & Case C–114/96 *Criminal proceedings against Kieffer and Thill* [1997] ECR I–3629.

[18] Case C–39/90 [1991] ECR I–3069. See also Case 35/76 *Simmenthal* v. *Italian Finance Administration* [1976] ECR 1871, [1977] 2 CMLR 1; Case 46/76 *Bauhuis* v. *Netherlands* [1977] ECR 5; Case 80–81/77 *Ramel* v. *Receveur des Douanes* [1978] ECR 927; Case 15/83 *Denkavit Nederland* v. *Hooftprodukschap voor Akkerbouwprodukten* [1984] ECR 2171, Case 37/83 *Rewe–Zentrale* v. *Landwirtschaftskammer Rheinland* [1984] ECR 1229, [1985] 2 CMLR 586; & Case C–114/96, n. 17 above at para. 37.

[19] See discussion of this point by Oliver, *Free Movement of Goods in the European Community*, 45–56, & Mortelmans, 'Excepties bij non-tarifaire intracommunautaire belemmering: assimilatie in het nieuwe EG-Verdrag?'.

[20] The ECJ may be persuaded to abandon such an anomaly as national markets integrate further and especially in light of the fact that in the context of non-contractual liability, it has held that the conditions for non-contractual liability of the Community under Art. 215 EC should be the same as those for the non-contractual liability of Member States since '[t]he protection of the rights which individuals derive from Community law cannot vary depending on whether a national authority or a Community authority is responsible for the damage': Cases C–46 & 48/93 *Brasserie du Pêcheur* v. *Germany/Factortame* (No. 3) [1996] ECR I–1029, [1996] 1 CMLR 889 at para. 42.

[21] Joined cases C–427/93, C–429/93 & C–436/93 [1996] ECR I–3457.

[22] First Council Directive 89/104 of 21 Dec. 1988 to approximate the laws of the Member States relating to trade marks [1989] OJ L40/1.

the Community' and therefore that 'any national measure relating thereto must be assessed in relation to the provisions of that directive and not Articles 30 to 36 of the Treaty'.[23] However, the ECJ went on to hold that 'Like any secondary legislation . . . the directive must be interpreted in the light of the Treaty rules on the free movement of goods and in particular Article 36.'[24] The ECJ proceeded to interpret Article 7 of the Directive to precisely the same extent as its case law on exhaustion which it had developed under Article 36.[25] On the other hand, the ECJ has recently held in *Kieffer and Thill*[26] that although the provisions of Regulation 3330/91 on the collection of statistics relating to the trading of goods between Member States[27] have restrictive effects with regard to the free movement of goods, the aim of the Regulation, namely to promote the completion of the internal market by establishing statistics on the trading of goods between Member States 'appears justified'.[28] The ECJ reached this conclusion since 'it does not appear that the obligation to make declarations imposed by the Regulation goes beyond what is necessary to achieve the objective pursued, especially since, as the Court has frequently stated, the Community legislature enjoys a discretion in the framework of its powers of harmonization'.[29] It is submitted that it would be more consistent with a genuine internal market for the ECJ to have adopted a more rigorous line in examining Community harmonization legislation subject to Articles 30 to 36 EC thereby bringing the discretion enjoyed by the Community legislator into line with that of the national legislator.

The application of this case law by the national courts will be examined in the remainder of this chapter in three sections. Firstly, national case law discerning whether Community legislation is exhaustive such that recourse to Article 36 is precluded; secondly, national case law examining the question of the compatibility of Community legislation with primary Treaty rules; and finally, national case law interpreting the legal mechanisms for the completion of the internal market.

2 EXHAUSTIVE COMMUNITY HARMONIZATION LEGISLATION PRECLUDING RECOURSE TO ARTICLE 36 EC

In most cases, the national courts have experienced little difficulty in ascertaining that a particular piece of Community harmonization legislation occupies the field exhaustively thereby precluding recourse to Article 36. The task of the French *Cour de Cassation* in *Hildbrand*[30] was greatly

---

[23] n. 21 above at para. 25.   [24] Ibid. at para. 27.
[25] See discussion of intellectual property rights in Ch. 8.   [26] n. 17 above.
[27] [1991] OJ L316/1.   [28] n. 17 above at para. 31.   [29] Ibid. at para. 37.
[30] *Cour de Cassation*, ch. crim, 17 Oct. 1994, Bull. Cass. Crim. 1994, no. 332 p. 809; Dalloz 1995, IR 26; JCP 1995, IV no. 294.

facilitated by the fact that the ECJ had already had opportunity to hold that the harmonization legislation at issue in that case constituted exhaustive harmonization, therefore precluding recourse to Article 36.[31] In *Procter & Gamble* v. *Productschap voor Groenten en Fruit*[32] on the other hand, the Dutch *CBB* was itself able to conclude that Article 7 of Directive 75/726 on the approximation of the laws of Member States concerning fruit juices[33] provided an exhaustive list of ingredients in order for a fruit juice to be labelled 'fruit nectar'. Equally, the Dutch *Hoge Raad* itself felt confident to conclude that Article 15(2) of Directive 79/112 on the approximation of the laws of the Member States relating to the labelling of foodstuffs[34] listed exhaustively the grounds upon which the application of non-harmonized national provisions prohibiting trade in foodstuffs may be justified.[35] This conclusion was subsequently confirmed by the ECJ in separate litigation.[36] On the other hand, in *Officier van Justitie* v. *G-D BV*,[37] the *Arrondissementsrechtbank* Arnhem came to the same conclusion with respect to Directive 79/112, but was less clear in its analysis of where and why the Directive was to be interpreted as constituting exhaustive harmonization. This lack of clarity was further confused by the fact that the *Arrondissementsrechtbank* Arnhem also mentioned that the application of Article 36 EC would yield the same result. Thus, although the result reached by the *Arrondissementsrechtbank* Arnhem is correct, it nevertheless failed to apply ECJ case law clearly and to first identify whether or not the legislation was exhaustive.

On the other side of the coin, the national courts have also had the opportunity to hold that certain Community harmonization legislation does not constitute exhaustive harmonization and thus that recourse to Article 36 was still possible. In many cases, the fact that particular harmonization legislation is not exhaustive derives from the simple fact that the Directive in question does not list the product at issue in an annex setting out those products covered by the Directive. In such straightforward cases, the national courts have encountered no difficulties.[38] Somewhat

---

[31] The case concerned Directive 76/768 on the approximation of the laws of the Member States relating to cosmetic products [1976] OJ L262/169 which had been held to constitute exhaustive harmonization by the ECJ in Case C–246/91 *Commission* v. *France* [1993] ECR I–2289.

[32] *CBB*, 18 June 1993, SEW 1994, 265 (with note by Mortelmans).

[33] [1975] OJ L311/40.   [34] [1979] OJ L33/1.

[35] *Openbaar Ministerie* v. *Ambtman BV*, *Hoge Raad* (*Strafkamer*), 30 Sept. 1986, NJ 1987, 299.

[36] Case C–241/89 *SARRP* v. *Chambre Syndicat des Raffineurs et Conditioneurs de sucre de France* [1990] ECR I–4695 at para. 15. See also Case C–17/93 *JJJ van der Veldt* [1994] ECR I–3537.

[37] *Arrondissementsrechtbank* Arnhem, 28 July 1987, NJ 1988, 736.

[38] See, e.g. the judgt of the President of the Dutch *Raad van State* (*Afd. Rechtspraak*) in *Van der Feesten* v. *Landbouw, Natuurbeheer en Visserij* (*Min.*), 14 Oct. 1992, M & R 1994, 24 (with note by Jans); AB 1994, 128 where the fact that the species of birds at issue were not listed in the annex to Directive 79/409 on the conservation of wild birds [1979] OJ L403/1 was held to

less satisfactory were three judgments of the French *Cour de Cassation* handed down on the same date[39] with respect to Directive 64/54 on the approximation of the laws of the Member States concerning preservatives authorized for use in foodstuffs intended for human consumption[40] and the judgment of the Dutch *Hoge Raad*[41] with respect to Directive 80/217 introducing Community measures for the control of classic swine fever.[42] In both sets of judgments, the national courts concluded that the Community legislation did not exhaustively occupy the field. While this conclusion appears to be uncontroversial, it is however regrettable that neither national court explained why it considered that this was the case.[43] It is submitted that in order to apply ECJ case law in this field competently, such an explanation should be regarded as a minimum requirement, *a fortiori* from national courts from which there is no further appeal within the national legal system.

The national courts have also carried out more controversial misapplications in this field. One such example is the judgment of the French *Cour de Cassation* in *The State* v. *Vituret & Chambion*[44] where it was held that the protection of animals in Article 36 could apply to justify a ban on the sale in France of woodcock paté imported from Belgium contrary to a French Order of 20 December 1983. Although the *Cour de Cassation* also mentioned and applied the provisions of Directive 79/409,[45] it neither cited nor applied the ECJ's judgment in *Gourmetterie Van den Burg*,[46] where the

---

exclude the application of that Directive and the case was decided on the basis of the protection of animals under Art. 36 EC. See further discussion of this case at p. 285. See also the judgment of the ECJ in *Nijman*, n. 16 above, and its implementation by the *Hoge Raad* (*Strafkamer*), 5 Mar. 1991, NJ 1991, 510 (with note by Van Veen). In fact, it has been argued that the fact that the Directive in this case (Directive 79/117, prohibiting the placing on the market and use of plant-protection products containing certain active substances [1979] OJ L33/36) was not exhaustive was so obvious that a reference to the ECJ should not have been necessary in the first place: see Meij, *Prejudiciële Vragen van Nederlandse Rechters en Hun Gevolgen*, 25.

[39] *Bellon; Crépin and Kugelmann, Cour de Cassation*, ch. crim., 27 Feb. 1995, Bull. Cass. Crim. 1995, 83; Ed. du Juris-Classeur, Droit Pénal 1995, no. 147; Dalloz 1995, IR 117.

[40] [1963–64] OJ Spec. Ed. 99.

[41] *Leffers* v. *De Staat der Nederlanden (Minister van Landbouw en Visserij), Hoge Raad*, 18 Jan. 1991, AB 1991, 241 (with note by van der Burg); Ars Aequi 1991, 656 (with note by van Buuren); RvdW 1991, 35; NJ 1992, 638 (with note by Brunner at [1992] NJ 639).

[42] [1980] OJ L47/11.

[43] It is true, however, that in *Leffers*, n. 41 above, a full discussion as to why the Directive in question was not exhaustive was carried out by Adv. Gen. Koopmans in his Opinion presented to the *Hoge Raad* in that case.

[44] *Cour de Cassation*, ch. crim., 2 Dec. 1992, [1995] 1 CMLR 185, Bull. Cass. Crim 1992, no. 401 p. 899.

[45] Council Directive on the conservation of wild birds [1979] OJ L 403/1. It may be noted that woodcock was mentioned in Annex III of the Directive and thus that the Directive was of application. This may be contrasted with the facts before the Dutch *Raad van State* (Afd. Rechtspraak) in *Van der Feesten* v. *Landbouw, Natuurbeheer en Visserij (Min.)*, n. 38 above.

[46] Case C–169/89, n. 15 above.

ECJ had held that Directive 79/409 'regulated exhaustively the Member States' powers with regard to the conservation of wild birds',[47] which precluded recourse to Article 36. It is submitted that by applying Article 36 in circumstances contrary to the ECJ's express judgment in *Gourmetterie Van den Burg* without itself making a preliminary reference, the *Cour de Cassation* was in breach of its obligations in Article 177(3) EC.[48]

A similarly striking misapplication was carried out by the English High Court in *R.* v. *Secretary of State for Social Services, ex p. The Wellcome Foundation*[49] where it held that possible infringement of trade mark rights was a relevant consideration which the national authorities may take into consideration in deciding whether to grant a product licence for the import of medicinal products into the United Kingdom. This the High Court held was consistent with the ECJ's interpretation of intellectual property rights under Article 36 EC. What is surprising in the context of the present discussion is that the High Court reached this conclusion in spite the clear provisions in Directive 65/65[50] that only public health considerations may be taken into account by a national authority when deciding upon authorization to market medicinal products. The High Court merely acknowledged that the provisions of Directive 65/65 led to the opposite conclusion, but held that 'Article 36 must prevail'.[51] It is regrettable that the High Court did not discuss, as it should have, whether the Directive was exhaustive or not. What is still more regrettable is that there was at that time explicit ECJ authority on this very point holding that Directive 65/65 should be interpreted as meaning that the authorization to import 'may not be refused, suspended or revoked save on the ground of the protection of public health as referred to by the Directive'.[52] Fortunately the matter was successfully appealed to the Court of Appeal which reversed the judgment of the High Court and applied the exhaustive provisions of the Directive to conclude that the national authority was not entitled to take into consideration the fact that the medicines might infringe trade mark rights in the United Kingdom.[53]

---

[47] Case C–169/89, n. 15 at para. 9.

[48] This is even more the case given that it is not clear why the *Cour de Cassation* assumed that the protection of animals in Art. 36 was applicable when the preamble to Directive 79/409 refers only to environmental concerns and the common heritage of the Community and is silent on the protection of animals as such.

[49] [1987] CMLR 333, [1987] RPC 220.

[50] [1965–1966] OJ Spec. Ed. 20.   [51] [1987] CMLR 333 at 347.

[52] Case 301/82 *SA Clin-Midy* v. *Belgian State* [1984] ECR 251, [1985] 1 CMLR 443.

[53] [1987] 3 CMLR 333; [1987] 2 All ER 1025; [1987] 1 WLR 1166. It may be noted that there was a further appeal in this case to the House of Lords which upheld the judgt of the Court of Appeal on the basis of English law alone, such that the case no longer turned upon the point of EC law: [1988] 3 CMLR 95, [1988] 2 All ER 684, [1988] 1 WLR 635. This judgt was noted by Morcom, 'Parallel Importation of Pharmaceutical Products in the Common Market' and by Barnard & Greaves, 'The Application of Community Law in the United Kingdom: 1986–1993'. For a judgt of the House of Lords to similar effect, see *R.* v. *Licensing Authority ex.*

A further unsatisfactory analysis before the English courts was carried out by the Queen's Bench Division of the High Court in *R. v. Minister of Agriculture, Fisheries and Food, ex.p. Roberts*.[54] The High Court was faced with an application for judicial review of a decision of the Minister of Agriculture not to refuse to grant export licences for the export of live lambs to France.[55] The objection to export was based on animal rights' grounds[56] following a number of horrifying incidents in France in which farmers had violently mistreated lambs imported from Britain which were being transported to destinations in France.[57] The applicants sought a declaration that the Minister of Agriculture was wrong in law to have stated in the decision that refusal of export licenses was likely to be contrary to Community law. The question of whether Article 34 was breached on those facts is discussed elsewhere in this work.[58] What is of interest in the context of the present discussion is that the High Court held that a ban on export would not be justified for the protection of animals under Article 36 and thus refused the declaration sought by the applicant. Popplewell J in the High Court reasoned that the Article 36 justification was not available since a ban could not be considered to be proportionate. The High Court reached this conclusion with respect to the proportionality of the measure since it noted that Article 4 of Directive 77/489 on the protection of animals during international transport[59] provided that Member States should 'take all necessary measures to avoid or reduce to a minimum the suffering of animals when strikes or other unforeseen circumstances in their territory impede application of this Directive'. Thus, concluded the High Court, a ban would have been disproportionate since the British authorities had complained to the French authorities which had a duty to comply with the Directive. It is submitted that while the result reached by the High Court in this case was correct, the reasoning was far from satisfactory. A

---

p. Smith Kline and French Laboratories [1989] 2 CMLR 137, [1989] 2 WLR 397 where it was again held that the case could be decided under English law such that the point of EC law became superfluous.

[54] [1991] 1 CMLR 555. It may be noted that there had been an earlier unsuccessful application for judicial review involving the same parties (High Court (QBD), 20 Sept. 1990, CO/1657/90, CO/1679/90 Transcr.: Marten Walsh Cherer, per Macpherson J). The CA subsequently ordered that the renewed application for leave to apply for judicial review should be granted. It is this renewed application which is the subject of discussion here.

[55] The decision of the Minister of Agriculture, Fisheries and Food was based on the Animal Health Act 1981, ss. 37(2) & 39 and Export of Animals (Protection) Order 1981, Art. 3.

[56] Roberts was representing the Royal Society for the Prevention of Cruelty to Animals (RSPCA).

[57] The incidents included putting lambs out on poisoned grass, burning them alive, and slaughtering them outside an abattoir.

[58] See discussion at pp. 138–9. See also discussion of this case in the context of the extraterritorial application of Art. 36 at pp. 286–8.

[59] [1977] OJ L200/10.

more appropriate course of reasoning would have been for the High Court to have examined whether the Directives at issue were exhaustive and thus whether recourse to Article 36 would have been precluded in the first place. This is firmly supported by the reasoning of the ECJ in *R. v. Ministry of Agriculture, Fisheries and Food, ex p. Hedley Lomas*[60] in which the analogous provisions of another animal welfare Directive[61] were held to exhaustively occupy the field precluding recourse to Article 36. The ECJ held that 'recourse to Article 36 is no longer possible where Community directives provide for harmonization of the measures necessary to achieve the specific objective which would be furthered by reliance upon this provision'.[62] It is therefore submitted that it would have been more satisfactory had the High Court in *Ex. p. Roberts* reasoned that the Directive provisions in that case made recourse to Article 36 impossible rather than concluding, as it did, that the Directive provisions made recourse to Article 36 disproportionate under the second sentence of Article 36.

The final case before the English courts which provides a particularly interesting axis for discussion concerns the facts raised in *R. v. London Boroughs' Transport Committee, ex.p. Freight Transport Association*. This case concerned an attempt by London Boroughs' Transport Committee (LBTC) to achieve noise controls by imposing a ban on night-time use of residential London streets by heavy goods vehicles without a permit. Permits were issued only if vehicles were fitted with air-brake noise suppressors, where they were capable of being fitted with such a device. Both the High Court[63] and the Court of Appeal[64] held that two Community Directives exhaustively occupied the field and since neither piece of legislation envisaged the use of noise suppressors, the LBTC requirement was an additional requirement which affected the free movement of goods and which did not comply with the Directives. The House of Lords[65] disagreed with the conclusion of the courts below and distinguished the Directives at issue. On the one hand, the House of Lords distinguished Directive 71/320 on braking devices ('the brake Directive')[66] by stating that that Directive only harmonized the technical and safety requirements of brakes on vehicles used in the Community, but did not impinge upon sound levels. On the other hand, Directive 70/157 on permissible sound levels and exhaust systems ('the sound level Directive')[67] was also distinguished on the basis that it harmonized only sound levels of vehicles and exhaust systems, but not the sound of air-brakes. The House of Lords thus concluded that given

[60] Case C–5/94 [1996] ECR I–2553.
[61] Council Directive 74/577 on stunning animals before slaughter [1974] OJ L316/10.
[62] Case C–5/94, n. 60 above at para. 18.
[63] [1990] 1 CMLR 229.   [64] [1990] 3 CMLR 495.
[65] [1992] 1 CMLR 5; [1991] 3 All ER 915; [1991] 1 WLR 828.
[66] [1971] OJ Spec. Ed. 746.   [67] [1970] OJ Spec. Ed. 111.

the LBTC requirement was outside the scope of the Community legislation, it was compatible with Community law. This judgment has been trenchantly criticized by Weatherill[68] who argues, *inter alia*, that there was at least scope for debate on the question of whether the two Community Directives were exhaustive or not, particularly in light of the ECJ's judgment in *Commission* v. *United Kingdom* (Re Dim Dip Vehicle Lights).[69] While Lord Templeman simply held that '[n]o plausible grounds have been advanced for a reference to the European Court of Justice',[70] Weatherill is surely correct to remark that 'one would have thought the arguments in favour of referral, let alone the obligation to refer, would have been strengthened by the fact that both the High Court and the Court of Appeal had decided the point of Community law in directly the opposite manner to that favoured by Lord Templeman'.[71] What is still more surprising is that, even if one assumes that the Directives could indeed be distinguished, the House of Lords should have then proceeded to apply Articles 30 to 36 EC. Regrettably, the House of Lords carried out no such analysis.[72]

The judgment of the House of Lords in *R.* v. *London Boroughs' Transport Committee, ex. p. Freight Transport Association* was thus far from satisfactory. The case does, however, highlight important shortcomings in a particular type of Community harmonization legislation. Both the Directives at issue constituted 'old style'[73] exhaustive (rather than minimum) harmonization which contained no safeguard procedures to adapt to technological advances.[74] The case thus touched at the heart of the difficulties of inflexible Community harmonization legislation. Many of these difficulties have now been addressed through development of new harmonization techniques. However, it remains the case that '[a] national court which chooses to improve on the Community legislator is likely severely to disrupt the uniform development of the Community legal order'.[75]

In sum, the national case law applying the ECJ's interpretation of exhaustive Community harmonization legislation has not been particularly satisfactory. The following problems may be identified. Firstly, the national courts have on occasion failed to first examine whether the

[68] Weatherill, 'Regulating the Internal Market: Result Orientation in the House of Lords'.
[69] Case 60/86 [1988] ECR 394.
[70] [1992] 1 CMLR 5 at 21.　　　　　　　　　　　　　[71] n. 68 above at 306.
[72] For an example before the Dutch courts, see *Leo Pharmaceutical Products BV* v. *De staatssecretaris van Landbouw, Natuurbeheer en Visserij, CBB,* 14 Sept. 1994, AB 1995, 204 where the court omitted to apply Art. 36 EC after the application of Directive 81/851 on veterinary medicinal products [1981] OJ L317/1 had been excluded.
[73] As opposed to Directives under the 'new approach' to technical harmonization. See n. 7 above.
[74] The air-brake noise suppressers at issue were alleged to halve the noise of the brakes of heavy goods vehicles for the relatively small cost of £30.
[75] Weatherill, n. 68 above at 305.

Community legislation was indeed exhaustive. Secondly, in cases where the national courts do conclude that such legislation is or is not exhaustive, no reasoning is offered as to why this is the case. Thirdly, national courts have applied Article 36 in cases where there is clear ECJ authority holding that a relevant Directive exhaustively harmonized the issue precluding recourse to that Article. Finally, in cases where the national court controversially concludes that Community legislation may be distinguished, it has failed to go on to apply the provisions of Articles 30 to 36 EC.

3 THE COMPATIBILITY OF COMMUNITY LEGISLATION WITH PRIMARY TREATY RULES

It has been noted in the introduction to this chapter that the necessary corollary to the fact that recourse to Article 36 EC is precluded once matters are exhaustively harmonized in Community legislation, is that the regime set up by the harmonizing legislation itself complies with the rigours of Articles 30 to 36 EC.[76] However, as has been discussed, the ECJ has hitherto taken a softer line in examining the compatibility of Community legislation with Articles 30 to 36 EC and takes the view that since the Community legislature acts in the general interest of the Community, it should enjoy greater freedom than that permitted for Member States under Articles 30 to 36.

Challenges to Community legislation for being in breach of Articles 30 to 36 are not common before the national courts. The English courts have dealt with such challenges and have purported to subject the substantive provisions of Community Directives to the rigours of Articles 30 to 36 without considering whether it was necessary to allow the Community legislator greater freedom.[77] On the other hand, the argument that Directive 84/631[78] on the supervision and control within the European Community of the trans-frontier shipment of hazardous waste was incompatible with Article 34 EC seems to have been completely ignored in a series of cases before the Dutch *Raad van State* (*Afdeling Geschillen van Bestuur*).[79] These cases concerned challenges to decisions of the Dutch

---

[76] n. 17 above.

[77] See, e.g. *R* v. *Moore and Cousins* [1995] 1 CMLR 654 (Crown Court), [1995] 3 CMLR 220 (CA) where it was held that the procedure for reclaim of excise duty set up under Directive 92/12 [1992] OJ L76/1 was compatible with Arts. 30 & 95 EC. The interpretation of Art. 30 in these cases is discussed critically at p. 13.

[78] [1984] OJ L326/31 as amended by Directive 86/279 [1986] OJ L181/13. Both Directives were repealed with effect from 6 May 1994 by Reg. 259/93 of 12 Feb. 1993 on the supervision and control of shipments of waste within, into, and out of the European Community ([1993] OJ L30/1).

[79] See *GMU Nederland BV* v. *Minister van Volkshuisvesting, Ruimtelijke Ordening en Milieubeheer*, Pres. *Raad van State* (*Afd. Geschillen van Bestuur*), 11 Dec. 1989, KG 1990, 72;

Ministry of Environment (*Volkshuisvesting, Ruimtelijke Ordening en Milieubeheer* (*VROM*)) refusing permission for the export of hazardous waste from the Netherlands to other Member States. The grounds of challenges were based on the proposition that Directive 84/631 had not been correctly implemented in the Netherlands by Article 16b of the *Wet Chemische Afvalstoffen* (*WCA*: Law on Chemical Waste) and that the refusal to issue an export licence constituted an infringement of Article 34 EC. While the *Raad van State* dealt with the compatibility of the implementation of the Directive by the Dutch legislation in detail,[80] it seems to have ignored the Article 34 EC point. It is submitted that it would have been desirable for the *Afdeling Geschillen van Bestuur* of the *Raad van State* to have remembered that even the rules in Community secondary legislation are subject to the Treaty rules on the free movement of goods.[81] The relationship between Article 34 EC and measurings concerning environmental protection prohibiting export has always been somewhat uncertain in ECJ case law.[82] It could be argued that a decision by a national authority to refuse permission to export waste is, according to the primary Treaty rules on free movement of goods, contrary to Article 34 (even on the *Groenveld*[83] interpretation of Article 34) and that the only possible justification is thus Article 36, which does not provide for justification of restrictions on grounds of the protection of the environment. Thus, it might be argued that any Directive provision that provides for the possibility for Member States to impose an export ban in specific circumstances according to environmental protection criteria, does not comply with the Treaty's rules on free movement of goods. On the other hand, now that the environment is

M & R 1990, 423 (with note by Addink and Jans); *Raad van State* (*Afd. Geschillen van Bestuur*), 6 Sept. 1990, AB 1991, 12 (with note by Drupsteen); M & R 1991, 37 (with note by Jans); RegelMaat 1991, 70 (with note by Drexhage); *Ecoservice Nederland* v. *VROM*, Pres. *Raad van State* (*Afd. Geschillen van Bestuur*), 16 Aug. 1990, KG 1990, 324; *Eldim BV* v. *VROM*, Pres. *Raad van State* (*Afd. Geschillen van Bestuur*), 14 Jan. 1992, AB 1992, 455 (with note by Drupsteen); M & R 1992, 486 (with note by Addink); *Raad van State* (*Afd. Geschillen van Bestuur*), 17 Feb. 1993, AB 1993, 424 (with note by Drupsteen); M & R 1993, 303 (with note by Addink); SEW 1993, 618 (with note by Jans) and *Edelchemie Panheel BV* v. *VROM*, *Raad van State* (*Afd. Bestuursrechtspraak*), 20 Jan. 1994, M & R 1994, 60 (with note by Jans).

[80] It may be noted that the conclusion of the *Raad van State* concerning the compatibility of the Dutch legislation with the Directive may be criticized for not having fully explored the possibilities of interpreting the Dutch legislation in conformity with the Directive on a case-by-case basis rather than holding that all administrative decisions based on the implementing legislation are incompatible with the Directive. See discussion by Drupsteen AB 1993, 424; Widdershoven, tB/S 1992, nr. 111; Jans, SEW 1993, 618; M & R 1993, 303; and idem *Milieurecht in Nederland*, 190–1. Furthermore, it appears that the interpretation of the substantive provisions of the Directive by the *Raad van State* in these cases was incorrect following the judgment of the ECJ in Case C–422/92 *Commission v Germany* [1995] ECR I–1097.

[81] See ECJ judgts cited n. 17 above.

[82] See discussion of this point in Ch. 4 sect. 4.

[83] Case 15/79, *Groenveld* v. *Produktschap voor Vee en Vlees* [1979] ECR 3409; [1981] 1 CMLR 207. See discussion of this case in Ch. 4.

an explicit and well-developed policy of the Community provided for in the Treaty, it is unlikely that the ECJ would hold such provisions in a Directive to be incompatible with Article 34 EC. The current authorities are not conclusive. In *Inter-Huiles*,[84] the ECJ held that French implementation legislation of Directive 75/439[85] on the disposal of waste oils, which provided for an implicit export ban for waste oils, infringed both the Directive and Article 34 EC. Furthermore, the same French legislation has also been held by the ECJ to be contrary to Article 34 on the grounds of Article 34 alone.[86] Finally in *ADBHU*,[87] the ECJ held that Directive 75/439[88] was compatible with the Treaty rules on free movement of goods but that 'they must nevertheless neither be discriminatory nor go beyond the inevitable restrictions which are justified by the pursuit of the objective of environmental protection which is in the general interest'.[89] It would thus seem that the ECJ is willing to test Community Directives against the vicissitudes of Article 34 and that environmental justifications will be allowed provided that the measure is part of a non-discriminatory programme.[90] The compatibility of Community environmental protection legislation with Article 34 nevertheless remains a complex point and one which, it is submitted, should have been discussed by the *Afdeling* Geschillen van Bestuur of the *Raad van State* more fully.

4 LEGAL MECHANISMS FOR THE COMPLETION OF THE INTERNAL MARKET

The major legal mechanism for the completion of the internal market is provided for in Article 100A EC which provides a legal basis for Community harmonization legislation for the establishment and functioning of the internal market. The addition of this legal basis aimed to make it possible to accelerate the completion of the internal market by substituting the unanimity in the Council of Ministers which is required under Article 100 EC, with qualified majority voting for legislation based on Article 100A. However, the latter Article also contains a compromise in that Article 100A(4) provides that

---

[84] Case 172/82 *Syndicat national des fabricants raffineurs d'huiles de graissage* v. *Groupement d'interêt économique (GIE) Inter-Huiles* [1983] ECR 555.

[85] [1979] OJ L194/23.   [86] See Case 173/83 *Commission* v. *France* [1985] ECR 491.

[87] Case 240/83 *Procureur de la République* v. *Association de defense des Bruleurs d'Huiles Usagées (ADBHU)* [1985] ECR 531.

[88] n. 85 above.

[89] n. 87 above at para. 15.

[90] See also the judgt of the ECJ in Case C–2/90 *Commission* v. *Belgium* [1992] ECR I–4431, [1993] 1 CMLR 365.

If, after the adoption of a harmonisation measure by the Council acting by a qualified majority, a Member State deems it necessary to apply national provisions on grounds of major needs referred to in Article 36, or relating to protection of the environment or the working environment, it shall notify the Commission of these provisions.

The Commission shall confirm the provisions involved after having verified that they are not a means of arbitrary discrimination or a disguised restriction on trade between Member States.

Thus, legislation adopted under Article 100A may be subject to individual derogations for particular Member States under Article 100A(4). This derogation has been the subject of much critical attention, which has perceived it to be a backward step holding the inherent danger that it would undermine the ECJ's case law interpreting Article 36 EC.[91] However, these fears have not been borne out in practice and the Article 100A(4) derogation has, in fact, only been used on a handful of occasions.[92] In any event, the ECJ has shown in the *PCP* case[93] that it is prepared to flex its muscles in subjecting the exercise of supervision by the Commission under Article 100A(4) to rigorous review.

The application of Article 100A(4) has arisen before the Dutch courts in *Conté Nederland B.V.* v. *Minister van VROM*[94] which concerned an appeal against the imposition by the Minister for the Environment (*Volkshuisvesting, Ruimtelijke Ordening en Milieubeheer (VROM)*) of a fine for infringement of Article 2(1) of the Cadmium Order Dangerous Substances Act (*Cadmiumbesluit Wet milieugevaarlijke stoffen*).[95] The applicant did not contest that it had infringed the provisions of the Cadmium Order, but argued that the standards contained therein were stricter than those provided for in Directive 91/338 on the approximation of the laws of the Member States relating to restrictions on the marketing and use of certain dangerous substances and preparations.[96] The Minister for the Environment argued that the Directive did not, for the particular substances at issue in that case, enter into force until 31 December 1995 (after the date of the judgment) and that, in any event, the Netherlands had voted against the Directive (which was based on Article 100A EC) in the Council and had sent a notification to the Commission on 20 May 1992 that the Netherlands intended to maintain its stricter provisions as permitted by Article 100A(4).[97] At the time of the judgment, the Commission had not yet responded to the notification. The President of the *Raad van State* (*Afdeling Bestuursrechtspraak*)

---

[91] See, e.g., Pescatore, n. 5 above, Flynn, 'How will Article 100A(4) work? A comparison with Article 93' (1987) 24 CMLRev 689.

[92] See Slot, n. 1 above, at fn 63.

[93] Case C–41/93 *France* v. *Commission* [1994] ECR I–1829.

[94] Pres. *Raad van State* (*Afd. Bestuursrechtspraak*), 19 Oct. 1994, SEW 1995, 444 (with note by van de Gronden and Mortelmans), KG 1995, 16.

[95] Stb. 1990, nr. 538.   [96] [1991] OJ L186/59.   [97] Stb. 1993, 422.

cited the judgment of the ECJ in *France* v. *Commission* ('the *PCP* case')[98] and held that 'In waiting for the decision of the Commission on the reliance by the Dutch Government on Article 100A(4) EC, the President is for the time being of the opinion that it is not unlikely that the legislation in question is justified for the necessity of protecting public health and the environment'. However, the President went on to hold that under Dutch law (Article 20(3) of the *Wet Milieubeheer* (Environment Protection Act)), the Minister for the Environment's decision should be annulled to the extent that it purported to be of immediate application (*terstond van kracht*). Nevertheless, the reasoning of the President with respect to Community law was far from clear. This lack of clarity arises from the fact that the President did not explicitly state that the Directive, in so far as it was applicable to the form of cadmium at issue in the case, had not yet entered into force. Furthermore, when the President stated that 'it is not unlikely that the legislation in question is justified for the necessity of protecting public health and the environment', it is not clear whether reference was being made here to Article 36 and the rule of reason or to Article 100A(4) itself. Clearly, if reference was indeed being made to Article 100A(4), this was misdirected as it is clear from the wording of Article 100A(4) itself that it is the Commission, rather that the national court, which is competent to 'confirm' the derogation under Article 100A(4). If, on the other hand, the President was applying the justifications to the provisions on free movement of goods in Article 36 and the rule of reason, it is not clear as to why either Article 30 or 34 may be held to have been infringed in the first place. As van de Gronden and Mortelmans point out,[99] the applicant was a Dutch undertaking operating in the Netherlands. The only provision of any relevance was thus surely Article 34 EC to the extent that the Dutch legislation may be held to restrict exports. However, it is difficult to see how on the *Groenveld*[100] interpretation of Article 34 there could be a breach of that Article since the Dutch legislation in question applied without discrimination as to the destination of the substance. Whatever the correct analysis, the point is that this judgment of the President of the *Raad van State* (*Afdeling Bestuursrechtspraak*) was far too brief and one is left to second-guess the reasoning of the President with respect to Community law.

It is submitted that the correct analysis would have been for the Court to have held that since the Directive had not, for the substances in question, yet entered into force, national law was applicable subject to the primary Treaty rules concerning the free movement of goods. As has been mentioned, it is unlikely that the latter rules were in fact infringed. It is submitted that this analysis is entirely consistent with the judgment of the ECJ in the *PCP* case where, although it held that a Member State may not

---

[98] Case C–41/93, n. 93 above.   [99] n. 94 above.   [100] Case 15/79, n. 83 above.

apply the stricter national provisions under Article 100A(4) until after it has obtained a decision from the Commission confirming them,[101] it also held that if a Member State wishes to continue to apply national provisions derogating from the Directive 'after the expiry of the time allowed for transposing, or after the entry into force of, a harmonization measure mentioned in Article 100A(1)'[102] it should notify the Commission. The clear implication is that the 'stand-still' requirement bites only after the provisions of the Directive have entered into force. Since none of these issues was discussed, let alone mentioned by the Dutch court in *Conté Nederland B.V.* v. *Minister van VROM*, the conclusion is undoubtedly that its judgment with respect to Community law was inadequately brief.

A further important legal mechanism to facilitate the completion of the internal market is Directive 83/189, which provides for an information procedure in the field of technical standards and regulations.[103] This important Directive provides for a 'stand-still' procedure under which Member States must notify any draft technical regulation to the Commission.[104] The Commission then circulates the proposal to all the other Member States and, after reactions have been received, prepares comments which the Member State concerned shall take into account 'as far as possible in the subsequent preparation of the technical regulation'.[105] Article 9 of the Directive obliges Member States to suspend the adoption of the draft technical regulation for three months from the date of notification and then for a further period of three or nine months depending on whether objections have been raised or whether Community legislation is envisaged.

Application of this Directive by the national courts necessarily begins with the question of whether the national provisions in question are 'technical specifications' within the meaning of the Directive.[106] However, the

---

[101] n. 98 above at para. 30. [102] Ibid. at para. 26.

[103] [1983] OJ L109/8. See amendments *inter alia* by Directive 88/182 [1988] OJ L81/75, Directive 94/10 [1994] OJ L100/30, and Decision 96/139 [1996] OJ L32/31. See also the proposal for a Directive consolidating the provisions for the information procedure in the field of technical standards: [1997] OJ C78/4.

[104] Art. 8(1) of the Directive. This notification requirement is of increasing importance in light of the current emphasis following the Sutherland Report on increased communication and administrative co-operation. See n. 11 above. See also Decision 3052/95 of the European Parliament and the Council of 13 Dec. 1995, establishing a procedure for the exchange of information of national measures derogating from the principle of the free movement of goods within the Community: [1995] OJ L321/1. See Fournier and La Pergola, 'La nouvelle procédure d'information mutuelle sur les mesures nationales derogeant au principe de libre circulation des marchandises à l'interieur de la Communauté' (1996) RMUE 145.

[105] Art. 8(2) of Directive.

[106] See, e.g., the judgments of the Belgian Court of Arbitration in Cases 7 & 8/95, judgts given on 2 Feb. 1995, Journal des tribunaux 1995, 470 & 474 and the Spanish Supreme Court (*Tribunal Supremo*), in the *Precious Metals* case, 14 Oct. 1992, Repertorio de Jurisprudentia Aranzadi 1992, no. 7892 where it was held that the national measures at issue were not technical specifications within the meaning of the Directive.

more important question is then whether the 'stand-still' requirements in Articles 8 and 9 of the Directive are directly effective and whether a national court is obliged to refuse to apply national technical regulations which have not been notified to the Commission in accordance with the Directive. In an important recent judgment, the ECJ has held in *CIA Security International* v. *Signalson*[107] that a breach of the obligation to notify under the Directive renders the technical regulations concerned inapplicable so as to be unenforceable against individuals, and furthermore that individuals may rely on this inapplicability before a national court which must decline to apply a national technical regulation which has not been notified in accordance with the Directive. This interpretation had been correctly anticipated by the Belgian *Conseil d'Etat* which reached the same conclusion before the ECJ's judgment in the *CIA Security* case.[108] Unfortunately, the same cannot be said for the Dutch *CBB* which, prior to the ECJ's *CIA Security* judgment, reached the opposite conclusion and held that the absence of notification did not mean that the national court had to decline to apply a national technical regulation which had not been notified in accordance with the Directive. In *Hema BV* v. *Minister van Verkeer en Waterstaat*,[109] the *CBB* held that the adoption of a test procedure in the Telecommunications Act (*Wet Telecommunicatievoorzieningen*) for type-approval of terminal equipment in the Netherlands was a technical requirement which should have been notified to the Commission under Article 8 of Directive 83/189. However, the *CBB* held that

It cannot be concluded, either from the wording or the purpose of the provisions of the Directive concerned, that when the Member States do not comply with the obligation for prior notification this automatically leads to the illegality (*onwettigheid*) of the applicable regulations.[110]

In reaching this conclusion, the *CBB* drew support from the ECJ's judgment in *Enichem Base* v. *Comune di Ciniselo Balsamo*[111] where the ECJ held that the obligation contained in Directive 75/442[112] for Member States to communicate to the Commission draft national rules falling within the scope of that Directive did not mean that failure by the Member States to observe this obligation rendered the national provisions unlawful. The *CBB* furthermore dismissed the importance of a Communication of the Commission of 1 November 1986[113] in which the Commission had expressed the opposite view with respect to Directive 83/189.

---

[107] Case C–194/94 [1996] ECR I–2201.   [108] Case 52.788, *Conseil d'Etat*, 12 Apr. 1995.
[109] *CBB*, 30 Jan. 1991, SEW 1991, 489 (with note by Mortelmans); Ars Aequis 1991, 8; NJB 1991, 756; UCB 1991, no. 8 (with note by Schipper-Spanninga). This same case had also been before the *CBB* in interim proceedings where the President of the *CBB* (judgt of 13 July 1989) only dealt with the matter under Arts. 30 to 36 EC: SEW 1989, 804 (with note by Mortelmans).
[110] SEW 1991, 489 at 491.   [111] Case 380/87 [1989] ECR 2491.
[112] [1975] OJ L194/39.   [113] [1986] OJ C245/4.

Following the judgment of the ECJ in the *CIA Security* case, the analysis of the *CBB* is, with hindsight, incorrect. Even if the point was at that time unclear, it should be remembered that the *CBB* is a court from which there is no possibility of further appeal within the meaning of Article 177(3) EC and that it is arguable that a reference to the ECJ was mandatory, especially given the fact that the *CBB* was effectively going directly against the views of the Commission which it had set out in its Communication.[114] It is true that the *CBB* went on to find that it was likely that the product in question did not, in any event, meet the essential safety requirements set out in Directives 88/301[115] and 86/361[116] and that the national provisions were compatible with Articles 30 to 36 (and consumer protection under the rule of reason in particular).[117] However, the ECJ's judgment in the *CIA Security* case makes it clear that this would not affect the conclusion that national provisions which have not been notified under Directive 83/189 were not enforceable. In *CIA Security* itself, the national court had also asked whether the national provisions at issue in that case infringed Article 30 EC. The ECJ simply held that this question did not need to be answered in light of the conclusion that the national provisions were not enforceable because they had not been notified to the Commission under Directive 83/189.[118] The judgment of the *CBB* in *Hema BV* v. *Minister van Verkeer en Waterstaat* can therefore be strongly criticized. It is true that the *CBB*'s conclusion was not wholly untenable following the ECJ's judgment in *Enichem Base*, and that the ECJ had to go to considerable lengths to distinguish that judgment in its *CIA Security* judgment.[119] Nevertheless, it is regrettable that the *CBB* chose to itself decide such an important question given the significant consequences for the uniform development of the internal market, without seeking the assistance of the ECJ pursuant to Article 177(3) EC. This judgment thus provides yet another warning that national courts should not be too hasty to conclude that the provisions of Community law are clear.[120]

[114] Ibid. [115] [1988] OJ L131/73. [116] [1986] OJ L217/21.

[117] See discussion of this aspect of the *CBB*'s judgment elsewhere in this work.

[118] On the other hand, the President of the *Rechbank* 's-Gravenhage has recently held that the very fact of notification to the Commission under Art. 9 of the analogous Directive 73/23 on the harmonization of the laws of Member States relating to electrical equipment [1973] OJ L77/29 had the result that there could be no breach of Art. 30 EC: *All-Line Incorporated* v. *Minister van Volksgezondheid, Welzijn en Sport*, Pres. *Rechtbank* 's-Granvenhage, 21 Aug. 1996, KG 1996, 301.

[119] Case C–194/94, n. 107 above paras. 49–50 of judgt.

[120] It may be noted that the consequences for the application of non-notified technical requirements has caused something of a commotion in the Netherlands after it became clear in June 1997 that the Dutch Government had overlooked the notification requirement in Directive 83/189 for several years. See Sevenster, 'Het Securitel-syndroom' NJB 1997, 1126. A further question on the extent of the non-applicability of non-notified national technical requirements has been referred to the ECJ by the *Arrondissementsrechtbank* Maastricht: Case C–226/97 *Lemmens*.

5 CONCLUSIONS

The application of Community legislation has caused many difficulties for the national courts. Community legislation aims, through harmonization, to clarify the provisions on the free movement of goods and it is ironic that its effect appears to have been to complicate, rather than to simplify, matters for the national courts. This state of affairs is also surprising since it is not that ECJ case law concerning the effect of Community harmonization legislation is particularly complex. The national courts are called upon to ask a simple question, namely whether the Community legislation applicable in an individual case is exhaustive or not. Those cases in which the national courts have failed altogether to ask this question are subject to the most severe criticism. However, even when the national courts do pose the correct question, it is essential that they set out more explicitly their reasoning for their conclusion that a particular piece of Community legislation is exhaustive or not. The national court judgments which have been discussed in this section have been unusually brief, inadequate and unclear. All too often one is left to second-guess the reasoning employed.

On the other hand, Community legislation does set up some complicated mechanisms and it must be admitted that the relationship between Articles 30 to 36 and Community secondary legislation is not always clear. This is not helped by the fact that there is a certain amount of circuitry: exhaustive legislation precludes recourse to Article 36 but the legislation itself is subject to the primary Treaty rules, including Article 36. Furthermore, the national courts have particular difficulties in assessing the application of national provisions when Community legislation requires prior notification. It is these procedural requirements which Community legislation introduces which give rise to the difficulties. In such cases, the national court is called upon to act more as a linesman than a referee in order to ensure that communication between the national authorities and the Commission is maintained according to the established procedures.

10

Remedies for Breach of Rules on the Free Movement of Goods Before National Courts

1 INTRODUCTION

The question of remedies for breaches of EC law before national courts has taken centre-stage in recent years.[1] This issue is of enormous practical importance given its position as the last link in the process towards effective and uniform application of EC law. The application of EC law by national courts may be seen in three stages. The first stage requires the national courts to accord provisions of EC law supremacy and direct effect in the national legal system. At the second stage, the national courts are called upon to apply the substantive provisions of EC law in accordance with the case law developed by the ECJ. The third and final stage concerns the provision of effective remedies for the breach of such substantive provisions. It is this third stage which forms the subject-matter of this chapter. The importance of the third stage is underlined by the fact that, should the national courts fail to provide effective remedies at the third stage, the benefits of correct application of EC law at the first and second stages will be negated. A Community right which can only be enforced through an ineffective remedy renders the right itself worthless.

Given the importance of remedies before national courts as a means to achieve the uniform application of EC law, it is surprising that the EC

---

[1] An exhaustive discussion of the question of remedies before national courts is beyond the scope of this work. See further Van Gerven, 'Bridging the Gap between Community and National laws: Towards a Principle of Homogeneity in the Field of Legal Remedies'; Caranta, 'Judicial Protection Against Member States: a new *jus commune* takes shape'; Bebr, 'Court of Justice: Judicial Protection and the Rule of Law' and Curtin & Mortelmans, 'Application and Enforcement of Community Law by the Member States: Actors in Search of a Third Generation Script', both in Curtin and Heukels (eds.), *Institutional Dynamics of European Integration, Essays in Honour of Henry G. Schermers*, vol. II (Martinus Nijhoff Publishers, 1995); Tash, 'Remedies for European Community Law Claims in Member States: Toward a European Standard'; Ruffert, 'Rights and Remedies in European Community Law: A Comparative View' (1997) 34 CMLRev 307; Brealey & Hoskins, *Remedies in EC Law*; D'Sa, *European Community Law and Civil Remedies in England and Wales*; Lonbay & Biondi (eds.), *Remedies for Breach of EC Law*; Steiner, *Enforcing EC Law*; Lewis, *Remedies and the Enforcement of European Community Law*. The issue of remedies before national courts is not new: see Hartley, 'The Effect in National Law of Judgements of the European Court of Justice'; Bridge, 'Procedural Aspects of the Enforcement of EC law Through the Legal Systems of the Member States'; Steiner, 'How to Make Actions Suit the Case: Domestic Remedies for Breach of EC Law'; Oliver, 'Enforcing Community Law Rights in English Courts'; Barav, 'Enforcement of Community Rights in National Courts: The Case for Jurisdiction to Grant Interim Relief'.

Treaty is silent on this issue. Faced with this silence, the ECJ has traditionally followed the principle of 'procedural autonomy' according to which:

In the absence of Community rules governing the matter, it is for the domestic
legal system of each Member State to designate the courts having jurisdiction and
to lay down the detailed procedural rules governing actions for safeguarding
rights which individuals derive from the direct effect of Community law.[2]

However, in a long series of cases, the ECJ has consistently held, drawing
on Article 5 EC,[3] that the principle of procedural autonomy is subject to
two provisos. Firstly, national rules must not be less favourable than those
governing similar domestic actions and secondly, such rules must not render virtually impossible or excessively difficult the exercise of rights conferred by Community law.[4] The ECJ has also held that the principle of
procedural autonomy has the result that there is no requirement for the
national courts to create new remedies.[5] In recent years, the facade of the
principle of procedural autonomy has been gradually eroded. This has
been in part due to the emergence of a further requirement in ECJ case law
for 'effective' remedies.[6] The latter requirement has driven a coach and
horses through the principle of procedural autonomy by requiring non-
discriminatory national remedies, which are no less favourable than those
governing similar domestic actions, to be set aside or substituted by remedies which protect EC law rights more effectively.[7] Furthermore, the ECJ

---

[2] Joined Cases C–430–431/93 *Van Schijndel* v. *Stichting Pensioenfonds voor Fysiotherapeuten*
[1995] ECR I–4705 at para. 17. The principle of 'procedural autonomy is a long-standing one:
see Case 6/60 *Humblet* v. *Belgium* [1960] ECR 559 & Case 28/67 *Mölkerei-Zentrale Westfalen* v.
Hauptzollamt Paderborn [1968] ECR 148, [1968] CMLR 187.

[3] Art. 5 EC provides: 'Member States shall take all appropriate measures, whether general
or particular, to ensure fulfilment of the obligations arising out of this Treaty or resulting
from action taken by the institutions of the Community. They shall facilitate the
Community's tasks. They shall abstain from any measure which could jeopardise the attainment of the objectives of the Treaty'. For a commentary on the role of Art. 5, see Temple Lang,
'Community Constitutional Law: Article 5 EEC Treaty' (1990) 27 CMLRev 645.

[4] See Case 33/76 *Rewe-Zentralfinanz* v. *Landwirtschaftskammer* [1976] ECR 1989, [1977] 1
CMLR 533; Case 45/76 *Comet BV* v. *Produktschap voor Siegerwassen* [1976] ECR 2043; Case
179/84 *Bozetti* v. *Invernizzi* [1985] ECR 2301, [1986] 2 CMLR 246; Case 68/79 *Hans Just* v.
Danish Ministry for Fiscal Affairs [1980] ECR 501; Case 199/82 *Amministrazione delle Finanze
dello Stato* v. *San Giorgio* [1983] ECR 3595, [1985] 2 CMLR 658; Joined Cases C–430–431/93, n.
2 above & Case C–312/93 *Peterbroek* v. *Belgium* [1995] ECR I–4599.

[5] Case 158/80 *Rewe-Handelsgesellsschaft Nord* v. *Hauptzollamt Kiel* [1981] ECR 1805, [1982] 1
CMLR 449 at para. 44.

[6] The requirement for national courts to provide effective remedies may also be seen as
implicit in the second proviso discussed above. See further, Fitzpatrick and Szyszczak,
'Remedies and Effective Judicial Protection in Community Law'; Szyszczak, 'Making Europe
More Relevant to Its Citizens: Effective Judicial Process' (1996) 21 ELRev. 351, Prechal, 'EC
Requirements for an Effective Remedy', & Jacobs, 'Enforcing Community Rights and
Obligations in National Courts: Striking the Balance' both in Lonbay and Biondi, n. 1 above.

[7] See Case 14/83 *von Colson* [1984] ECR 1891, [1986] 2 CMLR 430; Case 222/84 *Johnston* v.
Chief Constable of the RUC [1986] ECR 1651 [1986] 3 CMLR 240; Case C–213/89 *R.* v. *Secretary
of State for Transport, ex p. Factortame* [1990] ECR I–2433, [1990] 3 CMLR 1; Case C–271/91

has also proscribed that national remedies must have 'a real deterrent effect'.[8] The process of the erosion of the principle of procedural autonomy has come full cycle in recent years by the establishment by the ECJ of uniform Community-wide remedies in certain areas.[9]

The development in the ECJ's case law on remedies has taken place against a background of legislative inactivity. Legislative intervention in the field of remedies has been minimal.[10] While this is undoubtedly regrettable, it is submitted that the ECJ's boldness in developing remedies at Community level is to be commended. The principle of procedural autonomy is inadequate to service the long-term requirements for the administration of justice in the Community legal order. The obvious assumption underpinning the principle of procedural autonomy is that national procedures for obtaining legal redress will be adequate. However, this assumption is inaccurate since 'a particular legal situation which in some States would confer an individual right, may only amount to a mere interest or legitimate expectation in others'.[11] When different procedural rules

Marshall v. *Southampton and South West Area Health Authority* (No. 2) [1993] ECR I–4367, [1993] 3 CMLR 293; Case C–208/90 *Emmott* v. *Minister for Social Welfare* [1991] ECR I–4269, [1991] 3 CMLR 894. However, with respect to national time-limits, the ECJ has somewhat retreated; see Case C–338/91 *Steenhorst-Neerings* v. *Bestuur van de Bedrijfsvereniging voor Detailhandel, Ambachten en Huisvrouwen* [1993] ECR I–5475 & Case C–410/92 *Johnson* v. *Chief Adjudication Officer* [1994] ECR I–5483. See also Joined Cases C–430–431/93, n. 2 above at para. 19; Case C–312/93, n. 4 above at para. 14 where the ECJ reiterated the principle of procedural autonomy but nevertheless went on to hold that 'each case which raises the question whether a national procedural provision renders application of Community law impossible or excessively difficult must be analysed by reference to the role of that provision in the procedure, its progress and its special features, viewed as a whole, before the various national instances. In the light of that analysis the basic principles of the domestic judicial system, such as protection of the rights of the defence, the principle of legal certainty and the proper conduct of procedure, must, where appropriate, be taken into consideration.' For commentary, see Hoskins, 'Tilting the Balance: Supremacy and National Procedural Rules' & Szyszczak & Delicostopoulos, 'Intrusions into National Procedural Autonomy: The French Paradigm' (1997) 22 ELRev. 141.

[8] See Case 79/83 *Harz* v. *Deutsche Tradax* [1984] ECR 1921, [1986] 2 CMLR 430 at para. 23.

[9] See, e.g., Cases C–6 & 9/90 *Francovich and Bonifaci* v. *Italy* [1991] ECR I–5357, [1993] 2 CMLR 66; Cases C–143/88 & C–92/89 *Zuckerfabrik Süderdithmarschen* v. *Hauptzollamt Itzehoe* [1991] ECR I–415 & Cases C–46/93 & C–48/93 *Brasserie du Pêcheur* v. *Federal Republic of Germany*; *R.* v. *Secretary of State for Transport, ex parte Factortame Ltd* (No. 3) [1996] ECR I–1029; [1996] 1 CMLR 889.

[10] See, e.g., Council Directive 89/665 on the co-ordination of the laws, regulations and administrative provisions relating to the application of review procedures to the award of public supply and public works contracts [1989] OJ L395/33 and Directive 93/13 on remedies in procurement by the utilities [1992] OJ L76/14. See further, Weatherill, 'National Remedies and Public Procurement' (1990) 10 YEL 243; Gormley, 'Remedies in Public Procurement: Community Provisions and the United Kingdom' in Lonbay and Biondi (eds.), n. 1 above at 155 and Haguenau, *L'Application effective du droit communautaire en droit interne: Analyse comparative des problèmes recontrés en droit français, anglais et allemand* (Bruylant, 1995), 497–537. See also Council Resolution of 29 June 1995 on the effective uniform application of Community law and on the penalties applicable for breaches of Community law in the internal market [1995] OJ C188/1.

[11] Fernández Martín, *The EC Public Procurement Rules: A Critical Analysis* (OUP, 1996), 182.

in Member States lead to different results, the principle of procedural autonomy conflicts directly with the principle of uniformity which the ECJ has characterized as 'a fundamental requirement of the Community legal order'.[12]

With respect to the application of the provisions concerning the free movement of goods before national courts, two types of national remedy play a particularly important role. Firstly, the exercise of the discretion of the national judge in interlocutory proceedings to grant interim relief, and secondly, the liability of the State for its breaches of Articles 30 to 36 EC. Both of these issues will be examined in turn in this chapter.

2 INTERIM RELIEF BEFORE NATIONAL COURTS

Interim relief plays a crucial role in the good administration of justice by seeking to achieve effective judicial protection. The underlying principle is the maxim that 'justice delayed is justice denied'. From the point of view of parties to a legal dispute, reasons of urgency will often dictate that it is desirable to have the dispute settled as quickly as possible, even if this can only be achieved at the cost of thoroughness. The importance of interim protection is underlined by the fact that a great deal of litigation before the national courts does not proceed beyond the interim stage. Since national courts have an obligation to apply Community law as part of national law, it is obvious that they should do so both in interim proceedings and at full trial.[13]

It has long been established that a national court cannot declare acts of the Community institutions invalid.[14] The uniform application of Community law dictates that the validity of Community legislation should be determined at Community level and is therefore a matter within the ECJ's exclusive competence. However, in _Zuckerfabriek Süderdithmarschen_ v. _Hauptzollamt Itzehoe_,[15] the ECJ accepted that where interim measures are sought before a national court while a ruling from the ECJ on the validity of the Community measure is pending, a narrowly defined exception applies, allowing the national court to grant interim measures suspending the operation of a national measure adopted in implementation of the Community measure. The ECJ set out uniform criteria which the national courts must apply in exercising their discretion to grant

---

[12] Cases C–143/88 & C–92/89, n. 9 above at para. 26.
[13] See Case 106/77 _Amministrazione delle finanze dello stato_ v. _Simmenthal_ [1978] ECR 629, [1978] 3 CMLR 263.
[14] See Case 314/85 _Foto-Frost_ v. _Hauptzollamt Lübeck-Ost_ [1987] ECR 4199.
[15] Cases C–143/88 & C–92/89, n. 9 above.

interim relief in such circumstances.[16] Accordingly, national measures adopted in implementation of a Community measure may be suspended by a national court only:

(1) if that court entertains serious doubts as to the validity of the Community measure and, should the question of the validity of the contested measure not already have been brought before the ECJ, itself refers that question to the ECJ;

(2) if there is urgency and a threat of serious and irreparable damage to the applicant; and

(3) if the national court takes due account of the Community's interests.[17]

Importantly, however, the uniform criteria for the grant of interim relief set out by the ECJ in *Zuckerfabriek* do not apply in cases other than those in which the validity of Community legislation is called into question. While the ECJ in *R. v. Secretary of State for Transport, ex p. Factortame*[18] confirmed that interim relief must be available as a remedy even in cases where there is no challenge to Community legislation, it was silent on the question, which the House of Lords had referred to it, as to the criteria to be applied in exercising that discretion. The necessary implication is that, so long as the validity of a Community measure itself is not at issue, the ECJ is happy, subject to the usual provisos, for the national courts to apply national law criteria for the grant of interim relief in cases in which the compatibility of national provisions with Community law is at issue. This is in accordance with the principle of procedural autonomy and is based on the assumption that national procedures for granting interim relief are likely to be adequate.[19] However, it is somewhat anomalous that the ECJ was prepared in *Zuckerfabriek* to set strict conditions within which national courts may grant interim relief where the invalidity of Community legislation is at issue, whereas in *Factortame*, where the compatibility of national provisions with Community law was at issue, the ECJ did not

[16] The criteria which the ECJ set out are the same as those which the ECJ itself applies under Arts. 185 & 186 EC in granting suspension of the validity of a Community measure in direct actions. Ibid. at para. 27 of judgt.

[17] Ibid. at para. 33. It may be noted that the ECJ has reiterated and somewhat extended these criteria in Case C–465/93 *Atlanta Fruchthandelsgesellschaft* [1995] ECR I–3761 where it also held that the national courts are able to provide 'positive' as well as 'suspensory' interim relief. More recently, in Case C–68/95 *T. Port v. Bundesanstalt für Landwirtschaft und Ernährung* [1996] ECR I–6065, [1997] 1 CMLR 1 the ECJ held that in cases concerning interim protection in a situation where, by virtue of a Community Regulation, the existence and scope of a trader's rights had still to be established by a Commission measure which the Commission had not yet adopted, national courts had no jurisdiction to order interim measures pending action on the part of that institution and that judicial review of the alleged failure to act could be exercised only by the Community judicature.

[18] Case C–213/89, n. 7 above.

[19] See the Opinion of Adv. Gen. Tesauro in his Opinion to the ECJ in Case C–213/89, *Ex p. Factortame*, n. 7 above at 2464 of ECR.

specify the conditions applicable for the grant of interim relief by national courts.[20]

National case law dealing, at the interlocutory stage, with the compatibility of national provisions with the rules on free movement of goods in the EC Treaty will be discussed in the remainder of this section. The question at the heart of this discussion is whether or not the assumption that national procedures for the granting of interim relief are likely to be adequate is a correct one and furthermore, whether the absence of uniform criteria for the grant of interim relief leads in practice to a lack of uniformity in the application of EC law before national courts.

The discussion necessarily begins with a brief analysis of the prevailing criteria for granting interim relief in litigation before the French, United Kingdom, and Dutch courts respectively. This is then followed by a more detailed analysis of those cases before those courts in which the compatibility of national provisions with the free-movement-of-goods rules in the EC Treaty was dealt with at the interlocutory stage. Finally, the analysis will be synthesized and critically evaluated.

(A) Application of the provisions concerning the free movement of goods by the French courts in interim proceedings

Applications for interim relief in France are made to a *juge des référés*, the name given to a judge in summary proceedings.[21] The *juge des référés* is often referred to as the *juge de l'urgence*, the *juge du provisoire*, or the *juge de l'évident et l'incontestable de l'apparence*.[22] The powers of the *juge des référés* are governed by Article 809(1) of the New Code on Civil Procedure (*nouveau Code de procédure civile*) which provides that

The President in summary proceedings may always, even when faced with a serious dispute, prescribe interlocutory or restitutionary measures required either to

---

[20] See Sharpston, *Interim and Substantive Relief in Claims under Community Law* (Butterworths, 1993), 51 & idem. 'Interim Relief in the National Courts' at 48–50.

[21] For a discussion of the position of the *juge des référés* under French law, see Cavallini, *Le juge national du provisoire face au droit communautaire*, 12–67. See also Viatte, 'Les pouvoirs du juge des référés' Gaz. Pal. 1976, Doctr. 709; Normand, 'Notion et objet de la contestation sérieuse: obstacle aux pouvoirs du juge des référés' Rev. Trim. de Droit Civil 1979, 654; Blaisse, 'Quo vadis référés?' JCP 1982 I 3083; Rondeau-Rivier, 'L'évidence et la notion de contestation sérieuse devant le juge des référés' Gaz. Pal. 1991, Doctr. 355.

[22] For a general discussion of the application of Community law by the *juge des référés* see, Laurent, 'La fonction communautaire du juge judicaire français des référés'; Orsini, 'Le juge des référés et l'application des normes communautaires'; Goyet, Dalloz 1986, Jur. 161 & Parleani, 'Le juge des référés face au droit Communautaire'. See also Errera, 'French Courts and Article 177 of the Treaty of Rome' and Desmazières de Séchelles, 'Experiences and Problems in Applying the Preliminary Proceedings of Article 177 of the Treaty of Rome, as seen by a French advocate' in Schermers, Timmermans, Kellermann & Stewart Watson (eds.), *Article 177 EEC: Experiences & Problems*, at 86–8 & 148 respectively.

prevent imminent damage or to put an end to a mischief which is manifestly unlawful.[23]

The two key concepts in this provision are 'imminent damage' (*dommage imminent*) and 'a mischief which is manifestly unlawful' (*trouble manifeste-ment illicite*). At first sight, it would appear that the threshold for the plaintiff is rather high. If it has to be shown that a mischief is *manifestement* unlawful one might assume that if there is an element of doubt (for example, as to the compatibility of a national measure with Community law) the unlawfulness will no longer be manifest, such that interim measures should not be granted. However, the *Cour de Cassation* has interpreted *trouble manifestement illicite* such that the threshold is much lower than this.[24] It is widely assumed that urgency is an implied prerequisite for the application of this provision.[25]

It is not entirely clear whether the concepts of *dommage imminent* and *trouble manifestement illicite* in Article 809 apply cumulatively or in the alternative. On the one hand, the wording of Article 809 itself suggests that the latter is the case. However, Le Tallec has argued that the two concepts should be read cumulatively since there seems to be little need to grant an injunction to prevent a *dommage imminent* which is perfectly lawful.[26] The boundary between *trouble manifestement illicite* and *dommage imminent* can thus, in theory at least, be rather difficult to locate.

A huge volume of cases concerning the free movement of goods have been dealt with by *juge des référés* in France.[27] In fact, the volume of cases is such that they have been likened to '*une tempête jurisprudentielle*'.[28] The most important cases involving the application of the provisions concerning the free movement of goods before the *juge des référés* have concerned French legislation on resale price maintenance for books, on the minimum price for petrol, and on the protection of cinematographic works. The

---

[23] In the orginal French: '*Le président peut toujours, même en présence d'une contestation sérieuse, prescrire en référé les mesures conservatoire ou de remise in état qui s'imposent, soit pour prévenir un dommage imminent, soit pour fair cesser un trouble manifestement illicite*'. It may be noted that Art. 809, New Code on Civil Procedure applies only to a *juge des référés* sitting in a *Tribunal de grande instance*. An equivalent provision which applies to the *juge des référés* sitting in a *Tribunal de Commerce* is provided for in Art. 873(1), New Code on Civil Procedure.

[24] *Cour de Cassation*, ch. civ, 1re, 19 Feb. 1980 Gaz. Pal. II Pan jur. 359; *Cour de Cassation*, ch. civ, 3re, 12 May 1981 JCP IV 1981, 268; *Cour de Cassation*, ch. civ. 2e, 21 Apr. 1982, JCP 1982, IV 231; *Cour de Cassation*, ch. civ., 2e, 8 June 1983 JCP 1983, IV 258.

[25] See, e.g., note by Blaisse JCP 1987, II 20722. However, in *SA Argendis (Centre Leclerc) et Société ACDELEC* v. *Union syndicale des libraires de France et Syndicat des libraires professionels de Paris et de la région parisienne, Cour d'appel* Versailles, 1re ch. I, 30 May 1984, [1986] ECC 197 at 200 it was explicitly held that 'urgency is not required for the appliction of Article 809 of the New Code on Civil Procedure'.

[26] JCP 1986, I 3231. It may further be noted that while *dommage imminent* applies to something that has yet to occur, *trouble manifestement illicite* applies to an event which has already taken place.

[27] See commentaries cited at n. 22 above.   [28] Fourgoux, Gaz. Pal. 1984, II Jur. 58.

respective facts of these series of cases need not be rehearsed here.[29] What is of interest in the context of the present discussion is the exercise of the discretion by the *juge des référés* to grant interim measures. In all three series of cases, the compatibility of French legislation with the free-move-ment-of-goods provisions was raised. The *juge des référés* dealt with the discretion under Article 809 of the New Code on Civil Procedure[30] in a variety of ways.

(i) *Cases in which the* juge des référés *held that the breach of French law constituted a* trouble manifestement illicite *and that, until it was shown in an incontestable manner that the French provisions were contrary to Articles 30 to 36 EC, French law must apply*

In the majority of cases, the *juge des référés* simply applied the French pro-visions. In *SARL Debeaux, Pradier v. SA Ets Chautard,*[31] the *Tribunal de grande instance* of Dijon completely ignored the points on Community law and granted an injunction to stop a breach of the petrol-pricing legislation because it held that there was a *trouble manifestement illicite*. The *Tribunal* held that the *juge des référés* was the *'juge naturel'* for consumers and that they had a right to expect that their interests would be protected by the courts. In the context of the same legislation, the *Tribunal de grande instance* of Créteil[32] simply held that a breach of the French legislation constituted a *trouble manifestement illicite* and granted an injunction on the grounds that a *juge des référés* was only competent to enjoin the petrol retailers from further breaches. Similarly, in *CSNRA v. Sodialfo—Rennes Ouest,*[33] the *Tribunal de Commerce* of Rennes held that there was a conflict between the French provisions and the EC Treaty but that this *'contestation sérieuse'* could not be solved by a *juge des référés* without prejudicing the full trial and that in these circumstances, Article 809 of the New Code on Civil

---

[29] See discussion of the facts of the books cases at p. 165; of the petrol cases at pp. 83–4, and the cinema cases at p. 181. See further Cavallini, n. 21 above, 138–74.

[30] See n. 23 above.   [31] *TGI* Dijon (*Référés*), 18 Mar. 1983, Gaz. Pal. 1983, II Som. 346.

[32] *Maignam* v. *Sté Vitry-Distribution, TGI* Créteil (*Référés*), 26 Apr. 1984, Dalloz 1985, IR 273 (with note by Gavalda & Lucas De Leyssac).

[33] *Trib. comm.* Rennes (*Référés*), 12 July 1983, Gaz. Pal. 1983, II Jur. 585. See also to exactly the same effect: *CSNRA* v. *Paramé distribution, TGI* Saint-Malo (*Référés*), 5 July 1983, cited in note to Gaz. Pal. 1983, II Jur. 585; *CSNRA* v. *Distribution de Beauvais, Trib. corr.* Beauvais (*Référés*), 21 June 1983, cited in note to Gaz. Pal. 1983, II Jur. 585; *Hypermarché Continent* v. *CSNCRA, Tribunal de commerce* Meaux (*Référés*), 20 Mar. 1984, cited on appeal to *Cour d'appel* Paris 1re ch.A, 4 July 1984, Gaz. Pal. 1984, II Jur. 658; *Neudis (Centre Leclerc)* v. *SARL Mottet (Shell français), Trib. comm.* Lyon, 20 July 1983, cited on appeal to *Cour d'appel* Lyon, 1re ch., 4 Oct. 1984, [1985] 1 CMLR 247; *Chabrand* v. *SA Alpes distribution Aldis (Centre Leclerc), Trib. comm.* Manosque (*Référés*), 25 May 1984, cited on appeal to *Cour d'appel* Aix-en-Provence, 8e ch. civ., 21 May 1985, JCP 1987, II 20722; [1987] 2 CMLR 396; *SA Samu-Auchan, Cour d'appel* Lyon (*Référés*), 23 May 1984, cited on appeal to *Cour de Cassation*, ch. comm., 26 Nov. 1985, Journal du droit international 1986, 364 and *Dumoussaud* v. *Syndicat des artisans mécaniciens de l'automobile du Lot, Cour d'appel* Agen, 1re ch. (*Référés*), 28 Nov. 1984, cited on appeal to *Cour de Cassation*, ch. comm., 24 June 1986, Bull. Cass. Civ. 1986, IV 112.

Procedure required it to take all appropriate measures to prevent a *trouble manifestement illicite*. With respect to the book-pricing legislation, the *Tribunal de grande instance* of Bressuire held that

The deliberate breach of a statute, the conformity of which with international law and particularly with the EEC Treaty does not have to be examined of his own motion by a judge in summary proceedings, constitutes a manifestly unlawful mischief (*un trouble manifestement illicite*) . . . It is for the judge in summary proceedings to put a stop to such mischief and he has the jurisdiction to do so.[34]

It is submitted that these judgments by the *juge des référés* are contrary to the requirement under EC law for the national courts to provide effective remedies.[35] The *juge des référés* in these cases simply applied French law without examining in any depth whether Articles 30 to 36 EC were breached.[36] As such, it is submitted that the *juge des référés* did not perform their duty to act as Community courts.[37] Of yet more concern, however, are a string of judgments in interim proceedings where it was held that the breach of French provisions constituted a *trouble manifestement illicite* and that in such circumstances a *juge des référés* should effectively presume that French law applied. Thus in *SA Argendis*, the *Cour d'Appel* of Versailles held that

Undoubtedly a national court must observe the rules of Community law. It follows that if that law has a clear, specific provision prohibiting Member States from applying resale price maintenance to books, the national law should be ousted by that rule. On the other hand, if it is not shown manifestly that it is contrary to a rule of Community law, the national law must provisionally be observed by the parties and courts of summary jurisdiction in the Member State, until the court dealing with the main issue gives a decision on the compatibility or otherwise of the two systems, after obtaining a ruling from the European Court of Justice if necessary.[38]

---

[34] *Librairie 'Au Blé Vert'* v. *Association des centres distributeurs Edouard Leclerc, TGI* Bressuire (*Référés*), 11 Mar. 1982, [1982] 2 CMLR 568 at 570. See also *Association des centres distributeurs Edouard Leclerc* v. *Syndicat des librairies de Loire Océan, Cour d'appel* Angers (*Référés*), 17 Feb. 1983, cited in *Cour de Cassation*, ch. com., 15 May 1985, Bull. Cass. Civ. 1985, IV 133, Dalloz 1986, Jur. 159. See to similar effect *British Motors Wright* v. *SCP Boscher, Studer et Fromentin et Nado GmbH, Cour d'appel* Paris, 1re ch. A (*Référés*), 5 Nov. 1988, Gaz. Pal. 1989, I Jur. 159 (with note by Marchi) where it was held that a breach of a French law requiring a seller at a public auction to be registered at the place where the auction takes place constituted a *trouble manifestement illicite*. See further discussion of the substance of this case at p. 65.

[35] See discussion of this requirement at text at n. 6 above.

[36] The position of the *juge des référés* in these cases has also been criticized by Cavallini, n. 21 above, 142–3.

[37] In Case 106/77 *Amministrazione delle finanze dello stato* v. *Simmenthal* [1978] ECR 629, [1978] 3 CMLR 263 at para. 15 the ECJ held that 'any national court whose task it is as an organ of a Member State to protect, in a case within its jurisdiction, the rights conferred upon individuals by Community law'.

[38] n. 25 above at 201. See also to the same effect: *Haincourt* v. *Leclerc Service et SA des marchés et usines Auchan, TGI* Le Mans (*Référés*), 11 July 1983, Gaz. Pal. 1984, II Som. 121; Dalloz 1985, IR 273 (with note by Gavalda & Lucas De Leyssac); *Rosello* v. *Sodivar, Cour d'appel* Paris, 14e

This reasoning by the *juge des référés* has received some support in academic commentaries. Bertin has argued that the *juge des référés* is only called upon to give a provisional judgment and thus that '[w]hen a fire breaks out in the house, one does not begin by appointing an expert to investigate the causes; one puts it out'.[39] However, it is submitted that the position adopted by the *juge des référés* in these cases may be heavily criticized. The *juge des référés* claims to accept the supremacy of EC law where there is 'a clear, specific provision' prohibiting the national provisions. However, as Cavallini has pointed out, such a 'clear, specific provision' of Community law will seldom arise and *'par ce moyen, la norme nationale est assurée d'être toujous la norme qui s'impose immédiatement'*.[40] More serious is the fact that this approach contains a presumption that, until the full trial, the French law should prevail. It is submitted that this is contrary to the duty incumbent on the national court to apply Community integrally.[41] As the ECJ has held,

[A] national court which is called upon, within the limits of its jurisdiction, to apply the provisions of Community law is under a duty to give full effect to those provisions, if necessary refusing of its own motion to apply any conflicting provision of national legislation, even if adopted subsequently, and it is not necessary for the court to request or await the prior setting aside of such provision by legislative or other constitutional means.[42]

A *juge des référés* is a national judge and also a Community judge who has a duty to apply Community law as part of national law. The presumption that French law should apply in interim proceedings is thus a challenge to the proper functioning of the Community legal order.

(ii) *Cases in which the* juge des référés *held that the court was incompetent to resolve a serious dispute between French and EC law*

In several other cases, the *juges des référés* acknowledged that there was a serious dispute as to whether or not the French regulations were contrary to EC law and therefore that there could not be said to be a *trouble manifestement illicite*.[43] However, these courts went on to hold that a *juge des*

ch. A, 2 Nov. 1983, Gaz. Pal. 1984, I Jur. 47; *Garage Dehus* v. *Bouche Distribution, Cour d'appel* Paris, 14e ch. A (*Référés*), 2 Nov. 1983, [1984] 3 CMLR 452; Dalloz 1984, IR 257; *Stama* v. *Discar, Cour d'appel* Paris, 14e ch., 12 July 1983, Gaz. Pal. 1983, II Som. 343 and *Montgeron Distribution (Centre Leclerc)* v. *SA Garage Picot, Cour d'appel* Paris, 14e ch. C, 29 Mar. 1984, Gaz. Pal. 1984, II Som. 120.

[39] Bertin, 'Le juge des référés et le droit communautaire'. See also ibid., 'Un trouble manifestement illicite; la lutte contre la vie chère' Gaz. Pal. 1983, II Doctr. 419.

[40] Cavallini, n. 21 above, 161.

[41] Cavallini criticizes the presumption on validity of French legislation as being *'loin de servir les intérêts du droit communautaire'*, ibid., 157.

[42] Case 106/77, n. 37 above at para. 24.

[43] With respect to the French petrol-pricing provisions, see *Garage Dehus* v. *Bouche Distribution, TGI* Meaux (*Référés*), 6 July 1983, cited on appeal to *Cour d'appel* Paris, 14e ch. A,

référés was incompetent to resolve a serious dispute between French and EC law and on these grounds, refused to grant an injunction. Thus, while these judgments in interim proceedings at least acknowledged a serious conflict between Community and French law, by declaring themselves incompetent, the *juge des référés* may nevertheless be criticized for having failed to fulfil their duty to interpret Community law. Apart from being unsatisfactory from the point of view of Community law, it may also be argued that this position adopted by the *juge des référés* defeats the object of interim relief under national law. Cavallini points out that *'les opérateurs économiques sont souvent plus soucieux d'obtenir rapidement une décision même défavourable qu'un jugement tardif qui leur donnerait raison'*.[44] By declaring themselves incompetent, the *juge des référés* were thus serving neither the interests of the parties, nor those of Community law.

(iii) *Cases in which the* juge des référés *held that French law should be applied to avoid the emergence of a legal vacuum*

In *Editions Gallimard v. FNAC*,[45] the *Tribunal de grande instance* of Paris held in the context of the book-pricing legislation that the *juge des référés* must apply Community law, but that in case of conflict between Community and national law, and in the absence of a judgment of the ECJ, national law must be applied to avoid creating a 'legal vacuum' (*vide juridique*). It is submitted that this position is open to severe criticism since it implies that the *juge des référés* has no jurisdiction to solve such a conflict himself. While there is much to be said for a national court applying national law pending clarification by the ECJ, it is submitted that this is only acceptable after the national court has engaged in some balancing exercise, and that it is certainly not enough to simply apply national law to avoid creating a *vide juridique* without even starting to apply Articles 30 to 36 EC. It should also be pointed out that, by suspending the application of national legislation for being contrary to Community law, the *juge des référés* is not

---

2 Nov. 1983, [1984] 3 CMLR 452; Dalloz 1984, IR 257; *Monnet v. SA Somodis*, TGI Valence (*Référés*), 12 July 1983, Gaz. Pal. 1983, II Jur. 478; *Hoffmann v. Edouard Leclerc*, TGI Saint-Quentin (*Référés*), 4 Aug. 1983, Gaz. Pal. 1983, II Jur. 480; *CSNCRA v. SA Allouette Distribution*, *Trib. comm.* Tours (*Référés*), 2 Aug. 1983, Gaz. Pal. 1983, II Som. 342; *Bianchi v. Sarredis*, *Cour d'appel* Metz, ch. civ., 7 Feb. 1984, cited in judgt on appeal to *Cour de Cassation*, ch. comm., 15 May 1985, Bull. Cass. Civ. 1985, IV 131–2; Dalloz 1986, Jur. 159. With respect to the book-pricing provisions, see *Librairies présentes en Aquitaine et La machine à lire v. Carrefour Sogara*, TGI Bordeaux (*Référés*), 4 Apr. 1985, Gaz. Pal. 1985, I Jur. 340 (with note by Mauro); *Dammarie distribution (Centre Leclerc) v. FFSL*, *Cour d'appel* Paris, 1re ch. A, 10 Feb. 1988, Dalloz 1988, IR 81; *Syndicat national de l'édition v. SA Rocadis (Centre Leclerc)*, TGI Poitiers (*Référés*), 17 Apr. 1987, RTDE 1987, 555.

[44] Cavallini, n. 21 above, 174. See further at 167–74.

[45] TGI Paris (*Référés*), 4 June 1984, Gaz. Pal. 1984, I Jur. 603–4 (with note by Serna); JCP 1985, II 20357 (with note by Fourgoux).

creating a legal vacuum, but is merely according litigants their Community rights.[46]

(iv) *Cases in which the* juge des référés *carried out an effective balancing act between the provisions of French law and Articles 30 to 36 EC*

Although it is true to say that the less than satisfactory cases discussed in the sections above made up the majority of cases in the series, there were nonetheless some notable exceptions. For example, in the context of the petrol-pricing cases, the *Tribunal de commerce* of Melun recognized that there was a serious dispute between the French provisions and Articles 30 to 36 EC but, unlike in some of the cases discussed above, held that this fact did not remove the competence of the *juge des référés* under Article 809 of the New Code on Civil Procedure.[47] Accordingly, an injunction was refused and a reference was made to the ECJ pursuant to Article 177 EC.[48] Equally, with respect to the same French legislation, the *Cour d'Appel* of Lyon held that

[I]t seems doubtful whether the French regulations are compatible with the rules of Community law. . . The apparent contradiction between the Community rule and the national rule does not permit a court of summary jurisdiction to find the acts contrary to the national rule constitute a manifestly illegal mischief (*trouble manifestement illicite*) and to order interlocutory measures or restitution measures for putting an end to it.[49]

A similar line was taken by the *Cour d'Appel* of Paris in a 'second wave'[50] of cases after references had been made to the ECJ under Article 177 EC. For example, in *Hypermarché Continent* v. *CSNCRA*,[51] it was held that Community law was an integral part of national law and takes priority in the legal order in force on French territory and that the French courts had an obligation to apply these rules integrally and to protect the rights that they confer upon individuals, leaving inapplicable any national law which is contrary to Community law. The *Cour d'Appel* then held that the present case raised complex economic problems such that a decision by the ECJ was necessary, but noted that references had already been made to that

---

[46] See further criticisms of this position by Fourgoux, n. 45 above and Cavallini who comments that '[c]ette parade du "vide juridqiue" non seulement est artificielle mais surtout contraire au pouvoir interprétatif du juge', n. 21 above, 161.

[47] *Piszko and CSNCRA* v. *Carrefour supermarché*, Trib. comm. Melun (Référé), 12 Mar. 1984, Gaz. Pal. 1984, II Som. 126.

[48] Cases 114 & 115/84 [1985] ECR 2961.

[49] *Neudis (Centre Leclerc)* v. *SARL Mottet (Shell français)*, Cour d'appel Lyon, 1re ch., 4 Oct. 1984, [1985] 1 CMLR 247 at 248.

[50] Servan-Schreiber, 'EEC law in French Courts 1980–1984' at 169.

[51] *Cour d'appel* Paris, 1re ch. A, 4 July 1984, Gaz. Pal. 1984, II Jur. 658 (with note by Fourgoux). See also *Maignam* v. *Vitry-Distribution, Cour d'appel* Paris, 1re ch. A, 4 July 1984, Dalloz 1985, IR 273 (with note by Gavalda & Lucas De Leyssac) and *Dige-NCO* v. *Cora*, TGI Pontoise (*Référés*), 22 Feb. 1984, Gaz. Pal. 1984, I Jur. 296.

court by other French courts. In these circumstances, rather than declaring itself incompetent, the *Cour d'Appel* took the preliminary view that the French provisions were liable to compartmentalize the market contrary to the provisions concerning the free movement of goods and thus that their legality could be seriously contested such that it could not be said whether there was a *trouble manifestement illicite*. As a result, pending ECJ judgments on the question, the *Cour d'Appel* refused an injunction to enforce compliance with the French provisions.

A different approach was taken by the *Tribunal de grande instance* of Paris in the context of the cinematographic works cases.[52] In *Cinéthèque SA v. FNCF*,[53] the *Tribunal de grande instance* of Paris held that Community law was directly applicable in the courts of Member States and takes priority (according to Article 55 of the French Constitution) over national provisions. The *Tribunal de grande instance* then held that the *juge des référés* must apply Community law with immediate effect and, in case of a conflict between Community and national law, the *juge des référés* 'is bound, pending judgment at full trial settling the conflict substantively, to prevent actions causing damage and to take, as a result, preventative measures under Article 809 New Code on Civil Procedure entirely of an interlocutory nature'.[54] The *Tribunal de grande instance* then held that until the conflict between the Community and national law norms had been resolved, the *juge des référés* must follow 'the norm whose existence and interpretation seems to him immediately and directly possible' (*la norme dont l'appréhension et l'interprétation lui sont immédiatement et directement possibles*) and take appropriate measures to put an end to the *trouble manifestement illicite* or *dommage imminent*. According to this approach, no reference to the ECJ is made pursuant to Article 177 EC, but instead a vastly accelerated date is set for the full trial (the so-called '*passerelle*' procedure). In fact, in this case, the *Tribunal de grande instance* set a specific date for full trial only one month later.[55] This approach may be approved of as serving the interests of the good administration of justice.[56] Certainly, applying the interpretation which seems to be the most 'immediately and directly possible' is far more satisfactory than those cases in which the *juge des référés* merely declared itself to be incompetent to settle the dispute.

---

[52] n. 29 above.

[53] *TGI Paris (Référés)*, 15 Nov. 1983, Gaz. Pal. 1984, Jur. 49. See also *Editions René Château v. FNCF, TGI Paris*, 1re ch. I, 15 Feb. 1984, Gaz. Pal. 1984, I Jur. 231; RIDA 1984, no. 121 p. 181.

[54] Gaz. Pal. 1984, Jur. 49 at 50.

[55] *TGI Paris*, 1re ch. I, 15 Feb. 1984, Rev. juris. comm. 1984, 265 (with note by De Montblanc); Gaz. Pal. 1984, II 352. At the subsequent full trial, a reference to the ECJ was made, and the ECJ handed down its preliminary ruling in Cases 60 & 61/84 [1985] ECR 2605, [1986] 1 CMLR 365.

[56] See Guyot-Sionnest, 'Un vide juridique. Le problème des vidéo-cassettes'; Hassler Dalloz 1986, IR 243; Bertin Gaz. Pal. 1984, Jur. 50.

(v) *Evaluation of the exercise of the discretion to grant interim measures by the*
juge des référés

It has been argued that the approaches adopted by the *juge des référés* in the
cases discussed above are far from satisfactory. In particular, it is submitted that it is clearly contrary to Community law for the *juge des référés* to
hold that it is incompetent to resolve a serious dispute between French and
Community law. Furthermore, it seems that the *juge des référés* places far
too great a presumption on the application of French law in interim proceedings by holding that, until it is shown in an incontestable manner that
French provisions were contrary to Articles 30 to 36 EC, French law must
apply. Even less satisfactory was the conclusion that the *juge des référés*
should apply French law to avoid the emergence of a legal vacuum.
Regrettably, these difficulties remain largely unresolved. Many of the
judgments of the *juge des référés* discussed above were appealed to the *Cour
de Cassation*. However, by that time, the ECJ had handed down its judgments on the (in)compatibility of the French provisions in these cases. As
a result, the *Cour de Cassation* simply applied the clear findings of the ECJ
without commenting on the serious issues with respect to the discretion of
the *juge des référés* in interim proceedings.[57] A more helpful attitude after
the ECJ clarifications was taken by the *Cour d'Appel* of Aix-en-Provence
which, in the context of the petrol-pricing cases, held that 'a national court
is also a Community court and, in that capacity, it must apply directly the
legal rules contained in the Treaty of Rome and subsequent texts' and that
'a national court may not favour internal rules on the ground that
Community law is obscure or difficult to apply'.[58] Thus the *Cour d'Appel*
held that to decide whether national provisions are compatible with
Community law 'is within the competence of a court of summary jurisdiction which is required, like any other court, to state the grounds of its
decision and to determine whether the law invoked in support of the
application before it is applicable, the grant or dismissal of the application
depending on the authority and effect of the rule governing the *de facto* situation which the court is required to assess'.[59] The *Cour d'Appel* proceeded
to find that the French provisions were contrary to Articles 30 to 36 EC.

---

[57] See, *Edouard Leclerc* v. *Syndicat des librairies de Loire Océan, Cour de Cassation*, ch. comm.,
15 May 1985, Bull. Cass. Civ. 1985, IV 133; Dalloz 1986, Jur. 159 (with note by Goyet); *Gueret
distribution (Centre Leclerc)* v. *Maryan Martin, Cour de Cassation*, ch. comm., 15 May 1985, Bull.
Cass. Civ. 1985, IV 134, Dalloz 1986, Jur. 160; *Bianchi* v. *Sarredis, Cour de Cassation*, ch. comm.,
15 May 1985, Bull. Cass. Civ. 1985, IV 131–2; *SA Samu-Auchan, Cour de Cassation*, ch. comm.,
26 Nov. 1985, Journal du droit international 1986, 364; *Dumoussaud* v. *Syndicat des artisans
mécaniciens de l'automobile du Lot, Cour de Cassation*, ch. comm., 24 June 1986, Bull. Cass. Civ.
1986, IV 112.
[58] *Chabrand* v. *Alpes distribution Aldis (Centre Leclerc), Cour d'appel* Aix-en-Provence, 8e ch.
civ., 21 May 1985, JCP 1987, II 20722 (with note by Blaisse); [1987] 2 CMLR 396.
[59] [1987] 2 CMLR 396 at 398.

Although it did not cite the ECJ's judgment in *Cullet* v. *Centre Leclerc*,[60] it is clear that it was relying upon the ECJ's unequivocal judgment in that case that the French provisions infringed Articles 30 to 36 EC. Thus, while the positive clarification of the position of the *juge des référés* by the *Cour d'Appel* of Aix-en-Provence is to be welcomed, it should be remembered that it was easy for the *Cour d'Appel* to take such a view given that there was, by the time of its judgment, clear ECJ authority that the French provisions were contrary to Article 30 EC. The *Cour de Cassation* has subsequently held that the *juge des référés* may not simply declare itself incompetent to decide upon the compatibility of French provisions and Community law (*in casu* Article 86 EC) by leaving such a decision to the judge at full trial.[61] Again, although this is to be welcomed, it may be noted that the *Cour de Cassation* took this view only after a judgment of the ECJ clarifying the issue had been handed down.[62]

It therefore seems clear that the *juge des référés* may no longer simply declare itself incompetent and must apply Community law. However, the criteria for exercising the discretion has not yet been clarified to solve the difficulties highlighted in this section. In the absence of ECJ authority on the compatibility of French provisions with Articles 30 to 36 EC, the position of the *juge des référés* remains unclear.[63] It is a pity that the *Cour de Cassation* did not take the opportunity to be more expansive and clarify the exercise of the discretion of the *juge des référés*. However, it is submitted that the provisions of Article 809 of the New Code on Civil Procedure themselves are too inflexible and are ill-suited to dealing with interim relief when Community law is involved. The power to prevent a *trouble manifestement illicite* does not allow for a positive weighing up of the balance of convenience at the interim stage. The majority of cases discussed in this section suggest that the such inflexibility has not, to date, been compensated for by judicial flexibility on the part of the *juge des référés*. It is difficult to disagree with the conclusion of Cavallini that

---

[60] Case 231/83 [1985] ECR 305; [1985] 2 CMLR 524.

[61] *Bodson* v. *SA Pompes funèbres des régions libérées*, Cour de Cassation, ch. comm., 10 July 1989, Bull. Cass. Civ. 1989, IV 145; JCP 1989, IV 347; [1991] ECC 39. This judgment was warmly praised in Seventh Report to the European Parliament on Commission Monitoring of the Application of Community Law [1990] OJ C232/1 at 55 which describes it as a 'major development' in French courts as regards the *procédure de référé* 'which makes it possible to obtain a very rapid but interim judicial decision in cases where the obligation invoked cannot be seriously challenged or where a manifestly unlawful situation has to be brought to an end'.

[62] Case 30/87 *Bodson* v. *SA Pompes funèbres des régions libérées* [1988] ECR 2479. See note by Shaw (1988) 13 ELRev. 422.

[63] See notes by Blaisse, n. 58 above; Goyet, Dalloz 1986, Jur. 161 and Le Tallec, JCP 1986, I 3231. Cavallini, n. 21 above, 147 agrees and states that: '*il persiste toujours une incertitude sur l'appréhension du droit communautaire par le juge des référés*'.

[S]i le juge interne des référés a désormais l'obligation d'appliquer le droit communautaire dans le cadre de sa procédure nationale, ses règles de compétence sont loin d'avoir pris en compte l'émergence du droit communautaire. Il appartenait donc au juge interne des référés de procéder à une nouvelle interprétation de certains concepts, tels le 'trouble manifestement illicite' ou la 'contestation sérieuse' pour actualiser sa juridiction face aux bouleversements que se subissait le droit national.[64]

(B) The application of the provisions concerning the free movement of goods by United Kingdom courts in interim proceedings

Under English law, the jurisdiction to grant interim relief as a private law remedy is provided for in Section 37 of the Supreme Court Act 1981.[65] On the other hand, Order 53, Rule 3(10)(b) of the Rules of the Supreme Court, which is given statutory force by Section 31 of the Supreme Court Act 1981, provides for the grant of an interlocutory injunction in judicial review proceedings. The criteria for the grant of interim relief under these provisions were set out by the House of Lords in the leading case of *American Cyanamid* v. *Ethicon*.[66] According to those criteria, in deciding whether or not to grant interim relief, a court should not normally decide, even provisionally, the merits of the case. However, once the plaintiff has shown that there are some serious issues to be tried on the merits, the only questions for the court in deciding whether to grant an interlocutory injunction are whether damages to either party, rather than injunctive relief, would be an adequate remedy and, if not, whether the 'balance of convenience' favours the grant of an injunction, bearing in mind that the purpose of an interim injunction is to maintain the status quo until the full trial of the action. In order to obtain interim relief it is not therefore necessary to show a *prima facie* case for substantive relief. However, the existence of such a *prima facie* case may be a relevant factor in weighing the 'balance of convenience'.[67]

Under Scots law, injunctions ('interdicts') are designed to preserve the status quo or to prevent temporary or imminent wrongs. The grant of interim interdicts are a matter for the discretion of the Lord Ordinary

---

[64] n. 21 above, 207.

[65] The use of interim relief (usually in the form of injunctions) as a private law remedy has arisen before the English and Irish Courts primarily with respect to breaches of Arts. 85 & 86. See in particular *Garden Cottage Foods* v. *Milk Marketing Board* [1984] 1 AC 130, [1983] 2 All ER 770 (CA); *Cutsforth* v. *Mansfield Inns Ltd* [1986] 1 WLR 558 (CA); *ECS* v. *AKZO* [1986] 3 CMLR 273; *Plessey* v. *General Electric* [1990] ECC 384; *Holleran* v. *Daniel Thwaites* [1989] 2 CMLR 917; and *Patrick Dunlea* v. *Nissan Ireland Ltd* [1992] ECC 169 (Irish High Court). See also D'Sa, n. 1 above, 230–7; Brealy & Hoskins, n. 1 above, 87; and MacCulloch and Rodger, 'Wielding the Blunt Sword: Interim Relief for Breaches of EC Competition Law before the UK Courts' (1996) 7 ECLR 393.

[66] [1975] AC 396, [1975] 1 All ER 504.

[67] See *R.* v. *Secretary of State for Transport, ex p. Factortame* [1991] 1 AC 603 at 674 (HL per Lord Goff).

normally made according to the following criteria: title or interest to sue, a *prima facie* case and the 'balance of convenience'.[68] The criteria under Scots law are thus virtually identical to those under English law with the notable omission of an 'adequate remedy in damages' criterion under Scots law. In practice, however, even this difference is mitigated by the fact that Scottish courts will often be influenced by the availability of damages in weighing the 'balance of convenience' as a factor in refusing an interim interdict.[69]

For obvious reasons, the best-known case concerning interim relief in the United Kingdom is the infamous *Factortame* litigation.[70] The issue with respect to interim relief in that case was twofold: firstly, that as a matter of English law an Act of Parliament was assumed to be compatible with Community law (and therefore enforceable) unless and until it had been declared to be incompatible. As a result, in the event of uncertainty, it was not open to an English court to order an interim stay of the Act pending a determination of such compatibility. Secondly, the existence of the common-law rule that an interim injunction may not be granted against the Crown was at issue. On a reference from the House of Lords[71] the ECJ held that

[T]he full effectiveness of Community law would be just as much impaired if a rule of national law could prevent a court seized of a dispute governed by Community law from granting interim relief in order to ensure the full effectiveness of the judgment to be given on the existence of the rights claimed under Community law. It follows that a court which in those circumstances would grant interim relief, if it were not for the rule of national law, is obliged to set aside that rule.[72]

It is of interest to note that the House of Lords had also asked the ECJ which criteria it should apply in the event that it had to make available the possibility of granting interim relief against the Crown. Since the ECJ was silent on this point, the House of Lords implemented the ECJ judgment and applied the conventional *American Cyanamid* criteria, albeit with some modifications to take account of the public interest in ensuring that the law

[68] See *Argyll Group* v. *The Distillers Company* [1986] CMLR 764 (Court of Session) and *Hay* v. *Hay* [1968] SC 179. See Chisholm, 'Some Observations on the Use of Injunctions and Interdicts in the Enforcement of EC Law' in Lonbay & Biondi (eds.), n. 1 above at 73, 75 & 77.

[69] See *Argyll Group* v. *The Distillers Company*, n. 68 above and MacCulloch & Rodger, n. 65 above at 395.

[70] The series of litigation in *R.* v. *Secretary of State for Transport, ex p. Factortame* included no less than 3 references to the ECJ: on the substance Case C–221/89 [1991] ECR I–3905 [1991] 3 CMLR 589; on interim relief Case C–213/89 [1990] ECR I–2433; [1990] 3 CMLR 867 and on damages Case C–48/93 [1996] ECR I–1029. The facts of the litigation will not be rehearsed here and reference is made to annotations by Szyszczak (1990) 15 ELRev. 480; Craig (1991) 11 YEL 221 and Bonichot (1990) Rev. fr. dr. admin. 912.

[71] *R.* v. *Secretary of State for Transport ex p. Factortame* [1989] 3 CMLR 1; [1989] 2 All ER 692.

[72] Case C–213/89 [1990] ECR I–2433; [1990] 3 CMLR 867 at para. 21.

was enforced.[73] Subsequent cases make clear that those challenging an apparently authentic law must establish a better-than-even chance of eventual success in the substantive action.[74] More recently, in *R. v. Secretary of State for Health, ex p. Generics (United Kingdom) Ltd*,[75] the Court of Appeal held that in a case in which a reference had already been made to the ECJ pursuant to Article 177 EC[76] and where there were three rival interpretations of a provision of a Community Directive each having an equal chance of success before the ECJ, the familiar principles in *American Cyanamid v. Ethicon*, applying the 'balance of convenience', had no immediate application. The Court of Appeal reasoned that, in such an unusual case in which any one of three interpretations had equal chance of success, it would be wrong for the court in interim proceedings to lay down any general rule that, in applications for interim relief in such circumstances, one public interest should prevail over the other.

The *American Cyanamid*[77] criteria have been applied on several occasions in cases before English courts concerning the free movement-of-goods provisions. For example, in *Polydor Ltd v. Harlequin Record Shops Ltd*, Megarry VC held that, pending full trial, the balance of convenience favoured the grant of an injunction to prevent importation of pharmaceutical products from Portugal which infringed a United Kingdom patent.[78]

---

[73] [1991] 1 AC 603; [1990] 3 WLR 818; [1990] 3 CMLR 375. Lord Goff stated that '[P]articular stress should be placed upon the importance of upholding the law of the land, in the public interest, bearing in mind the need for stability in our society, and the duty placed upon certain authorities to enforce the law in the public interest . . . So if a public authority seeks to enforce what is on its face the law of the land, matters of considerable weight have to be put into the balance to outweigh the desirability of enforcing, in the public interest, what is on its face the law, and so as to justify the refusal of an interim injunction in favour of the authority, or to render it just or convenient to restrain the authority for the time being from enforcing the law. . . In the end, the matter is one for the discretion of the court, taking into account all the circumstances of the case. Even so, a court should not restrain a public authority by interim injunction from enforcing an apparently authentic law unless it is satisfied, having regard to all the circumstances, that the challenge to the validity of the law is, *prima facie*, so firmly based as to justify so exceptional a course being taken' [1991] 1 AC 603 at 673–4. See also *M. v. Home Office* [1993] 3 WLR 433. In Scotland, however, see *McDonald v. Secretary of State for Scotland* [1994] SLT 692 where the Court of Session held that litigants in Scotland do not have the right to obtain an interdict against the Crown.

[74] See, e.g., *R. v. Secretary of State for the National Heritage, ex p. Continental Television BV* [1993] 2 CMLR 333 (QBD), [1993] 3 CMLR 387 (CA). In *R. v. H.M. Treasury, ex p. British Telecommunications plc* [1994] 1 CMLR 621 the Court of Appeal (per Sir Thomas Bingham MR) emphasized that the strength of the plaintiff's case was only one of the factors relevant to the balance of convenience and that other issues concerning the public interest in not disapplying UK legislation, such as the number of people affected and the status quo, were also relevant. See further discussion in D'Sa, n. 65 above, 212–20 and Brealey & Hoskins, n. 1 above at 91–9 and Anderson, *References to the European Court*, 199–200.

[75] The Times, 25 Feb. 1997.

[76] Pending before the ECJ under C–368/96.　　　　　　　　　　　[77] n. 66 above.

[78] [1980] 1 CMLR 669 (Ch. D). It may be noted that the Court of Appeal took a different view of the balance of convenience and lifted the injunction and made a reference to the ECJ ([1980] 2 CMLR 413). The ECJ subsequently came to the same result as reached by Megarry

In *South Pembrokeshire District Council* v. *Wendy Fair Markets Limited*, the Chancery Division of the High Court applied the *American Cyanamid* criteria and held that damages would not be an adequate remedy for the plaintiff in that case if an injunction was not granted. The High Court then proceeded to apply the second part of the *American Cyanamid* criteria and held that the balance of convenience favoured the grant of an injunction to prevent the defendants opening their market contrary to an ancient (fourteenth-century) monopoly right held by the plaintiff Council.[79]

One of the most engaging problems which has arisen before the English courts with respect to the application of the provisions concerning the free movement of goods in interim proceedings is that of cross-undertakings in damages. It is common practice for English courts to make the grant of injunctive relief to a plaintiff subject to a cross-undertaking in damages should it be found at full trial that the plaintiff did not have such a right.[80] This issue arose before the English courts in the Sunday-trading cases.[81] Since the enforcement of the legislation prohibiting Sunday trading in England and Wales by a criminal sanction was ineffective as a deterrent,[82] local authorities attempted to obtain civil injunctions to restrain retailers.[83] However, the House of Lords had held in 1974 that the Crown could not be required to give cross-undertakings in damages when enforcing an Act of Parliament by injunction.[84] When the Article 30 EC defence surfaced, this became crucial because retailers were understandably concerned that, should the Shops Act be found to be contrary to Article 30 EC, they should have a right to damages from the local authorities for the period during which they were restrained from opening by injunction. The retailers therefore argued that if the English courts were to grant injunctions to restrain them from opening on Sundays, the local authorities should be

VC in the High Court but on different reasoning: Megarry VC conlcuded that the Free Trade Agreement between the EEC and Portugal did not allow free movement of goods in that case because of the difference in wording between Arts. 30 to 36 and Arts. 14(2) & 23 of the Free Trade Agreement. The ECJ reached this conclusion by stressing that the aims of the common market were different to those of an association agreement: Case 270/80 [1982] ECR 329; [1982] 1 CMLR 677. See note by Hicks (1980) EIPR 337.

[79] [1994] 1 CMLR 213 at 224–6. For a discussion of the substance of this case with respect to Art. 30 EC, see p. 103. See also *Smith Kline and French Labroratories* v. *Global Pharmaceuticals* [1986] RPC 394 (CA).

[80] *R.* v. *Secretary of State for the Environment, ex p. Royal Society for the Protection of Birds*, The Times, 10 Feb. 1995.

[81] The facts of the Sunday trading cases will not be rehearsed here. See full discussion in Ch. 6, sect. 4.

[82] Under s. 59, Shops Act 1950, trading on a Sunday was a criminal offence punishable by fine. The applicable fine rose to a maximum of £2,500: little deterrence to large retailers for whom the opportunity of considerably boosting their profits on a Sunday far outweighed the burdens of this criminal sanction.

[83] Under s. 222, Local Government Act 1972.

[84] *Hoffmann-La Roche* v. *Secretary of State for Trade and Industry* [1974] 2 All ER 1128, [1975] AC 295.

required to give cross-undertakings in damages.[85] In *Kirklees MBC v. Wickes Building Supplies*, the Court of Appeal[86] held that cross-undertakings in damages were indeed required and it is a matter of considerable interest that the Court of Appeal reached this conclusion explicitly on the reasoning that EC law required this. The nub of the Court of Appeal's reasoning was that the ECJ's judgment in *Amministrzione delle Finanze dello Stato* v. *Simmenthal SpA*[87] explicitly stated that the setting aside of incompatible national legislation 'must in every case have unrestricted retroactive effect so as to prevent the rights in question from being in any way adversely affected'.[88] This was of decisive influence as Dillon LJ concluded:

If therefore Wickes and B & Q are right that Section 47 of the Shops Act 1950 is incompatible with Article 30 of the EEC Treaty and is thereby overridden, they have a current right to open their stores for Sunday trading, and it is the duty of the national courts to protect that right.

If there is no cross-undertaking, the right to trade on Sunday will, assumedly, be established at the trial, but without the unrestricted retroactive effect required by the *Simmenthal* case. In that event, Wickes and B&Q will have been adversely affected by having been restrained by injunctions from Sunday trading pending the trial, without any compensation.

Consequently, in my judgment, the court is under European law bound to require cross-undertakings in damages from the plaintiff authorities if interlocutory injunctions to restrain Sunday trading until judgment or further order are to be granted.[89]

On appeal, the House of Lords[90] allowed the appeal and held that no cross-undertaking was necessary because 'such an undertaking would be superfluous'[91] as the ECJ's judgment in *Francovich*[92] makes the United Kingdom Government rather than the local authority liable for damages:

It is the government which would, on the hypothesis that Section 47 was invalid because it was inconsistent with Article 30, have failed to take necessary steps to ensure that Section 47 was amended or repealed as necessary.[93]

This was an extremely bold proposition. The ECJ's judgment in *Francovich* was indeed framed in broad terms.[94] However, at that time it was far from

---

[85] The implications of this were significant. A cross-undertaking in damages on behalf of the local authorities was clearly too onerous given their restricted budgets. In short, if they were required to give cross-undertakings, the Shops Act would in practice become unenforceable. It has been argued elsewhere in this work that it is here that the origins of the chaos in the Sunday-trading cases lay. See discussion in Ch. 6, sect. 4 (E) (*viii*) and Jarvis, 'The Sunday Trading Episode: In Defence of the Euro-Defence' 460–3.

[86] [1991] 4 All ER 240, [1991] 3 CMLR 82.   [87] Case 106/77, n. 37 above.
[88] Ibid. at para. 25.   [89] [1991] 4 All ER 240 at 247.
[90] [1992] 3 All ER 717, [1992] 2 CMLR 765.   [91] [1992] 3 All ER 717 at 735.
[92] Cases C–6/90 & 9/90, n. 9 above.
[93] [1992] 3 All ER 717 at 735 (per Lord Goff).
[94] See further discussion of the *Francovich* judgt in sect. 3.

clear whether or not that judgment included the type of position that the House of Lords assumed.[95] Clearly the conclusion reached by the House of Lords all but explicitly overrules the Court of Appeal's decision in *Bourgoin S.A.* v. *Ministry of Agriculture, Fisheries and Food*,[96] where the breach of Article 30 EC by a public body was characterized as giving rise to a public law right to have the violation terminated by judicial review but not, in the absence of misfeasance in public office, a private law right to damages. Lord Goff only went so far as to say 'there must now be doubt whether the *Bourgoin* case was correctly decided' but held that it was 'not necessary for the purpose of the present case for your Lordships' House to decide whether the *Bourgoin* case was correctly decided'.[97] With the greatest respect, this is regrettable. On the House of Lords' own reasoning, the cross-undertakings could only be set aside if the retailers could be certain to receive damages against the State should Section 47 of the Shops Act be found to be incompatible with Article 30 EC. In the absence of overruling *Bourgoin*, this would not be the case. It is submitted that it would have been much more desirable if their Lordships had overruled *Bourgoin* instead of using speculative notions of Community law (especially without seeking the assistance of the ECJ through an Article 177 EC reference) to reach its conclusion. This is all the more so since it is not entirely clear as to why the House of Lords assumed that the United Kingdom central government, rather than a local authority, would be liable to pay damages. After all, the ECJ's case law on 'emanations of the state' undoubtedly includes organs such as local government authorities.[98]

The issue of cross-undertakings in damages when the Crown is applying for an injunction thus remains, to a certain extent, unclear. Importantly, both the Court of Appeal and the House of Lords reached the same result. The right of the defendants to damages in the event that it was subsequently found that the English and Welsh legislation was contrary to Article 30 EC was secured according to the judgment of both courts. It is however submitted that, from the point of view of Community law, the reasoning of the Court of Appeal was more satisfactory than that of the House of Lords. In the light of the ECJ's judgment in *R.* v. *Secretary of State for Transport, ex p. Factortame*[99] it is surely the case that a rule of national

---

[95] See Ross, 'Beyond Francovich' (1993) 56 MLR 55, Lewis & Moore, 'Duties, Directives and Damages in European Community law' (1993) PL 151, and Craig, '*Francovich*, Remedies and the Scope of Damages Liability' (1993) 109 LQR 595. Even after the recent judgments of the ECJ concerning State liability, the liability of the State for breach of Art. 30 is by no means as automatic as Lord Goff seems to have assumed. See discussion of State liability in sect. 3.

[96] [1985] 3 All ER 585, [1986] QB 716.   [97] [1992] 3 All ER 717 at 734.

[98] See Case 152/84 *Marshall* v. *Southampton and South West Hampshire Area Health Authority* [1986] ECR 7233, [1986] 1 CMLR 6883; Case C–188/89 *Foster* v. *British Gas* [1990] ECR I–3313, [1990] 2 CMLR 833; Case 222/84, n. 7 above.

[99] Case C–213/89, n. 7 above (Re interim relief).

law which provides that the Crown could not be required to give cross-undertakings in damages when enforcing an Act of Parliament by injunction is contrary to the duty of national courts to ensure effective legal protection which individuals derive from directly effective provisions of Community law.

(C) The application of the provisions concerning the free movement of goods by Dutch courts in interim proceedings

In civil proceedings in the Netherlands, parties may apply for interim relief according to the *kort geding* procedure.[100] The powers of the court in *kort geding* cases is governed by Article 289 *et seq.* of the *Wetboek van Burgerlijke Rechtsvordering* (*Rv*: Code of Civil Procedure) which provides that

In all cases where an immediate, provisionally enforceable decision is required for reasons of urgency having regard to the parties' interests, a request may be made for a session to be held by the presiding judge for that purpose on such weekdays as shall be determined by him.[101]

Article 292 *Rv* provides that '[p]rovisionally enforceable decisions shall be without prejudice to the main issue in the case'.[102] In administrative courts, interim measures (*voorlopige voorzieningen*) may be granted under Article 8:81 of the *Algemene wet bestuursrecht* (*AWB*: General Administrative Law Act) if required for reasons of urgency having regard to the parties' interests (*indien onverwijlde spoed gelet op de betrokken belangen*).[103]

---

[100] On the *kort geding* procedure generally, see Groen, 'Het Kort Geding naar Nederlands Recht' (1991) 28 Tijdschrift voor Privaatrecht 1025; Korte, 'Prejudiciële verwijzingen (art. 177 EEG) in het kader van kort geding procedures door Nederlandse rechters (art. 289–97 Rv)'; Gisolf & Boer, *Kort geding en rechter* (WEJ Tjeenk Willink, 1993); Schenk & Blaauw, *Het kort geding* (Kluwer, 6th edn., 1996); and Asscher, *Onverwijlde spoed: het kort geding en andere spoedprocedures in het Nederlands recht* (WEJ Tjeenk Willink, 2nd edn., 1987). For summaries in English, see Brinkhof, 'Between Speed and Thoroughness: The Dutch 'Kort Geding' Procedure in Patent Cases' (1996) 9 EIPR 499 and idem 'Summary Proceedings and Other Provisional Measures in Connection with Patent Infringements' (1993) IIC 762.

[101] In the original Dutch: '*In alle zaken waarin uit hoofde van onverwijlde spoed, gelet op de belangen van partijen, een onmiddellijke voorziening bij voorraad wordt vereist, kan de vordering worden aangebracht op een terechtzitting, te dien einde door de president te houden op de daartoe door hem te bepalen werkdagen.*'

[102] In the original Dutch: '*De beslissingen bij voorraad brengen geen nadeel toe aan de zaak ten principale.*'

[103] See Langbroek, *Het bestuursrechtelijk kort geding: de voorlopige voorzieningsprocedure volgens titel 8.3 van de Algemene wet bestuursrecht* (VUGA, 1996) and Bots, *Op weg naar een zelfstandig bestuursrechtelijk kort geding?* (Kluwer, 1995). It may be noted that prior to the *AWB*, interim measures before the *Raad van State* were covered by Art. 107, *Wet op de Raad van State*. Under 107 the *Raad van State* had to examine whether the application of the contested administrative decision would cause '*onevenredig nadeel*' (disproportionate disadvantage) to one of the parties. See van der Hoeven, 'Het administratieve kort geding ex Art. 107 Wet op de Raad

Interpretation of these provisions by the courts makes clear that the crucial concept in interim proceedings is that of urgency (*onverwijlde spoed* which is often interpreted as *spoedeisend belang*). The usual remedy is an injunction and the President usually also orders that the defendant pay a penalty payment (*dwangsom*) for any subsequent breach of the injunction. Under Article 291 *Rv*, the presiding judge must be satisfied that, having regard to such matters as the nature and extent of the possible damage to the plaintiff, the case cannot be better dealt with in ordinary proceedings. Furthermore, the President may decline to give a judgment if the case cannot be dealt with in summary proceedings because of disagreement over crucial facts or the necessity for lengthy expert evidence.[104] In exercising his discretion, the presiding judge will evaluate whether the measure applied for is justified by an equitable consideration of the parties' interests. In carrying out such an evaluation, the judge may take into consideration the likelihood of success at full trial and the amount of damage suffered.[105] In cases concerning the compatibility of provisions of Dutch law with EC law, the Dutch courts have held that the Dutch provisions must apply unless it has been shown that they are 'unmistakably void' (*onmiskenbaar onverbindend*).

Several cases concerning the free-movement-of-goods provisions have been dealt with by the Dutch courts in interim proceedings. As has been set out above, the crucial concept before Dutch courts in interim proceedings is that of urgency (*onverwijlde spoed* or *spoedeisend belang*).[106] On the whole, judgments in interim proceedings before Dutch courts are

van State' in Asscher (ed.), *Onverwijlde spoed: het kort geding en andere spoedprocedures in het Nederlands recht* (WEJ Tjeenk Willink, 2nd edn., 1987) at 239. Interim measures under Art. 107 were granted on several occasions by the *Raad van State* in cases concerning the free movement of goods: see, e.g., *GMU Nederland BV* v. *Minister van Volkshuisvesting, Ruimtelijke Ordening en Milieubeheer*, Pres. *Raad van State* (*Afd. Geschillen van Bestuur*), 11 Dec. 1989, KG 1990, 72; M & R 1990, 423 (with note by Addink and Jans); *Ecoservice Nederland* v. *VROM*, Pres. *Raad van State* (*Afd. Geschillen van Bestuur*), 16 Aug. 1990, KG 1990, 324; *Eldim BV* v. *VROM*, Pres. *Raad van State* (*Afd. Geschillen van Bestuur*), 14 Jan. 1992, AB 1992, 455 (with note by Drusteen); M & R 1992, 486 (with note by Addink); *Claushuis Metaalmaatschappij* v. *VROM*, Pres. *Raad van State* (*Afd Geschillen van Bestuur*), 6 July 1993, AB 1994, 50 (with note by Drupsteen); *Verzinkerij Mook BV* v. *VROM*, Pres. *Raad van State* (*Afd. Bestuursrechtspraak*), 13 Dec. 1994; noted in Addink et al (eds.), *Europese milieurechtspraak, 104 nationale uitspraken met Europees milieurechterlijke aspecten*, 132–3 & 214; *Van der Feesten* v. *Landbouw, Natuurbeheer en Visserij* (*Min.*), Pres. *Raad van State* (*Afd. Rechtspraak*), 14 Oct. 1992, M & R 1994, 24 (with note by Jans); AB 1994, 128.

[104] *Eerste Twentse Behangselpapierindustrie NV* v. *Vereniging van Behangselpapierfabriekanten*, Hoge Raad, 8 Jan. 1965, NJ 1965, 162.

[105] See the Opinion of Adv. Gen. ten Kate in *Lotta Dieuwke Ruskamp* v. *Stichting ter bevordering van het welzijn van Surinamse in Nederland Walsuria*, Hoge Raad, 27 May 1983, NJ 1983, 758. See also *Pfizer* v. *Meditec BV*, Hoge Raad, 2 Apr. 1978, NJ 1979, 194.

[106] In the context of the free movement of goods, see, e.g. *Bakker Barendrecht Export* v. *Kwaliteitscontrole-Bureau voor Groenten en Fruit*, Pres. *Arrondissementsrechtbank* Haarlem, 3 July 1990, KG 1990, 249; SEW 1991, 203 (with note by Mortelmans).

extremely brief.[107] While this is hardly surprising given the very nature of interim proceedings, it is nevertheless submitted that the judge in interim proceedings should provide a minimum degree of explanation.[108]

The Dutch courts do take into account whether damages would be an adequate remedy at full trial. This was evident in the judgment of the President of the *Arrondissementsrechtbank* Almelo which, in the context of Dutch provisions on the minimum price for bread,[109] referred questions to the ECJ in interim proceedings and granted an injunction in the meantime to prevent Edah selling bread at below the minimum price. The Almelo court reasoned that, rather than pursuing their claim in the courts by challenging the Dutch provisions, Edah had ignored the provisions on a large and well-publicized scale to such an extent that damage to other bakeries could be fatal. The President then held that 'if the defendant is allowed to continue this campaign until the [ECJ's] judgment, much irreparable damage would befall bakeries, which, if the defendant is shown to be wrong, could not be repaired by damages'.[110] A further point of interest which was raised in the bread-pricing cases was the extent to which it was necessary to show that the Dutch provisions were 'unmistakably void' (*onmiskenbaar onverbindend*) before an injunction would be refused. In *Nederlandse Bakkerij Stichting* v. *Edah BV*,[111] the President of the *Arrondissementsrechtbank* Almelo commented that it would not have granted an injunction 'had the defendant demonstrated that the price requirements in question were clearly void (*kennelijk onverbindend*) . . . At most, one could say that the defendant's arguments are not hopeless or groundless (*kansloos of ongegrond*) as is demonstrated by the judgment of the *Hof* 's-Hertogenbosch of 26 February 1985, but this is not sufficient to justify the defendant's arguments.' The reference to the judgment of the *Hof* 's-Hertogenbosch is interesting because in that case, Edah was acquitted of breaching the Dutch provisions in criminal proceedings.[112] The Almelo court dismissed the relevance of this judgment by pointing out differences between the civil and criminal procedure. It was held that under criminal law, if it is not 'incontestable' that the law is valid, then the law cannot be applied, whereas in civil proceedings, by contrast, 'a balancing of the interests on a scale can lead to a decision against the defendant, even though the defendant's arguments regarding the validity of the Dutch price regulations are by no means hopeless or groundless'. This distinction

---

[107] See, e.g., *Cyanamid Benelux SA NV* v. *Minister van Landbouw en Visserij*, Pres. *CBB*, 28 Jan. 1988, SEW 1989, 791 (with note by Mortelmans).

[108] See Mortelmans, n. 107 above at 794.

[109] See discussion of the substance of this case at pp. 79–83.

[110] *Nederlandse Bakkerij Stichting* v. *Edah BV*, Pres. *Arrondissementsrechtbank* Almelo, 13 Mar. 1985, KG 1985, 86.

[111] Ibid.

[112] *Officier van Justitie* v. *Edah BV*, *Gerechtshof* 's-Hertogenbosch, 26 Feb. 1985.

between civil and criminal proceedings is interesting since different results may be reached on exactly the same facts at the interim stage, depending on whether the proceedings are criminal or civil.[113] In civil proceedings, at all events, the Dutch courts thus embark upon a balancing exercise according to which the defendant must show that the Dutch provisions are 'unmistakably void' (*onmiskenbaar onverbindend*).[114]

The question which arises is whether or not the requirement that the defendant contesting the compatibility of Dutch legal provisions as being contrary to Articles 30 to 36 EC demonstrate that those provisions are 'unmistakably void' (*onmiskenbaar onverbindend*) puts too heavy a presumption on the validity, in interim proceedings, of national law. It is submitted that this was the case in a judgment in interim proceedings by the President of the *CBB* in *Procter & Gamble Benelux BV* v. *Minister Volksgezondheid, Welzijn en Sport*.[115] This case concerned a refusal of permission, under Dutch legislation on the addition of vitamins to foodstuffs, to market a multi-vitamin drink imported from another Member State. The question was whether the Dutch provisions could be justified for the protection of health under Article 36 EC. The defendant argued that it was not justified on those grounds because there was clear evidence that the Government intended to amend the legislation. The *CBB* held that there was no urgency (*spoedeisend belang*) to justify the granting of interim relief in that case because it had not been shown that the present prohibition was '*onmiskenbaar onverbindend*'. The *CBB* held that the simple fact that the Minister had submitted draft legislation to an advice committee to amend the regime in force at that time did not make that legislation '*onmiskenbaar onverbindend*'. It is submitted that in this case, in interim proceedings, the *CBB* accorded too great a presumption on the applicability of the national law. The question was whether the Dutch provisions were objectively necessary for the protection of public health under Article 36 EC and the President of the CBB did not address this issue in his judgment.

A final point which has arisen before the Dutch courts with respect to the application of the provisions concerning the free movement of goods in interim proceedings, is the question of who is liable for the damages which accrue, if, at full trial, the judgment given at the interim stage is shown to have been an incorrect interpretation of Articles 30 to 36 EC. This

---

[113] On interim proceedings in criminal cases before the Dutch courts, see Blaauw, *Kort geding in strafzaken* (WEJ Tjeenk Willink, 1992).

[114] For a further case in which it was held that in *kort geding* proceedings it has to be shown that the national law is *onmiskenbaar onverbindend*, see *Bijou Brigitte Modische Accessoires AG* v. *Waarborg Platina, Goud en Zilver NV, Gerechtshof* 's-Gravenhage, 17 Mar. 1992, NJ 1993, 213.

[115] Pres. *CBB*, 2 Sept. 1994, KG 1994, 353.

issue arose before the *Hoge Raad* with respect to patent infringement.[116] The Hoge Raad held

> In order to answer the question at issue, it is important that the injunction ordered by the judge in interim proceedings is characterized as a temporary measure which, according to Article 292 of the Code of Civil Procedure, cannot in any way prejudice the full trial.
>
> On the one hand, the party who is subject to the interim judge's decision, must comply with the injunction as long as it is in force. . .
>
> On the other hand, it must in principle be assumed that the party which had compelled the opposing party by the threat of enforcement to comply with the injunction imposed in interim proceedings has acted unlawfully if it appears, from the decision at full trial, that he did not have the right to force the other party to refrain from the action in question. Furthermore, given the nature of interim proceedings, it must be assumed that the party which threatened enforcement knew, or at least ought to have known, that its actions were based on a provisional measure, such that in principle they must be deemed accountable for the damage caused by their actions. This solution is, from the point of view of society, more justified than the opposite conclusion, which would have the result that the party which, under threat of enforcement, complied with the injunction, would in principle have to bear the damage, even though it subsequently appeared that the right claimed by the plaintiff in interim proceedings did not exist.

Thus, instead of requiring a cross-undertaking in damages at the time of the interim judgment, Dutch law recognizes that if it subsequently transpires that the plaintiff was wrong, any damage suffered during the period between the granting of interim relief and the judgment at full trial, must be born by the plaintiff. The net result is therefore the same as if a cross-undertaking in damages had been issued at the time of the granting of the injunction.[117]

(D) Conclusions

It was noted at the outset that interim relief is fundamental to effective judicial protection. It has been shown that, so long as the validity of a Community measure itself is not at issue, the ECJ is happy, subject to the usual provisos, for the national courts to apply national law criteria for the

---

[116] *Ciba Geigy AG* v. *De Chemische Fabriek Brabant J. W. Voorbraak BV, Hoge Raad*, 16 Nov. 1984, NJ 1985, 547 (with notes by Heemskerk and Wichers Hoeth); BIE 1985, 30.

[117] The judgt of the *Hoge Raad* in this case was the culmination of a great deal of debate in the Dutch literature, in the course of which much ink has been spilled. See, e.g., Kamphuisen, NJB 1943, 21; Langemeijer, NJ 1965, 116 Van Schaik, *De aansprakelijkheid voor het executeren van een kort geding vonnis dat in de bodemprocedure terzijde wordt gesteld* (Deventer, 1987); Van Rossum, *Aansprakelijkheid voor de tenuitvoerlegging van vernietigde of terzijde gestelde rechterlijke beslissingen* (Kluwer, 1989); and Brinkhof, 'Summary Proceedings and Other Provisional Measures in Connection with Patent Infringements' (1993) IIC 762 at 772–3. See also *Kempkes* v. *Samson, Hoge Raad*, 22 Dec. 1989, NJ 1990, 434.

grant of interim relief in cases in which the compatibility of national provisions with Community law is at issue. As has been stated, this is in accordance with the principle of procedural autonomy and is based on the assumption that national procedures for granting interim relief are likely to be adequate. Is the latter assumption correct? How similar are the various criteria for the granting of interim relief in France, the United Kingdom and the Netherlands? Is there really very much difference between examining whether interim measures are necessary 'to put an end to a mischief which is manifestly unlawful' or whether the 'balance of convenience' favours the granting of interim measures?

At the outset, it is clearly possible to identify differences. For example, the criteria prevailing in France suggest that the *juge des référés* has to look at the merits of the case to decide whether there is a *trouble manifestement illicite*. By contrast the *American Cyanamid* criteria prevailing in the United Kingdom formally preclude evaluation of the merits of the case in favour of investigating whether there is a serious issue to be tried. However, such differences are more apparent than real when one considers that in weighing the 'balance of convenience', an English court is bound to carry out some analysis of the chance of success at full trial. To a certain extent, therefore, it must be the case that the criteria for the grant of interim relief, although at first sight heterogeneous, ultimately reach the same result. The latter view was argued by Advocate General Tesauro in his Opinion in *Factortame* where he commented that,

[I]t does not seem to me that the subject-matter allows much room for imagination or offers scope for revolutionary discoveries, since legal theory and positive law . . . have long specified the *prima facie* case (however designated) and the *periculum in mora* as the two basic pre-conditions for interim protection. The accent may be placed on one or the other according to the legal system in question, or what is a *prima facie* case may or may not perfectly coincide with the not manifestly ill-founded or the *prima facie* well-founded nature of the claim and so on, or it may be that in the assessment of the *periculum in mora*, apart from the traditional and necessary balancing of the respective interests of the parties (it must be ensured that the same interim measure does not in its turn cause irreparable damage to the other party), express consideration is also given to the public interest. All that forms part of the prudent appreciation by the national courts which, case by case, will carry out a just appraisal of the appropriateness or necessity of granting or refusing an interim measure for the interim protection of the rights claimed.[118]

However, even if it is likely that the national criteria for granting interim relief are sufficiently similar, it is submitted that it remains somewhat anomalous that the ECJ in *Zuckerfabriek*[119] was prepared to set strict conditions within which national courts may grant interim relief where the

---

[118] Case C–213/89, n. 7 above at para. 33 of Opinion.   [119] n. 12 above.

invalidity of Community legislation is at issue, whereas the ECJ does not specify the conditions applicable for the grant of interim relief by national courts where the compatibility of national provisions with Community law are at issue.[120] While in *Factortame*[121] the ECJ emphasized the importance of interim protection, in *Zuckerfabriek*, by contrast, emphasis was placed on the importance of upholding the validity of Community legislation. Why should the uniformity of criteria for interim relief throughout the Community be so important when Community legislation is at issue but not when national provisions are at issue?

In any event, the analysis of national case law applying the provisions concerning free movement of goods in this section does not suggest that the national law criteria are entirely satisfactory. The position of the *juge des référés* in France, in particular, has yet to adapt fully to the requirements of Community law. In certain respects the competence of the *juge des référés* under Article 809 of the New Code on Civil Procedure in France seems to be directly contrary to the requirement under EC law for the national courts to provide effective remedies. In particular, it is submitted that it is clearly contrary to Community law for the *juge des référés* to hold that it is incompetent to resolve a serious dispute between French and Community law. Even less satisfactory was the conclusion that the *juge des référés* should apply French law to avoid the emergence of a 'legal vacuum'. It is submitted that the provisions of Article 809 of the New Code on Civil Procedure themselves are too inflexible and are ill-suited to dealing with interim relief when Community law is involved. The power to prevent a *trouble manifestement illicite* does not allow for a positive weighing up of the balance of convenience at the interim stage.

The analysis of national case law in this chapter makes clear that national law criteria for the grant of interim relief place a clear presumption on the validity of national law. In the Netherlands, the Dutch courts have required the party contesting the compatibility of Dutch legal provisions as being contrary to Articles 30 to 36 EC to demonstrate that those provisions are 'unmistakably void' (*onmiskenbaar onverbindend*). In France, the *juge des référés* place a clear presumption on the application of French law in interim proceedings by holding that, until it is shown in an incontestable manner that the French provisions were contrary to Articles 30 to 36 EC, French law must apply. Equally, in the United Kingdom Lord Goff has held that 'a court should not restrain a public authority by interim injunction from enforcing an apparently authentic law unless it is satisfied, having regard to all the circumstances, that the challenge to the validity of the law is, *prima facie*, so firmly based as to justify so exceptional a course being taken'.[122] The question which arises is whether or not too

---

[120] See Sharpston, n. 20 above. [121] n. 7 above.
[122] *ex p. Factortame*, n. 73 above at 673–4 of AC report.

heavy a presumption is placed by the national courts in interim proceedings on the validity of national law. There are certainly examples in all three systems where it has been argued that this is the case. On this point therefore, it is submitted that it would be helpful for uniform criteria to be developed at Community level. In this way, the excesses of individual national courts may be checked.

It is clear that effective and uniform judicial protection would benefit from the development of uniform criteria at Community level on the exercise by national courts of the discretion to grant interim relief. This would be in line with the move towards homogeneity of Community remedies[123] and would be a next logical step in the procession away from the principle of procedural autonomy.

3 STATE LIABILITY FOR BREACH OF EC LAW

Given that Articles 30 to 36 EC are addressed to Member States,[124] liability for any damage suffered as a result of a breach of these provisions, will normally be directed towards the State or one of its organs. The discussion in this section will thus centre exclusively on State liability.[125] Furthermore, a detailed discussion of ECJ case law with respect to State liability is beyond the scope of this work.[126] As a result, the development

---

[123] Van Gerven, n. 1 above.

[124] See discussion of this point in Ch. 2, sect. 4.

[125] For a discussion of the liability of individuals for breach of EC law, see the Opinion of Adv. Gen. Van Gerven in Case C–128/92 *HJ Banks* v. *British Coal Corporation* [1994] ECR I–1209.

[126] See further Green & Barav, 'Damages in National Courts for Breach of EEC Law' (1986) 6 YEL 55; Dubouis, 'La responsabilité de l'Etat pour les dommages causés aux particuliers par la violation du droit communautaire' (1992) Rev. fr. dr. admin. 1; Haguenau, *L'Application effective du droit communautaire en droit interne: Analyse comparative des problèmes recontrés en droit français, anglais et allemand*, 455; Craig, '*Francovich*, Remedies and the Scope of Damages Liability', n. 95 above; Ross, 'Beyond *Francovich*' (1993) 56 MLR 55; Steiner, 'From Direct Effect to *Francovich*: Shifting Means of Enforcement of Community Law' (1993) 18 ELRev. 3; Schimke EuZW Heft 22/1993; Streinz EuZW Heft 19/1993; Ossenbül in Due, Lutter and Schwarze (eds.), *Festschrift für Ulrich Everling* (Baden-Baden: Nomos, 1995) pt II at 1031; Van Gerven, 'Bridging the Unbridgeable: Community and National Tort Laws after *Francovich* and *Brasserie*'; Betlem, 'Onrechtmatige Wetgeving: Overheidsaansprakelijkheid voor Schending van EG-recht in het post-Francovich Tijdperk' (1996) Regelmaat 128; Claes, 'Aansprakelijkheid van de Staat wegens schending van het gemeenscapsrecht' (1996) Jurisprudentie Bestuursrecht 226; von Danwitz, 'Die gemeinschaftsrechtliche Staatshaftung der Mitgliedstaaten' (1997) Deutsches Verwaltungsblatt 1; Wathelet and Van Raepenbusch, 'La responsabilité des États Membres en cas de violation du droit communautaire. Vers un alignement de la responsabilité de l'état sur celle de la communauté ou l'inverse?' (1997) 33 CDE 13; Craig, 'Once More Unto the Breach: The Community, the State and Damages Liability' (1997) 113 LQR 67; Fines, 'Quelle obligation de réparer pour la violation du droit communautaire?' (1997) 33 RTDE 69.

of Community law requirements in cases of State liability will only be analysed in this section in skeleton form.

The liability of Member States for their breaches of EC law has for some time been the focus of great attention. However, the concept itself is certainly not a novelty. In 1976, the ECJ held that

> It is for the national court to decide on the basis of the facts of each case whether an individual producer has suffered . . . damage.
>
> If such damage has been caused through an infringement of Community law the State is liable to the injured party of the consequences in the context of the provisions of national law on the liability of the State.[127]

However, it was the judgment of the ECJ in *Francovich*[128] which set the train firmly in motion, and that judgment has recently been clarified and extended in a series of important and long-awaited ECJ judgments. These recent developments are of considerable constitutional importance. The emerging principles governing State liability work in two directions: on the one hand they provide a strong incentive for Member States to comply with their Community obligations and, on the other, they improve and extend the possibilities open to individuals to secure effective remedies.

In *Francovich*, the ECJ explicitly required national courts to make available a claim for damages for breaches by a Member State of EC law. In that judgment, the ECJ held that 'it is a principle of Community law that the Member States are obliged to pay compensation for harm caused to individuals by breaches of Community law for which they can be held responsible'.[129] It is important that the ECJ expressly held that the principle of State liability was 'inherent in the system of the Treaty'[130] and was thus not simply a matter of protecting Community rights by means of existing national remedies. As is well known, the ECJ in paragraph 40 of the judgment in *Francovich* set out three minimal conditions of State liability for cases involving the non-implementation by that State of a Directive:

(1) the result prescribed by the Directive must entail the grant of rights to individuals;
(2) it must be possible to identify the content of those rights on the basis of the provisions of the Directive; and
(3) there must be a causal link between the breach of the State's obligation and the harm suffered by the injured parties.

The problem with the *Francovich* judgment was that it raised as many questions as it resolved. Most importantly, the judgment gave no indication as to the conditions which might apply to breaches of EC law by a

---

[127] Case 69/75 *Russo* v. *Azienda di Stato per gli interventi sub mercato agricolo (AIMA)* [1976] ECR 45 at paras 8–9.
[128] Cases C–6 and 9/90, n. 9 above.
[129] Ibid. at para. 37.   [130] Ibid. at para. 35.

Member State in a form other than the non-implementation or failure to comply with a Directive. Further references from national courts seeking clarification were thus inevitable.

Such clarification has now, to a significant extent, been provided by a series of recent judgments of the ECJ in *Brasserie du Pêcheur* v. *Federal Republic of Germany; R.* v. *Secretary of State for Transport, ex p. Factortame Ltd* (No. 3) (hereafter *Brasserie du Pêcheur*);[131] *R.* v. *H.M. Treasury, ex p. British Telecommunications plc* (hereafter *BT*);[132] *R.* v. *Minister of Agriculture, Fisheries and Food ex p. Hedley Lomas* (hereafter *Hedley Lomas*);[133] *Dillenkofer* v. *Federal Republic of Germany*[134] and *Denkavit International* v. *Bundesamt für Finanzen*.[135] In these cases, the ECJ had the opportunity make clear that the principle in *Francovich* that the State must be held liable for loss and damage caused to individuals as a result of breaches of Community law applies irrespective of the organ of the State whose act or omission was responsible for the breach; including the acts or omissions of the legislature.[136] Furthermore, the ECJ also explicitly opened up a parallel between its interpretation of the non-contractual liability of the Community under Article 215 EC and that of the Member States.[137] This is due to the compelling reason that the conditions under which the State may incur liability for damage should not differ from those governing the Community in like circumstances.[138]

The ECJ has now stated that Community law confers a right to reparation where three conditions are met:

(1) the rule of law must be intended to confer rights on individuals;
(2) the breach must be sufficiently serious; and

---

[131] Cases C–46/93 & C–48/93, n. 9 above. See case-notes by Dubouis (1996) Rev. fr. dr. admin. 583; Tridimas (1996) Camb. LJ 412; and Emiliou (1996) 21 ELRev. 399.

[132] Case C–392/93 [1996] ECR I–1631, [1996] 2 CMLR 217.

[133] Case C–5/94 [1996] ECR I–2553, [1996] 2 CMLR 391.

[134] Joined Cases C–178, 179 & 188–190/94 [1996] ECR I–4845, [1996] 3 CMLR 469.

[135] Joined Cases C–283, 291–292/94 [1996] ECR I–5063.

[136] Case C–46/93 & C–48/93, n. 9 above, paras. 16–36 of judgt.

[137] The non-contractual liability of the Community itself is governed by Art. 215(2) EC which provides: 'In the case of non-contractual liability, the Community shall, in accordance with the general principles common to the laws of the Member States, make good any damage caused by its institutions or by its servants in performance of their duties'. See the ECJ judgts applying Art. 215 EC in Case 5/71 *Aktien-Zuckerfabriek Schöppenstedt* v. *Council* [1971] ECR 975; Cases 83, 94/76, 4, 15, 40/77 *Bayerische HNL Vermehrungbetriebe GmbH* v. *Council and Commission* [1978] ECR 1209, [1978] 3 CMLR 566 & Case C–104/89 & C–37/90 *Mulder* v. *Council and Commission* [1992] ECR I–3061.

[138] Case C–46/93 & C–48/93, n. 9 above, para. 42 of judgt. It may be pointed out that, while a coherent approach is indeed desirable, the ECJ still has some way to go if the 2 sets of case law are to be satisfactorily reconciled. There is, furthermore, a potential difficulty arising from the split jurisdiction of the Court of First Instance in Art. 215 cases on the one hand, and the ECJ interpreting the liability of Member States by way of Art. 177 preliminary rulings on the other.

(3) there must be a direct causal link between the breach of the obligation resting on the State and the damage sustained by the injured parties.[139]

The second of the conditions set out above, namely that there be a sufficiently serious breach of Community law, will almost certainly be the decisive condition in practice for a finding of State liability.[140] The ECJ expanded on the meaning of this condition by explaining that a sufficiently serious breach of Community law arises where the Member State has 'manifestly and gravely disregarded the limits of its discretion'.[141] The national court may take into consideration the following factors: 'the clarity and precision of the rule breached, the measure of discretion left by that rule to the national or Community authorities, [and] whether the infringement and the damage caused was intentional or involuntary'.[142] The last factor, namely whether the infringement and the damage caused by the Member State was intentional or involuntary, implicitly incorporates the notion of fault. Nevertheless, the ECJ explicitly stated that any concept of fault going beyond that of a sufficiently serious breach of Community law cannot be a further condition for the right to reparation.[143]

The relationship between the three conditions set out by the ECJ in *Francovich* and those in *Brasserie du Pêcheur* was dealt with by the ECJ in its *Dillenkofer* judgment where it held that both sets of conditions are 'in substance' the same 'since the condition that there should be a sufficiently serious breach, although not expressly mentioned in *Francovich*, was nevertheless evident from the circumstances of that case'.[144] It seems therefore, that in cases concerning complete omissions on the part of a Member State to implement a Directive, there will by definition be a sufficiently serious breach of Community law. In all other cases, whether it be the incorrect implementation of a Directive,[145] a breach of EC law by a Member State exercising its rule-making powers[146] or a breach of EC law by the executive,[147] the *Brasserie du Pêcheur* conditions will be applicable.

As has been noted, the availability of remedies against a Member State for its breach of the provisions concerning the free movement of goods is of enormous practical significance. In particular, the recent ECJ judgments require the national courts to fashion existing remedies for the liability of

---

[139] Ibid., para. 51 of judgt.

[140] A 'sufficiently serious breach' of Community law was certainly the decisive condition in the *BT* & *Denkavit* cases, nn. 132 & 135 above respectively.

[141] Case C–46/93 & C–48/93, n. 9 above, para. 55 of judgt.

[142] Ibid., para. 56 of judgt.   [143] Ibid., para. 79 of judgt.

[144] Joined Cases C–178, 179 & 188–190/94, n. 134 above, para. 23. See also Joined Cases C–94–95/95 *Bonifaci* v. *INPS* [1997] ECR I–3969 and Case C–261/95 *Palmisani* v. *INPS* [1997] ECR I–4025.

[145] As in *BT* & *Denkavit*, nn. 132 & 135 above respectively.

[146] As in *Brasserie du Pêcheur* and *Factortame*, n. 131 above.

[147] As in *Hedley Lomas*, n. 133 above.

the State within the national context, to the vicissitudes of the ECJ conditions.[148] Clearly, the success of the system developed by the ECJ depends heavily upon the co-operation of the national courts.[149] The respective regimes for the liability of the State according to French, English, and Dutch law will be discussed in the remainder of this chapter. The key issues in the context of the present discussion are, firstly, how well the existing national law regimes fit into the conditions developed by the ECJ, and secondly, whether damage suffered as a result of specific breaches by the State of the free-movement-of-goods provisions are dealt with satisfactorily by the national courts.

(A) State liability for breach of EC law before the French courts

French administrative law regarding the liability of the State forms an autonomous body of law.[150] As such, it is entirely separate from the liability rules that apply in the French civil courts.[151] There are two types of State liability recognized by French administrative courts: liability based on *faute* and liability *sans faute*. Liability based on *faute*, in order to be founded, may either require *faute simple* or *faute lourde*, the latter being necessary when the task of the public service is particularly difficult or sensitive. The notion of *faute* is broad, encompassing any illegality on the part of the State, and 'is wider than common law concepts of trespass, negligence or misfeasance in public office'.[152] Liability *sans faute*, on the other hand, is based on the twin principles of 'risk' and 'equality'.[153] The theory of 'risk' is founded on the idea that the activities of the State, even when conducted without fault, may in certain circumstances constitute the

---

[148] For a poor example of such fashioning, see the judgment of the Italian *Corte di Cassazione* in *Presidente deel Consiglio dei Ministri* v. *Castellani*, judgt of 19 Jan. 1996, no. 401, *Il Foro Italiano* 1996, I 503 and note by Biondi, 'The Corte Cassazione and the proper implementation of Community law' (1996) 21 ELRev. 485.

[149] It may also be noted that the ECJ's judgment in *Brasserie du Pêcheur* has been implemented by the German *Bundesgerichtshof* in a judgt of 24 Oct. 1996, III ZR 127/91, EuZW 1996, 761; [1997] 1 CMLR 971 where it was held that the Federal Republic of Germany was not liable in damages firstly because the 'additives prohibition' in the German legislation was held not to constitute a sufficiently serious breach of Community law and secondly because there was held to be no causal connection between the loss suffered and the breach of Article 30 by the 'designation prohibition'.

[150] The discussion in this section draws upon the author's chapter 'Remedies for Breach of EC Law Before French Courts' in Lonbay and Biondi (eds.), *Remedies for Breach of EC Law*, 187.

[151] This may be contrasted with English and Dutch law under which, as a general rule, the liability of the State and other public authorities arises under the same rules of tort or contract as those applied to private individuals. See discussion of English and Dutch law in the sections which follow.

[152] Neville Brown and Bell, *French Administrative Law* (Clarendon Press, 4th edn., 1993), 181.

[153] See Errera, 'The Scope and Meaning of No-fault Liability in French Administrative Law' (1986) Current Legal Problems 171.

creation of a risk which, if it materializes and causes injury or loss, the State should make good. The second key concept is that of the 'equality of all citizens in bearing public burdens' (*égalité devant les charges publiques*). What is meant by this is that since the activities of the State are carried on in the interest of the entire community, the burdens that accrue should not weigh more heavily on some than on others. Thus, should State action result in individual damage to particular citizens, the State should make good that damage irrespective of whether or not there was a fault committed by the public officers concerned. Liability *sans faute* has been accepted by the French courts on the basis of 'risk' or 'equality' for damage suffered as a result of Acts of Parliament,[154] administrative regulations[155] and international conventions.[156] Traditionally, liability *sans faute* has only rarely been found to exist as the conditions regarding the level of seriousness required are strict.[157] Furthermore, the liability of the State to make good damage originating in international conventions is subject to the condition that 'neither the convention itself, nor the law which ratified the convention, can be interpreted as having been intended to exclude compensation'.[158]

The French administrative courts have held the French State liable for breaches of the free-movement-of-goods provisions on several occasions. Initially, it seemed that the French courts were going to favour founding the liability of the French State for a breach of its Community obligations on the principle of liability *sans faute*. This emerged in the *Henri Ramel* case[159] which formed part of a series of judgments in the context of '*la guerre du vin*'. Against a background of civil unrest perpetrated by French wine farmers against the import of cheap Italian wine, a number of local measures were undertaken to placate French wine farmers, amongst them an order of 17 March 1975 by the *Préfet* of Hérault forbidding all tankers, no matter what their nationality or origin, entry into the port of Sète. Les Fils d'Henri Ramel, a French company which owned Italian wine transported on a tanker which was prevented from entering the port, claimed that the administrative measure was contrary to Article 30 EC and thus sought damages. Responding to this claim, the *Conseil d'Etat* held that since the *Préfet's* order could be justified under Article 36 EC under the

---

[154] *Société des produits laitiers La Fleurette, Conseil d'Etat,* 14 Jan. 1938, Rec. Lebon 1938, 25.

[155] *Bovero, Conseil d'Etat,* Rec. Lebon 1963, 53.

[156] *Ass. Compagnie générale d'énergie radioélectrique, Conseil d'Etat,* 30 Mar. 1966, Rec. Lebon 1966, 257.

[157] The harm suffered must be shown to have been 'abnormal' or 'special': see *Caucheteux et Desmont, Conseil d'Etat,* Rec. Lebon 1994, 222 and *Ministre de la Culture et de la Communication, Conseil d'Etat,* Rec. Lebon 1981, 478.

[158] *Ass. Compagnie générale d'énergie radioélectrique,* n. 156 above.

[159] *SARL Les fils de Henri Ramel* v. *Ministre de l'interieur et Préfet de l'Hérault, Conseil d'Etat,* 7 Dec. 1979, Rec. Lebon 1979, 456; Dalloz 1980, Jur. 303; JCP 1981, II 19500 (with note by Pacteau); noted by Audeoud, Berlin & Manin (1982) 19 CMLRev. 289 at 295.

head of protection of public security,[160] there was no *faute de service* committed by the *Préfet*. The *Conseil d'Etat* nevertheless awarded damages to Ramel on the basis of no-fault liability since the damage was not a risk that Ramel knowingly undertook and the damages '*présentent un caractère de specialité qui justifie leur réparation par l'Etat*'.[161] The *Conseil d'Etat* in *Ramel* thus found State liability on the basis of 'risk' and 'equality' and thus *sans faute*.

The classic exposition of liability *sans faute* for breach of the provisions concerning the free movement of goods is, however, to be found in the judgment of the *Conseil d'Etat* in the infamous *Alivar* judgment.[162] Alivar was a French co-operative which undertook to sell potatoes to an Italian company. The contracts could not be carried out because the French public authorities refused to grant an export licence, having regard to the shortage of potatoes on the French market at the relevant time. In Article 169 infringement proceedings brought by the Commission against France, the ECJ declared that by making exports of potatoes conditional upon the production of an export certificate previously endorsed by the relevant agency, France had failed to fulfil its obligations under Article 34 EEC.[163] Alivar then commenced an action for damages against the French State before the administrative courts. After explicitly mentioning the ECJ's judgment establishing the French Republic's failure, the *Conseil d'Etat* went on to find liability *sans faute* in the following terms:

The task of determining whether the government decision and the refusal to issue an export licence are of such a nature as to render the State liable vis-à-vis the Alivar company falls upon the French administrative courts. It appears from the investigation that such measures were taken for reasons of general interest, resulting from the shortage situation on the potato market in France at the end of 1975 and in the beginning of 1976 which did not allow the grant of an export licence to Alivar. Therefore the French government may be held liable for damages to that company only on the grounds of no-fault liability if it could be shown that an abnormal and specific damage has been inflicted by the French Administration's intervention. Such a damage resulting from the acts of the said administration has been established in this case.

---

[160] This, in itself, was a highly contestable conclusion to have reached without making a preliminary reference to the ECJ under Art. 177 EC, given the ECJ's judgment in Case 231/83, n. 6 above. See extensive discussion of this point at p. 247.

[161] For a similar conclusion in the case of an export restriction which was equally controversially held to be justified on grounds of the protection of national treasures, see *Ministre de la culture* v. *Epoux Genty*, *Conseil d'Etat*, 7 Oct. 1987, Rec. Lebon 1987, 304; Dalloz 1988, Jur. 269; AJDA 1987, 768; Rev. fr. dr. admin. 1988, 861. See detailed dicussion of this case at p. 289.

[162] *Ministère du Commerce extérieur* v. *Société Alivar*, *Conseil d'Etat*, 23 Mar. 1984, Rec. Lebon 1984, 127; RTDE 1984, 341; La Semaine Juridique—éd. entreprise 1985, II 14547; AJDA 1984, 396; Gaz. Pal. 1984, I Jur. 329; JCP 1985, II 20423.

[163] Case 68/76 *Commission* v. *France* [1977] ECR 515.

Alivar and Henri Ramel will no doubt have been satisfied with the concrete result of these judgments since they both received the damages they sought. However, the legal basis upon which liability was founded has provoked much criticism from commentators.[164] An important criticism of the *Alivar* ruling was that the *Conseil d'Etat* unduly extended the concept of liability *sans faute* in French law which, according to well-established case law, will only exceptionally be found in cases of economic intervention by the State.[165] Perhaps more important, however, was the fact that by finding liability *sans faute*, the *Conseil d'Etat* was able to avoid answering the question of whether the administrative measure in question was lawful or not. The finding of State liability *sans faute* for breach of EC-law obligations was indeed far from satisfactory. Not only did it unduly extend and abuse the concept of liability *sans faute* in French law, it also contradicted the long-established principle that any illegality is *fautive*.[166] Finally, from the perspective of the effective enforcement of EC law, it was unduly onerous to the party claiming damages by requiring that the damage sustained was abnormal, specific, and directly attributable to the administrative acts.

In more recent years, there has been a discernible trend towards accepting and preferring the basing of French State liability for breach of the free movement of goods provisions on *faute*. On a number of occasions, the French administrative courts have found liability with *faute* and granted damages to compensate addressees of individual decisions which had been found to be incompatible with Articles 30 to 36 EC. For example, it has been held in cases concerning delays in French Customs in clearing imports of wine from Italy (which had been held by the ECJ to be disproportionate and contrary to Article 30 EC[167]) that '[b]y exceeding substantially this period (21 days) without furnishing any precise justification for such delay, the State has committed a fault such as to create liability'.[168] Similarly, the *Cour administrative d'appel* of Nancy in *Société Lefebvre*[169] held that the Finance Ministry's refusal to grant import licences in respect of

[164] See, e.g., Genevois, AJDA 1984, 396 who stated that the *Conseil d'Etat*'s judgment in *Alivar* put *'le commentateur dans l'embarras'*. See also Haguenau, n. 126 above, 474–6.

[165] See Roseren, 'The Application of Community law by French Courts from 1980 to 1993' (1994) 31 CMLRev. 315 at 337; Dantonel-Cor, 'La mise en jeu de la responsabilité de l'Etat français pour violation du droit communautaire' (1995) 31 RTDE 471 at 500; M.R.B., Gaz. Pal. 1984, I Jur. 331; Davignon, JCP 1985, II 20423 and Hubac & Schoettl, AJDA 1985, 536.

[166] Chapus, *Droit administratif général* (Monchrestien, 8th edn., 1994). See also, *Ville de Paris* v. *Sieur Draincourt*, Conseil d'Etat, 26 Jan. 1973, Rec. Lebon, 1973, 77.

[167] Case 42/82 *Commission* v. *France* [1983] ECR 1013.

[168] *Societé Tresch-Alsacaves* v. *Ministre de l'economie, des finances et du Budget*, Trib. admin. Strasbourg, 5 June 1984 [1986] 2 CMLR 625. See, to the same effect, *Societé vinicole Berard SA*, Trib. admin. Dijon, 15 Apr. 1986, Rec. Lebon 1986, 311; RTDE 1988, 112 (with note by Soler-Couteaux) and *Duault*, *CA'A* Nantes, 20 June 1991, Rec. Lebon 1991, 742; AJDA 1992, 172.

[169] *Ministre de l'économie, des finances et du budget* v. *Société Lefebvre*, CAA Nancy, 9 July 1991, Rec. Lebon 1991, 741.

bananas in free circulation in Belgium infringed Article 30 EC and, unlike in *Alivar*, this infringement of EC-law obligations was held to constitute a *faute* for which the State was liable to importers concerned for such damages sustained.[170]

The French ordinary courts (civil courts) have also held that the French State may be liable for a breach of the free-movement-of-goods provisions on the basis of liability for *faute*. The Commercial Chamber of the *Cour de Cassation* in *Sté United Distillers France* v. *Agent judiciaire du Trésor public*[171] has held that a circular issued by the French Minister of Justice encouraging public prosecutors to pursue criminal prosecutions for advertising alcoholic drinks contrary to Articles L. 17 and 18 of the *Code des débits de boissons* (Sale of Beverages Code) constituted a *faute lourde* under Article L. 781–1 of the *Code de l'organisation judiciaire* (Code on the Judiciary), since Articles L. 17 and 18 had been held by the ECJ to infringe Article 30 EC.[172]

The leading *Conseil d'Etat* authority establishing that the basis of liability for breach of EC law is *faute* is *SA Rothmans International France et SA Philip Morris France, Société Arizona Tobacco Products et SA Philip Morris France*.[173] This case did not, however, concern a breach of Articles 30 to 36 EC. Rather, the facts of the case concerned the fixing by the French State of the retail price of tobacco by a law of 24 May 1976[174] and a decree of 31 December 1976,[175] both introduced in order to implement Directive 72/464.[176] This implementation had, on two occasions, been held by the ECJ to be contrary to the Directive[177] and, on a claim for compensation from the French State for losses suffered, the *Conseil d'Etat* held that

[T]he ministerial decisions adopted pursuant to the Decree of 31 December 1976, refusing to fix the price of manufactured tobacco at the levels sought by the applicant companies for the period from 1 November 1982 to 31 December 1983, are illegal. Their illegality is such as to render the State liable.[178]

---

[170] See also *Aubin, Conseil d'Etat*, 20 Jan. 1988, Rec. Lebon 1988, 20; JCP 1989, II 21169 (with note by Moderne); AJDA 1988, 418 (with note by Prétot).

[171] *Cour de Cassation*, ch. comm., 21 Feb. 1995, Dalloz 1995, IR 100; noted by Mok SEW 1995, 548.

[172] Case 152/78 *Commission* v. *France* [1980] ECR 2299.

[173] *Conseil d'Etat*, 28 Feb. 1992, [1993] 1 CMLR 253; Rec. Lebon 1992, 78; Gaz. Pal. 1992, no. 355–7 p. 6; Rev. juris. fiscale 1992, 362; RTDE 1992, 426; AJDA 1992, 210. Noted by Errera (1992) PL 340 and Dutheil de la Rochère (1993) 30 CMLRev. 187.

[174] Law No. 76-448 JORF p. 3083.

[175] Decree no. 76-1324, JORF p. 189.

[176] Council Directive of 19 Dec. 1973 on taxes other than turnover taxes which affect the consumption of manufactured tobacco [1972] OJ L303/1.

[177] See Case 90/82 *Commission* v. *France* [1983] ECR 2011 & Case 169/87 *Commission* v. *France* [1988] ECR 4092.

[178] It may be noted that 7 years earlier, the *Conseil d'Etat* had, in the context of exactly the same French provisions, held in *International Sales and Support Corporation BV* v. *Ministre de l'economie et des Finances*, 13 Dec. 1985, Rec. Lebon 1985, 377; AJDA 1986, 174; RTDE 1988, 108 (with note by Soler-Couteaux) that it could not examine the compatibility of the French

This finding of State liability on the basis of 'illegality', has thus clearly established that the correct legal basis for a finding of liability for breaches by the French State of EC law is on the basis of *faute*.

A further challenge to French law on State liability raised by the ECJ's recent case law is the question as to whether the French legislature may be held liable for a breach of EC law.[179] The notion that the legislator can do no wrong is deeply rooted in the French republican tradition and has for many years created an insurmountable obstacle to the scrutiny by French courts of Acts of Parliament. In the *Rothmans* and *Société Arizona* cases discussed above,[180] the *Conseil d'Etat* was able to avoid answering this delicate question. A close reading of the *Conseil d'Etat*'s judgment, together with the conclusions of *Commissaire de gouvernement* Laroque (which the *Conseil d'Etat* followed), makes it clear that both the Conseil and its *Commissaire* explicitly avoided the question of liability of the State on the grounds of the illegality of the Act of 24 May 1976. Instead, the direct source of the damage was held to be found in the ministerial orders implementing the decree, rather than the Act itself.

While such a convenient construction to evade the issue was possible on the facts in *Société Arizona*, such was not the case in two subsequent judgments of the *Cour administrative d'appel* of Paris. While *Société Arizona* concerned an incorrect implementation of a directive, in *Société Jacques Dangeville*[181] the *Cour administrative d'appel* was confronted with complete absence of implementation of the Sixth VAT Directive[182] into French law. In a claim by an insurance broker for compensation for damages arising out of the imposition of VAT on its activities as an insurance broker under Article 256 of the *Code général des impôts* (General Code on Imports) when the Directive exempted such operations from VAT, the Paris court held:

It follows from the provisions of the EEC Treaty, particularly Article 5 of this Treaty, that the French State is obliged to adopt all measures in order to ensure the discharge of its Community obligations. One of these obligations is to make good the consequences of infringement of Community law, either directly, or by ensuring effective compensation for the damage resulting from the infringement.

legislation with the pre-dating EC law. With respect to the exercise of the powers of the Minister refusing to raise the retail price of that tobacco, the *Conseil d'Etat* held that this decision was taken in the general interest as a measure to fight inflation and was therefore compatible with EC law which, in the absence of *faute*, could not give rise to the liability of the State. Needless to say, this judgment was heavily criticized as yet another decision by the *Conseil d'Etat* refusing to accord supremacy to EC law over subsequent national legislation. See the Third Report to the European Parliament on Commission Monitoring of the Application of Community Law [1986] OJ C220 and Sixth Report [1988] OJ C330/1.

[179] See discussion of this question by Haguenau, n. 126 above, 478–80.
[180] n. 173 above.
[181] *CAA* Paris, Ass. Plén., 1 July 1992, Rec. Lebon 1992, 558; AJDA 1992, 768; Droit Fiscal 1992, No. 1665 p. 1420.
[182] Directive 77/388 [1977] OJ L145/1.

By awarding compensation for damage sustained by the applicant by reason of non-implementation of a Directive, the court in this case in effect found that the State was liable for Parliament's failure to implement the Directive. Similarly, in *Société John Walker*,[183] the same court allowed a claim for damages for loss sustained as a result of the application of French legislative provisions in the *Code général des impôts* relating to tax on certain spirits which had been held by the ECJ in a judgment under Article 169 EEC to infringe Article 95.[184]

One should not underestimate the boldness of the challenge advanced in these two judgments to the well-established French public-law principle of the infallibility of Parliament. Indeed, these judgments have not escaped without criticism. Prétot has described the *Dangeville* judgment as 'adventurous',[185] and points out that the conformity of statutes with the Constitution is a matter for the *Conseil constitutionnel* and that Article 55 of the French Constitution does not require a French court to declare a statute in conflict with EC law invalid, but only 'inapplicable'. It is not surprising therefore that in both *Dangeville* and *John Walker*, the *Cour administrative d'appel* avoided explicitly referring either to the liability of the French legislature for its failure to comply with EC law or to notions of *faute*. Instead, both judgments rather coyly and self-consciously refered to an 'illicit situation' which caused damage to the claimant. Nevertheless, the practical result reached by these two judgments was that an Act of Parliament, the content of which was contrary to EC law, was held to be capable of engaging the liability of the French State.

These recent judgments are to be welcomed, particularly in the light of the ECJ's judgment in *Francovich*.[186] Although the *Conseil d'Etat* in *Arizona Tobacco* and the Paris *Cour administrative d'appel* in *Dangeville* and *John Walker* did not explicitly refer to the *Francovich* ruling, the fact that the *Commissaires du gouvernement* in all three cases[187] mentioned and drew on that judgment, reinforces the conclusion that these cases were inspired by the spirit, if not the letter, of *Francovich*.

Paradoxically, however, these recent developments have also served to muddy the waters of State liability in French law. In none of these recent cases did the courts specify *faute*, but simply referred cryptically to an 'illicit situation' (*situation illicite*). As was noted above, this is not surprising given the bold challenge to the well-established principle of the infallibility of Parliament which was effectively being advanced in these cases. However, difficult questions are left unanswered. For example, it is not clear whether the French courts are slowly prising open a new category of

---

[183] *CAA* Paris, 12 Nov. 1992, Rec. Lebon 1992, 790; Dr. admin. 1993, Mar. no. 130.
[184] Case 168/78 *Commission v. France* [1980] ECR 347.
[185] Prétot, AJDA 1992, 768 at 770.   [186] n. 128 above.
[187] Laroque in *Arizona Tobacco*, Bernault in *Dangeville*, and Gipoulon in *John Walker*.

State liability for breaches of EC law or whether they are simply adapting the present law. It may be noted with dismay that all the courts were also careful to avoid specifying the precise nature of the illegality. The conclusion must be that the concept of *faute* in the French law on State liability for breach of EC law has become somewhat blurred.

These uncertainties have prompted some commentators to argue that the time is ripe for a more subtle approach, involving a re-writing of the categories for the recognition of State liability in France. Dantonel-Cor[188] points out that the term *faute*, with its pejorative connotations, is inappropriate in the context of State liability for breaches of Community law. Liability based on *faute*, she argues, should be reserved for knowing breaches of EC law by the State, while in most cases, liability could be founded on *'simple illégalité'* or *'erreur'*. Given that the ECJ has now, in *Brasserie du Pêcheur*,[189] explicitly stated that any concept of fault going beyond that of a sufficiently serious breach of EC law cannot be a further condition for the right to reparation,[190] it seems that a development in French law of State liability along the lines suggested by Dantonel-Cor would be fully in line with that judgment.

The *Conseil d'Etat* has recently overturned the judgment of the *Cour administrative d'appel* of Paris in *Dangeville*.[191] However, this overruling was based, not on the Paris court's reasoning with respect to State liability, but on the inadmissibility of the claim under French law principles that prior judgments are final (*l'autorité de la chose jugée*) and that litigation must be separated (*la distinction des contentieux*). The latter principles were relevant to the facts since the *Conseil d'Etat* had previously, by a judgment of 19 March 1986,[192] held that Dangeville could not invoke the Directive in question.[193] However, it is of interest to note that although *Commissaire du gouvernement* Goulard in this case had urged the *Conseil d'Etat* to overturn the judgment of the *Cour Administrative d'appel* of Paris on the grounds of admissibility set out above, he had also very coherently argued that the latter court's judgment with respect to the liability of the French State was

---

[188] 'La mise en jeu de la responsabilité de l'Etat français pour violation du droit communautaire' (1995) 31 RTDE 471 at 504.

[189] Case C–46/93 & C–48/93, n. 131 above.   [190] Ibid., at para. 79.

[191] *Ministre du Budget* v. *SA Jacques Dangeville, Conseil d'Etat*, Assemblée, 30 Oct. 1996 (1997) 33 RTDE 171.

[192] *SA Cabinet Dangeville, Conseil d'Etat*, 19 Mar. 1986, Rec. Lebon 1986, 465; RJF 1986, no. 553.

[193] It is respectfully submitted that the *Conseil d'Etat*'s reasoning on this point is subject to sharp criticism since the application of these two principles of domestic law made the *application* of EC law excessively difficult in practice. This is because the earlier judgment, which the *Conseil d'Etat* in *Dangeville* held was final, was based upon a misconceived view of the direct effect of EC law (drawing upon the *Cohn-Bendit* [*Conseil d'Etat*, 22 Dec. 1978, [1980] 1 CMLR 543; Rec. Lebon 1978, 524; AJDA 1979, 41] line of authority) which the *Conseil d'Etat* in any event abandoned by a judgment handed down on the same day (See *Cabinet Revert et Badelon, Conseil d'Etat*, Assemblée, 30 Oct. 1996 (1997) 33 RTDE 171).

correct.[194] The learned *Commissaire du gouvernement* took the view that in the *Arizona Tobacco* case,[195] the failure to transpose the directive at issue in that case was in fact imputable to the legislator, notwithstanding the fact that there were also ministerial orders (i.e. *un acte réglementaire*) implementing the French legislation. *Commissaire du gouvernement* Goulard argued that the same reasoning should be applied to the facts of the *Dangeville* case which concerned an individual decision (*une décision individuelle*) of the tax authorities applying the provisions of a French Act of Parliament which was incompatible with a Community Directive. To draw a distinction between cases in which there was an *acte réglementaire* and those in which there was a *décision individuelle* would, according to the *Commissaire du gouvernement*, not be based on any serious legal foundations. However, as has been noted, the *Conseil d'Etat* proceeded merely to accept the *Commissaire du gouvernement*'s conclusions with respect to the inadmissibility of the claim on French law grounds and did not comment on the wider question of State liability for acts of the legislator. As a result, the *Conseil d'Etat* has not yet expressed its views on the above matters, and it remains open for it to lay down some limitations in the future to the unbridled approaches of the *Cour administrative d'appel* of Paris in *Dangeville* and *John Walker*. However, now that the ECJ has unequivocally confirmed in *Brasserie du Pêcheur* that Member States may be held liable for legislative breaches of EC law,[196] it is submitted that the *Conseil d'Etat* would, according to EC law, be required to uphold the position adopted by the the Paris Administrative Appeals Court with respect to State liability.

(B) State liability for breach of EC law before the English courts

Under English law, it is indispensable to an understanding of the position of remedies against the State that the (relatively recent) distinction between rights in public and private law is fully appreciated.[197] The distinction is not an easy one, but can nevertheless be crucial. On the one hand, public law rights concern the right to have the law enforced and administered by a public authority properly and fairly and the duty is owed to the public at large.[198] Public law rights must be pursued by way of judicial review.[199] The essence of private law rights, on the other hand,

---

[194] (1997) 33 RTDE 171 at 173–5.   [195] n. 173 above.

[196] Cases C–46/93 & C–48/93, n. 131 above, at paras. 16–36.

[197] See discussion in Dutheil de la Rochère, Grief and Jarvis, 'L'Application du droit communautaire par les juridictions britanniques (1995–1996)'. See also Convery, 'State Liability in the United Kingdom After *Brasserie du Pêcheur*' (1997) 34 CMLRev. 603.

[198] *Bourgoin* v. *Ministry of Agriculture, Fisheries and Food* [1986] QB 716, [1986] 1 CMLR 267 at 283. See D'Sa, n. 1 above, 178.

[199] RSC Ord. 53; Supreme Court Act 1981, s. 31.

is a breach of a duty owed specifically to an individual. Private law rights must be pursued by way of ordinary civil action (a writ). If litigants can allege the commission of a tort or the existence of some other private law right (e.g. breach of a statutory duty) they should pursue the claim by means of a writ. The distinction between public and private law rights is of great practical significance because the so-called rule in *O'Reilly* v. *Mackman*[200] means that a public law right cannot, in general, be pursued by ordinary action since this will be considered to be an abuse of the process of the court and is liable to be struck out under the court's inherent jurisdiction.[201] Selection of either public or private law remedies can thus be crucial to the outcome of the case.[202] However, since most actions for damages arising from a breach of EC law for which the State is responsible will usually involve mixed issues of public and private law, it will usually be appropriate to proceed by ordinary action.[203]

If public law remedies are selected to pursue a claim against the State for breach of EC law, the remedy is judicial review. Although it is possible to claim damages in judicial review proceedings, it is a discretionary and exceptional remedy.[204] Thus, judicial review proceedings usually only yield a declaratory judgment. It is difficult to disagree with the Opinion of Advocate General Léger in *R.* v. *Ministry of Agriculture, Fisheries and Food, ex p. Hedley Lomas* that effective judicial protection is not guaranteed by a declaratory judgment delivered in judicial review proceedings.[205] Indeed, now that ECJ judgments themselves explicitly require the provision of reparation for the consequences of loss and damage, it is clear that judicial

---

[200] [1983] 2 AC 237, [1982] 3 WLR 1096, [1982] 3 All ER 1124.

[201] RSC O. 18 r. 19. By contrast, Scots law has attempted to avoid the procedural division between public and private rights: see *West* v. *Secretary of State for Scotland* [1992] SLT 636 and *Shetland Line* v. *Secretary of State for Scotland* [1996] SLT 653.

[202] It should be noted that the rigid procedural dichotomy set out in *O'Reilly* v. *Mackman* has been gradually relaxed: see *Roy* v. *Kensington and Chelsea and Westminster Family Practitioner Committee* [1992] 1 AC 624; *R.* v. *Secretary of State for Employment, ex p. EOC* [1995] 1 CMLR 391 and *Trustees of the Dennis Rye Pension Fund* v. *Sheffield City Council*, The Times 20 Aug. 1997, where Lord Woolf MR held that in considering whether a litigant should have brought judicial review proceedings or an ordinary action against a public body, the court should look at the practical consequences of the choice made rather than just technical questions concerning the distinction between public and private law rights.

[203] *An Bord Bainne Co-operative* v. *Milk Marketing Board* [1984] 2 CMLR 584. It has, however, been pointed out that in the event of doubt as to whether public or private law issues are dominant, it might be wise to apply for judicial review first since the time limits for bringing such an action are tighter than those applicable to bringing an ordinary civil action. See D'Sa, n. 1 above.

[204] RSC O. 53 r. 7, Supreme Court Act 1981, s. 31(4). In Scotland, the possibility of obtaining damages in judicial review proceedings is explicitly provided for. Under Chapter 58, Rule 58(4)(b) of the Rules of the Court of Session, on a petition for judicial review in Scotland, the court may make any order it thinks fit, including an order for 'payment (whether of damages or otherwise)'.

[205] Case C–5/94, n. 133 above, at para. 206 of Opinion of 20 June 1995.

review may no longer be regarded an effective remedy for the non-contractual liability of Member States for their breaches of EC law.

With respect to private law rights, it must be noted that under English law, there is no general theory of tortious liability. As a result, a case must be brought within the definition of a recognized tort if a remedy is to be obtained. The appropriate tort to accommodate the liability of the State for its breaches of Community law has, until recently, been an unresolved question in English law. The application by the Divisional Court of the ECJ's *Factortame* (No. 3) judgment has provided welcome clarification in this field.[206] However, before embarking upon a discussion of the latter judgment, it is instructive to first examine the approaches which have been considered by the English courts to date.

Firstly, the tort of *misfeasance in public office* was favoured by the majority of the Court of Appeal in *Bourgoin SA* v. *Ministry of Agriculture, Fisheries and Food*.[207] In order to found an action upon the tort of misfeasance in public office, it is necessary to prove either malice or actual knowledge by the defendant of the ultra vires or unlawful act, or at least a recklessness as to whether that is the case or not.[208] In other words, only a knowing or malicious breach of EC law would give rise to a private law right to damages for misfeasance. Again, in *R.* v. *Ministry of Agriculture, Fisheries and Food ex p. Hedley Lomas (Ireland) Ltd* Advocate General Léger concluded that misfeasance in public office could not be considered an effective remedy to repair breaches of EC law by Member States.[209] This has now been confirmed by the ECJ which in *Brasserie du Pêcheur* held that

[A]ny condition that may be imposed by English law on State liability requiring proof of misfeasance in public office, such an abuse of power being inconceivable in the case of the legislature, is also such as in practice to make it impossible or extremely difficult to obtain effective reparation for loss or damage resulting from a breach of Community law where the breach is attributable to the national legislature.[210]

In any event, it may be noted that in *Kirklees MBC* v. *Wickes Building Supplies*,[211] the House of Lords had already cast doubt upon the continued application of the judgment of the Court of Appeal in the *Bourgoin* case where Lord Goff went so far as to say that after the *Francovich* judgment

---

[206] Judgt of Divisional Court of 31 July 1997, The Times 11 Sept. 1997.

[207] n. 198 above. See also *An Bord Bainne Co-operative* v. *Milk Marketing Board* [1988] 1 CMLR 605 (CA).

[208] For a recent discussion of misfeasance in public office and EC law see the judgment of the English High Court in *Three Rivers District Council* v. *Bank of England* (No. 3) [1996] 3 All ER 558, [1997] 2 CMLR 429. See also *Bennett* v. *Commissioner of Police* [1995] 2 All ER 1, [1995] 1 WLR 488 and *Jones* v. *Swansea City Council* [1983] 3 All ER 162 (CA).

[209] Case C–5/94, n. 133 above, at para. 140 of Opinion delivered 20 June 1995.

[210] Cases C–46/93 & C–48/93, n. 131 above, at para. 73.   [211] n. 90 above.

'there must now be doubt whether the *Bourgoin* case was correctly decided'.[212]

A second possible private law right is the tort of *negligence*. Under this tort it would have to be argued that the negligent exercise of statutory power by the State gave rise to damages. Again, this tort would also seem to fail the effectiveness principle since it would, as the tort of negligence stands at present, require the national authorities to act unreasonably or in bad faith before it would apply. Liability for the negligent, but bona fide, exercise of discretionary power is unlikely to be accepted by the English courts as giving rise to damages, particularly in view of the fact that 'novel categories of negligence are now developed incrementally and by analogies with established categories'.[213]

A third and very much more viable possibility is the tort of *breach of statutory duty* discussed in the context of Article 86 EC by the House of Lords in *Garden Cottage Foods* v. *Milk Marketing Board*.[214] To allege the commission of this tort, it would have to be argued that a breach of a directly effective provision of EC law by the State may also be categorized as a breach of section 2(1) of the European Communities Act 1972 (the Act of Parliament which incorporated EC law in the United Kingdom upon its accession to the Community), thus constituting a breach of statutory duty giving rise to a civil cause of action. The use of this tort holds many attractions, especially for directly effective EC Treaty provisions (e.g. Article 30 or 52 EC) which can be said to be imposed for the protection of a limited class of the public and which were intended to give a right of action in the event of their breach. The use of this tort will not, however, be without problems. Indeed, a majority of the Court of Appeal has rejected the possibility that a breach of Article 30 EC by the United Kingdom administration could constitute a breach of statutory duty.[215] The principal difficulty is that the commission of this tort requires that the statutory duty was imposed for the protection of a limited class of the public and that Parliament intended to confer on members of that class a private right of action for breach of the duty.[216] It is difficult to construe the European

---

[212] [1992] 3 All ER 717 at 734. It should also be noted that the concerns of the majority of the CA in *Bourgoin* have now been met by the ECJ's judgment in *Brasserie du Pêcheur* (No. 3). The Court of Appeal had limited the liability of public authorities for their breach of EC law to misfeasance in public office since the damages regime would otherwise become too burdensome and would subject the State to a more onerous liability than the Community itself under Art. 215(2) EC. As has been shown, this concern has now been met since the ECJ now applies the same test for both State and Community liability and the requirement for a 'sufficiently serious breach' of EC law will prevent unduly burdensome liability.

[213] Brealy & Hoskins, n. 1 above, 78.

[214] [1984] AC 130, [1983] 2 All ER 770, [1983] 3 CMLR 43.

[215] *Bourgoin*, n. 207 above. See excellent analysis of this judgment in Green & Barav, 'Damages in the National Courts for Breaches of Community Law' (1986) 6 YEL 55 at 83–114.

[216] See *X.* v. *Bedfordshire CC* [1995] 3 All ER 353 at 364 per Lord Browne-Wilkinson.

Communities Act 1972 as meeting these criteria not least because, as the ECJ itself has stated,[217] the real duty to compensate is not found in the European Communities Act 1972 but is inherent in the EC Treaty itself. Furthermore, there would be difficult constitutional questions to be surmounted addressing the question of how Parliament can be considered to be in breach of its statutory duty.[218]

A final private law possibility is the creation of a so-called *'Euro-tort'* as was suggested by Lord Denning in *Application des Gaz* v. *Falks Veritas*.[219] Such a course of action would involve the invention by the British courts of a new cause of action or an 'innominate tort'. Although such an idea has received some support,[220] it has fallen on deaf judicial ears.[221] It is submitted that this is a pity. The above discussion of the other private law possibilities available demonstrates that none of the existing torts are altogether satisfactory. Following the recent ECJ judgments, the creation of an entirely new tort of 'breach of a Community obligation' seems the most sensible solution since the clear emphasis in the latter ECJ judgments is on the *sui generis* nature of EC law as a new legal order in which the requirement to provide compensation from a defaulting Member State is inherent to that legal order. The creation of a new tort also has the benefit that English law would be adapting to EC law rather than fitting EC law into rather ill-fitting existing national pigeon holes.

In the implementation of the *Factortame* (No. 3) judgment by the Divisional Court, a different solution has been favoured which is essentially a variant of the approach discussed in the previous paragraph.[222] The Divisional Court has in effect held that there is no necessity for a domestic method or classification for acknowledging EC law rights and remedies and has indicated that applicants are entitled to plead a direct claim based on the breach of a provision of the EC Treaty. Thus the Divisional Court held that

The whole *Factortame* litigation, and the various references to the ECJ which it has generated, owes its existence to the absence from English domestic law of any cause of action whereby a claim can be made for damage caused by the enactment of primary legislation in any circumstances or for damage caused by acts of the

---

[217] See for example, Case C–6 & 9/90, n. 9 above at para. 35.

[218] For further reasons why the tort of breach of statutory duty might not be a suitable remedy for breaches of substantive EC law by the State, see Steiner, 'How to Make the Action Suit the Case: Domestic Remedies for Breach of EC Law' at 108–10. Craig, 'Once More Unto the Breach: The Community, the State and Damages Liability' (1997) 113 LQR 67 at 88–9 has argued on the other hand that although the action for breach of statutory duty would have to be substantially adapted in this context, there is no reason why this could not be achieved.

[219] [1974] Ch. 4481, [1974] 2 CMLR 75, [1974] 3 All ER 51.

[220] See Usher, 'The Imposition of Sanctions for Breaches of Community Law'.

[221] See *Valor International* v. *Application des Gaz and EPI Leisure* [1978] 3 CMLR 87 at 100 and *Lonhro* v. *Shell* [1982] AC 173.

[222] n. 206 above.

Executive unless, perhaps, misfeasance can be established. Thus any remedy has to be imposed by Community law which, of course, applies to domestic law by virtue of the European Communities Act 1972.

This approach, in effect allowing the applicant to plead a direct claim based on the breach of a provision of the EC Treaty, is to be welcomed. It should also be noted that the Divisional Court also had to deal in *Factortame* (No. 3) with a claim for exemplary damages (which are essentially 'penal' damages). It will be remembered that the ECJ had held that 'it must be possible to award specific damages, such as the exemplary damages provided for by English law, pursuant to claims or actions founded on Community law, if such damages may be awarded pursuant to similar claims or actions founded on domestic law'.[223] As a result, the question which the Divisional Court had to resolve was whether, under English law, exemplary damages would be available in a similar claim founded on domestic law. This in turn required the Divisional Court to define under English law the correct nature of liability for a breach of Community law in order that a similar claim founded on domestic law could be assessed. In this context, the Divisional Court held that the similar domestic action in these circumstances was the tort of breach of statutory duty, and that since the European Communities Act 1972 did not expressly provide for exemplary damages, such damages were not available in this case. On the question of the correct remedy in English law for applicants to pursue in claims against the State for breaches of Community law, the Divisional Court held that 'whilst it can be said that the cause of action is *sui generis*, it is of the character of a breach of statutory duty'.

The conclusion following the judgment in this case appears to be that unless it is necessary to identify a similar claim founded on domestic law, English law allows applicants to plead a direct claim based on a breach of a provision of the EC Treaty, and hence the application of the conditions for liability set out by the ECJ in *Factortame* (No. 3)/*Brasserie du Pêcheur*, to the exclusion of any other conditions.[224] If, however, it is necessary to

---

[223] Para. 90 of judgt in *Factortame* (No. 3).

[224] It is interesting to note that the approach of the Divisional Court in *Factortame* (No. 3) had already been hinted at by Clarke J in *Three Rivers*, n. 208 above at 624 of the All ER report where the High Court noted that the ECJ's judgment in *Brasserie du Pêcheur* had laid down conditions for State liability for breach of EC law and held, *obiter dicta*, that '[t]hose criteria are different from the criteria which must be established on any view of the English tort of misfeasance in public office. It will be a matter for future consideration whether in such a case the claimant's remedy is properly to be regarded as a remedy for that tort. It appears to me that in such a case the claim should not be regarded as a claim for damages for the tort of misfeasance in public office, but rather as a claim of a different type not known to the common law, namely a claim for damages for breach of a duty imposed by Community law or for the infringement of a right conferred by Community law.' It is equally interesting to note that the Irish High Court in *Tate* v. *Minister for Social Welfare* [1995] 1 CMLR 825 has held that the

identify a similar claim founded on domestic law, the appropriate action is breach of statutory duty.

For the sake of completeness, it should be noted that the Divisional Court in *Factortame* (No. 3) held that although the United Kingdom acted in good faith, the breach of EC law by the British legislation at issue in that case constituted a 'sufficiently serious' breach in order to give rise to State liability. The Divisional Court cited four factors which led it to the conclusion that each of the conditions (nationality, domicile, and residence) constituted a sufficiently serious breach of Community law. Firstly, that discrimination on grounds of nationality was the intended effect of the British provisions; secondly, that the United Kingdom was aware that the imposition of the conditions would injure the applicants because they were intended to ensure that the applicants would no longer fish against the British quota; thirdly, that the United Kingdom decided to achieve its object through primary legislation which had the effect that applications for interim relief were precluded; and fourthly, that the Commission had made its view that the provisions were contrary to Community law known at an early stage.

In a further important recent judgment, the Court of Appeal in *R. v. Secretary of State for the Home Department, ex p. Gallagher*[225] also applied the criteria for State liability set down by the ECJ in *Brasserie du Pêcheur/Factortame* (No. 3). However, unlike the Divisional Court's application of the *Factortame* (No. 3) judgment, the Court of Appeal was able, according to the ECJ criteria, to exclude liability of the British Government on the facts of the case. The Court of Appeal held that the second and third conditions set out by the ECJ in *Brasserie du Pêcheur* were not met. Firstly, it was held that there was no causal connection between the breach of EC law and the loss suffered by the applicant.[226] Secondly, the Court of Appeal held that there was no 'sufficiently serious' breach of Community

non-implementation of a Directive by the Irish State (*in casu* Directive 79/7) gave rise to damages under the ECJ's *Francovich* judgt which was a right under Community law rather than one under national law. Carroll J held that '[i]n my opinion, the wrong committed by the State in continuing the discrimination by failing fully to implement the Directive is a wrong arising from Community law which has domestic effect. It is not a breach of constitutional rights; it is not a breach of statutory duty and it is not a breach of the duty of care. It is a breach of the duty to implement the Directive and it approximates to a breach of a constitutional duty.' See also *Coppinger* v. *Waterford County Council*, High Court of Ireland, 22 Mar. 1996 (per Geoghegan J) where it was held that the Irish State could be liable for damage suffered as a result of non-implementation of a Community Directive on the basis of the tort of 'actionable breach of a directive'. Travers, 'The Liability of Local Authorities for Breaches of Community Directives by Member States' (1997) 22 ELRev. 173 at 176 has commented that this judgment demonstrates 'the general willingness of Irish courts fully to enforce rights conferred by Community law, without being unecessarily concerned about the precise mode of fitting an action based on an alleged breach of such rights within the format of subsisting national causes of action'.

[225] [1996] 2 CMLR 951.   [226] Ibid. at 963–6.

law because, while the departure from the procedure required by Directive 64/221[227] might be 'manifest', it could not be described as 'grave', as the protection afforded by the United Kingdom's procedure could well be thought to be effective.[228] Since the Court of Appeal concluded that there was no liability, the issue of the correct remedy in English law did not therefore arise.

Finally, it may be noted that the House of Lords has expressed the view that in proceedings for liability for breach of EC law against the UK, it is the Attorney-General who would be the appropriate defendant. In *R.* v. *Secretary of State for Employment, ex. p. Equal Opportunities Commission,*[229] the House of Lords refused in judicial review proceedings to grant a declaration that the Secretary of State was in breach of EC law by failing to abolish incompatible national provisions because 'if there is any individual who believes that he or she has a good claim to compensation under the *Francovich* principle, it is the Attorney General who would be the defendant in any proceedings directed to enforcing it'.[230] More recently, the Court of Appeal has held that an industrial tribunal could not entertain a claim for damages on the basis of the *Francovich* judgment.[231] The Court of Appeal held that 'a *Francovich* claim for damages can be pursued in the same way as any other claim for damages in the ordinary courts' which in effect means the High Court or the County Court.

The recent judgments of the ECJ concerning State liability have thus had a considerable impact on English law. The decision of the Divisional Court in *Factortame III* to allow applicants to plead a direct claim based on Community law as the basis for liability is to be welcomed since it dispenses with the requirement to fashion existing national law remedies to the vicissitudes of the ECJ conditions. The Divisional Court's judgment constitutes a full, detailed, and competent application of the developing homogenization of national remedies which is being developed by the ECJ. The Divisional Court in this case performed its duty as a 'Community Court' to the full and has, in this way, made a positive contribution to the developing *jus commune* as far as effective national remedies is concerned. Furthermore, the Divisional Court's judgment is all the more remarkable from the perspective of English law since the United Kingdom was held to

---

[227] Council Directive on the co-ordination of special measures concerning the movement and residence of foreign nationals which are justified on grounds of public policy, public security or public health: [1963–64] OJ Spec. Ed. 117.

[228] Ibid. at 966–8.

[229] [1994] 2 WLR 409; [1995] 1 CMLR 391 (HL). Noted by Moore (1994) ELRev. 425.

[230] [1995] 1 CMLR 391 at 406. This has recently been confirmed by the House of Lords in *R.* v. *Secretary of State for Employment, ex p. Seymour-Smith* [1997] 2 All ER 273, [1997] 2 CMLR 904.

[231] *Potter and Mann* v. *Secretary of State for Employment* [1997] IRLR 21 (CA).

be liable in spite of the fact that it was explicitly found that it acted in good faith.[232]

(C) State liability for breach of EC Law before the Dutch courts

In the Netherlands, the ordinary courts (civil courts) have jurisdiction in matters of tort law even when the alleged tort has been committed by a public body. In other words, public bodies are, under Dutch law, submitted to the same tortious regime as private persons. This is particularly important when it is alleged that an Act of Parliament is contrary to Community law since actions for annulment of a generally binding measure (*algemeen verbindend voorschrift*) cannot be brought before the administrative courts.[233] As a result, any case concerning legislation in breach of EC law must be brought before the civil courts.

Under the Dutch Civil Code (*Burgerlijk Wetboek*), the law of tort or an 'illicit act' (*onrechtmatige daad*)[234] comprises a strict regime. The conditions under which the State may be held liable for *onrechtmatige daad* are: unlawfulness (*onrechtmatigheid*), attributability (*toerekenbaarheid*), damage (*schade*), causation (*causaliteit*) and relativity (*relativiteit*). The *Hoge Raad* has long recognized that the Dutch State may be held liable for *onrechtmatige daad* as a result of the actions of the legislative organs. In the *Tweede Pocketboek-arrest*,[235] the *Hoge Raad* held that the provisions of a Royal Decree (*ministeriële regeling*)[236] were incompatible with the freedom of expression provided for in Article 7 of the Dutch Constitution and that 'the nature of the legislative function of government does not have the result that Article 1401 has no or only limited application to illicit use that function'.[237] In recent years, it has become clear that the Dutch State may be

---

[232] A note of caution needs to be sounded in that although the Divisional Court in *Factortame* (No. 3) held that the UK committed a sufficiently serious breach of EC law sufficient to give rise to liability, the question of causation was not addressed. However, the causation issue is unlikely to provide a difficulty since the Divisional Court held that all 3 of the conditions in the UK legislation (nationality, domicile, and residence) constituted a sufficiently serious breach of Community law.

[233] Art. 8.1.1.2 General Administrative Law Act (*Algemeen wet bestuursrecht*). See Bok, 'Het Francovich-arrest en onrechtmatige wetgeving naar Nederlands recht' (1993) Tijdschrift voor Privaatrecht 37 at 37–8.

[234] Art. 6:162 Civil Code. Under the previous Civil Code this same Art. was numbered Art. 1401. The new Civil Code took effect from 1 Jan. 1992. Some of the cases discussed in this section arose before that date, and both Art. numbers will therefore be used interchangeably henceforth.

[235] *Hoge Raad*, 24 Jan. 1969, NJ 1969, 316; AB 1969, 194, AA 1969, 266. See van der Does and de Wijkerslooth, *Onrechtmatige Overheidsdaad* (Kluwer, 1985) at 63.

[236] *In casu: Vestigingsbeschikking boekverkopersbedrijf* 1958.

[237] In the original Dutch: '*de aard van de wetgevende functie van de overheid niet meebrengt dat Article 1401 bij onrechtmatig gebruik daarvan niet of slechts beperkt van toepassing zou kunnen zijn*'. See also *Staat* v. *LSV*, *Hoge Raad*, 1 July 1983, NJ 1984, 360 (with note by Scheltema). In the *Landbouwvliegersarrest*, *Hoge Raad*, 16 May 1986, NJ 1987, 251; AB 1986, 574; Asser-Hartkamp

held liable for *onrechtmatige daad* even in the absence of 'fault'.[238] For example, in *Van Gelder Papier*,[239] the *Hoge Raad* held that an administrative decision (*in casu* the *Uitvoeringsbesluit verontreiniging rijkswateren*) was contrary to an Act of Parliament (*in casu*, *Wet verontreiniging oppervlaktewatern*) and that 'fault' on the part of the State could simply be assumed. In *Van Gog* v. *Nederweert*,[240] the *Hoge Raad* held that

If an organ of the State commits an illicit act by taking and maintaining a decision which is subsequently annulled by the courts for infringing an Act of Parliament . . . the fault of the organ of the State is thereby in principle established.

Even when the organ of the State is subject to no blame, it must be held that this illicit act is in principle—in the terminology of Article 6:162 BW—attributable to the organ of the State.[241]

With respect to the provisions concerning free movement of goods, the Dutch courts have held, even before the ECJ's judgment in *Francovich*,[242] that the State could be held liable for a breach of Article 30. In *Roussell Laboratoria BV* v. *Netherlands State*, the *Arrondissementsrechtbank* Den Haag referred certain questions to the ECJ concerning the compatibility with Article 30 EC of a governmental Decree relating to the Prices of Registered Medicines (*Prijzenbeschikking registergeneesmiddelen*),[243] authorizing competent Ministers to fix maximum prices for imported pharmaceuticals.[244] After the ECJ had handed down its judgment in that case to the effect that the Dutch provisions were indeed incompatible with Article 30,[245] the *Arrondissementsrechtbank* Den Haag held the Dutch State was liable for the damage suffered by the applicant because the Government 'could and must have understood that it was treading very tricky ground, from the point of view of Community law, when it enacted the contested Prices Decree' and that 'by enacting the Prices of Registered Medicines Decree 1982, the defendant quite consciously laid itself open to the chance that the

---

III (1994) nr. 290I, the *Hoge Raad* held that the substantive provisions of an Act of Parliament can be held incompatible with unwritten legal principles (*ongeschreven rechtsbeginselen*). See also *Harmonisatiewet*, *Hoge Raad*, 14 Apr. 1989, NJ 1989, 469 and discussion by Betlem, 'Onrechtmatige Wetgeving: Overheidsaansprakelijkheid voor Schending van EG-recht in het post-Francovich Tijdperk' (1996) Regelmaat 128 at 138.

[238] The requirement of 'fault' may be read into the 'attributability' condition for liability mentioned above.

[239] *Hoge Raad*, 9 May 1986, NJ 1987, 252; AB 1986, 429.

[240] *Hoge Raad*, 31 May 1991, NJ 1993, 112 (with note by Brunner).

[241] In the original Dutch: '*Indien een overheidslichaam een onrechtmatige daad pleegt door een beschikking te nemen en te handhaven die naderhand door de rechter wordt vernietigd wegens strijd met de wet . . . is daarmede de schuld van het overheidslichaam in beginsel gegeven . . . Zelfs wanneer het overheidslichaam geen enkel verwijt treft, moet worden aangenomen dat deze onrechtmatige daad in beginsel—in de terminologie van artikel 6:162 BW—voor rekening van het overheidslichaam komt.*' See also *Staat* v. *Hoffmann-La Roche*, *Hoge Raad*, 26 Sept. 1986, NJ 1987, 253; AB 1987, 79.

[242] Cases C–6 & 9/90, n. 9 above. [243] Stcrt. 1982, no. 107 p. 7.

[244] Pres. *Arrondissementsrechtbank* 's-Gravenhage, 14 July 1982, [1983] 2 CMLR 340.

[245] Case 181/82 [1983] ECR 3849.

Decree would be deemed to be illegal owing to its incompatibility with Community law'.[246] This judgment underlines the breadth of State liability according to Dutch law. The *Arrondissementsrechtbank* Den Haag took no account of the nature of the illegality or the seriousness of the breach in establishing liability. Indeed, it seems unlikely that one could say that the public authority in question knew, at the time of issuing the decision, that it was acting unlawfully given that the *Arrondissementsrechtbank* Den Haag itself felt the need to refer a question for the interpretation of the provisions of Dutch law to the ECJ and when the Advocate General had reached the opposite conclusion in the case before the ECJ, opining that the legislation in question did not breach Article 30.[247]

In another case involving the free movement of goods before the *Francovich* judgment, the *Hoge Raad* held that a ban on production of pigs 'swill' was justified for the protection of public health under Article 36 EC.[248] However, the *Hoge Raad* held that in spite of the fact that the administrative acts were valid, and were manifestly issued in the general interest, the Dutch State was liable to pay damages for having committed an *onrechtmatige daad* under Article 1401 BW since the ban caused a 'special damage' to a limited group of citizens who were disproportionately affected by it ('*in onevenredige mate in haar belangen getroffen*'). Dutch law thus clearly also recognizes no-fault State liability on the basis of risk and equality.

Not surprisingly, commentators have agreed that the ECJ's *Francovich* judgment did not cause undue difficulties for Dutch law on State liability.[249] Indeed, the *Francovich* judgment has been explicitly applied by the Dutch courts. In *Lubsen-Brandsma* v. *Staat and Gemeente Abcoude*,[250] the *Rechtbank* Utrecht very commendably held that Article 4(1) of Directive 79/7[251] had not been correctly implemented into Dutch law and that the

---

[246] *Arrondissementsrechtbank* 's-Gravenhage, 18 July 1984 (transcr. summarized by Green and Barav (1987) 6 YEL 55 at 64–5).

[247] See discussion by Green and Barav, n. 215 above at 65.

[248] *Leffers* v. *De Staat der Nederlanden (Minister van Landbouw en Visserij)*, Hoge Raad, 18 Jan. 1991, AB 1991, 241 (with note by van der Burg); AA 1991, 656 (With note by van Buuren); NJ 1992, 638 (with note by Brunner). See also Van Male, RegelMaat 1991, 105 & Polak, Publiek Domein 1991, 245. The *Hoge Raad* held that relevant Community legislation in this field did not constitute exhaustive harmonization and thus that recourse to Art. 36 was still possible.

[249] See Bok, 'Het Francovich-arrest en onrechtmatige wetgeving naar Nederlands recht' (1993) Tijdschrift voor Privaatrecht 37 at 51 & 56 where the Dutch provisions for *onrechtmatige daad* are decribed as a 'good vehicle' to implement the *Francovich* liability requirements. For a discussion of the *onrechtmatige daad* conditions for State liability in the context of a breach of Community law before the ECJ's *Francovich* judgment, see Dekker, 'Diagonale werking van Europese richtlijnen?' (1991) SEW 782.

[250] *Rechtbank* Utrecht, 25 Oct. 1995, Jurisprudentie Bestuursrecht 1995, 305 (with note by Lefevere), Rechtspraak Awb 1996, 24 (with note by De Lange), Rechtspraak Nemesis 1996, 610 (with note by Senden).

[251] Council Directive on the progressive implementation of the principle of equal treatment for men and women in matters of social security [1979] OJ L6/24.

three conditions which the ECJ had set out in *Francovich* were met and thus that the Dutch State and the Municipality (*Gemeente*) Abcoude were liable in damages. In *Shapiro* v. *Staat*[252] on the other hand, the *Rechtbank* Den Haag held that an incorrect implementation of Directive 84/466[253] did not give rise to liability because the provisions in question did not intend to confer rights on individuals. In *Acciardi* v. *Gemeente Amsterdam*[254] the *Rechtbank* Amsterdam held that the Municipality (*Gemeente*) was liable in damages to the applicant for *onrechtmatige daad* after an administrative decision taken by it had been annulled by the administrative courts for having been based upon an Act of Parliament which was contrary to Community law.[255] The *Rechtbank* Amsterdam furthermore held that the Municipality could pass the costs of this damage on to the Dutch State because the latter was responsible for introducing the legislation which bound the Municipality and which was contrary to Community law. It may be noted that in *Lubsen-Brandsma* the *Rechtbank* Utrecht held that, in addition to central government, the Municipality might also liable,[256] whereas in *Acciardi* the *Rechtbank* Amsterdam held that the Municipality was liable to the applicant, but that the Municipality could pass the costs of this damage on to the Dutch State.[257]

---

[252] *Rechtbank* Den Haag, 14 Feb. 1996, Rechtspraak Algemene wet bestuursrecht 1996, 90 (with note by De Lange).

[253] Directive laying down basic measures for the radiation protection of persons undergoing medical examination or treatment [1984] OJ L265/1. However, the claim was rejected solely on the basis of Dutch law.

[254] *Rechtbank* Amsterdam, 11 Sept. 1996, Jurisprudentie Bestuursrecht, 1996, 237. See discussion of this judgment by Claes, 'Aansprakelijkheid van de Staat wegens schending van het gemeenscapsrecht' Jurisprudentie Bestuursrecht 1996, 226.

[255] The case concerned the incompatibility of Art. 5 of the *Wet Inkomensvoorziening Oudere en Gedeeltelijke Arbeidsongeschikte Werkloze Werknemers* (*IOAW*) with Art. 68(2) of Reg. 1408/71 as established by the ECJ in Case C–66/92 *Acciardi* v. *Noord-Holland* [1993] ECR I–4567.

[256] The *Rechtbank* Utrecht held that '[a]s an organ of the State, the Municipality, like the State, is bound to apply national legislation in conformity with Treaties and Directives. The Municipality is an organ with a separate legal personality and therefore liable in addition to the State on the grounds of having breached Community law, on the same grounds and in the same manner as has been expounded above in relation to the State.' This point of the judgment has been criticized by Lefevre, n. 251 above at 1105, for not providing satisfactory reasons why this was the case and without making a reference to the ECJ pursuant to Art. 177 EC.

[257] See further on this point Claes, n. 254 above at 976–7 and Keus, 'De post-Francovich-arresten en het Nederlandse overheidsaansprakelijkheidsrecht' Aansprakelijkheid & Verzekering 1997, 1 at 7. See more generally Prechal, *Directives in European Community Law* (Clarendon Press, 1995), 338–9. The view of the *Rechtbank* Utrecht is certainly not untenable given that the ECJ has held in Joined Cases 227–30/85 *Commission* v. *Belgium* [1988] ECR 1 at para. 9 that 'Each Member State is free to delegate powers to its domestic authorities as it considers fit and to implement directives by means of measures adopted by regional or local authorities. That division of powers does not however release it from the obligation to ensure that the provisions of the directive are properly implemented in national law.'

Commentators are also agreed that the ECJ's more recent judgments, starting with *Brasserie du Pêcheur*,[258] connect equally well with Dutch law on State liability and *onrechtmatige daad* under the Civil Code in particular.[259] Indeed, the reduction in the importance of the notion of 'fault' for ascertaining liability in the ECJ's judgment in *Brasserie du Pêcheur*[260] is, as has been discussed, familiar to Dutch law. The impact of the *Brasserie du Pêcheur* judgment on the Dutch legal order is thus likely to be very small.[261] This is all the more so given that the Dutch regime for State liability is, in many respects, broader than the ECJ conditions for liability set out in *Brasserie du Pêcheur*. For example, as has been discussed, the Dutch State may be held liable even if an administrative decision is annulled by the courts according to an interpretation of the law which was not foreseeable by that State organ at that time of the decision. This may be contrasted with the less strict condition under Community law according to which the national court, in examining whether there is a 'sufficiently serious' breach of Community law, may take into consideration 'the clarity and precision of the rule breached, the measure of discretion left by that rule to the national or Community authorities, whether the infringement and the damage caused was intentional or involuntary'.[262] The fact that Dutch law on State liability is wider than the Community requirements does not give rise to difficulties since the *Brasserie du Pêcheur* conditions are only minimum conditions and the ECJ explicitly recognized in that judgment the possibility that a Member State may incur liability 'under less strict conditions on the basis of national law'.[263] In fact, it is submitted that, according to the non-discrimination principle, a Dutch court would be positively required to apply the wider Dutch conditions in cases where they are less strict than the *Brasserie du Pêcheur* conditions.

The fact that Dutch law on State liability is wider than the Community requirements is not, however, without its difficulties. Keus has argued that it is rather unsatisfactory that Community and Dutch law on State liability are on certain points so out of step with one another.[264] In particular,

---

[258] Cases C–46/93 & C–48/93, n. 9 above.

[259] See Mok, TVVS 1996, 124 and SEW 1996, 278 and Betlem, 'Onrechtmatige Wetgeving: Overheidsaansprakelijkheid voor Schending van EG-recht in het post-Francovich Tijdperk' (1996) Regelmaat 128 at 139.

[260] Cases C–46/93 & C–48/93, n. 9 above, at paras. 75–80 of judgt.

[261] Betlem, n. 259 above at 139 notes that the one area where *Brasserie du Pêcheur* may have an impact is in cases in which there is a breach of Community law by a judgment of a national court. The *Hoge Raad* has always limited the liability of the State arising from a breach by one of its courts (see Hartkamp (ed.), *Mr C. Asser's Handleiding tot de beoefening van het Nederlands Burgelijk recht: Verbintenissenrecht*, Deel III (Tjeenk Willink, 9th edn., 1994) nr. 290j–k). However, the ECJ in *Brasserie du Pêcheur* (in paras. 34 & 35 of judgt) has now explicitly opened the possibility of liability of the State in such circumstances.

[262] Cases C–46/93 & C–48/93, n. 9 above, at para. 56 of judgt.

[263] Ibid. at para. 66 of the judgt.

[264] Keus, n. 257 above at 6.

Keus points out that the discrepancies may lead to undesirable results in practice when, for example, a national administrative authority applies a Community measure and the Community measure is subsequently held to be unlawful. In such a case, it might be that the national administrative authority may be held liable whereas the Community institutions, under the less strict Community liability regime under Article 215 EC, incurs no liability. Indeed, Keus calls into question whether Dutch law on State liability should not be reconsidered in order to bring it more into line with the Community regime.[265] Claes[266] notes that there may be scope for such reconsideration since, as has already been discussed, that Dutch courts have held that 'If an organ of the State commits an illicit act by taking and maintaining a decision which is subsequently annulled by the courts for infringing an Act of Parliament . . . the fault of the organ of the State is thereby *in principle* established'.[267]

The use of the words 'in principle' may provide scope for the Dutch courts to gradually open up exceptions to the strict regime. Any exceptions, however, would have to be applicable in a non-discriminatory way so as to be equally applicable in purely internal cases concerning the liability of the Dutch State.

(D) Conclusions

On a practical level, the discussion in this section illustrates that, when such actions have been brought, damage suffered as a result of specific breaches by the State of the provisions concerning the free movement of goods have led to compensation. Only in the *Bourgoin*[268] case before the English Court of Appeal was compensation for a breach of Article 30 EC refused.[269] In all the other cases in which such actions were brought for compensation arising from a breach of the free-movement-of-goods provisions, damages were granted under national law, albeit on the basis of various national law criteria. This necessarily gives rise to the question of whether uniform Community-wide rules for State liability are really necessary for the enforcement of the provisions concerning free movement of goods.

---

[265] Keus, n. 257 above at at 8. Cf. Wissink, 'De Nederlandse rechter en overheidsaansprakelijkheid krachtens Francovich en Brasserie du Pêcheur' (1997) SEW 78 who argues that the stricter Dutch conditions for State liability should be maintained and integrated into the EC law requirements.

[266] n. 257 above at 977–8.   [267] *Van Gog*, n. 241 above. Emphasis added.

[268] n. 198 above.

[269] It may, however, be noted that even in that case, the applicants received compensation in the form of an out-of-court settlement from the UK. See Parliamentary notice of this at [1987] 1 CMLR 169.

It is submitted that the latter question must be answered in the affirmative for two reasons. Firstly, it is notable that the respective regimes for the liability of the State according to French, English, and Dutch law encompass extremely varied conditions. At one end of the spectrum, English law has only a limited view of State liability requiring malice or actual knowledge that an act is incompatible with EC law. At the other extreme, under Dutch law, liability for acts incompatible with EC law is independent of fault or of the fact that there was no knowledge of the incompatibility with EC law at the time of the act. Given this wide range, uniform Community conditions are clearly necessary. Secondly, it is submitted that it is likely that the recent ECJ case law will lead to an increased awareness amongst litigants of the possibility of bringing an action for damages to compensate harm suffered as a result of a breach of the rules on the free movement of goods by a Member State. Increased awareness coupled with the opening up of clear uniform conditions should have the effect of overriding any reluctance which individuals may have hitherto had in suing national governments for damages.

The case law considered in this section has shown that the national courts are prepared to amend or adapt national legal regimes on State liability to those of the Community. As a result, the ECJ has clearly set in motion the gradual development of a *jus commune* in the field of State liability. In view of the clear signs that the national regimes for State liability are under review and are converging as a result of Community developments, the ECJ's bold approach towards creating uniform Community-wide remedies seems therefore to have been vindicated. The signs are that the ECJ may rely upon the co-operation of the national courts; the essential ingredient to the success of the system developed by the ECJ.

11

Preliminary References to the ECJ under Article 177 EC

1 INTRODUCTION

The contribution of the procedure on preliminary rulings contained in Article 177 EC to the development of the Community's legal order is widely recognized and celebrated. Article 177 provides for a mechanism whereby the national courts may, in cases pending before them, refer questions on the interpretation of EC law to the ECJ for a ruling.[1] After the ECJ's preliminary ruling, the case then returns before the national court where the interpretation of EC law handed down by the ECJ is applied to the facts of the case. The corner-stone of the Article 177 procedure has always been co-operation between the ECJ and the national courts in order to ensure the uniform application of EC law throughout the Community.[2] Article 177 therefore functions as a means to achieve a horizontal dialogue between the Community courts rather than providing for a hierarchical appellate procedure. The success of the preliminary-rulings procedure is underlined by the fact that the majority of the most important principles of EC law have been developed by the ECJ in preliminary rulings given pursuant to Article 177. Indeed, the ECJ has itself recently stated that '[t]he development of the Community legal order is largely the result of co-

---

[1] Art. 177 EC provides: 'The Court of Justice shall have jurisdiction to give preliminary rulings concerning: (a) the interpretation of this Treaty; (b) the validity and interpretation of acts of the institutions of the Community and of the ECB; (c) the interpretation of the statutes of bodies established by an act of the Council, where those statutes so provide.

Where such a question is raised before any court or tribunal of a Member State, that court or tribunal may, if it considers that a decision on the question is necessary to enable it to give judgment, request the Court of Justice to give a ruling thereon.

Where any such question is raised in a case pending before a court or tribunal of a Member State against whose decisions there is no judicial remedy under national law, that court or tribunal shall bring the matter before the Court of Justice.'

[2] See Case 13/61 *Kledingverkoopbedrijf de Geus en Uitdenbogerd* v. *Bosch* [1962] ECR 45, [1961] CMLR 1; Case 166/73 *Rheinmühlen-Düsseldorf* v. *Einfuhr- und Vorratsstelle für Geteide und Futermittel* [1974] ECR 33, [1974] 1 CMLR 523; Case 244/80 *Foglio* v. *Novello* (No. 2) [1981] ECR 3045, [1982] 1 CMLR 585, & Case 338/85 *Pardini Fratelli* v. *Ministero del Commercio con l'Estero* [1988] ECR 2041. In Case 16/65 *Firma Schwarze* [1965] ECR 877, the ECJ held that the preliminary reference procedure constitutes 'a special field of judicial co-operation which requires the national courts and the Court of Justice, both keeping within their respective jurisdiction, and with the aim of ensuring that Community law is applied in a unified manner, to make direct and complementary contributions to the working out of a decision'.

operation between the Court of Justice of the European Communities and national courts'.[3]

Any work on the application of EC law before national courts would be incomplete without some analysis of the role of the preliminary-rulings procedure. The Article 177 preliminary-rulings procedure is of immense importance in the process towards full application of EC law by the national courts since it is the single most important mechanism for fostering co-operation between the ECJ and the national courts.[4] Throughout this work, one of the central questions has been whether or not the national courts are applying the substantive provisions of EC law correctly and in conformity with the interpretation of those provisions in the case law of the ECJ. In all cases in which the application of EC law by a national court has appeared to be unsatisfactory or questionable, the reflex reaction has inevitably been to ask whether that national court would have been better advised to have addressed a reference to the ECJ pursuant to Article 177 EC. However, an exhaustive analysis of the preliminary-rulings procedure is clearly beyond the scope of this work. Given the importance of Article 177 in litigation before the national courts, there is a wealth of excellent literature on this subject to which reference is made.[5] Furthermore, a complete evaluation of the exercise by the national courts of the discretion to refer questions to the ECJ pursuant to Article 177 EC is equally beyond the scope of this work. The discussion in this chapter is therefore not intended to provide a comprehensive study on the discretion enjoyed by national courts to refer questions to the ECJ. Rather, the salient issues that have arisen before these courts, primarily in free movement of goods cases, will be discussed.

---

[3] See para. 1 of the *Note for Guidance on References by National Courts for Preliminary Rulings*, Weekly Proceedings No. 31/96 (1997) 22 ELRev. 55.

[4] Jacqué and Weiler have commented that Art. 177 EC 'is the instrument of integration *par excellence*': 'On the Road to European Union—A New Judicial Architecture: An Agenda for the Intergovernmental Conference' at 187.

[5] See esp. Anderson, *References to the European Court*; Chevallier & Maidani, *Guide Pratique Article 177 CEE* (Office of Official Publications of the European Communities, 1982); Schermers, Timmermans, Kellermann & Stewart Watson (eds.), *Article 177 EEC: Experiences and Problems*; Andenas (ed.), *Article 177 References to the European Court: Policy and Practice*. See also Lenaerts, 'Form and Substance of the Preliminary Rulings Procedure' in Curtin & Heukels (eds.), *Institutional Dynamics of European Integration, Essays in Honour of Henry G. Schermers*, vol. II (Martinus Nijhoff Publishers, 1995), 355; Arnull, 'References to the ECJ'; idem, 'The Evolution of the Court's Jurisdiction under Article 177 EEC'; Beaumont & Campbell, 'Preliminary Rulings'; Jacobs, 'When to Refer to the European Court'; Lenz, 'Rôle et fonctionnement de la procédure de décision préjudicielle en droit communautaire' (1995) JCP Doctrine 3834.

2 MANDATORY REFERENCES: THE OBLIGATION ON NATIONAL COURTS OF LAST RESORT TO REFER QUESTIONS OF EC LAW TO THE ECJ AND THE *ACTE CLAIR* DOCTRINE

Article 177(3) EC provides that where a question of interpretation of EC law is raised in a case before a court of a Member State 'against whose decision there is no judicial remedy under national law, that court or tribunal *shall* bring the matter before the Court of Justice' (emphasis added). In other words, national courts at the top of the judicial hierarchy in a Member State have an obligation, rather than discretion, to refer questions to the ECJ. However, the mandatory nature of Article 177(3) has been diluted. In *Da Costa* v. *Nederlandse Belastingadministratie*[6] the ECJ held that when a question raised is 'materially identical with a question which has already been the subject of a preliminary ruling in a similar case', such a reference under Article 177(3) is not mandatory. More importantly, in *CILFIT* v. *Italian Ministry of Health*,[7] the ECJ accepted the *acte clair* doctrine according to which national courts within Article 177(3) do not have to make a reference under that provision if 'the correct application of Community law [is] so obvious as to leave no scope for any reasonable doubt as to the manner in which the question raised is to be resolved'.[8] The question for the national court to decide, when dealing with a case for which there is no further appeal within the national legal system, is whether the point of EC law is 'so obvious as to leave no scope for any reasonable doubt'. It may also be noted that in recent years, the ECJ has placed greater emphasis on the form of the reference as a condition of the admissibility of the questions. In particular, the ECJ has stressed that national courts should ensure that the reference is drafted as clearly and precisely as possible so that the factual and legal context is clear.[9]

The French courts have earned a reputation, especially in the early years of Community law, for displaying a reluctance to refer questions to the ECJ. Indeed, the *Conseil d'Etat* applied the *acte clair* doctrine to refrain from referring questions to the ECJ long before that doctrine had been explicitly

---

[6] Case 28–30/62 [1963] ECR 31, [1963] CMLR 224.

[7] Case 283/81 [1982] ECR 3415.

[8] See Rasmussen, 'The European Court's *Acte Clair* Strategy in *CILFIT*' (1984) 9 ELRev. 242 and ter Kuile, 'To Refer or not to Refer: About the Last Paragraph of Article 177 of the EC Treaty' in Curtin & Heukels (eds.), n. 5 above, 381.

[9] See Joined Cases C–320–322/90 *Telemarsicabruzzo* v. *Circostel* [1993] ECR I–393 (noted by Arnull (1994) 31 CMLRev. 377); C–378/93 *La Pyramide SARL* [1994] ECR I–3999; C–458/93 *Saddik* [1995] ECR I–511; & C–167/94 *Grau Gomiz* [1995] ECR I–1023. See also *Note for Guidance*, n. 3 above and Bergerès, 'La CJCE et la pertinence de la question préjudicielle' (1993) Dalloz Chr. 245; Hatzopoulos, 'De l'arret *Foglia-novello* à l'arret *TWD Textilwerke*, la jurisprudence de la Cour de Justice relative à la recevabilité des renvois prejudiciels' (1994) 3 RMUE 195; Bergerès, 'Vade-mecum de la question préjudicielle de l'article 177 du Traité CEE' Dalloz, 1994 Chr. 181; Barnard & Sharpston, 'The Changing Face of Article 177 References'.

accepted by the ECJ in *CILFIT*.[10] Indeed, this caricature has been confirmed in several judgments of the *Conseil d'Etat* concerning applications
of the provisions concerning free movement of goods.[11] However, the
Cour de Cassation was also quick to apply the *acte clair* doctrine[12] and has,
on occasion, done so when the interpretation of Articles 30 to 36 EC has
arguably not been 'so obvious as to leave no scope for any reasonable
doubt'.[13] The Dutch courts, on the other hand, enjoy a reputation for being
very willing to refer questions to the ECJ.[14] However, the *Hoge Raad* did

[10] See *Soc. des Pétroles Shell-Berre*, *Conseil d'Etat*, Ass, 19 June 1964, Rec. Lebon 1964, 344. For
a description of the application of the *acte clair* doctrine in France, see Lagrange, 'Cour de justice et tribunaux nationaux' Gaz. Pal. 1971, I 130 and Buffet-Tchakaloff, *La France devant la
Cour de justice des Communautes européennes* 98–105. See also Berr, 'L'insertion dans les procès
français du mécanisme européen des questions préjudicielles' JCP 1967, Doctr. no. 2060 &
Lesguillons, 'Les juges français et l'article 177' CDE 1968, 253. See also Haguenau,
*L'Application effective du droit communautaire en droit interne: Analyse comparative des problèmes
recontrés en droit français, anglais et allemand*, 146–51, who writes: '*S'il faut regretter que le Conseil
d'Etat ait parfois méconnu l'article 177, il convient de noter une évolution encourageante de la
jurisprudence*' (at 151).
[11] See, e.g., the application of Arts. 30 to 36 EC in *Syndicat national des importateurs français
en produits laitiers et avicoles et Decker*, *Conseil d'Etat*, 27 Jan. 1967, [1968] 1 CMLR 81; AJDA
1967, 284; Rec. Lebon 1967, 41; RTDE 1967, 402 where the refusal to make a reference to the
ECJ has been described as an abuse of Art. 177 by Isaac, *Droit Communautaire général* (Masson,
3rd. edn., 1992) at 293. For other examples where the *Conseil d'Etat* refrained from making a
reference to the ECJ when the interpretation of Arts. 30 to 36 EC was not 'so obvious', see
Ministre de la culture v. *Epoux Genty*, *Conseil d'Etat*, 7 Oct. 1987, Rec. Lebon 1987, 304; Dalloz
1988, Jur. 269; AJDA 1987, 768; *Les fils de Henri Ramel* v. *Ministre de l'interieur et Préfet de
l'Hérault*, *Conseil d'Etat*, 7 Dec. 1979, Dalloz 1980, Jur. 303; Rec. Lebon 1979, 456; JCP 1981, II
19500 and *Association des centres distributeurs Edouard Leclerc*, *Conseil d'Etat*, 8 Feb. 1985, Rec.
Lebon 1985, 26.
[12] See e.g., *Ministère public* v. *Denise Deroche*, *Cour de Cassation*, ch. crim., 29 June 1966,
[1967] 1 CMLR 351; Dalloz 1966, Jur. 596; Gaz. Pal. 1966, I Jur. p. 297. See notes by Lauwaars
(1966) CMLRev. 339 and Desmazières de Séchelles, 'Experiences and Problems in Applying
the Preliminary Proceedings of Article 177 of the Treaty of Rome, as seen by a French advocate' in Schermers *et al.*, n. 5 above at 153.
[13] See, e.g., *Bernard Cambournac* v. *Union départementale des associations familiales des Alpes-
de-Haute-Provence et CNDCA*, *Cour de Cassation*, ch. crim., 16 June 1983, [1984] 2 CMLR 556;
JCP 1983, II 20044 (with note by Decocq); Dalloz 1984, Jur. 43 (with note by Ryziger) and
Ministère public v. *Théo Rossi di Montalera*, *Cour de Cassation*, ch. crim., 16 June 1983, RTDE
1983, 468 (with note by Isaac); *Malagutti* v. *Ministère public*, *Cour de Cassation*, ch. crim., 8 Jan.
1985, Bull. Cass. Crim. 1985, no. 15 p. 38; Dalloz 1985, Jur. 586; *Ministère public* v. *Norbert
Desolière*, *Cour de Cassation*, ch. crim., 18 Oct. 1988, Bull. Cass. Crim. 1988, no. 352 p. 945; Gaz.
Pal. 1989, I Jur. 683 and *Bocquin*, *Cour de Cassation*, ch. crim., 14 Oct. 1992, Bull. Cass. Crim.
1992, no. 326 p. 899.
[14] For discussion of the application of Art. 177 EC in the Netherlands, see Meij, *Prejudiciële
Vragen van Nederlandse Rechters en Hun Gevolgen*; Korte, Kellermann, Levelt-Overmars &
Possen, *Primus Inter Pares: The European Court and National Courts* (1990 EUI Working Paper
in Law no. 90/6); ter Kuile, 'De Hoge Raad en de prejudiciële verwijzing' (1978) NJB 212;
Mok, 'Experiences of the Netherlands Courts in Applying the Preliminary Proceedings of
Article 177 EEC', and Duk, 'Some Remarks of a Dutch Advocate on the Preliminary
Procedure of Article 177 EEC', both in Schermers *et al.*, n. 5 above; Franx & Mok, 'Prejudiciële
beslissingen op grond van verdragen' in *De Hoge Raad der Nederlanden, 1938–1988: Een portret*
(WEJ Tjeenk Willink, 1988), 187–98 and Baas, 'The Netherlands in Face of its Community
Obligations 1984–1995' (1996) 33 CMLRev. 1197 at 1238.

manifest a degree of early reluctance to refer questions to the ECJ.[15] In cases concerning the free movement of goods, there have also been instances where it has been argued that the *Hoge Raad* would have been better advised to have made an Article 177 EC reference.[16] The highest Dutch administrative court, the *Raad van State*, has also, in cases concerning Articles 30 to 36 EC, not even considered the possibility of making an Article 177 reference to the ECJ when the point was far from *acte clair* and when the opposite interpretation of Community law was reached in the same case at the interim stage.[17] However, it appears that most Dutch courts display commendable caution before applying the *acte clair* doctrine. For example, in *Chemische Fabriek Brabant J. W. Voorbraak BV* v. *Landbouw, Natuurbeheer en Visserij (Min.)*,[18] the *CBB*, which is a court against the judgments of which there is no appeal, only invoked the *CIL-FIT*[19] doctrine after it had examined the applicable ECJ authority in the Dutch, French, and English language versions.

The practice of the United Kingdom's courts with respect to Article 177 has been criticized by myriad authors.[20] This may be in part because the higher English courts have attempted to lay down guidelines for the exercise of the discretion to refer questions to the ECJ for a preliminary ruling.[21] The most recent formulation of such guidelines was carried out by

---

[15] See for example, *KIM* v. *Sieverding*, Hoge Raad, 13 Jan. 1961, NJ 1961, 245; SEW 1961, 324 where the *Hoge Raad* has been been criticized for not making a reference to the ECJ by Franx and Mok, n. 14 above 192 and by Korte *et al.*, n. 14 above, 31. See also *Constructa Werke GmbH* v. *De Geus & Uitdenbogerd NV*, Hoge Raad, 10 Apr. 1964, NJ 1964, 439 where the *Hoge Raad* refused to make preliminary reference even though the Adv. Gen. considered the Court to be under an obligation to do so. See also; *Nederlandse Spoorwegen*, Hoge Raad, 24 May 1978, BNB 1978, 175 where the Adv. Gen. concluded that the point of Community law was *acte clair*, whereas the *Hoge Raad* made a reference to the ECJ which interpreted the Community law point to reach a conclusion which was the opposite to that reached by the Adv. Gen. before the *Hoge Raad* (see Franx & Mok, n. 14 above, 192).

[16] See e.g., *Officier van Justicie* v. *Makro Zelfbedieningsgroothandel Nuth CV*, Hoge Raad, 4 Nov. 1986, NJ 1987, 384; SEW 1990, 674 and *Openbaar Ministerie* v. *Autohandel- en sloperij J. R. BV*, Hoge Raad (Strafkamer), 16 May 1995, NJ 1995, 567; M & R 1995, 108.

[17] See *Eldim BV* v. *VROM, Raad van State (Afd. Geschillen van Bestuur)*, 17 Feb. 1993, AB 1993, 424 (with note by Drupsteen); M & R 1993, 303 (with note by Addink); SEW 1993, 618 (with note by Jans) and the judgment in interim proceedings by the President of that same court of 14 Jan. 1992, AB 1992, 455 (with note by Drupsteen); M & R 1992, 486 (with note by Addink).

[18] *CBB*, 13 Nov. 1992, AB 1993, 273 (with note by Van Veen); SEW 1994, 450 (with note by Temmink).

[19] Case C–283/81, n. 7 above.

[20] See, e.g., Arnull, 'Use and Abuse of Article 177'; Dashwood and Arnull, 'English Courts and Article 177 of the EEC Treaty', and Burnside, 'La mise en oeuvre de l'article 177 au Royaume-Uni' CDE 1985, 3. See also Golub, 'The Politics of Judicial Discretion: Rethinking the Interaction between National Courts and the European Court of Justice', who uses empirical evidence to show that the UK's courts have consistently referred fewer questions to the ECJ under Art. 177 than have the courts of other Member States.

[21] See the judgt of Lord Denning in *Bulmer* v. *Bollinger* [1974] 2 CMLR 91. See also, *HM Commissioners of Customs and Excise* v. *Samex* [1983] 3 CMLR 194; [1983] 1 All ER 1042. For the

Sir Thomas Bingham MR in *R.* v. *International Stock Exchange, ex. p. ELSE*,[22] under which

> if the facts have been found and the Community law issue is critical to the court's final decision the *appropriate course is ordinarily to refer* the issue to the Court of Justice unless the national court can with *complete confidence* resolve the issue itself.[23]

The presumption in this formulation is to 'ordinarily refer' and this formulation is now widely accepted and applied as the correct test when deciding whether to refer.[24] With respect to cases concerning the free movement of goods, the House of Lords has respected the obligation to refer under Article 177 (3) EC.[25] However, in a handful of cases, the House of Lords has, rather controversially, avoided making a reference to the ECJ by deciding the case on English law points alone, so that the case no longer turned upon the point of interpretation of Articles 30 to 36 EC.[26]

3 THE WISHES OF THE PARTIES

Since it is the national court itself, rather than the parties, which makes the reference to the ECJ under Article 177, the views of the parties should not, strictly speaking, be a consideration for the national court in exercising the discretion to refer.[27] However, common-law practice often takes account of the interests of the parties to litigation. Thus, in *R.* v. *Secretary of State for*

---

influence of *Bulmer* in Scotland, see *Prince* v. *Younger* [1988] 1 CMLR 723 & *Procurator Fiscal, Elgin* v. *Cowie* [1990] 3 CMLR 445. Lord Denning's guidelines were undoubtedly influential: see, e.g., *R.* v. *Henn and Darby* [1978] 3 All ER 1190; [1978] 2 CMLR 688; [1978] 1 WLR 1031 (CA); *British Leyland Motor Corporation* v. *Armstrong Patents* [1982] FSR 481; *R.* v. *Inner London Education Authority, ex p. Hinde* [1985] 1 CMLR 716 and *R.* v. *Her Majesty's Treasury, ex p. Daily Mail and General Trust Plc* [1987] 2 CMLR 1.

[22] [1993] 2 CMLR 677. See note by Walsh, 'The Appeal of an Article 177 EEC Referral'.

[23] Emphasis added.

[24] See *R.* v. *Secretary of State for the National Heritage, ex p. Continental Television BV* [1993] 2 CMLR 333; *R.* v. *Ministry of Agriculture, Fisheries and Food, ex p. Portman Agrochemical Ltd* [1994] 3 CMLR 18; *R.* v. *Coventry City Council, ex p. Phoenix Aviation; R.* v. *Dover Harbour Board, ex p. Peter Gilder & Sons; R.* v. *Associated British Ports, ex p. Plymouth City Council* [1995] 3 All ER 37; *R.* v. *HM Commissioners of Customs and Excise, ex p. EMU Tabac* [1995] 3 CMLR 267, [1997] EuLR 153; & *R.* v. *Ministry of Agriculture, Fisheries & Food, ex p. British Agrochemicals Association* (transcr. available on Lexis).

[25] However, see *R.* v. *London Boroughs' Transport Committee (LBTC), ex p. Freight Transport Association (FTA)* [1992] 1 CMLR 5; [1991] 3 All ER 915; [1991] 1 WLR 828 (HL). See criticism of the substance of this case at pp. 354–5.

[26] See *Wellcome Foundation Limited* v. *Secretary of State for Social Services* [1988] 3 CMLR 95; [1988] 2 All ER 684; [1988] 1 WLR 635 (HL) and *R.* v. *Licensing Authority, ex p. Smith Kline and French Laboratories* [1989] 2 CMLR 137; [1989] 2 WLR 397 (HL).

[27] See Case 93/78 *Mattheus* v. *Doego Fruchtimport und Tiefkühlkost* [1978] ECR 2203, [1979] 1 CMLR 551.

Social Services, ex. p. Schering Chemicals Ltd,[28] the fact that neither party wanted a reference to the ECJ to be made, was a factor which the Queen's Bench Division of the English High Court took into account in its decision not to refer.[29] On the other hand, in *Rochdale BC* v. *Stewart Anders*,[30] the High Court at first refused to make a reference on the compatibility of the English and Welsh Sunday-trading rules with Article 30 EC because other references were already pending before the ECJ. However, after the parties had objected to this refusal, the High Court made a reference to the ECJ 'by consent'. A short time later, in *Portsmouth CC* v. *Richards & Quietlynn*, Kerr LJ warned against national courts making 'references by consent' which he thought 'should not creep into our practice'.[31]

4 A COURT AGAINST WHOSE DECISIONS THERE IS NO JUDICIAL REMEDY UNDER NATIONAL LAW

In the United Kingdom context, this question has given rise to controversy given that an appeal to the House of Lords is not a right but rather something for which leave is required. This gives rise to difficulties since, if the Appeals Committee of the House of Lords refuses to give leave to appeal, the lower court in effect becomes the court against whose decisions there is no judicial remedy under national law. However, by that stage, the case is no longer pending before the lower court which is then *functus officio* such that an Article 177 reference can no longer be made.[32] The English Court of Appeal has, however, consistently taken the view in several cases concerning the free movement of goods that that it does not, even if it itself refuses leave to appeal to the House of Lords, fall within Article 177(3) EC.[33] The reason offered to justify this position is that the unsuccessful

---

[28] [1987] 1 CMLR 277 (per MacPherson J).

[29] See also *R.* v. *Bow Street Magistrates' Court and Martin Dubbey, ex p. Noncyp* [1988] 3 CMLR 84 (QBD) at 94, where Woolf LJ held that 'I should make it clear that neither party considered that an application under Article 177 of the Treaty would assist'.

[30] [1988] 3 CMLR 431; [1988] 3 All ER 490 (QBD).

[31] [1989] 1 CMLR 673 at 708 (CA).

[32] See *Chiron* v. *Murex Diagnostics* (No. 2 & No. 8) [1995] All ER (EC) 88 (CA) at 93–4. This is what, in effect, occured in *SA Magnavision NV* v. *General Optical Council* (No. 2) [1987] 2 CMLR 262 (QBD) in which a certificate that a particular point was a point of law of general public importance was necessary to lodge a petition for leave to appeal with the House of Lords, and where the Divisional Court refused to issue such a certificate. The European Commission has expressed the view that the High Court in this case denied the plaintiff the opportunity of having the question of EC law examined by a court of final instance which was bound by Art. 177(3) EC: [1988] C310/44. The judgment of the Divisional Court has also been criticized by Staughton LJ in *Chiron* v. *Murex Diagnostics*, above, at 96. See also the judgt of the Irish High Court in *McNamara* v. *An Bord Pleanala and the Council of the County of Kildare and others* [1997] EuLR 110 (per Barr J).

[33] See *R.* v. *Secretary of State for Social Security, ex p. Bomore Medical Supplies* [1986] 1 CMLR 228 (CA); *R.* v. *Pharmaceutical Society of Great Britain and Secretary of State for Social Services,*

party still has the right to petition the Appeals Committee of the House of Lords for leave to appeal. It is submitted that this position is contrary to Article 177(3) since the 'right' to appeal to the House of Lords in such circumstances constitutes a mere possibility that leave to appeal will be granted.[34]

5 LENGTH OF TIME REQUIRED FOR A PRELIMINARY REFERENCE

The fact that a reference to the ECJ for a preliminary ruling under Article 177 will take between eighteen and twenty months will often make such a reference an undesirable option, particularly when such delay will frustrate the purpose of the litigation. It seems that the length of time required for a reference influenced the *Tribunal de grande instance* of Roanne in *Régie nationale des usines Renault* v. *Roland Thévenoux, SpA Maxi-Car*[35] to refrain from making a reference. Similarly, in *R.* v. *Cousins*, the English Court of Appeal held that '[w]e do not refer a question to the European Court of Justice, as the answer is clear to us, and delay and uncertainty would be damaging to all'.[36] Similarly, the Chancery Division of the English High Court in *Wychavon District Council* v. *Midland Enterprises (Special Event) Ltd* held that it would not make a reference to the ECJ pursuant to Article 177 in that case because: 'I am satisfied that the defendants' real concern is to obtain a two year delay so that they may continue to trade in infringement of the criminal law and at very great profit to themselves in the hope that the answers to these theoretical questions can be long delayed'.[37] Before the Dutch *Raad van State* in *Van der Feesten* v. *Landbouw, Natuurbeheer en Visserij (Min.),*[38] it was controversially held that the protection of animals in Article 36 was capable of having extra-territorial application to justify prohibiting the import into the Netherlands from Denmark of two birds belonging to endangered species. The *Raad van State* held that 'although in the light of the European Court of Justice's case law there is possible doubt (*mogelijke twijfel*) as to the defendant's defence in this case, we nevertheless assume that the defendants are entitled to refuse the licence applied for on the grounds mentioned in Article 36 EEC'. The *Raad van State* nevertheless

ex p. Association of Pharmaceutical Importers [1987] 3 CMLR 951 at 969 (CA); *R.* v. *Southwark Crown Court, ex p. Watts* [1992] 1 CMLR 446 at 456 (CA) and *Smith Kline and French Labroratories Ltd's (Cimetidine) Patents* [1990] 1 CMLR 416 at 434 (CA).

[34] See criticisms of the English courts' view on this matter by Demetriou (1995) 20 ELRev. 628. See also Anderson, n. 5 above, 155–63.

[35] TGI Roanne, 29 Apr. 1986, [1988] 3 CMLR 686; JCP 1987, II 20787.

[36] [1995] 3 CMLR 220 at 230 (CA).   [37] [1988] 1 CMLR 397 at 409.

[38] Pres. *Raad van State (Afd. Rechtspraak)*, 14 Oct. 1992, M & R 1994, 24 (with note by Jans); AB 1994, 128. See also Addink *et al.* (eds.), *Europese milieurechtspraak, 104 nationale uitspraken met Europees milieurechterlijke aspecten,* 152 & 197.

proceeded to decline to make a reference to the ECJ since 'making a preliminary reference to the [ECJ]—given that the applicant wishes to import
the birds in question in the short term—offers, in the framework of that
procedure, no result'. In other words, the delay which would be involved
with an Article 177 reference would, on the facts of the case, have made the
reference superfluous. If the importer could not import the birds in question at that time, the possibility that he could import the birds into the
Netherlands eighteen months later would be of no benefit. We therefore
see here a clear example of a case in which a national court refused to make
an Article 177 reference explicitly on the grounds that the length of time
involved in such a reference would make the application of little purpose
in practice.[39]

Finally, it may be noted that by the time the ECJ had handed down its
judgment in *Smanor*,[40] the judgment of the ECJ in that case could not assist
the applicant since it had already been declared bankrupt.

These cases before the national courts confirm the existing calls for the
length of the preliminary-rulings procedure to be substantially reduced.[41]
If such a reduction in time is not addressed, there is the danger that
national courts will lose confidence in the ECJ's ability to give a useful
reply within a reasonable period of time.[42]

6 APPEALS AGAINST DECISIONS TO REFER

Appeals against decisions to refer (or decisions refusing to refer) questions
to the ECJ concerning the provisions on the free movement of goods have
been made before the French,[43] the Dutch,[44] and the English courts.[45]

---

[39] For a similar case before English courts where the national court similarly refrained
from referring questions to the ECJ because the delay would empty the question of commercial meaning, see *Ex p. Portman Agrochemicals Ltd*.

[40] Case 298/87 [1988] ECR 4489.

[41] See, e.g., the Report of the British Institute of International and Comparative Law, *The
Role and Future of the European Court of Justice*, 1996 at 68–9 where it is suggested that the preliminary-rulings procedure should be reduced to not more than 12 months in the more
straightforward cases.

[42] Koopmans has commented that 'the system of Article 177 is ultimately based on confidence; it cannot work well if national courts lose their faith in the Court's capacity to give a
speedy reply' ('The Future of the Court of Justice of the European Communities' at 18).

[43] See, e.g. the referral to the ECJ in *Rosello* v. *Sodivar*, *TGI* Fontainebleau (*Référés*), 11 July
1983, Gaz. Pal. 1984, I Jur. 47 which was withdrawn on appeal to the *Cour d'appel* Paris, 14e
ch. A, 2 Nov. 1983, Gaz. Pal. 1984, I Jur. 47.

[44] See, e.g., appeal in *Pharmon* v. *Hoechst* from *Gerechtshof*'s-Gravenhage, 3e kamer, 3 Mar.
1982, RvdW 1984, no. 28; BIE 1986, 176; NJ 1986, 455 to the *Hoge Raad*, 1e kamer, 13 Jan. 1984,
RvdW 1984, no. 28; BIE 1986, 176; NJ 1986, 455.

[45] See, e.g., *R.* v. *International Stock Exchange, ex p. ELSE* [1993] 2 CMLR 677. In *Bulmer* v.
Bollinger [1974] 2 CMLR 91 at 125 it was stated (per Stamp LJ) that the CA would not not interfere with lower courts' discretion unless it was 'plainly wrong'.

However, the Irish Supreme Court has held that such appeals are not possible since, 'It is a matter of Irish law that Article 177 confers upon an Irish judge an unfettered discretion to make a preliminary reference to the European Court of Justice . . . [T]o fetter that right by making it subject to review on appeal would be contrary both to the spirit and letter of Article 177'.[46]

However, contrary to the vision of the Irish Supreme Court, the ECJ has always held that the application of national appeal procedures to decisions to refer is perfectly compatible with Article 177 EC.[47]

7 REPEAT REFERENCES

It may be noted that the French courts have in the past demonstrated a propensity to refer questions to the ECJ which are simply repeat references of questions which had been referred to the ECJ by other French courts. In the context of the petrol-pricing legislation in France, after the *Tribunal Commercial* of Toulouse had referred questions on the compatibility of this legislation with Articles 30 to 36 EC in *Cullet* v. *Centre Leclerc*,[48] there followed no less than nine further references from other French courts on precisely the same point.[49] It is submitted that such repeat references are easily avoided by better co-ordination within the national system, and are an unnecessary waste of ECJ resources, even if the ECJ is able to simply repeat its earlier ruling.

8 CONCLUSIONS

This chapter offers only a brief overview of the national court perspective in decisions to refer questions to the ECJ. The success of the Article 177

[46] *Campus Oil* v. *Minister for Industry and Energy* [1983] Irish Rep. 82 [1984] 1 CMLR 479.

[47] See Case 13/61 *Kledingverkoopbedrijf de Geus en Uitdenbogerd* v. *Bosch* [1962] ECR 45, [1961] CMLR 1 & Case 166/73 *Rheinmühlen-Düsseldorf* v. *Einfuhr- und Vorratsstelle für Geteide und Futermittel* [1974] ECR 33, [1974] 1 CMLR 523. See criticism of this position by O'Keeffe, 'Appeals Against an Order to Refer under Article 177' (1984) 9 ELRev. 87.

[48] Case 231/83 [1985] ECR 305; [1985] 2 CMLR 524.

[49] See references from: the *Cour d'Appel* Rennes, ch. corr., 13 June 1984 in *Ministère public* v. *Binet* (Case 149/84 [1985] ECR 2969); the *TGI* Briey, 14 Dec. 1983 in *Ministère public* v. *Gratiot* (Case 11/84 [1985] ECR 2907); the Trib. corr. Nanterre, 16 Dec. 1983 in *Ministère public* v. *Leclerc* (Case 34/84 [1985] ECR 2915); the *TGI* Verdun, 9 Mar. 1984 in *Ministère public* v. *Chabaud* (Case 79 & 80/84 [1985] ECR 2953); the Trib. comm. of Melun, 12 Mar. 1984, *Piszko* v. *SA Carrefour supermarché* (Case 114 & 115/84 [1985] ECR 2961); the *TGI* Orléans, ch. corr., 27 June 1984 in *Ministère public* v. *Gontier* (Case 201/84 [1985] ECR 2977); the *TGI* Versailles, ch. corr., 6 July 1984 in *Ministère public* v. *Héricotte* (Case 215/84 [1985] ECR 2993); the *TGI* Avignon, ch. corr., 26 July 1984 in *Ministère public* v. *Girault* (Case 202/84 [1985] ECR 2985); & the *TGI* La Roche-sur-Yon, ch. corr., 8 Oct. 1984 in *Ministère public* v. *Chiron* (Cases 271–274/84 and 6 & 7/85 [1986] ECR 529.

preliminary-rulings procedure is not disputed. However, in order that the co-operation which, as has been noted, is the corner-stone of this most important procedure, may be maintained, it is crucial that the length of time taken over preliminary rulings is reduced. The discussion in this chapter has brought attention to a number of clear instances when important points concerning the provisions on the free movement of goods have not been referred to the ECJ because the delay would empty the proceedings of commercial meaning. This is a potential threat to the uniform application of EC law and to the spirit of co-operation between the ECJ and the national courts.

From the national courts' perspective, a number of instances have also been highlighted in which it is arguable that an incorrect, or at least far from clear, interpretation of EC law was given without making a reference to the ECJ. This is all the more serious when it constitutes a breach of Article 177(3) EC. However, but for a few minor points, there is no sign that the Article 177 preliminary-rulings procedure is not functioning properly. Indeed it is submitted that, in the long term, Article 177 references should be the exception rather than the rule.[50]

---

[50] Tesauro has written that 'the national court is the natural forum for Community law, which it can and normally does apply; and it is right and proper that preliminary rulings should be sought from the Court of Justice only in exceptional cases, both because national proceedings are thereby considerably protracted, and because, at the present stage, Community law should by now be seen as a routine component of the rules applicable to everyday litigation, rather than an exotic excrescence upon the national legal order.' ('The Effectiveness of Judicial Protection and Co-operation between the Court of Justice and the National Courts' at 17). However, he goes on to add the caveat that this should not be at the cost of the spirit of co-operation between the ECJ and the national courts.

12

Conclusion

1 INTRODUCTION

As was noted at the outset, the decentralized system for the application and enforcement of EC law has the result that the national courts are the natural forum for the application of EC law. The volume of national case law applying the EC Treaty's free-movement-of-goods provisions confirms that the national judge is indeed the *'juge communautaire de droit commun'*. This is by no means a new awakening. The pivotal role played by the national courts, as the ordinary courts for the day-to-day application of substantive EC law, has become increasingly apparent in recent years.[1] The correct and loyal application of substantive EC law by the national courts is all to often presumed with little verification as to whether this is actually the case in practice. Thus, the central question to which the examination of the application of the provisions on the free movement of goods before the national courts gives rise is, whether the decentralized structure for the application of EC law is functioning satisfactorily. In more blunt terms, can the national courts be trusted to apply substantive EC law correctly? A further question which the study of national case law raises, is the extent to which the approach of the ECJ *itself* should be adapted to take into account problems of application of its own case law before national courts. The conclusions in this chapter will thus be centred around two points: firstly, the question of how the approach of the ECJ in interpreting Articles 30 to 36 EC should be altered in order to take into account the problems of application of the current case law before the national courts, and secondly, the question of whether the national courts may be trusted to apply EC law correctly.

---

[1] Maher has described the national courts as the 'judicial foot soldiers in the enforcement of EC law': Maher, 'National Courts as European Community Courts' 242. Barav has observed that '[n]ational courts are endowed with both prominence and omnipotence' 'Omnipotent Courts' in Curtin & Heukels (eds.), *Institutional Dynamics of European Integration, Essays in Honour of Henry G. Schermers*, 266.

1 HOW SHOULD THE APPROACH OF THE ECJ IN INTERPRETING THE PROVISIONS CONCERNING THE FREE MOVEMENT OF GOODS BE ALTERED IN ORDER TO TAKE INTO ACCOUNT THE PROBLEMS OF APPLICATION OF ITS CURRENT CASE LAW BEFORE THE NATIONAL COURTS?

The first point which emerges from the discussion in this work is that the national courts do not, perhaps understandably, seem to share the ECJ's emphasis on the need to interpret Article 30, as a basic freedom under the Treaty, as broadly as possible. While the national courts show no signs of dismissing the fundamental importance of the provisions on the free movement of goods, they are nevertheless very much more sober in their approach. For the national courts, Article 30 is a complex and at times technical legal provision which requires workmanlike application rather than expressions of expansive principle. As has been shown, the ECJ has until recently always advocated an extremely broad scope for Article 30 EC according to which any national rule that can be linked, even potentially, to an effect on trade is caught by Article 30 and subject to justification. While the striking breadth of the interpretation of Article 30 in the *Dassonville* formula[2] undoubtedly made a vital contribution to the elimination of barriers to trade, and consequently to achieving a truly integrated internal market, the experience of national courts in applying this approach has, however, given rise to difficulties. The discussion of national case law clearly illustrates that these courts have the expectation that Article 30 should have some limit of common sense. An unduly wide interpretation of Article 30 does not always conform to those expectations in the practical application of Article 30. As has been pointed out, this is important for two reasons. Firstly, the healthy development of EC law relies heavily on the co-operation of the national courts and thus the views of these courts should not be cast aside without careful consideration. Secondly, in view of the work load of the ECJ, it is desirable that the national courts be equipped with the 'tools' to weed out those cases where the integrationist merit is negligible. The requisite 'tool' to satisfy the two latter points is a clear body of case law on the scope of Article 30 for the national courts to apply. Before the landmark judgment of the ECJ in *Keck and Mithouard*,[3] such 'tools' were missing as ECJ case law reached the point of damaging inconsistency. National case law demonstrates that the practical effect of the inconsistent ECJ case law on the outer limits of Article 30 was to tie the hands of the national courts. This led to the damaging position in which legal certainty was reduced to nil and to the intol-

---

[2] Case 8/74 *Procureur du Roi* v. *Dassonville* [1974] ECR 837.
[3] Cases C–267 & 268/91 *Keck and Mithouard* [1993] ECR I–6097.

erably difficult circumstance in which reliance on one line of ECJ authority did not allow the national courts to satisfactorily distinguish the
authorities pointing in the opposite direction. It is clear that the national
courts were, pre-*Keck*, experiencing sufficiently serious difficulties in
locating the outer margins of Article 30 to merit a drastic reconsideration
by the ECJ of its case law. That something had to be done to clarify the
outer limits of Article 30 seems unchallengeable.

A further difficulty in the application of Article 30 before the national
courts has arisen from the fact that the ECJ has always rejected a *de minimis* principle for Article 30 and held that even a *potential* effect on the volume of imports was enough for Article 30 to bite. Such a position has led
to concern in the national courts in cases where no hindrance to inter-State
trade could be discerned. Some national courts have solved this problem
by simply ignoring the ECJ's rejection of a *de minimis* test. Others have
done so implicitly by requiring a 'restrictive effect', a 'disadvantage' or a
'clog' on the free movement of goods before they have found a breach of
Article 30. The conclusion is that the time seems ripe for the ECJ to reconsider its rejection of a role for a *de minimis* test in the light of the fact that
the national courts are *de facto* applying such a test by requiring a hindrance to trade before Article 30 will be held to apply.

The judgment of the ECJ in *Keck and Mithouard* represented an important
attempt by the ECJ to clarify the inconsistencies of its case law on the scope
of Article 30. From the point of view of legal certainty the rule-based
approach in *Keck*, under which non-discriminatory national 'selling
arrangements' fall outside the scope of Article 30, is an improvement.
Although the judgment in *Keck* may rightly be criticized for not making
clear which of its previous case law it was overruling, the ECJ has, in cases
subsequent to *Keck*, somewhat clarified the scope of that ruling by applying the *Keck* departure on a pragmatic case-by-case basis. Perhaps the
biggest advantage of the *Keck* approach from the national courts' perspective is that they can now avoid the difficult questions of justification
which, because of their subjectivity, have proved to be difficult to apply in
practice. These 'benefits' have, however, yet to filter through to the
national courts. The application of the *Keck* ruling before the national
courts to date has not been satisfactory. Rather, that judgment has been
applied by the national courts in a general fashion to exclude the application of Article 30. The national court judgments applying *Keck* to date,
therefore, confirm more the dangers than the advantages of that ruling. It
remains to be seen whether the national courts will reap the benefits of a
more consistent case law on the limits of Article 30 in the future.

With respect to the application of Article 30 more specifically, it has been
noted that the ECJ has not always maintained a rigorous distinction in
its Article 30 case law between 'quantitative restrictions' and 'measures

having equivalent effect'. This is usually of little consequence since both types of measure are in any event prohibited by Article 30. However, it was noted that the loose distinction between these two terms can lead to abuse before national courts which have, on occasion, analysed national measures as quantitative restrictions to the exclusion of measures having equivalent effect. A more tightly defined concept of quantitative restrictions can only reduce the possibility of such abuse. Similarly, the reference to 'trading rules' in the *Dassonville* formula of measures having equivalent effect has been rather liberally interpreted by the ECJ in subsequent cases. It was also noted that the term 'trading rules' has often been neglected and even omitted by the ECJ in subsequent judgments. The experience of national courts in applying Article 30 suggests that the ECJ should either abandon the reference to 'trading rules' altogether or at least define the meaning of the term more tightly. The reason for this is that the loose application of this term by the ECJ has opened up the possibility for abuse by the national courts. Thus, we have seen national courts, for example, excluding the application of Article 30 to national Sunday-trading legislation on the grounds that such legislation does not constitute a 'trading rule' within the *Dassonville* formula.[4] Such abuse could be avoided if the ECJ clarified the reference to 'trading rules'. Finally, the issue of whether Article 30 can impose obligations on individuals has never been conclusively settled by the ECJ. The reference to rules 'enacted by Member States' in the *Dassonville* formula strongly suggest that they cannot. The discussion of the case law of the judicial body the Dutch Advertising Standards Commission (*Stichting Nederlandse Reclame Code*) in particular (as to the application of Article 30 to advertising rules of self-regulation) demonstrates that more clarity on this question from the ECJ would indeed be desirable.

The interpretation by the ECJ of Article 34 relating to export restrictions has been characterized as rather eccentric since the ECJ has diverged from its interpretation of Article 30 by requiring discrimination before Article 34 will be applicable. The doctrinal underpinnings of such a divergence in the interpretation of two identically-worded Treaty Articles remains unexplained. Faced with this doctrinally difficult and at times illogical ECJ case law interpreting Article 34, the national courts could almost be forgiven for expressing confusion. Indeed, the national courts have described the interpretation of Article 34 by the ECJ in the *Groenveld* case[5] as 'decid-

---

[4] See discussion of the judgment of Peterborough Crown Court in *W. H. Smith Do-It-All and Payless DIY Ltd* v. *Peterborough City Council*, quoted in the judgment on appeal of the QBD of the High Court: [1990] 2 CMLR 577 and other judgments by national courts discussed in Ch. 2, sect. 4 (A).

[5] Case 15/79 *Groenveld* v. *Produktschap voor Vee en Vlees* [1979] ECR 3409; [1981] 1 CMLR 207.

edly unclear'.[6] In particular, they have found the application of *Groenveld* to export bans, and thus distinctly applicable measures, ambiguous. If it is the case that *Groenveld* does not apply in the latter case, it is unclear which interpretation does apply. Is it simply to be the *Dassonville* formula that applies in such circumstances? The experience of national courts in applying Article 34 thus suggests that the ECJ case law is in need of clarification. Pressure for reconsideration is also exerted by reason of the fact that the ECJ's interpretation of Article 34 has inevitably meant that reverse discrimination against national products cannot be prohibited by EC law since if non-discriminatory national restrictions on sale could be challenged by a national producer and potential exporter, the ECJ's interpretation of Article 34 would be rendered nugatory. The application of the ECJ's refusal to prohibit reverse discrimination has given rise to considerable difficulties before the national courts. In particular, the national courts have had difficulty in ascertaining whether national legislation, which has been found by the ECJ to infringe Articles 30 or 34, is still applicable to purely internal undertakings operating within that national territory. In practice, the line between purely national measures and measures which have a nexus with either importation or exportation is a difficult one to draw. This difficulty becomes even more apparent as national markets integrate further into a mature internal market. Furthermore, the refusal to prohibit reverse discrimination can give rise to inequality as an importer is treated more favourably under EC law than the domestic producer (and potential exporter) since a non-discriminatory national restriction on sale may be challenged by an importer (for example, because it has the effect of reducing the volume of imports in breach of Article 30 and cannot be justified under either the 'rule of reason' or Article 36) but not by a national producer. The French courts have on occasion concluded, sometimes explicitly contrary to ECJ judgments, that to allow such a distortion of competition would be illogical in a genuine common market and have drawn primarily on Article 3(g) EC to support the conclusion that EC law prohibited reverse discrimination. Such open challenges to the ECJ's case law by the national courts cannot be condoned. Nevertheless, it is submitted that the ECJ case law on Article 34 and the related absence of a prohibition on reverse discrimination is in need of reconsideration.

With respect to justifications for restrictions to the free movement of goods based on either the rule of reason or Article 36, the question which arises is whether it would be desirable, in order to ensure the uniform application of justifications for restrictions, for the ECJ to develop definitions of the concepts provided for in Article 36 or recognized under the rule of reason which would apply throughout the Community. The

---

[6] R. v. *Minister of Agriculture, Fisheries and Food, ex p. Roberts* [1991] 1 CMLR 555.

discussion of the application before the national courts of the heads of justification provided for in Article 36 in particular has demonstrated that in some of the categories mentioned in Article 36, a Community-wide definition is indeed essential. For example, the development of a Community-wide definition of 'national treasures' seems indispensable. However, in other fields, such as the protection of public health, it seems that the present approach of leaving the level of protection of public health, in the absence of harmonization, to the Member States (subject to the proportionality test) is a sensible one.

At the heart of application by national courts of justifications for restrictions to the free movement of goods is the application of the proportionality test. The application of this test is not an easy one and often puts national courts into difficult and sensitive positions. Consequently, the application of the proportionality principle has undoubtedly presented the national courts with difficulties. The discussion has shown that national courts have encountered difficulties in locating the 'objective' of national legislation which often represents a compromise between several highly charged political and social interests. Furthermore, the two-stage application of the proportionality test often gives rise to a conflict between the two limbs of the test. In particular, it has been shown that a conflict arises in cases concerning national measures for which the restrictive effect on inter-State trade is very small (thus satisfying the 'balancing' limb of the proportionality test) but for which there is no necessity because there are alternate means of achieving the objective in question (thereby failing the 'necessity test'). As has been shown, the problem with applying the proportionality test to such legislation is that a national court is obliged to examine the necessity of national regulatory measures whose effect on trade is so small as to be proportionate under the 'balancing' stage of the test. The judgments of national courts demonstrate that it is frequently only by giving dominance to the balancing limb of the proportionality test that it is possible to conclude easily that national regulatory provisions are proportionate. Given that it is the application of the proportionality principle that gives rise to the greatest difficulties before the national courts, it is imperative that the ECJ should be clearer in its guidance to the national courts as to how they should interpret and apply the proportionality principle in individual cases. It is submitted that the ECJ could do this by indicating to the national court which limb of the proportionality test should be given precedence in individual cases.

The balance of poor applications of the proportionality test by the national courts gives rise to the question as to whether it would be desirable for the ECJ to be encouraged to decide the proportionality of justifications raised to the facts of the cases referred to it. It has been noted that the ECJ has been somewhat erratic by deciding in some cases the proportionality of rule-of-reason justifications itself (and thus arguably overstepping its competence under Article 177 EC) while leaving it to the national court in others. When the ECJ decides the proportionality issue itself, the task of the national court in implementing the judgment is certainly made easier as it is very often left with little else to do than to rubber-stamp the judgment of the ECJ. Furthermore, if the ECJ itself applies the proportionality test to the facts, uniformity of application in the national courts is ensured. However, it is submitted that the discussion of the national-court experience in applying the justifications in both the rule of reason and Article 36 exposes serious dangers in cases in which the ECJ steps in to decide the proportionality issue itself rather than leaving it to the national court. One of these dangers arises from the fact that the ECJ's findings with respect to proportionality are necessarily of a generalized nature. As such, the dynamic application of the proportionality principle by the national courts on a case-by-case basis is precluded. This is all the more difficult when a finding of proportionality by the ECJ with respect to the legislation of one Member State is followed by a national court in another Member State. Further, the ECJ has neither the fact-finding capacity of the national courts nor the final word on the nuances of the national provisions involved. As a result, the ECJ's assessment of the facts often lacks subtlety,[7] is flawed,[8] and is liable to be too literally applied.[9] The national-court experience also demonstrates that the latter courts are undoubtedly much better placed to carry out an analysis of the facts in a dynamic fashion as opposed to the more generalized or 'broad brush' approach to which the ECJ is limited.[10] The conclusion is thus very firmly that the ECJ should not, under the present regime under Article 177 EC, be encouraged to decide the proportionality justifications raised to the facts of the cases referred to it.

The approach adopted by the ECJ in reconciling the free movement of goods in the EC with the existence of national intellectual property rights recognized in Article 36, is not based on the strongest of theoretical foundations. Nevertheless, it has been noted that the ECJ has developed a commendable body of case law which has proved to be both durable and flexible. In particular, the doctrine of 'exhaustion of rights' and the concept of 'consent' provide a simple rule of thumb for the national courts to apply. Consequently the ECJ case law, although based on shaky theoretical foundations, has the merit of having provided the national courts with

---

[7] See, e.g., discussion of the *Oosthoek* case at p. 192.

[8] See, e.g., discussion of ECJ case law interpreting the 'public morality' head of justification in Art. 36 in Ch. 7, sect. 2.

[9] See, e.g. the discussion of the 'public health' head of justification in Art. 36 in Ch. 7, sect. 4.

[10] See, e.g., discussion of the ECJ's judgments in Case 25/88 *Wurmser* [1989] ECR 1105, [1991] 1 CMLR 173 & Case 27/80 *Fietje* [1980] ECR 3839 at pp. 193–5.

practical and realistic tests to apply when faced with a conflict between the free movement of goods and national intellectual property rights. The pattern which emerges from judgments given by national courts and concerning intellectual property rights is that the application of the principles developed by the ECJ is being carried out in an accurate, straightforward, and competent fashion.

Remedies for breach of the provisions concerning the free movement of goods before the national courts is of fundamental importance. In particular, interim relief and damages against the State are crucial to effective judicial protection before the national courts. With respect to interim relief, it has been shown that, so long as the validity of a Community measure itself is not at issue, the ECJ is happy, subject to the usual provisos, for the national courts to apply national law criteria for the grant of interim relief in cases in which the compatibility of national provisions with Community law is at issue. As has been stated, this is in accordance with the principle of procedural autonomy and is based on the assumption that national procedures for granting interim relief are likely to be adequate. However, the discussion of the judgments of national courts applying the free-movement-of-goods provisions at the interim stage demonstrate that the latter assumption is misconceived. In particular, the position of the *juge des référés* in France has yet to adapt fully to the requirements of Community law. Furthermore, the various national regimes place varying degrees of presumption in interim proceedings on the validity of national law. It is clear that effective and uniform judicial protection would benefit from the development of criteria at Community level on the exercise by national courts of the discretion to grant interim relief. This would also solve the current anomaly according to which the ECJ in *Zuckerfabriek*[11] showed that it was prepared to set strict conditions within which national courts may grant interim relief where the invalidity of Community legislation is at issue, whereas the conditions applicable for the grant of interim relief by national courts where the compatibility of national provisions with Community law are at issue is left to national law. In the field of State liability on the other hand, the ECJ has begun the process towards developing uniform Community-wide rules. This is to be welcomed since the respective regimes for the liability of the State according to French, English, and Dutch law encompass extremely varied conditions. Furthermore, it is submitted that it is likely that recent ECJ case law will lead to an increased awareness amongst litigants as to the possibilities of bringing an action for damages to compensate harm suffered as a result of a breach of the rules on the free movement of goods by a Member State. Increased awareness coupled with the opening up of clear uniform condi-

[11] Cases C–143/88 & C–92/89 *Zuckerfabriek Süderdithmarschen* v. *Hauptzollamt Itzehoe* [1991] ECR I–415.

tions should have the effect of overriding any reluctance which individuals may have hitherto had in suing national governments.

3 CAN NATIONAL COURTS BE TRUSTED TO APPLY EC LAW CORRECTLY?

As was noted above, the correct and loyal application of substantive EC law by the national courts is all too often presumed with little verification as to whether this is actually the case in practice. The analysis in this work thus provides interesting insights into whether the decentralized structure for the application of EC law is functioning satisfactorily. In many respects, the answer to this question is an issue of confidence. In other words, does the experience of the national courts in applying the provisions on the free movement of goods give rise to confidence, or rather, to dismay? The discussion of this issue which follows will begin by centring around four points of concern. Firstly, those judgments before the national courts which display a hostility towards the application of EC law by handing down poor applications of Articles 30 to 36 EC. Secondly, attention will be focused on instances where the decentralized structure for the application of EC law before the national courts has led to irreconcilable judgments handed down by different courts in the Member States. Thirdly, the possibility and danger of the emergence of national precedents misapplying EC law will be discussed. Fourthly, attention will be devoted to the constitutional position of national judges in the application of EC law.

(A) Open hostility and poor applications of Articles 30 to 36 EC by the national courts

With respect to poor applications of Articles 30 to 36 EC, there are two overriding points which emerge from the national court experience to date. Firstly, prior to the ECJ departure in *Keck and Mithouard*,[12] the single most striking 'error' which the national courts made in applying Article 30 was to assume, contrary to the ECJ's *Cassis de Dijon* case law, that a national measure which applies equally to national products as it does to imports, is not capable of breaching Article 30. Time after time, national courts expressly stated that the indistinctly applicable nature of a particular national measure precluded the application of Article 30.[13] Since one of

---

[12] Cases C–267 & 268/91, n. 3 above.
[13] This view was expressed by the national courts primarily, though by no means exclusively, in cases concerning national restrictions on the time and place where goods may be sold and national rules restricting the advertising and promotion of products. The judgment

the most fundamental and long-standing principles of the ECJ's interpretation of Article 30 has been that that Article is capable of prohibiting national measures which apply indistinctly to national products as they do to imports, the views of the national courts in this respect are subject to sharp criticism.

The second overriding point which emerges from the experience of national courts is that the application by these courts of the proportionality principle in examining justifications to restrictions on the free movement of goods is extremely erratic. Applications before the national courts both under the rule of reason and the grounds of justification mentioned in Article 36 have given rise to examples in which these courts have been far too quick in deciding that a particular national measure is justified. This is largely due to a neglect on the part of these courts to perform a rigorous application of the proportionality principle. In effect, the national courts have often simply stated that the national measure is justified without proceeding to even mention the proportionality test, including whether there were any alternative means less restrictive of trade available to the Member State in question. In some national courts, the application of this principle of Community law has been complicated by an overlap with other similar, but not identical, concepts of national public law. For example, the English courts, in the Sunday-trading cases in particular, in effect refused to apply the proportionality test by replacing it with a test of reasonableness. However, it is the French courts which stand out for failing, on the face of their judgments, to give reasons for any applications of the proportionality test.[14] Clearly, criticism of insufficient reasoning on the part of national courts must be qualified by a care to appreciate the context of the national system. For example, the common-law expectation that judgments of courts of law should give reasons for and discuss the law in great detail cannot be applied *mutatis mutandis* to

---

of the ECJ in *Keck* has, to some extent, legitimated these 'errors' of the national courts, by holding that national measures which fall within the category of 'selling arrangements' no longer breach Art. 30 *unless* they are discriminatory.

[14] With respect to justification of French law affecting shop-opening hours, see *Joëlle Lenel, Cour de Cassation*, ch. crim., 20 Nov. 1990, Bull. Cass. Crim. 1990, no. 392 p. 989. With respect to justification for the protection of consumers under the rule of reason, see *Falck, Cour de Cassation*, ch. crim., 25 Oct. 1993, Bull. Cass. Crim. 1993, no. 309 p. 776; *Campin, Cour de Cassation*, ch. crim., 9 Nov. 1987, Bull. Cass. Crim. 1987, no. 394 p. 1038 and *Floch, Cour de Cassation*, ch. crim., 2 Feb. 1994, Bull. Cass. Crim. 1994, no. 51 p. 103. With respect to the protection of public health, see *Bocquin, Cour de Cassation*, ch. crim., 14 Oct. 1992, Bull. Cass. Crim. 1992, no. 326 p. 899; *Nauleau, Cour de Cassation*, ch. crim., 10 Mar. 1993, Bull. Cass. Crim. 1993, no. 108 p. 261 and *Republic (Conseil National de l'Ordre des Pharmaciens)* v. *Ruth, Cour de Cassation*, ch. crim., 25 May 1994, [1995] 1 CMLR 718, Bull. Cass. Crim. 1994, no. 202 p. 468. Finally, with respect to the protection of cultural expression under the rule of reason, see *Thorn-EMI Video France* v. *Fédération nationale des cinémas français, Cour de Cassation*, 1re ch. civ., 22 Apr. 1986, Bull. Cass. Civ. 1986, I no. 96 p. 96.

other legal traditions.[15] Nevertheless, the lack of motivation in some French court judgments is unsatisfactory since it is submitted that EC law *requires* the national court to provide explicit reasons as to why national measures restrictive of inter-State trade are justified. This is because ECJ case law on justifications for restrictions to the free movement of goods clearly emphasizes that these should be narrowly construed and therefore subject to a rigorous application of the proportionality test. Furthermore, national court application of justifications for restrictions to the free movement of goods is of particular interest since the granting of justifications under Article 36 or the rule of reason is at the sharp end of application of EC law by national courts. The granting of such justifications is the point at which the Community system entrusts the greatest amount of responsibility to the national courts. The fact that the national courts have been less than rigorous in this area does not therefore inspire confidence.

It is occasionally possible to detect a certain degree of hostility on the part of national courts to applying the free movement of goods provisions. For example in *British Leyland Motor Corporation* v. *T. I. Silencers*[16] Walton J in the Chancery Division of the High Court struck out certain 'Euro-defences' based on Articles 30 to 36 EC in the following terms:

[T]he defences in question have no merits whatsoever, being at the highest, purely technical defences which owe much more to the burning of midnight oil in Counsel's chambers than to any practical difficulty which the defendant will encounter in real life. The provisions of the Treaty of Rome are important, and the grand idea of the free movement of goods all over Europe is an important one, to be kept very much to the forefront of one's thinking; but the Treaty was never meant to afford a purely technical defence to infringers on specious and far-fetched grounds such as are set out in the defences herein. The more sweeping and important provisions of the Treaty, the more essential it is that all courts, in applying them, apply them to the matters to which they were intended to be applied and none other.[17]

It is of interest to note that, on appeal, the defences based on EC law were reinstated by the English Court of Appeal which commented that it was 'unable to accept such a simple, attractive but insular approach'[18] and went on to state that '[w]e have been warned, on more than one occasion, of the danger of assuming too much knowledge of the way in which the European Court interprets the Treaty of Rome'.[19] The approach of the

---

[15] See generally, Ranieri, 'Styles judiciaires dans l'histoire européenne: modèles divergents ou traditions communes' in Jacob, *Le juge et le jugement dans les traditions juridiques européennes*, 181; Sauvel, 'Histoire du jugement motivé' RDP 1955, 5; Goutal, 'Characteristics of Judicial Style in France, Britain and the USA' (1976) 24 Amer. J Comp. Law 43, Gillis Wetter, *The Styles of Appellate Judicial Opinions: A Case Study in Comparative Law* (Sythoff, 1960) & van Caenegem, *Judges, Legislators and Professors* (CUP, 1987).
[16] [1980] 1 CMLR 598.   [17] Ibid. at 608.   [18] [1981] 2 CMLR 75 at 78.
[19] Ibid. at 84.

French *Conseil d'Etat* has also provided examples of explicit hostility. The well-known and well-documented refusal of the *Conseil d'Etat* to accord supremacy to Community law over subsequent national legislation prior to its change of heart heralded by the *Nicolo* judgment,[20] led to several instances in which the latter approach resulted in a refusal to apply Articles 30 to 36 EC to French legislation enacted subsequent to the entering into force of the EC Treaty.[21] The *Conseil d'Etat* has now abandoned such an approach which undoubtedly amounted to hostility to EC law. In other cases, the *Conseil d'Etat* has held, on very unsatisfactory reasoning, that clear restrictions to the free movement of goods did not infringe Articles 30 to 36, but nevertheless mitigated this poor reasoning by awarding the applicants compensation from the French State on the basis of no-fault liability.[22] Similarly, it is submitted that the French *Cour de Cassation* displayed a certain degree of hostility in *Ministère public* v. *Théo Rossi di Montalera*[23] by holding, contrary to ECJ case law, that EC law prohibited reverse discrimination.

Cases in which the national courts display open hostility towards the application of EC law are, however, the exception. In the majority of cases, it is not so much open hostility as a question of confidence in the application of EC law. The discussion in this work is replete with examples of judgments of the national courts which have applied EC law in such a way that it would have been more appropriate for a reference to have been directed to the ECJ pursuant to Article 177 EC. More serious, of course, are those judgments in which an unsatisfactory application of Articles 30 to 36 was handed down by courts against whose decisions there is no further judicial remedy within the national legal system. Refraining from directing a reference to the ECJ in such circumstances is clearly an infringement of Article 177(3) EC. With respect to discerning a breach of Article 30, there are several instances where a reference to the ECJ would have been desirable given that the interpretation of Article 30 offered by the national court was neither convincing nor clear.[24] Such questionable applications were also handed

---

[20] *Conseil d'Etat*, 20 Oct. 1989, [1990] 1 CMLR 173, Rec. Lebon 1989, 190, AJDA 1989, 788.

[21] See, e.g., *Association des centres distributeurs Edouard Leclerc, Conseil d'Etat*, 8 Feb. 1985, Rec. Lebon 1985, 26; *International Sales and Support Corporation BV* v. *Ministre de l'economie et des Finances*, Conseil d'Etat, 13 Dec. 1985, Rec. Lebon 1985, 377; AJDA 1986, 174, RTDE 1988, 108 and *Bernard Carant et Cie* v. *Ministre de l'Economie, des Finances et de la Privatisation, Conseil d'Etat*, 27 Apr. 1988, Rec. Lebon 1988, 171.

[22] See *SARL Les fils de Henri Ramel* v. *Ministre de l'interieur et Préfet de l'Hérault, Conseil d'Etat*, 7 Dec. 1979, Rec. Lebon 1979, 456; *Ministère du Commerce extérieur* v. *Société Alivar, Conseil d'Etat*, 23 Mar. 1984, Rec. Lebon, 1984, 127 and *Ministre de la culture* v. *Epoux Genty, Conseil d'Etat*, 7 Oct. 1987, Rec. Lebon, 1987, 304.

[23] *Cour de Cassation*, ch. crim., 16 June 1983, RTDE 1983, 468.

[24] *Re Labelling of Dutch Poultry*, OBL Köln, 29 Apr. 1988, GRUR 1989, 694; [1990] 2 CMLR 104 (concerning *Pingo frisch* chicken); *SA Magnavision NV* v. *General Optical Council* (No. 1) [1987] 1 CMLR 887; *Extrude Hone Corporation's Patent*, [1981] 3 CMLR 379; [1982] RPC 361 (ChD); *Dirk van den Broek Supermarkten BV* v. *Leendert Arie Vente*, Pres.

down by courts at the top of the judicial hierarchy in the national systems.[25] Furthermore, as has already been mentioned, the application by the national courts of the *Keck and Mithouard*[26] judgment does not inspire confidence. For example, it has been seen how in the *Ex p. Mirza* case,[27] the *Keck* approach was abused to reach the result that Article 30 did not apply to technical requirements for taxis. In other national court judgments applying *Keck*, the application has been brief, with little or no discussion of whether and why the measures in question fell within the category of 'selling arrangements'. Furthermore, the two provisos set down in *Keck* have not been applied as rigorously as is desirable. With respect to export restrictions and Article 34, the *Groenveld*[28] interpretation of Article 34 has all too often been neglected by the national courts which have failed to recognize and explain the application of Article 34.[29] Finally, the national court case law applying the ECJ's interpretation of exhaustive Community harmonization legislation has equally not been particularly satisfactory.[30]

(B) Irreconcilable judgments: courts in one Member State faced with the compatibility of particular national legislation with the provisions concerning the free movement of goods but reaching different conclusions

The uniform application of Community law has been described by the ECJ as 'a fundamental requirement of the Community legal order'.[31] Indeed, it

---

Arrondissementsrechtbank Amsterdam, 2 June 1977, NJ 1980, 401; *Openbaar Ministerie* v. *Supermarket N.N. te Enschede, Economische Politierechter* Almelo, 6 Sept. 1977, SEW 1978, 157–9 (with note by Mok); *Officier van Justitie* v. *Edah BV, Arrondissementsrechtbank*'s Hertogenbosch (*Ec Raadkamer*), 5 Feb. 1985, NJ 1985, 308 and *Dommelsch NA België*, RCC, 10 Apr. 1991 and CvB, 28 Oct. 1991 both reported at RCC 1991, nr. 663 p. 79.

[25] *Syndicat national des importateurs français en produits laitiers et avicoles et Decker et Cie*, Conseil d'Etat, 27 Jan. 1967, Rec. Lebon 1967, 41; AJDA 1967, 284; [1968] 1 CMLR 81; *Smanor SA* v. *Syndicat national des fabricants de produits surgelés et congelés*, Conseil d'Etat, 19 Nov. 1986, Rec. Lebon 1986, 259, JCP 1987, II 20822; AJDA 1986, 714; RTDE 1988, 117; CDE 1989, 418 and *Openbaar Ministerie* v. *Autohandel- en sloperij J. R. BV*, Hoge Raad (*Strafkamer*), 16 May 1995, NJ 1995, 567; M & R 1995, 108 (with note by Hendriks).

[26] Cases C–267 & 268/91, n. 3 above.

[27] *R.* v. *Luton Borough Council, ex p. Mirza*, CA, 2 Feb. 1995 (transcr. available on Lexis).

[28] Case 15/79, n. 5 above.

[29] See, e.g., *R.* v. *Secretary of State for Health, ex p. United States Tobacco International* [1992] 1 All ER 212; [1992] 1 QB 353 and *Conté Nederland* v. *VROM*, 19 Oct. 1994, SEW 1995, 444 (with note by Mortelmans).

[30] See, e.g., *The State* v. *Vituret & Chambion, Cour de Cassation*, ch. crim., 2 Dec. 1992, [1995] 1 CMLR 185, Bull. Cass. Crim 1992, no. 401 p. 899 and *R.* v. *London Boroughs' Transport Committee, ex. p. Freight Transport Association*, [1992] 1 CMLR 5; [1991] 3 All ER 915; [1991] 1 WLR 828 (HL). For an incorrect interpretation of Directive 83/189 on an information procedure in the field of technical standards and regulations see *Hema BV* v. *Minister van Verkeer en Waterstaat*, CBB, 30 Jan. 1991, SEW 1991, 489 (with note by Mortelmans).

[31] Cases C–143/88 & C–92/89 *Zuckerfabrik Süderdithmarschen* v. *Hauptzollamt Itzehoe* [1991] ECR I–415 at para. 26 and Cases C–46 & 48/93 *Brasserie du Pêcheur/Factortame* (No. 3) [1996] ECR I–1029, [1996] 1 CMLR 889 at para. 33.

has also been remarked that 'Community law has to be interpreted and applied uniformly in all the Member States. The need for uniformity has often been stressed but the explanation is quite simply that, in the absence of uniformity, there would be no Community law.'[32] Thus, the survival of the Community legal order, and indeed the future of the European Union as a cohesive economic unit, would be undermined if the national courts of Member States reached different conclusions as to the compatibility of particular national legislation with the provisions on the free movement of goods. It should be noted that uniformity in this context has two meanings: firstly uniformity as between the national courts of different Member States and secondly uniformity of application as between such courts within a single Member State. Uniformity of application in both senses will be discussed in this section.

The analysis of the national case law in this work has given rise to instances where the potential for legal disunity has been exposed. For example, it has been discussed how the French courts have accorded a different (and broader) meaning to 'public policy' under Article 36 than either the ECJ or other courts in other Member States. Equally, it has been shown that until the ECJ clarifies the meaning of 'confusingly similar' trade marks under Article 4(1)(b) of the first trade mark Directive 89/104[33] there is a distinct danger to the uniformity of trade mark protection in the national courts of the Community. Furthermore, there are of course instances in which similar cases concerning Articles 30 to 36 are decided by the national courts of a single Member State to reach opposite conclusions despite the fact that the facts of the respective cases were virtually identical.[34]

The irreconcilable judgments mentioned above, although a threat to the uniform Community legal order in individual cases, do not, in the long term, pose insurmountable obstacles. The highlighted difficulties could be rectified, for example, when the ECJ has the opportunity to lay down in

---

[32] Jacobs, 'Remedies in National Courts for the Enforcement of Community Rights' in *Liber Amicorum for Diez de Velasco*, 969.

[33] [1989] OJ L40/1.

[34] In this regard, compare e.g. the judgment of the *TGI* of Créteil in *Roger Ruchat* v. *Ministère public*, TGI Créteil, 11e ch., 5 May 1987, La Semaine Juridique–éd. entreprise 1987, II 15041 with that of the Criminal Division of the *Cour de Cassation* in *Floch, Cour de Cassation*, ch. crim., 2 Feb. 1994, Bull. Cass. Crim. 1994, no. 51 p. 103 concerning the protection of consumers under the rule of reason. cf. also the judgt of the *Gerechtshof* Den Haag in *Richardson Vicks*, Gerechtshof 's-Gravenhage, 12 Feb. 1993, quoted in the subsequent judgment of the *Hoge Raad* (14 June 1994), NJB-katern 1994, 448 nr.182; transcr. 96.869 E with that of the President of the *CBB* in *Procter & Gamble Benelux BV* v. *Minister Volksgezondheid, Welzijn en Sport*, 2 Sept. 1994, KG 1994, 353 concerning the protection of public health under Art. 36. See also the variety of judgments by national court's before the French courts concerning French legislation restricting the advertising of alcoholic beverages in Ch. 5, sect. 2 and before the French and Dutch courts concerning national legislation on the disposal of waste in Ch. 4, sect. 4.

more detail Community-wide definitions for concepts such as public policy and 'confusingly similar' trade marks. Furthermore, the divergent decisions could in theory be settled by references by the national courts to the ECJ pursuant to Article 177 EC. A more difficult scenario arises, however, when national procedural rules intervene in litigation before the national courts to render the application of EC law inconsistent. The latter point is illustrated by looking at the now infamous application of Article 30 to English and Welsh Sunday-trading legislation. A closer look at the judgments of the English courts in this work reveals that the difficulties lay not so much in the divergent application of the proportionality test, but more in the problems thrown up by the duty upon the local authorities seeking injunctions to enforce the legislation to give cross-undertakings in damages should it subsequently have transpired that the national legislation was incompatible with Article 30. Indeed, it has been seen that, of the reported cases, there was only one case following the ECJ's judgment in *Torfaen*[35] in which it was concluded that the Shops Act was disproportionate to the objectives pursued by the English and Welsh legislation.[36] A similar pattern emerges from the French cases dealing with French legislation affecting shop-opening hours. After the *Torfaen* judgment, the French courts also came down almost uniformly (albeit on rather unsatisfactory reasoning) in favour of the proportionality of the French legislation.[37] It seems, therefore, that the often-stated view that the application of the proportionality principle caused a 'fragmentation of justice' should not be overstated. The French courts took control of the retailers, whereas the matter developed into a saga in England and Wales since the difficulties of English law with respect to the availability of injunctions rendered enforcement of the legislation by the local authorities impossible.

Similarly, the divergent conclusions of the French courts amongst the huge volume of cases during the 1980s concerning French legislation on resale price maintenance for books and on the minimum price for petrol was largely the result of the difficulties encountered under French law on the position of the judge in interim proceedings (*juge de référés*). Pending ECJ judgments in these cases some French courts in interim proceedings upheld the French legislation on the grounds that the breach of French law

---

[35] Case 145/88 *Torfaen BC* v. *B & Q* [1989] ECR 3851, [1990] 1 CMLR 337.

[36] *Shrewsbury & Atcham BC* v. *B & Q* [1990] 3 CMLR 535 (Shrewsbury Crown Court). The only other case known to the present writer in which this conclusion was reached before the English courts was the decision of a stipendiary magistrate at Pendle (unreported but referred to by Hoffmann J in *Stoke-on-Trent* v. *B & Q* [1991] 4 All ER 221 at 237) who identified the objective of the Shops Act as being to protect Sunday leisure activities and concluded that since many people regarded Sunday shopping in do-it-yourself and garden centres as a leisure activity, a ban on such shopping was disproportionate.

[37] There was only one divergent decision handed down by the Tribunal de Police of Narbonne in *Ministère public* v. *André Duhoux*, 22 Jan. 1990, D094/2 4/5 May 1990.

constituted a *trouble manifestement illicite*[38] and that, until it was shown in an incontestable manner that the French provisions were contrary to Articles 30 to 36 EC, French law must apply. On the other hand, other French courts in interim proceedings refused to uphold the French provisions since it was held that the *juge de référés* was incompetent to resolve a serious dispute between French and EC law. The important aspect of these judgments was that it was unclear limitations of *national law* which interfered with the application of substantive EC law by the national courts. For this reason, it is imperative that the ECJ develop uniform criteria for the grant of interim relief before the national courts in interim proceedings in cases where the compatibility of national provisions with EC law is at issue.

(C) The emergence of national precedents misapplying EC law

Under the common-law system of precedent, there is the latent danger that incorrect interpretations of EC law handed down by higher national courts in Member States of the common-law tradition will, over time, develop into precedents within the national system such that the incorrect precedent is subsequently followed by lower national courts without being corrected by the ECJ under the Article 177 EC preliminary rulings procedure. This danger has manifested itself before the English courts on two occasions discussed in this work.

Firstly, it was seen in cases before the English courts in which the policy of certain local councils in the United Kingdom requiring licensed taxis to be of the traditional London 'Black Cab' design (known as the FX4) was challenged as being incompatible with Article 30. It was argued that the technical specifications for taxis contained in these policies amounted to product requirements which restricted access to the market for licensed taxi vehicles manufactured in other Member States since in order to get access, these manufacturers would be put to the considerable expense of developing a vehicle which met these specifications. This argument was not fully developed in the first case before the English High Court but the Article 30 argument was nevertheless rejected by Glidewell J in *R. v. Metropolitan Borough Council of Wirral, ex. p. The Wirral Licensed Taxi Owners Association*.[39] In the context of the present discussion, it is of interest to note that in subsequent cases, that judgment of the High Court was used to assist in rejecting the Article 30 argument. For example, in *Hodgkinson v. Nottingham City Council*[40] the High Court's judgment in *Ex p. The Wirral Licensed Taxi Owners Association* was referred to as 'persuasive authority'

---

[38] New Code on Civil Procedure (*nouveau Code de procédure civile*), Art. 809(1).
[39] [1983] 3 CMLR 150. Critically noted by Gormley (1983) 8 ELRev. 141.
[40] [1993] 3 CMLR 503.

that Article 30 was not infringed.[41] The application of Article 30 by these courts has been criticized in detail elsewhere in this work, where it has been argued that the conclusion that Article 30 was not applicable to such national requirements was, at the very least, questionable.[42] This is thus a clear instance when national precedents were used to dismiss arguments based on Article 30 while at the same time refusing to refer questions to the ECJ under Article 177.

Secondly, cases decided by the English courts concerning the 'public morality' justification in Article 36 have also given rise to instances where a precedent within the national legal system was allowed to bind the decisions of further national courts as to the interpretation of EC law. In *R. v. Uxbridge Justices, ex. p. Webb*,[43] the High Court held the decision of the Court of Appeal in *R. v. Bow Street Magistrates' Court and Martin Dubbey, ex. p. Noncyp Ltd*,[44] was 'conclusive' authority for the argument that Article 36 allowed a ban on the importation of obscene material into the United Kingdom. Again it has been argued that the matter was in fact much more complex and that, in effect, a questionable national precedent was followed instead of referring questions to the ECJ under Article 177.[45]

(D) The constitutional position of national judges; Parliamentary sovereignty vs. the independence of the judiciary; free trade vs. national regulation of economic life

A final point of concern regarding the application of EC law by the national courts relates to the impact that such application has on the position of national judges within the national constitutional setting. The provisions concerning the free movement of goods have been remarkable for the extent of intervention which their application has involved in national regulation of economic life. The kind of national legislation to which these provisions apply tend to be highly sensitive in nature, often reflecting a broad spectrum of political issues about which feelings run deep. In most cases, the application of Articles 30 to 36 EC require the national court to investigate whether a particular national measure which is restrictive of intra-Community trade may nevertheless be justified. The application of justifications, whether under Article 36 or the rule of reason, often require the national judge to adjudicate on challenges launched by large commercial undertakings claiming that certain national legislation, which of itself comprises a political compromise, is not proportionate to that legislation's

---

[41] See also *R. v. Luton Borough Council, ex. p. Mirza*, QBD, 4 Nov. 1994 (transcr. available on Lexis).

[42] See discussion at pp. 73–6.   [43] [1994] 2 CMLR 288.

[44] [1990] 1 QB 123, [1989] 3 WLR 467, [1989] 1 CMLR 634.

[45] See discussion in Ch. 7, sect. 2.

objective. It will be evident that the application of the provisions on the free movement of goods is not completely value-free. Underlying much national legislation falling within the purview of Article 30 is a tension between regulation of economic life and market liberalization. An application of the proportionality principle under Article 36 or the rule of reason requires the national court to examine the choices made by the legislature and, in particular, to examine whether the same objectives could be achieved by alternate means. Consequently, large commercial enterprises are able to pose as the champions of free trade and the interests of consumers fighting against over-regulated national markets. It is for such cases that the free-movement-of-goods provisions are frequently called up as a reluctant conscript. As a result, the role played by EC law obliging national courts to investigate the proportionality of such legislation is extremely sensitive. Consequently, the application of Articles 30 to 36 brings the division within national constitutional settings between the legislature and judiciary under extreme pressure. This pressure is only increased by the fact that the ECJ has now unequivocally held that the State may be held liable for damage caused to individuals as a result of breaches of EC law through the acts or omissions of the legislature.[46] The position of the national judge *vis-à-vis* the legislature is thus significantly altered by the obligation to apply EC law and one should not underestimate the strain that this places upon the national courts in the national constitutional context.[47]

3 BALANCING THE SCALES: EVALUATION OF THE ADMINISTRATION OF JUSTICE IN THE COMMUNITY TAKEN AS A WHOLE

In any legal system, it will always be possible to identify individual judgments of courts which are 'incorrect'. Such judgments might be 'incorrect' for a number of reasons: because the reasoning is fundamentally flawed, because a certain text or precedent is clearly misconstrued, or simply because the judgment is subsequently overturned or clarified on appeal. The Community legal system is no exception to this. Consequently, it is to be expected that some national court judgments applying Articles 30 to 36 of the EC Treaty will, according to these terms, be considered 'incorrect'. In a case before the English High Court concerning the compatibility with Article 7a EC of frontier controls and passport checks on persons moving

[46] Cases C–46 and 48/93, n. 31 above.
[47] Barav has commented that '[i]t is undeniable that the increasingly intensive penetration of a patulous Community law into the fabric of the domestic legal system has brought about a dramatic alteration in the constitutional status of the national judicial authorities' 'Omnipotent Courts' n. 1 above, 301.

between Member States, McCullough J held that there was no such incompatibility and asked:

Am I . . . in any real doubt that this is the conclusion the European court of Justice would reach? I am not. I recognise, of course, that I may be wrong, but this is a commonplace of the judicial experience, even when one has no real doubt.[48]

It is thus submitted that in drawing conclusions as to the national court application of Article 30, care should be taken to balance the scales of poor applications with a realistic assessment of the judicial process which accepts that mistakes will be made. The application of EC law by national courts may be distinguished from the latter courts' application of their respective national laws by the fact that EC law has an extra dimension, namely that it must be applied uniformly in all the Member States. Nevertheless, it is submitted that there is no reason why the application of EC law by national courts should be judged by a higher standard than their application of domestic law. Furthermore, care should also be taken to avoid criticizing national courts' judgments with the benefit of hindsight.

It would be all too easy to take an extremely critical view of the application of the provisions concerning free movement of goods by the national courts. There are indeed ample examples to hand of incorrect or hostile applications of EC law. Furthermore, the real danger of irreconcilable judgments within a Member State and the emergence of national precedents misapplying EC law has manifested itself on a number of occasions. It would, however, be unfair to paint a picture of rampant misapplication. Such an analysis would take insufficient account of the balance of straightforward cases in which Articles 30 to 36 have been applied in a confident and competent fashion. In fact, the discussion of applications of Articles 30 to 36 by national courts demonstrates how effective their application of EC law can be. There is nothing more conducive to the establishment of a single market than when a Member State's own courts conclude that certain national provisions are restrictive of trade and are not objectively justified to protect, for example, mandatory requirements such as the protection of consumers. In this way, national provisions which are restrictive of trade are evaluated by a Member State's own courts on a case-by-case basis.

Moreover, it should not be forgotten that many of those judgments which consisted of questionable interpretations of EC law, were either corrected on appeal or subsequently referred to the ECJ. For example, everyone remembers that the English Court of Appeal in *R. v. Henn and Darby* handed down an incorrect interpretation of Article 30 by holding that a complete ban on import was not a 'quantitative restriction' within that

---

[48] *R. v. Secretary of State for the Home Department, ex. p. Flynn* [1995] 3 CMLR 397 at 415.

Article.[49] It should not, however, be forgotten that not only did the House of Lords overturn that judgment on appeal,[50] but it also directed a reference to the ECJ.[51] Similarly, while the English High Court in *British Leyland Motor Corporation* v. *T. I. Silencers* 'struck out' defences based on Articles 30 to 36 on unsatisfactory grounds,[52] the Court of Appeal allowed the appeal and reinstated the defences.[53] Again, while the High Court in *Thetford Corporation* v. *Fiamma SpA* 'struck out' so called 'Euro-defences' in that case[54] the Court of Appeal reinstated the defences[55] and even directed a reference to the ECJ pursuant to Article 177 EC.[56] The English High Court in *R.* v. *Pharmaceutical Society of Great Britain and Secretary of State for Social Services, ex. p. Association of Pharmaceutical Importers*[57] provides yet another such example. It will be recalled that that case concerned rules of a pharmacists' professional body in the United Kingdom which required pharmacists to supply the products specified in doctors' prescriptions so that, where a doctor prescribed a product by its trade-mark ('brand') name, only the product bearing that name could be supplied by the pharmacist. The (API) contended that the rule infringed Article 30. The High Court rejected this argument, holding that

whilst the effect of the measures sought to be challenged is no doubt to depress the level of intra-Community movement of parallel imports, it is in our judgment only designed to ensure that the customer gets what he specifies. Its adverse effect is in truth attributable not to any violation of Article 30 but rather to doctors failing to prescribe parallel imports.[58]

It has been submitted that this constituted a clear misapplication of ECJ case law in that the acceptance by the High Court that there was a reduction in intra-Community trade should have been enough for it to have concluded that Article 30 was breached and to move on to the question of possible justification. However, it is of interest in the context of the present discussion to note that on appeal to the Court of Appeal, Kerr LJ stated 'with the greatest respect for the reasoning of the Divisional Court' that its view was 'quite untenable'[59] and referred the case to the ECJ which confirmed that it could not 'exclude the possibility that, in the particular circumstances of the case, the said rule is capable of hindering intra-Community trade'.[60] In other words, the poor application of Article 30 was corrected and referred to the ECJ on appeal.

---

[49] [1978] 2 CMLR 688; [1978] 1 WLR 1031 (CA); [1978] 3 All ER 1190.
[50] [1979] 2 CMLR 495 (HL); [1980] 2 All ER 166.
[51] Case 34/79 [1979] ECR 3795; [1980] 1 CMLR 246.
[52] n. 16 above & [1980] 2 CMLR 332.   [53] [1981] 2 CMLR 75 (CA).
[54] Judgt 30 July 1985 (transcr. available on Lexis).   [55] [1987] 3 CMLR 266.
[56] Case 35/87 [1988] ECR 3585.   [57] [1987] 2 CMLR 504.
[58] Ibid. at 513 (per May LJ).   [59] [1987] 3 CMLR 951 at 965.
[60] Cases 266 & 267/87 *R.* v. *The Pharmaceutical Society, ex p. Association of Pharmaceutical Importers* [1989] ECR 1295 at para. 19.

Equally emphatic examples have arisen before the French and Dutch courts. By way of illustration, it was noted with dismay that the *Tribunal d'instance* of Bressuire, which was charged with implementing the judgment of the ECJ in *Draincourt* v. *Cognet*,[61] which it had itself referred to the ECJ, effectively ignored the ECJ's judgment in that case by holding, contrary to the express terms of the latter's judgment, that EC law prohibited reverse discrimination.[62] While this national court judgment may be criticized, it should nevertheless be recalled that the case was subsequently appealed through the French courts up to the *Cour de Cassation* which put the matter on a correct footing in line with the ECJ's ruling.[63] Likewise, before the Dutch courts, the President of the *Rechtbank* Haarlem in *Esge SA* v. *Alpha Trading BV and Wigo*[64] held in a passing-off (*slaafse nabootsing*) action that 'quantitative restrictions' provided for in Article 30 prohibited only legal or administrative provisions which restricted intra-Community trade and that 'judicial decisions holding that a ban such as that applied for in this case, are not covered by that term'. It has been submitted that this statement is, with respect, an incorrect application of Article 30 since ECJ case law clearly confirms that judicial decisions interpreting national legislation in such a way that the free movement of goods is restricted *are* capable of falling within the scope of Article 30.[65] Again, however, the incorrect interpretation of Article 30 was corrected following national avenues of appeal and the *Gerechtshof* Amsterdam subsequently had absolutely no hesitation in allowing the appeal and held that Article 30 was capable of being breached in such circumstances.[66]

The above instances consist of but a few examples illustrating the extent to which one can safely rely on avenues of appeal within the national legal system to put incorrect judgments with respect to EC law on a correct footing. The system for the administration of justice, even within the national context, is not a perfect one. Mistakes will be made by courts of law. Moreover, the accidents of litigation and the resources of litigants are both recognized limitations to the achievement of a pure and intellectually satisfying body of law as applied by the courts. On these terms, therefore, application of EC law by national courts is no less satisfactory than the application of national law.

---

[61] Case 355/85 *Draincourt* v. *Cognet* [1986] ECR 3231, [1987] 2 CMLR 942.

[62] *Tribunal d'instance* Bressuire, 10 Apr. 1987, RTDE 1987, 553.

[63] *Cour de Cassation*, ch. crim., 19 Dec. 1988, [1990] ECC 85; Bull. Cass. Crim. 1988, 1153.

[64] *Arrondissementsrechtbank* Haarlem, 29 Jan. 1980, BIE 1982, 87.

[65] See, e.g. Case 6/81 *BV Industrie Diensten Groep* v. *JA Beele Handelsmaatschappij BV* [1982] ECR 707, [1982] 3 CMLR 102 & Case 58/80 *Dansk Supermarked* v. *Imerco* [1981] ECR 181, [1981] 3 CMLR 590.

[66] *Gerechtshof* Amsterdam, 25 Sept. 1980, BIE 1982, 87.

5 TOWARDS A MATURE SYSTEM OF COMMUNITY COURTS

The national court is the natural forum for the application of EC law. As a result, it is submitted that the ordinary course of action for a national court faced with a question of EC law should be for that court to decide the matter of EC law itself. Tesauro has rightly pointed out that 'Community law should by now be seen as a routine component of the rules applicable to everyday litigation, rather than an exotic excrescence upon the national legal order'.[67] Under the current system, references to the ECJ should therefore be the exception rather than the rule.[68]

The Article 177 EC preliminary-rulings procedure has hitherto played a crucial role in fostering co-operation between the ECJ and the national courts. Indeed, this spirit of co-operation was vital in the early years of Community law in order to achieve acceptance by the national courts of a new legal order. However, it is submitted that as the Community develops further into a mature legal system, the Community's administration of justice system should likewise be amended to take these developments into account.[69] To this end it is submitted that while the Article 177 preliminary-rulings procedure was suitable in the early years of the development of Community law, the procedure in that Article should, in the longer term, be amended to introduce a more hierarchical court system with the ECJ as the Community Supreme Court.[70] What is proposed here is that Article 177 should be replaced by a provision which allows parties to appeal, as of right, to the ECJ only after national avenues of appeal have been exhausted.[71] This would replace the co-operation between the ECJ

---

[67] Tesauro, 'The Effectiveness of Judicial Protection and Co-operation between the Court of Justice and the National Courts' at 17.

[68] Vaughan has written that '[i]n a fully developed Community legal system many of the most important cases will be decided in national courts or tribunals, with only exceptional cases being referred to the European Court of Justice pursuant to Art. 177 of the EC Treaty', [1997] EuLR, editorial.

[69] It may be noted that there is ongoing discussion of possibilities for new judicial structures for the Community. However, the starting point of these discussions has invariably been a concern to reduce the work-load of the ECJ while maintaining the Art. 177 EC preliminary-rulings procedure. See Jacqué & Weiler, 'On the Road to European Union—A New Judicial Architecture: An Agenda for the Intergovernmental Conference'; Koopmans, 'The Future of the Court of Justice of the European Communities'; Arnull, 'Refurbishing the Judicial Architecture of the European Community', and Report of the British Institute of International and Comparative Law, *The Role and Future of the European Court of Justice*, 1996 at 98–125.

[70] The term 'Supreme Court' is used rather than 'Constitutional Court' since the ECJ's jurisdiction is not limited to strictly constitutional issues. Alternatively, Jacqué & Weiler, n. 69 above at 192, have suggested the name 'European High Court of Justice'.

[71] This is in line with the general principle in public international law that all domestic remedies must first be exhausted. This principle is founded in the belief that States must be afforded the opportunity to rectify any violations of their international obligations through domestic legal channels first. However, given that the Community constitutes 'a new legal

and the national courts with a more formalistic system suitable for a mature judicial system. Such a radical proposal is justified in the long term because the current procedure for preliminary reference is too limiting. Firstly, according to the terms of Article 177, the ECJ is limited to giving interpretations of EC law. In particular, the ECJ cannot decide on the facts or merits of a case nor act as a court of appeal. Consequently, it is the national court, rather than the ECJ, which has the task of implementing the ECJ judgment with the result that there is no guarantee of either effective or uniform application of EC law. Secondly, the preliminary-rulings procedure places too much reliance upon the national courts to exercise, in appropriate cases, their discretion to refer cases to the ECJ and on national court application of the *acte clair* doctrine. Thirdly, the current preliminary-rulings procedure does not offer any means for litigants to challenge incorrect applications of EC law handed down by courts of last resort within the national system. While it is true that the ECJ has explicitly opened up the possibility for damage suffered as a result of a breach of EC law by the national judiciary to give rise to State liability,[72] it is submitted that there are severe practical difficulties to that ever being carried out in practice.[73] Equally, the European Commission has always been reluctant to commence Article 169 EC infringement proceedings against a Member State in such circumstances in recognition of the independence of the judiciary.[74] Much more satisfactory, therefore, would be a provision which

order', the proposal advanced here is not based on this principle of international law. It is nevertheless interesting to note that under the European Convention for the Protection of Human Rights and Fundamental Freedoms (213 UNTS 222; ETS No. 5) the Commission (Art. 26) and the Court (Art. 35 of Protocol No. 11, ETS No. 155) 'may only deal with the matter after all domestic remedies have been exhausted, according to the generally recognised rules of international law, and within a period of six months from the date on which the final decision was taken'. See Gomien, Harris & Zwaak, *Law and Practice of the European Convention on Human Rights and the European Social Charter* (Council of Europe Publishing, 1996) at 55–9. It is equally interesting to note that Art. 2(2) of the Protocol concerning the interpretation by the Court of Justice of the Brussels Convention of 27 Sept. 1968 on jurisdiction and the enforcement of judgments in civil and commercial matters ([1990] OJ C189/25) withholds the facility of seeking guidance on the interpretation of the Convention from national courts of first instance. See criticism of this by Dashwood, Hacon & White, *A Guide to the Civil Jurisdiction and Judgments Convention* (Kluwer, 1987), 57. Note also that when the Treaty of Amsterdam enters into force, what will become Article 68 EC will restrict references on the interpretation of the new Title IV on visas, asylum, immigration and other policies related to the free movement of persons to national courts against whose decisions there is no judicial remedy. See also the new Article 35 TEV.

[72] Cases C–46 and 48/93, n. 31 above, at paras. 34–5.

[73] Such difficulties include the principle of the independence of the judiciary arising from the separation of powers between the legislature, the executive, and the judiciary; the principle of legal certainty and *res judicata*; and finally, the practical problem that it will sometimes be the the the same court which has to decide whether its own earlier judgt constituted a sufficiently serious breach of EC law which gives rise to State liability.

[74] e.g., in the Third Report to the European Parliament on Commission Monitoring of the Application of Community law it was stated that: 'As the Commission has made clear on a number of occasions in regard to cases in which national courts disregard the legal force and

would allow parties to appeal, as of right, to the ECJ after national avenues of appeal have been exhausted. Such an approach would, in principle, preclude national courts from deciding questions of EC law incorrectly while at the same time refusing to direct a reference to the ECJ. One would not then be relying upon the discretion of the national courts to refer or on national courts' conceptions of whether a matter is *acte clair*. Rather, the possibility for the parties to appeal the matter all the way up to the ECJ would always be open. The benefits would, moreover, be felt in a reduced case-load for the ECJ which would also have the advantage of the views of the national courts below.[75] Furthermore, the problem of irreconcilable judgments in different Member States could thereby be alleviated as the

the requirements of Article 177 of the EEC Treaty an infringement procedure may, where a national court fails to respect Community law, be initiated against the Member State in which the said court is situated. However such a procedure does not constitute the most suitable basis for co-operation between the national courts and the Court of Justice. For that reason, where circumstances permit, the Commission endeavours, in such cases, to induce the Member States to ensure, without impairing the independence of the judiciary, that Community law is respected, whether by recourse to primary or secondary legislation or to administrative means' [1986] OJ C220 at 27. See also to identical effect the Fourth Annual Report [1987] OJ C338 at 33 and the Fifth Annual Report [1988] OJ C310 at 43. In the Sixth Annual Report, it was stated that 'the Commission hesitates, given the universal principle of the independence of the judiciary, to find fault with a Member State on grounds of the conduct of one of its courts' [1989] OJ C330 at 53. The Commission has, however, occasionally begun, but never completed, infringement proceedings in such circumstances. For example, infringement proceedings were begun against France in connection with a judgment of the *Cour de Cassation*, ch. crim., 12 Nov. 1986 no. 85–95–751 which failed to apply the arrangements governing returned goods under Reg. 754/76. See the Sixth Annual Report, cited above. However, this case was settled following discussions between the French authorities and the Commission: see the Seventh Annual Report [1990] OJ C232 at 54. Similarly, with respect to the Hoechst inspection episode, the Commission began Art. 169 infringement proceedings against Germany since an order of a German court prohibiting the *Bundeskartellamt* from working with the Commission in its inspection was alleged to be in breach of Reg. 17/62. However, the proceedings only progressed to the reasoned Opinion stage, in light of the ECJ judgments in Case 46/87R *Hoechst AG* v. *Commission* [1987] ECR 1549 [1988] 4 CMLR 430 and Joined Cases 46/87 and 227/88 *Hoechst AG* v. *Commission* [1989] ECR 2859, [1991] 4 CMLR 410.

[75] In this respect, it is interesting to note that the withholding of the facility to make preliminary references to the ECJ concerning the Brussels Convention on jurisdiction and the enforcement of judgments in civil and commercial matters from national courts of first instance (see n. 71 above) is explained in the Jenard Report as desirable since questions of interpretation which are dealt with by first instance national courts ensures that the ECJ is fully informed: Jenard C59/68, para. 11(1). Equally, the US federal judicial system also has a 'Certification' procedure (strikingly similar to the Art. 177 EC preliminary-rulings procedure) whereby a lower Court (usually a Court of Appeals) may at any time certify to the Supreme Court a question of law in a civil or criminal case with respect to which instructions are desired. However, such certified questions are infrequently used and are discouraged by the Supreme Court in order to reduce the volume of its work and because it takes the view that it is the task of the Courts of Appeals to decide all properly presented cases before them. See annex on the US Federal Judicial System in the Report of the British Institute of International and Comparative Law, *The Role and Future of the European Court of Justice*, n. 69 above, 145–51. See also Jacobs & Karsk, 'The Federal Legal Order: The USA and Europe Compared, a Judicial Perspective' in Cappelletti, Seccombe & Weiler (eds.), *Integration Through Law*, vol. 1 bk. 1 (EUI, 1986) 169.

ECJ would then be competent to decide the proportionality question itself, when examining justifications advanced by Member States for restrictions to the free movement of goods. Indeed, the logical necessity for a central court of appeal within the Community was recognized as early as in 1975 by Graham J in the English High Court in *EMI Records* v. *CBS United Kingdom*, where he stated that

Unfortunately there is as yet no central court of appeal which is in a position to reconcile conflicting decisions emanating from different countries of the Community. Different decisions by the three countries concerned in the present case would lead to chaotic results and this shows the logical necessity for such a court.[76]

It is acknowledged that there are, of course, severe drawbacks to an amendment to Article 177 as proposed above. Firstly, it would remove the trust and co-operation between the ECJ and the national courts which has, hitherto, been the corner-stone of the system for the application of EC law before national courts. Secondly, points of EC and national law are often so intertwined that they cannot sensibly be separated, so that appeals to the ECJ might require the latter to rule on points of national law. Thirdly, the proposal outlined above may also increase costs if parties have to appeal their way up though the national system before they reach the ECJ. Indeed, it is often clear at the outset that some points of EC law will have to be resolved at ECJ level, and the current possibility of early referral is, in such cases, conducive to the good administration of justice.

These objections can, with varying degrees of success, be answered. With respect to the first objection, it should be noted that by taking away the possibility for lower national courts to refer questions to the ECJ, one is investing more, rather than less, trust in these courts to apply EC law. Indeed, the merit of the proposed amendment is that more trust is accorded to the national courts while at the same time improving the possibilities for litigants to correct incorrect national court judgments through appeals right up to the ECJ. The second objection could be avoided through employing a system of cassation under which individual cases are remitted to the national court. Furthermore, the second objection loses some of its force when one looks at the experience of the United States federal judicial system where the Supreme Court successfully sits not only at the apex of the pyramid of federal courts, but also as the final appellate court in cases involving federal law that arise in state courts.[77] The

---

[76] [1975] 1 CMLR 285 at 297.

[77] The Supreme Court may review decisions of the highest state courts only when a substantial federal question is raised and a balance is preserved by a number of self-restraining rules such as the rule that it will not review judgments of state courts unless federal questions have been raised early in the proceedings before the state courts. Furthermore, the Supreme Court has the ability to certify questions of state law to the highest state court for a decision; a kind of preliminary ruling in reverse which the Supreme Court uses enthusiastically: see *Lehman Brothers* v. *Schein* 1974, 94 S. Ct. 1741.

third point, concerning increased cost to the parties, can also be offset by recognizing that exactly the same is true of national law. Within national systems, parties do not have a right of direct appeal to supreme courts. The views of the lower courts up the national judicial hierarchy have first to be sought. In the national context, cases also arise where the need for resolution by the highest national court is likely at the outset. Nevertheless, avenues of appeal have to be followed. In this respect, it is proposed that EC law should be no different from national law. It is further submitted that the third objection could be mitigated by providing for a leap-frog procedure whereby a lower national court may issue a certificate after it has given judgment that a point of EC law of general public or Community importance is raised with the result that a direct appeal to the ECJ may be lodged.[78]

It is not here denied that there are no serious drawbacks to the proposed amendment. However, it is suggested that in the long term, the loss of the spirit of co-operation so precious to the current Article 177 procedure would be outweighed by the distinct advantages set out above.

In many ways, the question is not whether national courts can be trusted to apply EC law correctly. The need to trust them is an imperative of the decentralized Community system. It should be acknowledged that EC law is 'special' in the sense that it is a new legal order and is supra-national in nature and that there are certain features which distinguish EC law from national law, such as the added imperative with EC law, of less relevance with national law, that it is applied uniformly in several legal jurisdictions. However, much has been made of the necessity for national courts to treat EC law just as they do national law.[79] Seen in this light, EC law no longer needs to be treated with kid gloves. Moreover, a more hierarchical system would be a positive move towards a mature system for the application of Community law. The role of the ECJ would thus be reinforced while at the same time placing more trust in the national courts' abilities to apply the substantive rules of EC law. Most importantly, it would send out a clear signal that EC law is part of, and no different from, national law and should be applied as such. In this way, the courts of one Member State would be further encouraged to be less insular and to look to the judgments of the courts of other Member States which, it is submitted, would be a positive development for the Community legal system.[80]

---

[78] A provision to that effect exists under English law: see Administration of Justice Act 1969, s. 12.

[79] In Case 6/64 *Costa* v. *ENEL* [1964] ECR 585, [1964] CMLR 425 the ECJ held that Art. 37 EC had become 'an integral part of the legal system of the Member States' and 'forms part of the law of those States and directly concerns their nationals, in whose favour it creates individual rights which national courts must protect'. In Case C–2/88 *Imm. Zwartveld* [1990] ECR I–3365, [1990] 3 CMLR 457 the ECJ held that the EC legal system is 'an internal part of the legal systems of the Member States'.

[80] The necessity for more reporting of judgments by national courts which concern EC law would also be underlined by the proposed developments.

The development of substantive EC law may be likened to that of a child. In the early years, it is necessary to accord a young child special treatment and protection. However, as the child gets older, a parent has to learn when to let go and to allow the child to flourish independently. The same is true of EC law. In the early years it was necessary to treat EC law as a special creature. However, the time has now come to allow Community law to spread its wings.

Select Bibliography

Addink et al. (eds.), *Europese milieurechtspraak, 104 nationale uitspraken met Europees milieurechterlijke aspecten* (WEJ Tjeenk Willink, Zwolle, 1996).

Albers and Swaak, 'The Trouble with Toubon: Language Requirements for Slogans and Messages in the Light of Article 30 EC' (1996) 21 ELRev. 71.

Alter, 'The European Court and National Courts Doctrine and Jurisprudence: Legal Change in its Social Context. Explaining National Court Acceptance of European Court Jurisprudence. A Critical Evaluation of Theories of Integration' EUI Working Paper RSC No. 95/27 and other reports forming part of the Florence Project, incorporating reports from various Member States under the title, 'The European Court and National Courts—Doctrine and Jurisprudence: Legal Change in its Social Context', published as EUI Working Papers RSC No. 95/24 to 95/31.

Alves Viera, 'The Application of Community law by Portuguese Courts' (1991) 16 ELRev. 346.

Andenas (ed.), *Article 177 References to the European Court: Policy and Practice* (Butterworths, 1994).

Anderson, *References to the European Court* (Sweet & Maxwell, 1995).

Annual Reports to the European Parliament on Commission Monitoring of the Application of Community law: First COM (84) 181 final; Second COM (85) 149 final; Third [1986] OJ C220; Fourth [1987] OJ C338; Fifth [1988] OJ C310; Sixth [1989] OJ C330 (includes appendix on 'The Attitude of National Supreme Courts to Community Law'); Seventh [1990] OJ C232; Eighth [1991] OJ 1991 C338; Ninth [1992] OJ C250; Tenth [1993] OJ C233; Eleventh [1994] OJ C154; Twelfth [1995] OJ C254; Thirteenth [1996] C303.

Arnull, 'Use and Abuse of Article 177 EEC' (1989) 52 MLR 622.

—— 'References to the ECJ' (1990) 15 ELRev. 375.

—— 'What Shall We Do on Sunday?' (1991) 16 ELRev. 112.

—— 'The Evolution of the Court's Jurisdiction under Article 177 EEC' (1993) 18 ELRev. 129.

—— 'Refurbishing the Judicial Architecture of the European Community' (1994) 43 ICLQ 296.

Askham, Burke and Ramsden, *EC Sunday Trading Rules* (Butterworths, 1990).

Audeoud, Berlin and Manin, 'The Application of Community law in France: Review of French Court decisions from 1974 to 1981' (1982) 19 CMLRev. 289.

Baas, 'The Netherlands in Face of its Community Obligations 1984–1995' (1996) 33 CMLRev. 1197.

Bael, Van, 'The Role of the National Courts' (1994) 1 ECLR 3.

Bandrac and Momège, 'La Fermeture Dominicale et le Droit Communautaire' Gaz. Pal. 1990, III Doct. 552.

Barav, 'La fonction communautaire du juge national', unpubl. Ph. D. thesis, Strasbourg University, 1983.

Barav, 'Enforcement of Community Rights in National Courts: The Case for Jurisdiction to Grant Interim Relief' (1989) 26 CMLRev. 369.

—— 'La plénitude de compétence du juge national en sa qualité de juge communautaire' in *L'Europe et le droit: mélanges en hommage à Jean Boulouis* (Dalloz, 1991) p. 1.

—— 'Omnipotent Courts' in Curtin and Heukels (eds.), *Institutional Dynamics of European Integration, Essays in Honour of Henry G. Schermers* (Martinus Nijhoff Publishers, 1995) vol. II, 265.

Barnard, 'Sunday Trading: A Drama in Five Acts' (1994) 57 MLR 449.

Barnard and Sharpston, 'The Changing Face of Article 177 References' (1997) 34 CMLRev. 1113.

Barnard and Greaves, 'The Application of Community law in the United Kingdom: 1986–1993' (1994) 31 CMLRev. 1055.

Beaumont and Campbell, 'Preliminary Rulings' (1985) 53 Sc. Law Gaz. 62.

Bergerès, 'Vade-mecum de la question préjudicielle de l'article 177 du Traité CEE' Dalloz 1994, Chr. 181.

Bergstein, *Community law in the French Courts* (Martinus Nijhoff, 1973).

Bertin, 'Le juge des référés et le droit communautaire' Gaz. Pal. 1984, I Doctr. 48.

Betlem, 'Onrechtmatige Wetgeving: Overheidsaansprakelijkheid voor Schending van EG-recht in het post-Francovich Tijdperk' (1996) Regelmaat 128.

Bieber et al. (eds.), *1992: One European Market? A Critical Analysis of the Commission's Internal Market Strategy* (Nomos-Verl., 1988).

Bigot, 'Publicité et usage de la langue française: Réflexions sur la loi du 4 août 1994' Gaz. Pal. 1995, Doctr. 2.

Biondi, 'The Merchant, The Thief and The Citizen: The Circulation of Works of Art Within the European Union' (1997) 34 CMLRev. 1173.

Brealey and Hoskins, *Remedies in EC Law: law and practice in the English and EC courts* (Longman, 1994).

Bridge, 'Procedural Aspects of the Enforcement of EC Law Through the Legal Systems of the Member States' (1984) 9 ELRev. 28.

Brinkhorst, 'De Nederlandse rechter en het gemeenschapsrecht' SEW 1966, 65.

British Institute of International and Comparative Law, *The Role and Future of the European Court of Justice*, 1996.

Buffet-Tchakaloff, *La France devant la Cour de justice des Communautés européennes* (Economica, 1985).

Caranta, 'Judicial Protection Against Member States: a new *jus commune* takes shape' (1995) 32 CMLRev. 703.

Cavallini, *Le juge national du provisoire face au droit communautaire* (Bruylant, 1995).

Chalmers, 'Free Movement of Goods Within the European Community: An Unhealthy Addiction to Scotch Whisky' (1993) 42 ICLQ 269.

—— 'Repackaging the Internal Market—The Ramifications of the *Keck* Judgment' (1994) 19 ELRev. 385.

Chisholm, 'Some Observations on the Use of Injunctions and Interdicts in the Enforcement of EC Law' in Lonbay and Biondi (eds.), *Remedies for Breach of EC Law* (Wiley, 1997).

Claes, 'Aansprakelijkheid van de Staat wegens schending van het gemeenschapsrecht' (1996) Jurisprudentie Bestuursrecht 226.

Collins, *European Community Law in the United Kingdom* (Butterworths, 4th edn. 1990).

—— and O'Reilly, 'The Application of Community Law in Ireland 1973–1989' (1990) 27 CMLRev. 315.

Crossland, 'Community Law in German Courts: 1980–83' (1985) 10 ELRev. 462.

—— 'Community Law in German Courts: 1984–85' (1986) 11 ELRev. 473.

—— 'Community law in the German Courts 1986' (1989) 14 ELRev. 238.

—— 'Community law in the German Courts 1987' (1991) 16 ELRev. 334.

Curall, 'Some Aspects of the Relation between Articles 30–36 and Article 100 of the EEC Treaty With a Closer look at Optional Harmonisation' (1984) 4 YEL 169.

Curtin, 'The Decentralised Enforcement of Community Law Rights. Judicial Snakes and Ladders' in Curtin and O'Keeffe (eds.) *Constitutional Adjudication and National Law* (Butterworths, 1992), Ch. 5.

—— and O'Keeffe (eds.), *Constitutional Adjudication and National Law* (Butterworths, 1992).

Daintith, *Implementing EC Law in the United Kingdom* (Wiley, 1995).

Dantonel-Cor, 'La mise en jeu de la responsabilité de l'Etat français pour violation du droit communautaire' (1995) 31 RTDE 471.

Darmon and Calvet, 'Les juristes francais et le droit communautaire' Gaz. Pal. 1990, I Doctr. 197.

Dashwood and Arnull, 'English Courts and Article 177 of the EEC Treaty' (1984) 4 YEL 255.

Decocq, 'Le Nouvelles restrictions à la publicité en faveur des boissons alcooliques' JCP 1991, I 149.

Desmazières de Séchelles 'Experiences and Problems in Applying the Preliminary Proceedings of Article 177 of the Treaty of Rome, as seen by a French advocate' in Schermers, Timmermans, Kellermann & Stewart Watson (eds.), *Article 177 EEC: Experiences and Problems* (T.M.C. Asser Instituut North-Holland, 1986) at 153.

De Witte, 'Community Law and Constitutional Values' (1991) 2 LIEI 1.

Diamond, 'Dishonourable Defences: The Use of Injunctions & the EEC Treaty—Case Study of the Shops Act 1950' (1991) 54 MLR 72.

D'Sa, *European Community Law and Civil Remedies in England and Wales* (Sweet & Maxwell, 1994).

Duk, 'Some Remarks of a Dutch Advocate on the Preliminary Procedure of Article 177 EEC' in Schermers, Timmermans, Kellermann & Stewart Watson (eds.), *Article 177 EEC: Experiences and Problems* (T.M.C. Asser Instituut North-Holland, 1986).

Dutheil de la Rochère, Grief and Jarvis, 'L'Application du droit communautaire par les juridictions britanniques (1995–1996)' (1996) 32 RTDE 717.

Ehlerman, 'The Internal Market Following the SEA' (1987) 24 CMLRev. 361.

Errera, 'French Courts and Article 177 of the Treaty of Rome' in Schermers, Timmermans, Kellermann & Stewart Watson (eds.), *Article 177 EEC: Experiences and Problems* (T.M.C. Asser Instituut North-Holland, 1986) at 88.

—— 'The Scope and Meaning of No-fault Liability in French Administrative Law' (1986) Current Legal Problems 171.

Fitzpatrick and Szyszczak, 'Remedies and Effective Judicial Protection in Community Law' (1994) 57 MLR 435.

Gerven, Van, 'Bridging the Gap between Community and National laws: Towards a Principle of Homogeneity in the Field of Legal Remedies' (1995) 32 CMLRev. 679.

—— 'Bridging the Unbridgeable: Community and National Tort Laws after *Francovich* and *Brasserie*' (1996) 45 ICLQ 507.

Gjørtler, 'Community Law in Denmark, 1987–1988' (1989) 14 ELRev. 351.

Glaesner, 'The Single European Act' (1986) 6 YEL 283.

Goja, 'New Developments in a Continuing Story: The Relationship between EEC law and Italian law' (1990) 27 CMLRev. 83.

Golub, 'The Politics of Judicial Discretion: Rethinking the Interaction between National Courts and the European Court of Justice' (1996) 19 West European Politics 360.

Gormley, *Prohibiting Restrictions on Trade Within the EEC* (North Holland, 1985).

—— 'The Application of Community Law in the United Kingdom: 1976–1985' (1986) 23 CMLRev. 287.

—— 'Actually or Potentially, Directly or Indirectly? Obstacles to the Free Movement of Goods' (1989) 9 YEL 197.

—— 'Some Reflections on the Internal Market and Free Movement of Goods' [1989/1] LIEI 9.

—— 'Reasoning Renounced? The Remarkable Judgment of *Keck and Mithouard*' (1994) 5 EBLR 63.

—— 'Two Years After *Keck*' (1996) 19 Fordham Int. LJ 866.

Govaere, *The Use and Abuse of Intellectual Property Rights in EC Law* (Sweet & Maxwell, 1996).

Gravells, 'European Community Law in the English Courts' (1993) PL 44.

Green and Barav, 'Damages in National Courts for Breach of EEC Law' (1986) 6 YEL 55.

Grelon, 'La "*loi Lang*" sur le prix du livre et la discrimination à rebours' RTDE 1987, 405.

—— 'La Publicité sur le territoire français des Boisssons Alcooliques: Les incertitudes actuelles de la Loi Evin' Gaz. Pal. 1994, Jur. 638.

Grévisse and Bonichot, 'Les incidences du droit communautaire sur l'organisation et l'exercice de la fonction juridictionnelle dans les Etats membres' in *L'Europe et le droit*: *mélanges en hommage à Jean Boulouis* (Dalloz, 1991), 297.

Guy and Leigh, *The EEC and Intellectual Property* (Sweet & Maxwell, 1981).

Guyot-Sionnest, 'Un vide juridique. Le problème des vidéo-cassettes' Gaz. Pal. 1994, III Doctr. 203.

Haguenau, *L'Application effective du droit communautaire en droit interne: Analyse comparative des problèmes recontrés en droit français, anglais et allemand* (Bruylant, 1995).

Hartley, 'The Effect in National Law of Judgements of the European Court of Justice' (1980) 5 ELRev. 366.

Hoskins, 'Tilting the Balance: Supremacy and National Procedural Rules' (1996) 21 ELRev. 365.

Howells, (ed.), *European Business Law* (Dartmouth, 1996).

Ioannou, 'Recent Developments in the Application of Community law in Greece' (1989) 14 ELRev. 461.

—— and Anagnostopoulou, 'The Application of Community law in Greece (1989–1991)' (1994) 19 ELRev. 412.

Jacob, *Le juge et le jugement dans les traditions juridiques européennes* (LGDJ, 1996).

Jacobs, 'When to Refer to the European Court' (1974) 90 LQR 486.

—— 'Remedies in National Courts for the Enforcement of Community Rights' in *Liber Amicorum for Diez de Velasco* (Editorial Tecnos, 1993) at 969.

Jacqué, 'L'Acte Unique Européen' RTDE 1986, 575.

—— and Weiler, 'On the Road to European Union—A New Judicial Architecture: An Agenda for the Intergovernmental Conference' (1990) 27 CMLRev. 185.

Jans, *Europees Milieurecht in Nederland* (Wolters-Noordhoff, 1994).

—— 'Het beginsel van voorkeur voor binnenlandse afvalwerking' (1990) NJB 694.

—— 'Dutch Idiosyncracies and the Direct Effect of EC Law' (1996/1) LIEI 93.

Jarvis, M., 'The Sunday Trading Episode: In Defence of the Euro-Defence' (1995) 44 ICLQ 451.

—— 'Remedies for Breach of EC Law Before French Courts' in Lonbay and Biondi (eds.), *Remedies for Breach of EC Law* (Wiley, 1997), 187.

Joch and Wild, 'Application of EC law in Germany' (1981) 18 CMLRev. 79.

Kellermann, 'The Netherlands in Face of its Community Obligations' (1983) 20 CMLRev. 297.

—— Grondman & Tromm, 'Implementation of Community Law in the Netherlands' (1977) 2 ELRev. 392; (1977) 2 ELRev. 467 and (1979) 4 ELRev. 406.

Kerameus and Kremeis, 'The Application of Community Law in Greece 1981–1987' (1980) 17 CMLRev. 141.

Keus, 'De post-Francovich-arresten en het Nederlandse overheidsaansprake-lijkheidsrecht' Aansprakelijkheid & Verzekering 1997, 1.

Koopmans, 'The Future of the Court of Justice of the European Communities' (1991) 11 YEL 15.

Korte, 'Prejudiciële verwijzingen (art.177 EEG) in het kader van kort geding pro-cedures door Nederlandse rechters (Art. 289–297 Rv)' SEW 1990, 103.

—— Kellermann, Levelt-Overmars and Possen, *Primus Inter Pares: The European Court and National Courts. The Follow-up by National Courts of Preliminary Rulings ex Art. 177 of the Treaty of Rome: A Report on the Situation in the Netherlands*, 1990 EUI Working Paper in Law No. 90/6.

Kovar, 'Voies de droit ouverte aux individus devant les instances nationales en cas de violation des normes et décisions du droit communautaire' in *Les recours des individus devant les instances nationales en cas de violation du droit européen* (Institut d'études européennes de l'université libre de Bruxelles, 1978).

Laurent, 'La fonction communautaire du juge judiciaire français des référés' Gaz. Pal. 1984, II Doctr. 544.

Lenaerts, 'Application of EC Law in Belgium' (1986) 23 CMLRev. 253.

—— and Sunaert, 'Belgian Case Law Relating to Community law 1982–85' (1989) 14 ELRev. 434.

—— and Coppenholle, 'Belgian Case Law Relating to Community law 1986–88' (1990) 15 ELRev. 73.

—— 'The Application of Community Law in Belgium 1989–1992' (1992) 17 ELRev. 447.

Lewis, *Remedies and the Enforcement of European Community Law* (Sweet & Maxwell, 1996).

Lonbay and Biondi (eds.), *Remedies for Breach of EC Law* (Wiley, 1997).

Maher, 'National Courts as European Community Courts' (1994) 14 Legal Studies 226.

—— 'A Question of Conflict: The Higher English Courts and the Implementation of European Community Law' in Daintith, *Implementing EC Law in the United Kingdom* (Wiley, 1995), 303.

Mattera, *Le marché unique européen—ses règles, son fonctionnement* (Jupiter, 2nd edn., 1990).

—— 'La libre circulation des oeuvres d'art à l'intérieur de la Communauté et la protection des trésors nationaux ayant une valeur artistique, historique ou archéologique' (1993) RMUE 9.

—— 'De l'arrêt *Dassonville* à l'arrêt *Keck*: l'obscure clarté d'une jurisprudence riche en principes novateurs et en contradictions' (1994) RMUE 117.

McCarthy and Mercer, 'Language as a Barrier to Trade: The Loi Toubon' (1996) 17 ECLR 308.

McFarlane, 'Indecency and Obscenity: The View from Europe' (1990) NLJ 50.

McGee and Weatherill, 'The Evolution of the Single Market—Harmonisation or Liberalisation?' (1990) 53 MLR 578.

McMillan, 'La "certification", la reconnaissance mutuelle et le marché unique' (1991) RMUE 181.

Meij, *Prejudiciële Vragen van Nederlandse Rechters en Hun Gevolgen* (WEJ Tjeenk Willink, 1993).

Mok, 'Experiences of the Netherlands Courts in Applying the Preliminary Proceedings of Article 177 EEC' in Schermers, Timmermans, Kellermann & Stewart Watson (eds.), *Article 177 EEC: Experiences and Problems* (TMC Asser Instituut, North-Holland 1987).

Morcom, 'Parallel Importation of Pharmaceutical Products in the Common Market' (1988) 2 EIPR 47.

Mortelmans, 'Article 30 of the EEC Treaty and Legislation Relating to Marketing Circumstances: Time to Consider a New Definition?' (1991) 28 CMLRev. 115.

—— 'De interne markt en het facettenbeleid na het *Keck*-arrest: national beleid, vrij verkeer of harmonisatie' (1994) SEW 236.

—— 'Excepties bij non-tarifaire intracommunautaire belemmering: assimilatie in het nieuwe EG-Verdrag?' (1997) SEW 182.

Murphy, 'Community Law in Irish Courts 1973–1981' (1982) 7 ELRev. 331.

—— 'Community Law in Irish Courts 1982–85' (1986) 11 ELRev. 99.

—— 'Community Law in Irish Courts 1985–86' (1986) 11 ELRev. 479.

Nogueras and Barbero, 'The Judicial Application of Community law in Spain' (1993) 30 CMLRev. 1135.

Odle, 'Reclame en andere "verkoopmethoden" onder artikel 30 EG-Verdrag' IER 1994, 65.

Oliver, *Free Movement of Goods in the European Community* (Sweet & Maxwell, 3rd edn., 1996).

—— 'Enforcing Community Law Rights in English Courts' (1987) 50 MLR 881.

O'Neill, *Decisions of the ECJ and their Constitutional Implications* (Butterworths, 1994).

Orsini, 'Le juge des référés et l'application des normes communautaires' Gaz. Pal. 1985, II Doctr. 395.

Parleani, 'Le juge des référés face au droit Communautaire' Dalloz 1990, Ch. 65.

Pertek, 'L'enseignement du droit européen. Besoin et propositions' (1992) RMUE 159.

Pescatore, 'Some Critical Remarks on the "Single European Act" ' (1987) 24 CMLRev. 9.

Plehwe, von, 'European Union and the Free Movement of Cultural Goods' (1995) 20 ELRev. 431.

Prétot, 'Repos dominical et droit communautaire de la concurrence' (1991) Rev. juris. social. 483.

Quinn and MacGowan 'Could Article 30 Impose Obligations on Individuals?' (1987) 12 ELRev. 163.

Rasmussen, 'Denmark in face of Her Community Obligations' (1982) 4 CMLRev. 601.

Rawlings, 'The Euro-law Game: Some Deductions From a Saga' (1993) 20 Journal of Law & Society 309.

Reich, 'Protection of Diffuse Interests in the EEC and the Perspective of Progressively Establishing an Internal Market' (1988) Journal of Consumer Policy 395.

—— 'The "November Revolution" of the European Court of Justice: *Keck*, *Meng* and *Audi* Revisited' (1994) 31 CMLRev. 459.

Rideau (ed.), *Les États membres de l'Union européenne: Adaptations—Mutations—Résistances* (LGDJ, 1997).

Roseren, 'The Application of Community law by French Courts from 1980 to 1993' (1994) 31 CMLRev. 315.

Ross, '*Keck*—Grasping the Wrong Nettle', in Caiger and Floundas (eds.), *1996 Onwards* (Wiley, 1996), Ch. 4.

Roth, 'The Application of Community law in West Germany, 1980–90' (1991) 28 CMLRev. 137.

Rothnie, *Parallel Imports* (Sweet & Maxwell, 1993).

Santacruz, 'Spanish Adaptation to Community law: 1986–1988' (1991) 16 ELRev. 149.

Schermers, Timmermans, Kellermann & Stewart Watson (eds.), *Article 177 EEC: Experiences and Problems* (TMC Asser Instituut, North Holland 1987).

Servan-Schreiber 'EEC law in French Courts 1980–1984' (1986) 11 ELRev. 158.

Sharpston, 'Interim Relief in the National Courts' in Lonbay and Biondi (eds.), *Remedies for Breach of EC Law* (Wiley, 1997), 48.

Simon, 'Les exigences de la primauté du droit communautaire' in *L'Europe et le droit: mélanges en hommage à Jean Boulouis* (Dalloz, 1991) at 481.

Slot, 'Harmonisation' (1996) 21 ELRev. 378.

Slynn, *European Law and the National Judge* (Butterworth Lectures, 1991–2).

Steiner, *Enforcing EC Law* (Blackstone, 1995).

—— 'The Application of EEC law in National Courts: Problems, Pitfalls and Precepts' (1980) 96 LQR 126.

—— 'How to Make Actions Suit the Case: Domestic Remedies for Breach of EC Law' (1987) 12 ELRev. 102.

—— 'Drawing the Line: Uses and Abuses of Article 30' (1992) 29 CMLRev. 749.

Steyger, 'Nogmals het *Keck*-arrest: De nieuwe onduidelijkheid in de toepassing van artikel 30 EG-verdrag' (1995) NJB 933.

Szyszczak, 'Making Europe More Relevant to Its Citizens: Effective Judicial Process' (1996) 21 ELRev. 351.

Tallec, Le, 'Le soubassement juridique des affaires Leclerc carburants et Leclerc livres' JCP 1986, I 3231.

Tash, 'Remedies for European Community Law Claims in Member States: Toward a European Standard' (1994) 31 Col. J Transnat. Law 377.

Temmink, 'Reclamezelfregulering mag, maar er zijn Europeesrechtelijke grenzen' in Buren-Dee van, Hondius & Delft-Baas van (eds.), *Consument zonder grenzen: Opstellen aangeboden aan mr. M. van Delft-Baas ter gelegenheid van haar afscheid van het Molengraaff Instituut voor Privaatrecht* (Kluwer, 1996), 223.

Temple Lang, 'The Duties of National Courts under Community Constitutional Law' (1997) 22 ELRev. 3.

Tesauro, 'The Effectiveness of Judicial Protection and Co-operation between the Court of Justice and the National Courts' (1993) 13 YEL 1.

Thibaut de Berranger, *Constitutions nationales et construction communautaire* (LGDJ, 1995).

Travers, 'La jurisprudence italienne concernant le droit europeenne (annees 1984–87)' (1988) RMC 341.

Ullmann, 'Reconciling Trade Mark Decisions of National Courts and the European Court of Justice' (1996) 27 IIC 791.

Usher, *European Community law and national law: the irreversible transfer?* (Allen & Unwin, 1981).

—— 'Community Law and National Courts' in Vaughan (ed.), *Law of the European Communities Service* (Butterworths, loose-leaf since 1990), pt. 3.

—— 'The Imposition of Sanctions for Breaches of Community Law' UK Report to XV FIDE Congress, 1992.

Vaughan and Randolph, 'The Interface between Community Law and National Law: The United Kingdom Experience' in Curtin and O'Keeffe (eds.) *Constitutional Adjudication in European Community and National Law* (Butterworths, 1992) at 219.

VerLoren van Themaat, 'Gaat de Luxemburgse rechtspraak over de vier vrijheden en die over het mededingingsbeleid uiteenlopen?' SEW 1996, 398.

Vignes, 'The Harmonisation of National Legislation and the EEC' (1990) 15 ELRev. 358.

Vollebregt, 'De Reclame Code Commissie in Europees Perspectief: Artikel 85 van toepassing op de Reclame Code Commissie?' (1996) IER 137 and (1996) IER 98.

Voudouri, 'Circulation et protection des biens culturels dans l'Europe sans frontières' (1994) Rev. Dr. Pub. 479.

Walsh, 'The Appeal of an Article 177 EEC Referral' (1993) 56 MLR 881.

Weatherill, 'Regulating the Internal Market: Result Orientation in the House of Lords' (1992) 17 ELRev. 299.

—— 'After *Keck*: Some Thoughts on How to Clarify the Clarification' (1996) 33 CMLRev. 885.

—— and Beaumont, *EC Law* (Penguin, 2nd edn., 1995).

Whish, 'The Enforcement of EC Competition Law in the Domestic Courts of Member States' (1994) 5 EBLR 3, (1994) 2 ECLR 60.

White, 'In Search of the Limits to Article 30 of the EEC Treaty' (1989) 26 CMLRev. 235.

Wild and Joch, 'The Application of Community law in Germany: Review of Recent German Court Decisions' (1980) 17 CMLRev. 509.

Wils, *Prejudiciële Vragen van Belgische Rechters en Hum Gevolgen* (WEJ Tjeenk Willink 1993).

—— 'The Search for the Rule in Article 30 EEC: Much Ado About Nothing' (1993) 18 ELRev. 475.

Wissink, 'De Nederlandse rechter en overheidsaansprakelijkheid krachtens Francovich en Brasserie du Pêcheur' SEW 1997, 78.

Wyatt and Dashwood, *European Community Law* (Sweet & Maxwell, 3rd edn., 1993).

Wytink, 'The Application of Community law in Belgium: 1986–1992' (1993) 30 CMLRev. 981.

Index

advertising 30–6, 43, 59–64, 124
  alcoholic beverages, of 158–64, 277–8
agriculture, common market organizations
  and exports 149–52
aids, State, and measures of equivalent
  effect 10–12
animal health and Article (36) 280–8
  extra-territorial application 281–8
  proportionality, and 280–1, 287–8,
  welfare of animals 280
appellations of origin 325–6
  see also intellectual property rights
approximation of laws *see* internal market
archaeological value, goods of *see* treasures
artistic goods *see* treasures

books, and resale price maintenance
  165–8, 445
Brussels Convention 453 n

capital 7, 244–5
Cassis de Dijon case 53–4, 56, 58, 68, 71,
  104, 175–80, 439–40
  see also rule of reason
  and measures of equivalent effect 36
  application to exports 146–9
certificates of origin 21
coins 16–17
common commercial policy 23, 256 n
common customs tariff 7
common market 7, 162
common market organisations *see*
  agriculture
common origin principle 314–16
community legislation *see* harmonization
competition, unfair 50–1, 61, 195
competition law 10, 24, 36, 91 n, 110 n, 160,
  168, 232–3, 295
confusingly similar *see* trade marks
constitutional position of national judges
  see national courts
consumers, protection of 8, 31–2, 52, 68,
  124, 177, 183–95
copyright 108, 308–13
  television programme listings, and
  311–13
  see also intellectual property rights
cultural expression, protection of 177,
  180–3
cultural objects *see* treasures
customs duties 7, 289

and measures of equivalent effect 12
Dassonville formula 21, 23–4, 56, 58, 67, 86,
  89, 97, 102, 104, 116, 117, 121, 129, 432
  and exports 133–4, 140, 142, 149–50
de minimis rule
  absence of 97, 104–10, 130, 433
  exports, and 145
direct effect 3, 6, 30, 86, 93, 365
directly applicable measures *see* distinctly
  applicable measures
discrimination
  encouraging of 52–3
  nationality, on grounds of 163
  not a prerequisite for the application of
  Article (30) 36, 46, 54–5, 56, 61, 90
  prerequisite for the application of Article
  (34) 133, 146
  reverse discrimination *see* national
  measures
distinctly applicable measures 36, 37–53,
  141–2, 146, 180

emanations of the State *see* enacted by
  Member States
enacted by Member States 23–5, 28–36, 52,
  86, 296, 385, 434
encouraging discrimination *see* discrimination
environment, protection of 31, 177
  exports, and 145–9
equally applicable measures *see* indistinctly applicable measures
equal treatment 225
equivalent effect, measures of 20–3, *see*
  also import
  abusive recourse to Article 30 to
  circumvent national law 96
  advertising 59–64, 88
  encouraging national production 23
  exports, to *see* exports
  increasing imports 21–3, 69–71, 88
  limiting channels of distribution 47–9,
  57, 58
  obligatory origin marking 49–52
  potential effect on trade 10, 88–132
  presentation of goods 66–9, 88
  product requirements 71–6, 88
  requirement of qualified persons 56–9
  scope of *see* potential effect on trade
  time and place where may be sold 64–6,
  88